Peter,

Thanks for helping me get started with casewriting, and all the support you've given me at HBS.

FINANCIAL INSTRUMENTS AND MARKETS: A Casebook

George C. Chacko
Harvard Business School

Vincent Dessain
Harvard Business School

Peter A. Hecht
Harvard Business School

Anders Sjöman
Harvard Business School

WILEY

John Wiley & Sons, Inc.

Associate Publisher	Judy Joseph
Assistant Editor	Brian Kamins
Senior Production Editor	Sujin Hong
Design Director	Harry Nolan
Senior Designer	Kevin Murphy
Cover Photo	Sandra Baker/Photographer's Choice/Getty Images
Cover Design	David Levy

This book was set in 10/12 New Caledonia by Matrix Publishing and printed and bound by Hamilton Printing. The cover was printed by Phoenix Color.

This book is printed on acid free paper. ∞

Library of Congress Cataloging in Publication Data

Financial instruments and markets : a casebook / George C. Chacko . . . [et al.].
    p. cm.
  Includes index.
  ISBN-13: 978-0-471-73767-4 (cloth)
  ISBN-10: 0-471-73767-4 (cloth)
  1. Financial instruments. 2. Fixed-income securities. 3. Derivative
securities. 4. Capital market. I. Chacko, George.
  HG4521.F5584 2006
  332.63'2—dc22

                        2005028957

Printed in the United States of America

10 9 8 7 6 5 4 3 2 1

Acknowledgments

Teaching using the case method is a collaborative endeavor between teachers and students. Writing a casebook is an equally collaborative undertaking. We could not have completed this casebook without the generous assistance from colleagues at Harvard Business School and other academic institutions, students in our courses, practitioners in the field, and numerous other people. We owe any success this book might have to their kind participation, critical eyes, and well-formulated revisions. Any errors, however, remain our own.

It goes without saying that Harvard Business School contributed to this book in many ways. The Division of Research generously funded the research and case development efforts. The school also provided excellent research support in the form of skilled research assistants (Matthew Bailey, Daniela Beyersdorfer, Drew Blackburn, Marc Chennault, Jose-Abel Defina, Mei Hu, Andrew Kuhlman, Adam Plotkin, Eli Strick, Monika Stachowiak, Constantinos A Vingas), outstanding research staff (Chris Allen, Cynthia Churchwell, Jeffrey Cronin, Ann Cullen, Sarah Eriksen, Erika McCaffrey, Kathleen Ryan, Sarah Woolverton), and efficient case services support (Linda Olsen, Soebagio Notosoehardjo, Lillian Coltin, Sandra Frey, Patricia Hathaway, Ele Jeynes, Rosalyn Reiser, and Carol Sweet.) Above all, the school has given us a chance not only to test our cases but also to discuss our ideas and concepts with generations of MBA students. Their reactions in the classroom and their feedback have been invaluable for developing this casebook. For the cases in this book, we are particularly indebted to Kate Hao, Jacob Hook, Colin McGrady, Léonie Maruani, and George Nelson. Naturally, we would all have been utterly lost without the help of Dee Luther. Dr. Ross does not know what he is missing.

We are also grateful to the numerous professionals at various companies that have taken time and resources out of their schedules to help us develop these cases. Our specific thanks go to Ian Charles and Veeral Rathod at Cogent Partners.

In addition, **George** would like to thank Bala Dharan (Rice University), Hank Reiling (HBS), Marti Subrahmanyam (New York University), and Luis Viceira (HBS) for their contributions to cases in this book. Peter Tufano deserves special thanks. He not only contributed to several cases in the book, but he also actively encouraged George to begin writing cases, starting with including him as a co-author on two cases. It is safe to say that this casebook would never have come about without Peter's support and enthusiasm.

Vincent gives thanks from the bottom of his heart to Stéphanie.

Pete would like to thank the Harvard and University of Chicago Finance Departments, family, friends, and his wife, Brooke.

Finally, **Anders** would like to thank family, friends, and loved ones.

About the Authors

George C. Chacko is an Associate Professor at Harvard Business School (HBS) in the Finance Area, which he joined in 1997. He currently teaches a second-year course on Financial Instruments and Markets in the MBA program, and a Ph.D. course on Asset Pricing that is jointly offered by the Business School and the Harvard Economics Department. He has also taught courses in Capital Markets, Corporate Financial Engineering, and Corporate Finance in both the MBA program and the Executive Education program at HBS. As a researcher, Professor Chacko has published numerous articles in both academic and practitioner-oriented journals. Professor Chacko's research has focused on three areas: (1) transaction costs and liquidity risk in capital markets, particularly in the fixed income markets; (2) portfolio construction by institutions and individuals; and (3) the analysis and application of derivative securities. Professor Chacko holds a Ph.D. in Business Economics from Harvard University and dual Master's degrees in Business Economics (Harvard University) and Business Administration (University of Chicago). He holds a Bachelor's degree in Electrical Engineering from the Massachusetts Institute of Technology.

Vincent Dessain was appointed Executive Director of the Europe Research Center for Harvard Business School, based in Paris, in November 2001. The center he runs works with HBS faculty members on research and course development projects across the European continent. Previously, he was Senior Director of Corporate Relationships at INSEAD in Fontainebleau and on the school's Board of Directors. Mr. Dessain has been active as a management consultant with Booz-Allen & Hamilton in New York and Paris in the financial services field. His field of consulting was international market entry strategies, financial products, strategy, negotiation and implementation of cross-border alliances, financial restructuring, mergers and acquisitions. He has also been active as a Foreign Associate with the law firm Shearman & Sterling in New York in Banking and Finance and as an Advisor to the president of the College of Europe in Bruges, Belgium. A speaker of five European languages (French, English, German, Dutch, and Italian), Mr. Dessain holds a law degree from Leuven University (Belgium), a Business Administration degree from Louvain University (Belgium), and an MBA from Harvard Business School. Mr. Dessain is an avid mountain climber, marathon runner, and tennis player and will not miss a good art exhibition.

Assistant Professor **Peter A. Hecht** joined the Finance Unit at Harvard Business School in 2000. He teaches the required first-year Finance course in the MBA program and an advanced asset pricing course in the Business Economics Ph.D. program. Professor Hecht's research and publications cover a variety of areas within finance, including behavioral and rational theories of asset pricing, liquidity, capital market efficiency, complex security valuation, credit risk, and asset allocation. His experience prior to HBS has included work at investment banks J.P. Morgan and Hambrecht & Quist. In addition to advising financial institutions, Professor Hecht enjoys traveling, working out, and studying politics in his free time. He has an undergraduate degree in Economics and Engineering Sciences from Dartmouth College and an MBA and Ph.D. in Finance from the University of Chicago's Graduate School of Business.

Senior Researcher **Anders Sjöman** joined Harvard Business School at its Paris-based Europe Research Center in 2003. Mr. Sjöman works across management disciplines throughout Europe, conducting research and developing intellectual material for HBS. Previously, Mr. Sjöman worked five years in Boston for Englishtown.com, the world's largest online English school and an initiative by the EF Education Group. As Director of Production, he developed Englishtown's web services. A M.Sc.-graduate of the Stockholm School of Economics in his native Sweden and specialized in Information Management and International Business, Mr. Sjöman speaks Swedish, English, French, and Spanish. At least once a week, he can be found on a nearby squash court, playing in local tournaments or leagues.

Table of Contents

1

Introduction

This book contains material for a case-based course on financial instruments and markets. It covers the basics of financial instruments from terminology to pricing, and the markets in which these instruments trade, both organized exchanges (physical and electronic) and Over-the-Counter (OTC) markets. The securities covered in this book run the gamut of securities encountered in the financial markets, but the focus is on fixed income and derivative securities. Using real-life examples (the fundament for the case-based method), the main theme that runs throughout this book is how these securities accomplish risk transfer from actors who do not want risk to those who are willing to take it on—for a fee of course. The other main themes of this book are how to structure these risk transfers in a way that is efficient (from a tax, regulatory, etc. perspective) and how to price the risk transfers (including consideration of such frictions as liquidity risk) to arrive at a fair fee.

The book stems from a number of courses taught by the authors at the MBA and Executive Education levels at Harvard Business School (HBS), including Corporate Financial Engineering and Capital Markets.[1] The prerequisite for these courses is normally an introductory corporate finance course and an introductory investments course. These more basic courses should have covered the fundamentals of fixed-income mathematics, such as the definition and calculation of yield to maturity, and basic options concepts such as terminal payoff diagrams for European calls and puts.

Although they have been used extensively in other courses, the cases were primarily developed for a second-year MBA course at HBS called Capital Markets. The course covers primarily fixed income securities and derivatives. The course is designed to give second-year MBA students a more advanced treatment of fixed income (FI) securities than they would obtain during the first-year curriculum, from the mathematics of FI to the characteristics of the markets FI instruments trade in. It covers topics ranging from the application of duration and convexity, to asset/liability management, and to the creation of synthetic credit structures through securitization. At Harvard Business School, it is the main analytical course for students who intend to pursue careers in sales and trading, hedge funds, risk management, and so on. Along with fixed-income concepts, the course also provides a thorough introduction to derivative securities.

At HBS, courses are taught entirely by the case method. The cases in this book have been conceived to support the entire course we just described. They can therefore be used by instructors as the basis for an entire course. It does not mean, though, that the cases in this book have to be used together. Each case can be—and has been—successfully used on a stand-alone basis. We certainly expect, therefore, that some instructors will selectively pick cases in the book to supplement a lecture-based course

[1] Some of the cases are also used in courses covering investment management and corporate finance.

that is based on a traditional textbook. The cases would then serve to reinforce the material presented in lectures and text.

Before we go into more detail about the book's content and design, let's first address an important question: why should students worry about financial instruments in the first place?

WHY STUDY FINANCIAL INSTRUMENTS?

Economic Trends Breeding Financial Innovation

The last 35 years have seen an unprecedented pace of financial innovation. A whole new range of financial instruments are now available: from basic equity derivatives, such as single-stock calls and puts that trade on large organized exchanges (such as the Chicago Board Options Exchange and the International Securities Exchange) to more complicated products, like collateralized mortgage-backed securities and swaptions that trade directly between financial actors (in the over-the-counter, OTC, market.) The use of these instruments is not limited to obscure hedge funds, but has become standard operating procedure at most large- and mid-sized businesses, whether public or private, financial or non-financial. As a result, the modern business manager now needs to be well-trained in financial instruments and the capital markets. The enormous growth over the past decades in courses covering these subjects is testament to the importance of financial instruments.

At their base, all financial instruments were conceived to handle an overall increase in volatility in the financial markets. As markets became increasingly unpredictable, with several previously stable economic quantities fluctuating in ways not seen before, innovation in financial instruments was seen as a way to come up with tools to balance the new volatilities. Among the economic factors that grew increasingly unstable was for instance inflation volatility, which grew substantially in the 1960s and even more from the 1970s through the 1990s. Many reasons have been cited for this increase, including the suspension of the convertibility of dollars to gold. Figure 1 shows how inflation volatility has increased since the 1970s.

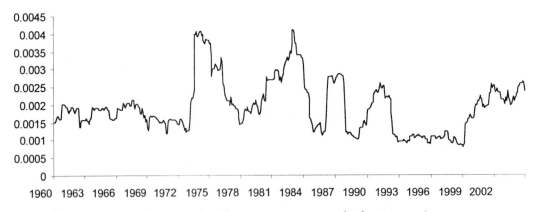

Figure 1 Inflation Volatility, 1960–2004 (based on U.S. Department of Labor Statistics)

Note: Calculated as rolling 20-month measures of Consumer Price Index for All Urban Consumers, monthly frequency.

Source: Consumer Price Index For All Urban Consumers, from U.S. Department of Labor: Bureau of Labor Statistics, ⟨http://www.bls.gov/⟩, accessed February 2005.

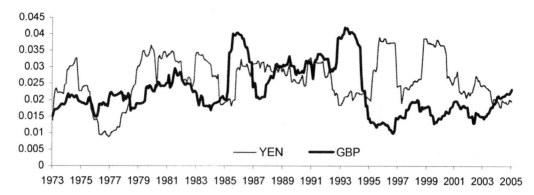

Figure 2   Exchange Rate Volatility: USD/GBP and JPY/USD: 1973–2005

Note: USD/GBP: Calculated as rolling 20-month volatility of U.S. /U.K Foreign Exchange Rate, monthly frequency.
JPY/USD: Calculated as rolling 20-month volatility of Japan/U.S. Foreign Exchange Rate, monthly frequency.
Source: Board of Governors of the Federal Reserve System, ⟨www.federalreserve.gov⟩, accessed February 2005.

Following the increase in inflation volatility, there was then also a rise in exchange rate volatility. The Bretton Woods agreement, which had fixed exchange rates between currencies, was dissolved in 1971. As a result, price risk for cross-border transactions grew forcefully, whether they were transactions in financial or real goods, as shown in Figure 2.

In addition to these two volatilities, interest rate volatility soon also presented itself, as the U.S. Federal Reserve Bank in 1979 ceased its policy of interest rate targeting and changed to a policy of money supply targeting. (The Fed believed this would be a better way of combating the rise in inflation witnessed during the past decade.) Financial institutions now saw an increase in volatility on both sides of their balance sheets. For example, banks could no longer safely finance long-term fixed-rate loans (to borrowing customers) with short-term floating rate deposits (from depositing customers) as short-term rates became more volatile than long-term rates. Figure 3 exemplifies this by showing the volatility of the 3-month Treasury Bill between 1965 and 2005.

Commodity prices, led by oil price volatility, reacted to the changes in economic fundamentals around the world and also increased in volatility. As an example, Figure 4 shows the volatility for crude materials between 1960 and 2005.

The cost of human capital also started to fluctuate, as seen in a higher volatility of unemployment (see Figure 5).

Ways to Handle Volatility: Financial Engineering Is Born

The reaction to all of this volatility was a demand by investors[2] for financial instruments that could transfer volatility to those economic institutions and investors that could best bear this risk. On the most basic level, there was an enormous increase in investors who

---

[2] By investors we mean generally all economic agents, from retail investors to financial institutions to corporations.

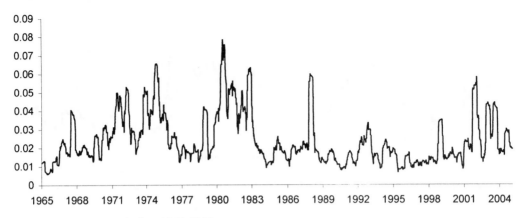

Figure 3 Interest Rate Volatility, 1965–2005

Note: Calculated as rolling 20-week volatility of 3-month Treasury Bill, weekly frequency.

Source: Board of Governors of the Federal Reserve System, ⟨www.federalreserve.gov⟩, accessed February 2005.

simply wanted to remove certain risks off their balance sheets entirely. These investors either found themselves with risks they did not want at all or with too heavy exposure to certain types of risk. (As most financial textbooks outline, the most basic way to reduce volatility is through diversification. Put simply, if you have too much of, say, interest rate risk, get rid of the investments that carry it and pick up other investments that are low on interest rate risk, but perhaps high on currency risk.) Therefore, the investors who found themselves too heavily invested in certain types of risks, and thus less than perfectly diversified, realized they were paying a premium in the form of opportunity costs for the additional risk they were bearing.[3] Thus, these investors were

[3] Rather than earning a risk premium on all of the risk they were bearing, the portion of risk that was diversifiable, or non-systematic, earned them zero risk premiums. They simply earned the risk-free rate on this risk. Thus, some of their risk capacity was essentially being underutilized or earning sub-par returns.

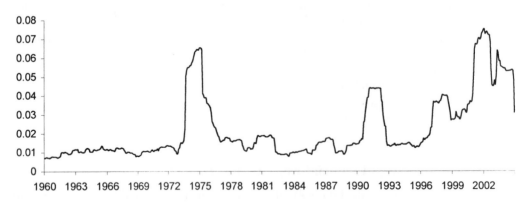

Figure 4 Commodity Volatility, 1960–2005 (based on Producer Price Index for Crude Materials for Further Processing)

Note: Calculated as rolling 20-week volatility of Producer Price Index: Crude Materials for Further Processing, monthly frequency.

Source: U.S. Department of Labor: Bureau of Labor Statistics, ⟨www.federalreserve.gov⟩, accessed February 2005.

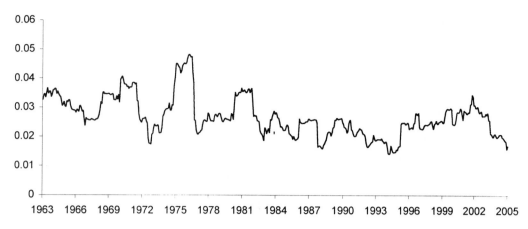

Figure 5   Unemployment Volatility, 1963–2005 (based on U.S. Department of Labor Statistics)

Note: Calculated as rolling 20-month measures of Unemployed: 16 Years & Over, monthly frequency.

Source: Unemployed: 16 Years & Over, from U.S. Department of Labor: Bureau of Labor Statistics, ⟨http://www.bls.gov/⟩, accessed February 2005.

willing to pay a small premium (less than the opportunity costs they were already bearing) to obtain risks that better diversified their assets.

The need to transfer risk resulted in an explosion of new financial instruments that were capable of "slicing and dicing" volatility and moving the individual slices to investors who could best make use of specific types of volatility. This process of creating financial instruments—of "slicing risk"—came to be known as "financial engineering."

As a result of the increase in risk and the number of instruments created to deal with this risk, it is now virtually impossible for a manager overseeing a substantial business, whether a financial or non-financial business, to be successful without a thorough understanding of these financial instruments and their value in hedging and diversifying. The use of complex financial instruments has risen substantially in most parts of the world—even among corporations. A recent survey found that well over 50% percent of non-financial businesses (public and private) in the United States and Europe used complex financial instruments of some form as part of their normal course of business.

Consequently, the demand for training in these instruments has witnessed an enormous increase. Programs cover everything from learning to decompose their structures to obtaining a basic understanding, and extend all the way to sophisticated valuation and hedging methodologies. Most business schools now offer multiple advanced courses in teaching about these instruments at the MBA and Executive Education levels. These courses typically have titles such as Financial Instruments, Capital Markets, Fixed Income Securities, Options and Futures, or Risk Management. In fact, many schools now offer specialized programs for those who want to train exclusively in these instruments and methods.[4] This book serves as an aid to such courses and programs.

---

[4] Many of these programs typically lead to a non-MBA degree such as a Master's in Financial Engineering.

TEACHING FINANCIAL INSTRUMENTS USING THE CASE METHOD

While it may seem unusual to teach quantitative material using the case method, the fixed-income course at HBS, Capital Markets, has been successfully taught using cases to many generations of students. If the main goal of teaching a course is simple presentation of formulas, then the case method is not ideal. However, if the course intends to present the topic of financial instruments in a solution-oriented manner that allows students to gain analytical, institutional, and functional knowledge and teaches them to employ this knowledge to solve new problems, then the case method is an excellent pedagogical approach.

In working through a case, the student not only must understand concepts at a formulaic level, but also needs to utilize these concepts to solve the problems presented in the case study. Almost always, working through these problems involves utilizing multiple concepts learned throughout the course. Moreover, real-world business situations usually require more than just financial skills to solve the problem at hand. Since students repeatedly have to deal with the question of "What would I do in this situation?" they have to combine their financial know-how with their skills in strategy, operations, marketing, negotiations, and so on. Thus, the case method not only reinforces and integrates the skills learned in other finance classes but also provides excellent cross-disciplinary training.

Most cases in this book range in length from six to fifteen pages of text, with up to fifteen more pages of exhibits. The exhibits normally present quantitative material, such as stock, bond, or option prices, as support for the students when discussing the case. The majority of the cases are so-called "field cases," where data and information were provided by the organization that is the focus of the case. (At times, some of this data may have been disguised or altered, either for teaching purposes or for confidentiality reasons.) Some "library cases" are also used; these draw their information fully from published material in the public domain. It is important to note that cases are not written to illustrate correct or incorrect handling of an administrative situation. They do not pretend to be descriptions of best practices. Furthermore, although they for the most part are based on actual events, cases never describe what happened. Instead, they focus on critical decisions that a company or an individual faced—and leave it up to students to discuss what decisions the protagonist could make.

In addition to cases, the book also makes limited use of so called "reading notes." Although concepts and theories for the most part are included in the cases themselves, reading notes are used to introduce basic concepts. The notes are short, always ending with short problem sets to help students practice.

Although many of the financial instruments described in this book originated in the United States and Europe, they are now utilized worldwide. The cases in this book reflect both the historical origin of financial engineering (with many cases set in the U.S. and Europe) as well as its international spread (with cases based in Korea, India, and elsewhere.) The cases can also be categorized by type of financial instrument that they cover and the type of financial institution that uses it. Table A shows the distribution of the cases in this book by these two variables.

BOOK STRUCTURE

The book consists of two sections: (1) fixed income securities and (2) derivative securities. A section includes several modules, each with several cases and reading notes.

TABLE A   Case Distribution by Financial Institution and Financial Instrument

Financial Instrument	Financial Institution					
	Investment Bank	Hedge Fund	Insurance Company	Corporate/ Government Treasury	Retail Bank	Financial Exchange
Bonds: Treasury Bonds	Deutsche Bank I and II (ICICI)			ICICI		
Bonds: Sovereign Bonds				Swedish Lottery Bonds (ICICI)		
Corporate Debt			Prudential Insurance	Tribune, Cox, DigaMem, ALZA		
Public Equities	Deutsche Bank II	Pine Street				(Deutsche Börse)
Private Equities						
Equity Derivatives	Sally Jameson	Ticonderoga, Nexgen (Pine Street)		Dell (Tribune, Dox, DigaMem, ALZA)		(Deutsche Börse, CBOE, ISE)
Securitized Products			Swiss Re	KAMCO	Bank Leu	
Market Structure						Deutsche Börse, CBOE, ISE
Real Options				RTY Telecom		
Interest Rate Derivatives	Enron, First Am Bank, Morgan Stanley (ICICI)			(ICICI)		(Deutsche Börse)

Note: Cases may cover more than one instrument and/or institution. Their secondary placements are indicated by putting the case name in parenthesis.

Each module normally begins with a set of concepts, introduced through a reading note (with a problem set). Then the module moves into applications, where case studies are used to introduce advanced securities and institutional features of the markets in which these securities trade. The cases all require students to analyze a new security. Students therefore develop a general framework for analyzing new financial instruments. This framework involves decomposing a security into simpler pieces, analyzing (pricing, hedging, etc.) each piece separately, and then putting these pieces back together for a unified analysis.

The common theme among these cases is how these securities enable risk structuring and transfer. Once a basic technical analysis is accomplished, it is easy to analyze the specific risk characteristics of the security. Then the question of how and why value is created through the risk structuring and transfer can be asked and answered. A proper discussion of this question is always the key to solving the case. Along the way, students also pick up institutional knowledge about the markets in which the securities trade, the security design process, and the role and motivation of financial intermediaries, such as commercial banks, investment banks, insurance companies, and hedge funds.

Section 1: Fixed-Income Securities

The fixed income securities section is broken up into two modules: Concepts and Applications.

Module FI-1: Concepts   Although the book assumes that a student has prior exposure to and knowledge of basic fixed income mathematics, the Concepts module covers this and more advanced concepts of duration and convexity in two reading notes. It starts with a reading note called **"Note on Bond Valuation and Returns"** that introduces the concept of compounding conventions (this also serves to review yield-to-maturity calculations) and conversions between the various compounding conventions. The following case, **"Deutsche Bank: Finding Relative-Value Trades,"** illustrates the use of these conventions in a trade being pitched by a fixed-income research group to customers. The case allows the student to learn how to analyze a trade in the Treasury market. It requires computation of yields and introduces the concept of a term structure model (though it does not require the student to develop such a model), and model-based arbitrage trading. The student also learns how the sales and trading business model functions in a typical investment bank.

After refreshing the basics of fixed income through the reading note and case, the module continues with the more advanced notions of duration and convexity. Again, a reading note, **"Note on Duration and Convexity,"** introduces the concepts, which measure interest rate sensitivity (risk) of a security. The note is followed by a case that directly uses the concepts from the reading note, **"Ticonderoga: Inverse Floating Rate Bond."** A very short case, it asks students to imagine that they are responsible for the fund's capital management overview, overseeing how the fund treats the various risks it takes on. In this particular case, Ticonderoga is considering an investment in a structured fixed income product: an inverse floating rate bond. The fund's policy is to hedge interest rate risk, maintaining a duration and convexity neutral portfolio—and the case allows students to plan and structure the hedge needed for this particular fixed-income product. The next case also ties into the concepts in the reading notes—it is an asset/liability management case called **"100-Year Liabilities at Prudential Insurance."** This case puts the student in the shoes of an asset/liability manager at an insurance company who is trying to hedge extremely long-maturity liabilities. It allows students to utilize their understanding of duration and convexity calculations and demonstrates the pitfalls of such calculations. The case also gives students a good understanding of the business model of an insurance company.

Module FI-2: Applications   A chance for more detailed practice follows in the Applications module, which is based on eight cases covering eight companies and eight different situations of risk structuring where fixed-income securities are used. The cases introduce a number of new securities (mortgage backed securities, catastrophe bonds, lottery bonds, collateralized debt obligations, and swaps.) While these cases may be done in any order, the ordering in the book is the order in which they are typically taught in the Capital Markets course at Harvard Business School.

The first case, **"Deutsche Bank: Discussing the Equity Risk Premium,"** looks at fixed income in a broader context by comparing the investment opportunity in U.S. Treasuries to that of U.S. equities. This case is also set at Deutsche Bank, where the chief fixed-income strategist is trying to decide how to advise clients on the equity to fixed-income asset allocation decision. The student needs to do a careful duration calculation to analyze this case, which demonstrates a common mistake made in the calculation of duration of equities. The case helps students further their understanding of duration and convexity and their applications, and also forces students to compare two of the largest markets in the world: the U.S. Treasury market and the U.S. equity market. Some institutional details about these markets are presented in addition to information about the sell-side business of a bank.

From the U.S. Treasury market, the book takes the student to the market for sovereign bonds in the next case: **"Swedish Lottery Bonds."** This case puts forth an unconventional bond used by Sweden's National Debt Office for its financing: a lottery bond. The student is asked to analyze how the country uses this bond and to evaluate whether the innovative nature of this bond makes it a good deal for the country or not. The case introduces students to analytical concepts such as bootstrapping a yield curve and institutional concepts such as the difference between sourcing financing from retail investors vs. institutional investors (differences in how they view risk) and introduces aspects of behavioral finance. A major part of this case is the notion of liquidity risk, and this turns out to be an important source of the value created by lottery bonds. The case also introduces the concept of credit risk, as lottery bond investors are exposed to sovereign default risk.

The next two cases switch the institutional focus from government bonds to the asset-backed securities markets. These two cases, which are closely related to each other (and ideally should be done sequentially), discuss the market for catastrophe bonds. The first case, **"Bank Leu's Prima Cat Bond Fund,"** takes the view of a buy-side institution (a fund within a private bank managing high net worth individuals' money), and the second case, **"Catastrophe Bonds at Swiss Re,"** takes the view of an issuer (a re-insurance company looking to securitize its re-insurance contracts). The cases provide an introduction to securitization, with an institutional overview of the process and some specific details about the process in the context of catastrophe risk.

The next three cases continue with the theme of securitization in the context of three other markets: the mortgage-backed securities, or MBS, market (**"Mortgage Backs at Ticonderoga"**), the market for collateralized loan obligations, CLOs, (**"KAMCO and the Cross-Border Securitization of Korean Non-Performing Loans"**), and the market for collateralized bond obligations, CBOs (**"Nexgen: Structuring Collateralized Debt Obligations (CDOs)"**).[5] The MBS case is from the perspective of a U.K. hedge fund that invests in MBSs; while the CLO case is from the perspective of the Korean government contemplating issuing CLOs; and the CBO case is from the perspective of a boutique investment bank in Paris that is putting together a structured solution for a client. Together these cases provide the student with a comprehensive introduction to securitization and structuring securitized products, allowing the development of

---

[5] The instructor should note that credit derivatives are both a fixed income security and derivatives security. As such, the case can be used in this section as well as the credit derivatives module of the derivatives securities section. If used in the fixed income section, detailed discussion of credit risk should be avoided, unless the students have been exposed to the Merton model on credit risk.

analytical skills and institutional knowledge. These cases also ground students in the concepts of risk structuring and transfer, as securitization is one of the most popular financial vehicles used these days for this purpose.

The final reading note and case introduces students to swaps. The reading note, **"Note on Forward Contracts and Swaps,"** develops the student's knowledge of forward contracts and introduces swaps as simply a portfolio of forward contracts. All of the needed analytical concepts are developed in this note. The case that follows, **"The Enron Odyssey (A): The Special Purpose of SPEs,"** utilizes the understanding of swaps developed in the reading note to analyze a set of complicated off-balance sheet swap transactions that Enron undertook to move asset risk. The case illustrates the uses of structured swaps in a practical setting and also allows students to gain institutional insights into the structuring process. The instructor can use these cases to demonstrate how structuring can be accomplished in both "proper" and "improper" ways, as some of the structures discussed in these cases led to the ultimate demise of Enron.

Section 2: Derivative Securities (DS)

The second major section of the book deals with derivative securities. It is intended to introduce students to the basic properties of options, their trading characteristics, and valuation techniques. The central focus of this section is a production-based framework for understanding derivative securities. This framework simply views all derivative products as simply outputs of a manufacturing process; the manufacturing process itself is the algorithm that accomplishes dynamic replication, and the inputs into the manufacturing process are the basis instruments of the cash markets that make up the replicating portfolio. For example, an equity option is the output from a manufacturing process that takes as inputs a short-term T-bill and the underlying stock; the manufacturing process is the replication algorithm laid out in Black-Scholes.

The section assumes very little prior background other than definitional knowledge of calls and puts. It starts with equity options because this is usually the most familiar context for students to study options. Special attention is then given to the fastest growing segment of this market: the market for credit risk derivatives. The next module introduces fixed-income derivatives. The last module covers the major derivatives markets of the world and the myriad issues facing these markets. The section then finishes with a case on real options.

Module DS-1: Equity Options: Concepts   After providing an introduction to equities, the section then moves to a module on basic equity option concepts that includes two reading notes and two cases. The first reading note, **"Note on Basic Option Properties,"** gives the definition of options, introduces payoff diagrams, and provides simple option comparative statistics such as how the value of an option is related to the underlying cash instrument's volatility. This note is then followed by a case, **"Dell Computer Corporation: Share Repurchase Program,"** which introduces a common practice employed by technology companies: selling puts and buying calls on their own stock. Students in this case are required to utilize their knowledge of option payoff diagrams and put-call parity to reframe this transaction into other economically equivalent forms. Students get their first sense of how financial engineering can be used to view transactions in a different form that gives greater insight about the economics of the transaction.

The second reading note covers the valuation of options and is followed by a case that requires students to immediately apply the concepts from the reading note. The reading note, **"Note on Option Valuation,"** begins with binomial valuation of European and American options and moves to the Black-Scholes/Merton model as a limiting case of the binomial model. This particular approach is taken for pedagogical reasons; students obtain a more intuitive feel for the Black-Scholes/Merton model once they understand and "get their hands dirty" with dynamic replication in a discrete-time setting. The binomial model is the simplest discrete-time setting, so this is the approach we start with. The case **"Sally Jameson—1999"** then covers a financial product known as a "stock loan" offered by a firm called Derivium Capital. The case requires the student to decompose the stock loan product into a set of options, drawing on the student's knowledge from the first reading note, and then to value these options, which requires the second reading note. After this set of reading notes and cases, the student should have a basic comprehension of options and their properties, including the valuation of plain-vanilla European options.

Module DS-2: Equity Options: Applications   An extended module on equity option applications then follows. This module covers a range of real-world applications and covers a number of different securities, with a particular emphasis on structured debt products, or debt-equity hybrids. Because of the emphasis on structured debt, the instructor can also use the module to reinforce some of the concepts introduced in the fixed-income section. However, as emphasized earlier, the fixed-income section is not a prerequisite for doing the options section.

The first case in the applications module, **"Pine Street Capital,"** takes place in the world of equity options, since it is often the easiest setting in which to learn about derivatives. The problem put forth in the case is that of a hedge fund facing a very unusual risk: a time-variation in market betas in its portfolio. The learning objective is then to help students understand that when there is a time-variation in betas, a simple linear hedge (such as the market) leaves the investor exposed to the nonlinearities in the time variation. The only way to hedge this is to use nonlinear instruments—and options are the perfect example of that. Students then learn that nonlinear risk is a great area in which to apply options. They are asked to solve exactly for the type of hedge that the hedge fund needs to implement. In so doing, students learn about concepts of delta and gamma hedging. Instructors should note that this is the main case in this book they can use to teach about the concepts of delta and gamma in an options setting. The concepts of duration and convexity in fixed income (which are the counterparts to delta and gamma in an equity context) were covered in the fixed-income section, which gives the instructor a chance to make the comparison between duration/convexity and delta/gamma.

The next three cases in this module cover structured debt products. The cases share a common approach: they are all about corporations that face a particular problem. In the case **"Tribune Company: The PHONES Proposal,"** the problem faced is taxes. In **"Cox Communications, Inc., 1999,"** the problem is taxes as well as fundraising. In **"DigaMem Inc.,"** the problem is purely one of raising financing. In all three cases, the proposed solution is a structured debt product—that is, a debt instrument with a rather complicated equity option embedded in it. In "Tribune," the proposed solution is known as "participating hybrid option note exchangeable securities", or PHONES. In the Cox case, the solution is a financial instrument called Feline Prides. In the DigaMem case, the solution is a floorless convertible. All three cases illustrate to students how options can solve a wide variety of general business and finance problems—and since these particular equity instruments are somewhat complicated, the students really have to rely on their fundamental knowledge of options to decompose the instruments into their fundamental parts. In essence, all three cases force students to work with the basics of financial engineering: to take a seemingly overwhelming problem, break it down into smaller and more manageable parts, and then solve each part separately, so that in combination they solve the larger problem. Any CFO can attest to this: new financial solutions are presented every day, but the actual heart of financial engineering is found in how you combine these solutions to solve larger business and finance problems.

Finally, the case **"ALZA and Bio-Electro Systems (A): Technological and Financial Innovation"** deals with synthetic debt. A biotech firm is trying to raise financing for a very risky project. The solution they propose to use is a complicated financial structure called SWORDS. Just as in the previous three cases, the student can decompose the structure into its basic blocks, and in doing so learn that the (at first seemingly unmanageable) structure is really nothing more than simple debt—that is, synthetic debt. Although at first glance the structure does not look like a bond, after further study and decomposing, the student realizes the structure works just like a bond. This case serves as the perfect setting in which to understand the basic Merton model of default risk, and therefore serves as a perfect transition to the next module on credit risk products.

Module DS-3: Credit Derivatives   In this module, you find one reading note and two cases. The reading note, **"Note on Credit Derivatives,"** gives the basic underlying model that can be used for the further credit risk analysis the student needs to do in this module. It also includes several examples such as asset swaps, credit default swaps, total rate of return swaps, and credit spread options.

The module's first case, **"First American Bank: Credit Default Swaps,"** focuses on credit default swaps (CDSs). The problem that First American Bank faces is one that every bank in the world encounters. To keep an important client, the bank needs to grant a loan to this client—but the bank does not want the credit risk that is associated with the loan. On the one hand, they want to keep the customer, but on the other hand, they abhor the extra credit risk. CDSs can then be used as an instrument to move the credit risk to other financial institutions. This case not only serves as an introduction to CDSs, but also requires the students to apply their knowledge of the Merton model (introduced in the reading note on Option Valuation) to the mechanics of a credit default swap. In so doing, students have to develop a thorough understanding of the Merton model, as well as of the mechanics of a CDS. The instructor should note that the case is extensive and is normally used on a two- or three-day basis at Harvard Business School.

While the First American Bank case is a very quantitative and mathematically involved case, the other case in this module, **"Morgan Stanley and TRAC-X: The Battle for the CDS Indexes Market,"** is more strategic and lends itself to a much more qualitative discussion. The First American Bank case looked at CDSs from a user's point of view; the Morgan Stanley and TRAC-X case looks at it from the perspective of a supplier. Morgan Stanley is one of the world's top players in credit default swaps and credit risk derivatives, and is running the CDS Index TRAC-X. However, TRAC-X is under attack by a competing index, iBoxx. Morgan Stanley now has to decide how to face this challenge: should they continue to compete and run two separate indexes; should they fold and leave the market to iBoxx; or should they pursue a merger? The case helps students learn about one of the fastest growing marketplaces in the world, the CDS market. The instructor can use the case to impart institutional knowledge about how sell-side firms function, about the financial innovation process (how new securities start and get traded first in the OTC market, and then gradually become a commodity and move to an exchange). In addition, the case can be used as strategy case.

Module DS-4: Interest Rate Derivatives   The book continues with a short module on Interest Rate Derivatives, consisting of one note and one case. The note, **"Introduction to Interest Rate Options,"** covers floors, caps, and swaptions. Floors and caps are introduced by analogy to equity calls and puts. As with calls and puts on equity, a put-call parity relationship is shown to exist between caps, floors, and swaps. The student, who already learned about the put-call parity in an equity context, should rather quickly grasp these concepts in an interest rate context. (It is important for the instructor to note that this note draws on the student's knowledge of the equity world, in a method we believe simple and intuitive but that is not often used in a teaching setting. The analogy that is used is that an equity put, an equity call, and stock in the equity world are exact analogies in the interest rate world to a floor, a cap, and a swap.)

The subsequent case, **"Advising on Currency Risk at ICICI Bank,"** reinforces the concepts learned in the reading note through a hedging example. ICICI Bank, India's second largest bank, has been approached by a client, India's Power Finance Corporation Ltd (PFC), for advice on their currency exposure. ICICI Bank proposes a hedge that involves multiple interest rates and currencies.

Module DS-5: Equity and Options Exchanges   The previous module concluded the book's coverage of financial instruments, and no new instruments are presented from this point on. Instead, the book now goes on to focus on *where* these instruments are traded. Such knowledge has so far been only summarily introduced, since a detailed understanding and discussion of the markets has not been needed or undertaken. However, in this module on equity and options exchanges, we discuss the evolution of financial markets, how they arise, the actors in the markets, and the major trends or market forces. This is done in the context of the major derivatives exchanges in the world, each one described in its own case: **"Deutsche Börse," "The Chicago Board Options Exchange (CBOE),"** and **"The International Securities Exchange: New Ground in Options Markets."**

German-based Deutsche Börse is the parent company of Eurex and the largest derivative exchange in the world. CBOE is the world's first option exchange, and was for a long time also the largest. The all-electronic ISE is an up-and-coming options exchange that very quickly has come to rival the CBOE in size and activity. In all three cases, students are put in the shoes of a senior executive at each of these exchanges and asked to deal with the various competitive issues that each exchange faces. All exchanges face issues such as the trends to automation, globalization, and consolidation. Through the cases, students learn about the specifics of those three aspects in how they pertain to each exchange. In the Deutsche Börse case, the exchange is contemplating an acquisition of Clearstream, a clearing, settlement, and custody company, and is trying to determine the synergies and costs such an acquisition would bring to Deutsche Börse's other businesses, especially Eurex, its derivatives exchange. In the CBOE case, the world's first and for a long term the largest derivatives exchange, CBOE, is discussing how to deal with competing exchanges that are highly automated. A possible strategic move would be to implement a hybrid solution that combines the traditional floor-based exchange with a floorless, electronic part. CBOE has to contemplate the pros and cons of such a move, as well as how they would implement it. In the ISE case, students meet an upstart exchange, which is purely automated, electronic, and floorless. The case contrasts the issues the students just faced in the CBOE case.

Module DS-6: Real Options   The section concludes with a case on real options, **"RTY Telecom: Network Expansion."** Real options have been a topic of significant discussion and research since the mid-1990s, but very few concrete examples of the application have emerged from practice. This case presents one such example: a telecommunications company is looking to expand its broadband capacity. It has two ways of doing so: it can either purchase the capacity as needed on the spot market, or it can buy a piece of equipment from Nortel, which would allow for easy and quick future upgrades in capacity at fixed prices. However, purchasing this piece of equipment is substantially more expensive than simply expanding capacity by purchasing in the spot market. The equipment, though more expensive, gives the company "optionality," just as a basic call option gives a company the right but not the obligation to purchase something. The question in the case is whether the optionality given to the company is worth the additional cost that the company has to pay for it. The case gives students a direct example of a real option and forces them to perform a real option valuation.

ALTERNATIVE WAYS TO WORK THROUGH THE BOOK

At HBS, the various courses that have used the material in this book have typically led off with the fixed-income securities section of the book—hence its place in the book. Starting with fixed-income securities will be more fruitful if students have already been introduced to some basic fixed-income mathematics. The concepts of duration and convexity hedging can then be taught early on in the course, which makes option replication an easier discussion in the second part of the course.

Alternatively, one could lead off with equity derivative securities, the second section of the book, where we assume constant interest rates, then go to fixed-income securities, where interest rates are implicitly assumed to be time-varying, and then come back to interest rate derivative securities. This approach would work successfully with students who have had some basic exposure to options.

It should also be noted that the two sections have been set up independently of each other. Therefore, a course focused exclusively on derivative securities, such as an options and futures course, could utilize the cases in the derivative securities section of the book without having done the cases in the fixed-income securities part of the course. Similarly, a course focused exclusively on fixed-income securities can use the cases in that section of the book independently from the cases in the derivative securities section.

In addition to the successful use of the cases in this book at the MBA level, the cases can be (and have been) used at the Executive Education level as well.[6] In writing this book, we have strived to balance the material in the cases so that investment bankers designing securities as well as corporate CFOs looking to apply securities to risk management problems will find something informative in every case. Naturally, some cases will appeal more to one audience than the other. Select groups of cases can therefore be combined and used for focused courses aimed at practitioners at the junior and executive levels on the buy-side, sell-side, or in corporate settings.

---

[6] While cases at HBS are taught to students with an undergraduate degree, we believe selective cases can also be used successfully at the undergraduate level with advanced business students.

Given how pervasive the use of sophisticated financial instruments has become, we have tried to make the cases in this book flexible enough to be accessible to managers and students in different educational settings and possessing varied backgrounds/experiences. This is simply a reflection of the evolution of business—as firms become more global, the goods and services markets across the world become more integrated, and as the number of sophisticated financial instruments available keeps growing, the need for flexible learning tools increases as well. We developed this casebook with this need for flexibility in mind, and we hope it will serve as a useful pedagogical tool in many settings and for many audiences.

Boston and Paris, November 2005

APPENDIX: CASE DESCRIPTIONS

Section 1: Fixed-Income Securities

Module FI-1   Fixed-Income Securities: Concepts

Reading Note: Note on Bond Valuation and Returns (HBS no. 205-008). All securities can be evaluated based on certain common characteristics: value, rate of return, risk, maturity, and so on. This note looks at how bonds are valued and how their rates of return are computed. It begins with basic definitions and features of fixed-income instruments and proceeds to basic bond mathematics. The note also provides an overview of the U.S. Treasury market as well as some national markets for other important domestic government bonds.

Case: Deutsche Bank: Finding Relative-Value Trades (HBS no. 205-059). Deutsche Bank's Fixed Income Research Group in the London office is looking for yield curve trades that they can pitch to clients as well as for their proprietary trading desk. The group has data on recent bond trades and a proprietary term structure model, which they can use to develop trading ideas. The case helps students understand how the sales-and-trading function works within an investment bank. It allows the instructor to have a qualitative discussion of the motivations and incentives of sell-side firms, of the various functions within these firms, and how these firms interact with clients. The case also allows the instructor to run a purely technical class on how to bootstrap a yield curve, construct term structure models, and spot potential arbitrage opportunities along the yield curve.

Reading Note: Note on Duration and Convexity (HBS no. 205-025). The note introduces two measures of price sensitivity for financial instruments: duration and convexity. These measures are normally used to gauge how sensitive a bond's price is to a change in interest rate levels. However, as concepts, both duration and convexity have wider application: they take into account any change for any risk factor affecting the price of any financial instrument.

Case: Ticonderoga: Inverse Floating Rate Bond (HBS no. 205-113). This case is a simple interest hedging exercise. The hedge fund Ticonderoga is considering an investment in a structured fixed income (FI) product—an inverse floating rate bond, or inverse floater—designed by a U.S. investment bank. Ticonderoga's normal policy is to hedge interest rate risk, maintaining a duration and convexity neutral portfolio. Because of the complicated nature of the structured product, the protagonist must now figure out how to hedge this product. The case requires students to first figure out how the structured product in question works, using fairly detailed no-arbitrage analysis. Students must then apply duration and convexity concepts that they have learned in the preceding note to decide how to structure interest rate risk.

Case: 100-Year Liabilities at Prudential Insurance (Not an HBS publication). Carlos Arrom, Managing Director of Asset Liability & Risk Management at Prudential Insurance, is contemplating the extremely long dated liabilities (some of over 100 years) that Prudential has. The firm has duration hedged these liabilities, but there seems to be substantial interest rate exposure left. Carlos is trying to analyze what is going wrong in the firm's duration hedging program. The case requires students to utilize their understanding of duration and convexity hedging; it demonstrates the assumptions behind these calculations; and also shows the pitfalls when these assumptions do not hold in the real world. The case also gives students a good understanding of the business model of an insurance company.

Module FI-2   *Fixed-Income Securities: Applications*

Case: Deutsche Bank: Discussing the Equity Risk Premium (HBS no. 205-040). Two members of Deutsche Bank's Fixed Income Research Group in London are discussing how to advise clients on asset allocation between equity and bonds. A critical aspect to this decision is the equity risk premium, and the case discusses a unique way developed by the bank for understanding the implications of the risk premium. The case furthers students' understanding of how a sales-and-trading group works within an investment bank. In addition to allowing the instructor to have a qualitative discussion of the motivations and incentives of sell-side firms, the case also allows the instructor to run a purely technical class on basic portfolio mathematics, estimation of the equity risk premium, and how the equity risk premium affects the bonds vs. equities asset allocation decision.

Case: Swedish Lottery Bonds (HBS no. 204-048). Profiling nonsystematic risk for a bond investor, the case describes lottery bond issues by the Swedish National Debt Office (SNDO). Swedish lottery bonds are a specific type of financial fixed-income instrument for Swedish retail investors. The distinctive feature of lottery bonds is that, unlike traditional institutional bonds, the normally guaranteed interest—the coupon—here only is paid as "wins" to bondholders selected in drawings. Anders Holmlund, head of the SNDO analysis group, is reviewing the proposal for the next lottery bond issue. While reviewing the features of the bond issue, he also considers the larger picture: What are the benefits to the Debt Office of issuing lottery bonds, especially in view of a recently launched Internet-based sales system that allows retail investors to take part in government bond auctions? Through the case, students reinforce bond math calculations and go through how to construct yield curves and forward curves. Students also explore the issue of systematic versus non-systematic risk and the effects of behavioral biases on the premium for systematic and non-systematic risk.

Case: Bank Leu's Prima Cat Bond Fund (HBS no. 205-005). In 2001, Bank Leu, a Swiss private bank, is considering creating the world's first public fund for catastrophe bonds. Cat bonds are securities whose payments depend on the probability of a catastrophe occurring, such as an earthquake or a hurricane. Cat bonds are traditionally issued by large insurance or reinsurance companies. The case outlines the traditional reinsurance market and securitization efforts that have taken place in the past, and then focuses on Bank Leu's decision as a buy-side participant in the cat bond market. The case explores how insurance risks can be transferred to the capital markets and how risks in general can be brokered, securitized, and traded.

Case: Catastrophe Bonds at Swiss Re (HBS no. 205-006). In 2002, Swiss Re, the world's second largest insurance company, is considering securitizing parts of its risk portfolio in the capital markets. This would be a first for the company, which, until then, had never transferred risk off its balance sheet. Peter Geissmann, head of the Retrocession Group, is considering catastrophe bonds as a way of transferring risk. Cat bonds are securities whose payments depend on the probability of a catastrophe occurring, such as an earthquake or hurricane. The case outlines the traditional reinsurance market and securitization efforts that have taken place in the past, and then focuses on Swiss Re's decision as a sell-side participant in the bond market. The case helps students explore how insurance risk can be transferred to the capital markets and how risks in general can be brokered, securitized, and traded.

Case: Mortgage Backs at Ticonderoga (HBS no. 205-122). Ticonderoga is a small hedge fund that trades in Mortgage Backed Securities (MBSs). MBSs are securities created from pooled mortgage loans. They often appear as straightforward so-called "pass-throughs," but can also be pooled again to create collateral for a mortgage security known as a Collateralized Mortgage Obligation (CMO). CMOs allowed the cash flows from the underlying pass-throughs to be directed, so that different classes of securities—"tranches"—with different maturities, coupons, and risk profiles were created. In April 2005, the general managers of Ticonderoga are looking at the market data, trying to construct a trade given their view on the prepayment speed of mortgages, versus the implied prepayment speed they derive from the CMOs in the market. The case helps students learn about the institutional details behind the MBS market, and covers both the actors as well as the mechanics (with special emphasis on the important prepayment feature.) It also requires students to go through the mathematics and calculations behind MBSs—in essence, students are asked to behave as if they worked at a mortgage back trading desk.

Case: KAMCO and the Cross-Border Securitization of Korean Non-Performing Loans (HBS no. 205-037). This case covers the first international non-performing loan (NPL) securitization done in Korea. The CEO of KAMCO is trying to dispose of a portfolio of nonperforming commercial loans that the organization acquired from a number of banks. A group of investment bankers have proposed securitizing the loans and selling them to institutional investors. Securitization of loans (or any other type of assets) is not common in Korea, so the CEO must think through several factors as he decides whether or not to accept this proposal, the most important of which is the recovery price. The case helps students explore financial securitization in depth, and both structuring and valuation principles.

Case: Nexgen: Structuring Collateralized Debt Obligations (CDOs) (HBS no. 204-135). Luc Giraud, CEO of the structured finance solutions provider Nexgen Financial Solutions, is asked by a client to put together a solution so that the client can add AAA-rated bonds to its portfolio. The client cannot find suitably priced top-rated bonds in the market, and is now wondering whether Nexgen can use lower grade bonds to create AAA equivalent instruments. The case's main teaching point is the role of securitization. The process of securitization packages together securities to create new securities with different risk and return profiles. In this case, the student is exposed to a situation in which a financial intermediary creates value by putting together a package of securities and offering the client a risk tranche that the client could not otherwise obtain. If the case is taught more from a credit risk point of view, there is an additional learning point—the impact of correlation in credit risk in portfolios of collateralized debt securities.

Reading Note: Note on Forward Contracts and Swaps (HBS no. 205-118). The note introduces forward contracts and derives the spot-forward parity graphically through basic arbitrage principles. The note then goes on to introduce swap contracts as simply a portfolio of forward contracts. It also covers briefly the mathematics behind swaps as an extension of spot-forward parity calculations.

Case: The Enron Odyssey (A): The Special Purpose of "SPEs" (HBS no. 204-009). The board has asked Ron Tolbert, an employee in the Risk Assessment and Control Group, to analyze three SPE (Special Purpose Entities) transactions executed by Enron executives: the Destec, Rhythms, and Fishtail/Bacchus transactions, which were prominently featured in the Examiner's Report in the ensuing Enron bankruptcy. Tolbert's job is to assess why Enron used SPEs for these transactions, whether risk was successfully transferred off the balance sheet, and whether risk transfer was the only motivation. SPEs are used in virtually all structured finance transactions. They are standard tools for accomplishing certain business objectives, such as risk isolation, ownership clarification, and so on. In this case, students learn how SPEs can add value in structured finance transactions, as well as how improper use of these vehicles can lead to substantial value destruction.

Section 2: Derivative Securities

Module DS-1   *Equity Options: Concepts*

Reading Note: Note on Basic Option Properties (HBS no. 205-105). Options are contracts that give the right, but not the obligation, to either buy or sell a specific underlying security for a specified price on or before a specific date. This note uses this fundamental option definition to cover the basics of options, such as their payoff schemes, parameters that influence their value (stock price, strike price, volatility, time-to-maturity, interest rate, and dividends), put-call parity, and upper and lower bounds of options prices.

Case: Dell Computer Corporation: Share Repurchase Program (HBS no. 200-056). Dell announced a share repurchase program shortly after a significant stock price drop. In this announcement, the company also stated that it would use options contracts. This case looks at the options transactions and how they relate to Dell's employee stock option program and the share repurchase program. It helps students develop basic financial engineering concepts utilizing put and call options.

Reading Note: Note on Option Valuation (HBS no. 205-106). For every option, a fair price has to be established—but how do you actually price an option? Assuming a basic knowledge of options, this note covers two pricing methods: the binominal tree and the Black-Scholes/Merton formula.

Case: Sally Jameson—1999 (HBS no. 200-006). Sally Jameson has a large block of appreciated stock, which she is contemplating selling to purchase a home. She is comparing an outright sale, borrowing against the stock, shorting against the box, and a stock loan proposed by a small financial services firm. The case helps students deal with basic option analysis, tax implications, various means of liquidating a portfolio, and credit risk inherent in dealing with financial intermediaries.

Module DS-2 *Equity Options: Applications*

Case: Pine Street Capital (HBS no. 201-071). A technology hedge fund is trying to decide whether and how to hedge equity market risk. Its hedging choices are short-selling and options. The fund has just gone through one of the most volatile periods in NASDAQ's history, and it is trying to decide whether to continue its risk management program of short-selling the NASDAQ index or switch to a hedging program that utilizes put options on the index. The case introduces students to the use of equity derivatives in the context of money management, particularly the use of delta-hedging using options. It also teaches how and why risk management decisions are made in a simple leveraged hedge fund.

Case: Tribune Company: The PHONES Proposal (HBS no. 205-087). The Tribune Company is considering issuing a structured note in order to monetize its investment in another company, America Online (AOL). Tribune originally invested in AOL in 1991 and currently has approximately 10 million shares left of that investment. However, these shares are worth over $1.5 billion now, and if Tribune sells these shares outright, the capital gain will be nearly this entire amount. In order to dispose of these shares in a more tax efficient manner, Merrill Lynch has suggested to Tribune's CFO that the firm issue a new convertible security known as PHONES, Participating Hybrid Option Note Exchangeable Security. This case teaches students how to analyze structured notes. It shows them how to decompose the securities, value them, and derive where the valuation for these securities is coming from. Additionally, the secondary trading characteristics of OTC issues can be discussed; because these securities are customized products, secondary trading of these securities will not be as broad as exchange-traded products. The effects of this lack of liquidity are an important consideration in the valuation of these securities and Merrill Lynch's motivation for underwriting them.

Case: Cox Communications, Inc., 1999 (HBS no. 201-003). The case covers the decision of how much external financing a firm needs and what securities the firm should use to raise this financing. Cox Communications is a major player in the cable industry in the United States, which is consolidating due to technological changes and capabilities brought about by the Internet. The corporate treasure of Cox needs to decide how much external financing is necessary to finance a series of intra-industry acquisitions that Cox has recently undertaken. The choices are plain-vanilla equity, debt, asset sales, and a new equity-linked derivative known as Feline Prides, offered by Merrill Lynch. The treasurer and his team must make this decision facing the usual market constraints. There are also some special constraints, including the need to maintain financial flexibility for further acquisitions and the need to limit the dilution of Cox's largest shareholder, who owns nearly 70% of the firm. The case helps students explore how to make long- and short-term financing decisions, taking into account specific business conditions and risk.

Case: DigaMem Inc. (HBS no. 203-003). Small high-tech companies have a very difficult time financing themselves. The main driver behind this difficulty is that the projects themselves are risky, and there is an enormous scope for information asymmetry because the projects typically involve very complicated technology, which is well understood by the managers of the firm but much less so by the typical investor. One solution to this problem is convertible bonds. This case explores why convertible structures are particularly useful in these situations. DigaMem is a semiconductor firm with a promising new technology, but its CEO faces a difficult financing problem. He is considering issuing a new security: a floorless convertible bond, also known as a "toxic" convertible.

Case: ALZA and Bio-Electro Systems (A): Technological and Financial Innovation (HBS no. 293-124). To develop the next generation of risky products, ALZA, a mature and profitable biotechnology firm specializing in drug delivery systems, must raise $40 million. Organizational constraints and competitive concerns demand that the work be done inside the firm. However, accounting considerations and concerns about shareholders' reactions to the introduction of new risks to the firm lead the CEO to consider off-balance-sheet means to finance the new venture. To do this, the firm creates a new financing vehicle: a unit consisting of callable common stock plus warrants. This case examines the CEO's decision leading up to the issue of the units and the establishment of a new research and development subsidiary.

Module DS-3   Credit Derivatives

Reading Note: Note on Credit Derivatives (HBS no. 205-111). This note gives the basic underlying model for credit risk analysis, as well as covers basic credit risk derivatives, such as asset swaps, credit default swaps, total return of rate swaps, and credit spread options.

Case: First American Bank: Credit Default Swaps (HBS no. 203-033). The case discusses a bank's ability to manage its credit exposure to a particular client using credit default swaps. The case gives students a basic understanding of credit risk and credit derivative mechanics.

Case: Morgan Stanley and TRAC-X: The Battle for the CDS Indexes Market (HBS no. 203-033). Morgan Stanley's credit derivatives business, specifically its CDO (Collateralized Debt Obligation) business, has been hugely successful. One of its leading offerings is the TRAC-X product, jointly created and marketed by Morgan Stanley and JP Morgan. However, a new competitor, iBoxx, has entered the picture by offering a similar synthetic CDO product. Lisa Watkinson at Morgan Stanley must now decide how to respond to this new competition. This case teaches students who have some familiarity with credit derivatives, specifically credit default swaps, about the institutional structure of how these instruments trade. Students learn to utilize their knowledge of credit derivatives in a practical setting.

Module DS-4   Interest Rate Derivatives

Reading Note: Introduction to Interest Rate Options (HBS no. 205-112). This very short note covers floors, caps, and swaptions. The note requires students to have a basic understanding of puts and calls in an equity context, as it introduces floors and caps by analogy to equity calls and puts. As with calls and puts on equity, a put-call parity relationship is shown to exist between caps, floors, and swaps.

Case: Advising on Currency Risk at ICICI Bank (HBS no. 205-074). In March 2003, the Markets Advisory Group at ICICI Bank, India's second largest bank, has been approached by a client about a hedging transaction. The hedge involves multiple interest rates and currencies. Shilpa Kumar, head of the Markets Advisory Group, now has to put together a recommendation for the client. In her recommendation she can choose from a number of financial instruments including swaps, options, and futures contracts on interest rates and currencies. This case teaches students how to apply their knowledge of financial derivatives such as options, futures, and swaps in a practical situation: a hedging decision by a corporation.

Module DS-5   *Equity and Options Exchanges*

Case: Deutsche Börse (HBS no. 204-008). The case focuses on how Deutsche Börse's (the German stock exchange based in Frankfurt) acquisition of a 50% stake in Clearstream International, a company specialized in clearing, settlement, and custody of securities across borders, may or may not confirm its position as the world's largest securities trading and related technologies powerhouse. Deutsche Börse has become a "transaction engine" and operates as an exchange, offering a wide range of financial services and products (cash market operations, derivatives, information products, clearing, and settlement custody). The company uses technology to support and fuel innovation. The case helps students explore the strategic implications and the synergies and costs that acquiring Clearstream would bring to Deutsche Börse's other businesses, especially Eurex.

Case: The Chicago Board Options Exchange (CBOE) (HBS no. 205-073). The CBOE must decide how to respond to new competition in the market for financial options. Options have typically been a very illiquid asset class, despite the fact that many single-name options are listed on the CBOE, the second largest option exchange in the world. In response to this illiquidity, new option exchanges have started up offering electronic trading, with the hope of making the markets more liquid and capturing market share and profitability from the CBOE. The CBOE must now decide whether to ignore the competition and continue with its floor-based model of trading, or switch to an all-electronic trading model or some type of hybrid model. This case teaches students who are familiar with the basics of equity options some of the institutional details behind how these options trade and introduces students to the strategic and operational issues that executives at options exchanges (and generally all financial exchanges) currently face.

Case: The International Securities Exchange: New Ground in Options Markets (HBS no. 203-063). The case covers the equity options market and studies the major parties involved in the options trading process. It takes an in-depth look at the path taken by the International Securities Exchange (ISE) as it entered a mature exchange industry and transformed itself into a major competitor. The case provides an introduction to securities markets. Students are exposed to concepts of liquidity and transaction costs and are asked to question the function and design of securities exchanges. Sufficient data is provided for students to analyze a substantial pilot study to advise the exchange on its strategy going forward.

Module DS-6   *Real Options*

Case: *RTY Telecom: Network Expansion (HBS no. 205-102).* This case requires real option analysis to analyze a capital expenditure decision by a large regional telecommunications firm. The firm needs to add network capacity for its broadband offering and is trying to decide how to do this. One approach is simply to purchase this capacity in the spot market, while another approach would be to buy an expensive piece of equipment from Nortel Networks. The protagonist in the case is trying to do an NPV analysis of this equipment. The specific way the equipment functions gives the firm a portfolio of real options on broadband capacity. Therefore, to do the NPV analysis correctly, the protagonist must identify what the real options are and determine how to value them.

FIXED-INCOME SECURITIES: CONCEPTS

2

Note on Bond Valuation and Returns

All securities can be evaluated based on certain common characteristics: value, rate of return, risk, maturity, and so on. In this note, we look at how bonds are valued in general and how their rates of return are computed. Beginning with basic definitions and features of fixed income instruments, we then go through some basic bond mathematics and introduce basic concepts regarding rates of return.[1] Finally, the note provides an overview of the U.S. Treasury market as well as some national markets for other important domestic government bonds.

CLASSIFYING BONDS

At first glance, bonds appear to be simple contracts between a lender and a borrower by which the borrower promises to repay a loan with interest. However, bonds can take on many additional features. The classification of a bond depends on its type of issuer, maturity, coupon rate, and redemption features. Figure A shows a possible classification.

Bond Issuers

The issuer of the bond is a major determinant of a bond's expected return and risk. Governments, municipalities, corporations, and many other entities issue various forms of debt to investors. The largest debt market in the world is the market for U.S. government bonds. Securities issued by the U.S. government are considered to have the lowest default risk of any issuer—the likelihood of the U.S. government defaulting on its bonds is considered extremely small.

Professors George Chacko and Peter Hecht, Executive Director of HBS Europe Research Center Vincent Dessain, and Research Assistant Monika Stachowiak prepared this note as the basis for class discussion.

[1] For a more basic review of fixed income securities, see Joshua D. Coval, Peter Tufano, and Ivo Welch, "Note on Credit Markets," HBS Case No. 203-069 (Boston: Harvard Business School Publishing, 2004).

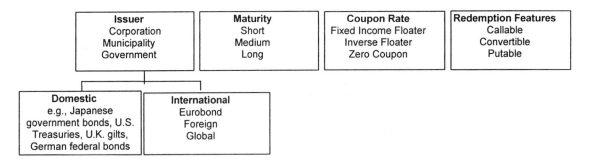

Figure A   Bond Classification

Source: Casewriter.

In addition to bonds being issued in the issuer's local currency, which will be the focus in this note, bonds may be issued in foreign currencies.

- A *eurobond* is denominated in a currency other than that of the country in which it is issued. For example, a euroyen bond is denominated in Japanese yen but issued in the U.S. (Note how the notation *euro* has no relation to either the continent Europe or the currency euro.) Eurobonds are popular debt instruments used by multinationals as well as foreign governments and supranationals (such as the World Bank).

- The issuers of *foreign bonds* are not domiciled in the country in which the bonds are sold and traded. These bonds are issued in the currency of the country in which they are sold. For example, Yankee bonds are dollar-denominated bonds that have been issued in the U.S. market by a foreign corporation or government. The Yankee market is typically dominated by foreign government issues or issues guaranteed by foreign governments.

- *Global bonds* are foreign bonds and eurobonds at the same time. They can be issued and traded as foreign bonds in some markets, while at the same time be registered and sold as eurobonds in other markets. This market is currently dominated by U.S. government agencies and corporations.

Term to Maturity

As with any loan, the issuer of a bond is a borrower that commits to return the principal amount at a predetermined time in the future, known as the *maturity*. Put differently, maturity is the time when the issuer will redeem the bond by paying the principal. Consequently, the *term to maturity* is simply the time during which the issuer agrees to meet the conditions of the bond's indenture.[2]

Generally, bonds with a maturity shorter than one year are considered short term. Bonds with a maturity between one and 10 years are viewed as intermediate term, and long-term bonds are those with a maturity of 10 years or more.

Principal and Coupon Rate

The actual amount issued in a bond is known as its principal. The principal value of a bond is what the issuer agrees to repay the bondholder at the maturity date.

For lending money to the bond issuer, the bondholder is compensated by periodic interest payments. These periodic payments are also known as coupon payments. The

---

[2] An indenture is simply the contract between the borrower and lender.

associated coupon rate can be thought of as the interest rate that the issuer agrees to pay each year on the principal amount. Mathematically, the coupon rate is multiplied by the principal amount of the bond to determine the coupon payment. Most bonds make periodic coupon payments, except for "zero-coupon" bonds, which make no coupon payments at all. The holder of a zero-coupon bond realizes interest by buying the bond substantially below the principal value (at a discount).

Most coupon payments are based on a fixed coupon rate. However, floating rate debt instruments also exist in which the coupon rate varies according to the movements of an underlying benchmark, such as the six-month Treasury-bill rate or six-month LIBOR.[3]

Redemption Features

Both investors and issuers are exposed to interest rate risk, since they are locked into either receiving or paying a set coupon rate over a specified period of time. For this reason, some bonds offer more flexibility for issuers or investors in terms of when they can choose to redeem the bond.

- *Callable* bonds give the bond issuer the right but not the obligation to redeem its issue of bonds before the bond's maturity. The issuer, however, must offer the bondholders a premium, normally expressed as a lower price. The optimal time for issuers to call their bonds is when the prevailing interest rate is lower than the coupon rate they are paying on the bonds. After calling its bonds, the company could then refinance its debt by reissuing bonds at a lower coupon rate.
- *Putable* bonds are the opposite of callable bonds. They give bondholders the right but not the obligation to sell their bond back to the issuer at a predetermined price.
- *Convertible* bonds give bondholders the right but not the obligation to convert their bonds into a predetermined number of equity shares at or prior to the bond's maturity. (This obviously only applies to corporate bonds.)

BOND PRICING

A bond is typically issued at par value of the principal amount. However, in the secondary market, the price of a bond can fluctuate greatly from its par value. The price of a bond, as with any asset, is determined by the present value of its expected cash flows and the discount rate used for each cash flow. The cash flows of a bond consist of:

1. Periodic coupon interest payments to the maturity date
2. The par value at maturity

Because a bond's cash flows occur at different points in time, the discount rate for each cash flow is generally different. If we define r_1 to be the discount rate for the first cash flow, r_2 to be the discount rate for the second cash flow, and so on, the price of a bond can then be computed using the following formula:

$$P = \frac{C}{1 + r_1} + \frac{C}{(1 + r_2)^2} + \frac{C}{(1 + r_3)^3} + \cdots + \frac{C}{(1 + r_n)^n} + \frac{M}{(1 + r_n)^n} \qquad [1]$$

[3] LIBOR (London Inter Bank Offered Rate) is the interest paid for dollars and euros at international markets in interbank borrowings. The LIBOR rate is fixed daily by the British Bankers' Association (BBA). It is similar to the U.S. Federal Reserve rate, in that it is used as a reference rate for other short-term interest rates.

where:

P = price

C = fixed coupon payment

M = maturity value

$r_1, r_2, r_3, \ldots, r_n$ = discount rates

n = number of periods

It is often more convenient to quote the price of a bond in terms of an interest rate rather than in some currency. However, in the formula above there are many interest rates that make up the price of a bond, so the question is, which one to use? The convention is to use a single interest rate called the *yield to maturity*. The yield to maturity is the single discount rate, which, if substituted for all of the discount rates in the valuation formula above, would give the same price of the bond. In mathematical terms:

$$r_1 = r_2 = r_3 = \ldots = r_n = y$$

where:

y = yield to maturity

The yield to maturity is the single interest rate that realizes the present value of the cash flows by holding the bond to a maturity equal to the price of that bond. Therefore, we can shorten our pricing formula to:

$$P = \sum_{t=1}^{n} \frac{C}{(1 + y)^t} + \frac{M}{(1 + y)^n} \qquad [2]$$

where:

t = time period when the payment is to be received

The formula above can be even further simplified:

$$P = C \left(\frac{1 - \dfrac{1}{(1 + y)^n}}{y} \right) + \frac{M}{(1 + y)^n} \qquad [3]$$

It is important to note that the yield to maturity is *not* the expected return of a bond. It is simply another way to quote a bond's price.

PRICE-YIELD RELATIONSHIP

A fundamental property of a bond is that its price changes in the opposite direction of the change in the interest rates. The reason is that the price of the bond is the present value of the cash flows; as the interest rate increases, the present value of the cash flows decreases, hence the price decreases. The opposite is true when the interest rate decreases; the present value of the cash flows increases, and therefore the price of the bond increases.

Let us go through a basic example to depict this general feature of all bonds; we will see how the price of a bond changes when the required yield varies. Let us calculate the price of a bond with a par value of $1,000 to be paid in 10 years, a coupon rate of 10%, and a required yield of 3%, 5%, 15%, and 25%. In our example we will assume that coupon payments are made annually to bondholders and that the next coupon payment is expected in 12 months.

When the required yield is 3%, you will see that the present value of the 10 annual coupon payments of $100 discounted at 3% is $1,597.11, calculated as

$$P = 100 \cdot \left[\frac{1 - \frac{1}{(1 + 0.03)^{10}}}{0.03} \right] + \frac{1000}{(1 + 0.03)^{10}} = \quad [4]$$

$$= 100 \cdot \frac{(1 - 0.744)}{0.03} + \frac{1000}{1.3439} =$$

$$= 100 \cdot 8.53 + 744.094 = \$1,597.11$$

If the required yield changes to 5% instead, we obtain:

$$P = 100 \cdot \left[\frac{1 - \frac{1}{(1 + 0.05)^{10}}}{0.05} \right] + \frac{1000}{(1 + 0.05)^{10}} = \quad [5]$$

$$= 100 \cdot \frac{(1 - 0.3861)}{0.05} + \frac{1000}{1.6289} =$$

$$= 100 \cdot 7.7217 + 613.91 = \$1,386.09$$

Then, for a required yield of 10%, we obtain:

$$P = 100 \cdot \left[\frac{1 - \frac{1}{(1 + 0.15)^{10}}}{0.15} \right] + \frac{1000}{(1 + 0.15)^{10}} = \quad [6]$$

$$= 100 \cdot \frac{(1 - 0.2471)}{0.15} + \frac{1000}{4.0455} =$$

$$= 100 \cdot 5.0187 + 247.18 = \$749.06$$

Finally, for a required yield of 15%, we obtain:

$$P = 100 \cdot \left[\frac{1 - \frac{1}{(1 + 0.25)^{10}}}{0.25} \right] + \frac{1000}{(1 + 0.25)^{10}} = \quad [7]$$

$$= 100 \cdot \frac{(1 - 0.8926)}{0.25} + \frac{1000}{9.3132} =$$

$$= 100 \cdot 3.57 + 107.37 = \$464.42$$

Using these calculations, we can depict the relationship between bond price and yield in a graph. The relationship looks like a curve, as shown in Figure B. The fact that a bond's price is not linearly related to its yield is termed "convexity." Because the slope of the curve increases as we move to the right (as yield increases), bonds are said to exhibit positive convexity.[4]

You have already seen how we calculate the price of a bond knowing its face value, coupon rate, term to maturity, and the required yield. However, in most cases investors

[4] For more on convexity and duration as measures of price sensitivity, see George Chacko et al., "Note on Duration and Convexity," HBS Case No. 204-155 (Boston: Harvard Business School Publishing, 2004).

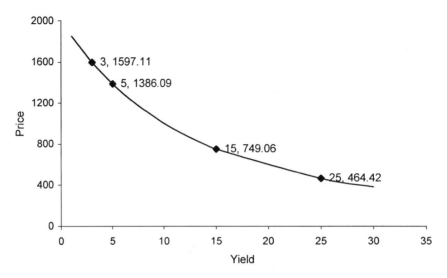

Figure B   Shape of Price-Yield Relationship

Source: Casewriter.

encounter the opposite situation. They can choose from a variety of bonds at set market prices that will most probably bring them different yields. Naturally, investors will be inclined to purchase the bond that bears the highest yield from a series of bonds that can be obtained at the same price.

Practically, however, the yield to maturity is an interest rate that must be calculated through trial and error. Of course, such a method of valuation is complicated and time consuming, so investors will typically use financial programs that quickly run through the process. But if you lack such a program, you can use an approximation method that does not require any serious mathematics. Consider the following example:

You hold a bond maturing in 36 months with a coupon of 5% and par value of $100. Currently the bond is priced at $95.26. What is the required yield on this investment?

So, every 12 months you would receive a coupon payment of $5. In total, you would receive three payments of $5, plus the future value of $100. Plugging the known amounts into the yield-to-maturity formula, you obtain:

$$\$95.26 = 5 \circ \left[\frac{1 - \dfrac{1}{(1 + y)^3}}{y} \right] + \frac{100}{(1 + y)^3} \tag{8}$$

Note that the bond is selling at a discount, that is, the bond price is less than its par value.[5] Therefore, you can expect that the required yield of the bond is greater than the coupon rate of 5%. The bond must sell at a discount to attract investors, who could find higher interest elsewhere in the prevailing market rates.

Now that we know this, we can calculate a number of bond prices by plugging various annual interest rates that are higher than 5% into the above formula. Ready-made tables exist to help with estimating the price according to the chosen interest rate. On the next page is such a table:

---

[5] The opposite situation would be a bond selling at a premium.

TABLE A

Annual interest rate	Bond price
10%	$87.56
9%	$89.87
8%	$92.27
7%	**$94.75**
6%	**$97.33**

Source: Casewriter.

Because our bond price is $95.26, our list shows that the interest rate we are searching for is between 6% and 7%. Now that we have found a range in which the interest rate lies, we can use another table that shows prices for interest rates in increments of 0.1% instead of 1%. Below we see the bond prices that result from various interest rates that are between 6% and 7%:

TABLE B

Annual interest rate	Bond price
7%	$94.75
6.9%	$95.00
6.8%	**$95.26**
6.7%	$95.51
6.6%	$95.77

Source: Casewriter.

We see then that the present value of our bond (the price) is equal to $95.26 when we have an annual interest rate of 6.8%.

COMPOUNDING CONVENTIONS AND CONVERSIONS

Compounding

In equation [2] for yield to maturity above, the period over which a discount rate applies is not restricted. In other words, the yield to maturity can be quoted in a number of different ways: as a one-year yield, a six-month yield, a three-month yield, and so on. Each of these is simply a different compounding convention, but all of these are valid ways to quote a yield for a bond. Therefore, when one is referring to the yield of a bond it is important to specify which compounding convention one means. However, regardless of which compounding convention one chooses to use, all of the resulting yields are nothing more than a way to quote the same price of an individual bond—while there are many ways to quote a bond in terms of yield to maturity, there can be only one price for a given bond.[6]

[6] For readers familiar with the concept of implied volatility from the options markets, implied volatilities and the price of an option have a similar relationship. An implied volatility can be quoted in many different ways (annual, semiannual, etc.), but all of these refer to the same price for the option (based on a pre-specified pricing model).

It is useful to be able to convert yields back and forth from various compounding conventions. The simple way to do this is to remember that no matter the compounding convention, the price of the bond must remain the same. For example, suppose that we wish to convert a 4% six-month yield to a three-month yield. Well, a zero-coupon bond paying $1 that matures in six months must have a price today of

$$\frac{\$1}{1 + 4\%} = 0.9615 \qquad [9]$$

using the formula [2] for yield to maturity from above. If we choose to use a three-month compounding convention, the price for that same bond must remain the same. So, if we let r_3 denote the three-month yield, the following equation must hold:

$$\frac{\$1}{(1 + r_3)^2} = 0.9615 \qquad [10]$$

This formula simply states that the bond's payoff discounted back at the three-month rate for two three-month periods (hence the exponent "2" in the denominator) must also give the bond's price, which must be the same price as that computed with the six-month rate. Solving for r_3, we find that the three-month rate is 1.98%. The key concept here is that when we define a specific yield (such as a six-month yield or a three-month yield), we are also setting the length of one period in the yield-to-maturity formula. So, if we are interested in a six-month rate, then one period is defined to equal six months. If we are interested in a three-month rate, then one period is now defined to equal three months, and the appropriate adjustment needs to be made to the exponents in the denominators of all the terms in the bond-pricing formula.

Compounding Conversion

Investors often need to compare effective yields on bonds quoted with different compounding conventions, so we need a general formula to convert a yield from one compounding convention to another. That formula is the following:

$$(1 + y_m)^{\frac{12}{m}} = (1 + y_n)^{\frac{12}{n}} \qquad [11]$$

where:

    y_m = yield in period m

    y_n = yield in period n

  m, n = numbers of months

This formula simply gives the future value of $1 invested today for the same amount of time (and therefore, the same interest rate), but the applicable interest rate is quoted using two different compounding conventions. Since we are putting in the same amount of money for the same amount of time for each interest rate, we must get the same dollar value at the end of the investment horizon. This is essentially what equation [11] above is stating.

In the example earlier, we started with a six-month yield of 4%, and we wanted to find the same yield but quoted on a quarterly (three-month) basis. So, using the conversion formula, $m = 6$ (the compounding period of the yield we know), and $y_m = 4\%$. The value for n is 3, and we now simply need to solve for y_n. This calculation yields

1.98%; in other words, the six-month (semiannual compounded) yield of 4% is equivalent to a three-month (quarterly compounded) yield of 1.98%.

By convention, market participants always annualize an interest rate before quoting it to others, regardless of which compounding convention is used. The simple way of annualizing is to take the m-period yield and multiply by $12/m$. So, the six-month yield of 4% in our example would always be quoted as 8% ($4\% \times 12/6$). This value of 8% is referred to as the annualized six-month yield. Similarly, the three-month yield of 1.98% would be quoted as 7.92% ($1.98\% \times 12/3$).

Certain annualized yields are quoted so often that they are given special names. For example, when a six-month yield is quoted on an annualized basis, the quote is referred to as the *bond equivalent yield*. This is typically the way that yields are quoted for semiannual coupon-paying bonds. In addition, when a one-month yield is quoted on an annualized basis (by multiplying the one-month yield by 12), it is referred to as an *annual percentage rate (APR)*. The interest rate associated with credit cards is typically quoted as an APR. In the above example, the APR associated with the six-month yield is 7.92%. This is found by first converting the six-month yield to a one-month yield using our conversion formula above. This gives 0.66%. We then multiply this one-month yield by 12 to get the APR.

Finally, one other commonly used term is the effective annual rate (EAR). This is simply the annual compounded rate. Because this is already an annual rate, a further step to annualize this rate is not needed. For example, the effective annual rate associated with the six-month yield of 4% is 8.16%. When quoting this rate to others, we would simply quote 8.16% as the annualized annual compounded rate.

$$EAR = (1 + 0.04)^2 - 1 = 1.0816 - 1 = 8.16\% \qquad [12]$$

PROBLEM SET

To practice the concepts in this reading note, here are some exercises.

Problem 1 On page 30, we said that equation [3] was a handy shortcut for pricing a bond and that it could be derived from equation [2]. In other words, we claimed:

$$P = \sum_{t=1}^{n} \frac{C}{(1 + y)^t} + \frac{M}{(1 + y)^n} = C \left(\frac{1 - \frac{1}{(1 + y)^n}}{y} \right) + \frac{M}{(1 + y)^n}$$

You should derive this result yourself, starting with the left side of the equation above, arriving at the right side. What does this result imply about the price of a bond with "infinite" maturity? (To help your calculations, note that $\sum_{t=0}^{\infty} a^t = \frac{1}{1 - a}$ for $0 < a < 1$.)

Problem 2 Consider a bond with a par value of $1,000 to be paid in seven years, a coupon rate of 5%, and a required annual yield of 12%. Assume that coupon payments are made annually to bondholders and that the next coupon payment is expected in 12 months. What is the current price of the bond?

Problem 3 For the bond described in problem 2, what is the new required annual yield if the bond price goes up 3%? If it goes down 3%?

Problem 4 On page 33–35, we discussed different compounding conventions. Now, to practice, what if the bond described in problem 2 was quoted on the market using an annualized one-month yield—or an annualized nine-month yield? Assuming the same bond price, what *are* the annualized one- and nine-month yields for that bond?

Problem 5 To continue practicing compounding conventions, what is the effective annual rate of a bond with a two-month yield of 1.1%?

APPENDIX—OVERVIEW OF BOND MARKETS

This appendix focuses on the five largest government bond markets: the U.S., Japan, Germany, France, and the U.K. The total amount of bonds outstanding worldwide in June 2003 accounted for $36,829 billion, an increase of 41% since 1997 (see Exhibit 1 for more details). Exhibit 2 then outlines fixed income securities by type of issuer in these five bond markets. Bonds issued by financial institutions have the highest share in the United States, whereas public sector issues account for the highest share in Japan and France. The U.K. has the most balanced situation with governments, financial institutions, and corporate bond issues relatively equally spread. In Germany, corporate bonds issued by German companies have so far played only a minor role.

The appendix concentrates on government securities, as they are generally perceived as a standard against which other bonds can be measured. Government bonds are considered to be a safe and secure investment option because the full faith and credit of the country's government guarantees that interest and principal payments will be paid on time. Also, most government securities are very liquid, meaning that they have a large secondary market, and so they can easily be sold for cash. Consequently, market participants view government bonds as having low credit risk.

Given their importance, government bonds have become benchmarks in fixed income securities markets. Most specifically, the benchmark bond is the latest issue within the given maturity with a comparable liquidity, issue size, and coupon.

EXHIBIT 1

DOMESTIC DEBT SECURITIES WORLDWIDE (AMOUNTS OUTSTANDING IN $ BILLION)

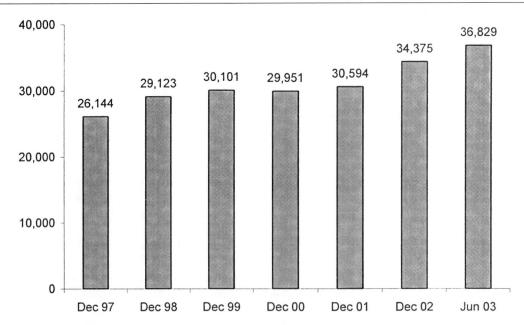

Source: Adapted from Bank for International Settlements, Statistics, http://www.bis.org/publ/qcsv/anx19a.csv, accessed February 26, 2004.

EXHIBIT 2

DOMESTIC DEBT SECURITIES—AMOUNTS OUTSTANDING (IN $ BILLION AS OF JUNE 2003)

	Governments		Financial Institutions		Corporate Issuers		Total	
U.S.	4,778	28%	9,754	57%	2,508	15%	17,040	100%
Japan	5,276	74%	1,111	16%	685	10%	7,072	100%
Germany	894	47%	932	48%	90	5%	1,916	100%
France	909	55%	522	32%	216	13%	1,647	100%
U.K.	470	41%	365	31%	326	28%	1,161	100%

Source: Adapted from "BIS Quarterly Review, December 2003," Bank for International Settlements Web site, http://www.bis.org/publ/qtrpdf/r_qa0312.pdf, accessed March 5, 2004.

United States

In the United States, government bonds are issued by the U.S. Department of the Treasury, and they are therefore called Treasuries.

Types of Treasury Securities

Fixed principal U.S. Treasuries are categorized as follows:

- Treasury bills[7] (or T-bills) with a maturity of less than one year
- Treasury notes with a maturity between two and 10 years
- Treasury bonds with a maturity longer than 10 years

Interest income from Treasury securities is subject to federal income taxes but is exempt from state and local income taxes.

In 1997, the U.S. department of the Treasury issued for the first time securities that adjust periodically for inflation. These securities are referred to as Treasury inflation protection securities (TIPS.) Using the consumer price index (CPI) as a benchmark, the value of the TIPS' principal is adjusted for inflation. A fixed interest rate is paid semiannually on the adjusted amount. At maturity, if inflation has increased the value of the principal, the investor receives the higher value. If deflation has decreased the value, the investor still receives the original face amount of the security. Worth noting is that the U.S. government has decided to tax the inflation adjustment each year.

Primary Market

Treasury securities are sold in the primary market through uniform-price, sealed-bid auctions.[8] Each auction is announced several days in advance by means of a Treasury Department press release or press conference.

---

[7] Bonds with a maturity less than one year are usually sold at a discount. Bonds with a maturity longer than one year offer coupon payments. This rule applies to all government bond markets.

[8] Also called "Dutch Auctions," in which the lowest price necessary to sell the entire offering becomes the price at which all securities offered are sold.

The Treasury Department determines the auctioning procedures for new Treasury securities, when to auction them, and what maturities to issue. The Treasury auctions on a regular basis T-bills with maturities of 4 weeks, 13 weeks, and 26 weeks. The Treasury auctions at more irregular intervals 2-year, 5-year, and 10-year Treasury notes. Treasury bonds are issued even more infrequently and irregularly.

The auctions for Treasury securities are conducted on a competitive bid basis that specifies the quantity sought and the yield at which the bidder is willing to purchase the auctioned security. By contrast, a noncompetitive bid indicates only the quantity that is sought at the yield determined by the auction process. In order to determine the results of an auction, after the quantity of total noncompetitive tenders is deducted from the total securities being auctioned, the remainder is awarded to competitive bidders. Competitive bids are arranged from the lowest-yield bid to the highest-yield bid submitted. Starting from the lowest-yield bid, all competitive bids are accepted until the amount to be distributed to the competitive bidders is completely allocated. The highest yield accepted by the Treasury is referred to as the stop-out yield.

Secondary Market

The secondary market for Treasury securities, a so-called over-the-counter (OTC) market, is characterized by a group of 23 U.S. government securities dealers, also known as "primary dealers,"[9] who offer continuous bid and ask prices on outstanding Treasuries.[10]

Bonds are also directly offered by the government through TreasuryDirect, which is available via phone, e-mail, and the World Wide Web. The Bureau of the Public Debt started TreasuryDirect so that individuals could buy bonds directly from the Treasury, thereby bypassing a broker. All transactions and interest payments are done electronically.

Japan

Similar to U.S. government bonds, coupon payments in Japan occur semiannually.

Types of Yen-Denominated Japanese Government Bonds (JGBs)

- Treasury bills with a maturity less than one year
- Bonds with maturities of two, four, five, and six years
- Bonds with maturities of 10, 15 (floating rate), 20, and 30 years

You can also buy three- and five-year discount government bonds that feature principal payment at maturity with no interest.

Primary Market

Underwriting by a syndicate has been the standard in the Japanese government bond primary market, with a specific goal of absorbing the full amount of new issues. Al-

---

[9] Their list can be found on the Web page of the Federal Reserve Bank of New York (http://www.ny.frb.org). Some of the financial institutions are Citigroup Global Markets Inc.; Goldman, Sachs & Co.; J. P. Morgan Securities, Inc.; Lehman Brothers Inc.; UBS Securities LLC.; Morgan Stanley & Co. Inc.; Barclays Capital Inc.; and CIBC World Markets Corp.

[10] The most recently auctioned issue is referred to as the on-the-run issue or the current issue. Other securities are called off-the-run issues.

though competitive auction features were built into the current syndicate underwriting, their utilization has been limited. Public auction systems (based on the multiple-price auctions) have been already introduced for the maturities of 2-, 4-, 6-, and 20-year bonds, but syndicate underwriting and noncompetitive auctions remain the major vehicle to absorb new issues of 10-year JGBs.

Currently, in the coupon-bearing category, 2-year, 5-year, and 10-year bonds are issued every month; 15-year bonds are issued quarterly; 20-year bonds are issued every other month; and 30-year bonds are issued twice a year. The government issued four-year bonds in February 2001 and six-year bonds in March 2001 but has no plan at this stage to issue these types of bonds in the future. With regard to discount government bonds, September 2000 marked the final issuance of five-year discount bonds, with no further plans for reissuance. The remaining type of three-year discount bonds, however, continue to be issued every other month through the syndicate underwriting system where bonds are allocated to syndicate members on a fixed-share basis.

As far as short-term securities are concerned, the Japanese government keeps on issuing six-month and one-year Treasury bills on a monthly basis.

Secondary Market

One characteristic feature of the JGB market is the lack of a primary dealer system. Instead, JGBs can be purchased at various financial institutions, such as banks, securities companies, Shinkin banks,[11] and post offices.

Germany

Germany has Europe's largest bond market with approximately $1,915 billion outstanding in June 2003.[12] The federal government offers euro-denominated securities with maturities ranging from six months to more than 30 years issued on its behalf by the German Finance Agency.

Types of German Federal Benchmark Securities

- Treasury papers ("Bubills"): six months
- Federal Treasury notes ("Schätze"): two years
- Five-year federal notes ("Bobls"): five years
- Federal bonds ("Bunds"): 10 years, sometimes 30 years

In recent years, listed federal securities (federal bonds, five-year special federal bonds, and federal Treasury notes) have reached a share of between 60% and 80% in the overall outstanding debt of the federal government.

---

[11] Shinkin banks are nonprofit credit associations established in accordance with the Shinkin Bank Law of 1951 (otherwise known as the Credit Association Law). These banks are small- and medium-sized financial institutions, organized in a membership structure, that aim to facilitate smooth financing for ordinary citizens (including small and medium-sized companies and their workers).

[12] "BIS Quarterly Review, December 2003," Bank for International Settlements Web site, http://www.bis.org, accessed March 5, 2004.

TABLE C **Monthly Average Trading Volume by Maturity (in Euro Thousands)**

Maturity	Trading Volume (€th)
2Y—"Schätze"	73,386,359
5Y—"Bobls"	78,414,039
10Y—"Bunds"	101,836,334

Source: Thomson Financial Datastream, accessed February 25, 2004.

Primary Market

Since 1998 primary bond issues have been auctioned under a uniform procedure through the Bund Issues Auction Group,[13] which consists of 42 financial institutions approved by the federal government. The list of members of the Bund Issues Auction Group is revised annually, and one of the major requirements is to guarantee a certain minimum placing power.

Secondary Market

Similarly to Japan, Germany has not adopted the primary dealer system in part because of its well-established bank-based financial system. However, the secondary market for German federal securities is considered to be one of the largest and most liquid markets for government bonds in the world. Federal bonds, five-year special federal bonds, and Treasury notes are traded actively on the German stock exchanges and over the counter in Germany and abroad.

France

Agence France Trésor (AFT) is the French government debt agency responsible for the issuance of French government securities.

Types of French Government Securities Benchmarks (Denominated in Euros)

- Negotiable fixed income Treasury bills (BTFs, or "Bons du Trésor à taux fixe et à intêrets précomptés"): less than one year
- Negotiable fixed rate medium-term Treasury notes with annual interest (BTANs, or "Bons du Trésor à taux fixe et à intérêts annuels"): two to five years
- Fungible Treasury bonds (OATs, or "Obligations assimilables du Trésor"): seven to 30 years

Inflation-indexed bonds (known by their abbreviations OATi, OAT€i) were introduced in 1998 and have been in high demand ever since. In 2002, for the first time, the AFT committed to issuing at least 10% of its medium- and long-term financing program in the form of indexed debt issues. The first type, OATi (the inflation-indexed

---

[13] Among others, Deutsche Bank AG, Dresdner Bank AG, Morgan Stanley Bank AG, Stadtsparkasse Köln, ABN AMRO Bank AG, BNP Paribas, CSFB Ltd., Goldman, Sachs & Co. oHG, J.P. Morgan Securities Ltd., Merrill Lynch Capital Markets Bank.

OAT) is a fixed real-rate coupon bond, where the principal is guaranteed at par, and protected against inflation, by an indexation to a daily inflation reference based on the French consumer price index. The second type, OAT€I, is the only government bond linked to the eurozone consumer price index. The July 2012 OAT€I, launched in October 2001, initiated the market of bonds indexed on eurozone inflation.

Primary Market

The principal method of issuing French government securities since 1985 has been a bid-price system. Participants compete in the auction on an equal footing through a transparent system of open bidding according to a planned issuance program.

This bid-price system consists of offering securities at the bid price or the effective bid rate as opposed to the marginal price or rate. This type of auction is known as a "multiple-price, sealed-bid auction," where highest bids are first served followed by lower bids until the AFT's target amount is reached.[14] Participants pay different prices, precisely reflecting their bids.

OATs and BTANs are auctioned monthly and BTFs weekly.

Secondary Market

In 2004, 22 primary dealers[15] ("Spécialistes en Valeurs du Trésor"—SVTs) have been actively trading in French government bonds in the secondary market.

United Kingdom

In the United Kingdom, the government-issued debt securities, called gilts, are denominated in pound sterling. The function of debt management was transferred in 1998 from the Bank of England to the newly created Debt Management Office (DMO).

Types of Benchmark Gilts

- Shorts: 0–7 years
- Mediums: 7–15 years
- Longs: over 15 years
- Undated: no fixed repayment date

In recent years the U.K. government has concentrated on issuing conventional gilts[16] of 5-, 10-, and 30-year maturities.

Index-linked gilts (IGs) accounted for 26% of the government's gilt portfolio at the end of March 2002. Both the interest payment and the capital repayment on redemption are adjusted in line with inflation (as measured by the Retail Prices Index—RPI).

---

[14] In contrast to the U.S. Treasuries uniform-price auction method.

[15] Among others, BNP Paribas, Deutsche Bank, Merrill Lynch Capital Markets France, Société Générale, Barclays Capital France, Dresdner Kleinwort Wasserstein, Morgan Stanley, Unicredito Banca Mobiliare, and Citigroup Global Markets.

[16] In contrast to inflation-indexed gilts.

TABLE D   Monthly Average Trading Volume by Maturity (in Pounds Thousands)

Maturity	Trading Volume (€th)
Shorts	6,210,310
Mediums	18,446,060
Longs	7,605,740

Source: U.K. Debt Management Office, Quarterly Reviews, issues 2003, DMO Web site, http://www.dmo.gov.uk/publication/f2qua.htm, accessed February 20, 2004.

Primary Market

New securities can be bought at the auction directly from the DMO via the Bank of England Registrar's Department, which maintains the main register of gilt-edged stock. Starting September 2003, all investors seeking to participate in gilt auctions need to be members of the DMO's "approved group" of investors.

Secondary Market

After the initial issue the gilts are traded on the secondary market by a group of primary dealers known as gilt-edged market makers (GEMMs). Sixteen GEMMs[17] deal continuously with major professional investors such as pension funds and insurance companies across the entire range of gilts. GEMMs, along with institutional investors and custodians who may hold stock on behalf of private investors, hold gilts in computerized form using the CREST settlement system.

Private investors can get access to the secondary bond markets through a stockbroker, a bank, or the brokerage service provided by the Bank of England.

---

[17] Among others, Deutsche Bank, JP Morgan Securities Limited, ABN AMRO Bank, Citigroup Global Markets, Goldman Sachs International.

3

Deutsche Bank: Finding Relative-Value Trades

It was the third week of August 2003, and Jamil Baz, head of Deutsche Bank's Fixed Income Research Group, gathered his research group for a morning meeting. "So, what are the markets telling us today?" he asked the group. "Are there any trends or news for new trade ideas?"

The Fixed Income Research Group that Baz led was Deutsche Bank's internal research and development (R&D) department for fixed income instruments. Their mandate was to look for untapped value across bond markets and interest rate derivatives. Long-term-oriented research findings were presented to clients, whereas immediate opportunities were suggested as trades to internal traders as well as clients. The success of the group was in part measured by how many of their trade suggestions actually turned into successful trades. So far, they had achieved an impressive 75% success rate.

A natural place to start looking for new trades was the latest prices on various U.S. Treasury bonds (see Exhibit 1 for data from August 15, 2003). The group's members consistently went through that data set, looking for possible trades to recommend. Typically relative-value trades took both long and short positions across different parts of the yield curve. Baz's standard weekly question just emphasized what they all knew: that it was time to scour through the numbers one more time to see if any such positions were available.

THE DEUTSCHE BANK FIXED INCOME RESEARCH GROUP

Headquartered in Deutsche Bank's London office, the company's Fixed Income Research Group consisted of about 50 analysts and strategists. (An additional 10 were

Professors George Chacko and Peter Hecht, Executive Director of the HBS Europe Research Center Vincent Dessain, and Research Associate Anders Sjöman prepared this case. This case deals with trade-specific advice activities of a research department and draws from "Deutsche Bank: Discussing the Equity Risk Premium," HBS Case No. 205-040, by the same authors. Case No. 205-040 deals with macro-level advice from the same research department. Some names and data have been disguised for confidentiality. HBS cases are developed solely as the basis for class discussion. Cases are not intended to serve as endorsements, sources of primary data, or illustrations of effective or ineffective management. This case is not intended as financial advice, and it should not be used as the basis for any investment decision, in whole or in part.

EXHIBIT 1

PRICES AND COUPON RATES OF VARIOUS U.S. TREASURY BONDS ON AUGUST 15, 2003

Coupon Rate (%)	Maturity Date	Current Price
3	2/15/2004	101.0544
2.125	8/15/2004	100.9254
1.5	2/15/2005	99.8942
6.5	8/15/2005	109.0934
5.625	2/15/2006	108.438
2.375	8/15/2006	99.7848
6.25	2/15/2007	111.7184
3.25	8/15/2007	101.0841
3	2/15/2008	99.1692
3.25	8/15/2008	99.271
5.5	2/15/2009	109.7707
6	8/15/2009	112.145
6.5	2/15/2010	114.9084
5.75	8/15/2010	110.3894
5	2/15/2011	105.2934
5	8/15/2011	104.7607
4.875	2/15/2012	103.4391
4.375	8/15/2012	99.2806
3.875	2/15/2013	95.0288
4.25	8/15/2013	97.7693
13.25	2/15/2014	174.3251
12.5	8/15/2014	168.9389
11.25	2/15/2015	157.0552
10.625	8/15/2015	152.4222
9.25	2/15/2016	140.0135
7.5	8/15/2016	123.3044
8.75	2/15/2017	136.0598
8.875	8/15/2017	137.504
9.125	2/15/2018	140.792
9	8/15/2018	139.9079
8.875	2/15/2019	138.7431
8.125	8/15/2019	130.7162

(Continued)

located in the bank's New York offices.) Global head of Fixed Income Research and in charge of the group was Baz, a managing director with Deutsche Bank since 2001. Previously at Lehman Brothers in London, Baz also held an M.S. in management from MIT and a Ph.D. in business economics from Harvard University.

As a part of a large financial institution, the research group was under constant pressure to monetize the ideas that they generated. The group presented its findings

EXHIBIT 1   (Continued)

PRICES AND COUPON RATES OF VARIOUS U.S. TREASURY BONDS ON AUGUST 15, 2003

Coupon Rate (%)	Maturity Date	Current Price
8.5	2/15/2020	135.2938
8.75	8/15/2020	138.3466
7.875	2/15/2021	128.4995
8.125	8/15/2021	131.7341
8	2/15/2022	130.4736
7.25	8/15/2022	121.58
7.125	2/15/2023	120.1744
6.25	8/15/2023	109.4538
7.5	2/15/2024	125.46
7.5	8/15/2024	125.4466
7.625	2/15/2025	127.1477
6.875	8/15/2025	117.5509
6	2/15/2026	106.3626
6.75	8/15/2026	116.1986
6.625	2/15/2027	114.7086
6.375	8/15/2027	111.4036
6.125	2/15/2028	108.0391
5.5	8/15/2028	99.633
5.25	2/15/2029	96.2876
6.125	8/15/2029	108.4062

Source: Adapted by casewriter from Datastream.

both internally to the Deutsche Bank traders, as well as externally to Deutsche Bank clients at the CEO, CFO, and Treasury level. Baz explained how the ideas were pitched:

> The final goal is to create a franchise with fixed income clients. So, for clients on the asset side, such as mutual funds, hedge funds, insurance companies, and pension plans, we help them generate high returns on their assets. We give specific ideas to be executed by the clients—hopefully with us, although that is never certain. However, even if we don't get a trade out of our recommendation, it is important enough that we maintain Deutsche Bank's presence at the client. Sometimes we also do bespoke—or customized—work, where we analyze their balance sheet and asset-liability mismatches for them, almost like technical financial consulting. In general, research alone will not give us clients, but research combined with pricing are the keys to building long-lasting relationships with external clients.

> Overall, we strive to push the frontiers of analytical finance when it comes to modeling interest rates, volatilities, and spreads. Owing to data availability and an intimate exposure to institutional market realities, we are often pushed to reach results ahead of academic finance journals.

On a group level, Deutsche Bank organized its fixed income activities in the global markets around three main pillars: investor coverage, issuer coverage, and research. The trading desks dealing in these areas were in turn divided into two groups: credit (with credit trading/credit derivatives, new issue syndicate, asset securitization, and emerging markets) and rates (with foreign exchange, money markets, fixed income, and interest rate derivatives).

The research efforts of the group were set up to match these organizational divisions. The Fixed Income Research Group was one of several research groups (as shown in Exhibit 2). All these groups were run under the banner of Global Markets Research. Research as a whole was headed by David Folkerts-Landau. Demand for direct meetings with Deutsche Bank's research groups had grown over the past few years, taken internally as a sign of increased respect for the bank's research output. In the last year, Baz's group alone had logged over 1,500 client meetings. All clients had access to the Deutsche Bank research in papers and newsletters that were available online. Internal traders also benefited from the research, which was a major influence behind much of the bank's proprietary—or "prop"—trading. Most members of the research group shared their time between external clients and traders, with more senior staff members working more with external clients and less with the trading floor.

In the end, measuring the research group's value to the organization was still difficult. Said Baz:

> Putting a value on the work we do, and the effect we have on the bank, is very hard. In fact, if you were to really measure it by attributing sales and trades back to us, the trading floor would be more reluctant to work with us. Instead, we are mostly evaluated by top management on three other factors. Firstly, overall market direction, which is how much of rate and spread moves did we catch in our advice. Secondly, the relative-value trades we originated. Thirdly, any customized business we have brought in from our client meetings.

EXHIBIT 2

DEUTSCHE BANK GLOBAL MARKETS RESEARCH ORGANIZATION

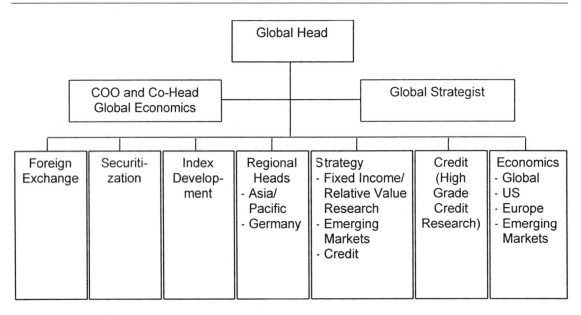

Source: Deutsche Bank.

Compensation to the members of the group was tied to the evaluation of the group as a whole. Individual bonuses were then given at the discretion of Baz as the group's manager, based on his qualitative impression of each member's contribution.

Strategic Advice and Relative-Value Activities

The group's activities were normally broken down into strategic advice on macro trends and relative value. The strategic advice activities built on long-term discussions with clients, where the group presented Deutsche Bank's view on macroeconomic trends to external clients. In these discussions, George Cooper, the group's global fixed income strategist, typically did not expect a quick monetary return. Cooper, a Ph.D. graduate in engineering at Durham University with experience from both Goldman Sachs and JP Morgan, explained:

> This type of activity does not generate a lot of money from a trade perspective. It generates brand value, though, and is especially appealing to insurance companies or asset-liability people, who appreciate the long-term view. We believe it serves more of an educational purpose. It gets the fund managers thinking. They are not looking for prescriptive research, where we tell them to "do this trade," but they look for interesting ideas. Of course, they then weigh our ideas against whatever Goldman Sachs or Morgan Stanley are saying. Our role is to come up with hopefully insightful but also informative new ways to look at things.

By contrast, the relative-value activities looked for more immediate opportunities by comparing different instruments and then recommending various trading strategies to clients and internal traders. Head of Relative Value Research for Europe was Jean Dumas, an engineer from ESME SUDRIA in France with a specialization in finance, who had worked with Relative Value Research for Deutsche Bank in Paris, Frankfurt, and Sydney before moving to London. Dumas explained his work:

> We come up with different types of trades all the time. The trade opportunities may be there for a week or two, sometimes longer. I look at different spreadsheets, listen to what traders are saying, watch the news, study different models. . . . Then I try to put everything together—and suddenly there is a trade opportunity. Our job is really grabbing things that don't seem to be related at first and see if there is a trade to be done.

The trade opportunities that the research group identified were published weekly in the newsletter "Deutsche Bank Fixed Income Weekly," which was distributed to Deutsche Bank traders as well as to clients. A frequent contributor to the newsletter was Dr. Nikan B. Firoozye, head of Global Quantitative Strategies and a Ph.D. graduate in mathematics from Courant Institute at New York University with experience from Alliance Capital, Sanford C. Bernstein, and Lehman Brothers. Firoozye explained:

> I write a piece on Euroland strategy every week where we suggest trades. Some of these are big trades that we don't change very often, such as curve-steepening trades. We can have the same trade off and on for a full year. We also summarize economic data as it impacts the bond markets. For instance, how structured trades could be influenced by the move in dollar versus yen, and how you should position for that.

In his role as head of Euroland Strategy, Firoozye also oversaw all strategic investments in Euroland bond markets. He was also involved in all modeling issues and wrote stand-alone papers on quantitative strategy.

LOOKING FOR A RELATIVE-VALUE TRADE

For the research group, one way to find relative-value trades was to compare the prices of traded securities against the prices that the group thought the securities *should* trade at. This subjective view was based on a proprietary model developed at Deutsche Bank. (Most banks used proprietary models as a base from which to evaluate the prices of traded securities.)

The models were built on the fact that the returns offered by fixed income instruments could be characterized by the yields that they offered. The yield was roughly seen as compensation for the risk borne by the holder of that security. There were many sources of risk in fixed income securities, such as interest rate risk, credit risk, and prepayment risk. Also, the yield of an instrument could be broken down into components. The components could be thought of as compensation for the different sources of risk. So, for example, the yield on a corporate bond could be thought of as being composed of a risk-free yield plus a credit spread. The risk-free yield represented compensation for interest rate risk in the bond, while the credit spread represented compensation for default risk in the bond.[1]

To understand the compensation for the interest rate risk alone, banks typically constructed "yield-curve models." These were models for the yields on zero-coupon Treasury securities, since Treasury instruments typically contained only interest rate risk. Models for the yield curve could be then used to compare the current and expected prices of U.S. Treasury instruments.[2]

The research group at Deutsche Bank had developed their own proprietary yield-curve model, a so-called three-factor affine model (see Exhibit 3 for a conceptual description of the model). Firoozye explained the fundaments of the model:

> We have three factors driving the yield curve that we see as analogous to the economy. In an economy, there is inflation, output gaps, and short rates. So first among our factors is a long rate, which is analogous to inflation. It is the slowest mean reverting of our three factors. In the fifties inflation was low, in the seventies it was extremely high, and now it is back down again. It takes 20 years to go through its cycle. It is very slow, very persistent, whereas the business cycle is much, much faster. You go through a business cycle in about seven years. So slope, our second factor, is then the measure of output gap. Slope mean reverts much more quickly than inflation. The third factor is the short rate, which mean reverts the fastest.

After estimating the variables of the three-factor model, the team calibrated the model to price the one-month, two-year, and 10-year zero-coupon bond.

After Baz's request at the weekly meeting, the analysts now used the latest numbers on various U.S. Treasury bonds to update and calibrate the model (see Exhibit 4 for the resulting output from Deutsche Bank's model). The idea was to then compare the actual zero-coupon yield curve against the predicted ones coming out of the model and see if any trade ideas presented themselves.

In fact, several trades seemed to come out of that comparison. Baz and the team now had to pick the trades with the highest profit potential.

---

[1] It should be noted that the notion of compensation here is approximate. The yield on a zero-coupon corporate bond is *not* the expected return of that bond. It is simply the *promised* return of that bond, or the return an investor would get if the bond did not default. Starting with this promised return and then factoring in the probability of default and a default risk premium leads to the expected return for that bond.

[2] More generally, yield-curve models could be used to price any interest rate-sensitive security. For example, the pricing of interest rate options starts with a yield-curve model.

EXHIBIT 3

DEUTSCHE BANK'S ZERO-COUPON YIELD MODEL

- **Key variables:** Short rate, slope, and long rate (or short rate, output gap, and inflation)
- **Model specified by a system of equations (in Q measure)**
  - Long rate mean reverts slowly (possibly to nonzero mean)
  $$dX_t = (\mu_X = k_X X_t)dt + \sigma_X dW_t^X$$
  - Slope mean reverts faster (to zero)
  $$dY_t = -k_Y Y_t dt + \sigma_Y dW_t^Y$$
  - In equilibrium short rate, r_t, follows the target $X_t + Y_t$ (an analogue of the Taylor rule)
  $$X_t + Y_t - r_t = 0$$
  - Short rate mean reverts fast in order to restore the equilibrium
  $$dr_t = k_r(X_t + Y_t - r_t)dt + \sigma_r dW_t^r$$

Source: Adapted by casewriter from "Quantitative Models for Fixed Income," Deutsche Bank presentation, October 2003.

EXHIBIT 4

OUTPUT FROM DEUTSCHE BANK'S ZERO-COUPON YIELD MODEL

Maturity (years)	Model Prediction (BEY)
1y	1.2443%
2y	1.8727%
3y	2.4110%
4y	2.9665%
5y	3.4454%
6y	3.8557%
7y	4.1996%
8y	4.4677%
9y	4.6528%
10y	4.7107%
15y	5.7160%
20y	5.9517%
25y	5.9315%

Note: The yields in this table are bond equivalent yields (BEY), that is, the semiannual yield multiplied by two.

Source: Adapted by casewriters from Deutsche Bank information.

4

Note on Duration and Convexity

When interest rates go up, bond prices fall.

All actors in the financial markets—money managers, traders, arbitrageurs—know this. But how do they compare how *much* prices will change between various financial instruments, before interest rates actually change? To inform their strategies, traders want to know, for instance, which bond will lose more in price given that interest rates rise 100 basis points: a 6% coupon bond with a 15-year maturity or one with a 30-year maturity—or maybe a 9% coupon bond with a 30-year maturity. To help estimate price sensitivity between bonds of different maturities and coupon rates, two measures are normally used: duration and convexity.

As measures, however, duration and convexity are not just limited to bonds. They apply to all financial instruments, fixed income and equity alike. They also measure price reaction to risk factors other than just interest rates. Therefore, put more generally, duration and convexity take into account *any* change for *any* risk factor affecting the price of *any* financial instrument. Although many examples in this note will center on their use for bonds regarding yield and interest rate changes, this larger application of duration and convexity should not be underrated.

The main difference between the two concepts is that duration focuses on small changes in risk factors, and convexity then builds on duration to adjust for larger changes. For bonds, for instance, the basic price-yield relationship of an option-free bond—a bond without any embedded options, such as being callable or putable—dictates that the bond price will change in the opposite direction of the change in the required yield.[1] (A more formal restatement of this note's first sentence.) When graphed, this correlation appears as a convex curve (see Exhibit 1). For small price changes, the line's curvature does not affect the relationship; a linear tangent can simply be fit as a first-order derivative for an approximate duration. For larger changes, however, the curvature comes into play and requires the addition of a second derivative, which leads to convexity.

Professors George Chacko and Peter Hecht, Executive Director of the HBS Europe Research Center Vincent Dessain, and Research Associate Anders Sjöman prepared this note as the basis for class discussion.

[1] For more on price-yield relationships, see George Chacko, Peter Hecht, Vincent Dessain, and Monica Stachowiak, "Note on Bond Valuation and Returns," HBS Note No. 204-154 (Boston: Harvard Business School Publishing, 2004).

EXHIBIT 1

RELATIONSHIP BETWEEN PRICE AND YIELD (FOR OPTION-FREE BONDS)

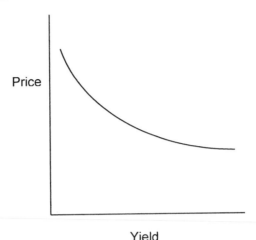

Source: Casewriter.

DURATION

Duration measures the sensitivity of any instrument to a small change in any of its underlying risk factors. For instance, it can measure the price volatility of a bond to a change in interest rates. Professional bond managers can, then, use duration to measure risk. Generally, instruments with a high duration will have a higher price fluctuation than instruments with a low duration. What is considered high and low naturally depends on the instrument and the market in which it is traded. It also depends on the interest rate that is being used: the one-year, two-year, and so on. As you use duration, be sure to define to which interest and maturity you refer.

To further confuse the situation, there also exist several different types of duration. Originally, the term "duration" was defined by Frederic Macaulay in 1938 to calculate the average time taken by the security, on a discounted basis, to pay back the original investment. The practice of quoting duration in years originates with Macaulay's definition. A "Macaulay duration" of eight years, then, simply means that it will take eight years until the original investment is paid back.

However, another definition uses duration to measure price elasticity or price volatility. This is the definition we use in this note: duration as the approximate *percentage* change in price for a small change in an underlying risk factor. Put mathematically:

$$\text{Duration} = -\frac{dP/P}{dY} \qquad [1]$$

It is important to remember that this definition—also known as "modified duration"—has nothing to do with the weighted average life of a financial instrument or with the absolute dollar change in price. It is the percentage change of price that interests us when we use modified duration.[2]

A duration of eight, then, means that an increase in yield of 10 basis points will result in a minus 8×10 basis points $= -0.8\%$ price change. Put algebraically, if $-dP/P$ over dY is 8, then

$$\frac{dP}{P} = -8 \circ dY = -8 \circ 10bps = -80bps = -0.08\% \tag{2}$$

We have already stated that duration is used for small changes to an underlying risk factor, whereas larger changes require the use of convexity. Although there is no generally established norm for what is considered small and large, an often-quoted baseline assumption is that small changes run in the 10-basis-point range, whereas 100 basis points might be considered a large change.

As has also already been stated, duration is a concept that can be used for any financial instrument, not just bonds. The examples below illustrate the versatility of the concept.

Duration for a Floating Rate Bond

The coupon of floating rate bonds adjusts automatically to the current interest rate level. Assuming we have a floating rate bond that pays continuous coupons, by definition the price of such a floating rate bond does not move with interest rates. The coupon simply absorbs all of the changes. That bond will trade every day at par value (or put in traders' jargon, "at 100"). Remember that duration is defined in this note as a percentage change in price with respect to a risk factor, such as the interest rate. Since the price does not change with a floating rate bond, then by definition duration is zero.

More realistically, a floating bond would not take continuous coupons but would have its coupons updated at regular intervals. Even so, its price volatility would still be very low.

Duration for Equity

Calculating duration for equity starts with the pricing model for equity. (How to calculate sensitivity for securities that do not have an explicit pricing formula is described in the section "Calculating Approximate Duration and Convexity" on page 57.) The price of equity is defined as:

$$P = \frac{CF}{1 + r} + \frac{CF(1 + g)}{(1 + r)^2} + \cdots \tag{3}$$

where:

   P = price of the equity

   CF = cash flow

   r = discount rate

   g = growth rate of cash flow

---

[2] In addition to Macaulay and modified duration, there is effective duration (which takes into account embedded options or redemption features) and key-rate duration (which calculates spot durations along a spot-rate curve). Both types are beyond the scope of this note.

Equation [3] above can be solved to show that:

$$P = \frac{\dfrac{CF}{1+r}}{1 - \dfrac{1+g}{1+r}} = \frac{CF}{r-g} \qquad [4]$$

Now, to calculate how a small change in the discount rate affects the price, we calculate the first derivative of the equation above with respect to the required yield:

$$\frac{dP}{dr} = -\frac{CF}{(r-g)^2} \qquad [5]$$

To get the percentage change—again, the modified duration—we divide by P (price), which we know from above is the same as $CF/(r-g)$. This gives:

$$\text{Modified duration: } -\frac{dP/P}{dr} = \frac{\dfrac{CF}{(r-g)^2}}{\dfrac{CF}{r-g}} = \frac{1}{r-g} \text{ assuming } r > g \qquad [6]$$

Example. Substituting the actual discount rate (r) and the growth rate (g) in the equation above would give the modified duration. For example, if we assume $r - g$ to be around 4% for the aggregate stock market, we find the duration of equity to be around **25**.

Duration for a Fixed Rate Bond

Just as with equity, calculating duration for a fixed rate bond starts with the price model of the instrument. The price of an option-free bond is calculated as the present value of its cash flows plus the present value of the principal at maturity. Put mathematically:

$$P = \sum_{t=1}^{n} \frac{C}{(1+y)^t} + \frac{M}{(1+y)^n} \qquad [7]$$

where:

P = price of the bond

C = coupon interest (in dollars, euros, or any currency) per period, normally semi-annually for bonds

y = annual yield to maturity or required yield divided by number of periods per year[3]

n = number of periods (number of years times periods per year)

M = maturity value (in dollars, euros, or any currency)

The price can then be rewritten for its two components, stating the present value of an annuity (where the annuity is the sum of the coupon payments) and

---

[3] This "y" was called bond equivalent yield in the previously mentioned Chacko et al., "Note on Bond Valuation and Returns."

the present value of the par (or maturity) value. The price of a bond can also be expressed as:

$$P = C\left[\frac{1 - \dfrac{1}{(1+y)^n}}{y}\right] + \frac{M}{(1+y)^n} \qquad [8]$$

To approximate how a small change in yield affects the price, we calculate the first derivative of the equation above with respect to the required yield and divide by price (*P*). For mathematical completeness, the formula is also multiplied by a minus one.

$$\text{Modified duration} = -\frac{\dfrac{C}{y^2}\left[1 - \dfrac{1}{(1+y)^n}\right] + \dfrac{n(M - C/y)}{(1+y)^{n+1}}}{P} \qquad [9]$$

Example. To illustrate, take a 30-year 5% bond, with semiannual coupons, selling at 75.055 to a yield of 7%. Using the formula above, this gives:

- $C = 0.05 \times 100 \times 1/2 = 2.5$
- $y = 7\% \times 1/2 = 0.035$
- $n = 60$
- $P = 75.055$
- $M = 100$

Substituting these numbers into equation [9] above gives:

$$\text{Modified duration} = \frac{\dfrac{2.5}{0.035^2}\left[1 - \dfrac{1}{(1.035)^{60}}\right] + \dfrac{60(100 - 2.5/0.035)}{(1.035)^{61}}}{75.055} = 26.54067 \qquad [10]$$

Remember that the coupons for this bond were semiannual. "*C*" in the formula was therefore divided by two—which means that the modified duration above is by half year. We do, however, want to get an annual number for the modified duration, and so we divide by two. Our annual modified duration is then **13.27**.

In fact, the Macaulay duration that we discussed above can be expressed by multiplying the modified duration by $(1 + y)$. In this example, multiplying by 1.035 gives a Macaulay duration of 13.73 years.

CONVEXITY

As we stated earlier, duration works well with small changes to interest rates (or other underlying risk factors). However, with large changes, duration does not estimate well how prices will change. As a first-order derivative, duration implies a linear relationship and simply does not take into account the convex relationship between an instrument's price and its cash flow or yield (see Exhibit 2). For larger changes, the curvature of the relationship has to be taken into account. We therefore use convexity, the second derivative of price with respect to yield. By adding convexity to the duration estimate, we get better approximations of the true relationship between price and yield.

EXHIBIT 2

DURATION CREATING A CONVEXITY ERROR FOR LARGE CHANGES

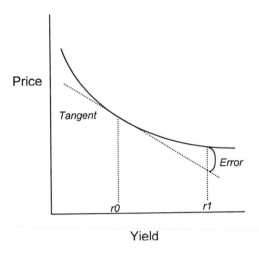

Note: When yield changes from r0 to r1, using the first derivative (duration) will result in a faulty approximation of the new price. Adding a second derivative—convexity—helps adjust the error.

Source: Casewriter.

We can also use a Taylor series to illustrate how convexity adds to the exactness of our sensitivity estimations. The price of any security can be affected by any number of risk factors. A Taylor series lays out the factors; the more of these factors we can approximate, the more accurate our estimates of price change will be. Even if we do not know all factors, knowing how the change in one risk factor affects the overall price will help us make better-informed decisions.

The Taylor series for a change in price looks like this:

$$dP = \frac{dP}{dy} \, dy + \frac{1}{2} \frac{d^2P}{dy^2} \, (dy)^2 + \frac{1}{6} \frac{d^3P}{dy^3} \, (dy)^3 + \cdots \qquad [11]$$

Dividing both sides of the equation by price (*P*) gives us the percentage price change:

$$\frac{dP}{P} = \frac{dP}{dy} \frac{1}{P} \, dy + \frac{1}{2} \frac{d^2P}{dy^2} \frac{1}{P} \, (dy)^2 + \frac{1}{6} \frac{d^3P}{dy^3} \frac{1}{P} \, (dy)^3 + \cdots \qquad [12]$$

Now, look carefully at the first term on the right-hand side. This is the percentage change in price given a change in yield—or, simply put, duration. (Expressed more mathematically correct: the minus of duration.) If we supposed this was the only risk factor that affected the price of our instrument, we could roughly calculate the percentage price change, or the duration. However, using just duration ignores all the other factors of the Taylor series. The more terms we can include in our estimate, the more accurate our calculations will be. In practice this means that people add a second term—using it as a measure of convexity.

Returning to our three earlier examples, let us see how adding convexity changes our estimations.

Convexity for a Floating Rate Bond

We established above that duration for a floating rate bond with continuous coupons was zero. The bond price was constant, so there was no need to add convexity; the result remains zero.

Convexity for Equity

In the case of equity, convexity is the second derivative of the equity price equation [4] above:

$$\frac{d^2P}{dr^2} = \frac{2CF}{(r-g)^3} \qquad [13]$$

This second derivative is then divided by price (P) to obtain a convexity measure:

$$\text{Convexity measure: } \frac{\dfrac{2CF}{(r-g)^3}}{\dfrac{CF}{r-g}} = \frac{2}{(r-g)^2} \qquad [14]$$

Example. If we, as above for duration, assume that $r - g$ roughly equals 4%, convexity for equity will then be around **12.5**.

Convexity for a Fixed Rate Bond

For the fixed rate bond, let's start with the second derivative of the price equation [7] above:

$$\frac{d^2P}{dy^2} = \sum_{t=1}^{n} \frac{t(t+1)C}{(1+y)^{t+2}} + \frac{n(n+1)M}{(1+y)^{n+2}} \qquad [15]$$

Similarly, the rewritten price equation [8] above can also be taken to its second-order derivative. This gives us a simpler mathematical formula with which to work:

$$\frac{d^2P}{dy^2} = \frac{2C}{y^3}\left[1 - \frac{1}{(1+y)^n}\right] - \frac{2Cn}{y^2(1+y)^{n+1}} + \frac{n(n+1)(M-C/y)}{(1+y)^{n+2}} \qquad [16]$$

This second derivative is then divided by price (P) to obtain a convexity measure:

$$\text{Convexity measure (by period): } \frac{\dfrac{2C}{y^3}\left[1 - \dfrac{1}{(1+y)^n}\right] - \dfrac{2Cn}{y^2(1+y)^{n+1}} + \dfrac{n(n+1)(M-C/y)}{(1+y)^{n+2}}}{P} \qquad [17]$$

The convexity measure is in terms of periods squared. To convert convexity measures for coupons that, for instance, were semiannual into an annual figure, you would therefore need to divide by four.

Example. To exemplify, we return to the fixed bond from above: a 30-year 5% bond, with semiannual coupons, selling at 75.055 to a yield of 7%. Using equation [17], we obtain a semiannual convexity measure:

$$\frac{\frac{2(2.5)}{(0.035)^3}\left[1 - \frac{1}{(1.035)^{60}}\right] - \frac{2(2.5)(60)}{(0.035)^2(1.035)^{61}} + \frac{60(61)(100 - 2.5/0.035)}{(1.035)^{62}}}{75.055} = 1121.4662 \quad [18]$$

Since the coupon is semiannual, we annualize the measure by dividing by four (since the convexity measure above is in terms of periods squared) to obtain an annualized convexity of **280.36**.

USEFUL CONCEPTS AND TOOLS

Calculating Approximate Duration and Convexity for Any Security

Above we showed how to calculate duration and convexity for equity securities, floating rate bonds, and fixed rate bonds. Common to all three is that they each have their own pricing formula. However, many instruments do not have explicit pricing formulas. For these instruments there are, however, approximations of duration and convexity that can be used. The method builds on taking a baseline price and then simply moving the risk factor up and down a certain amount.

To approximate duration, take a bond with a given price (P_0). Decrease the yield of that bond by a small number of basis points. Determine the new higher price (P_{hi}) of the bond. Then increase the original yield of the bond by the same number of basis points. Determine that lower new price (P_{lo}). Finally, approximate the duration with the following formula:

$$\text{Approximate duration} = \frac{P_{lo} - P_{hi}}{2(P_0)(dy)} \quad [19]$$

where:

P_{lo} = new lower price

P_{hi} = new higher price

P_0 = original price

dy = change in yield

What the formula measures is the average percentage price change relative to the initial price per one basis point change in yield.

We can also approximate the convexity measure with a similar formula:

$$\text{Approximate convexity measure} = \frac{P_{hi} + P_{lo} - 2P_0}{P_0(dy)^2} \quad [20]$$

Example. To exemplify how good the approximations are, let us return to our previous fixed rate bond example: a 30-year 5% bond, with semiannual coupons, selling at 75.055 to a yield of 7%. Increasing the bond yield by 10 basis points, from 7% to 7.1%, gives a new price of 74.070. Decreasing the yield by the same 10 basis points gives us a new price of 76.062.

With these numbers, we can substitute in both equation [19] and [20] to give:

$$\text{Approximate duration} = \frac{76.062 - 74.070}{2(75.055)(0.001)} = 13.27 \qquad [21]$$

$$\text{Approximate convexity measure} = \frac{74.070 + 76.062 - 2(75.055)}{75.055(0.001)^2} = 293.1 \qquad [22]$$

Our earlier estimations (given the more complicated formulas) were 13.27 for duration and 280.36 for convexity. The approximations are not far off, although more accurate for duration than convexity.

Delta and Gamma: Dollar Duration and Dollar Convexity

We have insisted throughout this note on discussing *percentage* change in price for a change in an underlying risk factor. We defined, for instance, duration as dP/dY divided by P. However, if we do not divide by price, we are left with dP/dY, or, in non-mathematical terms, the absolute dollar change. In the market, this is called dollar duration, or simply *delta*. (This equals the numerator of equation [9].)

The same holds true for convexity. Focusing on the absolute dollar change, we could have left the formula as d^2P/y^2, without dividing by P. This is called dollar convexity, or *gamma*. (This equals the numerator of equation [17].)

Example. For the fixed rate bond that we have used as an example all along (the 30-year 5% bond, with semiannual coupons, selling at 75.055 to a yield of 7%) we could use the numerators of equations [9] and [17] to calculate the delta and gamma.

However, since we already have calculated duration and convexity for this bond, let us just multiply back the price to reach the same result:

$$\text{Delta} = 13.27 \,^\circ\, 75.055 = \$996.00 \qquad [23]$$
$$\text{Gamma} = 280.36 \,^\circ\, 75.055 = \$21,042.91 \qquad [24]$$

PROBLEM SET

For the problems below, consider a bond with a par value of $1,000 to be paid in four years, a coupon rate of 6%, and a current annualized six-month yield of 9%. Assume that coupon payments are made semiannually to bondholders and that the next coupon payment is expected in six months.

Problem 1 What is the bond's duration (annualized)? Compare this with the approximate duration.

Problem 2 What is the bond's convexity (annualized)? Compare this with the approximate convexity.

Problem 3 What is the bond's delta (annualized)?

Problem 4 What is the bond's gamma (annualized)?

Problem 5 If the bond's annualized six-month yield decreased by 20 basis points, what would be the bond's realized return (percentage price change)? Compare this with the approximate realized return using the first two terms of equation [12] on page 55. Recalculate the answers for problems one through four using the new annualized six-month yield.

5

Ticonderoga: Inverse Floating Rate Bond

Late in the evening on December 17, 2004, David Talbot, founder and partner of London-based hedge fund group Ticonderoga Management, stepped into the office of Greg Bower, responsible for the fund's capital management overview. Like all hedge funds, Ticonderoga had a capital management function that monitored the trading risk of the hedge fund's portfolio. Many trades that entered the hedge fund's portfolio came with risk types that the hedge fund was not comfortable holding—and it was Bower's role to make sure such risks were hedged out and fully passed on.

When deciding which risks to hedge out, Bower followed a policy put in place by Ticonderoga's Investment Committee, which was made up by the fund's partners. The policy's main rule was that the fund should not take any bets on interest rates; all interest rate exposure should be completely hedged out. The fund implemented this policy by duration and convexity hedging its portfolio. It typically utilized cash instruments in addition to interest rate derivatives to accomplish this hedge.

This evening, Bower had an interesting story to tell Talbot. A recently proposed trade would bring with it some fairly large interest rate exposure, and Talbot was trying to figure out how to hedge the interest rate exposure and what the consequences of a hedge might be. He explained,

> It is a trade that has been proposed to us by a small merchant bank and Shannon at the trading desk would like us to take it on. It concerns buying a inverse floating rate bond [or simply an "inverse floater"]. Shannon believes the bond is mispriced given the current level of interest rates, and she is certain that we can make a excellent return on capital on the trade if we bought it—but the numbers will only work if we can hedge out the interest rate risk portion. Otherwise we would need to commit a lot of capital to the trade, and the resulting reduction in ROE would make the trade not worthwhile.

Professor George Chacko and Research Associate Anders Sjöman of the HBS Europe Research Center prepared this case. HBS cases are developed solely as the basis for class discussion. Certain details are disguised. Cases are not intended to serve as endorsements, sources of primary data, or illustrations of effective or ineffective management.

The trade that the merchant bank had proposed built on the bank taking a 20-year U.S. Treasury Bond, which had been issued 18 years ago, and now had two years left to maturity. When the bond was issued, it was issued at par and paid a coupon of 7.29%. The bank had taken the bond and split it into two pieces: one floating rate bond that paid LIBOR, and one inverse floating rate bond that paid 7.29% minus LIBOR. However, although the bond paid semi-annual coupons, the two derivative products paid their investors on a daily basis. Essentially, the merchant bank would use its balance sheet to convert the two semi-annual payments into a much smoother stream of payments.

The bank had offered Ticonderoga's trader a long position in the inverse floater—and the trader was now keen on taking on the trade, since she believed that the merchant bank had mispriced the inverse floater relative to the floater. Ideally, she wanted to take a long-short position: long the inverse floater and short the floater and then hedge out any residual interest rate risk. This would isolate the pricing discrepancy and allow Ticonderoga to commit the least amount of capital to the trade and still fully take advantage of the profit opportunity.

BOWER'S TASK: HEDGE INTEREST RATE RISK

The apparent mispricings amused both Talbot and Bower, who like most of their colleagues were proud of their strong quantitative approach. (The fund was run by a number of senior industry professionals, all trained at Harvard University in fields ranging from economics to applied math, including a founder with a Ph.D in Economics.) They were certain that they wanted to take on the trade—but before green-lighting the trade, Bower had to figure out a hedge that would get rid of the interest rate exposure in the long-short position. In order to figure out the appropriate hedging transaction, he had pulled up today's market data (see Exhibit 1 for the yield curve, Exhibit 2 for the interest rate swap rates, and Exhibit 3 for Eurodollar deposits).

Bower began constructing his hedge.

EXHIBIT 1

US TREASURY YIELDS FOR DECEMBER 17, 2004

Maturity	Yield
1 month	1.98
3 month	2.21
1 year	2.66
2 year	3.00
3 year	3.18
5 year	3.54
7 year	3.85
10 year	4.16
20 year	4.80

Source: Adapted by case authors from data provided by the Board of Governors of the Federal Reserve System, http://www.federalreserve.gov/releases/h15/data.htm, accessed April 2005.

EXHIBIT 2

SWAP RATES FOR DECEMBER 17, 2004

Maturity	Rate
1 year	3.02
2 year	3.35
3 year	3.56
4 year	3.75
5 year	3.92
7 year	4.22
10 year	4.55
30 year	5.18

Source: Adapted by case authors from data provided by the Board of Governors of the Federal Reserve System, http://www.federalreserve.gov/releases/h15/data.htm, accessed April 2005.

EXHIBIT 3

EURODOLLAR DEPOSIT RATES FOR DECEMBER 17, 2004

Maturity	Interest Rates
1 month	2.35
3 month	2.44
6 month	2.63

Source: Adapted by case authors from data provided by the Board of Governors of the Federal Reserve System, http://www.federalreserve.gov/releases/h15/data.htm, accessed April 2005.

6

100-Year Liabilities at Prudential Insurance

At first glance, Carlos Arrom, Managing Director of Asset Liability & Risk Management at Prudential Insurance, saw nothing particularly unusual about the $3.6 billion bond portfolio he used to match Prudential Insurance's structured settlement liabilities. The structured settlement liabilities represented long-term payment streams that Prudential Insurance promised to pay over the following 100 years to winners of lotteries or lawsuits such as those related to tobacco. The set of structured settlement liabilities had a duration of 14.86 years, matching the duration of the bond portfolio Arrom used to collateralize the liabilities. However, the durations of the liabilities and assets became frequently and significantly mismatched, requiring more and more of Arrom's time as he repeatedly had to rebalance the assets to mirror the duration of the liabilities.

Arrom called Anne Fifick, Vice President of Asset Liability & Risk Management at Prudential Insurance, to help him investigate the problem. Could it be that the dramatically low interest rates of March 2003, driven by a sluggish economy and the start of a war with Iraq, created some aberration in the markets? Was there something unusual about this relatively newly-constructed bond portfolio that Arrom did not realize? Could there be something unique about the structured settlement liabilities that Arrom had overlooked? Arrom was certain that he and Fifick, with a combined 25 years of experience in asset-liability management, would uncover the cause—and a solution—to the constant headache caused by the frequent rebalancing of the structured settlements portfolio.

U.S. LIFE INSURANCE INDUSTRY IN 2003[1]

The insurance industry in the United States was generally categorized into two sectors: life insurers, which offered products such as life insurance and annuities, and property and casualty insurers, which offered products such as insurance against theft and accidents. At the end of 2002, over 55,000 life insurance policies were in force in the United States totaling $16.3 trillion in coverage. There were approximately 1,200 life insurers in business in the U.S. at year-end 2002, a number that had been steadily decreasing since

Professors George Chacko and Peter A. Hecht and Research Associate Akiko M. Mitsui (MBA '01) prepared this case. This case was developed from published sources. The authors would like to thank the management at Prudential for helpful discussions in developing this case. This case was developed solely as the basis for class discussion. It is not intended to serve as endorsement, source of primary data, or illustration of effective or ineffective management.

[1] This section draws in part from "Life Insurers Fact Book 2003," American Council of Life Insurers.

the late 1980s due to consolidations and acquisitions. Among these companies, the three largest players—MetLife, AIG and Prudential Insurance—accounted for almost 20% of all industry assets, and the top 25 companies accounted for 75% of industry assets. (See Exhibit 1 for list of largest life insurers by total assets as of year-end 2002).

Life insurers were regulated in the U.S. by states, with little direct federal government oversight. Insurers applied for and received licenses from each state in which they conducted business. Under the National Association of Insurance Commissioners (NAIC), insurance regulators from around the country developed uniform or complementary policies around certain issues. For instance, the NAIC's uniform financial reporting standards applied to insurance companies throughout the U.S. In addition, the NAIC established capital requirements for insurance companies based on the riskiness of different assets held by insurance companies. Capital measured in this manner was often referred to as "regulatory capital," as opposed to capital measured as equity or retained earnings on the balance sheet.

EXHIBIT 1

LARGEST LIFE INSURERS IN U.S. BY TOTAL ASSETS, 12/31/02

Rank	Company Name	Assets (USD billion)
1	Metropolitan Group	246.1
2	American International Group	233.8
3	Prudential Financial Group	205.7
4	AEGON USA Group	144.9
5	TIAA Group	144.7
6	Hartford Life Group	136.8
7	ING Group	126.0
8	New York Life Group	121.9
9	Northwestern Mutual Group	102.9
10	Nationwide Group	87.4
11	Mass Mutual Financial Group	84.2
12	John Hancock Group	79.3
13	AXA Financial / Equitable Group	79.3
14	Principal Life	78.0
15	GE Financial Assurance Group	77.3
16	Citigroup/Travelers	75.0
17	CIGNA Group	72.3
18	Lincoln National Group	71.0
19	Allstate Group	63.8
20	American Express Group	55.1
21	Pacific Life Group	52.0
22	Jackson National Group	49.4
23	Manulife Financial Group	48.7
24	Sun Life of Canada Group	47.2
25	American Family Corporation	36.4

Source: Adapted from "Life Insurers Fact Book 2003," American Council of Life Insurers.

Life insurers were organized as stock companies or mutual companies. Stock life insurers issued stock and were owned by their stockholders. Mutual companies were owned by the policyholders and did not issue publicly traded stock. Mutual life insurers and stock life insurance companies were subject to the same insurance industry regulations with regard to amount of capital and reserves, but mutual life insurers, as privately-owned companies, were not required to issue the quarterly financial reports according to GAAP that were required for public companies. Likewise, Wall Street analysts closely followed the quarterly performance of the larger public life insurers. Starting in the late 1990s, several of the largest mutual companies, including Prudential Insurance, "demutualized" and changed from mutual companies to stock companies with initial public offerings of stock. In doing so, their existing policyholders received cash or shares of the new public company. While several large life insurers were still organized as mutual companies in 2003, over 90% of U.S. life insurers were stock companies.

Life insurance companies faced several competitive pressures in early 2003. In late-1999, historic financial services legislation, the Graham-Leach-Bliley Act of 1999, also called the Financial Modernization Act, removed longstanding barriers that required insurance and securities firms to be separated from banking businesses. Some insurance companies became affiliated with banks and asset managers, notably exemplified by the Citicorp acquisition of Travelers Insurance. In connection with competition from diversified financial companies and demand by consumers to share in equity market gains of the late 1990s, some insurers diversified their product offerings by introducing more market-based products such as variable annuities, or expanding their asset management functions.

Assets of Life Insurers

Life insurers collected premiums from policyholders and in return stood ready to pay the future benefits promised to these policyholders. Life insurance companies invested money collected from policyholders until the policy expired or a payment was made to the policy beneficiary.

Investment strategies of life insurers were conservative—the assets were generally matched to mirror the liabilities for which the assets were collateralizing. This investment strategy was driven by several factors, including regulatory capital requirements and risk ratings assigned by rating agencies. Among other things, rating agencies evaluated insurance companies' asset/liability match. As insurance companies had no implicit or explicit government guarantee, consumers buying life insurance policies relied heavily on these ratings to purchase policies.

A counterforce to purely conservative investment policies was insurance companies' drive to increase income through investments. The two main sources of income for an insurance company were premium income and investment income. In 2002, premium income represented 70% of total income for the industry, investment income represented 25%, and other income was 5%.[2]

Life insurers were major players in the U.S. capital markets. At year-end 2002 life insurers held over $3.3 trillion in financial assets. Life insurers were the largest single sector owner of corporate and foreign bonds outstanding in the United States at year-end 2002, with approximately $1.5 trillion of corporate and foreign bonds. This was about one-fourth of the $6.2 trillion of such bonds outstanding.[3] With long-dated lia-

---

[2] "Life Insurers Fact Book 2003," American Council of Life Insurers.

[3] "Flow of Funds Accounts of the United States, First Quarter 2003," Federal Reserve Board, June 5, 2003, Tables L.117, L.212.

EXHIBIT 2

**FINANCIAL ASSETS OF U.S. LIFE INSURERS
(GENERAL AND SEPARATE ACCOUNTS), 12/31/2002**

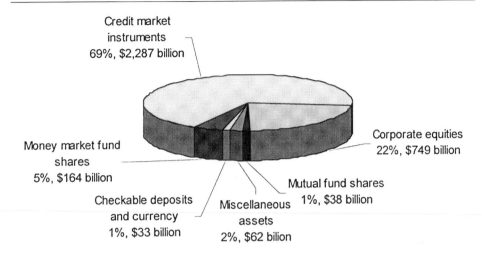

Credit market
instruments
69%, $2,287 billion

Corporate equities
22%, $749 billion

Money market fund
shares
5%, $164 billion

Mutual fund shares
1%, $38 billion

Checkable deposits
and currency
1%, $33 billion

Miscellaneous
assets
2%, $62 bilion

Source: Adapted from "Flow of Funds Accounts of the United States, First Quarter 2003," Federal Reserve Board.

---

bilities, life insurers were especially active investors of long-term bonds. Almost one-third of insurers' bonds had maturities of over 10 years, and over 60% had maturities of over five years.[4] (See Exhibit 2 for financial assets held by life insurance companies as of December 31, 2002.)

Assets of life insurers were held in two accounts, a general account for assets used as collateral against future policy payments, and a separate account for assets in which the customer accrued the investment risk and rewards of the assets, such as for pension funds or variable annuities. State insurance laws allowed assets in separate accounts to be invested without the restrictions usually placed on assets in general accounts. In aggregate, assets in separate accounts were much more highly weighted in equities than those in general accounts, with 74% of separate account assets in equities at year-end 2002 compared with 73% of general account assets invested in bonds.[5] Almost all bonds invested in the general account were high quality, investment grade bonds.

PRUDENTIAL FINANCIAL, INC. HISTORY AND RECENT DEVELOPMENTS

The roots of Prudential Financial, Inc. trace back to 1873, as a company that sold life insurance to industrial workers in New Jersey. In 2003 Prudential Financial, Inc.'s flagship subsidiary, Prudential Insurance, was the third largest life insurance company in the United States ranked by assets. In addition to insurance, Prudential Financial had

---

[4] "Life Insurers Fact Book 2003," American Council of Life Insurers.

[5] "Life Insurers Fact Book 2003," American Council of Life Insurers.

a large investment division derived from their 1981 purchase of a securities company. Prudential Financial also had significant international operations. A mutual company since the 1940s, in 1998 Prudential announced plans to change to a stock ownership company. The initial public offering was one of the largest in the insurance industry, and raised $3 billion in December 2001 at a price of $27.50 per share. (See Exhibit 3 to Exhibit 5 for Prudential Financial, Inc.'s income statement, balance sheet and cash flow statements, respectively, and Exhibit 6 for stock price history since the company's demutualization.)

As a public company, Prudential Financial, Inc. focused on cutting costs, streamlining operations, and concentrating on core businesses, which Prudential identified as insurance, investments and international. For instance, Prudential divested itself of investment banking, property and casualty insurance, and other businesses while using its newly-issued stock as currency to purchase other life insurance companies and investment businesses.

ASSET LIABILITY AND RISK MANAGEMENT AT PRUDENTIAL INSURANCE

Organization and General Principles

Prudential Insurance sold a variety of insurance products, including term life, group life, whole life, and annuity products. Prudential Insurance collected premiums and other payments for these policies. These payments were invested in the general account for policies in which Prudential absorbed all the investment risk, and in the separate account for policies in which the policyholder bore the investment risk of the assets.

The primary responsibility of the Asset Liability & Risk Management (AL&RM) division, headed by Arrom, was the investment management of Prudential Insurance's general account and insurance subsidiaries. AL&RM worked closely with Prudential's product areas and with Prudential's investment management function to establish investment policies and implement investment strategies. The five key functions of the investment process for the general account were:

- Investment policy, which was driven by the product mix, expectations concerning investment returns, leverage/risk and exposures. It was heavily weighted on a philosophy of asset-liability matching.
- Planning, which involved the selection of managers and specific allocation plans reflecting comparative strengths.
- Strategy and tactics, which reflected AL&RM's outlook for investment markets and changing investment opportunities.
- Performance management, which focused on two primary objectives: (1) total return vs. market benchmarks, and (2) GAAP and statutory investment income vs. plans.
- Risk control encompassed the entire investment process and was monitored by a separate risk management group.

In its 2002 10-K filing, Prudential Insurance considered "risk management to be an integral part of our core business." In this regard, Prudential identified and measured various forms of risk, established risk thresholds, and created processes to maintain risks within the thresholds while maximizing returns on the underlying assets or liabilities.

EXHIBIT 3

PRUDENTIAL FINANCIAL, INC. INCOME STATEMENTS (GAAP), 1998–2001

	As of or for the Year Ended December 31,				
	2002	**2001**	**2000**	**1999**	**1998**
	(in millions, except per share and ratio information)				
Income Statement Data:					
Revenues:					
Premiums	$ 13,531	$ 12,477	$ 10,181	$ 9,528	$ 9,048
Policy charges and fee income	1,653	1,803	1,639	1,516	1,465
Net investment income	8,832	9,138	9,479	9,348	9,436
Realized investment gains (losses), net	−1,358	−671	−266	924	2,641
Commissions and other income	4,017	4,324	5,299	5,095	4,299
Total revenues	**26,675**	**27,071**	**26,332**	**26,411**	**26,889**
Benefits and expenses:					
Policyholders' benefits	13,658	12,752	10,640	10,226	9,786
Interest credited to policyholders' account balances	1,846	1,804	1,751	1,811	1,953
Dividends to policyholders	2,644	2,722	2,724	2,571	2,477
General and administrative expenses	8,443	9,346	9,875	9,396	8,916
Capital markets restructuring	—	—	476	—	—
Sales practices remedies and costs	20	—	—	100	1,150
Demutualization costs and expenses	—	588	143	75	24
Total benefits and expenses	**26,611**	**27,212**	**25,609**	**24,179**	**24,306**
Income (loss) from continuing operations before income taxes	**64**	**−141**	**723**	**2,232**	**2,583**
Income tax expense (benefit)	−192	−34	398	1,033	964
Income (loss) from continuing operations	256	−107	325	1,199	1,619
Income (loss) from discontinued operations, net of taxes	−62	−47	73	−386	−51
Net income (loss)	**$ 194**	**$ −154**	**$ 398**	**$ 813**	**$ 1,106**
Basic and diluted income from continuing operations per share—Common Stock(1)	$ 1.36	$ 0.07			
Basic and diluted net income per share—Common Stock(1)	$ 1.25	$ 0.07			
Basic and diluted net income (loss) per share—Class B Stock(1)	$ −264	$ 1.5			
Dividends declared per share—Common Stock	$ 0.4				
Dividends declared per share—Class B Stock	$ 9.625				
Ratio of earnings to fixed charges(2)	1.04		1.23	1.79	1.83

Source: Adapted from company 2002 10-K.

EXHIBIT 4

PRUDENTIAL FINANCIAL, INC. BALANCE SHEET (GAAP), 1998–2002

	As of or for the Year Ended December 31,				
	2002	**2001**	**2000** (in millions)	**1999**	**1998**
Balance Sheet Data:					
Total investments excluding policy loans	$ 174,267	$ 157,264	$ 140,469	$ 151,338	$ 148,837
Separate account assets	70,555	77,158	82,217	82,131	80,931
Total assets	**292,746**	**293,030**	**272,753**	**285,094**	**279,422**
Future policy benefits, policyholders' account balances and unpaid claims and claim adjustment expenses	140,168	133,732	104,130	102,928	104,301
Separate account liabilities	70,555	77,158	82,217	82,131	80,931
Short-term debt	3,469	5,405	11,131	10,858	10,082
Long-term debt	4,757	5,304	2,502	5,513	4,734
Total liabilities	**270,726**	**271,887**	**252,145**	**265,803**	**259,027**
Guaranteed beneficial interest in Trust holding solely debentures of Parent	690	690	—	—	—
Equity	**21,330**	**20,453**	**20,608**	**19,291**	**20,395**

Source: Adapted from company 2002 10-K.

Risk mangers also established investment risk limits for exposures to any issuer, geographic region, and type of security or industry.

Investment Policy and Asset Liability Management

A key component of determining the asset investment policy for any given set of liabilities was to understand the design and anticipated cash flows for the product generating the liabilities. AL&RM worked closely with Prudential Insurance's business groups to understand the cash flow characteristics of insurance products sold by Prudential. The duration of each products' cash flows, as well as the need for current income vs. capital gains for the product, generally pointed to a certain mix of fixed assets vs. equity assets. In addition to duration and convexity matching, several other factors were considered in designing the investment policy for a product. Some of these factors included analyzing the effect of certain assets on regulatory capital, determining how asset volatility could affect GAAP earnings, and maximizing the expected economic return of the portfolio. (See Exhibit 7 for diagram of different considerations affecting investment policy.) Given the many considerations involved in investment policy, one of the most important of which was duration and convexity matching, Prudential's predominant asset invested in the general account was fixed income. (See Exhibit 8 for composition of Prudential's general account assets as of September 30, 2001, the latest publicly available data.)

EXHIBIT 5

PRUDENTIAL FINANCIAL, INC. STATEMENT OF CASH FLOWS, 1998–2002

	31-Dec-2002	31-Dec-2001	31-Dec-2000	31-Dec-1999	31-Dec-1998
Net Income (SCF)	194	−154	398	813	1,106
Depreciation	559	433	740	689	337
Other Non-Cash Items	−486	−482	−419	100	−9
Other Operating Cash Flows	9,714	285	7,146	−1,040	−4,020
Cash from Operations	**9,981**	**82**	**7,865**	**562**	**−2,586**
Other Investing Cash Flows	−14,052	12,458	−1,973	−219	5,803
Cash from Investing	**−14,052**	**12,458**	**−1,973**	**−219**	**5,803**
Dividends Paid	−192	0	0	0	0
Purchase or Sale of Stock	−781	4,167	0	0	0
Purchase and Retirement of Debt	−2,590	−3,604	−3,270	1,369	3,944
Other Financing Cash Flows	−1,004	−2,243	−1,373	−2,864	−4,130
Cash From Financing	**−4,567**	**−1,680**	**−4,643**	**−1,495**	**−186**
Exchange Rate Effects	0	0	0	0	0
Net Change in Cash	**−8,638**	**10,860**	**1,249**	**−1,152**	**3,031**
Cash Interest Paid	458	638	1,040	824	864
Cash Taxes Paid	57	466	248	−344	163

Source: Adapted from company 2002 10-K.

EXHIBIT 6

PRUDENTIAL FINANCIAL, INC. MONTHLY CLOSING STOCK PRICE VS. (REBALANCED) S&P 500

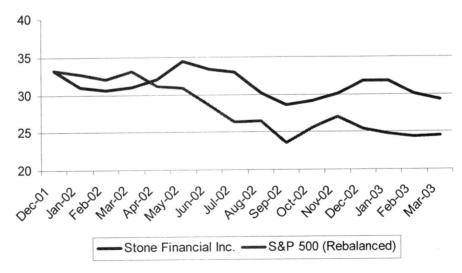

Source: Data provided by OneSource® Business BrowserSM, an online business information product of OneSource Information Services, Inc. ("OneSource"), accessed November 2003, and by Global Financial Data, accessed November 2003.

EXHIBIT 7

FACTORS AFFECTING INVESTMENT POLICY FOR PRODUCTS

Investment Policy Construction: Asset-Liability Management

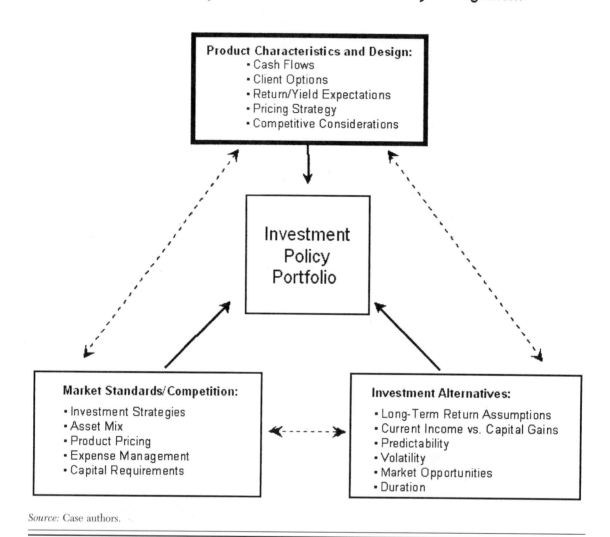

Source: Case authors.

Duration and Convexity Matching

One of the primary ways Prudential Insurance managed its investment portfolio was to calculate duration and convexity of liability cash flows, and invest in assets that closely matched these characteristics. According to company documents:

With respect to non-variable life insurance products, fixed rate annuities, the fixed rate options in our variable life insurance and annuity products, consumer banking products, and other finance businesses, we incur market risk primarily in the form of interest rate risk. We manage this risk through asset/liability management strategies that seek to match the

EXHIBIT 8

PRUDENTIAL INSURANCE GENERAL ACCOUNT ASSETS, SEPTEMBER 31, 2001

$ millions	Amount	% Total
Fixed maturities:		
Public available for sale, at fair value	61,832	48%
Public held to maturity, at amortized cost	336	0%
Private available for sale, at fair value	32,874	25%
Private held to maturity, at amortized cost	60	0%
Trading account assets, at fair value	8	0%
Equity securities, at fair value	1,911	1%
Mortgage loans, book value	15,046	12%
Other long term investments	4,335	3%
Loans to owners of insurance policies	8,337	6%
Short term investments	4,304	3%
Total investments	129,043	100%

Source: Adapted from Company 2002 Annual Report.

interest rate sensitivity of the assets to that of the underlying liabilities. Our overall objective in these strategies is to limit the net change in value of assets and liabilities arising from interest rate movements. . . . We use duration and convexity analyses to measure price sensitivity to interest rate changes. . . . We seek to manage our interest rate exposure . . . by matching the relative sensitivity of asset and liability values to interest rate changes, or controlling "duration mismatch" of assets and liabilities.[6]

Risk-Based Capital Requirements

Insurance regulators expected insurance companies to have minimum risk-based capital ratios of 100% to maintain solvency and avoid regulatory action. Most regulators followed the model risk-based capital rules established by the NAIC, whereby each asset was assigned with a risk-weighting to determine "risk-based assets." An insurance firm's total capital divided by risk-based capital determined the risk-based capital ratio. An insurance company's risk-based capital measure was one of several important capital-related considerations that determined investment policy. (See Exhibit 9 for risk weightings established by the NAIC for different asset classes.) Most insurance companies, including Prudential, aimed to have risk-based capital ratios that were multiples of the minimum 100%, in order to maintain strong ratings from insurance rating agencies. The risk-based capital ratio for the U.S. insurance industry at year-end 2002 was 325%.[7] Such risk-based capital ratios were generally considered to be within the range of an AA rating from insurance rating agencies. (See Exhibit 10 for a sample of how much capital a company would need to hold, with a target risk-based capital ratio of 325%, for investments in different assets.)

[6] Company 2002 10-K.

[7] "Life Insurers Fact Book 2003," American Council of Life Insurers.

EXHIBIT 9

NAIC INSURANCE COMPANY ASSET RISK FACTORS TO DETERMINE REGULATORY CAPITAL

Asset Class	Asset	Risk Factor, %
Bonds	NAIC CLASS 0 (EXEMPT)	0.0
	NAIC CLASS 1 (Aaa, Aa, A)	0.3
	NAIC CLASS 2 (Baa)	1.0
	NAIC CLASS 3 (Ba)	3.4
	NAIC CLASS 4 (B)	7.4
	NAIC CLASS 5 (C and lower)	17.0
	NAIC CLASS 6 (In or near default)	19.5
Short term bonds	NAIC CLASS 0 (EXEMPT)	0.0
	NAIC CLASS 1	3.0
	NAIC CLASS 2	1.0
	NAIC CLASS 3	3.4
	NAIC CLASS 4	7.4
	NAIC CLASS 5	17.0
	NAIC CLASS 6	19.5
Mortgages	IN GOOD STANDING	2.4
	90 DAYS OVERDUE	13.3
	IN FORECLOSURE	17.0
Preferred stock	NAIC CLASS 1	0.8
	NAIC CLASS 2	2.2
	NAIC CLASS 3	5.3
	NAIC CLASS 4	11.1
	NAIC CLASS 5	18.4
	NAIC CLASS 6	19.5
Common stock	UNAFFILIATED-PUBLIC	18.9
	UNAFFILIATED-PRIVATE	19.5
Real estate	COMPANY OCCUPIED	9.75
	INVESTMENT	9.75
	FORECLOSED	14.95

Source: Adapted from Company Annual Report 2002 and Company 2002 10-K.

Other Measures

Other measurement tools used by Prudential in asset/liability management were key rate duration, value-at-risk, stress-testing, and credit default models. These tools were used simultaneously with duration and convexity measurements to determine investment policies. Assets were also evaluated with respect to risk-based capital implications, total return expectations for different asset classes, and the volatility of asset classes. Investment income was an important source of revenue for insurance companies, and higher returns on the assets in the investment portfolio made products more profitable, or enabled products to be priced more competitively to consumers. At the same time, the higher volatility that was typical of most higher-return assets could expose an insurance company to year-to-year risk of missing capital targets or to volatility in income statements.

EXHIBIT 10

THEORETICAL EXAMPLE OF CAPITAL REQUIRED FOR $100 OF DIFFERENT ASSETS ASSUMING A TARGET RISK-BASED CAPITAL RATIO OF 325%

Asset	Book Value	NAIC Risk Factor	Risk-Adjusted Asset Value	Capital Required to Invest in Asset and Maintain 325% Risk-Based Capital Ratio
U.S. Treasury Bond (NAIC Class 0)	$100	0.0%	$ 0.00	$ 0.00
AA Corporate Bond (NAIC Class 1)	$100	0.3	0.30	0.90
B Corporate Bond (NAIC Class 4)	$100	7.4	7.40	22.20
Common Public Stocks	$100	18.9	18.90	56.70

Source: Casewriter estimates.

PRUDENTIAL INSURANCE'S 100-YEAR LIABILITY PORTFOLIO

Arrom and Fifick collected all the data he thought he would need to evaluate the structured settlements liabilities and the bonds that were used to defease these liabilities. While the structured settlement product did not represent a large part of Prudential's business to date, Arrom expected growth in structured settlements. Structured settlements referred to Prudential's business of guaranteeing future payments of lottery winnings and litigation settlements. A structured settlement policy, for instance, could arise from a state government winning a lawsuit against a tobacco company. The tobacco company may agree to pay the settlement over several years. However, if the state did not want to accept the risk of default by the tobacco company, an insurance company can in effect write a policy to take the liability off of the balance sheet of the tobacco company, and onto the balance sheet of the insurance company. The insurance company would be responsible for paying the liabilities to the state government, and for investing the premiums paid by the tobacco company.

A cash flow model that represents Prudential's expected payments arising from their structured settlements products is shown in Exhibit 11.[8] Typically, such an expected cash flow model would be used by AL&RM to construct an asset portfolio with similar duration. However, in this case, the cash flow model was adjusted to reduce the 100-years of cash flows into a more manageable, equivalent 30-year model. The adjusted cash flow model was created by first discounting the cash flows in years 31 to 100 at the prevailing 30-year Treasury yield to a single cash flow in year 31. This method of adjustment was considered to be reasonable because the present values of the original and amended cash flow models were the same. In addition, for practical purposes of choosing an investment portfolio, yield curves were generally flat after 20–30 years. So discounting the year 31–100 cash flows using the 30-year Treasury was appropriate. Exhibit 12 shows the amended cash flow model for the structured settlements portfolio, used by Arrom and Fifick, to develop an investment policy for the portfolio. The amended liabilities, using the 30-year Treasury yield prevailing on March 31, 2003 of

---

[8] Although representative, the numbers in this cash flow model are created by the case authors for the purposes of this case.

EXHIBIT 11

REPRESENTATIVE LIABILITY CASH FLOWS FOR STRUCTURED SETTLEMENTS PORTFOLIO

Year	Cash Flow, $ mill	Year	Cash Flow, $ mil	Year	Cash Flow, $ mil	Year	Cash Flow, $ mil
1	200	26	187	51	129	76	72
2	198	27	169	52	125	77	69
3	194	28	160	53	126	78	65
4	196	29	165	54	124	79	62
5	208	30	168	55	125	80	58
6	208	31	163	56	119	81	54
7	197	32	154	57	117	82	49
8	201	33	149	58	117	83	45
9	200	34	156	59	115	84	41
10	204	35	159	60	113	85	36
11	207	36	158	61	111	86	32
12	199	37	150	62	109	87	28
13	192	38	147	63	108	88	25
14	192	39	144	64	105	89	21
15	204	40	148	65	102	90	18
16	226	41	148	66	100	91	15
17	203	42	141	67	98	92	13
18	186	43	137	68	95	93	11
19	205	44	141	69	93	94	9
20	192	45	139	70	90	95	7
21	190	46	137	71	87	96	6
22	178	47	133	72	85	97	5
23	175	48	136	73	82	98	4
24	189	49	136	74	79	99	3
25	178	50	133	75	76	100	2
						101	2
						102	1
						103	1

Source: Casewriter estimates.

4.93%, had a present value of approximately $3.6 billion, and a duration of approximately 14.86 years.

Arrom noted that the portfolio of bonds used to collateralize the structured settlements also had a duration of 14.86 years. As interest rates started declining rapidly in 2000, the value of the bond portfolio did not increase as much as the value of the structured settlements. It was suggested to Arrom and Fifick that the rapid and historic low interest rates might have created some aberration in the markets, resulting in the mismatched portfolios. (See Exhibit 13 for 10-year Treasury yields from January 2000 to March 2003.)

EXHIBIT 12

AMENDED LIABILITY CASH FLOWS FOR STRUCTURED SETTLEMENTS PORTFOLIO

Year	Cash Flow, $ mill	Year	Cash Flow, $ mil	Year	Cash Flow, $ mil	Year	Cash Flow, $ mil
1	200	11	207	21	190	31	2,636
2	198	12	199	22	178		
3	194	13	192	23	175		
4	196	14	192	24	189		
5	208	15	204	25	178		
6	208	16	226	26	187		
7	197	17	203	27	169		
8	201	18	186	28	160		
9	200	19	205	29	165		
10	204	20	192	30	168		

Source: Casewriter estimates.

EXHIBIT 13

10-YEAR U.S. TREASURY YIELDS, JANUARY 2000–MARCH 2003: COMPANY 2002 10-K

Source: Adapted from Global Financial Data, accessed November 2003.

EXHIBIT 14

ROLLING 30-YEAR TOTAL RETURN ON S&P 500 INDEX, 1918–2002

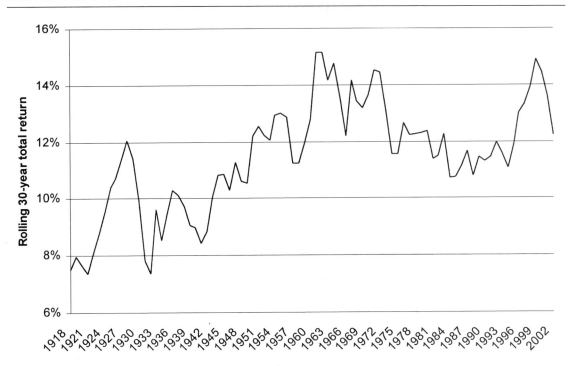

Source: Adapted from Global Financial Data, accessed November 2003.

In this context, Arrom and Fifick wondered whether bonds were the right matching asset for the structured settlements portfolio. Since the U.S. government discontinued new issues of 30-year Treasury bonds in 2001, it was relatively difficult to find a large supply of long-duration bonds other than some types of mortgage related bonds. Alternatively, equities could be considered to be long duration assets. Since Prudential's structured settlement liability cash flows beyond 30 years were discounted at about 5%, Arrom and Fifick simply needed a very long-term asset that was expected to return around 5–6% per year to be well-hedged. As a rule, Prudential was not investing in new real estate. Arrom noted that over rolling 30-year periods, equities had performed well against the 6% standard, and indeed, returned more than 6% consistently. (See Exhibit 14 for total returns of the S&P 500 index over rolling 30-year periods from 1918–2002.)

FIXED-INCOME SECURITIES: APPLICATIONS

7

Deutsche Bank: Discussing the Equity Risk Premium

Jamil Baz, global head of fixed income research at Deutsche Bank, sat down at the conference table in his office with George Cooper, the group's global fixed income strategist. It was August 2003, and for the better part of two years, the two had been discussing with their clients the danger of overstating the equity risk premium (ERP) when comparing bonds and equities. Cooper had now put together a presentation to justify this argument. Both Baz and Cooper believed that their advice added value to their clients' activities. They just wanted to go through the presentation one last time, making sure the arguments were well presented for their target audience.

THE DEUTSCHE BANK FIXED INCOME RESEARCH GROUP

Baz joined Deutsche Bank in 2001 as a managing director. The Fixed Income Research Group, which he headed, was Deutsche Bank's internal research and development (R&D) department for fixed income instruments. Their mandate was to look for untapped value across bond markets and interest rate derivatives. Based in Deutsche Bank's London office, the research group consisted of about 50 analysts and strategists. (Of these, about 10 were located in the bank's New York offices.)

As a part of a large financial institution, the research group was under constant pressure to monetize the ideas that they generated. Immediate opportunities were suggested as trades to internal traders as well as clients, whereas long-term-oriented research findings were presented to clients at the CEO, CFO, and Treasury level. Baz, who previously had been a managing director at Lehman Brothers in London and also held an M.S. in management from MIT and a Ph.D. in business economics from Harvard University, explained how the ideas were pitched:

Professors George Chacko and Peter Hecht, Executive Director of the HBS Europe Research Center Vincent Dessain, and Research Associate Anders Sjöman prepared this case. This case deals with the macro-level advice activities of a research department and draws from "Deutsche Bank: Finding Relative Value Trades," HBS Case No. 205-059, by the same authors. Case No. 205-059 deals with trade-specific advice from the same research department. Some names and data have been disguised for confidentiality. HBS cases are developed solely as the basis for class discussion. Cases are not intended to serve as endorsements, sources of primary data, or illustrations of effective or ineffective management. This case is not intended as financial advice, and it should not be used as the basis for any investment decision, in whole or in part.

The final goal is to create a franchise with fixed income clients. So, for clients on the asset side, such as mutual funds, hedge funds, insurance companies, and pension plans, we help them generate high returns on their assets. We give specific ideas to be executed by the clients—hopefully with us, although that is never certain. However, even if we don't get a trade out of our recommendation, it is important enough that we maintain Deutsche Bank's presence at the client. Sometimes we also do bespoke—or customized—work, where we analyze their balance sheet and asset-liability mismatches for them, almost like technical financial consulting. Overall, research alone will not give us clients, but research combined with pricing are the keys to building long-lasting relationships with external clients.

Overall, we strive to push the frontiers of analytical finance when it comes to modeling interest rates, volatilities, and spreads. Owing to data availability and an intimate exposure to institutional market realities, we are often pushed to reach results ahead of academic finance journals.

On a group level, Deutsche Bank organized its fixed income activities in the global markets around three main pillars: investor coverage, issuer coverage, and research. The trading desks dealing in these areas were in turn divided into two groups: credit (with credit trading/credit derivatives, new issue syndicate, asset securitization, and emerging markets) and rates (with foreign exchange, money markets, fixed income, and interest rate derivatives).

The research efforts of the group were set up to match these organizational divisions. The Fixed Income Research Group was one of several research groups (as shown in Exhibit 1). All these groups were run under the banner of Global Markets Research.

EXHIBIT 1

DEUTSCHE BANK GLOBAL MARKETS RESEARCH ORGANIZATION

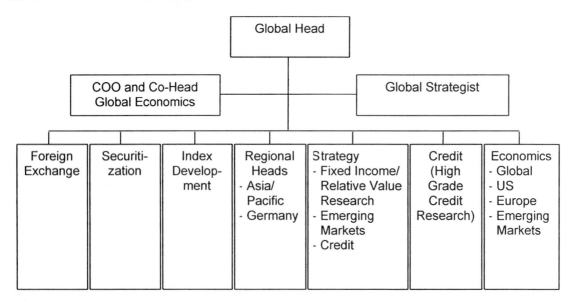

Source: Deutsche Bank.

Research as a whole was headed by David Folkerts-Landau. Demand for direct meetings with Deutsche Bank's research groups had grown over the past few years, taken internally as a sign of increased respect for the bank's research output. In the last year, Baz's group alone had logged over 1,500 client meetings. All clients had access to the Deutsche Bank research in papers and newsletters that were available online. Internal traders also benefited from the research, which was a major influence behind much of the bank's proprietary—or "prop"—trading. Most members of the research group shared their time between external clients and traders, with more senior staff members working more with external clients and less with the trading floor.

In the end, measuring the research group's value to the organization was generally hard. Said Baz:

> Putting a value on the work we do, and the effect we have on the bank, is very hard. In fact, the minute you really start measuring it by attributing sales and trades back to us, the trading floor would be more reluctant to work with us. Instead, we are mostly evaluated by top management on three other factors. Firstly, overall market direction, which is how much of rate and spread moves did we catch in our advice. Secondly, the relative-value trades we originated. Thirdly, any customized business we have brought in from our client meetings.

Compensation to the members of the group was tied to the evaluation of the group as a whole. Individual bonuses were then given at the discretion of Baz as the group's manager, based on his qualitative impression of each member's contribution.

The group's activities were normally broken down into relative-value and strategic advice on macro trends. In relative-value, the group looked for opportunities by comparing different instruments and then recommended trading strategies to clients and internal traders. The trade opportunities that the research group identified were published weekly in the "Deutsche Bank Fixed Income Weekly" newsletter that was distributed to traders and clients. Head of Relative Value Research for Europe was Jean Dumas, an engineer from the ESME SUDRIA in France with a specialization in finance, who had worked with Relative Value Research for Deutsche Bank in Paris, Frankfurt, and Sydney before moving to London. Dumas explained his work: "We come up with different types of trades all the time. The trade opportunities may be there for a week or two, sometimes longer. I look at different spreadsheets, listen to what traders are saying, watch the news, study different models. . . . Then I try to put everything together—and suddenly there is a trade opportunity."

By contrast, the macro and strategic advice activities dealt with more long-term discussions, presenting Deutsche Bank's view on macroeconomic trends to external clients. In these discussions, the group typically did not expect a quick monetary return. Cooper, a Ph.D. graduate in engineering at Durham University and previously a fixed income portfolio manager for both Goldman Sachs Asset Management and JP Morgan Investment Management, explained:

> This type of activity does not generate a lot of money from a trade perspective. It generates brand value, though, and is especially appealing to insurance companies or asset-liability people, who appreciate the long-term view. We believe it serves more of an educational purpose. It gets the fund managers thinking. They are not looking for prescriptive research, where we tell them to "do this trade," but they look for interesting ideas. Of course, they then weigh our ideas against whatever Goldman Sachs or Morgan Stanley are saying. Our role is to come up with hopefully insightful but also informative new ways to look at things.

EQUITY RISK PREMIUM, AND FIXED INCOME VERSUS EQUITIES

An ongoing discussion that the research group had held over the past few years with its clients was that the investor community should not overstate the equity risk premium (ERP) when comparing bonds and equities. ERP was traditionally defined as the expected return on the stock market in excess of the return on a risk-free bond. Obtaining a reasonable estimate of ERP was important, since portfolio managers often used this estimate to help guide their funds allocation between stocks and bonds.

In the presentation package that Cooper had just given Baz (see Exhibit 2 for the full presentation), he had included two alternative ways to estimate ERP. The first method was based on a traditional approach; the second was more novel. However, the two methods actually resulted in rather different ERP measures. Baz and Cooper would have to decide how to handle this apparent difference when meeting clients.

EXHIBIT 2

BONDS VERSUS EQUITIES—A FEW THOUGHTS ON THE EQUITY RISK PREMIUM

Slide 1: Bonds vs. Equity: Method #1—Dividend discounting

	U.S.
Dividend Yield	1.64%
+	
Real Dividend Growth	3.30%
Real Equity Yield	4.94%
−	
Real Bond Yield	2.47%
= Equity Risk Premium	2.47%
ERP Duration	*61 years*

Slide 2: Equity risk premium: has risen but still a long way to go

The equity risk premium has risen in the past few months...

But it is still low compared to historical average of 4.46*

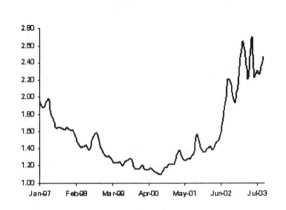

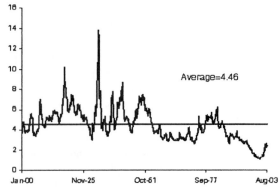

Based on data from January 1900 - October 2003

The first method built on using a dividend discount model, the so-called Gordon Growth Model. The model held that the total return of a stock investment would equal its dividend yield plus its dividend growth rate. In algebraic terms, R (return) = D (dividend)/P (current share price) + G (dividend growth rate). Cooper walked Baz through Slide 1 of the presentation:

EXHIBIT 2   (Continued)

BONDS VERSUS EQUITIES—A FEW THOUGHTS ON THE EQUITY RISK PREMIUM

Slide 3: Dividend yields: low levels in the U.S. . . .

• Dividend yields in the U.S. are low compared to historical average

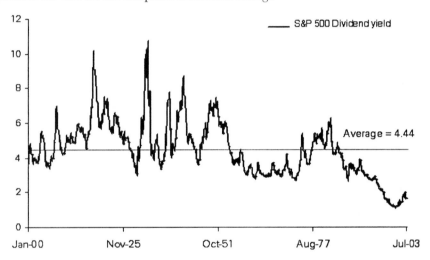

Slide 4: But close to fair value in Euroland

• However, in Euroland, dividend yields are close to their historical average

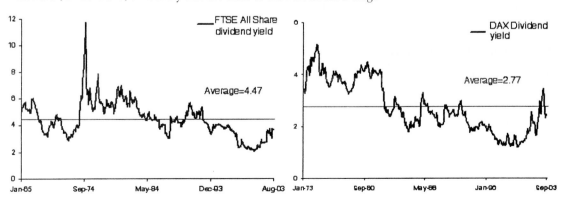

(Continued)

EXHIBIT 2   (Continued)

BONDS VERSUS EQUITIES—A FEW THOUGHTS ON THE EQUITY RISK PREMIUM

Slide 5: Equity risk premium: what does it imply for the future?

• Equity risk premium is mean reverting with a half life of approx. 4 years

• ERP likely to increase in the future

• We expect the ERP to increase by 40bp and 100bp in 1 year and 3 years respectively

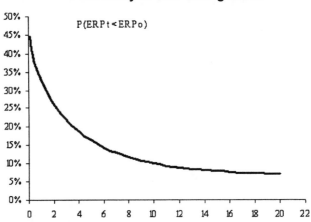

Probability of ERP falling is low

Slide 6: Defined benefit asset liability mismatch: bad news is really bad news

• The equity market sell-off has changed the balance sheet picture of corporate defined benefits plans from over-funded to underfunded

	1st Jan 2002				23rd October 2003°		
A			L	A			L
Equity	55	Defined benefits	100	Equity	50	Defined benefits	110
Bonds	45	Overfunding	0	Bonds	48	Overfunding	(−12)

• Asset liability mismatch equals nearly two years of corporate earnings

• Mismatch to result in corporate earnings being reduced by 6% to 20% annually

Slide 7: Defined benefits pension plans: problem is worse than you think

• But this is understanding the mismatch
  –Defined benefits plans periodically rebalance their portfolios
  –Assets of defined benefits pension plans declined by 13% in 2002, and not just 8% which this simple model would suggest

• Add to this problems of accounting for stock options, accounting irregularities . . .

(Continued)

EXHIBIT 2 (Continued)

BONDS VERSUS EQUITIES—A FEW THOUGHTS ON THE EQUITY RISK PREMIUM

Slide 8: S&P 500 and bonds: crises correlation pattern

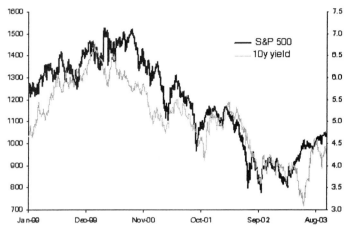

Source: DB Global Markets Research, Bloomberg

Correlation between 10y
Treasury yield and S&P 500

Period	Correlation
1990–1999	-0.702
1999–Aug 2003	0.901

Slide 9: Method #2: Earnings yield vs. real bond yield

- It can be shown that the earnings yield is the real equity yield°
- Thus the equity risk premium (ERP) can be expressed as

$$ERP = Earnings\ yield - real\ bond\ yield$$

Slide 10: Equity risk premium—adjusting to a realistic scenario

- We adjust the P/E to more realistic levels by correcting for presumed distortions

Influencing factor	Correction factor	P/E
• I/B/E/S estimate		19.3
• Historical over-prediction of IBES estimates to actual values	12%	21.4
• Defined benefits pension funds asset liability mismatch	10%	23.8
• Stock options	10%	26.4
• Accounting irregularities	10%	29.3

Slide 11: Equity risk premium using Earnings yield

	U.S.
Earnings yield	3.41%
Real bond yield	2.47%
Equity risk premium	**0.94%**

(Continued)

EXHIBIT 2 *(Continued)*

BONDS VERSUS EQUITIES—A FEW THOUGHTS ON THE EQUITY RISK PREMIUM

Slide 12: U.S.: Probability of outperformance of stocks vs. bonds

Probability of Outperformance of Equity versus Bonds

$$\phi\left[\left(\frac{ERP}{vol} - \frac{vol}{2}\right)\sqrt{T}\right]$$

Where *ERP* is the Equity Risk Premium, *vol* is the volatility of equity index, *T* is the horizon

Example of the S&P 500

Equity Risk Premium = 0.94%

Volatility = 20%

Probability of Outperformance of Equity versus TIPS over 20 years

$$= \phi\left[\left(\frac{0.94\%}{20\%} - \frac{20\%}{2}\right)4.5\right] = \phi(-24\%) = 40.6\%$$

Source: Deutsche Bank.

U.S.: Probability of Outperformance of Stocks versus Bonds

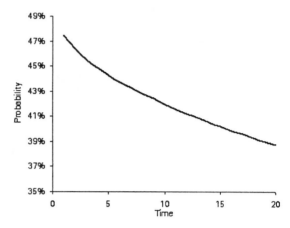

Source: DB Global Markets Research, Bloomberg

With the Gordon Growth Model, we input the current dividend yield for the stock market. When I put this presentation together, it was about 1.64%. You add onto that some estimate for forward-looking growth of dividends. A reasonable assumption would be that they will grow in line with GDP [gross domestic product]—so we take a consensus forecast for real GDP growth of 3.3%. That gets us to the real equity yield of 4.94%. We take away a riskless long-term real yield, which we take from the 30-year TIPS[1] market, which at the time was about 2.5%. We then arrive at a reasonable measure of a forward-looking equity risk premium, at about 2.5%. You can compare that to the historic ERP in the U.S., which has been slightly north of 4%.

Baz nodded in agreement with Cooper's explanation and browsed though the remaining slides until he reached Slide 9. Here, the other ERP estimation method was presented. To Cooper, this method represented one of the "new ways to look at things" that the research group should strive to find. He explained:

> If we take a macro view of the stock market, imagine a company that pays out half its earnings as dividends and retains half of its earnings. It then has to choose what to do with these retained earnings. Let's say that its choices are to buy its own stock, build a new factory, or buy a new company. Let's also assume that the potential returns available on all three options are in equilibrium. The new factory is the same cost as buying a competitor, which is the same cost as buying its own stock. In that case, if everything is basically in equilibrium with buying its own stock, then it is going to reinvest the retained earnings at whatever its own quoted P/E [price-to-earnings] ratios are. And this means that that the company's real return, or equity yield, is equal to E over P, the earnings yield.

[1] Treasury inflation-protected securities (TIPS) are a special form of U.S. Treasury notes and bonds, where the coupons and principal amount are adjusted periodically for inflation.

Turning to Slide 10 and Slide 11, Cooper presented the numbers that followed that line of reasoning. He said, "So, if we take the market-adjusted P/E of 29.3, that gives us an earnings yield—and thus an equity return—of 3.41%. Subtracting the 30-year TIPS yield of 2.5%, we get an ERP of 0.94%."

Baz reacted immediately, "But that is quite different from the number we got from the first method: 2.67% versus 0.94%. Also, the second method implies that bonds have a higher chance of outperforming stocks, especially as your holding period increases [see Slide 12]."

While appreciating the reasoning that Cooper had put forth, Baz now had to decide how to handle this information in a client meeting. Which of the two methods should he emphasize in the client meetings? Should he emphasize one over the other at all? If he didn't, how could he best explain the apparent difference in the results of the two methods?

8

Swedish Lottery Bonds

"The Newest and Largest Money Lottery in the World is the Swedish State's Lottery Bond."

—Advertising from the Stockholm Exchange Office, early 1920s

Anders Holmlund brushed the snow off his feet as he stepped into the offices of the Swedish National Debt Office (SNDO) in Stockholm. It was March 31, 2003 and Holmlund's priority this morning was a planning meeting for the next lottery bond issue. The lottery bond (or *premieobligationer* in Swedish) had for 80 years been an important instrument for the Debt Office in attracting Swedish households to invest in the nation's debt. Holmlund still had an hour before the meeting to review the proposed issue, prepared by Joy Sundberg and Magnus Andersson of his analyst group.

Lottery bonds were of course just a part of Holmlund's responsibility. As Head of Analysis for the SNDO, he also worked with more traditional instruments, such as government bonds and treasury bills. The SNDO was the Swedish government's agency for managing central government debt, and they did their borrowing from both institutional investors (insurance companies, capital funds and large companies) and the retail market (private individuals, and small companies and organizations). Holmlund's team defined the structures of the SNDO bond issues—and today they were setting the parameters for the first lottery bond 2003 with the Retail Market group, who would handle the marketing and sales of the bond.

Sweden had been the first country in the world to use lottery bonds as an instrument for retail investment. It was still one of the few who used the tool. Lottery bonds were different from traditional bonds in that a normally guaranteed interest—the coupon—only was paid as "wins" to bondholders selected in drawings. Although all investors got their principal investment back, it was only a small number of holders, determined by the pyramid scheme of the lottery that actually received a coupon on their bond.

Holmlund knew well that the retail market only accounted for a small portion of the Swedish national debt (4.9% in 2002). However, the Debt Office had recently allowed retail investors to participate directly in government bond auctions, using an

Professors George Chacko and Peter Hecht, Director of the HBS European Research Center Vincent Dessain, and Research Associate Anders Sjöman prepared this case. HBS cases are developed solely as the basis for class discussion. Cases are not intended to serve as endorsements, sources of primary data, or illustrations of effective or ineffective management.

internet-based system, giving individuals and small organizations access to investment opportunities that previously had been reserved for institutional investors. The Debt Office planned to expand this system and start selling treasury bills and inflation-linked bonds as well during 2003.

How this new opportunity would affect investor appetite for lottery bonds was still unclear. At the Debt Office, some feared that the household investor would lose interest in lottery bonds. In that case, the bonds might as well be taken off the market. Lottery bonds had a clear baseline objective, set by the Swedish government, which stated that borrowing from the retail market should be done at a lower cost than from the institutional market. This objective might be harder to meet should the interest in lottery bonds drop. In earlier discussions, Christine Holm, Director of the Retail Market Department, that handled the sales and marketing of all retail instruments, had told Holmlund: "We have generated a profit each year with the lottery bonds, I know. But in essence we could push that funding into the institutional market. It wouldn't matter at all. Plus, Swedes are hard to get to buy bonds. Over the last years, they have been more into stocks. They are very risk-seeking." However, both Holm and Holmlund understood the historical importance of lottery bonds, financially as an alternative source of funding and socially as a means for citizens to invest in their own country.

The meeting this morning was the last one before releasing the next lottery bond. The analysts from Holmlund's group and the team from the Retail Department had already shaped most of the bond, for example the number of drawings, the distribution of "wins" and an approximation of the bond amount. All that was left now was to set the coupon rate. But although Holmlund knew he should focus on the details of the upcoming issue, he couldn't stop thinking about the larger picture, and about the future of Swedish lottery bonds.

THE SWEDISH NATIONAL DEBT OFFICE (SNDO)

The activities of the SNDO—or *Riksgäldskontoret* in Swedish—had changed many times over the years. From financing wars in the 18th century to railways in the 20th century; and from lending surplus funds to European neighbors wrecked by world wars to borrowing abroad in times of international recessions. As the Swedish government's financial administration, the SNDO now had three main responsibilities: managing the central government debt, issuing central government guarantees and acting as the central government's internal bank.

The SNDO followed the overall objective of all central government debt management: to minimize the long-term cost of the debt while taking into account the risks inherent in such management. The Swedish Government set annual guidelines, the State Debt Policy, for the SNDO on how to manage the debt. The guidelines included strategic decisions such as the allocation between debt denominated in Swedish Kronor (SEK) and in foreign currencies, the pace of foreign currency debt amortization and the duration of the overall debt. The SNDO then established more detailed objectives for the operative management of the central government debt.

The Swedish Central Government Debt

At the close of 2002, the Swedish central government debt had amounted to SEK 1,160 billion (approx. USD 136 billion, given an exchange rate of 8.48 SEK/USD). Institutional investment, including foreign currency, accounted for approx 95% of the debt. Lottery bonds made up SEK 40.9 billion (3.52%) of the debt. With the addition of other retail market instruments, such as the National Debt Savings system—*riksgäldsspar* in Swedish—the retail market contributed 4.9% to the national debt. Exhibit 1 breaks down the debt by the instruments used (treasury bonds, lottery bonds, etc).

The 2002 government debt was the equivalent of about 50% of the Gross Domestic Product (GDP). After reaching a peak of 80% in 1994, this percentage had diminished throughout the 1990s, in part driven by European Union requirements for countries belonging to the European Economic and Monetary Union (EMU). Although not using the Euro currency, Sweden, as a member of the EMU had to maintain a central government debt that did not exceed 60% of the gross national product. Exhibit 2 details the development of the Swedish national debt since 1975, as well as describes the relationship between lottery bonds, Swedish national debt and the Swedish GDP.

Swedish Tax Structure

Contrary to popular belief, Swedish tax levels in 2003 were competitive with those of other West European countries. Although historically a high-taxation country, Swedish tax rates had been lowered after the 1991 tax reform (in Swedish media frequently called "The Tax Reform of the Century"). The tax base also changed during the 1980s and 1990s, where e.g. taxes paid by the lowest income groups had increased. Further, the assessed incomes of high-income earners rose, since some previously untaxed employment benefits were made taxable, but at the same time the tax rates applied to those incomes were lowered considerably. A primary goal for the 1991 tax reform had been to lower marginal tax rates on income, which in 1980 had reached 81% for high-income taxpayers. In 2000, it was at 56%. (For a historical overview of direct taxes as a percentage of assessed income in Sweden, see Exhibit 3.)

The Swedish tax system comprised three categories: income, capital and business revenue. Income tax had two parts, the local (municipal) tax and the state tax. The local income tax varied between municipalities, with the lowest rates generally found in well-to-do suburbs of the large cities, and the highest rates in the rural north or in municipalities hit by industrial decline. In 2002, local taxes ranged between 27.50% and 33.30%, with an average of 30.52%. State income tax only applied to taxable incomes above a threshold, which in 2002 was 20% after an income of SEK 290.100. (A second threshold of 25% was applied to income over SEK 430.900.) The marginal income tax

EXHIBIT 1

THE SWEDISH NATIONAL DEBT 2002

	SEK millions		Percentage of total debt
Treasury Bonds and Bills	770,300		66.39%
Inflation-linked bonds	135,100		11.64%
Foreign currency incl. Swaps	197,800		17.05%
Retail (household) market	57,100		4.92%
—Lottery bonds		40,900	3.52%
—Other retail market instruments		16,200	1.40%
	1,160,300		

Source: SNDO Annual Report 2002.

EXHIBIT 2

RELATIONSHIP LOTTERY BONDS, SWEDISH CENTRAL GOVERNMENT DEBT AND GROSS DOMESTIC PRODUCT (MSEK)

Year	Lottery Bonds	Central Gov. Debt	GDP	Lottery bonds/ Central Gov. Debt,%	Central Gov. Debt/ GDP,%
1975	8,175	73,467	301,102	11.1%	24.4%
1976	10,200	80,411	340,725	12.7%	23.6%
1977	11,900	97,982	369,743	12.1%	26.5%
1978	13,950	131,175	412,500	10.6%	31.8%
1979	17,600	175,146	462,127	10.0%	37.9%
1980	21,225	229,589	531,456	9.2%	43.2%
1981	21,525	295,590	581,870	7.3%	50.8%
1982	23,225	377,089	635,901	6.2%	59.3%
1983	28,050	460,196	712,378	6.1%	64.6%
1984	34,050	534,622	796,754	6.4%	67.1%
1985	38,100	595,695	867,096	6.4%	68.7%
1986	53,800	630,784	947,123	8.5%	66.6%
1987	53,400	622,272	1,023,474	8.6%	60.8%
1988	55,000	609,940	1,115,064	9.0%	54.7%
1989	48,900	600,047	1,232,129	8.1%	48.7%
1990	46,800	618,570	1,359,495	7.6%	45.5%
1991	45,600	692,958	1,446,676	6.6%	47.9%
1992	49,400	880,802	1,441,574	5.6%	61.1%
1993	55,800	1,132,267	1,497,708	4.9%	75.6%
1994	60,200	1,286,596	1,596,273	4.7%	80.6%
1995	64,800	1,386,165	1,713,430	4.7%	80.9%
1996	60,100	1,411,193	1,757,401	4.3%	80.3%
1997	61,332	1,432,076	1,824,301	4.3%	78.5%
1998	58,700	1,448,859	1,973,922	4.1%	73.4%
1999	54,400	1,374,180	2,078,941	4.0%	66.1%
2000	50,200	1,279,205	2,197,947	3.9%	58.2%
2001	44,100	1,156,827	2,259,428	3.8%	51.2%
2002	40,900	1,160,329	2,329,978	3.5%	49.8%

By end of decade

Year	Lottery Bonds	Central Gov. Debt	GDP	Lottery bonds,%	Central Gov. Debt/ GDP,%
1940	403	4,518	18,441	8.9%	24.5%
1950	1,425	12,464	32,124	11.3%	38.8%
1960	2,103	22,770	72,057	9.2%	31.6%
1970	3,740	36,155	172,167	10.3%	21.0%
1980	21,225	229,589	531,456	9.2%	43.2%
1990	46,800	618,570	1,359,495	7.6%	45.5%
2000	50,200	1,279,205	2,197,947	3.9%	58.2%

Source: Adapted from SNDO website, and EcoWin (www.ecowin.com).

EXHIBIT 3

DIRECT TAXES AS PERCENTAGE OF ASSESSED INCOME (YEAR 2000 PRICES)

Total assessed income	1980	1989	1991	2000
0,000–50,000	9%	14%	19%	21%
1,000,000–150,000	29%	33%	27%	30%
200,000–250,000	36%	36%	29%	34%
500,000–	54%	58%	39%	41%
All (age 18 or older)	**33%**	**36%**	**29%**	**35%**
Highest marginal income tax rate (based on average local income tax rate)	85%	73%	51%	56%

Note: In this context, direct taxes include income and property taxes paid by individuals, together with social security contributions not paid by employers as payroll taxes.

Source: Swedish National Tax Board, *Taxes in Sweden 2002* (Stockholm: Riksskatteverket, 2003) p. 17.

for any one taxpayer then depended on the municipality and whether or not the individual had passed the threshold for state income tax. Although the threshold levels changed at times, the overall income tax pressure had not fluctuated much in the 1990s.

The capital income tax rate in 2002 was a flat rate of 30% and had been since the 1991 tax reform.

Sweden's credit rating was in 2003 stable at a high level. Exhibit 4 shows the ratings by Moody as well as Standard & Poor's.

The Institutional Government Bond Market

In Sweden, it was the government, banks, municipalities and large companies that issued bonds to borrow money. For the government, the SNDO issued fixed income instruments (government bonds, inflation-linked bonds and treasury bills) on a regular basis, normally every second week for government bonds and every other second week for treasury bills. The issue amount and date were announced ahead of time, and the issue was then carried out as an auction. Institutional investors, such as insurance companies,

EXHIBIT 4

SWEDEN'S CREDIT RATING, FALL 2002

Borrowing in SEK	Long term
Moody's	Aaa
Standard & Poor's	AAA

Borrowing in foreign currencies	Long term
Moody's	Aaa
Standard & Poor's	AA+

Source: SNDO, *Handbok om statspapper*, (Stockholm: Riksgäldskontoret, 2002), p 28.

capital funds and large companies, bid a specific interest rate for a specific volume. A primary dealer, normally one of the large Swedish banks, did the actual bidding.

Naturally, the SNDO was interested in borrowing money to as low a rate as possible, which meant that the investor that had offered the lowest interest rate was first awarded bonds. The SNDO would then move to the next lowest rate offer, and so on, until the issue had been fully subscribed. Upon completion, the Debt Office published the result and average interest rate of the auction. (Exhibit 5 shows government bond auction results for 2002 and first quarter of 2003.)

Starting in the fall of 2002, a small additional part of each government bond issue was earmarked for retail investors. This novelty allowed individuals and small companies to take part in the auctions, which previously had been reserved for investors capable of investing hundreds of millions of Swedish Kronor. Retail investors could now use an internet-based system to participate at the issue's average interest rate, and give a nominal volume offer, minimum SEK 25,000 Kronor and maximum SEK 5 million Kronor. (If offers from the retail investors exceed the allotted amount, all investors were given bonds in relation to the size of their bid.) The new retail system was expected to grow to include inflation-linked bonds and treasury bills later in 2003.

As in any financial market, companies and banks actively traded their own and their clients' bonds to the fixed income instruments that earned the largest yield at any given moment. In Sweden, this secondary market trading took place on the Stockholm Exchange (*OM Stockholmsbörsen*), where in 2002 government bonds were traded daily for SEK 20–30 billion Kronor and treasury bills for SEK 10–15 billion. (By comparison, the daily stock trade amounted to about SEK 15 billion.) The trade was carried out through banks or fund commissioners, who normally charged a small percentage of the trade amount for their services (0.5%–1.0% for the retail investor or through a spread for the institutional investors).

Capital gains, such as coupons and net gains on sales, were taxed at a flat 30%, applicable to all bond types, except specifically for lottery bond coupons. These "wins" were tax exempt.

LOTTERY BONDS AS AN INSTRUMENT FOR RETAIL MARKET BORROWING

To borrow money from the Swedish retail market, the SNDO had issued lottery bonds since 1918. Although small in size compared to the institutional market, the retail market had been considered important, especially during recessions. "The retail market was for instance very important in the nineties, especially between 1992 and 1997. We needed to use every channel available then," explained Holm of the Retail Market Department.

History of Lottery Bonds

Lottery bonds were born in 1918 out of a necessity to explore new funding channels. With a world war ending, Sweden had to issue more bonds domestically. Lottery bonds, the brainchild of then SNDO Director General Karl Hildebrand, was thought of as a good alternative to the traditional instruments. The first lottery bond issue was at SEK 100 million, with a two percent coupon, with annual drawings of SEK 2 million and a nominal price of SEK 50. Already by the second issue, the new bond form was gaining momentum.

It appears though that the investors in the early days did not see it as taking part in the bond market. They were simply buying lotteries. Although the Swedish word for the bond type does not have the actual word "lottery" in it, the new bonds were simply accepted as a form of state-run lottery. Seemingly comfortable with the misconception, the

EXHIBIT 5

SWEDISH NOMINAL GOVERNMENT BONDS, AUCTION RESULTS 2002–2003, Q1

Auction Date	Loan no	Coupon %	Maturity	Offered (mSEK)	Tendered (mSEK)	Issued (mSEK)	Subscription ratio	No. of bids	No. of accepted bids	Yield ave.	Low	High	Price ave. (SEK)
2003 Q1													
2003-01-15	1046	5.50%	2012-10-08	4,500	11,173	4,499	2.48	73	27	4.806%	4.799%	4.810%	105.262
2003-01-29	1046	5.50%	2012-10-08	4,500	13,170	4,499	2.93	71	15	4.516%	4.510%	4.523%	107.556
2003-02-12	1041	6.75%	2014-05-05	4,500	13,494	4,500	3.00	70	21	4.554%	4.545%	4.560%	118.937
2003-02-26	1041	6.75%	2014-05-05	4,500	9,375	4,497	2.08	66	34	4.511%	4.504%	4.519%	119.299
2003-03-12	1043	5.00%	2009-01-28	5,000	12,131	4,997	2.43	60	24	3.934%	3.925%	3.940%	105.473
2003-03-26	1043	5.00%	2009-01-28	5,000	14,834	5,000	2.97	59	12	4.345%	4.339%	4.348%	103.294
No. Loans: 6				**Sum** 28,000	**Sum** 74,177	**Sum** 27,992	**Ave** 2.65	**Ave** 67	**Ave** 22				
2002													
2002-01-16	1037	8.00%	2007-08-15	2,000	8,095	2,000	4.05	40	3	4.864%	4.864%	4.864%	114.930
2002-01-30	1045	5.25%	2011-03-15	2,000	2,953	2,000	1.48	33	23	5.318%	5.309%	5.318%	99.503
2002-02-13	1037	8.00%	2007-08-15	2,000	4,189	1,995	2.09	29	14	5.225%	5.215%	5.230%	112.905
2002-02-27	1037	8.00%	2007-08-15	2,000	8,350	2,000	4.18	42	1	5.247%	5.247%	5.247%	112.707
2002-03-13	1046	5.50%	2012-10-08	2,000	5,420	1,999	2.71	40	12	5.690%	5.680%	5.695%	98.484
2002-03-14	1046*	5.50%	2012-10-08	6,000	23,909	5,999	3.98	76	25	5.697%	5.693%	5.699%	98.431
2002-03-15	1046*	5.50%	2012-10-08	4,000	9,679	3,997	2.42	49	13	5.724%	5.722%	5.726%	98.225
2002-03-18	1046*	5.50%	2012-10-08	6,000	14,038	6,000	2.34	58	19	5.703%	5.701%	5.704%	98.386
2002-03-19	1046*	5.50%	2012-10-08	4,000	9,230	3,999	2.31	44	18	5.673%	5.669%	5.678%	98.615
2002-03-21	1046*	5.50%	2012-10-08	6,000	8,038	5,997	1.34	40	34	5.724%	5.721%	5.725%	98.229
2002-04-10	1046	5.50%	2012-10-08	2,000	4,490	2,000	2.25	31	8	5.655%	5.653%	5.656%	98.765
2002-04-24	1046	5.50%	2012-10-08	2,000	7,778	2,000	3.89	39	1	5.675%	5.675%	5.675%	98.615

(Continued)

EXHIBIT 5 *(Continued)*

SWEDISH NOMINAL GOVERNMENT BONDS, AUCTION RESULTS 2002–2003, Q1

Auction Date	Loan no	Coupon %	Maturity	Offered (mSEK)	Tendered (mSEK)	Issued (mSEK)	Subscription ratio	No. of bids	No. of accepted bids	Yield ave.	Low	High	Price ave. (SEK)
2002-05-07	1037	8.00%	2007-08-15	2,000	7,705	1,999	3.85	35	8	5.372%	5.369%	5.374%	111.721
2002-05-22	1037	8.00%	2007-08-15	2,000	10,210	2,000	5.11	30	3	5.422%	5.420%	5.424%	111.410
2002-06-05	1046	5.50%	2012-10-08	2,000	2,860	2,000	1.43	22	15	5.628%	5.618%	5.634%	98.984
2002-06-19	1037	8.00%	2007-08-15	2,000	7,650	2,000	3.83	31	4	5.182%	5.179%	5.183%	112.410
2002-07-03	1046	5.50%	2012-10-08	2,000	3,536	1,999	1.77	33	20	5.429%	5.429%	5.417%	100.562
2002-08-07	1037	8.00%	2007-08-15	2,000	5,830	1,999	2.92	33	6	4.757%	4.755%	4.760%	114.158
2002-08-21	1046	5.50%	2012-10-08	2,000	2,920	2,000	1.46	24	15	5.177%	5.174%	5.184%	102.477
2002-09-04	1037	8.00%	2007-08-15	2,000	6,185	2,000	3.09	25	1	4.659%	4.659%	4.659%	114.418
2002-09-18	1046	5.50%	2012-10-08	2,000	3,555	2,000	1.78	19	1	4.859%	4.859%	4.859%	104.996
2002-10-02	1037	8.00%	2007-08-15	3,000	7,800	3,000	2.6	22	3	4.552%	4.549%	4.553%	114.701
2002-10-16	1046	5.50%	2012-10-08	3,000	5,525	3,000	1.84	32	9	5.143%	5.139%	5.155%	102.724
2002-10-30	1037	8.00%	2007-08-15	3,000	11,940	3,000	3.98	35	1	4.597%	4.597%	4.597%	114.280
2002-11-13	1035	6.00%	2005-02-09	3,000	14,595	3,000	4.87	41	9	4.089%	4.085%	4.092%	103.966
2002-11-27	1035	6.00%	2005-02-09	3,000	10,500	2,999	3.5	33	13	4.135%	4.133%	4.139%	103.805
2002-12-11	1046	5.50%	2012-10-08	3,000	3,995	3,000	1.33	34	28	4.955%	4.944%	4.970%	104.133
No. Loans:	**27**			Sum	Sum	Sum	Ave	Ave	Ave				
				76,000	210,975	75,982	2.83	36	11				

Note: All dates in format YYYY-MM-DD.

Source: SNDO Website ⟨http://www.rgk.se/scripts/cgiip.exe/rgk/emission/listbonds.w?Year=2003⟩, and ⟨http://www.rgk.se/scripts/cgiip.exe/rgk/emission/listbonds.w?Year=2002⟩, accessed 3 April 2003.

Debt Office did not actively work to change the adoption of the new bonds as lottery instruments, and in fact often pitched the issues as lotteries in their marketing.

In 1931, however, the SNDO started questioning the practice of lottery bonds. Hildebrand himself thought the time was ripe to return completely to more traditional interest bearing bonds. His arguments were based on scandals surrounding the lottery bonds, where intermediaries had been caught embezzling funds, and on the fact that the same bond could be passed as loan collateral between several individuals, to the point that it was completely without value to the original holder. To top it off, international finance experts recommended Sweden to discontinue the use.

Still, when public opinion caught wind of the possible cancellation, it quickly became clear just how popular the lottery bonds were with the Swedes. Leading politicians also supported the lottery bonds, as they provided a means for the Debt Office to reach a part of the Swedish society that otherwise would be excluded. Some also feared that money would start pouring out of Sweden, as investors turned to other international options. In the end, the lottery bonds were kept.

In October 1939, with a new world war breaking out, the Debt Office was asked by the Central Bank of Sweden to issue a large bond that would target not the institutional investors, but the retail market. For inflation reasons, the bank wanted to dampen the purchasing power of households in the coming war times. Although the central bank held no jurisdiction over the Debt Office, the SNDO did agree to issue a bond, which from then on was referred to as the Defense Loan of 1939.

A second Defense Loan was issued in 1942, and marketing for both loans built heavily on nationalistic themes, and on the importance of maintaining Swedish neutrality in war times. Full-page ads portrayed Swedes saying: "In my family we were going to renovate our small home this year. We now gladly cancel this; every penny we can spare will go to the Defense Loan. What do we need new furniture for, if the war would destroy our home?"

After the war, the lottery bonds were never again the subject for any public questioning or discussions. On the practical side, however, they underwent some modification. The drawings were for instance computerized in 1965, and from 1996 bonds were no longer issued on paper, but only registered with the Swedish Settlement Institute (*Värdepapperscentralen, VPC*).

The Typical Lottery Bond Investor

Although institutional investors were able to invest in lottery bonds, they typically stayed away from the instrument. The typical investor instead was an individual or a small household. In 2002, investor demographics broke down as follows:

- 54% were women
- 60% did *not* live in one of Sweden's three larger cities (Stockholm, Göteborg or Malmö).
- 78% were older than 50 years. (See Exhibit 6 for a detailed age distribution.)
- 57% had 1-49 bonds; 76% had 1-99 bonds.
- 45-50% of investors in each issue already held lottery bonds ("return" or "loyal" investors).
- About 50% of the bondholders held consecutive series (which guaranteed wins at some of the drawings, discussed in more detail below) although this varied between bond issues. Exhibit 7 details the distribution of bondholders with consecutive and mixed series.

EXHIBIT 6

AGE DISTRIBUTION OF LOTTERY BOND HOLDERS, MARCH 2003

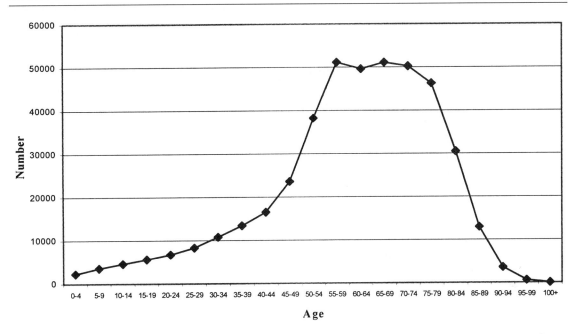

Source: SNDO.

EXHIBIT 7

DISTRIBUTION OF BOND HOLDERS WITH CONSECUTIVE SERIES

Lottery bond		Consecutive series	Customers with 1 consecutive series		Customers with 2 consecutive series		Customers with >2 consecutive series		Remaining (Mixed series)		Total no. of customers
1996	1	20	26,923	29%	6,439	7%	16,323	17%	44,708	47%	94,393
	2	20	24,116	37%	4,935	8%	10,081	16%	25,399	39%	64,531
1997	1	20	43,139	42%	8,401	8%	15,154	15%	35,654	35%	102,348
	2	20	31,662	46%	4,900	7%	7,549	11%	24,081	35%	68,192
1998	1	25	50,559	62%	8,911	11%	9,792	12%	12,266	15%	81,528
	2	25	45,606	48%	11,551	12%	9,970	10%	28,130	30%	95,257
1999	1	25	12,001	13%	24,329	26%	29,723	32%	27,556	29%	93,609
2000	1	0							122,133	100%	122,133
	2	0							124,865	100%	124,865
	3	50	30,420	55%	4,965	9%	1,545	3%	18,704	34%	55,634
2001	1	50	1,610	4%	3,676	8%	934	2%	38,066	86%	44,286
	2	50	23,064	35%	5,010	8%	1,312	2%	35,818	55%	65,204
2002	1	50	23,686	43%	4,730	9%	1,232	2%	25,225	46%	54,873
	2	50	28,073	34%	6,899	8%	2,002	2%	45,941	55%	82,915

Source: SNDO Retail Market Department, casewriters.

EXHIBIT 8

OUTSTANDING LOTTERY BONDS

Bond	Amount (mSEK)	Coupon rate (%)	Guarantee-order	Guarantee-win (%)
1996:1	4,500	5.10	20	3.0
1996:2	2,400	4.20	20	3.0
1997:1	3,700	3.75	20	2.4
1997:2	2,100	3.75	20	2.6
1998:1	3,400	3.75	25	2.1
1998:2	3,900	3.30	25	1.4
1999:1	3,700	2.00–6.00	25, 50, 100	1.0–1.4
2000:1	2,500	3.30	—	—
2000:2	2,500	3.30	—	—
2000:3	1,500	2.80	—	—
2001:1	2,000	2.90	50	1.0
2001:2	2,700	2.80	50	1.0
2002:1	2,500	3.50	50	1.4
2002:2	3,500	2.80	50	1.0
14	**40,900**			

Note: Bond 1999:1 was constructed as a floating interest rate loan where the coupon varied with the 180 days government treasury bill, with a floor of 2 percent and a cap of 6 percent.

Source: SNDO.

ISSUING LOTTERY BONDS

In January 2003, the SNDO had fourteen lottery bonds outstanding, at a total debt amount of SEK 40.9 billion. Exhibit 8 details the amount for each lottery bond, and Exhibit 9 goes on to show their traded prices in the secondary market during the last week of March 2003. For comparison, Exhibit 10 and Exhibit 11 show prices for institutional government bonds (nominal and inflation-linked) during the same time period, in both Sweden and the US. In addition, for the currency market, Exhibit 12 displays the forward prices for Swedish Kronor in U.S. Dollars.

A new lottery bond was normally issued when an old reached its maturity date, as the Debt Office sought to maintain the same outstanding amount, or at least minimize the decrease in outstanding lottery bonds. This normally meant two new lottery bonds per year, issued spring and fall.

Coupons, Drawings and Guaranteed "Wins"

Lottery bonds were coupon bonds, where the coupons were paid two to six times a year. The aggregate coupon for each bond was normally fixed.[1] For instance, the aggregate

---

[1] Floating interest rates could be used, but had been done so sparingly. Of the bonds outstanding in early 2003, only Bond 99:1 (the first bond for 1999) was constructed as a floating interest rate loan where the coupon varied with the 180 days government treasury bill, with a floor of 2 percent and a cap of 6 percent.

EXHIBIT 9

CLOSING PRICES FOR LOTTERY BONDS TRADED ON THE SECONDARY MARKET, MARCH 28, 2003[a]

Year/ issue	Issue year	Maturity Date[b]	Coupon rate (%)	Next three drawings	Loan series[c]	Total trading volume (kSEK)	Bid	Offer
001	2000	2003-04-15	3.30		Mixed	90	994	1000
			3.30		Cons 100	100	994	1005
002	2000	2003-04-15	3.30	2003-04-07	Mixed	—	—	—
			3.30		Cons 100	—	—	—
003	2000	2004-03-15	2.80	2003-04-14, 06-23, 08-18	Mixed	42	488	500
			2.80		Cons 50	125	500	502
011	2001	2005-03-04	2.90	2003-05-26, 08-25, 11-24	Mixed	—	995	1000
			2.90		Cons 50	347	990	993
012	2001	2004-09-24	2.80	2003-06-10, 09-08, 12-15	Mixed	113	981	989
			2.80		Cons 50	934	990	999
021	2002	2005-03-04	3.50	2003-05-05, 07-07, 09-01	Mixed	20	995	1011
			3.50		Cons 50	504	996	1020
022	2002	2007-06-15	2.80	2003-04-07, 06-02, 08-04	Mixed	—	—	—
			2.80		Cons 50	—	—	—
961	1996	2003-10-27	5.10	2003-06-16, 10-20	Mixed	211	1004	1014
			5.10		Cons 20	344	1005	1013
			5.10		Cons 100	402	1005	1017
962	1996	2003-04-15	4.20	2003-04-07	Mixed	—	—	—
			4.20		Cons 20	—	—	—
971	1997	2004-03-15	3.75	2003-07-14, 11-17, 03-15	Mixed	95	986	1003
			3.75		Cons 20	399	997	1000
972	1997	2004-05-14	3.75	2003-05-12, 09-15, 2004-01-12	Mixed	70	997	1005
			3.75		Cons 20	61	1010	1015
981	1998	2006-06-16	3.75	2003-06-23, 10-27, 2004-02-23	Mixed	—	995	1000
			3.75		Cons 25	278	1010	1015
982	1998	2008-12-12	3.30	2003-06-02, 12-01, 2004-06-07	Mixed	14	950	965
			3.30		Cons 25	457	960	965
991	1999	2007-11-09	2.00-6.00	2003-05-05, 11-10, 05-17	Mixed	52	470	475
			2.00-6.00		Cons 25	12	472	480
			2.00-6.00		Cons 50	—	476	485
			2.00-6.00		Cons 100	—	484	489

Notes: a. All trading of a specific lottery bond paused six stock exchange days before drawing. Drawings most often take place on Mondays, meaning that trading normally ceases the Friday one week earlier. Trading is resumed six stock exchange days after the drawing.

     b. Dates in format YYYY-MM-DD.

     c. Loan series could either mixed order numbers, or consecutive (cons) series of 20, 25, 50 or 100 bonds.

Source: Adapted from the Stockholm Stock Exchange (OM Stockholmsbörsen).

EXHIBIT 10

SWEDISH GOVERNMENT BONDS (NOMINAL BONDS, INFLATION-LINKED BONDS, AND TREASURY BILLS) TRADED ON THE SECONDARY MARKET (BOTH EXCHANGE AND TRADER TO TRADER), MARCH 28, 2003

Short name[a]	Coupon (%)	Maturity[b]	Next Coupon Date[b]	Bid	Ask	Trading Volume (kSEK)	Volume Issued (mSEK)	Notes
SO-1035	6.00	2005-02-09	2004-02-09	104.206	104.243	5,182,200	69,293	Benchmark
SO-1044	3.50	2006-04-20	2003-04-20	99.176	99.233	1,517,300	61,595	Benchmark
SO-1037	8.00	2007-08-15	2003-08-15	115.648	115.734	2,126,000	64,716	Benchmark
SO-1040	6.50	2008-05-05	2003-05-05	110.675	110.771	2,540,300	54,783	Benchmark
SO-1043	5.00	2009-01-28	2004-01-28	103.679	103.783	978,000	60,138	Benchmark
SO-1045	5.25	2011-03-15	2004-03-15	104.647	104.782	305,090	45,532	Benchmark
SO-1046	5.50	2012-10-08	2003-10-08	106.152	106.309	2,695,400	55,726	Benchmark
SO-1041	6.75	2014-05-05	2003-05-05	116.460	116.646	1,209,900	46,726	Benchmark
SSV-0304	0.00	2003-04-16		99.854	99.855	182,000	0	
SO-1033	10.25	2003-05-05	2003-05-05	100.582	100.585	8,945	9,592	
SSV-0305	0.00	2003-05-21		99.529	99.533	512,500	0	
SSV-0306	0.00	2003-06-18		99.271	99.277	3,390,300	11,103	
SSV-0309	0.00	2003-09-17		98.443	98.456	3,052,900	11,103	
SSV-0312	0.00	2003-12-17		97.631	97.651	6,814,200	0	
SO-1042	5.00	2004-01-15	2004-01-15	101.142	101.166	959,535	17,845	
SSV-0403	0.00	2004-03-17		96.801	96.828	1,639,700	0	
SO-3002	0.00	2004-04-01		111.385	111.439	500	4,483	Infl. linked
SO-1044E	3.50	2006-04-20	2003-04-02				2,650	Euro
SO-1038	6.50	2006-10-25	2003-10-25	107.933	108.053		1,750	
SO-3101	4.00	2008-12-01	2003-12-01	123.630	123.946	182,000	35,516	Infl. linked
SO-1043E	5.00	2009-01-28	2004-01-28				3,000	Euro
SO-1034	9.00	2009-04-20	2003-04-02	124.298	124.478		1,518	
SO-3001	0.00	2014-04-01		83.584	84.033		11,195	Infl. linked
SO-3105	3.50	2015-12-01	2003-12-01	116.293	116.892	110,000	37,663	Infl. linked
SO-3102	4.00	2020-12-01	2003-12-01	129.565	130.409	10	20,699	Infl. linked
SO-3103	3.50	2028-12-01	2003-12-01	116.584	121.559		3	Infl. linked
SO-3104	3.50	2028-12-01	2003-12-01	117.498	118.515		27,360	Infl. linked

Notes: a. SO = Government bonds (Statsobligationer), SSV = Treasury bills (Statsskuldväxlar),
b. Dates in format YYYY-MM-DD.

Source: Adapted from the Stockholm Stock Exchange (OM Stockholmsbörsen).

coupon for the second lottery bond issued in 2001—named 2001:2—had been at 2.80%. With a total issue of 2.7 billion SEK, that gave a coupon return of 75.6 million SEK.

Unlike traditional bonds, however, the coupon distribution for lottery bonds was not known at the time of issue, as it was determined by lottery drawings throughout the life span of the bond. Each buyer's return was therefore never known ahead of the

EXHIBIT 11

BID/ASK PRICES FOR INDIVIDUAL U.S. TREASURY SECURITIES ON MARCH 28, 2003

U.S. Treasury Bills[a]	Maturity Date[b]	Coupon	Bid Discount	Ask Discount
	2003-06-26	NA	1.11	1.10
	2003-09-25	NA	1.12	1.11

U.S. Treasury Notes/Bonds[c]	Maturity Date	Coupon	Bid Price	Ask Price
	2004-03-31	$3\,^5/_8$	102-13	102-15
	2005-03-31	$1\,^5/_8$	100-05	100-05
	2006-02-15	$9\,^3/_8$	120-21	102-23
	2007-02-15	$6\,^2/_8$	113-31	113-31
	2008-02-15	3	100-27	100-27
	2009-05-15	$5\,^4/_8$	112-23	112-25
	2010-02-15	$6\,^4/_8$	118-23	118-25
	2011-02-15	5	109-08	109-10
	2012-02-15	$4\,^7/_8$	107-30	108-00
	2013-02-15	$3\,^7/_8$	99-25	99-26
	2015-02-15	$11\,^2/_8$	165-15	165-17
	2018-11-15	9	148-03	148-05
	2023-02-15	$7\,^1/_8$	127-21	127-22
	2031-02-15	$5\,^3/_8$	106-30	106-31

U.S. Treasury Strips	Maturity Date	Coupon	Bid Price	Ask Price
	2003-06-30	NA	99.71	99.73
	2003-09-30	NA	99.43	99.43
	2004-03-31	NA	98.87	98.87
	2005-03-31	NA	97.00	97.00
	2006-04-15	NA	93.83	94.11
	2007-02-15	NA	90.64	90.71
	2008-02-15	NA	86.91	86.99
	2009-02-15	NA	82.47	82.56
	2010-02-15	NA	77.95	78.05
	2011-02-15	NA	73.68	73.80
	2012-02-15	NA	69.62	69.74
	2013-02-15	NA	65.60	65.72
	2013-02-15	NA	57.48	57.68
	2018-02-15	NA	47.04	47.25
	2023-02-15	NA	34.11	34.31
	2031-02-15	NA	22.92	24.86

Notes: a. Based on a discount yield, relating the return as a percent of the T-Bill's face value, rather than the purchase price.
b. Dates in format Y YYY-MM-DD.
c. Prices quoted as a percent of the bond's face value (or par value), expressed in 32nds of a point. A bid price of 102-13 means that the bond can be sold for 102 13/32% of the face value.

Source: Adapted from "PX1 Screen, Historical Prices, Price Table," BLOOMBERG, Accessed 17 May 2003.

EXHIBIT 12

FORWARD PRICES OF SWEDISH KRONOR IN U.S. DOLLARS

| | SEK/USD FORWARD | | | |
Trade date	1 month	3 months	6 months	12 months
2003-03-24	8.6582	8.6898	8.7378	8.8272
2003-03-25	8.6588	8.691	8.7399	8.8299
2003-03-26	8.6578	8.6918	8.7391	8.8287
2003-03-27	8.6454	8.6784	8.7269	8.8183
2003-03-28	8.6165	8.6493	8.6976	8.7918
2003-03-31	8.5166	8.5499	8.5987	8.6925

Note: Current exchange rate SEK/USD on March 31, 2003: 8.4711.

Source: Adapted from Sveriges riksbank (Sweden's Central Bank)—Based on midpoint of bid and ask quotes.

---

drawings. However, bondholders could be guaranteed a minimum of "wins"—or more accurately, a minimum return—corresponding to a fixed rate of interest if they purchased a series of consecutive bonds, normally either 25 or 50 bonds. (As opposed to buying "mixed" or non-consecutive bonds.) Using bond 2001:2 as an example again, this issue (which had 2.7 million bonds) was split into 54,000 lots of 50 consecutively numbered bonds (numbered 1–50, 51–100, 101–150, etc.). Investors who bought all of the bonds in one of these lots were guaranteed a 1% coupon, which was given at two of the four annual drawings. Practically, this was arranged by having one drawing—the guarantee drawing—where one bond in each lot was drawn as a winner. Therefore, if an investor owned all of the bonds in a lot, he was guaranteed a win because at least one of his bonds would be drawn during the guarantee drawing. In addition, investors with guarantee series were also eligible to win money in the other, "regular," drawings in addition to the guarantee drawing.

Before Issue . . .

Defining the Bond

At the Debt Office, defining a new bond issue was a joint effort between the Analysis group of the Debt Management department, which Anders Holmlund headed, and the Retail Market department. (The SNDO was organized around four main departments, with a General Director overseeing the whole organization. Exhibit 13 outlines the organizational structure.) The analysts in Holmlund's group performed the financial analysis, whereas the retail group planned the sales and marketing activities for the bond issue. The retail group was also responsible for after-sales customer support and system management.

In a first meeting, the group defined the core features of the bond issue, such as the maturity, number of drawings per year, the guaranteed amount, and number of consecutive bonds required to obtain the guaranteed "win." Maturity and face value did not change much from issue to issue, where a five-year maturity and a SEK 1000 face value had been used for most of the recent issues. The lottery bonds were always sold at par.

EXHIBIT 13

SNDO ORGANIZATION (SELECTED OVERVIEW)

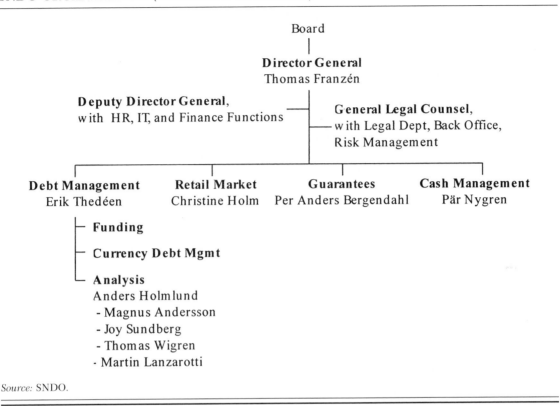

Source: SNDO.

Over the years, the Debt Office had tried various structures for the drawings. For instance, they had at one point included a SEK 1 million win for every SEK 1 billion in the bond amount. "However," described Joy Sundberg of the Analyst Group, "we now just offer 1 million-kronor win per drawing, regardless of the bond amount. Instead, we include many smaller wins, which has been very popular." In 2000, they also experimented with issuing two bonds during the spring, where holding bonds from both issues gave access to a third combined drawing. As to guarantee series, the standard lately had been to set them at 50 consecutive bonds.

In this first planning meeting, the group did however *not* decide on the coupon rate, as this had to be set as close as possible to the start of the sales period (although clearly the coupon rate would have to be higher than a regular bank savings rate, to attract the investors.) The meeting resulted in an internal memo, describing the new lottery bond, which the SNDO Director General had to approve.

Marketing

In the Retail Department, one person was in charge of marketing the lottery bonds, working in cooperation with an advertising and ad placement agency. Marketing activities normally included ads in the daily press and on TV, Internet, billboards and bus stops posters, and direct mailings to all registered previous investors. "About

SEK 17 million is put on marketing per year," explained Sundberg. The marketing message normally focused on the fact that lottery bonds were risk-free investments, with a chance to win. A recent campaign played the concepts of risk and chance against each other with the slogans "The only risk you take is winning" and "Highest risk to win: 1 million!" (See Exhibit 14 for ad samples.)

Setting the Coupon Rate

Two days before the sales start, the members of the Lottery Bond group met again, this time to decide the actual coupon rate. (This was the meeting that Holmlund was preparing for on March 31, 2003.) When setting the coupon, the overriding principle was, as always, that borrowing from the retail market should be carried out at a lower cost than the corresponding cost in the institutional market. Therefore, the analysts used the yield of a comparable government bond to set the ceiling of the coupon rate of the new lottery bond. (Coupons were paid tax-free to the investor, whereas bond sales were subject to a flat capital tax rate of 30%.)

EXHIBIT 14

LOTTERY BONDS SAMPLE ADS

Online ad for Lottery Bond 2003:1. In translation:

"**The only risk you take is to win.** Buy Lottery Bond 03:1 before April 15! Read more and book."

Other ads in the same campaign had more detailed information. One ad carried the text:

"**The only risk you take when you buy Lottery Bonds is the risk to win.** Everything else is safe and secure. With Lottery Bond 03:1 you have six chances every year, for five years, to win between one thousand and one million Kronor. Tax-free! It is as guaranteed as buying 50 consecutive bonds will get you a guaranteed win, corresponding to a bank interest of 1.4%. And your investment is securely kept too. When all the drawings are done, you get all your invested money back. This year's first Lottery Bond 03:1 costs 1,000 Kronor and is on sale only until April 15. Order it from 020-780 250, www.rgk.se or from your bank or fund commissioner."

Source: SNDO, casewriters.

However, when calculating the coupon, there were always two unknown factors. Firstly, the Debt Office did not limit the volume, so the tendered amount was in fact unknown prior to the close of the sales period. The concept of a "fully subscribed" issue did therefore not apply.[2] Naturally, the SNDO made assumptions about the amount, based on past sales experience and on outstanding bonds that were maturing, assuming that approximately 50% of previous bond holders would buy new ones as their old ones matured.

The second unknown factor came from the fact that the Debt Office had to announce the coupon rate at the beginning of the sales period, but that the comparable market rate could still fluctuate during the sales and settlement periods of four weeks. As interest rates and yields could move during these four weeks, the coupon calculations always had a built-in buffer. This was also the motivation for setting the coupon rate as close to the start of the sales period as possible. (Exhibit 15 shows rate fluctuations for recent sales periods. Exhibit 16 presents interest rate development of Swedish 5-year government bonds during the 1990s, and Exhibit 17 shows Standard Deviations for the same bonds.)

Given these considerations, Holmlund and his team then ran scenarios of different volumes against possible coupons rates to find the best coupon rate. Naturally, only coupon rates with a positive net present value (NPV) were considered. To counter the two unknown factors, the NPV also had to be large enough to still be positive if an

---

[2] During the early 1990s, the Debt Office did set a maximum limit to bond issues, keeping subscription lists for potential investors. Few bonds were ever fully subscribed though, and so the max limit served no purpose, and was abandoned.

EXHIBIT 15

RATE FLUCTUATIONS DURING LOTTERY BOND SALES PERIODS

Bond	Rate movement in basis points (bps)
1996:1	27
1996:2	−55
1997:1	66
1997:2	0
1998:1	−23
1998:2	−34
1999:1	−37
2000:1	5
2000:2	−33
2000:3	−21
2001:1	21
2001:2	−1
2002:1	−3
2002:2	−14

Source: SNDO.

EXHIBIT 16

INTEREST RATE DEVELOPMENT, SWEDEN 5-YEAR GOVERNMENT BOND, CLOSE DAILY

Source: Adapted from EcoWin (www.ecowin.com).

EXHIBIT 17

SWEDISH 5-YEAR GOVERNMENT BOND, ROLLING 20-DAY STANDARD DEVIATIONS (ANNUALIZED)

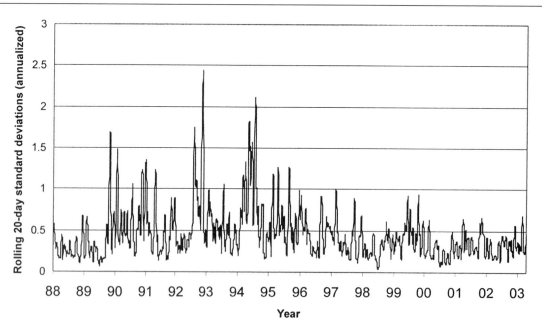

Note: On March 28, 2003, the 5-year Swedish Government Bond closed at 4.130, with a 20 day rolling average of 0.6881. The average volatility over the past five years (March 27, 1998—March 28, 2003) had been 0.3322.

Source: SNDO, casewriters.

interest rate reduction occurred (normally assumed to be 20 basis points, but at times of high volatility sometimes increased to 30 basis points) between the day that the coupon rate is fixed and the issue date and if an unexpectedly low volume was sold.

To the calculations of financial cash flows were finally added administrative costs, e.g. marketing costs and stock exchange fees, of about 7% to reach the full cost for the Debt Office.

Sales and Stock Exchange Registration

What the purchaser finally saw as a description of the lottery bond is exemplified in Exhibit 18 for lottery bonds 2001:2, 2001:1 and 2002:2.

The sales period was normally fourteen days, during which the SNDO sold bonds directly through its own sales department. They also worked with dealers, primarily banks and financial institutions. This distribution channel came with its own complications. Holm commented: "We have to force them a bit to market our products, since lottery bonds are just one of their offerings, besides trust funds, mutual funds, etc."

At the end of the sales period, the lottery bond was quoted on the Stockholm Stock Exchange.

Timeline for a Sample Bond

The time plan for a full issue was about two months. A sample timeline for Lottery Bond 2002:2 is described in Exhibit 19.

After Issue . . .

Drawings and After-Sales Support

A typical bond had two to six yearly drawings (six being the standard). The computer-based drawings were supervised by the National Lottery Inspection and carried out at the SNDO. Since all bonds were registered digitally with the Swedish Settlement Institute (VPC), wins were automatically deposited in the clients' accounts. Results were published on the SNDO website, through an automated phone service, and printed lists were available upon request. Bondholders often contacted the Debt Office after a drawing to comment and sometimes plain out gripe. "You hear people claim that 'it's only people from Stockholm who win' or better still 'it's only *rich* people from Stockholm who win," explained Sundberg. Other customers wondered why the coupon rates had dropped so much since the 1990s, not understanding how interest rates in general affected the lottery bond coupons.

Secondary Market Trading

After issue, bonds could be traded on the Swedish Stock Exchange. Although relatively little trading went on, the price of a lottery bond did normally go up prior to a drawing, only to drop directly after. Purchasers could however never see which numbers of a series that were for sale, thus eliminating the opportunity of consolidating mixed series into consecutive series. Secondary market prices for lottery bonds were published in the daily newspapers in Sweden, and also on the Stock Exchange website. The SNDO did not make a point out of actively following the secondary trading, as analysts considered that secondary trading was almost non-existent because of the capital gains tax.

At maturity, finally, SNDO redeemed the bonds at their nominal value.

EXHIBIT 18

LOTTERY BONDS 2001:2, 2002:1, 2002:2

Lottery bond	2001:2	2002:1	2002:2
Loan date (Issuance date)	16 Oct, 2001	7 May, 2002	26 Nov, 2002
Redemption date (Maturity)	24 Sep, 2004	4 Mar, 2005	15 Jun, 2007
Loan amount (mSEK)	2,700	2,500	3,500
Nominal amount (SEK)	1,000	1,000	1,000
Number of bonds	2,700,000	2,500,000	3,500,000
Sales period start	19 Sep, 2001	10 Apr, 2002	30 Oct, 2002
Sales period finish	2 Oct, 2001	23 Apr, 2002	12 Nov, 2002
Return/year (tax free)[a]	2.80%	3.50%	2.80%
Guarantee[b]	50 consecutive series	50 consecutive series	50 consecutive series
Guarantee coupon rate	1.00% (tax free)	1.40% (tax free)	1.00% (tax free)
Drawings			
Drawings held in:	Mar, Jun, Sep, Dec	Jan, Mar, May, Jul, Sep, Nov	Feb, Apr, Jun, Aug, Oct, Dec
Guarantee wins paid for drawings:[c]	Mar, Sep	Jan, Jul	Feb, Aug
Total no. drawings	12	17	27
Drawing dates (format YYYY: Marsh & McLennan-DD)	2001: 12-03 2002: 03-04, 06-10, 09-09, 12-16 2003: 03-10, 06-10, 09-08, 12-15 2004: 03-08, 06-14, 09-20	2002: 07-01,09-02, 11-04 2003: 01-13,03-03, 05-05, 07-07, 09-01,11-3 2004: 01-12, 03-01, 03-03, 07-05, 09-06, 11-08 2005: 01-10, 02-28	2003: 03-02, 04-07, 06-02, 08-04, 10-06,12-01 2004: 02-02. 04-05. 06-07, 08-02, 10-04, 12-06 2005: 02-07, 04-04, 06-07, 08-01, 10-03, 12-05 2006: 02-06, 04-03, 06-07, 08-07, 10-02,12-04 2007: 02-05, 04-02, 06-11

Wins per drawing (with guarantees)	**Mar, Sep**		**Jan, Jul**		**Feb, Aug**	
% return per drawing	0.770%		0.910%		0.800%	
No. of wins × amount	1	× 1,000,000	1	× 1,000,000	1	× 1,000,000
	3	× 50,000	2	× 50,000	1	× 50,000
	30	× 10,000	249	× 5,000	754	× 5,000
	125	× 5,000	2905	× 1,000	5,680	× 1,000
	5,215	× 1,000	50,000	× 350	70,000	× 250
	54,000	× 250				
Total wins—	59,374	20,790,000	53,157	22,750,000	76,436	28,000,000
Total amount (SEK)	wins	SEK	wins	SEK	wins	SEK

Wins per drawing (regular)	**Jun, Dec**		**Mar, May, Sep, Nov**		**Apr, Jun, Oct, Dec**	
% return per drawing	0.630%		0.420%		0.300%	
No. of wins × amount	1	× 1,000,000	1	× 1,000,000	1	× 1,000,000
	3	× 50,000	2	× 50,000	2	× 50,000
	99	× 10,000	747	× 5,000	780	× 5,000
	332	× 5,000	5,665	× 1,000	5,500	× 1,000
	13,210	× 1,000				
Total wins—	13,645	17,010,000	6,415	10,500,000	6,283	10,500,000
Total amount (SEK)	wins	SEK	wins	SEK	wins	SEK

Notes: a. Total annual return in drawings. E.g. for bond 2001:2, 2.80% (of 2.7 bnSEK) are given as wins (equals 75.6 mSEK.)

b. If investors buy a series of 50 sequentially numbered bonds, they are guaranteed a win at selected drawings.

c. During the guarantee drawings, one of the payouts is set such that one of every 50 sequentially numbered bonds wins. E.g. for bond 2001:2, investors with consecutive series received a guaranteed winning equal to a 1% coupon rate. In addition, they were eligible to win money in the drawings as well.

Source: SNDO.

EXHIBIT 19

TIME PLAN LOTTERY BOND 2002:2

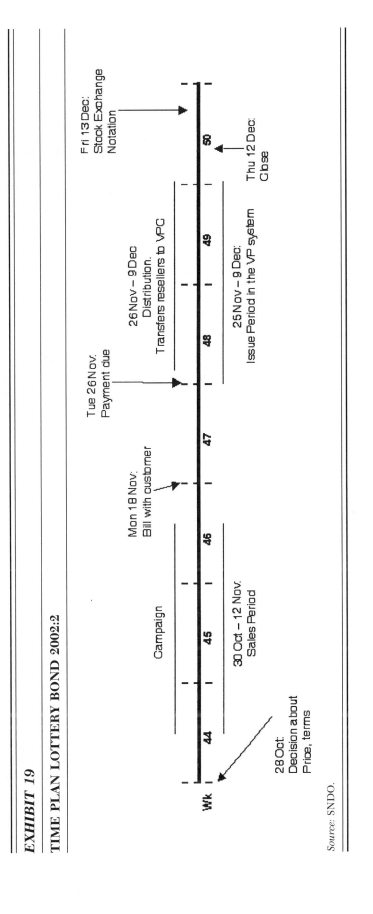

Source: SNDO.

LOTTERY BOND 2003:1—TO BE OR NOT TO BE

The new Internet-based system, that allowed retail investors to participate in the institutional market, had Holmlund thinking, "We have always provided a sort of social good with the lottery bonds. Now, we've taken this to another level." Would the typical lottery bond investor abandon the old instrument in favor of the new? Granted, the minimum amount for an institutional bond was higher at SEK 25,000 compared to SEK 1,000 for the lottery bond. In any case, government bonds should be due for an upswing during the current global economic situation. In the past, bond issues had sometimes been viewed as deadly boring by the market, but a guarantee to receive the principal back was now a welcomed feature.

As he went into the lottery bond meeting on the morning of March 31, 2003, to set the coupon rate, Holmlund realized that the issue needed to be a success. During the spring, outstanding bonds would mature to a value of SEK 7.4 billion, an unusually large amount. Since the Debt Office always sought to keep the lottery bonds' share of the Swedish debt constant, they had quite a gap to fill. If they reached SEK 4 billion it would be thought of as a successful issue. The calculations, however, would be based on an expected volume of SEK 3 billion.

Holmlund sat down with his colleagues to set the coupon rate for Lottery Bond 2003:1. The sales period was set to the first two weeks of April (April 2–15, 2003). The corresponding bond—a government bond named 1040, maturing on May 5, 2008, with a coupon of 6.50%—had at 9.05AM that morning been quoted on the Stockholm Stock Exchange at a spread of 10 tics, which would give the group the comparable yield on which to base the calculations. The drawings had been set to six a year, with two of the drawings earmarked for the guaranteed wins of 1% per year. (See Exhibit 20 for the proposed drawing plan.)

As they started doing the numbers, however, Holmlund's mind drifted back to the general question of whether to issue lottery bonds or not. The retail market was after all not only small but also relatively difficult to serve. Although seemingly healthy, did the 80-year old financial instrument really have a future?

EXHIBIT 20

DRAWING PLAN 2003:1

Drawings and Wins	2003:1
Drawings held	Jan, Mar, May, Jul, Sep, Nov
Guarantee wins paid during drawings in:	May, Sep
Total no. drawings	30
Drawing dates	2003: 07-07, 09-08, 11-10
	2004: 01-12, 03-08, 05-10, 07-12, 09-13, 11-08
	2005: 01-10, 03-07, 05-09, 07-11, 09-12, 11-14
	2006: 01-09, 03-13, 05-15, 07-10, 09-11, 11-13
	2007: 01-08, 03-12, 05-07, 07-09, 09-10, 11-12
	2008: 01-14, 03-10, 05-05

Note: Dates in format YYYY: MM-DD.

Source: SNDO.

9

Bank Leu's Prima Cat Bond Fund

In the summer of 2001, Matthias Weber, head of investment research and consulting at Bank Leu, knew he was onto a good thing; the question was *how* good. Since May 2001, Zürich-based Bank Leu had run a small but popular in-house fund, called the Prima Cat Bond Fund. The fund packaged so-called catastrophe bonds—"cat bonds"—which were sold exclusively to the bank's private clients. Cat bonds were securities whose coupon and principal payments depended on the probability of a catastrophe occurring, such as an earthquake or hurricane. It was traditionally large insurance and reinsurance companies that offered cat bonds, looking to transfer risk to the capital markets. The returns on the bonds were therefore completely tied to events covered by insurance policies.

It was clear to Weber that the asset class was new to both investors and issuers, with unclear regulatory treatment. Initially, all cat bond issues were underwritten as private placements, following the U.S. securities regulation Rule 144A. Although this permitted fewer filing requirements with the Securities and Exchange Commission (SEC), it prevented the cat bonds from being marketed to most individuals. In Switzerland, it was only recently that the country's Federal Tax Administration had determined the tax treatment of cat bonds. Still, individual investors could not invest in cat bonds except through a mutual fund—but to date, no such retail fund existed.

Therefore, Weber considered making the Prima Fund a public offering, available to all interested investors and not exclusive to the bank's clients. Such a fund would be the world's first cat bond retail fund. He anticipated that investor interest would be high, given the current poor performance of traditional asset classes, such as equities. For Bank Leu, inviting investors other than existing bank clients would provide diversification and

Professors George Chacko and Peter Hecht, Executive Director of the HBS Europe Research Center Vincent Dessain, Research Associate Anders Sjöman, and Adam J. Plotkin (MBA '04) prepared this case. The authors gratefully acknowledge the help of Daniel Hausammann, Bank Leu. This case draws heavily from "Catastrophe Bonds at Swiss Re," HBS No. 205-006, by the same authors. HBS cases are developed solely as the basis for class discussion. Cases are not intended to serve as endorsements, sources of primary data, or illustrations of effective or ineffective management.

growth benefits. For Weber personally, a public cat bond fund fit nicely with his mandate to grow the profitability of the firm's assets. The bank was undergoing a major strategic reposition to move its image from "the oldest Swiss bank" to one of "competence and innovation," a premier private bank for the twenty-first century.

However, Weber wondered exactly how lucrative an opportunity it was for the bank to make catastrophe bonds available to retail investors other than Bank Leu's private clients. He was concerned about going against the grain of the competition in entering this asset class. If there were a significant loss, Weber would be on his own in justifying his recommendation.

THE INSURANCE AND REINSURANCE MARKETS

Traditionally, insurance companies offered a variety of insurance products to their customers, such as life, health, property, and auto insurance. Coverage for large natural catastrophes such as hurricanes and earthquakes was also available. These types of events were by their very nature more unpredictable and hazardous than other events, and insurance products were tailored accordingly.

Just as insurance companies served businesses and individuals, reinsurance companies in turn acted as insurance companies to insurers. A primary insurer that wanted to limit its exposure to an insured type of risk would seek reinsurance coverage by selling a portion of the risk to a reinsurer. This limited the primary insurer's potential loss to some fixed and manageable amount. Additionally, insurers were required by regulations to maintain reserves against possible future payouts to customers. Reinsurance allowed for the release of some of these required capital reserves, making it available to underwrite new policies. Primary insurers often entered into multiple reinsurance contracts for the same risk. In turn, reinsurers sometimes sought reinsurance themselves, so-called retrocession.

Reinsurance was usually purchased in layers corresponding to different loss amounts. For example, an insurance company could reinsure itself for Florida hurricane risk for damages in excess of $450 million, not to exceed $750 million, that is, $300 million of reinsurance. The price of reinsurance was based on the probability of the insured event occurring, or its "actuary attachment." The price was normally called the rate online (ROL) and was expressed as a percentage of the risk exposure that was covered. For example, if a company had to pay an insurance premium of $45 million in order to obtain the above-mentioned $300 million payout in the event of a hurricane, the ROL would be 45 divided by 300, or 15%.

According to an assessment by Swiss Re, the world's second-largest reinsurance company, the worldwide insurance market, life and nonlife, wrote direct premiums in 2000 for $2.408 billion.[1] Catastrophe reinsurance capacity that year amounted, according to another assessment, to $65 billion in the five largest markets (United States, Japan, United Kingdom, Canada, and France).

CATASTROPHE BONDS

The 1992 hurricane Andrew was at the time the biggest insurance event in history at $20 billion. Around 60 insurers declared bankruptcy from the resulting claims. The price,

---

[1] http://www.financialservicesfacts.org/financial2/insurance/insurance/wim/, Swiss Re's *sigma*, accessed October 1, 2003.

EXHIBIT 1

LARGEST INSURANCE CLAIMS OF PAST 30 YEARS

Event	Insured Damage ($ millions, at 2001 prices)	Year	Region
Hurricane Andrew	20,129	1992	U.S.
Northridge earthquake	14,894	1994	U.S.
Typhoon Mireille	7,284	1991	Japan
Winter storm Daria	6,204	1990	Europe
Hurricane Hugo	5,974	1989	Puerto Rico
Winter storm Lothar	4,746	1999	Europe
Storms and floods	4,656	1987	Europe
Winter storm Vivian	4,311	1990	Europe
Hurricane Georges	3,820	1998	U.S., Caribbean
Typhoon Bart	3,143	1999	Japan
Oil platform Piper Alpha	2,986	1995	North Sea

Source: Bank Leu.

or ROL, for certain risks increased dramatically as a result. Since then, no major catastrophes of similar magnitude had occurred, and ROLs had dropped considerably. However, if a major new catastrophe occurred, Weber fully expected these ROLs to rise dramatically again (Exhibit 1 details the largest insurance claims of the past 30 years, and Exhibit 2 shows the change in catastrophe reinsurance prices after large catastrophes).

Due to the number of reinsurers that went bankrupt due to Andrew, the reinsurance industry looked for alternative risk-financing sources in the mid-1990s in order to better share the risks of a major catastrophe. As one option, they turned to the capital

EXHIBIT 2

CATASTROPHE PRICE INDEX AND EVENTS

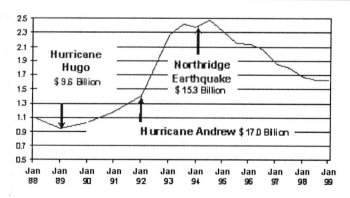

Source: Bank Leu.

markets, exploring various forms of insurance-linked securities (ILSes). The approach was new, as it required the participants to understand both capital and insurance markets, markets that until then had had very little to do with each other. Of several attempts, including futures and options on catastrophe claims, only cat bonds managed to get off the ground. The first cat bond was issued in 1994 by Hanover Re, and the market began in earnest in 1997.

Cat bonds normally took over part of a layer of risk from traditional reinsurance insurance coverage. Exhibit 3 exemplifies how by showing how United Services Automobile Association (USAA), a Texas-based insurance company, issued the cat bond "Residential Re" in 2001, which assumed $150 million, or 30%, of the risk for U.S. Gulf and East Coast hurricanes for a specific risk layer that began (or "attached") at 1.12% and ended (or "exhausted") at 0.41%.[2] The attachment level represented the risk that *some* amount would have to be paid out, the exhaustion level that the *entire* amount would default.

Issuing Cat Bonds

The typical cat bond issue is outlined in Figure A on the following page. It involves an insurance or reinsurance company (the "sponsor") that incorporated a special-purpose

[2] For a detailed look at a specific cat bond issuance, see Kenneth Froot and Mark Seasholes, "USAA: Catastrophe Risk Financing," HBS Case No. 298-007 (Boston: Harvard Business School Publishing, 1997).

EXHIBIT 3

EXAMPLE OF A CAT BOND: RESIDENTIAL RE 2001

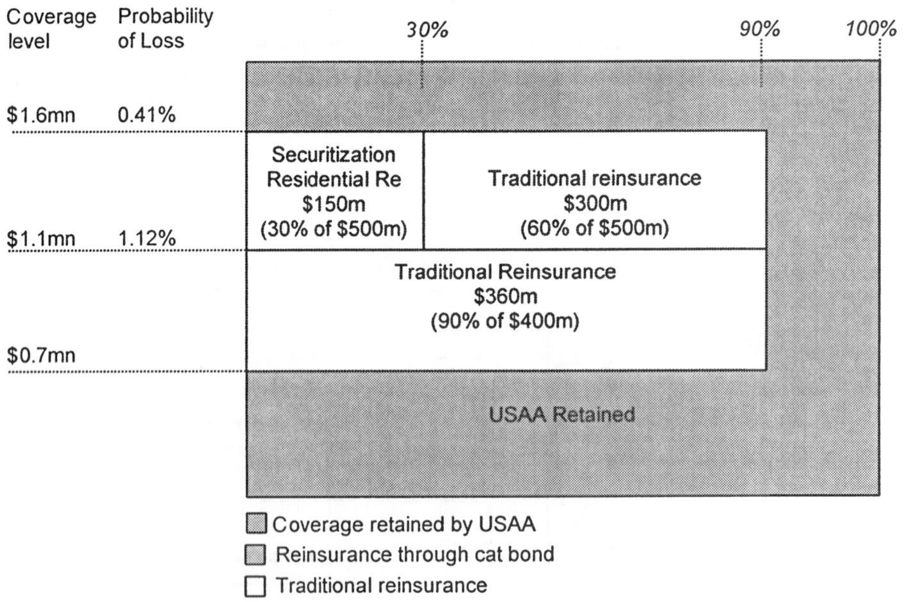

Note: The insurance company USAA created the cat bond issuer Residential Re for the specific purpose of transferring insurance risk related to U.S. East and Gulf Coast hurricanes to the capital markets.

Source: Adapted from Cochran, Caronia Securities.

reinsurance vehicle (SPV) in a tax-advantaged jurisdiction, such as Bermuda or the Cayman Islands. The SPV's purpose was to transfer insurance risk into the capital markets through the issuance of cat bonds. The SPV assumed the risk of a defined type of natural event from the sponsor through a reinsurance or retrocedence contract. In return, the SPV received payments of insurance premiums from the sponsor.

a. Transaction

b. Possible end position

Figure A   Structural Overview of Cat Bond Issuance

Source: Adapted from Bank Leu.

The SPV then issued bonds to the fixed-income capital markets for investors to purchase. The nominal capital paid by the investors, their principal, was invested by the SPV in low-risk securities, and the income from these investments was paid to investors in the form of a quarterly coupon, provided of course that the insured event did not occur. The coupon was normally set to be that of comparable U.S. Treasury bonds plus a premium spread. This premium typically ranged between 300 and 600 basis points.[3] The premium component of the coupon paid to investors came from the payments made by the sponsor to the SPV.

When the term expired at maturity, the principal was repaid to the investors. However, if the insured event did occur, the SPV paid out the principal in full or in part to cover losses by the sponsor. The investors in the SPV, therefore, made money (the return on the low-risk securities plus the reinsurance premium) if no catastrophe occurred but lost money if a catastrophe occurred. Catastrophe risk was therefore transferred to the investors in the SPV.

Pricing Cat Bonds: Ratings, Attachment, and Payment Triggers

A cat bond's price was expressed as LIBOR[4] plus a spread. The pricing of cat bonds was affected by numerous variables but, above all, by the rating given to it by one of the three

---

[3] A basis point represents 1/100 of 1%, or 0.01%.

[4] LIBOR (London Inter Bank Offered Rate) is the interest paid for dollars and euros at international markets in interbank borrowings. The LIBOR rate is fixed daily by the British Bankers' Association (BBA). It is similar to the U.S. Federal Reserve rate, in that it is used as a reference rate for other short-term interest rates.

large rating agencies, Standard & Poor's, Moody's, and Fitch. Cat bonds were typically rated under the same system as corporate bonds and were mostly given noninvestment-grade BB ratings or less. Sponsors often argued that rating agencies biased their ratings of cat bonds downward due to their focus on the "peak peril" of the associated catastrophes, that is, the worst-case losses in the event of a cat. Since the risk of a cat bond lay entirely in the occurrence of an insured event, sponsors believed that the rating agencies were overconcerned with this peak-peril aspect, rather than looking at expected losses.

At any rate, most industry specialists agreed that cat bonds were well suited for these "peak perils." Traditional reinsurance programs often did not cover one in 100 events (the top 1% loss events). Reinsurers felt they had limited ability to diversify away these high-peril, low-probability risks. Cat bonds instead provided a new type of transfer for risk that attached at the one-in-100-year events and exhausted at the one-in-250-year events (0.4% per year). Above the one-in-250-year events, only a very small portion of the total catastrophe risk was normally reinsured, as these risks were considered extremely remote.

The investment banks that underwrote cat bonds prepared detailed presentations for the rating agencies to explain the risks intrinsic to the bonds, much as they would accompany a corporate bond issuer to the rating agencies. The rating for corporate bonds was generally determined by the rating agency's evaluation of the risk of financial distress or bankruptcy of the bond issuer. The probability of bankruptcy had as its rough analogs in the cat bond market the probability of the insured event occurring (or its probability of "attachment") and expected loss.

For assessments of the attachment and expected loss, the industry relied primarily on full-risk evaluations, carried out by third-party expert scientific modeling firms. Three such firms were commonly used: Applied Insurance Research (AIR), EQECAT (EQE), and Risk Management Solutions (RMS).

The costs resulting from an event, and the resulting payments due to the sponsor from the SPV, were calculated using various methods, often referred to as "payment triggers." Put differently, the triggers determined whether a natural catastrophe qualified for coverage. Triggers included indemnity, industry index, parametric index, and modeled loss.

The most straightforward method was indemnity-based triggers, where payouts were based on the actual and verified size of the losses. This approach, however, required that the sponsor disclose potentially confidential details about the protected portfolio to investors. It also required the investors to fully understand the sponsoring company's portfolio, which was both time consuming and difficult.

As an alternative, so-called index triggers were commonly used. Index triggers followed one of two broad approaches: industry-loss indices, and parametric indices. Industry-loss indices were triggered by an estimate of the aggregate insurance industry loss in a catastrophe. The estimates were derived from either a reporting service such as Property Claim Service (PCS) or through the use of a catastrophe model, a so-called modeled loss. A modeled loss was calculated by running an event's physical parameters, for example, wind speed of a hurricane or magnitude of an earthquake, against the modeling firm's database of industry exposures. The resulting number was the modeling firm's estimate of an industry loss. The payment would then be calculated by multiplying the total estimated losses by a prespecified percentage. Parametric triggers worked similarly but were even more simplified. Here, payouts were triggered simply by the occurrence of an event with certain defined physical parameters, for instance, wind speeds or Richter measurements above a certain level. The resulting loss was just assumed, based on industry experience and historical data.

As mentioned, the different types of triggers offered a range of levels of basis risk (the risk that the paid amount and the actual amount required as coverage differed) and transparency to investors (as illustrated in Exhibit 4). (Exhibit 5 then shows all cat bond issues since 1997.)

THE CAT BOND MARKET IN 2001

In 2001, cat bonds were usually issued with a three-year maturity. Among the underlying risks that had been securitized using cat bonds were California earthquakes, U.S. East and Gulf Coast hurricanes, European earthquakes, Florida hurricanes, French windstorms, German windstorms and hail, Japanese earthquakes, and European property. (Exhibit 6 breaks down the outstanding cat bonds by underlying peril.) An individual cat bond could either cover one peril or multiperil transactions. It seemed as if sponsors preferred issuing multiperil bonds, since covering many territories in a single bond minimized issuance and administration costs. Investors, on the other hand, preferred the single-peril bond approach, which gave them freedom to assemble a risk portfolio according to their own investment preferences.

Advantages to Investors

By early 2001, cat bond investors included life insurance companies, investment advisors, hedge funds, mutual funds, banks, property and casualty insurance companies, as well as reinsurers. Investors in catastrophe risk securities liked the asset class, since it provided them with a number of diversification benefits and represented exposures that differed significantly from those of high-yield corporate bonds. Above all, they were seen by most as completely uncorrelated with the economic cycle. Investors were also attracted by the yield spread for a cat bond (its promised returns in excess of Treasury

---

EXHIBIT 4

TRADE-OFF BETWEEN BASIS RISK AND TRANSPARENCY

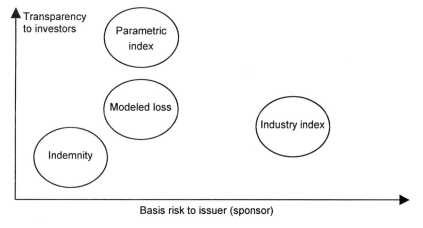

Source: Adapted from "Insurance-Linked Securities," Swiss Re, 2003, p. 8.

EXHIBIT 5

ALL CAT BOND TRANSACTIONS (1997–EARLY 2001)

Year	Transaction/ SPV	Sponsor	Lead Managers	Tranche	Size ($ 000)	Term (yrs)
2001	Residential Re 01	USAA	GS, LB, ML	Notes	150,000	3
2000	PRIME Cap.	Munich Re	GS, LB	Notes	129,000	3
				Units	3,000	3
				Shares	6,000	3
	PRIME Cap. Hurricane Ltd.	Munich Re	GS, LB	Notes	159,000	3
				Units	3,000	3
				Shares	6,000	3
	Mediterranean Re	AGF	GS	Class A	41,000	5
				Class B	88,000	
	NeHi	Vesta	Aon	Notes	41,500	3
				Shares	8,500	3
	Residential Re 00	USAA	GS, LB, ML	—	200,000	1
	Alpha Wind 2000-A Ltd.	State Farm	GS	Notes	52,500	1
				Shares	32,500	1
	Halyard Re Renew	Sorema	Aon	—	17,000	1
	Atlas Re	SCOR	GS	Class A	70,000	3
				Class B	30,000	3
				Class C	100,000	3
	Seismic Ltd.	Lehman Re	LB	Notes	145,500	2
				Shares	4,500	2
1999	Namazu Re	Gerling	Aon, GS	—	100,000	5
	Gold Eagle Capital Ltd.	American Re	AR	Class A	50,000	1.25
				Class B	126,600	1.25
				Shares	5,500	1.25
	Kelvin Ltd.	Koch Energy	GS	1st Event	21,608	3
				2nd Event	23,000	3
	Juno Re	Gerling	GS	—	80,000	3
	Residential Re 99	USAA	GS, ML, LB	—	200,000	1
	Circle Maihama	Oriental Land	GS	—	100,000	5
	Concentric Ltd.	Oriental Land	GS	—	100,000	5
	Halyard Re	Sorema	ML, Aon	—	17,000	3
	Domestic Inc.	Kemper	Aon	Notes	80,000	3
				Shares	20,000	3
	SECTRS 1999	Gerling	GS	Class A	€245,500	3
				Class B	€127,500	3
				Class C	€82,000	3
	Mosaic Re 2	St. Paul/ F&G Re	GS, EWB	Units	1,400	1
				Class A	24,300	1
				Class B	20,000	1
	Trinity Re 1999	Centre Solutions	GS	Class A-1	5,000	1
				Class A-2	51,615	1

(Continued)

EXHIBIT 5   *(Continued)*

ALL CAT BOND TRANSACTIONS (1997–EARLY 2001)

Risk	Region	Trigger	Attach Prob (%)	Exhaust Prob (%)	E{L} (%)
Hurricane	U.S. Gulf/ East Co.	Indemnity	1.12	0.41	0.68
Earthquake & Windstorm	California & Europe	Parametric	1.69	1.07	1.33
Hurricane	New York area & Miami area	Parametric	1.46	1.08	1.27
Earthquake & Windstorm	France & Monaco	Modeled Loss	0.28	0.17	0.22
			1.47	0.93	1.16
Hurricane	Northeast/Haw	Indemnity	0.87	0.56	0.70
			1.00	0.87	0.93
Hurricane	U.S. East /Gulf Co	Indemnity	0.95	0.31	0.54
Hurricane	Florida	Indemnity	0.99	0.38	0.63
	Florida		2.08	0.99	1.46
Typh, EQ, Wind	Europe, Japan	Indemnity	0.84	0.40	0.60
Earthquake,	U.S., Japan,	Indemnity	0.19	0.05	0.11
Windstorm	Europe		0.29	0.19	0.23
			5.47	1.90	3.24
Earthquake	California	Index –	1.13	0.47	0.73
		Ind. Loss	1.13	1.13	1.13
Earthquake	Japan	Ind. – Mod.	1.00	0.32	0.75
Hurricane,	U.S. East &	Ind. – Mod.	0.17	0.17	0.17
Earthquake	Gulf Coast,	Modeled	0.78		0.63
	U.S. Midwest & CA		0.17	0.17	0.17
Weather	U.S. Nationwide	Index	12.10	0.50	4.45
			4.05	NA	0.60
Hurr. (Multi Event)	U.S. Gulf/East Co.	Indemnity	0.60	0.33	0.45
Single Hurricane	U.S. Gulf/East Co.	Indemnity	0.76	0.26	0.45
Earthquake	Japan	Ind. - Param.	0.64	NA	NA
Earthquake	Japan	Ind. - Param.	0.64	NA	0.42
Typh, EQ, Wind	Europe, Japan	Indemnity	0.84	0.45	0.63
Earthquake	U.S. Midwest	Indemnity	0.58	0.44	0.50
			0.62	0.58	0.60
Insolvency	Europe	Index	NA	NA	NA
			NA	NA	NA
			NA	NA	NA
Aggregate	U.S.	Indemnity	NA	NA	NA
Cat	Nationwide		1.15	0.12	0.42
			5.25	1.15	2.84
Hurricane (Multiple Event)	Florida	Indemnity	1.20	0.49	0.00
			1.20	0.49	0.77

(Continued)

EXHIBIT 5 *(Continued)*

ALL CAT BOND TRANSACTIONS (1997–EARLY 2001)

Year	Moody's	S&P	Fitch	Sharpe Ratio	Spread	Modeling Firm
2001	Ba2	BB+	NA	0.68	L+499	AIR
2000	Ba3	BB	BB-	0.62	L+750	RMS
	Ba3	BB+	BB	0.55	L+650	RMS
	Baa3	BBB+	BBB	0.69	L+260	EQE
	Ba3	BB+	BB+	0.51	L+585	
	Ba2	NA	BB-	0.55	L+410	AIR
				0.48	L+450	AIR
	Ba2	BB+	NA	0.70	L+410	AIR
	NA	BB+	NA	0.74	L+456	RMS
	NA	BB	NA	0.65	L+700	RMS
	NA	NA	NA	0.87	L+600	RMS
	NA	BBB+	BBB	1.13	L+270	EQE
	NA	BBB-	BBB-	0.91	L+370	EQE
	NA	B	B-	0.72	L+1400	EQE
	Ba2	BB+		0.58	L+450	RMS
	NA					RMS
1999	NA	BB		0.56	L+450	EQE
	Baa3		BBB-	0.84	L+295	RMS
	Ba2		BB		L+540	RMS
				2.18	L+850	RMS
	NR	NR	NR	0.79	15.70%	RMS
	NR	BB	BB+		8.70%	RMS
	NA	BB	BB+	0.70	L+420	AIR
	Ba2	BB	NA	0.64	L+366	AIR
	NA	A	NA		L+75	EQE
	Ba1	BB+	NA		L+310	EQE
	NA			0.76	L+450	RMS
	Ba2	BB+	NA	0.56	L+369	AIR
	NR	NR	NR	0.59	L+450	AIR
	Aa2	AA	NA		E+45	D&B
	A2	A	NA		E+85	D&B
	Baa2	BBB+	NA		E+170	D&B
	NA	NA	NA		L+190	AIR
	NA	NA	NA	0.85	L+400	AIR
	NA	NA	NA	0.42	L+825	AIR
	Aaa	NA	AAA		L+175	RMS
	Ba3	NA	BB	0.22	L+417	RMS

(Continued)

EXHIBIT 5   (Continued)

ALL CAT BOND TRANSACTIONS (1997–EARLY 2001)

Year	Transaction/ SPV	Sponsor	Lead Managers	Tranche	Size ($ 000)	Term (yrs)
1998	Gemini Re	Allianz Risk	GS	Notes	150,000	3
	X.L./	X.L./	GS	Class A	45,000	1
	MidOcean Re	MidOcean Re		Class B	55,000	1
	Gramercy Place	TMCC	GS	Class A	60,680	3
				Class B	283,130	3
				Class C-1	122,470	3
				Class C-2	100,000	3
	Mosaic Re	St. Paul/	GS, EWB	Units	18,000	1
		F&G Re		Class A	15,000	1
				Class B	21,000	1
	Pacific Re	Yasuda Fire	Aon	Notes	80,000	5
	Residential Re 98	USAA	ML, GS, LB	—	450,000	1
1997	Mutual	NPI	WDR, DKB,	Class A-1	£140,000	14
	Securitisation		GS	Class A-2	£120,000	24
	Trinity Re 1998	Centre	GS0	Class A-1	22,000	1
		Solutions		Class A-2	61,500	1
	Parametric Re	Tokio	GS, SR	Units	20,000	10
		Marine & Fire		Notes	80,000	10
	SR Earthquake	Swiss Re	SR, CSFB	Class A-1	42,000	2.25
	Fund			Class A-2	20,000	2.25
				Class B	60,000	2.25
				Class C	15,000	2.25
	Residential Re 97	USAA	ML, GS, LB	Class A-1	163,800	1
				Class A-2	313,180	1

(Continued)

bonds). (Exhibits 7 to 11 provide more detail on cat bond spreads, corporate bond spreads, default probabilities, and recovery rates.)

The overall risk-return trade-off for cat bonds appealed to many investors, since the ratio of expected excess return to volatility (the so-called Sharpe ratio) was significantly higher for catastrophe risk securities than other alternatives (see Exhibit 12). Introducing catastrophe-linked securities to an investment portfolio would therefore raise the slope of the "capital market line," which maps expected return against risk in a fully diversified and efficient portfolio. In other words, not only would cat bonds most likely increase the expected returns of the portfolio, but they would also lower its volatility due to their low or absent correlation with other financial instruments, thus affecting both sides of the Sharpe ratio.

Still, investors at times struggled to understand the nature and mechanisms of cat bonds, since their primary concern was easy-to-understand, intelligible, and verifiable definitions of risks.

Advantages to Sponsors

In the early days of the cat bond market, issuers as a rule had not known how to work in the capital markets. Indeed, for insurance companies, working with capital market

---

EXHIBIT 5   (Continued)

ALL CAT BOND TRANSACTIONS (1997–EARLY 2001)

Year	Risk	Region	Trigger	Attach Prob (%)	Exhaust Prob (%)	E{L} (%)
1998	Windstorm & Hail	Europe	Indemnity	6.40	2.05	3.61
	Cat	U.S.	Indemnity	0.61	0.23	0.39
	(Multiple) Event	Nationwide		1.50	0.61	1.05
	Auto Lease	U.S.	Indemnity	NA	NA	NA
	Residual	Nationwide		NA	NA	NA
				NA	NA	NA
				NA	NA	NA
	Aggregate	U.S.	Indemnity	1.13	NA	0.28
	Cat	Nationwide		1.13	0.05	0.55
				4.40	1.21	2.60
	Typhoon	Japan	Indemnity	0.94	0.82	0.88
	Single Hurricane	U.S. Gulf/East Co.	Indemnity	0.87	0.32	0.58
1997	Life	U.K.	Modified	NA	NA	NA
	Insurance		Indemnity	NA	NA	NA
	Hurricane	Florida	Indemnity	1.53	0.44	0.39
	Multiple Event			1.53	0.44	0.83
	Earthquake	Japan	Index –	1.02	0.00	0.35
			Ind. Loss	1.02	0.41	0.70
	Earthquake	California	Index –	1.00	0.52	0.46
			Ind. Loss	1.00	0.52	0.46
				1.00	0.52	0.76
				2.40	2.40	2.40
	Single	U.S. Gulf/East Co.	Indemnity	1.00	0.39	0.34
	Hurricane			1.00	0.39	0.62

(Continued)

participants was very different from working with their traditional reinsurance partners. Nevertheless, capital markets offered an attractive alternative for insurers and reinsurers looking to transfer catastrophe risk. The cat risk securities markets offered multi-year coverage, almost eliminated credit risk concerns, and also brought a more stable and diversified source of investors. Further, pricing of the securities better represented the underlying risk due to greater risk transparency.

Industry analysts estimated the all-in cost of issuance for catastrophe bonds at approximately 80 basis points for a three-year cat bond issue. (For example, for a cat bond issue of $100, the issuer's cost would be $0.80.) The cost of structuring the issuance included fees to lawyers (about $600,000), modeling agencies (about $400,000), rating agencies (five basis points of the issued amount), and distributors. This issuance cost was seen by some market participants, notably large reinsurance companies, as prohibitive. To them, only multiyear issuances in excess of $100 million would even be worth considering.

A large investment bank attempted to take the analysis a bit further by putting a value on all benefits associated with issuing cat bonds, relative to the traditional reinsurance markets. It found savings of 125 basis points, broken into four different parts.

EXHIBIT 5   (Continued)

ALL CAT BOND TRANSACTIONS (1997–EARLY 2001)

Moody's	S&P	Fitch	Sharpe Ratio	Spread	Modeling Firm
B3	NA	BB	0.33	L+822	RMS
NR	NR	NR		L+412	AIR
NR	NR	NR		L+590	AIR
Aa2	AA	NA		L+23	
A2	A	NA		L+45	
Ba2	BB	NA		L+325	
Ba2	BB	NA		T+360	
NA	NA	NA	0.75	L+216.5	AIR
NA	NA	NA	0.77	L+444	AIR
NA	NA	NA	0.43	L+827	AIR
Ba3	NA	BB	0.36	L+370	RMS
Ba2	BB	BB	0.57	L+416	AIR
A3	A-	NA		G+140	WatsonWyatt
A3	A3	NA		G+170	
Aaa	NA	AAA	0.33	L+153	RMS
Ba3	NA	BB	0.40	L+367	RMS
Baa3	NA	NA		L+206	EQE
Ba2	NA	NA	0.53	L+430	EQE
Baa3	NA	BBB-	0.38	L+255	EQE
Baa3	NA	BBB-	0.42	L+280	EQE
Ba1	NA	BB	0.52	L+475	EQE
NR	NR	NR	0.27	L+625	EQE
Aaa	AAA	AAA	0.76	L+273	AIR
Ba2	BB	BB	0.75	L+576	AIR

Lead managers: Aon = Aon Capital Markets; AR = AR Insurance; DKB = Dai-Ichi Kangyo Bank Ltd.; CSFB = Credit Suisse First Boston; SR = Swiss Re; GS = Goldman Sachs; LB = Lehman Brothers; ML = Merrill Lynch; WDR = Warburg Dillon Read

Source: Adapted from Goldman Sachs.

The first part, "credit risk," included the reduction of counter-party risk when a sponsor did not have to contract with a reinsurance company that might not be able to honor its obligations and instead contracted with an SPV, whose investments were required to be of the highest commercial paper rating quality. Furthermore, cat bonds helped the issuers to move the credit risk off the balance sheet, since with an SPV, they received the money up front from the issuing SPV. The investment bank assigned a benefit of 50 basis points to this part.

The second part, "term structure," brought a saving of 50 basis points. It represented savings to the insurer by enabling it to sell multiple years of risk at once without being exposed to the refinancing risk of having to sell it each year. However, a direct risk of multiyear contracts, for example, one of three years, was that in year three the market rate of reinsurance could be lower than in year one. The locked-in price would then be higher than current market prices and in fact would become a loss, not a saving, to the cat bond issuer.

EXHIBIT 6

OVERVIEW SECURITIZATIONS RISK CATEGORIES

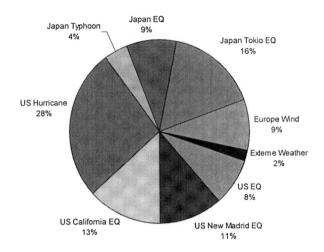

Source: Adapted from Goldman Sachs.

The third part, "strategic benefit," was the result of having lower overall costs as an insurer by having a new market to turn to for reinsurance. The hardest to which to assign an actual value, the part was estimated at 50 basis points by a large investment bank. Finally, the fourth part, "contract features," worked *against* the previous savings by about 25 basis points, since trading in the capital markets required standardized contracts, which meant losing the flexibility of custom contracts in the reinsurance market.

EXHIBIT 7

SPREAD COMPARISON

Investment	Rating	Spread, mid-2001	Loss Probability (LP)	Risk Coverage (=Spread/LP)
Corporate Bonds BB+	BB+	3.52%	0.53%	6.6x
Cat Bonds Redwood Capital I	BB+	5.50%	0.53%	10.4x
Corporate Bonds BB	BB	4.73%	1.66%	2.8x
Cat Bond Namazu	BB	5.31%	0.75%	7.1x
Corporate Bonds BB−	BB−	4.83%	3.42%	1.4x
Cat Bond CalQuake & Euro Wind	BB−	8.50%	1.33%	6.4x
Corporate Bonds B+	B+	5.78%	6.75%	0.9x
Cat Bond Atlas C	B+	16.83%	3.24%	5.2x

Source: Bank Leu documents.

EXHIBIT 8

COMPARATIVE YIELDS ON JUNE 1, 2001 FOR CORPORATE BONDS OF DIFFERENT RATINGS AND MATURITIES

Maturity	AAA	AA	A+	A	A−	BBB+	BBB	BBB−	BB+	BB	BB−	B+
3 Month	4.08	4.14	4.28	4.4	4.71	5.08	5.08	5.5	6.37	6.52	6.74	7.17
6 Month	4.15	4.21	4.31	4.43	4.65	4.98	5.06	5.47	6.24	6.51	6.75	7.12
1 Year	4.27	4.3	4.48	4.62	4.79	5.11	5.15	5.68	6.7	6.89	7.14	7.50
2 Year	4.75	4.8	5.07	5.17	5.35	5.59	5.72	6.27	7.12	7.44	7.73	8.10
3 Year	5.15	5.28	5.51	5.74	5.76	6.09	6.23	6.65	7.53	7.78	8.1	8.54
4 Year	5.43	5.57	5.79	5.99	6.06	6.35	6.49	6.89	7.77	8.02	8.44	8.79
5 Year	5.67	5.76	6.00	6.18	6.27	6.48	6.6	7.05	8.01	8.23	8.77	9.04
7 Year	5.96	6.16	6.35	6.51	6.63	6.91	6.93	7.39	8.2	8.45	8.98	9.20
8 Year	6.07	6.3	6.44	6.64	6.74	7.00	7.00	7.47	8.28	8.49	9.09	9.31
9 Year	6.1	6.36	6.42	6.64	6.76	7.04	7.05	7.52	8.41	8.6	9.19	9.40
10 Year	6.14	6.35	6.43	6.68	6.82	7.04	7.06	7.56	8.47	8.74	9.31	9.53
15 Year	6.43	6.61	6.81	7.05	7.3	7.45	7.5	8.01	8.87	9.12	9.66	9.88
20 Year	6.7	6.9	7.1	7.37	7.59	7.72	7.79	8.23	9.02	9.27	9.89	10.13
25 Year	6.69	6.91	7.05	7.35	7.53	7.73	7.76	8.16	9.12	9.30	9.95	10.26
30 Year	6.64	6.87	7.03	7.24	7.34	7.63	7.66	8.06	9.04	9.26	10.00	10.34

Note: Ratings by Standard & Poor's.

Source: Bloomberg LP, accessed on May 1, 2004.

In addition, industry insiders valued cat bonds for the short time (about two to three weeks) it took after an event to receive the actual coverage, referring to the "short tail" of cat bonds.

Trading Cat Bonds in the Secondary Market

At the end of 2000, $1.5 billion of catastrophe risk was placed in the capital markets, representing about 1% of catastrophe reinsurance capacity. In addition to cat bonds, the asset class of insurance-linked securities (ILSes) included catastrophe risk exchange (CATEX) swaps, insurance-related derivatives and options, catastrophe equity puts (CAT-E-Puts), contingent surplus notes, and weather derivatives.

EXHIBIT 9

YIELD CURVE RATES ON JUNE 1, 2001 FOR U.S. TREASURIES

3-mo	6-mo	1-yr	2-yr	3-yr	5-yr	7-yr	10-yr	20-yr	30-yr
3.67	3.61	3.67	4.22	4.49	4.94	5.24	5.39	5.89	5.71

Source: Adapted from U.S. Treasury Web site, http://www.ustreas.gov/offices/domestic-finance/debt-management/interest-rate/yield20010601.html, accessed February 3, 2004.

EXHIBIT 10

HISTORICAL FIVE-YEAR CUMULATIVE DEFAULT PROBABILITIES FOR VARIOUS CREDITS

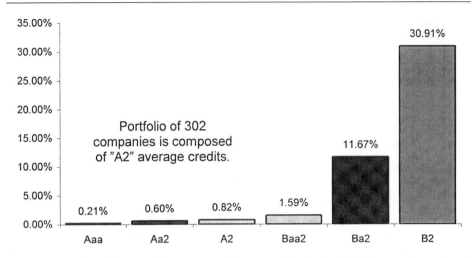

Source: "Historical Default Rates of Corporate Bond Issuers, 1920–1996," Moody's Investor Service. Based on cohorts formed since 1970.

EXHIBIT 11

RECOVERY RATE ON DEBT INSTRUMENTS OF VARYING SENIORITY

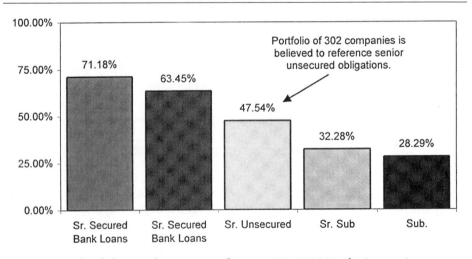

Source: "Historical Default Rates of Corporate Bond Issuers, 1920–1996," Moody's Investor Service.

EXHIBIT 12

SHARPE RATIOS

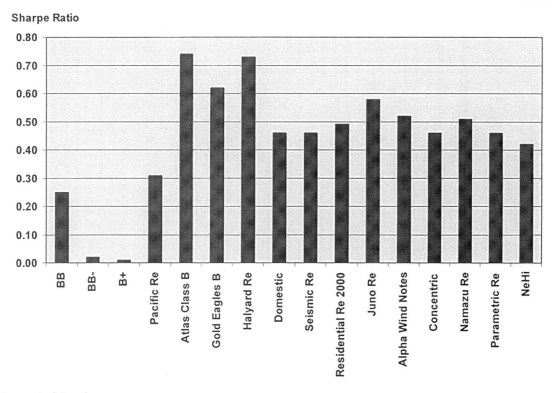

Sharpe Ratio

Source: Bank Leu documents.

Active trading and bid prices were made available by Goldman Sachs, Swiss Re Capital Markets, Aon Capital Markets, Lehman Brothers, and American Re. Often, the bids posted differed across market makers and were indicative rather than representative of any actual trades executed. (Exhibit 13 lists examples of bid differentials.)

To date, there had not been a single catastrophic event to actually cause a full or even partial loss of principal.

BANK LEU AND CAT BONDS

Based in Zürich, Switzerland, Bank Leu, Ltd. was a legally independent member of Credit Suisse Group and was part of the Credit Suisse Private Banking business unit. Founded in 1755 as "Leu et Compagnie," Bank Leu was the oldest bank in Switzerland and had initially served Swiss aristocrats. In 1793 the bank executed its first transfer of money to the United States, and soon money transfers developed into one of Bank Leu's major business activities within Europe also. In 1883, the bank was listed on the Zurich Stock Exchange. The modern Bank Leu took shape in 1990, when the Swiss banking sector was swept by a wave of mergers and acquisitions and Bank Leu

EXHIBIT 13

SAMPLE SECONDARY MARKET TRADING (MARCH 14, 2001)

Bond	Bid Price	Ask Price	Bid Spread	Ask Spread	Expected Loss
California Quake #2	99.31	99.59	5.35%	5.00%	73
California Quake #3	99.47	99.97	5.40%	5.10%	55
Europe multiperil A	99.63	100.59	2.70%	2.45%	22
Europe multiperil B	99.78	100.28	5.90%	5.78%	116
Florida Wind notes	100.69	100.81	0.90%	0.35%	63
Florida Wind preference shares	101.13	101.25	1.10%	0.50%	146
Japan Quake #1	100.19	100.47	3.10%	3.00%	41
Japan Quake #2	98.84	99.16	4.85%	4.75%	75
Japan Quake #3	101.97	103.00	3.95%	3.75%	70
U.S. Wind #1	100.59	100.97	3.90%	3.60%	45
U.S. Wind #3	100.66	100.78	0.90%	0.35%	54
World multiperil #1 A	99.81	100.13	2.80%	2.65%	11
World multiperil #1 B	99.81	100.09	3.80%	3.65%	23
World multiperil #2	99.53	100.63	7.70%	7.25%	133

Notes: 1. Exact name of bonds disguised and replaced by the primary peril covered by the bond.
  2. The average bid/ask spread for both sets of data is 30bp.

Source: Swiss Re Capital Markets.

became a member of Credit Suisse Holding. In 2000, Bank Leu reorganized its business activities as an independent private bank within the Credit Suisse Group, concentrating on private banking. The bank employed about 600 people.

Weber had joined Bank Leu in 1995 with a degree from the University of Sankt Gallen and professional experience with A.C. Nielsen as a market research analyst and his own entrepreneurial activities. At Bank Leu, he started as a bond analyst, progressing to become head of the bank's investment research and consulting.

Weber explained Bank Leu's current charter: "Our core business is private banking for Swiss and international clients, which means investment advisory and asset management services for high-net-worth private clients. As a specialist for the Swiss financial market, we are also an issuer of derivative products and a market maker, serving professional and institutional clients in Switzerland and abroad."

These clients were provided with specialized services in the fields of securities trading and custody, as well as foreign exchange, money market, and precious metals. In addition to branches in Geneva and Nassau (Bahamas), Bank Leu had a number of representative offices and associated companies abroad through which it conducted private banking business.

In 2000, Bank Leu posted its best results to date, as total operating profit rose from 169 million Swiss francs (CHF) (about US$121 million) to CHF 241 million (about $173 million). The bank represented approximately CHF 30 billion (about $22 billion) in client assets. (Exhibit 14 gives more financial details on Bank Leu.)

EXHIBIT 14

BANK LEU FINANCIAL STATEMENTS

a. Bank Leu Income Statement, 1999–2000 (all numbers in CHF 1,000)

Income and Expense from Ordinary Banking Business	2000	1999	Change	Change (%)
Net income from interest operations:				
Interest and discount income	473,707	263,055	210,652	80
Interest and dividend income from financial assets	3,450	5,561	−2,111	−38
Interest expense	−360,585	−176,969	−183,616	104
Subtotal, net income from interest operations	**116,572**	**91,625**	**24,947**	**27**
Net commission and fee income:				
Commissions from lending business	1,520	967	553	57
Commissions from securities & investment business	277,372	222,035	55,337	25
Other commission and fee income	2,376	2,034	342	17
Commission expense	−7,547	−1,078	−6,469	600
Subtotal, net commission and fee income	**273,721**	**223,958**	**49,763**	**22**
Net income from trading	**96,375**	**51,337**	**45,038**	**88**
Other ordinary net income:				
Net income from the sale of financial assets	200		200	n/a
Income from investments in associates	911	340	571	168
Other ordinary income	913	483	430	89
Other ordinary expense	−345	−200	−145	73
Subtotal, other ordinary net income	**1,679**	**623**	**1,056**	**170**
Total operating income	**488,347**	**367,543**	**120,804**	**33**
Operating expense:				
Personnel expense	137,584	103,813	33,771	33
General administrative expense	109,855	95,182	14,673	15
Subtotal, operating expense	**247,439**	**198,995**	**48,444**	**24**
Operating profit	**240,908**	**168,548**	**72,360**	**43**
Net profit				
Operating profit	240,908	168,548	72,360	43
Depreciable/write-downs on noncurrent assets	489	209	280	134
Value adjustments, provisions and losses	11,937	8,753	3,184	36
Net profit before extraordinary items and taxes	**228,482**	**159,586**	**68,896**	**43**
Extraordinary income	3,498	20,294	−16,796	−83
Extraordinary expense	−127	−708	581	−82
Taxes	−52,500	−44,085	8,415	19
Net profit	**179,353**	**135,087**	**44,266**	**33**

Source: Bank Leu.

(Continued)

EXHIBIT 14 (Continued)

BANK LEU FINANCIAL STATEMENTS

b. Bank Leu Balance Sheet, 2000 (all numbers in CHF 1,000)

Balance Sheet	Dec. 31, 2000	Dec. 31, 1999	Change	Change (%)
Assets				
Cash and cash equivalents	164,601	182,159	−17,558	−10
Money market paper	550,127	959,778	−409,651	−43
Due from banks	4,273,297	3,022,864	1,250,433	41
Due from clients	1,377,940	1,679,386	−301,446	−18
Mortgage loans	1,158,923	972,112	186,811	19
Securities and precious metals trading assets	1,389,851	1,253,483	136,368	11
Financial assets	41,740	101,642	−59,902	−59
Investments in associates	6,395	6,475	−80	−1
Property and equipment	468	624	−156	−25
Accrued income and prepaid expenses	38,223	29,595	8,628	29
Other assets	579,881	485,409	94,472	19
Total assets	**9,581,446**	**8,693,527**	**887,919**	**10**
Total subordinated assets	0	37,993	−37,993	−100
Total amounts receivable from shareholder & group companies	1,092,279	679,148	413,131	61
Liabilities and shareholders' equity				
Due to banks	2,726,608	2,082,531	644,077	31
Client savings and investment deposits	348,477	452,422	103,945	−23
Other balances due to clients	5,130,974	4,947,447	183,527	4
Bonds and mortgage bonds issued	100,000	100,000	0	0
Accrued expenses and deferred income	108,534	75,002	33,532	45
Other liabilities	571,415	498,728	72,687	15
Value adjustments and provisions	114,154	111,466	2,688	2
Reserves for general banking risks	14,102	14,102	0	0
Share capital	200,000	200,000	0	0
General statutory reserves	87,785	76,385	11,400	15
Profit carried forward	44	357	−313	−88
Net profit for the year	179,353	135,087	44,266	33
Total shareholders' equity	481,284	425,931	55,353	13
Total liabilities and shareholders' equity	**9,581,446**	**8,693,527**	**887,919**	**10**
Total subordinated liabilities	130,000	130,000	0	0
Total amounts payable to shareholder and group companies	1,074,801	443,365	631,436	142

Source: Bank Leu.

The Genesis of the Prima Cat Bond Fund

In May 2000, after following the development of the cat bond market for a while and realizing there were no retail funds for cat bonds, Weber and his group thought that it might be time to launch a cat bond mutual fund. After gaining internal approval, both from the bank's chief investment officer and its CEO, the group approached the Swiss Banking Commission (SBC), which accepted the new fund type with the limitation that it was offered only to Bank Leu's in-house customers. So, in May 2001 Bank Leu launched the Prima Cat Bond Fund as a pure in-house fund, exclusively for the clients of Bank Leu. The fund quickly attracted investors, since other asset classes, such as equities, were performing poorly at the time, and soon reached about CHF 60 million.

Looking forward, Weber saw potential in taking the fund public. For instance, in-house fund clients had to sign a managed-mandate contract, which was difficult to obtain from offshore clients. Taking the fund public would simplify administration—and above all help broaden the investor base. Bank Leu would, however, obtain approval from the SBL to change the stature of the fund. Such an approval would be the external stamp of approval that could help launch the cat bond fund more widely. Weber explained:

> Where else can you find an investment that makes it so easy to ensure there is no dependence between yields and the events on other financial markets? There had to be an interest in the larger public for a retail fund of such securities. It is also a very easy product to explain to investors: They receive LIBOR plus, say, 4% to 6%, as long as there's no major earthquake or catastrophe. The instrument is also backed by an AAA rating.

From a diversification point of view, Weber welcomed the opportunity to expand the investor base to clients outside of Bank Leu. However, the new instrument might still require some explaining to convince investors of its benefits. Weber therefore put together a presentation of a sample portfolio of cat bonds. The sample portfolio assumed that cat bonds as an instrument had existed for more than 100 years, and with it Weber tried to answer the questions, "What would happen if the cat bond fund was started in 1900, taking into account the worst natural events of the last 100 years? Given the current density of population and asset values in the affected regions, what value and annual returns would such a fund produce?"

Weber started at year 1900, and for every year he looked to see if a natural disaster had occurred that would have been covered by one of the bonds in the existing in-house Prima Fund. If a disaster occurred, he calculated the impact of that event on the securities in the current portfolio. For the bonds that were not affected that year, he put in an assumed fixed return of 11%. For each year, he took off 50 basis points, representing Bank Leu's management fee to its customers.

Exhibit 15 shows the sample Prima Fund from Weber's scenario, as well as the outcome, using the 14 worst natural disasters of the past century. While U.S. equities had experienced negative returns in 25 of those 99 years, the sample portfolio experienced negative returns in only three. The maximum loss of 16% was, however, considerable and occurred very suddenly, which Weber realized might be regarded as a disadvantage. On the other hand, natural events were individual events. There was no domino effect, in contrast to what often happened in the financial markets. Analyzing the sample portfolio, Weber also remarked that it was extraordinarily unlikely for a cat event to impact returns in the first three years of operation.

Taking the Prima Fund Public

Sitting in his office at Bank Leu's headquarters on Bahnhofstrasse in central Zürich in the early summer of 2001, Weber worried about the obstacles in taking the Prima Fund public. First, the regulatory environment for this type of mutual fund was quite uncertain. While recent regulatory findings in the United States cleared the way for American institutional investors to invest in catastrophe risk securities without tax or governance concerns, the SBC would have to approve Bank Leu's offering in advance. The

EXHIBIT 15

PRIMA FUND SAMPLE PORTFOLIO

a. Composition

Type of Risk	% in Portfolio
Multi Risk & Euro Wind	15%
Atlas B	12%
Halyard	3%
U.S. Weather	8%
Kelvin	8%
U.S. Earthquake	24%
Seismic	14%
Domestic	10%
U.S. Wind	26%
Residential Re	8%
NeHi	8%
Alpha Shares	10%
Japan Earthquake	12%
Concentric	4%
Namazu	8%
Japan Typhoon	15%
Pacific	15%

b. Largest Natural Disasters

Year	Disaster	Loss to Principal
1900	Galveston Hurricane	0%
1906	San Francisco Earthquake	−18.0%
1923	Great Kanto Earthquake, Tokyo	−15.6%
1926	Great Miami Hurricane	0%
1930	Tanna Earthquake Japan	0%
1938	"Long Island Express" Hurricane	0%
1944	East Coast Hurricane	0%
1961	Typhoon Nancy	−7.9%
1976–78	Extreme Weather	−1.4%
1989	Hurricane Hugo	0%
1992	Hurricane Andrew	0%
1994	Northridge California Earthquake	0%
1995	Kobe Earthquake	0%
1999	Orcan Lothar	0%

c. Historical Performanc

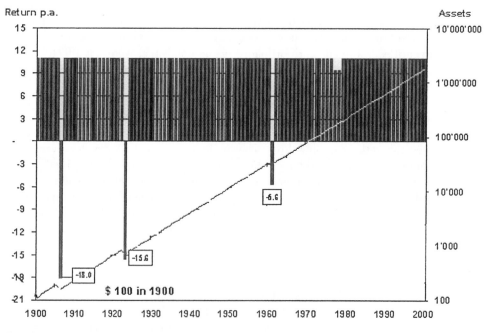

Source: Adapted by casewriters from Bank Leu, Goldman Sachs.

banking commission typically devoted its attention to traditional equity and debt secu-rities and would require a lot of coaching to understand the structure of catastrophe risk securities.

Second, Weber was concerned with accepting investments in various currencies. Some of Bank Leu's customers preferred Swiss franc-denominated investments, while others preferred euro- or U.S. dollar-denominated investments.

EXHIBIT 16

RESIDENTIAL RE 2001

a. First Page of Prospectus

Subject to Completion, dated May 7, 2001.

$150,000,000

Residential Reinsurance 2001 Limited

Variable Rate Notes Due June 1, 2004

The Variable Rate Notes (the "Notes") of Residential Reinsurance 2001 Limited (the "Company") are scheduled to mature on June 1, 2004 (the "Scheduled Maturity Date"). The maturity date of the Notes may be extended to December 1, 2004 (the "Final Maturity Date"), if United Services Automobile Association, a reciprocal inter-insurance exchange organized under the laws of Texas, USAA Casualty Insurance Company, a Texas corporation and USAA Texas Lloyd's Company, a Texas Lloyd's plan insurer (collectively, the "Ceding Insurer"), elect to extend the period (the "Extended Claims Period") in which they may present a Proof of Loss Claim under the Reinsurance Agreement to be entered into on the Closing Date with the Company (the "Reinsurance Agreement"). The Company's obligation to repay the original principal amount of the Notes will be reduced by an amount (each such amount, a "Principal Reduction") equal to the amount of any payment by the Company to the Ceding Insurer of any amount owed to the Ceding Insurer under the Reinsurance Agreement.

Interest on the Notes will be payable quarterly, on the first day of each quarter commencing on September 1, 2001, until the Scheduled Maturity Date or the Early Termination Date, as applicable, or, if the Ceding Insurer elects the Extended Claims Period, the Final Maturity Date, in each case, if such day is not a Business Day, on the next succeeding Business Day (each, an "Interest Payment Date"). The interest rate for the Notes will be three-month LIBOR plus [ ]% per annum during the period from the Closing Date to the Scheduled Maturity Date or the Early Termination Date, as applicable. If the Ceding Insurer elects the Extended Claims Period, unless a Reduced Interest Event occurs, the interest rate for the Notes during the period from the Scheduled Maturity Date to the Final Maturity Date will be three-month LIBOR plus 3.00% per annum. If a Reduced Interest Event occurs before the beginning of the Extended Claims Period, the interest rate for the Notes will be three-month LIBOR plus 0.30% per annum for the Extended Claims Period. If a Reduced Interest Event occurs during the first Interest Accrual Period of the Extended Claims Period, the interest rate for the Notes will be three-month LIBOR plus 0.30% per annum for the second Interest Accrual Period of the Extended Claims Period. Interest will be calculated on the Net Principal Amount of the Notes as of the first day of the related Interest Accrual Period after giving effect to any Principal Reduction made on such date; provided, however, that for all Interest Accrual Periods prior to June 1, 2002, interest will be calculated on the original principal amount of the Notes.

Source: Adapted from "Residential Reinsurance 2001 Ltd." proposal.

(Continued)

EXHIBIT 16   *(Continued)*

RESIDENTIAL RE 2001

---

b. Prospectus in Summary

	Residential Re 2001 Ltd.
Ceding Insurer	USAA
Closing Date	June 1, 2001
Amount	$150 million
Composition	$150 million FRN
Maturity – Initial	June 1, 2004
Maturity – Extended	November 30, 2004
Extension Notice Date	5 days prior to May 31, 2004
Risk Period To:	May 31, 2002, 2003 and 2004
Capital Exposed	100%
Cedant Retention	10% (may be less in year 2 and 3)
Covered Events	Category 3 or greater Hurricane loss in 20 Gulf and Atlantic coastal states, and Washington D.C.
Cover Form	Reinsurance
Coverage	30% of $500 million in excess of $1.1 billion
Trigger: Indemnity or Index	Indemnity
Occurrence	Single in each risk period (at discretion of USAA)
Interest rate – pa	L3 + 499 bps
Interest Pay Date	March 1, June 1, September 1, December 1
SPV	Residential Reinsurance 2001, Ltd.
SPV Location	Cayman Island
SPV Capitalization	$5,000 common
Charitable Trust	Yes
Charitable Trustee Administrator	HSBC Financial Services (Cayman) Ltd.
Fiscal Agent	None
Indenture Trustee	Chase Manhattan Bank
Reinsurance Trust	Yes
Reinsurance Trustee	Bankers Trust Company
Claims Review	KPMG (Cayman)
Attorney – Placement Agent	Skadden, Arps
Attorney – SPV	Skadden, Arps
	Maples & Calder (Bermuda)
Accountant – Principal	KPMG
Accountant – SPV Local	KPMG (Cayman)
Rated	S&P Moody Fitch
	BB+ Ba2
Loss Estimates	AIR
Placement Agent/Underwriter	Goldman Sachs; Merrill Lynch; Lehman Brothers
Comments	- Refinancing of Residential Re IV but for lower amount and for a three-year term.
	- AIR will remodel layer, trigger and exhaustion amounts for years 2 and 3 using updated USAA data and fixed probabilities.
Attachment Probability	1.12%
Exhaustion Probability	0.41%
Expected Loss	0.68%

Source: Adapted from "Residential Reinsurance 2001 Ltd." proposal.

Third, catastrophe risk securities were new and therefore thinly traded. In a mutual fund, an investor can redeem his or her shares at the posted net asset value (NAV) at periodic intervals, typically daily. Weber was concerned that the lack of deep secondary markets might pose problems in calculating a daily NAV, or worse, that in the event of a large number of simultaneous redemptions, the fund would not be able to liquidate its inventory of securities at a reasonable price.

Public or not, Weber would still need to keep the fund running for the bank's private clients. The discussions on which cat bond issues to include in the fund would be ongoing. For instance, on his desk Weber had the prospectus for a cat bond issue from the American insurer USAA, named "Residential Re 2001." (See Exhibit 16 for a summary of its prospectus.) He still had to evaluate if and how much the Prima Fund should invest in that specific issue.

Despite all of the obstacles to taking the fund public, catastrophe risk securities provided a valuable source of additional return, with risk that exhibited limited correlation with other available investment vehicles. Weber considered past experiences where he had learned that his customers did not always know they wanted a certain asset class before it was made available to them. This asset class, though, was more novel than anything he had presented before. Could Bank Leu convince investors of the benefits of cat bonds? Or, what if the demand for the fund exceeded the presently miniscule capacity of the market?

10

Catastrophe Bonds at Swiss Re

It was March 2002, and Peter Giessmann, head of Swiss Re's Retrocession Group in ZÅrich, Switzerland, looked at the documents strewn across his desk. A few months earlier, the Swiss Re board of management had made the strategic decision to try to securitize parts of their risk portfolio in the capital markets. They had given Giessmann the mandate to operationalize the decision: Which would be the best way to transfer risk to the capital markets, to the benefit of both Swiss Re and its clients? After researching the market, Giessmann now had to make a proposal.

For the 139-year old reinsurance company, the decision to securitize risk marked a turning point. Never before had Swiss Re, the world's second largest reinsurer, transferred significant parts of the risk it held on its balance sheet. The management board now believed, though, that large natural catastrophe risks—such as Florida hurricanes, European gale storms or Tokyo earthquakes—could not be well diversified within traditional global risk portfolios. These so called "peak risks," and their disproportionate need for capital if they occurred, were expensive to cover for reinsurers, insurers—and ultimately the insurance takers themselves.

In addition, population and value growth in some regions were projected to increase strongly, while capacity in the insurance industry had just been badly hit by claims resulting from the September 11-event and declining equity markets. In this context, ceding risks to other reinsurers (so called "retrocession") did not make sense to the Swiss Re management. Instead, transferring peak risks to the much larger capital markets seemed like an obvious strategic long term solution.

Giessmann knew that securitization could be done through so called catastrophe bonds, or "cat bonds." Cat bonds were securities whose coupon and principal payments depended on the probability of a catastrophe occurring, such as an earthquake or a hurricane. Their returns were therefore completely tied to events covered by insurance policies. Swiss Re had in fact issued two cat bonds some years earlier, but had found

Professors George Chacko and Peter Hecht, Executive Director of the HBS Europe Research Center Vincent Dessain, and Research Associate Anders Sjöman prepared this case. Some names and data have been disguised for confidentiality. This case deals with the sales side of the cat bond market and draws heavily from "Bank Leu's Prima Cat Bond Fund," Case No. 205-005, by the same authors. Case No. 205-005 provides a buy side perspective on the cat bond market. HBS cases are developed solely as the basis for class discussion. Cases are not intended to serve as endorsements, sources of primary data, or illustrations of effective or ineffective management.

them costly. Giessmann knew he had to find a cost-efficient way to issue cat bonds, allowing Swiss Re to at least break even on its bond issues, as compared to traditional retrocession. The recent rise in reinsurance prices might actually create an opportunity for this. At any rate, Swiss Re would have to play an active role in developing the fledgling cat bond market.

THE INSURANCE AND REINSURANCE MARKETS

Traditionally, insurance companies offered a variety of insurance products to their customers, such as life, health, property and auto insurance. Coverage for large natural catastrophes like hurricanes and earthquakes was also available. These types of events were by their very nature more unpredictable and hazardous than other events, and insurance products were tailored accordingly.

Just as insurance companies served businesses and individuals, reinsurance companies in turn acted as insurance companies to insurers. A primary insurer that wanted to limit its exposure to an insured type of risk would seek reinsurance coverage, by selling a portion of the risk to a reinsurer. This limited the primary insurer's potential loss to some fixed and manageable amount. Additionally, insurers were required by regulations to maintain reserves against possible future payouts to customers. Reinsurance then released some of the required capital reserves, making it available to underwrite new policies. Primary insurers often entered into multiple reinsurance contracts with more than one reinsurer for the same risk. In turn, reinsurers sometimes sought reinsurance themselves, so called retrocession.

Reinsurance was usually purchased in layers corresponding to different loss amounts. For example, an insurance company could reinsure itself for Florida Hurricane Risk for damages in excess of $450 million, not to exceed $750 million, i.e., $300 million of reinsurance. The price of reinsurance was based on the probability of the insured event occurring, or its "actuary attachment." The price was normally called the Rate Online (ROL) and was expressed as a percentage of the risk exposure that was covered. For example, if a company had to pay an insurance premium of $45 million in order to obtain the above-mentioned $300 million payout in the event of a hurricane, the ROL would be 45/300 = 15%.

According to an assessment by Swiss Re, the worldwide insurance market, life and non-life, wrote direct premiums in 2000 for $2.408 billion. Catastrophe reinsurance capacity that year amounted, according to another assessment, to $65 billion in the five largest markets (USA, Japan, United Kingdom, Canada and France).

CATASTROPHE BONDS

The 1992 hurricane Andrew was at the time the biggest insurance loss event in history at $20 billion. Around 60 insurers declared bankruptcy from the resulting claims. The price, or ROL, for certain risks increased dramatically as a result. Since then, no major catastrophes of similar magnitude had occurred and ROLs had dropped considerably. However, if a major new catastrophe occurred, industry analysts fully expected these ROLs to rise dramatically again (Exhibit 1 details the largest insurance claims of the past 30 years, and Exhibit 2 shows the change in catastrophe reinsurance prices after large catastrophes).

After the large losses caused by Andrew, the reinsurance industry looked for new risk-financing sources in the mid-1990s to better share the risks of major catastrophes.

EXHIBIT 1

LARGEST INSURANCE CLAIMS OF PAST 30 YEARS

Event	Insured Damage (mUSD, at 2001 prices)	Year	Region
Hurricane Andrew	20,129	1992	U.S.
Northridge earthquake	14,894	1994	U.S.
Typhoon Mireille	7,284	1991	Japan
Winter storm Daria	6,204	1990	Europe
Hurricane Hugo	5,974	1989	Puerto Rico
Winter storm Lothar	4,746	1999	Europe
Storms and floods	4,656	1987	Europe
Winter storm Vivian	4,311	1990	Europe
Hurricane Georges	3,820	1998	U.S., Caribbean
Typhoon Bart	3,143	1999	Japan
Oil platform Piper Alpha	2,986	1995	North Sea

Source: Bank Leu.

As one option, they turned to the capital markets, exploring various forms of insurance-linked securities (ILS). The approach was new, and required the participants to understand both capital and insurance markets, markets that until then had very little to do with each other. Of several attempts, including futures and options on catastrophe claims, only cat bonds managed to get off the ground. The first cat bond was issued in 1994 by Hanover Re, and the market began in earnest in 1997.

EXHIBIT 2

CATASTROPHE PRICE INDEX AND EVENTS

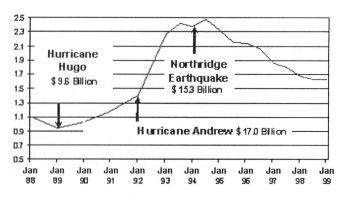

Source: Bank Leu.

EXHIBIT 3

EXAMPLE OF A CAT BOND: RESIDENTIAL RE 2001

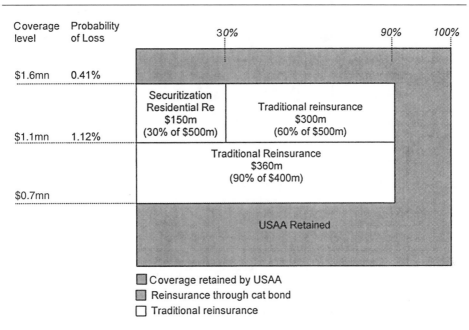

Note: The insurance company USAA created the cat bond issuer Residential Re for the specific purpose of transferring insurance risk related to U.S. East and Gulf Coast Hurricanes to the capital markets.

Source: Adapted from Cochran, Caronia Securities.

Cat bonds normally took a part of a risk layer from traditional reinsurance coverage. As an example, Exhibit 3 shows how United Services Automobile Association (USAA), a Texas-based insurance company, issued the cat bond "Residential Re" in 2001.[1] The bond took $150 million, or 30%, of the risk for U.S. Gulf and East Coast Hurricanes for a risk layer that began (or "attached") at a probability of 1.12% and ended (or "exhausted") at 0.41%. The attachment level represented the risk that *some* amount would have to be paid out; the exhaustion level that the *entire* amount would default.

Issuing Cat Bonds

The typical cat bond issue is outlined in Figure A on the following page. It involved an insurance or reinsurance company (the "sponsor") that incorporated a special purpose reinsurance vehicle (SPV) in a tax-advantaged jurisdiction, such as Bermuda or the Cayman Islands. The SPV's purpose was to transfer insurance risk into the capital markets through the issuance of cat bonds. The SPV assumed the risk of a defined type of natural event from the sponsor through a reinsurance or retrocedence contract. In return, the SPV received payments of insurance premiums from the sponsor.

---

[1] For a detailed look at a specific cat bond issuance, see Kenneth Froot and Mark Seasholes, "USAA: Catastrophe Risk Financing," HBS Case No. 9-298-007 (Boston: Harvard Business School Publishing, 1997).

a. Transaction

b. Possible end position

Figure A Structural Overview of Cat Bond Issuance

Source: Adapted from Bank Leu.

The SPV then issued bonds in the fixed income capital markets for investors to purchase. The nominal capital paid by the investors, their principal, was invested by the SPV in low-risk securities, such as AAA short term treasuries or corporate bonds, which yielded a return about equal to LIBOR.[2] The income from these investments, plus a premium, was paid to investors in the form of a quarterly coupon, provided of course that the insured event did not occur. The premium component of the coupon came from the payments made by the sponsor to the SPV for the retrocedence agreement. This premium ranged between 180 and 1400 basis points.[3]

When the term expired at maturity, the principal was repaid to the investors. However, if the insured event did occur, the SPV paid out the principal in full or in part to cover losses by the sponsor. The investors in the SPV, therefore, made money (the return on the low-risk securities plus the reinsurance premium) if no catastrophe occurred, but lost some or all of their money if a catastrophe occurred. Catastrophe risk was therefore transferred to the investors in the SPV.

Pricing Cat Bonds: Ratings, Attachment and Payment Triggers

A cat bond's price was expressed as LIBOR plus a spread. The pricing of cat bonds was affected by numerous variables, but, above all, by the rating given to it by one of the three large rating agencies: Standard & Poor's, Moody's and Fitch. Cat bonds were typically rated under the same system as corporate bonds, and were mostly given non-investment grade BB ratings. Sponsors often argued that ratings agencies biased their ratings of cat bonds downwards, due to their focus on the "peak-peril" of the catastrophes, i.e., the worst-case losses in the event of a cat occurrence. Since the risk of a cat bond lay entirely in the occurrence of an insured event, sponsors believed that the ratings agencies were over-concerned with this peak-peril aspect, rather than looking at expected losses.

---

[2] LIBOR (London Inter Bank Offered Rate) is the interest paid for dollars and euros at international markets in inter bank borrowings. The LIBOR rate is fixed daily by the British Bankers' Association (BBA). It is similar to the U.S. Federal Reserve rate, in that it is used as a reference rate for other short term interest rates.

[3] A basis point represents 1/100 of 1%, or 0.01%.

At any rate, most industry specialists agreed that cat bonds were well suited for these "peak perils." Traditional reinsurance programs often did not cover 1-in-100 events (the top 1% loss events). Reinsurers felt they had limited ability to diversify away these high-severity, low probability risks. Cat bonds instead provided a new type of transfer for risk that attached at the 1-in-100-year events and exhausted at the 1-in-250-year events (0.4% per year). Above the 1-in-250-year events, only a very small portion of the total catastrophe risk was normally reinsured, as these risks were considered extremely remote.

The investment banks that underwrote cat bonds prepared detailed presentations for the rating agencies to explain the risks intrinsic to the bonds, much as they would accompany a corporate bond issuer to the rating agencies. The rating for corporate bonds was generally determined by the rating agency's evaluation of the risk of financial distress or bankruptcy of the bond issuer. The probability of bankruptcy had as its rough analogs in the cat bond market the probability of the insured event occurring (or its probability of "attachment") and expected loss.

For assessments of the attachment and expected loss, the industry relied primarily on full-risk evaluations, carried out by third-party expert scientific modeling firms. Three such firms were commonly used: Applied Insurance Research (AIR), EQECAT (EQE), and Risk Management Solutions (RMS).

The costs resulting from an event, and the resulting payments due to the sponsor from the SPV, were calculated using various methods, often referred to as "payment triggers." Put differently, the triggers determined whether a natural catastrophe qualified for coverage. Triggers included indemnity, industry index, parametric index and modeled loss.

The most straight-forward method was indemnity-based triggers, where payouts were based on the actual and verified size of the losses incurred by the sponsor. This approach however required that the sponsor disclosed potentially confidential details about the protected portfolio to investors. It also required the investors to fully understand the sponsoring company's portfolio, which was both time-consuming and difficult.

As an alternative, so called "index triggers" were commonly used. Index triggers followed one of two broad approaches: industry-loss indices and parametric indices. Industry-loss indices were triggered by an estimate of the aggregate insurance industry loss in a catastrophe. The estimates were derived from either a reporting service such as Property Claim Service (PCS) or through the use of a catastrophe model, a so-called "modeled loss." A modeled loss was calculated by running an event's physical parameters, e.g., wind speed of a hurricane or magnitude of an earthquake, against the modeling firm's database of industry exposures. The resulting number was the modeling firm's estimate of an industry loss. The payment would then be calculated by multiplying the total estimated losses by a pre-specified percentage. Parametric index triggers worked similarly, but were more transparent to the investors. Here, payouts were triggered simply by the occurrence of an event with certain defined physical parameters, for instance winds speeds or ground acceleration measurements. Since most of the covered regions had a high resolution network of official measuring stations, the loss incurred to the sponsor could be estimated using a predefined formula.

As mentioned, the different types of triggers offered a range of levels of basis risk (the risk that the paid amount and the actual amount required as coverage differed) and transparency to investors, as illustrated in Exhibit 4.

Advantages to Investors

By early 2001, cat bond investors included life insurance companies, investment advisors, hedge funds, mutual funds, banks, property and casualty insurance companies as

EXHIBIT 4

TRADE-OFF BETWEEN BASIS RISK AND TRANSPARENCY

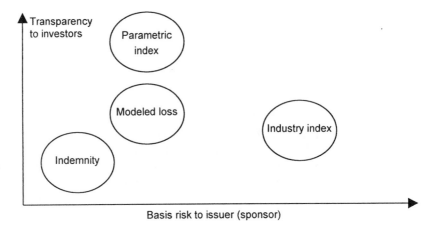

Source: Adapted from Swiss Re, "Insurance-Linked Securities," 2003, page 8.

well as reinsurers. Investors in catastrophe risk securities liked the asset class since it provided them with a number of diversification benefits, and represented exposures that differed significantly from those of high-yield corporate bonds. Above all, they were seen by most as completely uncorrelated with the economic cycle. Investors were also attracted by the spread for a cat bond (its promised returns in excess of treasury bonds). Exhibits 5–9 provide more detail on cat bond spreads, corporate bond spreads, default probabilities and recovery rates.

EXHIBIT 5

SPREAD COMPARISON

Investment	Rating	Spread, mid-2001	Loss Probability (LP)	Risk Coverage (=Spread/LP)
Corporate Bonds BB+	BB+	3.52%	0.53%	6.6x
Cat Bonds Redwood Capital I	BB+	5.50%	0.53%	10.4x
Corporate Bonds BB	BB	4.73%	1.66%	2.8x
Cat Bond Namazu	BB	5.31%	0.75%	7.1x
Corporate Bonds BB−	BB−	4.83%	3.42%	1.4x
Cat Bond CalQuake & Euro Wind	BB−	8.50%	1.33%	6.4x
Corporate Bonds B+	B+	5.78%	6.75%	0.9x
Cat Bond Atlas C	B+	16.83%	3.24%	5.2x

Source: Bank Leu documents.

EXHIBIT 6

COMPARATIVE CREDIT SPREADS ON JUNE 1, 2001 FOR CORPORATE BONDS OF DIFFERENT RATINGS AND MATURITIES

Maturity	AAA	AA	A+	A	A−	BBB+	BBB	BBB−	BB+	BB	BB−	B+
3 Month	4.08	4.14	4.28	4.4	4.71	5.08	5.08	5.5	6.37	6.52	6.74	7.17
6 Month	4.15	4.21	4.31	4.43	4.65	4.98	5.06	5.47	6.24	6.51	6.75	7.12
1 Year	4.27	4.3	4.48	4.62	4.79	5.11	5.15	5.68	6.7	6.89	7.14	7.50
2 Year	4.75	4.8	5.07	5.17	5.35	5.59	5.72	6.27	7.12	7.44	7.73	8.10
3 Year	5.15	5.28	5.51	5.74	5.76	6.09	6.23	6.65	7.53	7.78	8.1	8.54
4 Year	5.43	5.57	5.79	5.99	6.06	6.35	6.49	6.89	7.77	8.02	8.44	8.79
5 Year	5.67	5.76	6.00	6.18	6.27	6.48	6.6	7.05	8.01	8.23	8.77	9.04
7 Year	5.96	6.16	6.35	6.51	6.63	6.91	6.93	7.39	8.2	8.45	8.98	9.20
8 Year	6.07	6.3	6.44	6.64	6.74	7.00	7.00	7.47	8.28	8.49	9.09	9.31
9 Year	6.1	6.36	6.42	6.64	6.76	7.04	7.05	7.52	8.41	8.6	9.19	9.40
10 Year	6.14	6.35	6.43	6.68	6.82	7.04	7.06	7.56	8.47	8.74	9.31	9.53
15 Year	6.43	6.61	6.81	7.05	7.3	7.45	7.5	8.01	8.87	9.12	9.66	9.88
20 Year	6.7	6.9	7.1	7.37	7.59	7.72	7.79	8.23	9 .02	9.27	9.89	10.13
25 Year	6.69	6.91	7.05	7.35	7.53	7.73	7.76	8.16	9.12	9.30	9.95	10.26
30 Year	6.64	6.87	7.03	7.24	7.34	7.63	7.66	8.06	9.04	9.26	10.00	10.34

Note: Ratings by Standard & Poor's.

Source: Bloomberg LP, accessed on May 1, 2004.

The overall risk-return trade-off for cat bonds appealed to many investors, since the ratio of expected excess return to volatility (the so called "Sharpe ratio") was significantly higher for catastrophe risk securities than other alternatives (see Exhibit 10). Introducing catastrophe linked securities to an investment portfolio would therefore raise the slope of the "capital market line," which maps expected return against risk in a fully diversified and efficient portfolio. Or in other words, not only would cat bonds most likely increase the expected returns of the portfolio, but they would also lower its volatility, due to their low or absent correlation with other financial instruments, thus affecting both sides of the Sharpe ratio.

EXHIBIT 7

YIELD CURVE RATES ON MARCH 1, 2002 FOR U.S. TREASURIES

3-mo	6-mo	1-yr	2-yr	3-yr	5-yr	7-yr	10-yr	20-yr	30-yr
1.78	1.77	1.91	2.33	3.18	3.73	4.43	4.82	4.98	5.70

Source: Adapted from U.S. Treasury website, ⟨http://www.ustreas.gov/offices/domestic-finance/debt-management/interest-rate/yield20020301.html⟩, accessed 3 February 2004.

EXHIBIT 8

HISTORICAL FIVE-YEAR CUMULATIVE DEFAULT PROBABILITIES FOR VARIOUS CREDITS

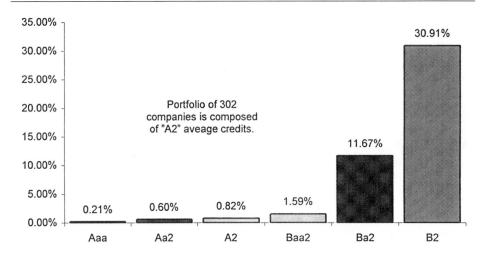

Source: Moody's Investor Service, Historical Default Rates of Corporate Bond Issuers, 1920–1996. Based on cohorts formed since 1970.

EXHIBIT 9

RECOVERY RATE ON DEBT INSTRUMENTS OF VARYING SENIORITY

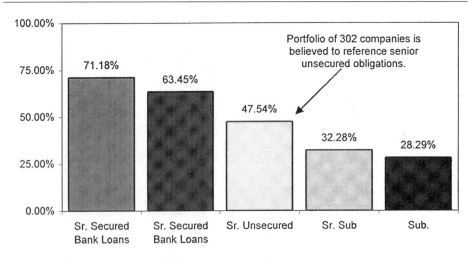

Source: Moody's Investor Service, Historical Default Rates of Corporate Bond Issuers, 1920–1996.

EXHIBIT 10

SHARPE RATIOS

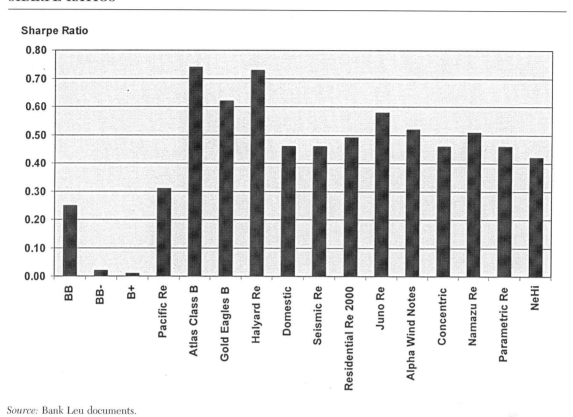

Source: Bank Leu documents.

Still, investors were at times struggling to understand the mechanisms of cat bonds, since as always their primary concern were easy-to-understand, intelligible and verifiable definitions of risks.

Advantages to Sponsors

In the early days of the cat bond market, issuers as a rule had not known how to work in the capital markets. Indeed, for insurance companies, working with capital markets participants was very different from their traditional reinsurance partners. Exhibit 11 describes the issuer community in 2002. Nevertheless, capital markets offered an attractive alternative for insurers and reinsurers looking to transfer catastrophe risk. The cat risk securities markets offered multi-year coverage, almost eliminated credit quality concerns, and they also brought a more stable and diversified source of investors. Further, the pricing of the securities better represented the underlying risk due to the increased transparency of the risk.

Although there was no consensus in the industry as to the actual all-in costs of issuing catastrophe bonds, some analysts had made an estimate. Their estimate landed at a cost of around 80 basis points per year for a three-year cat bond issue. The cost of

EXHIBIT 11

RISK-LINKED SECURITIES MARKET SHARE BY ISSUER (2002)

Transaction Sponsor	Nature of Sponsor	Amount Outstanding (mUSD)	Issues outstanding	Market share
Swiss Re	Reinsurer	806.5	4	29.1%
SCOR	Reinsurer	350.0	2	12.6%
Munich Re	Reinsurer	300.0	2	10.8%
USAA	Insurer	275.0	2	9.9%
Vivendi Universal	Corporate	175.0	1	6.3%
Lehman Re	Reinsurer	165.0	1	6.0%
Zürich Reinsurance	Insurer	161.9	1	5.8%
AGF IART	Insurer	129.0	1	4.7%
Oriental Land Company	Corporate	100.0	1	3.6%
Yasuda Fire & Marine	Insurer	80.0	1	2.9%
Tokio Marine & Fire	Insurer	80.0	1	2.9%
Nissay Dowa General Insurance	Insurer	70.0	1	2.5%
Vesta Fire Insurance	Insurer	41.5	1	1.5%
Hiscox	Reinsurer	33.0	1	1.2%
Totals		2.767	20	100%

Note: Issues Outstanding aggregates tranches of securities into the main SPV, therefore, the number of issues is less than the number of securities.

Source: Cochran, Caronia Securities.

structuring the issuance included fees to lawyers (about $600,000 for an average size issue), modeling agencies (about $400,000), rating agencies (5 basis points of the issued amount per agency; the average issuance used two agencies) as well as distribution costs (a variable cost of about 1%–1.5% of the issue volume).[4] For a three-year $100 million bond, this would come out at about $2.2 million–$2.7 million.

This issuance cost was seen by some market participants, notably some of the large reinsurance companies, as prohibitive for issuing cat bonds. To them, only multi-year issuances in excess of $100 million would even be worth considering.

Analysts at a large investment bank attempted to take the comparison of cat bonds to retrocession a bit further. They put a value on all benefits associated with issuing cat bonds, relative to the traditional reinsurance markets. They found savings of 125 basis points, broken into four different parts. The first part, "Credit Risk," included the reduction of counter party risk when a sponsor did not have to contract with a reinsur-

[4] The distribution cost did indeed account for almost half the cost of an issue. For issuers with an in-house distribution network—as was the case for Swiss Re—the distribution cost could to a certain degree be ignored. By comparison, the distribution costs associated with traditional retrocession, which was placed through brokers, amounted to about 10% of the premium annually.

ance company that might not be able to honor its obligations and instead contracted with an SPV, whose investments were required to be of the highest commercial paper rating quality. Furthermore, cat bonds also helped the issuers to move the credit risk off the balance sheet, since with an SPV, they received the money up-front from the issuing SPV. The investment bank assigned a benefit of 50 basis points to this part.

The second part, "Term Structure," brought a saving of 50 basis points. It represented savings to the insurer by being able to sell multiple years of risk at once, without being exposed to the "refinancing" risk of having to sell it each year. However, a direct risk of multi-year contracts, e.g. three years, was that in year three the market rate of reinsurance could be lower than in year one. The "locked-in" price would then be higher than current market prices, and in fact would become a loss, not a saving, to the cat bond issuer.

The third part, "Strategic Benefit," was the result of having lower overall costs as an insurer by having a new market to turn to for reinsurance. The hardest to assign an actual value, the part was estimated at 50 basis points by a large investment bank. Finally, the fourth part, "Contract Features," worked *against* the previous savings by about 25 basis points, since trading in the capital markets required standardized contracts, losing the flexibility of custom contracts in the reinsurance market.

In addition, industry insiders also valued cat bonds for the short time (about two to three weeks) it took after an event to receive the actual coverage, referring to the "short tail" of cat bonds.

Trading Cat Bonds in the Secondary Market

In 2001, the worst underwriting year in the history of the insurance industry, cat bonds still returned 9.45% for the year, outperforming the Merrill Lynch High Yield Master II Index by almost 500 basis points. Exhibit 12 goes on to compare cat bonds versus high yield bonds in 2002 and Exhibits 13 and 14 then compare risk-linked securities in general with various financial instruments. Cat bonds also performed better than the stock market average.

Active trading and bid prices were made available by Goldman Sachs, Swiss Re Capital Markets, Aon Capital Markets, Lehman Brothers, and American Re. Often, the bids posted differed across market makers and were indicative, rather than representative of any actual trades executed. According to one trader, the cat bond market saw only about half a dozen trades a week at most. The common buy-and-hold attitude of cat bond investors compounded the problem of low liquidity.

Exhibit 15 lists example bid differentials and Exhibit 16 market trading volume for one market maker, Swiss Re. Exhibit 17 displays the secondary spread trends for a selected sample of cat bonds.

THE CAT BOND MARKET BY YEAR END 2001

Since the cat bond market began in earnest in 1997, a little over $5.5 billion had been placed in cat bonds. Exhibit 18 details all cat bonds issued from 1997 until the end of 2001. In addition to cat bonds, the asset class of Insurance Linked Securities (ILS) also included catastrophe risk exchange (CATEX) swaps, insurance related derivatives and options, catastrophe equity puts (CAT-E-Puts), contingent surplus notes and weather derivatives.

EXHIBIT 12

RISK-LINKED SECURITIES VS. HIGH YIELD BONDS (MERRILL HIGH YIELD MASTER) IN 2001

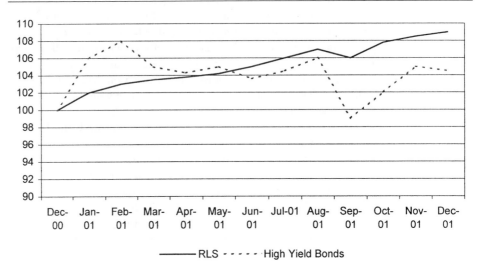

Note: In their quarterly update on Insurance Linked Securities, February 2003, Swiss Re carried out the same type of comparison against Lehman Brothers BB High Yield Index. Their numbers were 9.23% and –1.79% respectively.

Source: Cochran, Caronia Securities, Review of the Year 2001, page 8.

EXHIBIT 13

RISK-LINKED SECURITIES VS. VARIOUS FINANCIAL INSTRUMENTS (2002)

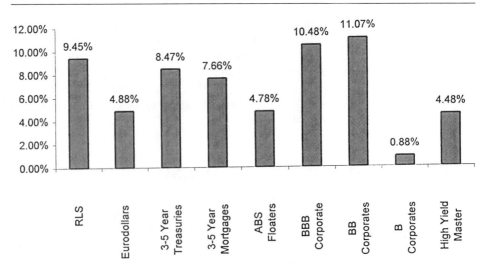

Source: Cochran, Caronia Securities, Review of the Year 2001, page 9.

EXHIBIT 14

RISK-LINKED SECURITIES 2002 OVERVIEW
(TOTAL RETURN BY MONTH)

Security	Jan-02	Feb-02	Mar-02
Atlas Re A	0.45%	0.33%	0.47%
Atlas Re B	1.08%	0.36%	0.29%
Atlas Re C	2.96%	1.79%	1.27%
Atlas Re II A	0.72%	0.18%	0.62%
Atlas Re II B	0.43%	0.49%	0.75%
Concentric	1.43%	0.72%	0.64%
Gold Eagle 2001	0.55%	0.24%	0.35%
Halyard Re	0.86%	0.41%	0.45%
Juno Re	0.76%	0.30%	0.28%
Mediterranean A	0.22%	0.67%	0.20%
Mediterranean B	2.73%	1.11%	0.67%
Namazu Re	2.87%	0.76%	0.90%
NeHi Notes	0.29%	0.48%	0.08%
Pacific Re	0.38%	0.52%	0.08%
Parametric Re	3.75%	0.94%	0.99%
Prime CalEuro	3.53%	0.95%	0.75%
Prime Hurricane	0.58%	0.45%	−0.04%
Redwood Capital I	0.39%	0.98%	0.34%
Residential Re 2001	0.98%	0.67%	0.47%
SR Wind A-1	2.21%	1.18%	0.09%
SR Wind A-2	1.67%	1.19%	−0.29%
St. Agatha Re	—	—	—
Trinom A-1	3.29%	0.67%	0.58%
Trinom A-2	0.82%	0.55%	0.66%
Western Capital	1.08%	1.02%	0.31%
	1.44%	**0.74%**	**0.48%**

Source: Cochran, Caronia Securities.

Cat bonds were usually issued with a three year maturity. Among the underlying risks that had been securitized using cat bonds were California earthquakes, U.S. East and Gulf Coast hurricanes, European earthquakes, Florida hurricanes, French windstorms, German windstorms and hail, Japanese earthquakes, and European property. An individual cat bond could either cover one single peril or several perils simultaneously, so called "multi-peril" coverage. It seemed as if sponsors preferred issuing multi-peril bonds, since covering many territories in a single bond minimized issuance and administration costs and provided additional capital relief. Investors, on the other hand, preferred the single-peril bond approach, which gave them freedom to assemble a risk portfolio according to their own investment preferences.

EXHIBIT 15

SECONDARY MARKET TRADING (MARCH 14, 2001 COMPARED TO MARCH 8, 2002)

Bond	Bid Price	Ask Price	Bid Spread	Ask Spread	Expected loss
March 14, 2001					
California Quake #2	99.31	99.59	5.35%	5.00%	73
California Quake #3	99.47	99.97	5.40%	5.10%	55
Europe multiperil A	99.63	100.59	2.70%	2.45%	22
Europe multiperil B	99.78	100.28	5.90%	5.78%	116
Florida Wind notes	100.69	100.81	0.90%	0.35%	63
Florida Wind preference shares	101.13	101.25	1.10%	0.50%	146
Japan Quake #1	100.19	100.47	3.10%	3.00%	41
Japan Quake #2	98.84	99.16	4.85%	4.75%	75
Japan Quake #3	101.97	103.00	3.95%	3.75%	70
US Wind #1	100.59	100.97	3.90%	3.60%	45
US Wind #3	100.66	100.78	0.90%	0.35%	54
World multiperil #1 A	99.81	100.13	2.80%	2.65%	11
World multiperil #1 B	99.81	100.09	3.80%	3.65%	23
World multiperil #2	99.53	100.63	7.70%	7.25%	133
March 8, 2002					
California Quake #1	100.19	100.31	5.25%	5.10%	53
California Quake #3	99.94	100.15	5.15%	4.90%	55
Europe multiperil A	100.60	101.22	2.40%	2.25%	22
Europe multiperil B	98.71	99.19	6.25%	6.10%	116
Europe Wind	100.55	101.43	5.05%	4.75%	68
Japan Quake #1	100.09	100.71	3.05%	2.80%	41
Japan Quake #2	100.23	100.74	4.40%	4.25%	75
Japan Quake #3	100.24	100.94	4.25%	4.10%	70
Japan typhoon	100.90	101.23	2.95%	2.70%	88
US Multiperil	100.22	100.25	2.35%	1.90%	63
US Wind #1	100.80	101.05	1.28%	0.50%	45
US Wind #2	100.32	101.00	6.30%	5.92%	127
US Wind #4	101.18	101.85	5.33%	5.10%	76
World multiperil #1 A	100.60	100.75	2.10%	2.00%	11
World multiperil #1 A - Series II	100.73	101.15	2.10%	1.95%	5
World multiperil #1 B	101.13	101.42	2.60%	2.35%	23
World multiperil #1 B - Series II	99.48	100.75	6.95%	6.45%	90
World multiperil #2	100.37	100.98	7.27%	6.91%	133
World multiperil #3 A	99.40	100.64	8.27%	7.68%	111
World multiperil #3 B	100.42	101.17	3.80%	3.45%	67

Notes: 1. Exact name of bonds disguised, and replaced by the primary peril covered by the bond.
    2. The average bid/ask spread for both sets of data is 30bp.

Source: Swiss Re Capital Markets.

EXHIBIT 16

APPROXIMATE CAT BOND TRADING VOLUMES FOR SWISS RE CAPITAL MARKETS

Month	Amount ($)
Sep, 2001	14,750,000
Oct, 2001	5,750,000
Nov, 2001	35,500,000
Dec, 2001	43,000,000
Jan, 2002	36,700,000
Feb, 2002	6,000,000
Mar, 2002	18,950,000
Grand total	**160,650,000**
Monthly average	**22,950,000**

Note: Numbers are for Swiss Re Capital Markets (SRCM) only and therefore not representative of the entire secondary market volume. SRCM was estimated to be one of three major broker-dealers in March 2002, in addition to numerous smaller dealers and/or end-users trading in cat bonds.

Source: Swiss Re Capital Markets.

Of the cat bonds issues since 1997, approximately $2.08 billion of cat bonds were still outstanding in the capital markets in 2001 (up from $1.73 billion the year before). To date, there had not been a single catastrophic event to actually cause a full or even partial loss of principal.

Primary insurers, with roughly 60% of the issuances, dominated as cat bond sponsors, compared to reinsurers. With the rise in reinsurance premiums, the capital markets were apparently becoming economically attractive for primary insurers. Early 2002 had also seen the second-ever corporate-sponsored transaction. French media conglomerate Vivendi Universal issued a $175 million, 42-month bond to provide protection against earthquake damage to its Universal Studios holdings in Southern California.

It seemed, however, as if several reinsurers still were not convinced of the attractiveness of cat bonds. These companies seemed to consider cat bonds as too expensive and administratively too time-consuming to issue than taking out traditional retrocession cover. They claimed that a single bond could take months to put together, and that the legal and underwriting costs, combined with the high spreads usually demanded by investors, made it difficult for cat bonds to compete on price. In fact, both SCOR, France's largest reinsurer, and Munich Re, the world's largest reinsurer and a previous cat bond issuer, were currently not considering cat bonds as an alternative for risk transfer.

Industry observers sometimes believed that large reinsurer's were downplaying the importance of cat bonds for fear that the primary insurers would start turning directly to the capital markets for their reinsurance needs.

SWISS RE, A 139-YEAR-OLD REINSURER

Swiss Re had been an early participant in the insurance-linked securities market, creating Swiss Re Capital Markets Corporation in 1995 and sponsoring one of the first cat

EXHIBIT 17

SECONDARY SPREAD TRENDS

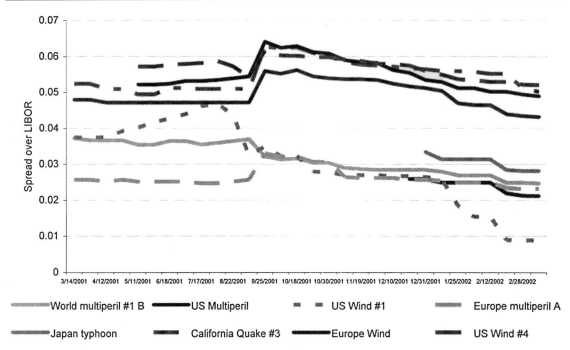

Note: Although theoretically, there should be no correlation between cat bonds and the September 11-events, Swiss Re Capital Markets did notice that general sentiment at the time, plus some investors who suddenly needed liquidity, raised spreads for a few weeks after September 2001, as evident in the diagram above. The "anomaly" disappeared rapidly. Furthermore, cat bonds linked to windstorms and hurricanes have a seasonal character, since the risk is not evenly distributed over the year, but concentrated in a few periods. This leads to seasonal adjustments in spreads, to "follow the risk." E.g. hurricane spreads are lowest in December, which is the end of the hurricane season.

Source: Swiss Re Capital Markets.

bond transactions, SR Earthquake Ltd. in 1997. It had seemed a wise move for the company to familiarize itself with the securities market, although, as Giessmann described it, the company back then had not yet made a full commitment to securitizing in the capital markets.

Founded in 1863 as Schweizerische Rueckverischerungsgesellschaft, Swiss Re reinsured life, health, property, motor, and liability insurance. As the world's second largest reinsurer after Munich Re, they operated 70 offices in over 30 countries, and had a strong track record of earnings growth. However, that record had been interrupted in 2001 with a net loss of CHF 165 million, largely due to the September 11-event. Although their property and casualty results were improving so far in 2002, falling equity markets would keep its net income in the red for the next year. See Exhibit 19 for Swiss Re's 2001 and 2000 financials.

Swiss Re offered its asset management services to small and medium-sized insurers looking to outsource their funds management. The company had also recently created weather derivatives aimed at power utilities and heating oil and gas distributors that could have their profits undercut by unseasonable weather.

The company was organized around three large groups: the Property & Casualty Group; the Life & Health Business Group, which included life, health and disability reinsurance; and finally the Financial Services Business Group, which included risk solutions, credit solutions, capital markets and advisory, and asset management business units.

The Strategic Decision: Turning to the Capital Markets

In the fall of 2001, Swiss Re's board of management decided after long discussions that the company should try to securitize parts of their risk portfolio in the capital markets. Until now, the company had not seriously contemplated passing on parts of their risk. Explained Giessmann,

> For 139 years, Swiss Re had taken risk onto the balance sheet and never given it way away. Swiss Re, like some other reinsurers, was founded in the second half of the 19th century, when a few devastating fires destroyed entire cities. These catastrophes revealed that the risk landscape had changed as a result of the industrial revolution and the resulting concentration of assets into one location. Local insurance companies were not capable to take these rare, but catastrophic risks anymore. They needed a pool or a new, national entity to which they could cede these risks.

> Today, it seems we may have reached a similar point. Florida and California, as an example, are highly exposed to natural catastrophes. Yet these states show a strong population and value growth—a trend which is predicted to continue over the next 10 years. As a result, these large risks become increasingly difficult to diversify with other risks and therefore use up a disproportionate amount of capital. This makes these risks expensive to cover for reinsurers, insurers and ultimately the insurance taker.

> We have a few options to improve the situation. We could decrease on the front-end, or simply put, take less peak peril business. That option does not interest us. Instead, we could move the risks off our balance sheets. It would mean the first time in Swiss Re's history that we seriously look for retrocession. Although retrocession is fine for smaller reinsurers, for a large company like ours, there are really only three or four companies to go to. And they are normally our competitors. Retroceding to them would mean giving them control of a part of Swiss Re, since they for example get information on our risk profile. So traditional retrocession has never been an option. Now, though, there is securitizing in the capital markets.

Giessmann had joined Swiss Re four years earlier, with a Ph.D. in biophysics and close to two years of management consultant experience at the Boston Consulting Group. In the summer of 2001, he was coming off another corporate strategy project, as Swiss Re's Chief Financial Officer called him into his office. On behalf of the board of management, the CFO gave Giessmann the mandate to investigate ways that Swiss Re could transfer risk to the capital markets.

The Tactical Decision: Going with Cat Bonds

Giessmann's first order of business was to look at which of Swiss Re's lines of business were well suited for securitization in the capital markets. Explained Giessmann,

EXHIBIT 18

SELECTED CAT BOND TRANSACTIONS

Year	Transaction/ SPV	Sponsor	Lead Managers	Tranche	Size ($ 000)	Term (yrs)
2001	SR Wind, Ltd. 1	Swiss Re	SR, LB	Notes	58,200	4
				Shares	1,800	
	SR Wind, Ltd. 2	Swiss Re	SR, LB	Notes	58,200	4
				Shares	1,800	
	Halyard Re III	Sorema	Aon	—	17,000	1
	Gold Eagle 2	American Re	AR, LB, ML	Notes	125,000	1
				Shares		
	Western Cap Lid	Swiss Re Capital Mkts	GS, SR	Notes	97,000	2
					3,000	2
	Residential Re 01	USAA	GS, LB, ML	Notes	150,000	3
2000	PRIME Cap	Munich Re	GS, LB	Notes	129,000	3
				Units	3,000	3
				Shares	6,000	3
	PRIME Cap Hurricane Ltd.	Munich Re	GS, LB	Notes	159,000	3
				Units	3,000	3
				Shares	6,000	3
	Mediterranean Re	AGF	GS	Class A	41,000	5
				Class B	88,000	
	NeHi	Vesta	Aon	Notes	41,500	3
				Shares	8,500	3
	Residential Re 00	USAA	GS, LB, ML	—	200,000	1
	Alpha Wind 2000-A Ltd.	State Farm	GS	Notes	52,500	1
				Shares	32,500	1
	Halyard Re Renew	Sorema	Aon	—	17,000	1
	Atlas Re	SCOR	GS	Class A	70,000	3
				Class B	30,000	3
				Class C	100,000	3
	Seismic Ltd.	Lehman Re	LB	Notes	145,500	2
				Shares	4,500	2
1999	Namazu Re	Gerling	Aon, GS	—	100,000	5
	Gold Eagle Capital Ltd	American Re	AR	Class A	50,000	1.25
				Class B	126,600	1.25
				Shares	5,500	1.25
	Kelvin Ltd	Koch Energy	GS	1st Event	21,608	3
				2nd Event	23,000	3
	Juno Re	Gerling	GS	—	80,000	3
	Residential Re 99	USAA	GS, ML, LB	—	200,000	1
	Circle Maihama	Oriental Land	GS	—	100,000	5
	Concentric Ltd.	Oriental Land	GS	—	100,000	5
	Halyard Re	Sorema	ML, Aon	—	17,000	3
	Domestic Inc.	Kemper	Aon	Notes	80,000	3
				Shares	20,000	3
	SECTRS 1999	Gerling	GS	Class A	€245,500	3
				Class B	€127,500	3
				Class C	€82,000	3
	Mosaic Re 2	St. Paul/ F&G Re	GS, EWB	Units	1,400	1
				Class A	24,300	1
				Class B	20,000	1
	Trinity Re 1999	Centre Solutions	GS	Class A-1	5,000	1
				Class A-2	51,615	1

(Continued)

EXHIBIT 18 *(Continued)*

SELECTED CAT BOND TRANSACTIONS

Risk	Region	Trigger	Attach Prob (%)	Exhaust Prob (%)	E{L} (%)
Windstorm Second Event	France Possibly Florida	Parametric	1.07	0.44	0.68
Hurricane Second Event	Florida Possibly France	Parametric	1.13	0.53	0.76
Typh,earth,wind	Japan, Europe	Indemnity			0.60
Hurricane, Earthquake	U.S. East & Gulf Coast, N. Madrid	Index	1.18	0.51	0.75
Earthquake	California	Index – Ind. Loss	0.82	0.34	0.55 0.82
Hurricane	U.S. Gulf/ East Co.	Indemnity	1.12	0.41	0.68
Earthquake & Windstorm	California & Europe	Parametric	1.69	1.07	1.33
Hurricane	New York area & Miami area	Parametric	1.46	1.08	1.27
Earthquake & Windstorm	France & Monaco	Modeled Loss	0.28 1.47	0.17 0.93	0.22 1.16
Hurricane	Northeast/Haw	Indemnity	0.87 1.00	0.56 0.87	0.70 0.93
Hurricane	U.S. East /Gulf Co.	Indemnity	0.95	0.31	0.54
Hurricane	Florida Florida	Indemnity	0.99 2.08	0.38 0.99	0.63 1.46
Typh, EQ, Wind	Europe, Japan	Indemnity	0.84	0.40	0.60
Earthquake, Windstorm	U.S., Japan, Europe	Indemnity	0.19 0.29 5.47	0.05 0.19 1.90	0.11 0.23 3.24
Earthquake	California	Index – Ind. Loss	1.13 1.13	0.47 1.13	0.73 1.13
Earthquake	Japan	Ind – Mod.	1.00	0.32	0.75
Hurricane, Earthquake	U.S. East & Gulf Coast, U.S. Midwest & CA	Ind – Mod Modeled	0.17 0.78 0.17	0.17 0.17	0.17 0.63 0.17
Weather	U.S. Nationwide	Index	12.10 4.05	0.50 NA	4.45 0.60
Hurr. (Multi Event)	U.S. Gulf/ East Co.	Indemnity	0.60	0.33	0.45
Single Hurricane	U.S. Gulf/ East Co.	Indemnity	0.76	0.26	0.45
Earthquake	Japan	Ind - Param.	0.64	NA	NA
Earthquake	Japan	Ind - Param.	0.64	NA	0.42
Typh, EQ, Wind	Europe, Japan	Indemnity	0.84	0.45	0.63
Earthquake	U.S. Midwest	Indemnity	0.58 0.62	0.44 0.58	0.50 0.60
Insolvency	Europe	Index	NA NA NA	NA NA NA	NA NA NA
Aggregate Cat	U.S. Nationwide	Indemnity	NA 1.15 5.25	NA 0.12 1.15	NA 0.42 2.84
Hurricane (Multiple Event)	Florida	Indemnity	1.20 1.20	0.49 0.49	0.00 0.77

(Continued)

EXHIBIT 18   (Continued)

SELECTED CAT BOND TRANSACTIONS

Year	Moody's	S&P	Fitch	Sharpe Ratio	Spread	Modeling Firm
2001	NA	BB+	BB+	0.70	L+525	EQE
	BB	BB				
	NA	BB+	BB+	0.71	L+575	EQE
	BBB					
	NA	NA	NA		L+550	RMS
	Ba2	BB	NA	0.71	L+550	RMS
	Ba2	BB+	NA	0.77	L+ 510	EQE
					L+635	
	Ba2	BB+	NA	0.68	L+499	AIR
2000	Ba3	BB	BB−	0.62	L+750	RMS
	Ba3	BB+	BB	0.55	L+650	RMS
	Baa3	BBB+	BBB	0.69	L+260	EQE
	Ba3	BB+	BB+	0.51	L+585	
	Ba2	NA	BB−	0.55	L+410	AIR
				0.48	L+450	AIR
	Ba2	BB+	NA	0.70	L+410	AIR
	NA	BB+	NA	0.74	L+456	RMS
	NA	BB	NA	0.65	L+700	RMS
	NA	NA	NA	0.87	L+600	RMS
	NA	BBB+	BBB	1.13	L+270	EQE
	NA	BBB-	BBB-	0.91	L+370	EQE
	NA	B	B-	0.72	L+1400	EQE
	Ba2	BB+		0.58	L+450	RMS
	NA					RMS
1999	NA	BB		0.56	L+450	EQE
	Baa3		BBB-	0.84	L+295	RMS
	Ba2		BB		L+540	RMS
	NA			2.18	L+850	RMS
	NR	NR	NR	0.79	15.70%	RMS
	NR	BB	BB+		8.70%	RMS
	NA	BB	BB+	0.70	L+420	AIR
	Ba2	BB	NA	0.64	L+366	AIR
	NA	A	NA		L+75	EQE
	Ba1	BB+	NA		L+310	EQE
	NA			0.76	L+450	RMS
	Ba2	BB+	NA	0.56	L+369	AIR
	NR	NR	NR	0.59	L+450	AIR
	Aa2	AA	NA		E+45	D&B
	A2	A	NA		E+85	D&B
	Baa2	BBB+	NA		E+170	D&B
	NA	NA	NA		L+190	AIR
	NA	NA	NA	0.85	L+400	AIR
	NA	NA	NA	0.42	L+825	AIR
	Aaa	NA	AAA		L+175	RMS
	Ba3	NA	BB	0.22	L+417	RMS

(Continued)

EXHIBIT 18 *(Continued)*

SELECTED CAT BOND TRANSACTIONS

Year	Transaction/ SPV	Sponsor	Lead Managers	Tranche	Size ($ 000)	Term (yrs)
1998	Gemini Re	Allianz Risk	GS	Notes	150,000	3
	X.L./	X.L./	GS	Class A	45,000	1
	MidOcean Re	MidOcean Re		Class B	55,000	1
	Gramercy Place	TMCC	GS	Class A	60,680	3
				Class B	283,130	3
				Class C-1	122,470	3
				Class C-2	100,000	3
	Mosaic Re	St. Paul/	GS, EWB	Units	18,000	1
		F&G Re		Class A	15,000	1
				Class B	21,000	1
	Pacific Re	Yasuda Fire	Aon	Notes	80,000	5
	Residential Re 98	USAA	ML, GS, LB	—	450,000	1
1997	Mutual	NPI	WDR, DKB,	Class A-1	£140,000	14
	Securitisation		GS	Class A-2	£120,000	24
	Trinity Re 1998	Centre	GS0	Class A-1	22,000	1
		Solutions		Class A-2	61,500	1
	Parametric Re	Tokio	GS, SR	Units	20,000	10
		Marine & Fire		Notes	80,000	10
	SR Earthquake	Swiss Re	SR, CSFB	Class A-1	42,000	2.25
	Fund			Class A-2	20,000	2.25
				Class B	60,000	2.25
				Class C	15,000	2.25
	Residential Re 97	USAA	ML, GS, LB	Class A-1	163,800	1
				Class A-2	313,180	1

(Continued)

For something to be securitizable, you firstly want it to be short-tailed, meaning that you know the claims pretty much right away after an event. You couldn't securitize for instance liability insurance, where it can take up to 20–30 years to determine the claims. Secondly, you need independent modeling agencies to calculate probabilities and risks. These are the two feasibility criteria. The third criterion is economical: you want peak risks, because then the industry already has shown a willingness to pay extra for coverage.

Applying the criteria to Swiss Re's product portfolio, Giessmann ruled out products from the liability, motor, life, aviation, marine, and most of the property business. In the end, the natural catastrophe part of property reinsurance seemed most suitable for securitization in the capital markets. This naturally led to cat bonds, and served as a confirmation of the cat bond interest Swiss Re already had shown. Giessmann also knew from before that the risk officers at Swiss Re liked cat bonds. Bruno Porro, Chief Risk Officer, had for instance explained to the press, "[In traditional retrocession,] there is a substantial credit risk, especially for these rare event covers. With cat bonds, the money is paid up-front, so there is no credit risk for Swiss Re if one of the events is triggered."

However, the general sentiment seemed to be that cat bonds were expensive to issue and provided low margins, compared to traditional reinsurance and retrocession. Giessmann reflected,

EXHIBIT 18 *(Continued)*

SELECTED CAT BOND TRANSACTIONS

Year	Risk	Region	Trigger	Attach Prob (%)	Exhaust Prob (%)	E{L} (%)
1998	Windstorm & Hail	Europe	Indemnity	6.40	2.05	3.61
	Cat	U.S.	Indemnity	0.61	0.23	0.39
	(Multiple) Event	Nationwide		1.50	0.61	1.05
	Auto Lease	U.S.	Indemnity	NA	NA	NA
	Residual	Nationwide		NA	NA	NA
				NA	NA	NA
				NA	NA	NA
	Aggregate	U.S.	Indemnity	1.13	NA	0.28
	Cat	Nationwide		1.13	0.05	0.55
				4.40	1.21	2.60
	Typhoon	Japan	Indemnity	0.94	0.82	0.88
	Single Hurricane	U.S. Gulf/ East Co.	Indemnity	0.87	0.32	0.58
1997	Life	UK	Modified	NA	NA	NA
	Insurance		Indemnity	NA	NA	NA
	Hurricane	Florida	Indemnity	1.53	0.44	0.39
	Multiple Event			1.53	0.44	0.83
	Earthquake	Japan	Index –	1.02	0.00	0.35
			Ind. Loss	1.02	0.41	0.70
	Earthquake	California	Index –	1.00	0.52	0.46
			Ind. Loss	1.00	0.52	0.46
				1.00	0.52	0.76
				2.40	2.40	2.40
	Single	U.S. Gulf/East Co.	Indemnity	1.00	0.39	0.34
	Hurricane			1.00	0.39	0.62

(Continued)

Most likely, for a hurricane risk with 1% attachment probability, the prices, or rather the spread premium, would be 5% in traditional reinsurance, 5.5% in retrocession, and then 6% for cat bonds. After that you have to add to the price the administration costs. In retrocession, you usually have a broker in between who takes 10% of the premium per year. In cat bonds, the cost is about 250 basis points as a one time up-front fee, which can be amortized over the duration of the bond.

Giessmann further believed the market would have to mature much more for cat bonds to be actually economical for the issuer. He agreed with his colleagues' view, that the market was still in its infancy, marked by uneven supply of issues and low secondary market trading. If Swiss Re wanted to really make cat bonds a profitable alternative, they would most likely have to help develop the actual market.

Clearly, the insurance claims from the September 11-event had struck Swiss Re and the entire insurance industry hard. At the same time, they did however also mean that reinsurance prices went up dramatically. Internally, Swiss Re predicted that property and casualty premium rates would continue to rise in the years to come. This would be the only way for insurers to remain profitable, given the industry pressures they were

EXHIBIT 18   (Continued)

SELECTED CAT BOND TRANSACTIONS

Moody's	S&P	Fitch	Sharpe Ratio	Spread	Modeling Firm
B3	NA	BB	0.33	L+822	RMS
NR	NR	NR		L+412	AIR
NR	NR	NR		L+590	AIR
Aa2	AA	NA		L+23	
A2	A	NA		L+45	
Ba2	BB	NA		L+325	
Ba2	BB	NA		T+360	
NA	NA	NA	0.75	L+216.5	AIR
NA	NA	NA	0.77	L+444	AIR
NA	NA	NA	0.43	L+827	AIR
Ba3	NA	BB	0.36	L+370	RMS
Ba2	BB	BB	0.57	L+416	AIR
A3	A-	NA		G+140	WatsonWyatt
A3	A3	NA		G+170	
Aaa	NA	AAA	0.33	L+153	RMS
Ba3	NA	BB	0.40	L+367	RMS
Baa3	NA	NA		L+206	EQE
Ba2	NA	NA	0.53	L+430	EQE
Baa3	NA	BBB-	0.38	L+255	EQE
Baa3	NA	BBB-	0.42	L+280	EQE
Ba1	NA	BB	0.52	L+475	EQE
NR	NR	NR	0.27	L+625	EQE
Aaa	AAA	AAA	0.76	L+273	AIR
Ba 2	BB	BB	0.75	L+576	AIR

Lead managers: Aon = Aon Capital Markets; AR = AR Insurance; DKB = Dai-Ichi Kangyo Bank Ltd; CSFB = Credit Suisse First Boston; GS = Goldman Sachs; LB = Lehman Brothers; ML = Merrill Lynch; SR = Swiss Re; WDR = Warburg Dillon Read

Source: Adapted from Goldman Sachs.

facing. Even though more than $20 billion had been raised since the World Trade Center attack and credit losses from Enron and similar situations, capital resources were still dramatically contracted. The four top players—Munich Re, Swiss Re, Berkshire Hathaway (including GenRe) and Lloyd's Market—had already an estimated $9.1 billion in pretax losses. The whole insurance/reinsurance industry was projected to have losses of $40 billion in total. By comparison, the largest natural catastrophe loss ever—Hurricane Andrew in 1992—had resulted in costs of $20.5 billion, half of the projected.

At the same time, capital markets were declining. Giessmann saw it as a chance to increase the economic attractiveness of cat bond issues. He explained, "For Swiss Re to be interested, which means that we can reach at least break-even, then the spreads [the price] have got to come down at least 100 basis points." In addition, Giessmann also believed that traditional retrocedence in general was still a viable option for securitizing smaller amounts. "For cat bonds, you want multiyear issues worth over $100 million," he said.

EXHIBIT 19

SWISS RE FINANCIAL STATEMENTS 2001 AND 2000

Income Statement (Swiss Francs, millions)[5]	2000	2001	Change
Revenues			
Premiums earned	22081	25219	14%
Net investment income	4802	5765	20%
Net realized investment gains	4275	2665	−38%
Other revenues	395	455	15%
Total revenues	**31553**	**34104**	**8%**
Expenses			
Claims and claim adjustment expenses	−12153	−16266	34%
Life and health benefits	−7478	−8532	14%
Acquisition costs	−4883	−5658	16%
Amortization of goodwill	−310	−368	19%
Other operating costs and expenses	−3074	−3384	10%
Total expenses	**−27898**	**−34208**	**23%**
Income / loss before income tax expense	**3655**	−104	−103%
Income tax expense	−689	−61	−91%
Net income / loss	**2966**	**−165**	**−106%**
Earnings / loss per share	10.39°	−0.57	−106%

Balance sheet (CHF millions)	2000	2001	Change
Assets			
Investments			
Fixed income securities	50472	61079	21%
Equity securities	23224	19013	−18%
Mortgages and other loans	6920	7796	13%
Other invested assets	8968	11234	25%
Total investments	**89584**	**99122**	**11%**
Cash and cash equivalents	3433	6046	76%
Reinsurance assets	28985	37637	30%
Deferred acquisition costs	3155	3836	22%
Goodwill and other intangible assets	8491	11961	41%
Other assets	8992	11628	29%
Total assets	**142640**	**170230**	**19%**
Liabilities and shareholders' equity			
Liabilities			
Unpaid claims and claim adjustment expenses	59600	68618	15%
Liabilities for life and health policy benefits	29300	41370	41%
Unearned premiums	6131	6399	4%
Funds held under reinsurance treaties	4247	4504	6%
Reinsurance balances payable	3697	3958	7%
Other liabilities	11820	15465	31%
Long-term debt	5058	7318	45%
Total liabilities	**119853**	**147632**	**23%**
Total shareholders' equity	**22787**	**22598**	**−1%**
Total liabilities and shareholders' equity	**142640**	**170230**	**19%**

Source: ⟨http://www.swissre.com/INTERNET/pwswpspr.nsf/alldocbyidkeylu/SSTR-5SNPCA?OpenDocument⟩, accessed February 3, 2004.

---

[5] In March, 2002, 1 Swiss Francs CHF = 0.602704 USD.

On the investor side, the market held about 20–30 regular investors. From Giessmann's point of view, these could be broken into three categories. The first group included insurers and reinsurers, the earliest ones to join the cat bond market. With rising insurance and reinsurance prices after September 11, these buyers were gradually leaving the market to use their capital to acquire business at their own front-end. The second group was the money managers. Commented Giessmann,

> These are the opportunistic investors, and currently make up about 50% of the investor base. The group we want to attract, however, is the third, which are the fund managers dedicated to the cat bond sector. Here in ZÅrich, for instance, Bank Leu launched the first ever public retail fund for cat bonds. There are also hedge funds specifically investing into this asset class. We talk a lot with this type of investor to understand what their concerns and investment preferences are for cat bonds.

From his discussions with the investor community, Giessmann learned several things: they preferred single peril risk bonds over multi-peril, physical trigger indices over other types, and maximum three to four year terms. These preferences aside, however, their main perceived problem was the lack of steady supply. They even assured Giessmann that they would welcome if Swiss Re led the way in reducing spreads. Although it would provide less return on each cat bond issue, it would create dynamics that could allow the market to grow, primarily because more companies would be interested in issuing cat bonds if spreads came down. Still, even at a lower spread, Giessmann worried that single cat bond issues at best reach would break-even.

However, as Giessmann well knew, the cost of cat bond issuance compared to traditional reinsurance varied according to the insurance underwriting cycle. In some periods, such as after a major disaster, industry capital was in short supply—a "hard" market—pressuring insurers and reinsurers to increase rates in order to rebuild surplus. During a hard market, cat bonds (as well as other insurance-linked securities) could be somewhat less expensive than reinsurance for certain risks. In contrast, when there was excess capacity in the industry—a "soft" market—insurers aggressively competed for business by lowering rates and the cost of reinsurance tended to fall, making cat bonds relatively less attractive. Therefore, from a sponsor's perspective, conditions on the insurance and reinsurance markets had considerable impact on the attractiveness of cat bonds.

On the cost side, an average size issue normally passed the $1.5 million-mark in administration and issuance costs. This amount, plus the overall need to lower the spread, made Giessmann believe that it would be almost impossible to reach break-even with simple single-issuances. When discussing his dilemma with colleagues, he was however reminded of a program from another division: the European Medium Term Note (EMTN) program. The EMTN was applied to Swiss Re's regular issues of operational debt to provide working capital. Issuing these corporate bonds individually was rather costly and took time, and so the EMTN program had been constructed. The program was effectively a platform from which to launch bond issues on an on-going basis, called a "shelf offering." EMTN pre-registered an amount of capital with the Securities and Exchange Commission (SEC), but without issuing right away. A standard documentation framework was however put in place, governing all future issues, so when the market conditions were right, issues could be launched from this amount and offered quickly to the market. Each issue was also completely flexible when it came to amounts, maturity, and issue price. Giessmann wondered if issuing cat bonds could be done in a similar way.

At any rate, Giessmann decided to lay down one ground-rule for Swiss Re's cat bond issues: the price of the cat bond (its spread over LIBOR) would be fixed, but the volume of the issue would not be. This was the complete opposite of how cat bonds had been issued until then. Giessmann said:

> We must avoid pricing at the last dollar, where an opportunistic investor may try to break us for the last dollars. Instead, we will go to the markets and say, "This is our price. Take it or leave it." Some will take it, and some won't. It will probably turn away a lot of the category two-type of investors. In the end, we may not get the volume off Swiss Re's balance sheet that we looked for, but we did get the price. Thankfully, top management does not give me any pressure to reach a certain volume, since their long term goal is to develop the market.

The Operational Decision: How to Best Issue Cat Bonds

Giessmann wanted to be able to go to cat bond investors and say, "This is our price. We don't haggle over it. But we will provide a steady supply and help you grow the market." That price should allow Swiss Re to use cat bonds as an economically attractive risk management tool, meaning that the price, as measured in spread, had to be small.

At his desk, looking at all the industry reports and his notes from talking to colleagues and investors, Giessmann wondered what to do next.

11

Mortgage Backs at Ticonderoga

On an early spring morning in April 2005, David Talbot came in to the offices of London-based hedge fund group Ticonderoga Management and, before even taking off his coat, asked, "So, Margaret, how are the Fannies, Freddies and Ginnies doing today? Any possibilities out there?"

Coming from careers in large investment banks, Talbot and Margaret Stanway had recently founded Ticonderoga Management. Focused on trading in traditional fixed income instruments, such as corporate and sovereign bonds, the fund had recently also begun to trade in mortgage-backed securities (MBS). MBSs were securities created from pooled mortgage loans. As the underlying mortgages were paid off by the homeowners, the investors received periodic payments of interest and principal. Most such pooled mortgage securities in the U.S. were issued by one of three U.S. government agencies, known by their nicknames Ginnie Mae, Fannie Mae or Freddie Mac. These securities, called "pass-throughs," could then be pooled again to create collateral for a more complex type of mortgage security known as a Collateralized Mortgage Obligation (CMO). CMOs allowed the cash flows from the underlying pass-throughs to be split up so that different classes of securities—so called "tranches"—with different maturities, coupons and risk profiles were created.

Ticonderoga had experienced good luck in raising capital since its founding, and founders Talbot and Stanway had gathered a small team of seasoned professionals to invest this capital. A recent recruit had brought with him experience in the MBS market, and the group had therefore started a new investment style, going for relative prepayment risk for MBSs. For the time being, they were only using the founders own funds to invest in the market. The group now followed the daily trading going on with mortgage backs in the market place, trying to identify new trade opportunities. This day, Stanway actually believed they were on to a new interesting trade idea. As Talbot took off his coat, she began to explain the idea to him.

Professors George Chacko and Peter Hecht, Executive Director of the HBS Europe Research Center, Vincent Dessain, and Research Associate Anders Sjöman prepared this case. Some names and data have been disguised for confidentiality. HBS cases are developed solely as the basis for class discussion. Cases are not intended to serve as endorsements, sources of primary data, or illustrations of effective or ineffective management.

ASSET BACKED SECURITIES (ABS)

Theoretically, any asset with a revenue stream—and not just mortgages or similar house loans—could be transformed into marketable debt securities or asset-backed securities. The collateral for an ABS could be mortgage loans, credit card receivables, car-loan payments, leasing payments, project finance loans, student loans, or home-equity loan cash flows. ABSs were normally issued by financing institutions, who sold their loans to underwriters, who in turn pooled the loans and sold them to investors. For the lending institutions, selling off the original loans—getting them "off the books"—removed the risk of potential defaults, and also freed up money to lend to borrowers. The underwriter, who repackaged the assets as ABSs for sale, was usually a Special Purpose Vehicle (SPV), a legal entity created for just that transaction and completely separate from the originating financial institution.[1]

Different classes for ABSs had evolved over the years, and now included Collateralized Loan Obligation (CLOs, based on loans to corporate clients); Collateralized Bond Obligation (CBOs, based on corporate bonds); Collateralized Debt Obligation (CDOs, based on corporate loans and securities); and Mortgage Backed Securities (MBSs, for either private or commercial mortgage loans.) Even more specialized classes existed, for instance royalties payable to rock stars from a pool of their works. For example, in 1998, a $55 million bond issue was collateralized by royalties from songs by David Bowie. The MBS sector aside, the largest segment of the ABS market was made up by home-equity loans, credit cards, auto loans to consumers and manufactured-housing ("mobile homes") contracts.

ABSs were generally considered to be on the riskier side of the investment spectrum for two reasons. First, the asset value fluctuated inversely with changes in interest rate levels, creating high volatility. Second, defaults on the loans were normally highly unpredictable.

MORTGAGE BACKED SECURITIES

Due to its size, the MBS market was often treated apart from the ABS market. In 2003, it was generally considered one of the world's largest financial markets, with about $7 trillion outstanding. The first pass-through mortgage security had been issued in 1970 by the Government National Mortgage Association (GNMA). Derivative products, such as Collateralized Mortgage Obligations, were introduced in the 1980s, helping the market to grow.

A Typical Pass-Through

An MBS was a type of ABS that represented ownership in a group of mortgages. MBSs comprised of loans on real estate property issued by mortgage bankers, commercial banks, savings-and-loan banks, service banks and other financial institutions. For the typical U.S. mortgage, a home owner borrowed funds from an institution to pay for a home. The lender kept a secured interest in the property, and could foreclose if the borrower failed to pay. The borrower made monthly payments, consisting of both interest and principal

---

[1] SPVs were mostly incorporated in offshore tax havens, such as the Cayman Islands. The originators themselves would not own the SPV, to avoid having the loans consolidated back onto their balance sheet. Instead, a number of SPV management companies had sprung up to run SPVs, including providing autonomous boards of directors.

payments. (See Exhibit 1 for a typical mortgage cash flow.) Mortgages existed in a variety of terms (e.g. 15- and 30-year terms) and interest rates (fixed and floating rates).

To create an MBS out of mortgage loans, a federal agency or mortgage banker bought mortgages in the whole-loan market and pooled loans with similar features to create securities. Most pass-throughs were backed by fixed-rate mortgage loans, although adjustable-rate mortgage loans (ARMs) could be used. For the selling institution, this represented a pure sale of the asset, a complete removal off the balance sheet. (In contrast to regular ABSs, no SPV was involved.) The issuer then collected monthly payments directly from the homeowners and "passed through" the cash flow to investors in monthly payments which represented both interest and repayment of principal. The security was known as a Pass-Through or Participation Certificate (PC). (Exhibit 2 outlines the process.)

In addition to issuing the pass through, most issuers also guaranteed the timely payment on all of its mortgage securities. For their services, the issuers charged a servicing spread of about 40–75 basis points (bps). The pass-through coupon rate (PT) that the final MBS holder earned was thus the gross-mortgage coupon minus the servicing fee. Payments also depended upon how much an investor owned of a specific mortgage pool. For instance, if 1,000 certificates had been issued for a pool, and the investor held 100 certificates, the investor would receive 10% of each payment in the pool.

MBS investors received payments on a monthly basis—unlike standard U.S. Treasury bonds with their semi-annual payments—reflecting the underlying monthly payments of the mortgage holders. The payments consisted of both principal and interest.

Issuing Pass-Throughs: Ginnie, Fannie and Freddie

The largest mortgage pass-through issuers were three U.S. government related agencies. The U.S. government had long seen mortgage securities as crucial in promoting home ownership. Having public agencies participate in the capital markets linked the capital markets and home owners, and helped create a continuous flow of mortgage capital. The system also ensured that mortgage funds were available throughout the United States, minimizing regional differences.

EXHIBIT 1

TYPICAL SCHEDULED MORTGAGE CASH FLOW

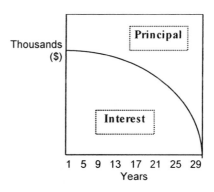

Source: Casewriters.

EXHIBIT 2

CREATING MORTGAGE BACKED SECURITIES

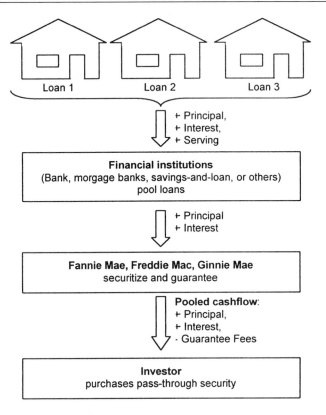

Loan 1   Loan 2   Loan 3

⊢ Principal,
⊢ Interest,
⊢ Serving

Financial institutions
(Bank, morgage banks, savings-and-loan, or others)
pool loans

⊢ Principal
⊢ Interest

Fannie Mae, Freddie Mac, Ginnie Mae
securitize and guarantee

Pooled cashflow:
⊢ Principal,
⊢ Interest,
- Guarantee Fees

Investor
purchases pass-through security

Source: Casewriters.

Of the three, the Government National Mortgage Association (GNMA or "Ginnie Mae") was the oldest, created in 1968. Ginnie Mae served low-to-moderate-income homebuyers by supporting a public market for residential mortgages. The agency only pooled mortgages insured or guaranteed by the Federal Housing Administration (FHA), the Veterans Administration (VA) and the Rural Housing Service (RHS). Since the first Ginnie Mae pass-through security in 1970, the agency had dominated the pass-through securities market.

Ginnie Mae's two smaller cousins were not government agencies, but government-sponsored private enterprises. The Federal National Mortgage Association (FNMA, "Fannie Mae") and the Federal Home Loan Mortgage Corporation (FHLMC, "Freddie Mac") were owned by shareholders, but had their charter set by the US Congress. Fannie Mae and Freddie Mac, through their close ties to the government, were seen as having minimal credit risk, almost as good as Ginnie Mae that was backed by the full faith and credit of the U.S. government. Fannie and Freddie also had a line of credit with the federal government, which so far never had been tapped. All three agencies normally received AAA ratings for their securities from the credit rating agencies.

The majority of pass-throughs were backed by these three agencies. However, some private institutions issued mortgage securities, for instance, Prudential Home, CitiCorp Housing, and GE Capital. These issues were known as "private label" or "non-agency" mortgage securities, and were typically given AAA or AA ratings. Non-agency mortgage pass-throughs must be registered with the Securities and Exchange Commission (SEC). Exhibit 3 compares securities based on their issuer.

The Complexity of Prepayments

To an investor, the value of a pass-through security depended in large part on its cash flow. However, mortgage cash flows were notoriously hard to predict, since they not only included scheduled interest and principal repayments, but also *unscheduled* payments, known as prepayments. Prepayments simply meant that the borrower sent in more money than required, up until fully paying back the loan in advance. (Full prepayments normally carried a penalty fee for the privilege of paying off the loan early.) Partial prepayments, when a home owner put a little extra into the monthly check, were known as curtailments.

Prepayments typically occurred when house owners sold their property, refinanced into lower mortgage rates, refinanced to take out a larger mortgage (so called "cash-out refinance") or if they just defaulted on the loan. The primary influence on these actions was the current interest rate level. If interest rates dropped, prepayments increased as people looked to refinance their homes. Borrowers prepaid for other reasons too, such as professional (relocating to a new area), demographic changes (growth of the family), or investment and tax reasons. Prepayments followed a seasonality with higher turnover during the summer months. Older (or "seasoned") loans were also more likely to be prepaid. Home owners were also influenced by loan size and their credit standing with banks.

EXHIBIT 3

COMPARISON OF MORTGAGE SECURITIES CHARACTERISTICS

Security	Guarantee	Minimum Investment
Ginnie Mae I And Ii	Full and timely payment of principal and interest, backed by the full-faith-and-credit guarantee of the U.S. government	$25,000 minimum; $1 increments
Ginnie Mae Platinum	As above	As above
Fannie Mae MBS	Full and timely payment of principal and interest guaranteed by Fannie Mae	$1,000 minimum; $1 increments
FREDDIE MAC PC (75-Day PC)	Full and timely payment of interest and ultimate payment of principal guaranteed by Freddie Mac	$1,000 minimum; $1 increments
Freddie Mac Gold Pc	Full and timely payment of interest and scheduled principal guaranteed by Freddie Mac	$1,000 minimum; $1 increments

Source: Adapted by casewriters from "An Investors Guide to Pass-Through and Collateralized Mortgage Securities," pp. 16–17, available from ⟨http://www.investinginbonds.com/info/igmbs/pass-through.htm⟩, accessed 16 December 2003.

Prepayments were at the root of many of the complexities surrounding mortgage securities. For example, imagine mortgage rates declining. The price of any traditional U.S. Treasury bond would in that situation increase. However, for a pass-through security, the price increase will not be as high, since with lower mortgage rates, prepayment rates will increase, which dampens the price impact on the mortgage security. In the industry, this was known as "negative convexity." Further, with higher prepayment rates, the investors would receive their principal back sooner than expected, which they then would have to reinvest at current, lower, market interest rates. This was known as the "contraction risk" of pass-throughs.

On the other hand, when mortgage rates rose, homeowners were less likely to refinance, and prepayment rates slowed down. Pass-through holders now found their principal committed for a longer period of time, and themselves unable to invest at now higher market rates. Also, with higher rates, the value of future payments was lower. These effects were known as the "extension risk."

Further adding to the complexity was the fact that mortgage securities—as all amortizing securities—were not traded in terms of maturity dates, like corporate bonds. For a pass-through, the maturity only represented the last in a series of payments. Instead, they traded in terms of their "average life." In fact, since pass-throughs represented a pool of mortgages, they were described in terms of their combined average life, or weighted average maturity (WAM). The WAM weighed the number of months left to maturity for each mortgage loan in the pool by the mortgage amount outstanding. The WAM was naturally affected by prepayment rates. If the prepayment speed increased, the WAM would shorten; conversely, if the speed slowed down, WAM extended. WAM was expressed in months, for instance, 357 months for a 3-month old 30-year loan. In addition, pass-throughs were also described in terms of a weighted average coupon rate (WAC). The WAC weighed the rate of each mortgage loan in the pool by the mortgage amount outstanding.

Quoting Conventions for Prepayments

When trading in mortgage securities, the industry used quoting conventions, presented as prepayment rate benchmarks. The benchmarks, combined with the yield of a bond, helped traders arrive at a price of the bond. However, market participants knew that the benchmarks were not solid enough to generate good forecasts. More elaborate prepayment models were used for forecasting, and so the quoting conventions were used by traders more as a convenient short-hand to quote trades. The two most commonly used conventions were the Conditional Prepayment Rate (CPR) and the Public Securities Association (PSA) Prepayment Benchmark.

CPR gave the proportion of the remaining mortgage balance that was prepaid each month on an annual basis, given the characteristics of the pool, such as its past prepayment speed, and the current and future economic environment. For the first 30 months of a mortgage, CPR was calculated as:

$$CPR = (Month/30) \circ 6\%$$

Past 30 months, it was assumed that CPR was fixed at 6% (as explained in more detail later on). Since CPR was an annual rate, SMM (Single Monthly Mortality Rate) was derived as the monthly version of CPR, as expressed by the formula

$$SMM = 1 - (1 - CPR)^{1/12}.$$

Using numbers, a SMM of 5% meant that 5% of the remaining mortgage balance for a month, after deduction of the scheduled payment for that month, would prepay that month.

CPR and SMM were not enough alone to calculate prepayments. An assumption also had to be made about how quickly loans were paid back. Since prepayment rates were affected by the age of the loan (where older loans were more likely to prepay quicker), the PSA curve was then used to account for the seasoning, or aging, of residential loans. The curve was the result of a study by the Public Securities Association, which suggested that prepayment rates seemed to level off after about 30 months. The PSA curve assumed that for a 30-year (360 months) mortgage the prepayment rate started at 0.2% CPR for the first month and then increased 0.2% per month until month 30, after which the speed was a constant 6% per year. (This is reflected in the CPR formula above.) This baseline model was referred to as the 100% PSA model or "100 PSA." The PSA model could then be modified for different prepayment speeds. For example, if interest rates dropped, the PSA model could be turned up to 150% PSA, meaning 1.5 times higher CPR then the 100 PSA. Conversely, in times of higher interest rates, a 50% PSA could be more appropriate. (Exhibit 4 shows the curves for two different PSAs.) As reference, for 100 PSA, the average time a 30-year mortgage was held was 17 years. For 225 PSA, it was 8 years.

EXHIBIT 4

PSA PREPAYMENT CURVES

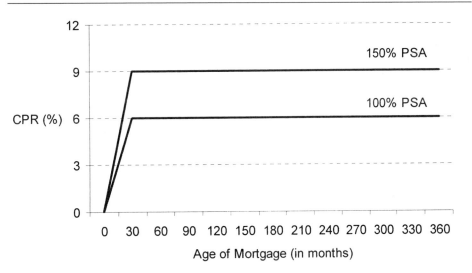

Note: Mathematically, the 100% PSA could be expressed as:
- If $t \cdot 30$: CPR = 6% $(t/30)$
- If $t > 30$: CPR = 6%

Source: Compiled and adapted by casewriters from general descriptions of PSA, e.g. at Investopedia ⟨http://www.investopedia.com/terms/p/psa.asp⟩ and Mathworks, ⟨http://www.mathworks.com/products/demos/fixedincome/mbscf/mbscf.htm⟩, both accessed 20 December 2003.

By combining CPR, SMM and PSA, traders could then obtain a prepayment number for any given month of a mortgage. For instance, assuming a 150 PSA for month 40 of a mortgage (where the CPR is assumed at 6% since the loan is past month 30) would give a PSA of:

$$150 \text{ PSA} = 1.5 \,^\circ\, 0.06 = 0.09$$

and a SMM of:

$$\text{SMM} = 1 - (1 - 0.09)^{1/12} = 0.007828$$

Obviously, the PSA assumption was key to any calculation, and traders kept their own valuations close to themselves. Where one trader believed prepayments were would often contrast with another trader's opinion—and this is where the mortgage market was created. Based on their PSA assumption, pass-throughs traders would construct a monthly cash flow for any pass-through. The cash flow would then consist of three components: interest (from the pass-through rate), the regular principal repayments and the prepayments based on the PSA assumption. Exhibit 5 gives examples of how to calculate the cash flow of a mortgage portfolio using all these variables.

EXHIBIT 5

EXAMPLES OF PROJECTED CASH FLOW OF MORTGAGE PORTFOLIOS

Definitions
- Mortgage portfolio: F_0
- Prepayment speed assumptions: PSA
- Weighted average coupon rate: WAC
- Weighted average maturity: WAM
- Pass-through rate: PT

Note: The PT rate was lower than WAC, with the difference going to the MBS issuer.

Formulas:

- Monthly mortgage payment:
$$p = \frac{F_0}{\dfrac{1 - 1/(1 + \text{WAC}/12))^{WAM}}{\text{WAC}/12}}$$

- Interest without pass-through rate:
$$i = \frac{\text{WAC}}{12} \,^\circ\, F_0$$

- Interest with pass-through rate:
$$i = \frac{\text{PT}}{12} \,^\circ\, F_0$$

- Scheduled principal:
$$p - i$$

- Conditional prepayment rate:
$$\text{CPR} = \frac{\text{Month}}{30} \,^\circ\, 6\% \text{ (Past 30 months, CPR fixed at 6\%.)}$$

- Single-monthly mortality rate: $\text{SMM} = 1 - [1 - \text{CPR}]^{1/12}$
- Prepaid principal: Prepaid principal $= \text{SMM} \,^\circ\, [F_0 - \text{Scheduled principal}]$
- Cash flow: $\text{CF} = \text{Interest} + \text{Scheduled principal} + \text{Prepaid principal}$

(Continued)

EXHIBIT 5   (Continued)

EXAMPLES OF PROJECTED CASH FLOW OF MORTGAGE PORTFOLIOS

Examples

	Example 1: 100% PSA	Example 2: 150% PSA with 7.5% Pass-Through Rate
Mortgage portfolio (mUSD)	100	100
WAC (%)	8.00%	9.00%
WAM (months)	360	357
PT Rate		7.500%
Prepayment (%PSA)	100	150
First month		
Month WAM	1	4
P (mUSD)	0.7338	0.80595
Interest (mUSD)	0.67	0.625
Scheduled Principal (mUSD)	0.0671	0.05595
Estimated prepaid principal		
CPR (%)	0.002	0.012
SMM (%)	0.0001668	0.0010055
Prepaid Principal (mUSD)	0.01667	0.10050
Cash Flow (mUSD)	0.750435	0.781451
Second month		
Month WAM	2	5
Beginning balance month 2 (mUSD)	99.9162	99.8435
P (mUSD)	0.733642	0.805143
Interest (mUSD)	0.67	0.62402
Scheduled Principal (mUSD)	0.067534	0.05632
Estimated prepaid principal		
CPR (%)	0.004	0.015
SMM (%)	0.0003339	0.00126
Prepaid Principal (mUSD)	0.033344	0.125600
Cash Flow (mUSD)	0.766986	0.805938

Source: Casewriters.

CREATING COLLATERALIZED MORTGAGE OBLIGATIONS (CMO)

Not all investors were willing to accept all the prepayment risk inherent in pass-through. Banks for instance normally sought short duration assets, whereas insurance companies looked for long duration assets. Other investors still were more adverse to contraction risks, whereas others objected to expansion risks. Pass-throughs could therefore be structured as fixed income derivatives, known as Collateralized Mortgage Obligations (CMOs).[2] A CMO had as its collateral a pool of pass-through securities, and it divided

---

[2] CMOs were also known as REMICs. The Tax Reform Act of 1986 allowed mortgage securities pools to elect the tax status of a Real Estate Mortgage Investment Conduit (REMIC). Most new CMOs were issued in REMIC form to create tax and accounting advantages for the issuers. In daily use, both terms were used interchangeably.

the cash flow from the underlying mortgages into new classes. These classes, or "tranches," could all have different average lives, coupons and risk profiles, to attract new and different investors. (Exhibit 6 compares characteristics of CMOs based on their issuer.)

IO/PO Bonds

In its most basic form, a CMO separated the cash flow from a pass-through into a principal and an interest part. This type of CMO was known as a Stripped MBS or "mortgage strips." The two parts (also known as tranches) were referred to as Principal Only (PO), and Interest Only (IO). Investors who believed that interest rates would go down, and prepayment rates increase, would buy POs, since they would receive their principal back quicker than otherwise. Conversely, if investors believed rates would increase, their appetite would change to IOs, since the prepayment rate would drop and coupons would continue to be paid out for a longer time.

Sequential Pay Bonds (SEQ)

From that simple concept of two tranches, the CMO market had evolved. A more advanced form of CMO—although still known as a "plain vanilla" CMO—was the Sequential Pay Bond (SEQ). Here several tranches were used to distribute the cash flow, with the tranches prioritized in terms of the order in which they received payments. The first priority tranche's principal had to be paid entirely, or "retired," until the next tranche received payments, and so on. Through sequential-pay tranches, some tranches would obtain average lives longer than the underlying MBS collateral, and some that were shorter. The lower the average life of a tranche, the lower its rate sensitivity and consequently its prepayment risk. For traders, such as hedge funds, this type of structure simplified duration management.

EXHIBIT 6

COMPARISON OF CMO CHARACTERISTICS

Security	Guarantee	Minimum Investment
Ginnie Mae Remic	Full and timely payment of principal and interest, backed by the full-faith-and-credit guarantee of the U.S. government	$1,000 minimum; $1 increments
Freddie Mac Remic	Full and timely payment of interest and scheduled principal, guaranteed by Freddie Mac.	$1; $1 increments
Fannie Mae Remic	Full and timely payment of interest and scheduled principal guaranteed by Fannie Mae (collateral of Fannie Mae "G" series is also backed by the full faith and credit of the U.S. government).	$1,000 minimum; $1 increments
Agency-Backed,	Collateral guaranteed by Ginnie Mae, Fannie Mae or Freddie Mac.	Varies
Private-Label Cmo/Remic	Structure provides basis for AAA rating, but these securities carry no explicit government guarantee.	
Whole-Loan Backed, Private-Label Cmo/Remic	Credit support provided by some combination of issuer or third-party guarantee, letter of credit, over-collateralization, pool insurance, and/or subordination. Generally rated AA or AAA.	Varies

Source: Adapted from "An Investors Guide to Pass-Through and Collateralized Mortgage Securities," ⟨http://www.investinginbonds.com/info/igmbs/pass-through.htm⟩, accessed 16 December 2003.

Accrual Tranche of a SEQ Bond

At times, the final tranche of a SEQ bond was set up to *not* receive any current interest at all. Instead, its interest was used to pay down the principal on the other tranches. This tranche type was known as an "accrual" tranche, or a Z-bond (because of its similarity to U.S. Treasury zero-coupon bonds). The existence of an accrual tranche stabilized the cash-flow patterns in the other tranches, as well as reduced their average lives. However, the originator of the CMO was often unable to sell this highest risk tranche, and would have to keep the Z-Bond on its own balance sheet.

Floaters and Inverse Floaters

In addition to turning one tranche into an accrual tranche, other classes could be turned into floating rate tranches. With floating rate tranches, the spectrum of potential investors increased considerably, compared to only having fixed-interest bonds. Floating rate tranches built on taking one fixed-interest tranche of a SEQ bond, and dividing it up into two new tranches. The first tranche becomes a floating rate tranche and the second one became an inverse-floating rate class.

Planned Amortization Classes (PAC)

Even with an accrual tranche, the prepayment risk of SEQ bonds was considerable. A different type of bond could therefore be used, where some tranches were set up to have zero or minimal prepayment risk. Such Planned Amortization Classes bonds then received a promised cash flow each month. Their characteristic was that—within a specified range of prepayments—the cash flow pattern was completely known. PAC bondholders simply took priority over all other classes when it came to receiving principal payments. However, this meant that the other classes in the CMO issue had to absorb all the prepayment risk. These classes were referred to as support or companion bonds. When prepayment rates were slow, the companion bond received no principal. The entire principal went to the PAC tranches, which made them very stable. Conversely, with higher prepayment rates, the companion bond would "jump to the front" and take all the principal cash coming in, while the PAC tranches stayed on schedule. Naturally, PAC bonds traded at lower yields than the companion bonds.

In short, the various forms of CMOs allowed for tranches with short, intermediate, or long maturities; or for one tranche to be made less interest rate sensitive than another. Moreover, prepayment risks were transferred between tranches, giving some tranches improved prepayment stability. All the differing aspects of the tranches helped meet specific investment objectives of various investors.

TRADING IN MORTGAGE BACKS

The MBS market was in 2005 one of the world's largest financial markets, although after two record-breaking years, issuance had in 2004 been affected by higher volatility in mortgage rates and a slower refinancing speed among mortgage holders. It was estimated that issuance of mortgage related securities (including agency and private-label pass-throughs as well as CMOs) would reach about $1.6 trillion in 2004.[3]

---

[3] The Bond Market Association, http://www.bondmarkets.com/assets/files/US_Mkt_Outlook_0105.pdf, accessed April 2005.

In the primary market, investors bought agency or private label MBSs either directly from the issuer or through dealers. Most buyers were institutional investors. On the secondary market, as with any fixed-income security, the yield of an MBS depended on the purchase price in relation to the coupon rate and the length of time the principal was outstanding. However, since the notion of maturity was not applicable to mortgage securities, with their prepayment and cash flow complexities, assumptions on prepayment speeds were key to all traders. Yields were in the end determined by market interest rates and the traders' individual views on prepayment rates. The difference in where two traders believed that, say, a 1998 Fannie Mae 6% would prepay is what generated trades. However, for exactly that same prepayment reason, MBSs were generally considered to be one of the most complicated fixed-income instruments around to price. As a result, they offered yields higher than most other fixed-income securities of comparable credit quality.

Secondary trading was done completely over-the-counter (OTC) between buyers and sellers; no standardized exchange trading existed. Most pass-through securities traded in the TBA (To Be Announced) market.[4] TBA trading enhanced liquidity by commoditizing MBS pass-throughs. As an alternative to the TBA-market, pass-through securities could also be traded on the Specified Pool Market, where investors knew or specified the characteristics of the underlying pool. The specified pools were then traded at a premium compared to TBA securities. Trades on the Specified Pool Market normally involved large pools of securities, seasoned pools or pools with so called Alt-A securities (where the loan takers carried a low credit rating). Mortgage securities were quoted in the same way as U.S. Treasuries. A quote of 95-10 meant 95 and 10/32s of the security's par value. However, as described earlier, traders in mortgage securities often used just the yield and the prepayment assumption, expressed in PSA, when quoting trades.

Generally, CMOs provided better cash flow certainty than regular pass-throughs, while still giving the same credit quality and yield advantage—an attractive feature for investors. CMOs were however also less liquid on the secondary market than standard MBSs, because of the uniqueness of each security.

In Europe, the mortgage securities market almost exclusively traded in American mortgage backs. With few exceptions, all of the European mortgage markets primarily used floating loans, based on LIBOR.[5] With floating mortgage loans, there was little incentive for home owners to refinance their homes; and without refinancing, there was no prepayment; and consequently no MBS market.

Trades That Could Take Hedge Funds Out of Business

Although the market was full of successful trades, it also had some examples of some that had been less than successful. In 2002, one particular trade had in fact brought down another hedge fund. Talbot and Stanway at Ticonderoga had tried to reconstruct what had happened based on the media coverage. As far as they could tell, the story had started when the other fund had found an interesting CMO, a Companion Inverse Floater, which was backed by a 6% Fannie Mae 30-year. As all inverse floaters, the

---

[4] The TBA market is a forward market, where the exact details of the mortgage pool sold was not specifically determined prior to settlement. Only the coupon and agency type were specified on trade date. (The TBA market thus showed similarities to the "When Issued" Treasuries market.)

[5] LIBOR (London Inter Bank Offered Rate) is the interest paid for dollars and euros at international markets in inter bank borrowings. The LIBOR rate is fixed daily by the British Bankers' Association (BBA). It is similar to the U.S. Federal Reserve rate, in that it is used as a reference rate for other short term interest rates.

EXHIBIT 7

NEGATIVE CONVEXITY CAN BE FATAL

a. Situation on July 1, 2002

	Long: FHR 2389 S	Short: UST 10-year note
Description	Companion Inverse Floater, backed by 30-year 6s, 6.59% WAC, 348 WAM	Treasury Bullet Bond
Coupon	20.25% − 3 × LIBOR = 16.1%	4.875%
Price	$91-11	$100-22
Yield	17% @ 165% PSA	4.78%
Average Life	25 years @ 100% PSA 0.4 years @ 40% CPR	9.6 years
Duration	24 years	7.9 years

b. The Trade

Duration Neutral trade on July 1, 2002:

- Buy $35 million face value Inverse Floater at $91-11, financed with 24% haircut.
- Sell $95 million face value U.S. Treasury 10-year notes at $100-22, financed with 2% haircut

Equity applied is $100 million.

c. Development over time

Date	Jul 1, 2002	Jul 31, 2002	Aug 30, 2002	Sep 30, 2002
10-year yield	4.78%	4.46%	4.14$	3.59%
Price (Inverse Floater)	$91-11	$95-30	$100-07	$101-31
Duration (Inverse Floater)	24 years	19 years	11 years	4 years
Price (UST, 10-year)	$100-22	$103-06	$105-28	$110-08
Duration (UST, 10-year)	7.9 years	8.0 years	8.0 years	8.1 years
Net Trade Duration (U.S. 10-year equivalent)	$0 mn	−$6 mn	−$14 mn	−$22 mn
Cumulative Total Return	**0%**	**−7%**	**−18%**	**−54%**

Source: Casewriters

bond had huge interest rate sensitivity. That said, it was still backed by triple-A rated bonds, and since the coupon was 16%, the price 91, and the yield about 17%, the hedge fund found it to be a very interesting trade opportunity. So on July 1, 2002, the hedge fund bought $35 million of the Inverse Floater. (Exhibit 7 outlines the full timeline of the trade.) To hedge against the duration risk[6] of this long trade, they went short with a very liquid security, a 10-year U.S. Treasury note with duration of 8 years and a yield of 4.78%. After borrowing to finance the purchase, the hedge fund put up a total equity of $100 million, for which they were short $95 million in treasuries.

[6] Duration measures of the sensitivity of a security to changes in e.g. the interest rate. For more on duration and measurements of price sensitivity, see George Chacko, Peter Hecht, Vincent Dessain, and Anders Sjöman, "Note on Duration and Convexity," Harvard Business School Note No. 205-009 (Boston: Harvard Business School Publishing, 2004).

Talbot and Stanway saw the trade as the hedge fund betting on how the market rates would develop. They hoped rates would increase. However, during July, interest rates fell 32 basis points on the 10-year treasuries. The inverse floater went up in price to nearly $96, and so the trade was now minus $6 million. At this point, the hedge fund could have decided to either hedge with $6 million 10-year treasuries, or they could have just left the trade, taking the loss. They chose however to keep the trade on, assuming that rates could not fall anymore. However, rates fell another 32 basis points in August. Then Fannie Mae announced in September that the agency was short the equivalent of $100 billion 10-year treasury notes, which made the rates of 10-year notes fall even further, to a historic low of 3.59%. The trade that the fund had put on had by now lost $22 million. The nosedive made it lose over 40% of its investor capital in one month—and forced the fund out of business.

TRADING MORTGAGE BACKS AT TICONDEROGA

Ticonderoga Group managed a set of hedge funds which invested in various fixed income sectors, including U.S. and global corporate debt, and various asset-backed securities. The group had been formed in the spring of 2004 with funding for various trading strategies, of which the mortgage-backed fund was their largest. The funds all employed considerable leverage to amplify small pricing discrepancies they found in the market. Trading in the MBS fund started in the summer of 2004. For the time being, Ticonderoga's MBS activities targeted only agency MBSs and CMOs. The basic idea was to identify and exploit non-systematic arbitrage opportunities that appeared in the MBS market.

As they gathered experience, Talbot and Stanway also started to develop a risk management approach. They wanted to emphasize non-systematic risk, meaning running their trades duration neutral. They also ran their trades yield curve neutral, with plus/minus 1 year. At the end, the only risk they found acceptable was credit risk. They also implemented their normal policy of having a stop-loss limit on every trade that they did; if a trade started losing money and reached the limit, they would immediately stop the trade, accept the losses and move on to the next trade. As a simple way to define the stop-loss limit, they simply picked it as the negative opposite of what they estimated the profit potential in any given trade to be.

Talbot explained their trading approach so far,

> In the most basic form, we just look for relative value trades. You buy a Ginnie, short a Fannie, etc. However, we also look for relative prepayment arbitrages. Say that we find a security that we think will prepay slower than the market seems to believe, such as an IO. You then hedge that IO with another security that you think will prepay faster, say a PO. So you combine the two securities, and then sell the underlying against them.

In the one common office of Ticonderoga, the members of the group scoured their financial data screens daily in search for new trade ideas. They followed the development of the Ginnies, Fannies and Freddies, the various pass-throughs, and also the different CMOs trading in the market. On this particular morning in April 2005, Stanway had noticed something in the market that she thought might be a good trade. She had found a CMO which was based on a pass-through with pooled mortgages of $600 million. The pass-through rate for the pool was 5.20%, the WAC was 6.75% and the WAM was at 357 months. The CMO that had been formed with the pass-through as the underlying security had four separate tranches: tranches A–D. It was a so called Z-PAC

CMO, in that one of its tranches (tranche B) was a PAC (with its boundaries set between PSA 100 and PSA 600), and that the D tranche was an accrual tranche (or Z-tranche). The tranches were priced at $212,846,852 for Tranche A, $92,167,402 for Tranche B, $143,567,072 for Tranche C and $131,292,782 for Tranche D.

Then, for the underlying pass-through, Stanway calculated an implied PSA rate, which she found to be PSA 198. However, this implied PSA rate appeared high to Stanway, and when she told Talbot, he agreed. In their opinion, inflation in the economy was increasing, which would lead to interest rate levels also going up. This, in turn, they took as a sign that prepayments would slow down. In fact, as part of company policy, Ticonderoga frequently discussed future prepayment speeds in regular staff meetings, and set their official view on PSA speeds for every month. Their current view was that prepayment levels should be much lower than the implied PSA 198 they had found for this particular CMO. They discussed why that could be, believing that it could be the slightly unusual structure—a CMO with both a PAC and a Z tranche—that made the market misprice it.

Regardless of why, however, they believed there was a trade opportunity between the implied PSA level for this CMO and their own view on prepayment speeds. They would now look to construct a trade which took advantage of that difference in view on prepayments. Based on their view, Stanway and Talbot would take a position on one of the tranches in the CMO. This meant that they first would have to figure out which of the tranches to actually invest in. They decided to invest about $10 million in this long position.

They did, however, want to hedge out part of the risk that came with such an investment. In addition to the prepayment risk, the tranche they picked would also carry interest rate risk. As a general rule, Ticonderoga only felt comfortable accepting prepayment risk, and so they would want to hedge out changes in interest rates, by duration hedging. The hedge would most likely be done using U.S. Treasuries. (See Exhibit 8 for U.S. treasury yields.)

Stanway and Talbot sat down to start the calculations which would help them decide both which tranche to invest in, and to estimate the interest rate risk that would have to be hedged out.

EXHIBIT 8

U.S. TREASURY YIELDS FOR APRIL 19, 2005

Maturity	Yield
3 month	2.8900
6 month	3.1199
2 year	3.5728
3 year	3.6973
5 year	3.9198
10 year	4.2665
30 year	4.5958

Source: Bloomberg LP, accessed April 2005.

12

KAMCO and the Cross-Border Securitization of Korean Non-Performing Loans

Chung Jae-Ryong closed the door to his office. It was late April 2000 in Seoul, and the Chairman and CEO of the Korea Asset Management Company (KAMCO) had an important document to review: a securitization proposal for some of the distressed Korean debt that KAMCO held on its balance sheets. "Bad debt" was a common phenomenon for all South Korean banks since the country's 1997 financial crisis. As a government agency, KAMCO played an important role in rehabilitating the country's banking system. Its mandate was to acquire non-performing loans (NPLs) from troubled financial institutions and dispose of them as quickly as possible.

Several months ago Chung had asked bankers at UBS Warburg and Deutsche Bank to think about offering securitized distressed Korean debt on the Luxembourg exchange. The resulting proposal that Chung now had before him was a complex structured offering that involved dollar denominated notes secured by restructured loans to Korean companies with various forms of credit enhancement. If successful, the $367 million-deal would be the largest Korean Asset Backed Securitization (ABS) offering ever— and the first international non-performing loan securitization in Asia outside of Japan. Such a deal ought to build international interest in Korean debt, helping to develop both the distressed loan and ABS markets. The offering would also raise KAMCO's regional profile as an NPL specialist and help the bank's plans for international expansion.

However, there were several issues Chung had to consider. For instance, how would investors respond to the notes and their pricing? Also, what were the risks inherent in

Professor George Chacko, Jacob Hook (MALD '04, Fletcher School), Vincent Dessain, Executive Director of the HBS Europe Research Center, and Research Associate Anders Sjöman prepared this case. The authors thank Professors Patrick Schena and Laurent Jacque of the Fletcher School of Law and Diplomacy, Tufts University, for their valuable input and advice. HBS cases are developed solely as the basis for class discussion. Cases are not intended to serve as endorsements, sources of primary data, or illustrations of effective or ineffective management.

the deal and how well had the underwriter's structure overcome these? Comparing the costs of the securitization with more traditional alternatives was also important. Finally, Chung had to consider how the ABS offering fit into KAMCO's overall strategy for resolving Korea's non-performing loan problem.

KOREA'S FINANCIAL CRISIS AND NON-PERFORMING LOAN PROBLEM

South Korea's dramatic financial collapse in 1997 had its roots in the same development and policy patterns that had underpinned its earlier rapid growth (averaging above 6% annually) since the 1970s.[1] The country had relied on large family owned conglomerates known as *chaebol* as the primary locus of investment and engine of economic development. Supported by industrial policy and financial regulation that ensured a flow of subsidized funds from the banking sector, the *chaebol* pursued exporting and growth across multiple industries. This aggressive strategy helped pull the country from the ranks of least developed countries in the 1950s to OECD membership in 1996.

Unfortunately, the aggressive growth strategy also led to over-investment in uneconomical projects and the country built up extremely high levels of debt. Even when government-directed policy lending was scaled back after the 1970s, banks remained heavily exposed to their major borrowers. Bankers had little power relative to their corporate borrowers and found it hard to obtain comprehensive financial disclosure, making effective credit control difficult.[2] Lax regulatory oversight also allowed concentration of credit risk and excessive flexibility in loan classification and loss provisioning.[3] In fact, many *chaebol* groups established their own non-bank financial institutions (NBFIs) to circumvent any government attempts to tighten the credit supply. By the end of 1997 such NBFIs comprised 30% of the financial sector and included merchant banks, investment trust companies, securities companies, savings institutions, and insurance companies.[4] Most NBFIs were controlled by *chaebol* groups and existed primarily to channel funds to the parent firms or other group members. The NBFIs paid little regard to borrower credit quality or risk management.

As a result, Korean corporations developed a very high level of debt dependence. The leverage ratios of the major *chaebol* in the 1990s often exceeded 400%, compared to averages of 150% in the US and 210% in Japan. Several top firms had ratios as high as 500% in 1997 and operating cash flows that only covered 80% of interest payments in 1996.[5] To be able to carry their debt, the *chaebol* depended upon strong macro-level growth and continued rolling over of loans and provisioning of new funds from the financial sector. This made both the *chaebol* and the banking sector very vulnerable to shocks to corporate earnings. (See Exhibit 1 for pre-crisis leverage ratios for major Korean corporates.)

Partial financial liberalization during the early 1990s brought further structural imbalances.[6] Capital account regulations for short-term foreign borrowing were relaxed, while limits on long-term foreign lending and participation in domestic capital markets were retained. Korean corporations also remained unable to directly approach foreign financing sources, and had to go through domestic banks. Korean financial intermediaries took the chance to finance long-term won-denominated[a] lending to domestic firms with short-term foreign currency loans from offshore banks. International enthusiasm for Korea's growth prospects and a lack of lender prudence ensured a steady flow of cheap

---

[a] The local currency, the Korean Won (KRW), was in April 2000 valued at $1 USD = 1,105.15 KRW.

EXHIBIT 1

CHAEBOL LEVERAGE RATIOS—FINANCIAL STATUS OF LISTED CHAEBOL (KOREAN WON BILLION)

Group	No. of Listed Cos.	1997					First Half 1998				
		Total Equity	Total Liabilities	Net Debt	Liab. to Equity (%)	Net Debt to Equity (%)	Total Equity	Total Liabilities	Net Debt	Liab. to Equity (%)	Net Debt to Equity (%)
Hyundai	17	7,467	44,761	26,898	599	360	8,293	46,852	31,077	565	375
Samsung	12	11,321	38,463	24,323	340	215	12,839	36,164	19,732	282	154
LG	11	6,113	29,185	19,751	477	323	5,943	28,656	20,430	482	344
Daewoo	10	7,745	29,929	19,520	386	252	9,630	37,025	25,920	384	269
SK	7	4,762	16,875	11,435	354	240	4,903	16,145	11,150	329	227
Ssangyong	6	2,632	8,410	5,272	320	200	2,657	8,050	5,476	303	206
Hanjin	6	1,716	15,552	4,783	906	279	2,105	14,689	4,565	698	217
Hanwha	4	1,293	7,483	4,762	579	368	1,533	7,794	5,389	508	351
Lotte	4	398	1,735	778	436	196	526	1,724	678	328	129
Kumho	4	1,120	4,402	3,100	393	277	1,060	4,548	3,274	429	309
Halla	4	437	4,425	3,259	1,013	746	368	4,703	3,252	1,278	884
Dongah	2	551	1,650	906	299	164	500	1,543	835	308	167
Doosan	7	697	3,866	2,469	555	354	587	3,734	2,725	638	464
Daelim	7	944	4,050	2,413	429	256	995	4,120	2,226	414	224
Hansol	6	790	2,598	1,890	329	239	806	3,127	1,885	388	234
Hyosun	4	432	2,491	1,722	576	398	399	2,314	1,640	580	411
Dongkuk Steel	6	1,004	2,887	1,470	288	146	1,361	3,118	1,467	229	108
Jinro	3	287	1,774	1,260	619	440	282	2,184	1,690	775	599

(*Continued*)

EXHIBIT 1 *(Continued)*

CHAEBOL LEVERAGE RATIOS—FINANCIAL STATUS OF LISTED CHAEBOL (KOREAN WON BILLION)

Group	No. of Listed Cos.	1997					First Half 1998				
		Total Equity	Total Liabilities	Net Debt	Liab. to Equity (%)	Net Debt to Equity (%)	Total Equity	Total Liabilities	Net Debt	Liab. to Equity (%)	Net Debt to Equity (%)
Kolon	4	823	2,975	1,672	362	203	830	3,024	1,669	364	201
Kohap	3	797	3,485	2,942	437	369	334	4,516	3,677	1,352	1,101
Dongbu	4	901	3,006	1,908	334	212	1,174	3,474	2,159	296	184
Tongyang	2	525	1,900	1,373	362	262	753	2,267	1,622	301	215
Haitai	3	192	2,453	1,676	1,278	873	14	361	275	2,579	1,964
Anam	2	92	3,259	1,781	3,542	1,936	91	3,223	1,762	3,542	1,936
Hamil	2	245	1,915	1,444	782	589	25	1,868	1,485	7,472	5,940
Keopyung	4	73	443	310	607	425	48	235	156	490	325
Daesand	4	396	1,383	905	349	229	1,164	1,828	482	157	41
Shinho	6	42	1,483	784	3,531	1,867	195	1,788	1,036	917	531
Total	**154**	**53,796**	**242,838**	**150,806**	**451**	**280**	**59,414**	**249,081**	**157,732**	**419**	**265**
Top-five Chaebol	57	37,409	159,213	101,928	426	272	41,607	164,842	108,308	396	260

Source: Korea Stock Exchange and Goldman Sachs, as reported in Goldman Sachs' analyst report "Korea Chaebol Restructuring II – Incomplete Conquest," December 4, 1998, Table 2, page 6.

foreign credits. While most investment needs were long-term, the regulatory constraints to long-term international financing combined with a low risk premium on short-term loans encouraged the build up of short-term debt.[7] Many financial institutions, particularly NBFIs, developed asset-liability mismatches in terms of both currency and maturity. For example, in 1997 short-term assets covered only 55% of commercial bank short-term liabilities and only 25% for merchant banks.[8] The aggregate foreign liabilities of domestic financial institutions at this point were approximately $160 billion, up from $40 billion at the end of 1993, with the majority of these funds invested domestically.[9]

The 1997 Collapse

The precarious positions of both the corporate and financial sectors were laid bare in the summer of 1997. A global economic slowdown, combined with the collapse of the Thai baht, had foreign lenders starting to loose faith in Korea. In August 1997, they began to cut off lines of credit and stop rolling over outstanding loans. A currency slump, with the won dropping from around 900 to almost 2000 to the dollar, compounded the problems for banks highly exposed to exchange rate risk. Korean banks found themselves forced to tighten the supply of credit to the corporate sector, causing overnight call rates to rise to over 25% at the peak of the crisis. The sudden credit cut-off, together with falling domestic and international sales, tipped many major *chaebol* into deep financial distress. By the end of the year, 13 of the top 30 firms were bankrupt, along with large numbers of SMEs. (See Exhibit 2 for distressed *chaebol* groups.) Sol-

EXHIBIT 2

FINANCIALS FOR BANKRUPT CHAEBOL IN 1997
(WON BILLION; FINANCIALS AT TIME OF BANKRUPTCY)

Group	Default Date	Asset	Equity	Sales	Net Profits	Borrowings
Hanbo	1/23/97	4,470	224	333	−90	4,091
Sammi	3/19/97	2,515	−78	1,492	−252	875
Jinro	4/28/97	3,898	90	1,594	−214	1,917
Daenong	5/28/97	1,759	−65	1,366	−302	1,172
Hanshin Con.	6/2/97	1,326	177	1,058	−3	502
Kia	7/15/97	14,186	2,775	12,144	−129	6,624
Ssangbangwool	10/15/97	1,420	175	812	−6	595
Taeil Media	10/24/97	1,102	254	797	−4	588
Haitai	11/1/97	3,397	448	2,716	36	3,046
Newcore	11/4/97	2,803	212	1,828	20	1,215
Soosan Heavy	11/26/97	1,267	220	618	−20	639
Halla	12/5/97	6,627	306	5,294	23	6,453
Chunggu	12/27/97	1,897	325	1,099	−4	728
Total		**46,667**	**5,063**	**31,151**	**−945**	**28,445**

Source: Korea Financial Supervisory Commission, as quoted in Goldman Sachs' analyst report "Korea Chaebol Restructuring II—Incomplete Conquest," December 4, 1998, Table 7, page 29.

vent firms also began to default on their obligations with increasing frequency, bringing aggregate NPLs to an estimated 35% of total loans outstanding (about 35% of 1997 GDP).[10] The net worth of Korean financial institutions fell low, with more than half of all commercial banks having capital adequacy ratios (CARs) below the Bank for International Settlements (BIS) recommended minimum of 8%, and two being technically insolvent. A complete systemic collapse was on the horizon, and far-reaching government intervention became necessary.

With the assistance of the IMF and the World Bank, the Korean government put in place strategies to provide both immediate relief and longer term rehabilitation of the financial sector. The very first emergency measures were designed to restore confidence in the banking system. In mid-November the government announced that it would guarantee all deposits with financial institutions until 2000 and would provide temporary liquidity support as needed.[11] To build international confidence, the Bank of Korea deposited about $23 billion of foreign reserves with the overseas branches of Korean commercial banks which might not meet their foreign commitments.[12] The measures reduced immediate fears of bank runs and systemic insolvency, so the government could look to longer term reforms. Key reform principles included minimizing costs to the public; taking action to minimize the effects of the inevitable credit crunch on the real economy; and avoiding moral hazard by ensuring that shareholders, managers, and employees shared the pain of restructuring.[13]

The most important reform policy, however, was ensuring that all financial institutions met minimum standards of capital adequacy. To achieve this, the most insolvent banks were closed or nationalized, and salvageable institutions were merged with stronger ones. Further, there were induced equity issues and limited use of public funds for recapitalization or NPL purchases. In 1998 16 out of 30 merchant banks had their licenses revoked and their assets and liabilities rolled into a public bridge bank.[14] Two insolvent but systemically important commercial banks were affected: Korea First Bank was nationalized and sold to a foreign investor (NewBridge Asia) and Seoul Bank was eventually merged with domestic HANA Bank in 2002, after failed acquisition talks with Deutsche Bank. In February the newly formed Financial Supervisory Service (FSS) required 12 commercial banks with BIS capital adequacy ratios of less than 8% to submit management and capital enhancement plans or face exit.[15] Five of these institutions failed to convince the FSS of their ongoing viability and were taken over by stronger banks under purchase and assumption agreements supported by the government. Other banks were required to seek private sources for additional capital, generally in the form of foreign strategic investors. The government encouraged further mergers between relatively healthy institutions in order to create soundly capitalized lead banks that could compete internationally. (See Exhibit 3 for summarized restructuring plans.) By year end 1999 there were only 17 commercial banks in the country, down from 26 before the onset of the crisis.[16] The aggregate BIS capital adequacy ratio for Korea's nationwide commercial banks rose from 6.66% in 1997 to 10.52% in 2000.[17] (Exhibit 4 shows individual bank BIS ratios before and after the crisis.)

The total cost of these efforts to overhaul the financial sector was estimated at 21.5% of GDP by the government and 25-30% of GDP by foreign analysts.[18] Approximately half of the expenditures were for recapitalization, deposit payments, and auxiliary expenses, with the rest going toward the purchase of NPLs.[19] Two government agencies, KAMCO and the Korea Deposit Insurance Company (KDIC), were charged with providing immediate balance sheet relief to restructuring banks. The mandates of the two agencies differed: KAMCO was to acquire NPLs directly from financial institutions in order to dispose of them, whereas KDIC assisted financial institutions in raising their

---

EXHIBIT 3

**SAMPLE MANAGEMENT IMPROVEMENT PLANS FOR
7 CONDITIONALLY IMPROVED BANKS 1998**

Bank	Recommendation
CBK, Hanil	Merger, capital reduction and injection of public funds by the government
Chohung, KEB	Raise capital by introduction of foreign investors
Peace	Withdraw from international business and large value loan business over 5 billion won
Kangwon	Capital increase and merge with a related institution Hyundai Merchant Bank
Chungbuk	Capital increase

Source: Kim, D., 1999. "Bank Restructuring in Korea" in Bank Restructuring in Practice. Policy Paper No. 6. Bank for International Settlements: Basel, Page 152.

---

capital adequacy ratio, without explicitly acquiring the NPLs. The government hoped that using centralized Asset Management Companies to deal with the distressed asset problems rather than requiring banks to individually sell off their impaired loans would yield faster and more efficient overall recoveries.

THE KOREA ASSET MANAGEMENT COMPANY (KAMCO)

KAMCO was established in 1962 to manage and dispose of bad debts from the state-owned Korea Development Bank. It also provided fee-based services to private banks. In the 1980s and 1990s it began managing and disposing of assets acquired by the Ministry of Finance and Economy (MOFE) and the Taxation Office. Until the financial crisis struck, the agency had maintained a staff of only a few hundred and a relatively small balance sheet.

As the financial crisis deepened, the government issued the "Act on Efficient Management of Non-Performing Loans (NPLs) of Financial Institutions and Establishment of KAMCO" in November 1997. Through the Act, KAMCO was charged with managing the newly established Non-Performing Asset Management Fund (discussed below) in order to acquire and dispose of distressed assets of Korean financial institutions. KAMCO's official goal was "to expedite efficient disposal of NPLs for the betterment of liquidity and soundness of financial institutions, thus contributing to the development of financial industry and national economy."[20]

In August 1998, KAMCO underwent a functional and organizational overhaul inspired by the U.S. Resolution Trust Company, the agency responsible for resolving the U.S. Savings and Loan Crisis during the 1990s.[21] Additional activities—including lending, debt equity swaps, and extension of payment guarantees—were authorized so that KAMCO could act as a public sector "bad bank."[22] The agency was further divided into 13 departments: planning, general affairs, computing, audit and inspection, funds management, corporate management, asset management (three divisions), overdue loan management, property disposition, tax disposition, and national property management.[23] KAMCO's staff grew to more than 1,500 employees, mostly hired from the private sector.[24] The reform of KAMCO also extended to its capital structure: its funding base

EXHIBIT 4

KOREAN BIS (BANK FOR INTERNATIONAL SETTLEMENTS) CAPITAL RATIOS (IN %)

Bank	1996	1997	1998	1999	2000
Cho-Hung Bank	8.48%	6.50%	0.93%	9.80%	9.78%
Hanvit Bank	—	—	12.05%	8.67%	10.26%
(Commercial Bank of Korea)	9.25%	7.62%	—	—	—
(Hanil Bank)	8.89%	6.90%	—	—	—
Korea First Bank	9.14%	Δ2.70%	Δ1.47%	11.44%	13.40%
Seoul Bank	8.56%	0.97%	Δ0.88%	10.41%	10.08%
Korea Exchange Bank	9.16%	6.79%	8.06%	9.76%	9.19%
Kookmin Bank	8.46%	9.78%	10.09%	11.38%	11.18%
Korea Housing & Commercial Bank	—	10.29%	10.79%	11.74%	9.92%
Shinhan Bank	10.03%	10.29%	14.69%	13.85%	12.30%
KorAm Bank	8.80%	8.57%	15.21%	12.14%	8.67%
Hana Bank	8.71%	9.29%	13.10%	12.33%	10.45%
Peace Bank	8.92%	5.45%	Δ1.79%	5.15%	10.09%
Nationwide Commercial Banks	**8.97%**	**6.66%**	**8.22%**	**10.79%**	**10.52%**
Daegu Bank	9.93%	11.25%	11.42%	12.12%	11.69%
Pusan Bank	8.58%	9.66%	9.25%	11.45%	10.53%
Kwangju Bank	11.27%	10.65%	10.12%	8.63%	10.12%
Bank of Cheju	14.95%	12.13%	9.65%	7.85%	10.14%
Jeonbuk Bank	15.13%	13.27%	12.94%	13.36%	10.87%
Kyongnam Bank	9.41%	12.27%	11.87%	12.39%	10.06%
Regional Banks	**10.15%**	**9.60%**	**8.31%**	**11.36%**	**10.77%**
Domestic Commercial Banks	**9.14%**	**7.04%**	**8.23%**	**10.83%**	**10.53%**
Korea Development Bank	—	—	—	17.6%	11.4%
Industrial Bank of Korea	—	—	—	10.9%	11.0%
Export-Import Bank of Korea	—	—	—	24.4%	18.6%
National Agricultural Cooperative Federation	—	—	—	8.6%	10.2%
National Federation of Fisheries Cooperatives	—	—	—	−4.6%	−40.7%
Specialized Banks	**—**	**—**	**—**	**13.9%**	**10.6%**
Banks	**—**	**—**	**—**	**11.7%**	**10.6%**

Note: 1) The figures are calculated on the condition that Allowance for Valuation of Securities and Credit Losses are made no less than 100% from 1997.

Source: Korea Financial Supervisory Service 2002 "BIS Ratios," available at http://www.fss.or.kr. Last accessed March 2004.

deepened to provide additional working capital and to more fully share funding costs with market participants. Following the reorganization, the agency was owned 38% by the government, 31% by the Korea Development Bank (KDB), and 31% by 24 commercial banks.[25] By the end of 1999 KAMCO had total assets of KRW 876 billion (about $755 million), mostly consisting of working capital and assets acquired for disposal. Total paid-in capital was KRW 130 billion with the bulk coming from long-term government guaranteed borrowing.[26] (See Exhibit 5 for KAMCO's financials.)

EXHIBIT 5

KAMCO BALANCE SHEET AND INCOME STATEMENT, YEAR ENDED DEC 31, 1999 (SUMMARIES OF AUDITED NON-CONSOLIDATED FINANCIAL STATEMENTS)

Income Statement Data	KRW thousands	USD thousands
Operating Revenue	183,979,739	160,625
Operating Expenses	158,756,606	138,604
Operating Income	25,214,133	22,013
Other Income	8,655,141	7,556
Ordinary Income	33,869,274	29,570
Income before Income Taxes	33,869,274	29,570
Income Taxes	24,226,274	21,151
Net Income	9,643,000	8,419

Balance Sheet Data (as of Dec 31, 1999):		
Total Current Assets	780,057,007	681,035
Total Investments	59,834,372	52,239
Property and Equipment	36,221,240	31,623
Total Assets	876,112,619	764,897
Total Current Liabilities	158,917,263	138,744
Total Long-Term Liabilities	576,359,277	503,195
Total Liabilities	735,276,540	641,939
Total Stockholders' Equity	140,836,079	122,958

Source: KAMCO (Korea Asset Funding 2000-1 Limited Prospectus).

KAMCO was managed by a 7 member board of directors and an 11 member management supervisory committee, representing the Ministry of Finance and Economy (MOFE), the Financial Supervisory Service, and major shareholding banks.[27] Chairman and CEO Chung Jae-Ryong, the agency's head since January 1999, was a former vice-minister of the MOFE.[28] Despite KAMCO's political ownership, its top management felt they were able to operate independently.[29] Transparency in asset acquisition, management, and disposition activities was emphasized with audited annual financial statements for both KAMCO and the Non-Performing Asset Management Fund.[30]

The Non-Performing Asset Management Fund

The Non-Performing Asset Management Fund (the Fund) was an entity legally independent from KAMCO and wholly owned by the government. KAMCO used the fund's resources to purchase NPLs and then manage or dispose of these on behalf of the Fund as efficiently as possible.[b] The Fund was initially financed by financial institutions (KRW

---

[b] The majority of the NPL business that KAMCO carried out was conducted on behalf of the Fund, however, KAMCO still had a small quantity of NPLs on its own books remaining from its traditional asset management activities before the crisis.

573.4 billion), borrowings from the Korea Development Bank (KRW 500 billion), and by government guaranteed Non-Performing Loan Management Fund Bonds (KRW 20.5 trillion). The Non-Performing Loan Management Fund Bonds were both sold directly to the capital markets and used as payment to banks for NPL acquisitions.

As of December 31, 1999, total Fund assets stood at approximately KRW 17.5 trillion while liabilities were KRW 18.8 trillion, making for a total deficit of KRW 1.3 trillion.[31] The deficit came from Fund losses in 1998 and 1999. (The Fund's financials are presented in Exhibit 6.) Although KAMCO had successfully sold NPLs for greater than acquisition cost during this period, such gains had been more than offset by interest charges and loan loss provisions.[32] Most analysts assumed that the government would eventually cover any remaining deficit after KAMCO had disposed of all the Fund's assets, despite the lack of explicit assurances on this matter.[33] Approximately 80% of Fund assets were NPL inventories awaiting sale or rehabilitation. Proceeds from the sale of such assets were used to purchase additional distressed loans and to pay down debts.

KAMCO's Activities

By March 31, 2000 KAMCO had acquired NPLs with a total face value of KRW 67 trillion, paying KRW 26 trillion.[34] (See Exhibit 7 for a purchase summary.) Loans were purchased from commercial banks, government owned policy banks, and non-bank financial institutions. Initially, discounts from face value were negotiated between KAMCO and the seller and then adjusted after KAMCO had assumed and analyzed

---

EXHIBIT 6

NON-PERFORMING ASSET FUND BALANCE SHEET AND INCOME STATEMENT, YEAR END DEC 31, 1999

Income Statement Data	KRW thousands	USD thousands
Total Operating Revenue	6,514,457,292	5,687,496
Total Operating Expenses	6,954,806,893	6,071,946
Operating Loss	440,349,601	384,451
Non-Operating Income	5,421,301	4,733
Loss before Income Tax Expense	434,928,300	379,717
Income Tax Expense	39,943,816	34,873
Net Loss	474,872,116	414,591

Balance Sheet Data (as of):		
Total Assets	17,494,121,058	15,273,373
Long-Term Borrowings	2,122,142,009	1,852,752
Total Non-Performing Asset Fund Bonds	15,418,390,726	13,461,140
Total Liabilities	18,810,323,328	16,422,493
Contributed Funds	573,380,000	500,594
Accumulated Deficit	−1,902,073,174	−1,660,619
Total Deficit	−1,316,202,270	−1,149,120

Source: KAMCO (Korea Asset Funding 2000-1 Limited Prospectus).

EXHIBIT 7

KAMCO PURCHASES (KRW TRILLION, AS OF MARCH 2000)

	Face Value (A)	Purchase Price (B)	B/A (%)
Ordinary Loans (Secured)	10.50	6.50	61.9
Ordinary Loans (Unsecured)	11.88	1.50	12.6
Restructured Loans with Recourse	18.69	10.04	53.7
Restructured Loans without Recourse	7.43	1.61	21.7
Daewoo Bonds from ITCs	16.50	5.72	34.7
Guaranteed Loans	1.60	0.69	43.2
Total	**66.60**	**26.06**	

Note: ITCs: Investment trust companies.

Source: Fitch Analyst Report, "Korea Asset Funding 2000-1 Limited," 10 July 2000, page 4.

the assets. In September 1998 this cumbersome approach was replaced by a standardized formula that set the purchase price for defaulted loans not subject to a restructuring agreement at 45% of any unpledged collateral value for secured loans and 3% of par for unsecured obligations.[35] Secured loans undergoing court restructuring were sold at 45% of face value with the price later adjusted to reflect expected cash flows once a final settlement was reached. The 45% rate was chosen to reflect KAMCO's historical recovery experience. Payments were made initially with a mix of cash and Fund bonds, and then entirely in the form of bonds after February 1998.[36]

Valuing NPLs

The aggregate principle value of the NPLs purchased consisted of KRW 22.3 trillion of secured and unsecured defaulted loans, KRW 26 trillion of restructured corporate loans, and KRW 16 trillion of commercial paper issued by the failed Daewoo conglomerate[c] and purchased from investment trust companies.[37] The majority of the loans were denominated in won. Roughly 70% of restructured loans were purchased with full recourse[d] to the originating banks. In 1999 the portfolio consisted of 170,000 loans which were managed in-house, of which 32,000 were secured. An additional 233,000 loans (less than 15% of the total portfolio value) were serviced externally. Of the 30,000 total borrowers, the largest 1,500 accounted for 90% of total obligations. [38]Each of the large obligors[e] was individually analyzed so that alternative exit strategies could be assessed and minimum acceptable sale prices set. KAMCO was prepared to reduce borrower obligations in exchange for equity if there was potential for high returns through value-adding workout programs. In general, however, the agency preferred quick disposal of loans.[39] Chung explained:

[c] The Daewoo Group, created in 1967, was one of South Korea's leading trading groups. It was declared defunct in 2000, with parts of the group later saved from complete bankruptcy and restructured.

[d] Recourse loans are sold with an option to return all outstanding principal to the originating bank, normally at a discount.

[e] Also called debtor, an obligor is an individual or company that owes debt to another individual or company (the creditor).

The key reason for our success was probably the expeditious handling of distressed assets while selling them at reasonable prices. Actually this was a Catch 22 situation as time is needed to obtain the right price, but waiting only accumulates more distressed assets. Also if we sell the assets too cheaply, again we will come in for criticism. Between the two alternatives, I chose to dispose of the assets quickly as I believed that the handling of distressed assets was a fight against time. In the case of normal debt, volume increases arithmetically but distressed assets on the other hand increase geometrically.[40]

Disposing NPLs

KAMCO employed various methods for liquidating NPLs. It used domestic and international auctions, private sales, workout and collection, exercise of recourse and domestic ABSs. Overall, KAMCO had disposed of approximately 34% of the total principal value of loans acquired. Total recoveries to date stood at KRW 14.3 trillion for loans with an aggregate face value of KRW 25.8 trillion and represented 111% of the purchase price of these loans.[41]

International auctions accounted for approximately KRW 3.5 trillion of total principal sold. American investment banks and private equity funds such as Goldman Sachs and Texas-based Lone Star Fund competed aggressively for prepackaged loan bundles.[42] KAMCO had issued its first domestic ABS in June 1999 and had since brought several more such securities to the market, disposing loans to a face value of KRW 3.4 trillion. Asset securitization was a relatively new practice in the Korean financial markets and the NPL backed securities had proved popular with domestic institutional and individual investors.[43] In fact, in the years to come, Won Young Yon, who took over as KAMCO CEO from Chung in January 2002, continued to issue asset back securities. In 2003, for instance, he issued two ABSs, extending the underlying asset range to include restructuring loans and workout loans. (Appendix 1 discusses the use of securitization as a means of disposing of NPLs and Appendix 2 provides background on the development of the securitization market in Korea.)

In addition, foreclosure auctions (KRW 2.6 trillion), domestic public auctions (KRW 411 billion), and individual loan sales (KRW 38 billion) were used.[44] Repayments by loan obligors retired a further KRW 2.3 trillion. However, the majority of collections (more than KRW 13 trillion of face value) were accounted for by cancellations, voluntary buy-backs, and KAMCO's exercise of recourse options that allowed it to return certain loans to the originating banks in the event of further obligor default.[45] (Exhibit 8 details some of KAMCO's major loan disposal transactions.)

Future Challenges

Its impressive recovery rate of 111% had attracted widespread attention, including the naming of KAMCO as "Best Financial Restructuring Agency 1999" by International Financial Review Asia. However, there was still much work to be done. Furthermore, some analysts believed that the agency had selectively sold off its most attractive assets, and that future recovery rates could be much lower.[46]

Another challenge was ensuring that the Fund had enough cash to continue purchasing NPLs. Recent outlays on the assets of investment trust companies had pushed the Fund's cash reserves below KRW 5 trillion. Meanwhile, the government had instructed KAMCO to purchase a further KRW 3.2 trillion of Daewoo commercial paper and KRW 2.3 trillion of Daewoo's foreign debts.[47]

Chung's plans for 2000 included recovering at least KRW 8 trillion on KRW 17 trillion of NPLs. Recoveries at this level would require intensive efforts to maintain and

EXHIBIT 8

SELECTED MAJOR KAMCO LOAN DISPOSITION TRANSACTIONS

a. International Bidding for Corporate Restructured Loans (Unit: KRW billion)

Date	Portfolio	Face Value	Purchasing Price	Sales Price	Purchased by
01-09-1998	KAMCO 98-1	207.5	2.8	25.4	Goldman Sachs
27-05-1999	KAMCO 99-1	772.4	71.7	123.8	Goldman Sachs & Others
10-11-1999	KAMCO 99-2	811.2	97.7	170.5	Morgan Stanley Dean Witter & Others
26-07-2000	KAMCO 2000-1	1,097.5	228.9	322.8	Goldman Sachs & Others
Total		**2,888.6**	**401.1**	**642.5**	

b. International Bidding for Secured Loans (Unit: KRW billion)

Date	Portfolio	Face Value	Purchasing Price	Sales Price	Purchased by
09-12-1998	KAMCO Secured NPL 98-1	564.6	238.8	201.2	Lonestar Fund
22-06-1999	KAMCO Secured NPL 99-1	1,038.8	554.5	525.9	Lonestar Fund
08-12-1999	KAMCO Secured NPL 99-2	1,022.6	379.6	439.3	Morgan Stanley Dean Witter
Total		**2,626.0**	**1,172.9**	**1,166.4**	

c. ABS Issuance (Unit: KRW billion)

ABS	Date	Face Value	Purchasing Price	Amount
Mirae Bond 99-1	15-06-1999	305.1	268.0	320
Mirae Bond 99-2	30-08-1999	384.9	299.6	360
Mirae Bond 99-3	09-11-1999	237.7	201.9	223
Mirae Bond 99-4	27-12-1999	291.5	221.7	265
Mirae Bond 2000-1	19-01-2000	365.6	337	340
Mirae Bond 2000-2	03-04-2000	320.7	342.5	330
Mirae Bond 2000-3	27-04-2000	414.0	367	375
Total		**2,319.5**	**2,037.7**	**2,213**

Source: KAMCO.

deepen KAMCO's "hard earned overseas and domestic distressed asset markets."[48] KAMCO would continue its aggressive marketing at investment forums in Korea and abroad, as well as undertake a strategic move from low value-added wholesaling of NPLs to more focused sales of smaller blocks to generate higher returns.[49] Specifically, Chung hoped to increase returns and develop KAMCO's knowledge base by handing over about KRW 3 trillion to seven new Asset Management Companies. These would be joint ventures, established with foreign fund managers and investment banks as equity partners.[50]

KAMCO's senior management also wanted to define the agency's mission more broadly than just management and disposal of the NPLs held by the Non-Performing Asset Management Fund. Although the Fund was due to wind down by November of 2002, KAMCO itself had no legislative sunset and its accumulated experience could still be put to good use after this point.[f] Chung felt that there was significant potential for leveraging KAMCO's expertise in the Southeast Asian and Chinese distressed debt markets. "We would like to turn ourselves into an investment bank like Goldman Sachs or Morgan Stanley, specializing in distressed assets," he said.[51] KAMCO had already signed an agreement to begin providing assistance to one Chinese Asset Management Company and was engaged in working-level discussions with three other Chinese AMCs and one in Japan.[52] An Asian NPL conference was also to be held in Seoul later in 2000 to showcase KAMCO's successes and strengthen relationships with other agencies in the region.

THE CROSS-BORDER NPL SECURITIZATION PROPOSAL

One method that Chung hoped to use in 2000 was to replicate KAMCO's domestic ABS issues on the international market. Given the success of both these issues and the international NPL auctions, Chung felt that securitizing distressed loans for sale to foreign investors would enable KAMCO to tap new funding sources as well as raise its international profile. He asked investment bankers at Deutsche Bank and UBS Warburg to put together a proposal for such an offering. The proposal they came back with was a complex structured offering comprised of dollar denominated floating rate notes issued via multiple special purpose corporations (SPCs)[g] and secured by a portfolio of non-performing loans sold to one of the SPCs by KAMCO.[53] The deal incorporated currency and interest rate hedges, recourse to the originating banks in the event of loan obligor default, subordinated tranching and an irrevocable credit facility from the Korea Development Bank. The bankers' analysis had suggested that the notes could be priced at LIBOR[h] plus 200 basis points (bp).[i]

The Securitized Asset

The underlying asset to be securitized was a static portfolio of 135 non-performing loans to Korean corporations with an aggregate outstanding principal amount of $395.3 million.[j] The loans were denominated in U.S. dollars (90.9% of total value) and Japanese yen (9.1%) and had been purchased by KAMCO in 1998. The originating banks were

---

[f] Indeed, the NPL acquisitions through the NPA public fund were terminated on November 22, 2002. However, KAMCO continued to acquire NPLs on its own account.

[g] Also known as Special Purpose Vehicles (SPVs), SPCs were mostly incorporated in offshore tax havens, such as the Cayman Islands. An originator would not own the SPC, to avoid having the loans consolidated back onto its balance sheet. Instead, a number of SPV management companies had sprung up, whose services included providing autonomous boards of directors.

[h] LIBOR (London Inter Bank Offered Rate) is the interest paid for dollars and euros at international markets in inter bank borrowings. The LIBOR rate is fixed daily by the British Bankers' Association (BBA). It is similar to the U.S. Federal Reserve rate, in that it is used as a reference rate for other short term interest rates.

[i] A basis point represents 1/100 of 1%, or 0.01%.

[j] Because several of the loans in the pool initially had zero principal outstanding but were to assume accrued but unpaid interest on other loans as their principal over the life of the deal the total principal to be repaid was actually $419 million.

the Korea Development Bank, Kookmin Bank, Shinhan Bank, Hanvit Bank, Cho Hung Bank, and the Korea Exchange Bank. All of the 45 loan obligors were or had been involved in formal restructuring proceedings and were believed to be insolvent.[54] In its pre-offering analysis, Fitch Ratings assumed that nearly 75% of the obligors would default again within the first few years of the deal.[55] Borrower concentration was high, with 37% of the portfolio's aggregate principal accounted for by the top three borrowers and 75% by the top ten. (See Exhibit 9 and 10 for details on the major obligors.) Interest payments on the loans were based on a variety of indices. More than half of the dollar denominated loans paid the U.S. dollar prime rate of the lending bank, with the rest paying fixed rates or LIBOR. The majority of the yen loans paid fixed rates or were zero-coupon obligations. (Exhibit 11 details the portfolio's interest rate exposure.)

The Deal Structure

The proposed legal structure of the deal followed a detailed outline. At the closing date KAMCO would sell the loan portfolio and associated recourse rights (discussed below) to a Korean incorporated SPC called Korea 1st International ABS Specialty Co., Ltd. This SPC would finance the purchase by issuing a $367 million Purchaser Senior Floating Rate Note due February 2009 and a $52,960,997 Purchaser Subordinated Fixed

---

EXHIBIT 9

TEN LARGEST LOAN OBLIGATORS

Loan Obligor	Outstanding principal amount (USD)	% of all Loan Transactions	% of Put Option Price by Put Option bank[a]
Pan Ocean Shipping Co., Ltd	63,506,393	16.1%	KEB (47.0%) Hanvit (30.8%) Chohung (22.2%)
Kia Heavy Industrial Co., Ltd	47,070,745	11.9%	KDB (100%)
Taeil Media Co., Ltd	37,304,897	9.4%	Chohung (70.4%) KEB (23.7%) Shinhan (5.9%)
Dooray Air Metal Co., Ltd	25,716,355	6.5%	KDB (94.0%) Hanvit (6.0%)
Cho-il Paper Co., Ltd	24,581,391	6.2%	KDB (96.4%) KEB (3.6%)
Hwan Young Steel Co., Ltd	23,921,210	6.0%	KDB (100%)
Heung-A Shipping Co., Ltd	22,281,444	5.6%	KDB (100%)
Punghan Co., Ltd	20,567,124	5.2%	KEB (100%)
Daedong Shipbuilding Co., Ltd	17,684,348	4.5%	KDB (100%)
Dooyang Shipping Co., Ltd	15,125,429	3.8%	KDB (100%)
Total	**297,759,336**	**75.3%**	

Note: (a) Indicates percentage of the Put Option Price for each Loan Obligor that would have been payable by each Put Option Bank on the Cut-Off Date if each Put Option had been exercised.

Source: KAMCO (Korea Asset Funding 2000-1 Limited Prospectus).

EXHIBIT 10

DISTRIBUTION OF LOAN OBLIGATORS BY INDUSTRY (USING MOODY'S INDUSTRY CATEGORIES)

Industry Category	Outstanding Principal for Loan Transactions (USD)	% of all Loan Transactions
Cargo, transport	129,316,835	32.7%
Mining, Steel, Iron and Non-precious Metals	73,099,253	18.5%
Machinery (Non-agriculture, Non-construction, Non-electronic)	48,244,602	12.2%
Electronics	38,789,156	9.8%
Textiles and Leather	32,686,820	8.3%
Printing, Publishing and Broadcasting	26,027,568	6.6%
Automobile	14,581,765	3.7%
Buildings and Real Estate	14,801,315	3.7%
Diversified/Conglomerate Service (Gross-Trade Company)	6,723,946	1.7%
Healthcare, Education and Childcare	5,278,072	1.3%
Beverage, Food and Tobacco	2,828,000	0.7%
Diversified/Conglomerate Manufacturing	1,785,050	0.5%
Chemicals, Plastics and Rubber	1,122,623	0.3%
Broadcasting	165,989	0.0%
Total	**395,450,993**	**100.0%**

Source: KAMCO (Korea Asset Funding 2000-1 Limited Prospectus).

Rate Note due 2019. The larger Purchaser Senior Note was then sold to Korea Asset Funding 2000-1 Limited, a Cayman Islands based SPC, specifically incorporated for the purposes of the transaction. Korea Asset Funding 2000-1 in turn would issue $367 million of Secured Floating Rate Notes (the Issuer Notes) with a maturity of 8.5 years in $50,000 denominations. The Issuer Notes were to be listed on the Luxemburg Stock Exchange and marketed to international institutional investors. Interest and principle would be paid semiannually in U.S. dollars. (Exhibit 12 graphically depicts the structure.)

The cash flow waterfall for the structure would begin with KAMCO acting as master servicer for the underlying loans. KAMCO would collect interest and principal payments as they fell due and pass these on to the Korean SPC. Monies received would then be used to service the Senior Purchaser Note, with fees and interest payments taking priority and any additional funds used to pay down the principal. (See Exhibit 13 for the expected principal amortization schedule.) Upon receiving Purchaser Note payments Korea Asset Funding 2000-1 would settle its own outstanding fees and distribute interest and principal to the holders of the Issuer Notes.

Recourse and Repurchase

If a borrower defaulted on its obligation, the Korea 1st International ABS Specialty Co had recourse to the originating bank. A loan was considered defaulted if the borrower

EXHIBIT 11

LOAN TRANSACTIONS

a. Dollar Loan Transactions

Interest Rate Index	Outstanding Principal for Dollar Loan Transactions (USD)	% of all USD Loan Transactions
No interest	7,095,639	2.0%
Fixed	77,978,769	21.7%
Floating Rate		
3M Libor	27,046,903	7.5%
6M Libor	65,783,175	18.3%
Prime Rates	181,417,763	50.5%
Total Floating Rate	274,247,841	76.3%
Total	**359,322,249**	**100.0%**

Note: The interest rates for 50.5% of loan transactions are prime rates. Such rates consist of USD prime rates quoted by KDB, Hanvit, Chohung, and KEB. Certain banks use higher prime rates for small and medium sized companies compared to the rates used for larger companies.

b. Yen Loan Transactions

Interest Rate Index	Outstanding Principal for Yen Loan Transaction (Y)	% of all Yen Loan Transactions
No interest	1,024,928,000	27.6%
Fixed	2,152,885,158	58.0%
Floating Rate – Prime Rate	535,694,300	14.4%
Total	**3,713,507,458**	**100.0%**

Note: The interest rates in relation to 14.4% of loan transactions above are prime rates. Such prime rates consist of Yen prime rates quoted by KDB, and in the case of one Yen transaction, the prime rate quoted by Hanvit.

Source: KAMCO (Korea Asset Funding 2000-1 Limited Prospectus).

was delinquent on any amount of interest or principal due for more than six months. KAMCO, as the master servicer, also had discretion to declare default should it deem payment impossible due to a cancellation of restructuring proceedings or if other loan defects should be discovered. If a default occurred, KAMCO, acting as the agent of the SPC could oblige the originating bank to repurchase it for a pre-determined price. In capital markets terminology this arrangement represented a put option on the underlying loan granted to the SPC by the banks.

The repurchase prices were defined in settlement agreements between KAMCO as the original purchaser and the selling bank. At the time of settlement each expected cash flow on a given loan was assigned a present value.[56] The applicable discount rate was determined by starting with a base rate (the then prevailing five-year interest rate of the National Housing Fund) plus a maturity premium (0.5% > five years, 1.0% > 10 years, 1.5% > 15 years) and a bank credit-risk premium (0.5% for KDB, 1.0% for

EXHIBIT 12

SECURITIZATION STRUCTURES

a. The Securitization Transaction Structure—at Closing

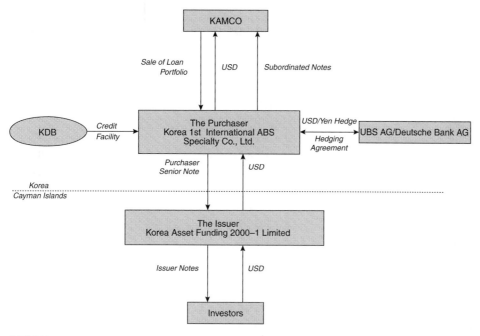

KAMCO–Korea Asset Management Corp. KDB–Korea Development Bank, USD–US dollar.

b. The Securitization Transaction Structure–Post-Closing

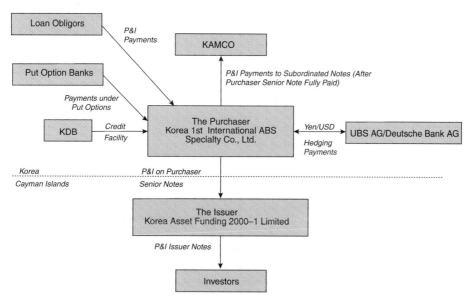

KAMCO–Korea Asset Management Corp. KDB–Korea Development Bank, P&I–Principal and interest, USD–US dollar.

Source: Fitch Analyst Report, "Korea Asset Funding 2000-1 Limited," 10 July 2000, p. 5.

EXHIBIT 13

CUMULATIVE PRINCIPAL AMOUNTS OF PAYMENTS DUE (USD)

Year	Cumulative principal amount (USD)[1]	% of all Loan Transactions
2000	12,161,649	2.9%
2001	50,715,331	12.0%
2002	117,592,859	27.9%
2003	167,037,564	39.6%
2004	213,779,482	50.6%
2005	259,342,048	61.4%
2006	304,017,433	72.0%
2007	342,805,473	81.2%
2008	370,776,351	87.8%
2009	391,704,640	92.8%
2010	402,506,404	95.4%
2011	410,643,437	97.3%
2012	416,115,721	98.6%
2013	419,819,806	99.5%
2014	420,277,312	99.6%
2015	420,734,819	99.7%
2016	421,192,326	99.8%
2017	421,649,833	99.9%
2018[2]	422,107,340	100.0%

Notes: (1) Each Loan Obligor is required to meet a payment schedule which has been set in accordance with the repayment plan in relation to the Relevant Loan Transaction. The table shows the cumulative amount of principal payments due in respect to all Loan Transactions according to such repayment plans, by reference to year.

(2) There are seven Loan Transactions in relation to Kia Heavy Industrial Co., Ltd which have zero principal amounts outstanding as of the Cut-Off Date. Interest accrued from other Loan Transactions of the same Loan Obligor is to be capitalized into those seven Loan Transactions and, accordingly, the principal amount outstanding increases over time. The difference between the cumulative principal payment due in 2018 (US$422,107,340) and the principal amount outstanding as of the Cut-Off Date (US$385,450,993) arises from this increase in principal amount outstanding.

Source: KAMCO (Korea Asset Funding 2000-1 Limited Prospectus).

Shinhan and Kookmin, 1.5% for KEB, Cho Hung, and Hanvit).[k] To calculate the repurchase price for a loan, the settlement date present values of all outstanding payments would be summed and interest for the number of days between December 30, 1999 and the repurchase date would be applied to the aggregate amount at the rate of three-month US LIBOR plus 1%. Yen denominated loans would be repurchased with

[k] The aggregate put option value for a given loan could be higher or lower than the outstanding principal. For example, if the discount rate was lower than the loan yield then the put option value would be higher than the outstanding principal amount.

U.S. dollars, with settlement present values translated at the rate of US$1.00 = ¥102.785.[57] (Exhibit 14 shows the impact of exercises of the put options on the average life of the notes under various default scenarios.)

Credit Facility

Beyond recourse to the originating banks, the deal structure built on an irrevocable $110 million credit facility from the Korea Development Bank. The credit could be drawn upon when cash flows from the underlying loans or obligor repurchases were insufficient to meet the outstanding fee, interest or principal payments. The size of the facility reduced as the Notes amortized, and was equal to the lesser of $110 million or the remaining principal outstanding, to a floor of $36.7 million. Interest on the facility was to be LIBOR plus 2% prior to August 2005, LIBOR plus 2.5% from then until August 2010, and LIBOR plus 3% thereafter.[58] A commitment fee of 1.375% also applied. Interest and principal repayments on the credit facility were subordinated to the Purchaser Senior Note, but had priority over the Purchaser Subordinated Note.

EXHIBIT 14

ESTIMATED AVERAGE LIFE OF THE NOTES

Default Scenario	% outstanding principal amount of Loan Portfolio Assets	Estimated Average Life	Final Life
No Loan Obligor Defaults	0.0%	4.64	8.5
Only Largest Loan Obligor Defaults[1]	16.1%	4.37	8.5
Only Two Largest Loan Obligors Default[2]	28.0%	3.91	8.5
Only Three Largest Loan Obligors Default[3]	37.4%	3.79	8.5

Assumptions:

(a) no prepayment of principal is made by any Obligor;

(b) no Put Option is exercised in respect of any Loan Transaction with respect to any of the Loan Obligors specified in the Default Scenario until any amount of principal or interest thereunder has been overdue for at least six (6) months according to the terms and conditions of such Loan Transaction and that the relevant Put Option is then exercised;

(c) the relevant Put Option Bank pays the Put Option Price in respect of the Defaulted Loan Transactions in accordance with the Settlement Agreement;

(d) the Notes carry a rate of interest of 6-month LIBOR (which is and remains at 6.9325%) plus a margin of 2%;

(e) all of the Loan Transactions of Loan Obligors specified in the Default Scenario become Defaulted Loan Transactions on their first payment dates after the Closing Date.

Notes: (1) Pan Ocean Shipping Co., Ltd: largest amount of principal outstanding (US$63,506,393) as of Cut-Off Date.

(2) Kia Heavy Industrial Co., Ltd: second largest amount of principal outstanding (US$47,070,745) as of Cut-Off Date.

(3) Taeil Media Co., Ltd: third largest amount of principal outstanding (US$37,304,897) as of Cut-Off Date.

Source: KAMCO (Korea Asset Funding 2000-1 Limited Prospectus).

Hedging

Because the Notes were to pay a LIBOR based rate and principal in U.S. dollars while the underlying assets were based on a variety of indices in both dollars and yen, hedging arrangements were required to mitigate currency, interest rate, and basis risks. The hedging mechanisms were interest rate and currency swaps with Deutsche Bank and UBS Warburg as counterparties. Yen exposures to fixed, floating, and zero-coupon loans were transformed into U.S. dollar LIBOR payments through an interest rate cum currency swap. The swap was arranged around a pre-agreed payment and amortization schedule but it was sufficiently flexible to allow the SPC to make delayed payments with interest if an obligor did not make its payments in time. In the event that recourse rights to the originating banks were exercised, all future swap transactions related to the loans in question were accelerated and the counterparty was obliged to accept payment in dollars. For the dollar denominated portion of the portfolio, 75% of the fixed rate exposures were swapped into LIBOR. Payments on the prime rate loans, however, were left unhedged. The lending banks set their prime rates on the basis of their funding costs, which had historically been substantially higher than LIBOR. Over the previous four years the spread between the banks' prime rates and U.S. dollar LIBOR had been between 175 and 400 basis points.[59] (Exhibits 15 and 16 give further data on these spreads.) The bankers therefore felt that the prime rate exposures could be left unhedged without jeopardizing the structure's ability to make LIBOR based payments. The interest rate swap was due to terminate in 2007 while the yen swap could be optionally terminated on specified dates between 2007 and 2009. Payments made during the last two years of the Notes' lives were thus left unhedged.

EXHIBIT 15

U.S. DOLLAR SIX-MONTH LIBOR/KOREAN BANKS' PRIME SPREADS

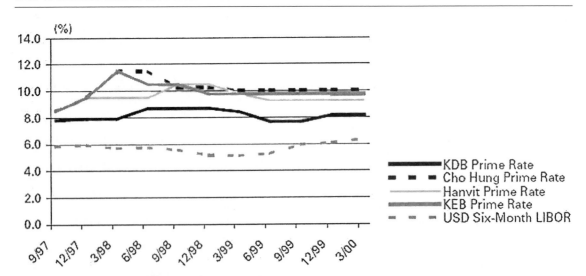

Note: KDB = Korea Development Bank; KEB = Korean Exchange Bank; LIBOR = London Interbank Offered Rate.

Source: Fitch Analyst Report, "Korea Asset Funding 2000-1 Limited," 10 July 2000, page 8.

EXHIBIT 16

VARIOUS KOREAN BANK RATES, APRIL 15, 2000

Name		Rate
KO Corporate Bond Yield	- 3 Year	10
KO Interest Rate On Loans Of Nationwide Commercial Banks		8.57
KEPCO Bond 3 year	- Red. Yield	9.3
Korea Call Overnight	- Middle Rate	4.81
Korea Short Term Ben. Cert. 180 days	- Middle Rate	7.25
Korean Commercial Paper 91 days	- Middle Rate	7.3
Korean Treasury Bond 1 Year	- Red. Yield	8.38
Korean Treasury Bond 3 Year	- Red. Yield	9
Korean Treasury Bond 5 Year	- Red. Yield	9.34
South Korean Won To Euro (WMR)	- Exchange Rate	1062.323
South Korean Won To UK £ (WMR)	- Exchange Rate	1763.649
South Korean Won To US $ (WMR)	- Exchange Rate	1111.1
South Korean Won To 100japan.Yen (KO)	- Exchange Rate	1049.08

Source: Datastream.

Initial discussions with representatives from Fitch Ratings and Moody's had indicated that the Issuer Notes should be able to secure a BBB+/Baa2 rating.[1]

The Originating Banks

Each of the six originating banks was to be responsible for repurchasing the loans it had sold to KAMCO if obligors defaulted. (Exhibit 17 displays each bank's credit rating and its proportion of the NPLs.) The recourse obligations ranked *pari passu*[m] with any other unsecured debt of the banks and were reported in their accounts as contingent liabilities.[60] There was no obligation to raise loan loss provisions for such liabilities although Korean banks tended to make modest provisions against them (approximately one-fifth coverage) on a voluntary basis.[61]

---

[1] In analyzing such transactions, rating agencies took numerous factors into account, including: quantitative and qualitative characteristics of the obligor's credit worthiness; obligor diversification; recovery rates; timing of defaults and recoveries; maturity and average life of the securities; liquidity needs; collateral manager capabilities; and the legal robustness of the structure. Various cash flow scenarios were run on the basis of historical data on comparable assets. When asset pools were not sufficiently large or diverse to allow for meaningful statistical projections a "weakest link" approach was taken. Stress tests would be conducted to see what impact the default of specific obligors or groups of obligors would have on the structure. Finally, in the case of deals in emerging market countries, the agencies imposed 'sovereign ceilings' to reflect country-level risk factors such as currency convertibility and earnings repatriation. In general, sovereign ceilings meant that a deal within a particular jurisdiction could not attain a rating higher than that of the relevant sovereign.

[m] Latin meaning "with equal step," or more freely "at an equal pace or rate."

EXHIBIT 17

PUT OPTION BANK CONCENTRATION

Put Option Bank	Put Option Price in U.S. dollars	% of Total Put Option Price	Moody's	Fitch
KDB	243,182,287	59.9%	Baa2	BBB+
KEB	76,928,090	19.0%	Ba1	BBB−
Chohung	48,860,100	12.0%	Ba1	BBB−
Hanvit	25,226,530	6.2%	Ba1	BBB−
Shinhan	9,199,992	2.3%	Baa3	BBB
Kookmin	2,318,827	0.6%	Baa3	BBB
Total	405,715,825	100.0%		

Notes: The table shows
(i) the proportion of the total Put Option Prices as of the Cut-Off Date recoverable from each Put Option Bank in the event that such Put Options were exercised;
(ii) lists the long-term foreign currency credit ratings currently ascribed to the Put Option Banks by Moody's and Fitch. The Fitch ratings in relation to Chohung, Shinhan, and Kookmin are shadow ratings.

Source: KAMCO (Korea Asset Funding 2000-1 Limited Prospectus).

The most important originator was the Korea Development Bank, which accounted for almost 60% of the loans in the portfolio. The KDB was a public financial institution established in 1954 to provide credit to industries deemed strategically important. The bank's act defined its role as to "furnish and administer funds for the financing of major industrial projects in order to expedite industrial development and expansion of the national economy."[62] The KDB's total asset value was KRW 75.6 trillion in 1999. Completely owned by the government, KDB was financed by equity of KRW 6.2 trillion and also through bond issues, deposits and off-shore borrowing. Its average cost of debt was approximately 90bp above LIBOR.[63] Because of explicit government guarantees of support, the credit quality of the KDB was inherently linked to that of the sovereign, which paid very similar yields in the market. The 1997 crisis had left the Korea Development Bank with a substantial distressed assets problem. During 1998 the bank had sold NPLs with KRW 3 trillion in aggregate principal to KAMCO with recourse for KRW 1.3 trillion.[64] Over the following year approximately two thirds of the loans had been repurchased under recourse arrangements, leaving KRW 1 trillion in aggregate principal outstanding. At year end 1999 non-performing loans comprised approximately 17% of the total loan book.[65]

Like the KDB, the other five originating banks were among the largest in the country and together represented a major part of the financial system. As such the banks had great systemic importance and analysts felt that they enjoyed implicit governmental support and would be likely to receive external assistance in the event of financial distress.[66] However the individual performances of the banks were highly correlated and closely related to that of the economy as a whole. This meant that the simultaneous collapse of multiple banks in a new financial crisis was a scenario that credit analysts had to consider. In such a case the government's resources might be insufficient to rescue all of the troubled banks and it would be forced to prioritize. After the legally guaranteed KDB, Hanvit Bank and Cho Hung Bank would be the most likely to receive support as they made up 15% and 10% of the commercial bank market respectively.[67] The Korea Exchange Bank, although slightly smaller than Cho Hung, would also have a strong claim on the basis of its close relationship with the central bank and its important role in facilitating Korea's foreign trade. Even if an originating bank were to default and not be supported by the government, some recovery of monies owed could still be made by the servicer from both the bank and the obligor. Fitch's conservative estimate of recoveries for a large, systemically important bank was 40% after 18 months.[68] (Exhibit 18 summarizes financials and operating details for all six originating banks.)

THE DECISION

Chung sat back to ponder the possible consequences of going ahead with the deal. How would investors react? How would they conceive of and price the inherent credit and other risks? Were the investment bankers realistic in estimating a par yield of 200bp over LIBOR? The bankers had suggested that such a yield would allow the Notes to be marketed as "cheap Korea," yet an argument could be made that this spread was narrower than that on similar ABS offerings.[69] Although close comparables were hard to find, asset-backed bonds with BBB+/Baa2 ratings were currently yielding between 245bp and 270bp over LIBOR. (See Exhibit 19 for average default rates and Exhibit 20 for a history of Korean sovereign ratings.) The underlying assets for such securities tended to be of high credit quality, which was clearly not the case for the loans in KAMCO's pool. The would-be underwriters had responded to these concerns by pointing out that the senior ranking and other credit enhancements of the Notes gave them a pricing advantage over most ABS offerings, which tended to be subordinated. They also contended that investors would react well to the fact that deteriorations of credit quality would reduce the average life of the notes rather than extend it, which was generally the case for asset-backed paper. Even if he could assume that the target pricing would be achieved, Chung still had to ask himself what the effective costs to KAMCO would be. Would these costs accurately reflect the agency's cost of capital and could the deal be structured differently in order to reduce them? Alternatively, would it be cheaper to keep the loans on KAMCO's books for a longer period of time, or even to sell them to investors outright in an international auction?

Some of Chung's advisors had pointed out that the proposed securitization relied very heavily on the credit quality of KDB, yet the expected yield was well above that on the bank's unsecured bonds. They suggested that perhaps the NPLs in question could be more efficiently financed by having KDB issue bonds directly and then lend the money to KAMCO. The agency could then use the funds to pay down debt and purchase further NPLs, exactly as they would if the loans had been sold to the SPC and securitized. The NPLs could be held on KAMCO's books until they matured, or until they defaulted and were put back to the originating banks. Chung wondered if this might be a cheaper way to finance the loans. Even if it were cheaper, how could he reconcile this option with his belief that the most efficient means of handling NPLs was disposing of them rapidly?

Aside from securitizing or holding the loans, a third option was selling them off in another auction. The key advantage of employing auctions was that they allowed large amounts of assets to be presented to the market while minimizing overhead costs.[70] Previous auction costs had represented roughly 1% of the assets' sale price.[71] KAMCO's transparent auction processes had impressed foreign investors and substantial interest

EXHIBIT 18

SUMMARY FINANCIAL AND OPERATING DETAILS OF THE ORIGINATING BANKS

a. Korea Development Bank

	Won (millions)	USD
Consolidated Balance Sheet 1999		
Assets	80,582,875	70,353,479,000
Loans	44,862,352	39,167,411,000
Other	35,720,523	31,186,068,000
Liabilities	73,232,254	63,935,965,000
Equity	6,294,506	5,495,465,000
Total Liab. + Equity	79,526,760	69,431,430,000
Consolidated Income Statement 1999		
Interest Income	5,323,571	
Interest Expense	5,677,820	
Net Income	141,517	

Branches as of Dec 31, 1999	**Domestic**	**Overseas**
	35	10

Principal Activities
- Corporate restructuring
- Investment banking
- Direct investments: venture business and SMEs
- Capital markets transactions: Samurai bond, 144A bond, Euro MTNs
- Foreign exchange transactions in the international money markets
- Trade finance
- Lending and Project finance
- M&A and financial consulting services
- Mutual fund investment
- Trust business

b. Hanvit Bank

	Won (millions)	USD
Consolidated Balance Sheet 1999		
Assets	72,825,644	63,580,971,000
Loans	40,597,618	35,444,053,000
Other	32,228,026	28,136,918,000
Liabilities	70,149,474	61,244,521,000
Equity	2,419,801	2,112,625,000
Total Liab. + Equity	72,569,275	63,357,146,000

Branches as at Dec 31, 1999	**Domestic**	**Overseas**
	699	8

Principal Activities
- Consumer banking
- Middle market banking (for small- and medium-sized enterprise)
- Corporate banking
- International banking
- Investment banking

(Continued)

EXHIBIT 18   (Continued)

SUMMARY FINANCIAL AND OPERATING DETAILS OF
THE ORIGINATING BANKS

c. Korea Exchange Bank

	Won (millions)	USD
Consolidated Balance Sheet 1999		
Assets	47,468,294	41,442,548,000
Loans	27,192,532	23,740,643,000
Other	20,275,762	17,701,905,000
Liabilities	45,903,819	40,076,671,000
Equity	1,414,761	1,235,168,000
Total Liab. + Equity	47,318,580	41,311,893,000
Consolidated Income Statement 1999		
Interest Income	3,917,478	
Interest Expense	2,988,308	
Net Income	−823,411	

Branches as at Dec 31, 1999	Domestic
	305 (includes overseas)

Principal Activities
- Corporate banking
- Merger and acquisitions transactions
- Asset securitization
- Custody business
- Fund administration services to mutual funds and pension funds
- Retail banking, incl. electronic banking
- Trust business
- Credit card operations

d. Shinhan Bank

	Won (millions)	USD
Consolidated Balance Sheet 1999		
Assets	42,635,552	37,223,286,000
Loans	24,489,871	21,381,064,000
Other	18,145,681	15,842,222,000
Liabilities	39,714,066	34,672,661,000
Equity	2,853,762	2,491,498,000
Total Liab. + Equity	42,567,828	37,164,159,000
Consolidated Income Statement 1999		
Interest Income	3,283,348	
Interest Expense	2,544,164	
Net Income	113,927	

Branches as at Dec 31, 1999	Domestic	Overseas
	328	8

Principal Activities
- Retail banking
- Corporate banking (SMEs and large corporations)
- International banking

(Continued)

EXHIBIT 18 *(Continued)*

SUMMARY FINANCIAL AND OPERATING DETAILS OF THE ORIGINATING BANKS

e. Chohung Bank

	Won (millions)	USD
Consolidated Balance Sheet 1999		
Assets	46,939,185	40,980,605,000
Loans	24,899,471	21,738,669,000
Other	22,039,714	19,241,936,000
Liabilities	44,746,082	39,065,900,000
Equity	2,135,863	1,864,731,000
Total Liab. + Equity	46,881,945	40,930,631,000
Consolidated Income Statement 1999		
Interest Income	3,608,603	
Interest Expense	2,572,270	
Net Income	−746,322	

Branches as at Dec 31, 1999	Domestic	Overseas
	401 (+ 75 depository offices)	6

Principal Activities
- Deposit products, Won-denominated and foreign currency loans and overdraft facilities to large corporations that are affiliated with chaebol, small and medium sized enterprises
- Deposit products, consumer loans, credit card ervices, incl. credit card loans and electronic banking to retail customers
- Capital markets related businesses

f. Kookmin Bank

	Won (millions)	USD
Non-consolidated Balance Sheet 1999		
Assets	66,181,488	57,780,241,000
Loans	38,872,332	33,937,779,000
Other	27,309,156	23,842,462,000
Liabilities	62,609,607	54,661,784,000
Equity	3,371,881	3,118,457,000
Total Liab. + Equity	65,981,488	57,780,241
Non-consolidated Income Statement 1999		
Interest Income	6,122,100	
Interest Expense	4,215,645	
Net Income	107,901	

Branches as at Dec 31, 1999	Domestic	Overseas
	587	5

Source: KAMCO (Korea Asset Funding 2000-1 Limited Prospectus).

EXHIBIT 19

MOODY'S AVERAGE CUMULATIVE DEFAULT RATES FROM 1 TO 8 YEARS (PERCENT)

In Percent	Year 1	Year 2	Year 3	Year 4	Year 5	Year 6	Year 7	Year 8
Aaa	0.00	0.00	0.00	0.07	0.24	0.33	0.45	0.59
Aa1	0.00	0.00	0.00	0.28	0.28	0.47	0.47	0.47
Aa2	0.00	0.00	0.07	0.25	0.56	0.68	0.82	0.99
Aa3	0.08	0.13	0.23	0.36	0.50	0.68	0.68	0.68
A1	0.00	0.04	0.42	0.67	0.85	1.06	1.15	1.26
A2	0.00	0.03	0.18	0.49	0.75	0.99	1.13	1.55
A3	0.00	0.17	0.32	0.44	0.51	0.68	1.00	1.12
Baa1	0.05	0.33	0.67	1.07	1.46	1.71	2.16	2.53
Baa2	0.05	0.22	0.29	0.79	1.31	1.94	2.40	2.59
Baa3	0.35	0.85	1.45	2.41	3.09	3.90	4.91	5.89
Ba1	0.71	2.36	4.14	6.63	8.98	11.60	13.31	14.94
Ba2	0.59	2.93	5.69	8.41	10.79	12.59	14.35	15.49
Ba3	2.71	7.32	12.32	17.09	21.67	25.64	29.28	33.26
B1	3.75	9.77	15.97	21.74	27.28	32.84	37.78	41.32
B2	6.73	13.30	19.95	25.32	29.38	32.50	34.33	35.18
B3	13.20	21.91	28.48	33.10	37.44	40.47	43.01	47.54
Caa-C	19.42	26.07	30.59	34.01	37.72	42.91	42.91	48.92
Investment-Grade	**0.04**	**0.15**	**0.35**	**0.63**	**0.89**	**1.15**	**1.38**	**1.62**
Speculative-Grade	**4.37**	**9.07**	**13.65**	**17.83**	**21.67**	**25.14**	**27.98**	**30.63**
All Corporates	**1.41**	**2.91**	**4.35**	**5.67**	**6.80**	**7.80**	**8.59**	**9.32**

Source: Moody's Investors Service, "Historical Default Rates of Corporate Bond Issuers, 1920–1997," February 1998, Exhibit 29, page 28.

seemed to remain in the market.[72] Bidding in June 1999 had attracted 13 domestic and overseas participants, a previously unheard of level of competition.[73] As a result, the successful auction bidding ratio had been almost double that of the year before, with the most recent sale of secured loans realizing 43% of face value.[74] Chung wondered though whether auction sale would be an appropriate disposition method for this pool of loans given that it came with attached put options. Most of the loans previously auctioned did not have recourse to the originators. Would auction investors value the put options appropriately? How much would they be willing to pay for the entire pool? And would KAMCO be passing up an opportunity to make significant strides in developing the market for securitized NPLs if it sold these loans in an auction?

Chung also felt it important that he take a broader view on how the decision at hand fitted into KAMCO's overall plans for resolving Korea's non-performing loan problem. What was the long-term market potential for securitization of Korean NPLs, both for KAMCO and for private Korean financial institutions—and for public asset management agencies in other parts of Asia? What kind of a catalyst would it be for the de-

EXHIBIT 20

HISTORY OF KOREAN SOVEREIGN RATINGS: FITCH

Date	Long-term	Short-term	Outlook/Watch	Long currency rating long-term
29 Mar 2000	BBB+	F2	—	A
24 Jun 1999	BBB	F2	—	A−
26 Apr 1999	BBB−	F3	Rating Watch positive	A−
19 Jan 1999	BBB−	F3	—	A−
22 Dec 1998	BB+	B	Rating Watch positive	A−
19 Jun 1998	BB+	B	—	A−
3 Feb 1998	BB+	B	Rating Watch positive	A−
21 Jan 1998	B−	B	Rating Watch positive	BBB−
23 Dec 1997	B−	B	Rating Watch negative	BBB−
12 Dec 1997	BBB−	F3	Rating Watch negative	A
11 Dec 1997	BBB−	F3	Rating Watch negative	AA
26 Nov 1997	A	F2	—	AA
18 Nov 1997	A+	F1	—	AA+
27 Jun 1996	AA−	F1+	—	AAA

Source: Adapted from Fitch Ratings "Fitch—Complete Sovereign Rating History." Available at http://www.fitchratings.com/shared/sovereign_ratings_history.pdf. (Version accessed March 2004.)

velopment of the Korean distressed debt and ABS markets? How sustainable was cross-border securitization as a strategy for financing NPLs? Chung further wondered about the use of recourse obligations in the proposed deal and in KAMCO's other activities. How important were the put options to the success of the proposed offering? Were there any disadvantages to their use? What impact did they have on KAMCO's fulfillment of its mission and what role should they play in future purchase and disposition activities? Finally, how would a cross-border securitization affect Chung's aspirations to grow KAMCO into a world-class distressed debt specialist capable of competing with the leading international investment banks?

APPENDIX 1: THE LOGIC AND HISTORY OF SECURITIZING NON-PERFORMING LOANS

Securitization is the act of transforming illiquid assets into tradable securities.[75]

Securitization begins with a financial institution or corporation selling income-generating assets to a special purpose corporation (SPC), also known as a special purpose vehicle (SPV). The SPC, which exists solely for the purpose of the transaction, then sells securities to investors to finance the asset purchase. Over time the cash flows from the assets are collected by an appointed servicer and used to compensate the security owners for their investment. Because the assets have been legally separated from their original owner (the originator) the investors can assess the risks inherent in the asset cash flows without concern for the overall financial condition of the originator. For this separation of assets from originator to be effective the SPC must be bankruptcy remote and the asset transfer must qualify as a true sale so that the securitized assets cannot be claimed by the originator's estate in the event of a bankruptcy. Investors are also often granted default protection via the provision of various forms of credit enhancement including guarantees from the originator or third parties, irrevocable letters of credit from banks, subordinated tranches of securities that take the first losses, or an over-collateralized asset pool capable of generating more than the minimum necessary cash flows.

The advantage of this rather convoluted process of securitization is that it can realize economic gains for both the originator and the investor. This "alchemy of securitization" works through the exploitation of market inefficiencies.[76] By separating "asset risks" from "entity risks," securitized assets can often be financed more cheaply than if they were left on the balance sheets of originating firms.[77] Separation of risks reduces the informational disadvantage of investors who can more easily analyze the stand-alone assets than the overall operations of a firm.[78] Adding credit enhancements further reduces the yield required by investors and—in markets that are not perfectly efficient—the cost of providing such enhancement may be less than the savings it generates. Even if the required market inefficiencies are not present, securitization can still benefit originators by providing new sources of funding, and in the case of financial institutions, by moving assets off balance sheet to reduce regulatory capital requirements.[79] From the point of view of investors, securitized assets can offer yield pick-ups over straight debt instruments of comparable risk as well as providing new sources of portfolio diversification.[80]

Securitization technology was originally developed in the context of the mortgage market in the US during the 1970s, but was later expanded for use with many kinds of different assets. For securitization to make sense the underlying assets must be homogenous and their cash flows predictable. The focus of securitization tended to be on high quality performing assets. However, securitization also offers potential as an innovative source of financing for impaired assets.

Analytically, a securitization transaction for non-performing loans must meet certain conditions if it is to be successful.[81] Most important is having information on the underlying loans. Historical default and recovery rates that allow for future projections are necessary. The key is predictability rather than good rates per se because any level of delinquency can be accounted for in the asset-backed security (ABS) rating and pricing process so long as market participants feel they can make accurate forecasts. The cost of gathering and analyzing default rate information can be minimized if the loans are relatively homogenous in their terms, delinquency characteristics, and the nature of their obligors. Recovery rate information is even more important than default rates because it is safe to assume that a very high proportion of an NPL pool will default during the life of a deal. Recovery rates are easiest to predict if the obligations are collateralized by highly liquid assets such as well-located real estate and marketable securities.

The importance of loan homogeneity and liquid collateral suggests that securitization may be more appropriate in the case of non-performing residential mortgage loans than for tainted corporate paper. Indeed, even securitization of performing loans to all but the biggest and most well know corporations is a difficult process that has yet to be performed on a significant scale precisely because of the issues of default and recovery predictability.[82] Finally, it is critical that the pool of underlying loans be large and diverse enough to allow default and recovery predictions to be statistically meaningful. Over-concentration of obligors should also be avoided to ensure statistical accuracy.

If the above conditions are not met then securitization of NPLs may still be possible if a structure incorporates sufficient credit enhancement to overcome the unpredictable cash flow characteristics and obtain an acceptable credit rating.[83] Credit enhancements that involve guarantees or lines of credit from third parties can help to "take the story out of the deal" by allowing investors some leeway to ignore the complex and unpredictable underlying assets and concentrate instead on the credit quality of the enhancement provider.[84] Credit enhancement provided by originators can also facilitate successful NPL securitization by providing guarantees or recourse options that allow investors to analyze ABS offering in the same manner as the corporate bonds of the issuer. However, some commentators note that deals backed by originators do not qualify as 'pure' securitization because they do not transfer asset risk away from the originator.[85]

The use of securitization for disposing of non-performing loans was pioneered by the U.S. government agency Resolution Trust Corporation (RTC). The RTC was charged with resolving thrifts that had failed during the Savings and Loan Crisis in the 1990s. Despite the enormity of its task the RTC performed well during its six years of operation, resolving 747 failed thrifts and recovering $395 billion USD from assets with a face value of $456 billion USD.[86] Although the majority of the agency's recoveries came from bulk asset sales, auctions and performing mortgage securitizations, non-performing loan securitizations were also employed to open up new sources of funding and to spread the risks of NPLs to market participants willing to bear them in return for suitable compensation. The first such deal was the "N-1" NPL securitization of December 1992.[87] In this deal the RTC sold non-performing mortgage loans with a book value of US$ 350 million to an SPC. The SPC financed the purchase with $110 million USD in debt raised by Lehman Brothers. A 50% equity interest in the remaining asset cash flows was sold to Bankers Trust and Soros Realty, with the RTC providing the rest of the equity financing. With a debt to assets ratio of only 31%, this deal clearly made heavy use of the subordinated equity tranche as a means of enhancing the credit quality of the debt financing. Although the sale price of the equity was undisclosed it is likely that it was valued at substantially less than book value because of the poor asset quality, thus indicating considerable over-collateralization as well. However, although this deal broke new ground in applying securitization technology to NPLs, the high equity stake retained by the RTC suggests that the N-1 deal did not harness the full potential of securitization for removing asset risks from an originator's balance sheet. For this reason it may be more appropriate to describe the RTC's offering as a loss sharing arrangement than a true securitization.[88]

Securitization of "bad loans," following the RTC example, has occurred several times since the 1990s. "Bad banks" employing ABS techniques been used both for whole industries (such as Sweden's banking industry in the late 1990s) and for specific companies (such as German retail bank Dresdner Bank in 2001).

APPENDIX 2: SECURITIZATION IN KOREA

Unlike the United States, which possesses a common law system that proved fertile for the development of securitization, Korea's civil code prevented this financing technique until special legislation was passed.[89] While common law systems allow the application of new financial technologies so long as they are not prohibited by existing laws, civil codes prevent such activities until they have been explicitly authorized. For example, before the financial crisis in Korea it was impossible to set up a bankruptcy remote SPC that had unalienable ownership of the assets transferred to it by the originator. Therefore, in September 1998 the Korean government issued the Act on Asset Backed Securitization as part of its broader endeavors to improve the soundness of the financial system. The Act granted bankruptcy remoteness to SPCs used solely for securitization transactions registered with the Financial Supervisory Service (FSS).[90] Assets eligible for securitization include debt claims, real estate claims, and other property rights. In Korea, only certain governmental entities, financial institutions and major corporations are entitled to register securitizations. Registration requires the submission of a securitization plan to the FSC that provides information on the assets, their disposition, and the parties involved in the transaction. The plan must also appoint a qualified servicer who will manage the assets of the SPC without mixing them with its own assets and trustees who will discharge other required business functions. Once a plan has been approved for registration, the SPC will enjoy relief from restrictions on debt issuance that apply under the Commercial Code as well as breaks on property, acquisition, dividend and value-added taxes.[91] Withholding taxes on foreign currency bonds issued by Korean SPCs are also waived.[92]

One of the most important features of the ABS Act was that it clarified issues of true sale and perfection in the case of asset transfers to an SPC. Prior to the Act, the law did not easily differentiate between a true sale and a security interest.[93] This distinction is important because it determines whether the originator's estate may have a claim on the securitized assets in the event of bankruptcy. Application of the ABS law removes this uncertainty and makes the transfer a true sale so that the originator no longer has power over the assets and the purchaser fully bears their risks.[94] An exception is made in the case of contractual provisions that call for the originator to bear the asset risks for a specified period. Perfection of asset sales to SPCs is also facilitated by the ABS law. Asset transfers are considered perfected against third parties as soon as a securitization is registered. Perfection vis-à-vis obligors occurs as soon as the originator provides them with notice of the transfer of their obligations.[95] Obligor consent is not required for the transfer to be perfected.

Although the ABS Act has eliminated many of the legal impediments that previously prevented securitization in Korea, some complications remain in early 2004, particularly in terms of international ABS issuance. Because of several overlapping laws (the Secured Bond Trust Act of 1962 and the Securities and Exchange Act 1972, the Foreign Exchange Transaction Act 1998 and Foreigners Land Acquisition Act 1998) there are numerous complex restrictions on Korea SPCs with security interests in Korean assets issuing securities to foreigners.[96] To get around the onerous compliance requirements, dual SPC structures can be used with a Korean SPC only issuing notes to an offshore SPC that will in turn issue notes to multiple foreign investors who will enjoy the benefit of the security granted by the Korean SPC to the offshore SPC.

The effect of the ABS Act on the domestic securitization market was dramatic. From almost nothing in 1998, total ABS issuance grew to about KRW 6 trillion in 1999 and KRW 49 trillion in 2000.[97] Banks and government entities attempting to clean up impaired balance sheets by selling off non-performing assets were the dominant originators during this period. NPL deals made up 42.2% of total securitization in 1999.[98] Other assets packaged into ABS offerings by the financial sector included performing offshore loans owned by the Korea Export-Import Bank and Industrial Bank of Korea,[n] automobile leases originated by Samsung Finance Company, and residential mortgages held by the Korean Mortgage Company.[99] The corporate sector was also quick to take advantage of the opportunities presented by securitization. ABS offerings went from 14.5% of public corporate bonds issued in Korea in 1999 to around 70% in 2000.[100] The key drivers behind corporate interest were low credit ratings and a credit crunch that made sub-investment grade debt very expensive. At the peak of the crunch in late 2000 the spread between A+ and BBB-bonds was approximately 100bp wider than historical norms, creating a major incentive to issue highly rated ABS debt.[101]

Despite the enthusiastic adoption of foreign ABS techniques, securitization in Korea has tended to differ from the United States and Europe in its heavy dependence on originator and third party guarantees.[102] The offshore loan pool securitized by the Korea Export Import Bank in 1998 for example was 90% covered by governmental and bank guarantees.[103] The Industrial Bank of Korea's ABS issue was fully wrapped by an international monoline insurer.[104] Indeed, most Korean ABS offerings in the years immediately following the introduction of the ABS Act were heavily supported by guarantees.[105] While credit enhancement of securitizations via guarantees was common in many markets, the unique Korean feature was the almost complete reliance on these arrangements for the viability of a deal. Because guarantees tended to cover all or almost all of an asset pool, investors had no need to closely scrutinize the underlying claims and in effect made their lending decisions as if buying the bonds of the guarantor.[106] As a result contingent asset risk remained with ABS issuers to a greater extent than in Western markets.

---

[n] Offshore loans denominated in foreign currency were particularly attractive assets for securitization because they could be sold to foreign investors without currency risk complications. It was more difficult to securitize long-term won denominated assets for sale in foreign markets because risk management tools such as won-dollar swaps were not available for periods of greater than three years.

END NOTES

1. For discussions of Korea's financial crisis and its roots refer to Lindgren, C., et. al. 1999 "Financial Sector Crisis and Restructuring: Lessons from Asia," IMF Occasional Paper 188, International Monetary Fund: Washington, D.C.; and Balino, T. and Ubide, A., 1999. "The Korean Financial Crisis of 1997—A Strategy of Financial Sector Reform," IMF Working Paper WP/99/28. International Monetary Fund: Washington, D.C.

2. Lindgren, C., et. al. 1999. Pages 68–9.

3. Lindgren, C., et. al. 1999. Page 70.

4. Lindgren, C., et. al. 1999. Page 68.

5. Balino, T. and Ubide, A., 1999. Page 20.

6. Lindgren, C., et. al. 1999. Page 69.

7. Lindgren, C., et. al. 1999. Page 69.

8. Balino, T. and Ubide, A., 1999. Page 22.

9. Lindgren, C., et. al. 1999. Page 69.

10. Cooke, D., and Foley, J., 1999. "The Role of the Asset Management Entity: An East Asian Perspective." In Asian Development Bank, 1999. *Rising to the Challenge in Asia: A Study of Financial Markets*. Volume 2 Special Issues Asian Development Bank: Manila. Page 4.

11. Lindgren, C., et. al. 1999. Page 71.

12. Lindgren, C., et. al. 1999. Page 71.

13. Kim, D., 1999. "Bank Restructuring in Korea" in *Bank Restructuring in Practice*. Policy Paper No. 6. Bank for International Settlements: Basel. Page 144.

14. Kim, D., 1999. Page 147.

15. Kim, D., 1999. Page 149.

16. Deutsche Bank and UBS Warburg 2000. Korea Asset Funding 2000-1 Offering Prospectus. Page 71.

17. Korea Financial Supervisory Commission 2002 "BIS Ratios" available at http://www.fsc.go.kr. Last accessed March 2004.

18. Root, et. al., 2000, "Financial Sector Restructuring in East Asia" in Adams, C., Litman, R., Pomerleano, M., eds. *Managing Financial and Corporate Distress: Lessons from Asia*. Brookings Institution Press: Washington, DC. Page 207.

19. Kim, D., 1999. Page 157.

20. Cooke, D., and Foley, J., 1999. Page 35.

21. Lindgren, C., et. al. 1999. Page 72.

22. KAMCO, 2001. "Korea Asset Management Company Annual Report 2001." KAMCO: Seoul. Page 13.

23. Cooke, D., and Foley, J., 1999. Page 36.

24. Schuman, M., 1999 "Seoul's Bad-Loan Agency Dreams Big—KAMCO Does Well on Debt, But Critics See Hurdles; Goldman Sachs Is Model." *Wall Street Journal* (Eastern edition). November 2 1999. New York. Page A20.

25. Agrawala, A., et. al., 2000. "Korea Asset Funding 2000-1 Limited." Fitch Ratings. Available at ⟨www.fitchratings.com⟩. Last accessed November 2003. Page 4.

26. Deutsche Bank and UBS Warburg 2000. Pages 51–52.

27. Cooke, D., and Foley, J., 1999. Page 36.

28. Business Korea, 2000. "Success from Distress." *Business Korea*. February 2000. Vol. 17, Iss. 2. Seoul. Page 26.

29. Cooke, D., and Foley, J., 1999. Page 36.

30. Fung, B. et. al. 2004 "Public Asset Management Companies in East Asia: A Comparative Study" Financial Stability Institute Occasional Paper No. 3. Bank for International Settlements: Basel. Page 18.

31. Deutsche Bank and UBS Warburg 2000. Pages 51–52.
32. Agrawala, A., et. al., 2000. Page 4.
33. Agrawala, A., et. al., 2000. Page 4.
34. Deutsche Bank and UBS Warburg 2000. Page 53.
35. Cooke, D., and Foley, J., 1999. Page 37.
36. Cooke, D., and Foley, J., 1999. Page 36.
37. Agrawala, A., et. al., 2000. Page 4.
38. Cooke, D., and Foley, J., 1999. Pages 37, 58.
39. Cooke, D., and Foley, J., 1999. Page 37.
40. Business Korea, 2000.
41. Deutsche Bank and UBS Warburg 2000. Page 53.
42. Cooke, D., and Foley, J., 1999. Page 37; Business Korea, 2000; Deutsche Bank and UBS Warburg 2000. Page 53.
43. Business Korea, 2000.
44. Deutsche Bank and UBS Warburg 2000. Page 53.
45. Agrawala, A., et. al., 2000. Page 4.
46. Cooke, D., and Foley, J., 1999. Page 37.
47. Davies, M. "News—Asia: KAMCO's coming" *Asset Securitization Report*. July 3, 2000. Available at ⟨www.asreport.com⟩. Last accessed March 2004.
48. Business Korea, 2000.
49. Business Korea, 2000.
50. Business Korea, 2000.
51. Schuman, M., 1999.
52. Business Korea, 2000.
53. The following details of the ABS offering are taken from Deutsche Bank and UBS Warburg 2000.
54. Deutsche Bank and UBS Warburg 2000. Page 54.
55. Agrawala, A., et. al., 2000. Page 2.
56. Agrawala, A., et. al., 2000. Pages 6–7.
57. Deutsche Bank and UBS Warburg 2000. Pages 60–61.
58. Deutsche Bank and UBS Warburg 2000. Page 20.
59. Agrawala, A., et. al., 2000. Page 8.
60. Kothari, V. 2000. "Chat on Securitization of Non-Performing Loans (Special Reference to KAMCO)." Available at ⟨www.vinodkothari.com⟩. Last accessed April 2004.
61. Fitch, 2002. "Korean Banks' Asset Quality: Fact or Fiction" Fitch Ratings. Available at ⟨www.fitchratings.com⟩, last accessed March 2004. Page 3.
62. Liang, T., and Loh, M., 2002. "Korea Development Bank" ABN-AMRO: Singapore. Page 1.
63. Kothari, V., 2000.
64. Deutsche Bank and UBS Warburg 2000. Page 63.
65. Liang, T., and Loh, M., 2002. Page 11.
66. Agrawala, A., et. al., 2000. Page 9.
67. Agrawala, A., et. al., 2000. Page 9.
68. Agrawala, A., et. al., 2000. Page 10.
69. Wright, C., 2000. "KAMCO leads region with ABS landmark," *AsiaMoney*. September 2000. Available at ⟨www.asiamoney.com⟩. Last accessed November 2003.
70. Lim, A., 1998. "The S&L Crisis Revisited: Exporting An American Model To Resolve Thailand's Banking Problems." *Duke Journal of Comparative and International Law*. Fall 1998. Page 358.

71. Casewriter's estimate.

72. Song, K., 2003. "Looking Beyond Korea's Bad Debt." *Far Eastern Economic Review*. July 31, 2003. Vol 166. Iss. 30. Hong Kong. Page 36.

73. Business Korea, 2000.

74. Business Korea, 2000.

75. This analytical discussion of securitization is drawn mostly from Giddy, I., 2000. "Asset Securitization in Asia," available at ⟨http://pages.stern.nyu.edu/~igiddy/ABS/absasia.pdf⟩, last accessed in March 2004.

76. Schwarcz, S., 1994. "The Alchemy of Asset Securitization." *Stanford Journal of Business and Finance 1*, 133, 154.

77. Dvorak, Y. 2001. "Transplanting Asset Securitization: Is the Grass Green Enough on the Other Side?" *Houston Law Review* (38) 51. Page 550.

78. Giddy, I., 2000. Page 17.

79. Giddy, I., 2000. Page 17.

80. Giddy, I., 2000. Page 20.

81. The discussion of NPL securitization requirements is drawn from Cao, H., 2003. "Asset Securitization: Is it a Resolution Options for China's Non-Performing Loans?" *Brooklyn Journal of International Law* (28) 565. Page 584.

82. See the discussion of Fremont Financial Corporation in Crane, D. 1995. "The Transfer of Economic Resources" in Crane, D. et. al. eds. *The Global Financial System: A Functional Perspective*. Harvard Business School Press: Boston.

83. Cao, H., 2003. Page 585.

84. Giddy, I., 2000. Page 9.

85. Giddy, I., 2001. "Financial Institution Risk Management: The Impact of Securitization." Paper Presented at Seminar on Risk Management in Financial Institutions, Sogang University, Seoul, October 2001. Available at ⟨http://giddy.org/riskandabs.htm⟩. Last accessed April 2004.

86. Foust, D., 1996 "The RTC's Epitaph: It Worked." *Business Week*. January 15, 1996, No. 3458. Page 29.

87. Cao, H., 2003. Page 588.

88. Marshall, J., 1993. "Learning from the RTC." *United States Banker*. September 1993. Vol. 103, Iss. 9. New York. Page 28.

89. Cao, H., 2003. Pages 589–90.

90. Cao, H., 2003. Page 593.

91. Lester, T., Asaria, M., and Van der Linden, U., 2002. "Securitization: Korea and Taiwan follow Japanese lead." *International Financial Law Review*, Oct 2002 v21 i10 p22(5).

92. Lester, T., Asaria, M., and Van der Linden, U., 2002.

93. Yoon. E., and Gilligan, P., 2000. "Investment Grade Korea Revives Securitization." *International Financial Law Review*, Feb 2000 v19 i2 p34(4).

94. Yoon. E., and Gilligan, P., 2000.

95. Yoon. E., and Gilligan, P., 2000.

96. Lester, T., Asaria, M., and Van der Linden, U., 2002.

97. Jong-Goo Yi, 2001. "Trends and issues in securitization in Korea." *International Financial Law Review* (2425), April 1, 2001.

98. Lee and Ko "Securitization in Korea" available at ⟨http://www.lawleeko.com/pdf/Article_MHL_1.pdf⟩, last accessed March 2004.

99. Yoon. E., and Gilligan, P., 2000.

100. Jong-Goo Yi, 2001.

101. Kim Young-Min, 2001 "New borrowing options through ABS." *Business Korea*: Seoul. Vol. 18, Iss. 4; 26 (2).

102. Korea Industry Update, 2000. "Finance: Korea's Problem Assets Still Hanging Around, S&P Reports." *Korea Industry Update.* August 18, 2000, Page 11.

103. Yoon. E., and Gilligan, P., 2000.

104. Yoon. E., and Gilligan, P., 2000.

105. Chu, V., 2000 "Korean Banks Press on with NPLs." *Asset Securitization Report.* January 31, 2000; and Chu, V., 1999 "Domestic ABS Takes Off in Asia—Well, Kind of." *Asset Securitization Report.* September 20, 1999.

106. Kim Young-Min, 2001; Chu, V., 1999; Chu, V. 2000.

13

Nexgen: Structuring Collateralized Debt Obligations (CDOs)

Luc Giraud, CEO of the structured finance solutions provider Nexgen Financial Solutions, put down the phone. It was January 2004, and he had just received a request from the bank ABC. The call had concerned a client that ABC couldn't fully serve on its own. They hoped Nexgen could help with one of its tailor-made solutions.

ABC's client wanted to add AAA-rated bonds to its portfolio, but ABC had not been able to find suitably priced top-rated bonds in the market. Instead of buying the bonds directly from the market, ABC now wondered if Nexgen couldn't find a solution. Giraud's contact at ABC had explained the situation, "There are not enough triple-As out there since most are held by buy-and-hold investors. We do however own plenty of lower-grade bonds already. Could you find a way to increase their credit quality? We want to be able to give our client returns as if they held top grade bonds."

Nexgen had been founded three years earlier and marketed structured capital solutions with a focus on tailor-made financing and risk transfer services. An assignment like this was exactly what they were created to do and Giraud was certain they could find a solution for ABC's client. Once they found a structure, though, they would also have to figure out what a fair fee for their services would be.

NEXGEN FINANCIAL SOLUTIONS

Nexgen Financial Solutions was established in Dublin in April 2001 by Luc Giraud and Ravi Viswanathan. The two founders brought experience from the structured finance

Professors George Chacko and Peter Hecht, Professor Marti G. Subrahmanyam of the Stern School of Business at New York University, Executive Director Vincent Dessain, and Research Associate Anders Sjöman of the HBS Europe Research Center prepared this case. Some names and data have been disguised for confidentiality. HBS cases are developed solely as the basis for class discussion. Cases are not intended to serve as endorsements, sources of primary data, or illustrations of effective or ineffective management.

industry and especially M&A firms in London and Paris. As a structured finance solutions provider, Nexgen's marketing focused on tailor-made financing and risk transfer solutions to clients that it believed were not well served by the traditional investment banks. The company positioned itself between the banking and the reinsurance sectors, with a staff of about 50 people that came from structured finance, equity and commodity derivatives, as well as reinsurance markets. The group's solutions then mixed techniques from these sectors into multi-layered transactions.

The client base consisted primarily of large international companies, insurance firms, European and Asian mid-market companies and high net worth individuals. Nexgen's transactions normally came from mergers and acquisition activities, the treasury or corporate finance departments of companies, or private financing situations. Some solutions helped clients undertake strategic equity acquisitions or disposals, using equity swaps or variable share forward structures. Other solutions were meant to raise collateralized financing without affecting the client's balance sheet. Nexgen combined techniques from both the capital and the insurance market, like strategic equity structures and alternative risk transfer.

However, the company stayed away from taking any directional views, and instead structured its solutions on financial engineering and risk management skills. The group also carried out arbitrage and financial transactions on its own account in order to raise its commercial and risk expertise. These transactions were almost always comparable to those that might come out of work that the company did with its clients.

At year end 2002, the Nexgen group had a total capitalization of $194 million. Exhibit 1 shows the group's financials.

Group and Ownership Structure

The Nexgen group was organized around Dublin-based holding company Nexgen Financial Holdings. (See Exhibit 2 for group structure.) The main subsidiaries were Nexgen Re that engaged in financial reinsurance; Nexgen Capital, the group's operating arm for capital markets transactions, which also carried on its balance sheet the various risks from the transactions; and Nexgen Financial Solutions, the marketing arm that structured and prepared transactions for the other subsidiaries. The group had its head office in Dublin, with principal branches in Paris and Singapore.

Given these varied locations, staff members had to obtain relevant licenses from the Central Bank of Ireland, the Department of Employment, Trade and Enterprise of Ireland, or the Monetary Authority of Singapore. The various companies in the group were likewise authorized by Irish or Singaporean financial regulatory authorities.

Funding for the group had originally come from GK Goh Holdings, an Asian investment services group, and Singapore Technologies, now Temasek Holdings, a diversified industrial group and the investment arm of the Singaporean state. In addition, the individual founders had also contributed funds. In April 2002, the group had brought on two further strategic investors: Luxembourg-based Athena Private Equity and Ixis-CIB, now a subsidiary of the French Double-A rated mutual bank Groupe Caisse d'Epargne. The new investors gave Nexgen an injection of $104 million in additional capital. By the end of 2003, staff still held 22% of the capital, with all shareholders locked into non-sale agreements until the end of 2005. Exhibit 3 shows the full ownership situation.

Business Model

Nexgen's business model was based on the group's ability to realize value from the solutions that it implemented for its clients. This in turn built on the group's financial and

EXHIBIT 1

NEXGEN FINANCIALS

Consolidated Balance Sheet	31-Dec-03	31-Dec-02	31-Dec-01
Assets			
Cash at Bank and in hand	5,209	3,172	938
Deposits with financial institutions	117,048	123,516	81,243
Trading securities	394,672	123,629	40,297
Derivative financial instruments	102,436	43,607	3,056
Reinsurer's share of technical provision	—	745	—
Debtors	2,179	3,112	679
Tangible fixed assets	913	1,162	1,248
Total Assets	622,457	298,943	127,461
Liabilities			
Trading securities - short positions	112,555	30,746	3,981
Derivative financial instruments	90,301	45,670	9,335
Loans from financial institutions	211,384	22,575	25,587
Reinsurance liabilities	—	1,208	—
Creditors	5,996	4,963	1,933
Total Liabilities	420,236	105,162	40,836
Net Assets	202,221	193,781	86,625
Capital and reserves: Preference shares	—	—	277
Non-equity interests	—	—	277
Called up share capital	1,861	1,861	589
Share premium	187,632	187,632	85,635
Profit and loss account	12,664	4,248	154
Other reserves	64	40	−30
Equity shareholder's funds	202,221	193,781	86,348
Total shareholders' funds	**202,221**	**193,781**	**86,625**

Cash Flow	Year ended 31 Dec 02	Year ended 31 Dec 02	Year ended 31 Dec 01
Net cash outflow from operating activities	−3,368	−57,812	−5,359
Returns on investment and servicing of finance			
Interest income	—	—	1,871
Taxation			
Taxation paid	−748	−278	—
Capital expenditure			
Additions to tangible fixed assets	−315	−395	−1,409
Acquisitions and disposals			
Net cash outflow	—	—	−1,561
Cash acquired with subsidiary undertaking	—	—	21
Cash outflow bef. mgmt of liquid resources & financing	−4,431	−58,485	−6,437
Management of liquid resources			
Increase in short term bank deposits	6,468	−42,273	−79,126
Financing			
Issue of preference shares	—	−277	27,667
Issue of equity shares	—	103,269	58,834
Increase in cash			
Cash at bank	2,037	2,234	938

Source: Nexgen Annual Reports 2002 and 2003.

EXHIBIT 2

NEXGEN GROUP STRUCTURE

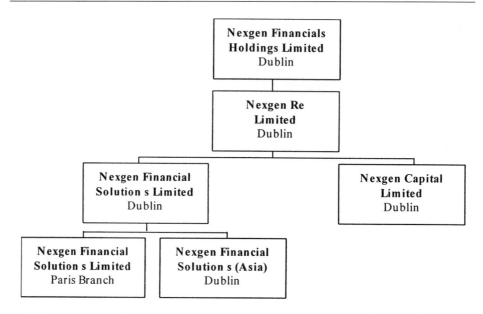

Note: The main operating companies incorporated and regulated in Ireland. All companies 100% owned by Nexgen Financial Holdings Limited.

Source: Nexgen, http://www.nexgenfs.com/a_structure.htm, accessed 16 January 2004.

EXHIBIT 3

SHAREHOLDER STRUCTURE

Share holder	% Voting rights	No. Shares
Ordinary shares		
Ixis-CIB	38.70%	90,000,000
Singapore Technologies	20.64%	48,000,000
GK Goh	15.05%	35,000,000
Athena	4.10%	9,523,810
Nexgen employees	1.51%	3,500,00
Founders share		
Nexgen founders	20.00%	110,708

Source: Nexgen Directors' Report and Financial Statements 2002.

organizational capacity to act as a principal, accepting risks on behalf of its clients. In fact, Nexgen took most of the risk from its transactions onto its *own* balance sheet, and did not try to push it on. This approach was a key part of the company's business model. The executive managers believed it made Nexgen more credible in the eyes of its clients. Explained Giraud, "As a company, confidentiality is everything for us—and we can guarantee it since we don't pass on the risk directly."

Still, according to the Nexgen management, the company managed to keep an overall satisfactory return/risk profile by unbundling the various risks of a transaction and keeping only the ones it was comfortable holding. Explained Charles Monneron of Nexgen's Singapore office,

> Typically, a well-structured transaction will be able to stand strong stressing of parameters governing the residual risks in the balance sheet without entering into negative territory. In other words, the transaction creates its own capital cushion.

Compared to more traditional investment banks, Giraud believed that Nexgen differed in several ways. He explained,

> We provide clients with customized risk management solutions. We start from the basis of what they need and not from the product. All our products are tailored to clients' particular situations. We also have an additional edge over bigger commercial and investment banks that do structured finance, since this is the *only* thing we do. Our clients know that we have no conflict of interest. We don't do business across the board like the banks; we don't do lending, dealing and financial management. We also don't try to maximize each individual deal, looking for cheap quick profits. Instead, since almost everyone who works here is a shareholder in the company, we take more of a long term view.
>
> Some people sometimes refer to us as a hedge fund. This is wrong, we think. We are in-between an investment bank and a hedge fund. I am convinced hedge funds are going to be the new investment banks. It will happen whenever the fed starts to regulate hedge funds.

With customized solutions and risk management techniques playing such an important role, the founding managers put a high value on mathematics and quantitative analysis. They believed that innovations came from combining the research done in universities with the problems encountered in the commercial world.

Risk Management Principles

Even though the management did not refer to the company as a hedge fund, risks that affected hedge funds also played a role for Nexgen in its transactions. Typical risks included correlation, liquidity, volatility and model risk. For whatever risk that Nexgen took on its own balance sheet, it used hedging techniques to hedge out as much of the risk as possible. Its risk management policy was to eliminate as much risk as possible from the transactions that the company entered into. In the end, the group wanted to be left with only the two risks with which it was comfortable holding on its own balance sheet: correlation risk and model risk.

The basic principle for managing risk was to unbundle the various risk components of a transaction, so that these could be handled by specialized units in the Nexgen organization. These units were also independent from the structuring or trading teams.

Before entering into any transaction, all present and anticipated risks of that transaction were analyzed in detail by the Nexgen teams. A proprietary in-house valuation and reporting system, in addition to external risk management software tools, had been designed to price, measure and hedge the risks of any type of structure whatever the underlying instrument.

For risks that could be traded on the market—hedgeable risks—the group studied how the risk most effectively could be hedged, given the liquidity of the market. Different techniques were used to mitigate counterparty credit risk and concentration risks, including credit default swaps (CDSs), and special purpose vehicles, SPVs. (SPVs were legal entities especially set-up for specific transactions, and normally incorporated in offshore tax havens, such as the Cayman Islands.)

After the execution and initial hedging of the principal transactions, resulting risks were managed and controlled within a system of limits. Each identifiable risk (equity, interest rate, foreign exchange, volatility, correlation, credit, etc) was given a maximum risk limit. Sensitivities for hedgeable risks and stress tests for diversifiable risks were closely monitored. Nexgen was currently also implementing a Value-at-Risk (VaR) system, with measurements of the maximum losses likely to incur on portfolios during a certain period.

The risk limits were managed and controlled through the group's risk management process. A specific Risk Management unit monitored the risks and executed market transactions required to keep the risks within their limits. A separate Risk and Results Reporting unit monitored the limits and produced Profit-and-Loss analyses for each trade. Higher up, the Board of Directors approved all limits, and also appointed in-house Risk Controllers to monitor compliance with the limits.

COLLATERALIZED DEBT OBLIGATIONS (CDOS) AND CREDIT DEFAULT SWAPS (CDSS)

One of the instruments that Nexgen frequently used for its customized financial solutions was Collateralized Debt Obligations. CDOs were generally defined as a securitization of corporate obligations or credit risk, and were normally based on corporate loans and securities. The instrument helped the issuer pool diverse risks, regroup them, and then disperse them into the capital markets.

More than anything else, it was the underlying asset that defined a CDO. CDOs were normally based on commercial loans, corporate bonds, emerging market debt and also on other CDOs. As a term, CDO also included several other fixed income instruments, such as Collateralized Loan Obligation (CLOs, based on bank loans to corporate clients); Collateralized Bond Obligation (CBOs, based on bonds); and Collateralized Mortgage Obligations (CMOs, based on private or commercial mortgage loans).

The risks that came from the underlying assets in the CDO were diversified by creating several layers of securities, so called "tranches." Each tranche would have its own risk and return profile, as well as a different priority in the event of default. By offering tranches with different risk profiles, an issuer could attract various types of investors. Investors could then in turn customize their credit risk exposure by risk, reward and maturity. The highest rated tranches of a CDO issue were known as senior fixed or floating rate notes, followed by mezzanine fixed or floating rate notes. The last tranche was known as subordinated notes. (See Exhibit 4 for a typical transaction setup.)

Depending on the motivation of the sponsor of the transaction, CDOs could be classified in one of two ways: as balance sheet or arbitrage CDOs. Balance sheet CDOs could be initiated by, for instance, a commercial bank that wanted to sell assets or trans-

EXHIBIT 4

GENERIC CDO STRUCTURE

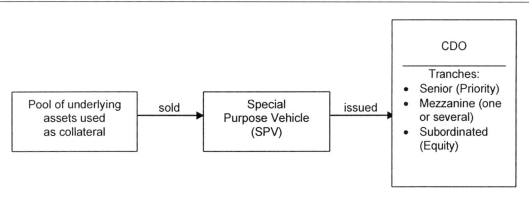

Source: Casewriters.

fer the risk of the assets. In this way the bank moved the risks off the balance sheet and freed up capital for further lending or to meet regulatory capital requirements. Arbitrage CDOs, in contrast, had as their primary purpose to earn the sponsor a spread between the yield offered on the collateral and the payments made to the various tranches in the structure.

In addition to CDOs, Nexgen also often made use of another credit derivative, known as Credit Default Swap (CDS).[1] In a CDS agreement, a party looked for protection against a credit event, such as a default. The party used the CDS to buy protection from another party for this credit event. The CDS thus shifted the credit risk exposure from the credit protection buyer to the seller. (In industry jargon, the party buying the protection was going short the credit; conversely the party selling the protection was going long the credit event risk.) In exchange for receiving protection, the protection buyer paid a periodic fee to the protection seller until the contract expired or a credit event occurred. If a credit event occurred, the protection seller would have to pay out the initial amount.

FINDING A SOLUTION

With the needs of ABC's client in mind, Giraud and his team set out to find a solution that would give the client "synthetic" AAA-bonds, or bonds that although they were not literal AAA-bonds would have similar risk/return characteristics. Using a CDO structure seemed like an obvious solution for this problem. ABC had a number of lower grade bonds (see Exhibit 5 for a complete list) from which Nexgen could create the CDO. Actually creating the CDO meant setting up a Special Purpose Vehicle (SPV), which would issue the actual CDO, using the lower-grade bonds as collateral.

[1] For a detailed look at credit default swaps, see George Chacko and Eli Peter Strick; "First American Bank: Credit Default Swaps," HBS Case No. 9-203-033 (Boston: Harvard Business School Publishing, 2002).

EXHIBIT 5

NEXGEN SAMPLE BOND PORTFOLIO

Legal name	Spread 5 year	Recovery Rate	Default Probability	Industry Sector	Rating
Akzo Nobel NV	24.8	0.45	2.2343%	Chemicals, Plastics & Rubber	A−
Alcoa Inc	26	0.4	2.1480%	Mining, Steel, Iron & Nonprecious Metals	A−
Ambac Financial Group Inc	29.3	0.35	2.2336%	Insurance	AA
AMP Group Holdings Limited	22	0.3	1.5616%	Insurance	A−
Anglo American Plc	26.8	0.5	2.6514%	Mining, Steel, Iron & Nonprecious Metals	A−
AT&T Wireless Services Inc	23.8	0.45	2.1450%	Telecommunications	A
Australian Gas Light Co.	21.5	0.4	1.7789%	Oil & Gas	A
Axa SA	24.8	0.35	1.8932%	Insurance	A
BAA PLC	18	0.3	1.2791%	Personal Transportation	A+
Bank of America Corp	17.5	0.5	1.7378%	Banking	A+
Bayer AG	25.5	0.45	2.2968%	Chemicals, Plastics & Rubber	A
BCE Inc	26.5	0.4	2.1889%	Telecommunications	A
Bear Stearns Companies Inc	29.3	0.35	2.2336%	Finance	A
Boeing Capital Corp	26.8	0.3	1.8997%	Finance	A
Boots Group Plc	60.5	0.5	5.9054%	Retail Stores	A+
Bristol-Myers Squibb Co	19.8	0.45	1.7871%	Healthcare, Education & Childcare	A+
BT Group Plc	52.8	0.4	4.3232%	Telecommunications	A−
Cargill Inc	15.5	0.35	1.1866%	Farming & Agriculture	A+
Carnival Corp	27.5	0.3	1.9489%	Personal Transportation	A−
Centrica Plc	28.3	0.5	2.7981%	Utilities	A
Chubb Corp	26.5	0.45	2.3860%	Insurance	A
CIT Group Inc	34.3	0.4	2.8258%	Finance	A
Compagnie de Saint-Gobain	28.8	0.35	2.1958%	Containers, Packaging & Glass	A−
Computer Sciences Corp	20.5	0.3	1.4557%	Electronics	A
Countrywide Home Loans Inc	46.5	0.5	4.5643%	Banking	A
CVS Corp	19.5	0.45	1.7602%	Retail Stores	A−
Diageo Plc	25.8	0.4	2.1316%	Beverage, Food & Tobacco	A
Diamond Offshore Drilling Inc	30.8	0.35	2.3469%	Oil & Gas	A−
Dow Chemical Co	26	0.3	1.8434%	Chemicals, Plastics & Rubber	A−
Dresdner Bank AG	16	0.5	1.5898%	Banking	A
E.ON AG	19.5	0.45	1.7602%	Chemicals, Plastics & Rubber	AA−
EnCana Corp	37	0.4	3.0455%	Oil & Gas	A−
Endesa SA	28.3	0.35	2.1580%	Oil & Gas	A
Energie Baden-Wuerttemberg	20.3	0.3	1.4416%	Utilities	A
EADS NV	28	0.5	2.7688%	Aerospace & Defense	A

(Continued)

EXHIBIT 5 *(Continued)*

NEXGEN SAMPLE BOND PORTFOLIO

Legal name	Spread 5 year	Recovery Rate	Default Probability	Industry Sector	Rating
Exelon Corporation	31.5	0.45	2.8310%	Utilities	A−
Export-Import Bank Of Korea	32.5	0.4	2.6792%	Finance	A−
Federal National Mortgage	20.3	0.35	1.5518%	Finance	AAA
General Electric Capital Corp	24.5	0.3	1.7378%	Finance	AAA
Goldman Sachs Group Inc	28.8	0.5	2.8470%	Finance	A+
Hammerson Plc	37	0.45	3.3187%	Finance	A−
Hannover Rueckversicherungs	23	0.4	1.9020%	Insurance	AA−
Hartford Finl. Services Group	42	0.35	3.1893%	Insurance	A−
Hewlett-Packard Co	25.5	0.3	1.8082%	Electronics	A−
Honeywell International Inc	17.3	0.5	1.7181%	Aerospace & Defense	A
Hutchison Whampoa Ltd.	53	0.45	4.7262%	Diversified/Conglomerate Manufacturing	A−
Iberdrola SA	21.8	0.4	1.8035%	Utilities	A+
International Lease Finance	37	0.35	2.8139%	Insurance	AA−
JP Morgan Chase & Co	29	0.3	2.0543%	Banking	A+
Korea Electric Power Corp	30.8	0.5	3.0423%	Utilities	A−
Korea Highway Corp	38	0.45	3.4071%	Buildings & Real Estate	A−
Korea Tobacco & Ginseng	27	0.4	2.2298%	Beverage, Food & Tobacco	BBB
Kraft Foods Inc	24.5	0.35	1.8705%	Grocery	A−
Lehman Brothers Holdings Inc	28	0.3	1.9841%	Finance	A
MBIA Insurance Corp	32.5	0.5	3.2080%	Insurance	AAA
Merrill Lynch & Co Inc	27.5	0.45	2.4751%	Finance	A+
National Grid Transco Plc	26.8	0.4	2.2135%	Utilities	A
Omnicom Group Inc	25.5	0.35	1.9462%	Diversified/Conglomerate Service	A−
Petroliam Nasional Bhd	24	0.3	1.7026%	Oil & Gas	A−
Peugeot SA	26	0.5	2.5731%	Personal Transportation	A−
POSCO	32	0.45	2.8754%	Mining, Steel, Iron & Nonprecious Metals	A−
Prudential Financial Inc	30	0.4	2.4751%	Insurance	A−
Publishing & Broadcasting Ltd	27.5	0.35	2.0976%	Broadcasting & Entertainment	A−
Radian Group Inc	44.3	0.3	3.1245%	Insurance	A
Reed Elsevier Plc	28.3	0.5	2.7981%	Printing & Publishing	A−
Reuters Group Plc	28.5	0.45	2.5642%	Diversified/Conglomerate Service	A
Rio Tinto Plc	20	0.4	1.6556%	Mining, Steel, Iron & Nonprecious Metals	A+
RWE AG	20.5	0.35	1.5670%	Utilities	A+

(Continued)

EXHIBIT 5 *(Continued)*

NEXGEN SAMPLE BOND PORTFOLIO

Legal name	Spread 5 year	Recovery Rate	Default Probability	Industry Sector	Rating
Samsung Electronics Co Ltd	30.3	0.3	2.1456%	Electronics	A−
SBC Communications Inc	28.5	0.5	2.8177%	Telecommunications	A
Schlumberger Ltd	19	0.45	1.7154%	Oil & Gas	A+
Scottish Power Plc	23.8	0.4	1.9677%	Utilities	A−
Siemens AG	15.3	0.35	1.1714%	Diversified/Conglomerate Manufacturing	AA−
Singtel Optus Pty Limited	22	0.3	1.5616%	Telecommunications	A+
Sk Telecom Co Ltd	33.3	0.5	3.2859%	Telecommunications	A
Skandia Forsakrings AB	50	0.45	4.4636%	Insurance	BBB
Solvay SA	20.5	0.4	1.6967%	Chemicals, Plastics & Rubber	A
Southwest Airlines Co	39.5	0.35	3.0018%	Personal Transportation	A
Statoil ASA	16.8	0.3	1.1943%	Oil & Gas	A
STMicroelectronics NV	27.8	0.5	2.7493%	Electronics	A−
Suez	29	0.45	2.6087%	Utilities	A−
Telenor SA	18.8	0.4	1.5569%	Telecommunications	A−
Tesco Plc	16.3	0.35	1.2476%	Grocery	A+
Textron Financial Corp	26	0.3	1.8434%	Diversified/Conglomerate Manufacturing	A−
Textron Inc	23	0.5	2.2789%	Aerospace & Defense	A−
Transocean Inc.	35	0.45	3.1416%	Oil & Gas	A−
Unilever NV	16	0.4	1.3262%	Personal, Food, and Misc. Services	A+
Universal Corp	25.5	0.35	1.9462%	Beverage, Food & Tobacco	A−
UST Inc	25.8	0.3	1.8293%	Beverage, Food & Tobacco	A
Vattenfall AB	26.8	0.5	2.6514%	Utilities	A−
Verizon Global Fdg Corp	24	0.45	2.1629%	Telecommunications	A+
Viacom Inc	38	0.4	3.1268%	Broadcasting & Entertainment	A−
Volkswagen AG	63.5	0.35	4.7901%	Automobile	A−
Wachovia Corp	16.5	0.3	1.1730%	Banking	A
Washington Mutual Inc	38	0.5	3.7427%	Banking	A−
Wells Fargo & Co	17	0.45	1.5359%	Banking	AA−
Woodside Petroleum Limited	26	0.4	2.1480%	Oil & Gas	A−
Wyeth	45.3	0.35	3.4364%	Healthcare, Education & Childcare	A
XL Capital Ltd	39.5	0.3	2.7898%	Insurance	A+
Zurich Insurance Co	30.3	0.5	2.9935%	Insurance	A

Source: Adapted by case authors from Nexgen material.

EXHIBIT 6

S&P DEFAULT RATES (AVERAGE RATES FOR 2003)

Maturity	4	5	7	10
AAA	0.19	0.30	0.52	0.99
AA	0.57	0.78	1.20	1.99
A	0.81	1.14	1.81	3.04
BBB	1.81	2.52	3.94	6.08
BB	9.49	11.06	14.20	17.47
B	21.45	23.02	26.15	28.45

Note: 5 year rate interpolated between 4 and 7 year rates by Nexgen.

Source: Adapted by casewriters from Nexgen and Standard & Poor's.

Creating the different tranches of the CDO was key to the success of the solution. Each tranche would carry its own risk and reward profile, based on its probability of default. The highest tranche should have close to no credit risk, giving it a triple-A grade. This tranche would then go to the ABC client, who thus effectively received the AAA-notes that it wanted. The lower tranche, which held a higher risk of default, would be given to Nexgen to keep on its balance sheet.[2]

The primary task for Nexgen was to decide on the structure of the CDO, with the main objective of giving the top tranche the equivalent of an AAA-rating. (See Exhibit 6 for Standards & Poor's default rates for bonds of various ratings.) One important input into this decision seemed to be the correlation structure among the various bonds in the CDO.

Secondly, Nexgen would have to determine the value of the lowest equity-like tranche that it would keep on its balance sheet. In essence, the value of this tranche was the fee that Nexgen would receive for its services. Giraud and his team wondered if that fee would be sufficient.

---

[2] In reality, Nexgen would probably hedge all or part of what it held on its balance sheet using CDSs. For the purposes of this teaching case, however, a simplifying assumption has been made that Nexgen keeps the whole tranche unhedged on its balance sheet.

14

Note on Forward Contracts and Swaps

Forward contracts and swaps are among the most common examples of financial derivatives. A derivative is a financial instrument whose value depends on another product (known as the underlying), which can be financial (such as bonds or currencies) or physical (such as wheat, oil or other commodities). The underlying of a forward contract is an asset of some sort, and the contract specifies the delivery of that asset at a fixed time in the future at a certain price between the parties of the contract. Farming companies, for instance, use forward contracts to fix a price for their upcoming crop before the crop has been harvested. As to swaps, the underlying is normally a financial instrument, such as interest rates, currencies or a financial index. In its most basic form, a swap is an agreement in which two counterparties agree to exchange future cash flows. The cash flows are determined by the performance of the underlying. This can be done, for instance, to transform a floating-rate loan into a fixed-rate or vice versa.

When discussing "forwards," a related term that often appears is "futures." Although similar in many aspects, the two derivatives differ in one key aspect. While forward contracts are settled at their expiration, futures are settled every day during the lifespan of the contract. In this note, for simplicity, we will not distinguish between forwards and futures, but will use the term "forward contract" exclusively.[1]

FORWARD CONTRACTS

Forward contracts are agreements between a buyer and a seller, calling for delivery of a specified amount of a specified asset at a specified, future date.[2] The party that is obligated to buy takes a long position; the party that sells takes a short position. The dis-

---

Professors George Chacko and Peter Hecht, Executive Director of the HBS Europe Research Center Vincent Dessain and Research Associate Anders Sjöman prepared this note as the basis for class discussion.

[1] It can be shown that forward prices and futures prices are very close to each other if interest rates have very low volatility.

[2] Although forward contracts appear similar to options at a first glance, note an important difference: forwards carry an obligation for *both* parties, whereas options only oblige one party, the option writer.

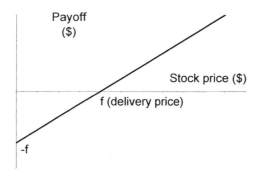

Figure 1   Payoff Diagram for Holder of Forward Contract

tinction between the **trade date** (when the contract is agreed upon and traded) and the future **delivery date** is fundamental to forward contracts. It allows the parties to agree on prices and settlements ahead of time, so that instead of trading using today's **spot price,** they agree on a **forward price** (sometimes known as **delivery price**). The difference between the spot and the forward price is the **forward premium**. This separation between now and then is what makes forward contracts efficient in controlling different types of risk, such as currency exposure in the financial markets or weather fluctuations in the commodities markets.

A typical forward contract covers the product, its quantity, its price and its delivery time. Take for instance a forward contract where you agree to buy 100 shares of Acme at $5 per share three months from now. The Acme stock today happens to be trading at $4.95. You agree on the contract—but no money or assets actually change hands before the maturity or delivery date that is agreed upon in the contract. The value of a standard forward contract is therefore generally said to be zero at inception.[3] It is over time that you will either gain or lose money, depending on how the value of the underlying asset changes.

Your motivation to enter into this long contract could be one of several. Perhaps it is speculative: you believe that Acme shares will be worth much more than $5 in three months and you want to benefit from the difference. (The seller then obviously has the opposite view of how the Acme stock will develop.) Or perhaps you are a portfolio manager looking to hedge risk: Acme stock is just one part of your portfolio, and the risk profile of the portfolio calls for guaranteed stock prices.[4]

Payoff for a Forward Contract

Regardless of why you hold a forward contract, its payoff diagram can be shown graphically as in Figure 1.

Using our previous example, when the price of the underlying stock is equal to the delivery price, the position breaks even. As the stock price grows larger than the delivery price, the forward contract starts paying off. If the stock price drops below the delivery price, the long position starts losing money, and the maximum loss occurs if the

---

[3] Although less common, a forward contract can be structured to have nonzero value at inception.

[4] Note how in this example a call option, which gives the right but not the obligation to buy, could also be used. In coming examples, when the underlying asset is not a stock, the difference between options and forward contracts will be clearer.

Figure 2 Payoff for stock

stock loses *all* its value. (The opposite situation, when being the seller in a forward contract, or "going short the forward," results in the opposite payoff diagram, where the forward contract pays off up *until* the stock price reaches the delivery price.)

Payoffs for Stocks and Bonds

For completeness, let's add the payoff for stocks (equity) and risk free bonds (debt).[5] Figure 2 shows the profit potential that comes from owning stock in a company. As the stock price increases, the payoff increases just as much; if the stock goes up by $50, the profit also increases by $50. The slope of the payoff line is in other words 1.

The payoff for a bond is different. Figure 3 shows the profit potential of a zero-coupon bond (one that makes no interest payments to the bondholder). As the line shows, no matter how the stock price changes, the bondholder only receives the principal value of the bond when the bond matures. Since the stock price has no impact on the bond value, the line is flat.

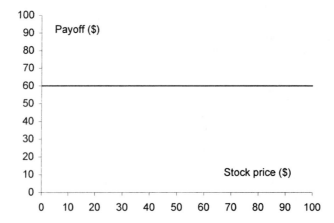

Figure 3 Payoff for bonds

[5] Unless otherwise stated, the bonds in this note are assumed to be risk free.

Figure 4   Spot-Forward Parity Explained Graphically

SPOT-FORWARD PARITY

We have now looked at the payoff schemes for forward contracts, stocks and bonds. Combining these schemes will help illustrate an important derivatives concept known as *spot-forward parity*.[6] As the word "parity" conveys, there is a type of equivalence between spot and forward rates. It can most easily be shown by using a portfolio containing a bond and a stock to replicate the exact payoffs of a forward contract. We can replicate the payoff of a standard forward contract by combining the payoffs from shorting bonds with a face value equal to the delivery price and buying stock with those proceeds. Figure 4 above shows how owning the underlying asset and shorting the bond, i.e. borrowing money, replicates the payoff from buying a forward contract. Since there were no upfront costs associated with the stock-bond portfolio that replicated the forward payoff, this standard forward contract has zero value at inception.

Described differently, you own an asset in the form of the stock, which has an inherent value. However, you also have a cost of owning, or carrying, that asset. This "cost-of-carry" is primarily the interest you are paying on the loan you had to take (or bonds that you had to issue) to buy the asset in the first place. If the asset is a physical commodity, your cost-of-carry also includes the cost of physically storing the good.

Now, this can be put mathematically as:

$$S - PV(f) = 0 \tag{1}$$

where:

S = stock price today (or spot price)

PV = present value

f = bond face value (or delivery price)

This can also be expressed as[7]

$$S = \frac{f}{(1 + r)^T} = 0 \tag{2}$$

[6] As a concept, the spot-forward parity is similar to the put-call parity applied to option valuation. For a description of the put-call parity, see for instance George Chacko, Peter Hecht, Vincent Dessain, and Anders Sjöman, "Option Valuation," Harvard Business School Note No. 205-106 (Boston: Harvard Business School Publishing, 2005).

[7] Note that $PV(f)$ is the value of a bond that has a face value of "f."

where:

r = risk-free rate

T = time-to-expiration of forward contract

Further rearranging this formula gives:

$$f = S(1 + r)^T \qquad [3]$$

which in fact is the spot-forward parity.

The spot-forward parity illustrates that you can get the delivery price (the forward price) by simply taking the spot rate of an asset and using the risk-free interest rate as a measurement of the cost-of-carry. In practice, the forward price is sometimes viewed as the market's estimation of an asset's future price.

Example. Assume that the Acme stock is trading today at $10. You are interested in buying a three-month forward contract on that stock and are also interested in the fair forward price for that contract. The current risk-free annual compounded interest rate is estimated at 5%. This gives us:

$$f = 10(1 + 5\%)^{3/12} = 10.12 \qquad [4]$$

$10.12 then is the forward price for the stock.

Forward-Neutral Valuation

Above we rather nonchalantly said that we could take the risk-free interest rate as a measurement of the cost-of-carry. We had previously also used the risk-free rate as a discount rate when calculating the present value of a bond. What allows us to do this (instead of using a more complicated discount rate that takes into consideration various sorts of risks) is an important concept when valuing forward contracts: *the forward-neutral measure*. The forward-neutral measure gives us the ability to equate today's value of the cashflow from a financial derivative with its future value discounted back by the risk free rate.[8]

The forward-neutral measure can be explained mathematically by taking equation [3] and rearranging it until it becomes:

$$\frac{f}{(1 + r)^T} = S \qquad [5]$$

In other words, if you can figure out the forward price or forward cash flows for an asset, you can simply discount those cash flows/assets at the risk-free rate and you'll arrive at a valuation. This is forward-neutral valuation.

Let's exemplify using a commodity good: oil. You are involved in an oil excavation project and have found an area with large oil reserves. You have estimated how many barrels of oil the excavation should give you over the next five years. All you have to do now is drill for the oil. You'll pump up a certain amount in the first year, another amount in the second year, etc. and sell each amount each year on the market at the spot price. The only uncertainty you have over the next five years is what the spot price at each

---

[8] A formal derivation of this concept is beyond the scope of this note.

given time will be. You now want to find out the value of your oil supply. Instead of trying to estimate the cash flows in the future and discounting at the appropriate risk-adjusted discount rate, you can calculate using the forward rates. The forward rates, according to equation [5], can simply be discounted at the risk-free rate; and forward rates are easy to find for widely traded commodities, like oil. So, to figure out the value today of your oil supply, you simply take the amount of excavated oil at any given point times the forward price of oil for that day and discount back by the risk free rate.

ADJUSTMENTS TO SPOT-FORWARD PARITY

The spot-forward parity relationship that we developed in equation [3] may at times need to be adjusted. That relationship was derived from the fact that if we take the pay-off diagram for a stock and a short bond, we can replicate the payoff of a forward contract. Taking the present value of the replicating portfolio and the forward contract, we then get the spot-parity relationship. However, in taking the present value of the stock, we have to be careful to adjust for any cash inflows to or outflows from the stock during the life of the forward contract.

Convenience Yield

The convenience yield is a cash inflow to the stock. It is commonly defined as the premium or benefits that an investor accrues from holding the actual underlying, in this case the stock, rather than the forward contract. In taking the present value of the stock's payoff, the accrued dividends and any other cashflows to the owner of the stock between the current time and the expiration of the forward contract need to be included. If we then consider the convenience yield as a fixed percentage, y, of the stock price, then we can modify our original spot-forward parity from equation [3] to:

$$f = S(1 + r)^{T}/(1 + y)^{T} \qquad [6]$$

where in addition to our previous parameters

y = convenience yield

Cost-of-Carry

In the case that the cashflows from holding the underlying security are negative, i.e., there is a cost to holding the security, the cashflows are then referred to as a cost-of-carry. The cost-of-carry needs to be reflected in the spot-parity relationship. Similar to the convenience yield, if we consider the cost-of-carry as a fixed percentage, c, of the stock price, then we can modify [6] to:[9]

$$f = S(1 + r)^{T}/(1 + y - c)^{T} \qquad [7]$$

where the new parameter is:

c = cost-of-carry

Example. Let's exemplify by continuing with the example we used when we discussed the spot-parity relationship (see equation [4]). In addition to what we already

---

[9] Note that these equations can be expressed in different forms depending on the timing conventions.

know, we now assume that Acme stock pays a dividend yield of 2% per annum and that everyone has to pay a custodial fee of 0.1% per annum to a broker in order to safekeep their stock certificates. Using equation [7] gives us:

$$f = 10(1 + 5\%)^{3/12}/(1 + 2\% - 0.1\%)^{3/12} = 10.08 \qquad [8]$$

The forward rate for the Acme stock, when adjusting for the convenience yield and cost of carry, becomes $10.08, compared to the $10.12 when not adjusting for these in- and outflows of cash.

FORWARD CONTRACT ON COMMODITIES AND BONDS

Up until now we have been using a forward contract on stocks as our main example. However, although stocks are good to use when explaining forward contracts, forwards on equity are actually fairly uncommon. Let's instead generalize what we have learned to the two areas where forward contracts are used the most: bonds and commodities.

Bonds

Forward contracts on bonds follow the same general principles as the ones we have just covered: spot-forward parity, convenience yield and cost-of-carry. One major difference, however, is that traders don't talk about forward prices for bonds. Instead, they use *forward interest rates*.

Forward Interest Rates

For a bond, the spot rate is the actual interest rate on that bond today. The forward interest rate (or just "forward rate") is then an agreed-upon interest rate for a bond that will be issued at a future date—or put differently; the forward rate is the interest rate, fixed today, on a loan that is made at a fixed time in the future.

Let's exemplify. You have money that you want to invest for three years, and you have two ways to invest it. Your first option is to invest all your money in a zero-coupon 3-year treasury bond that yields 3%. Your other option is to invest the money in a zero-coupon 2-year treasury. At maturity, after two years, you take the proceeds and roll them over into a one-year treasury. It is obvious that your two investment options are not identical, since the interest rate will differ. With the first option—the three-year bond—you know exactly what you will get back. However, with the 2 + 1 year bonds, you don't know the 1-year rate two years from now. You simply don't know how much money you will make on the second investment. But what if someone was willing to give you a contract today (for a fee of course) that guaranteed a specific one-year interest rate in two years? This would remove all uncertainty: you cold invest in the two year bond, then at its maturity roll it over into the one year investment with the locked in rate. So, today, you know exactly how much money you will get three years from now.

If you know the one year rate in two years already today, then the risk of that investment strategy is the same as for the three-year bond. So as long as you invest the same amount in either investment strategy today, you should end up with the same amount in the future—since the risks are identical, the return must be the same.

Example of Forward Interest Rate Calculation

The "one-year guaranteed rate" that we mentioned above is simply the forward interest rate. Forward rates are available in the markets for all maturities. Conceptually, they are also easy to calculate. Say that the 3-year bond's yield is 3% and that the 2-year yield is 2.5%. Let's figure out what the 1-year forward rate will be two years from now. Setting up the following equation and solving for the forward rate, f, does the trick:

$$(1 + 3\%)^3 = (1 + 2.5\%)^2 \cdot (1 + f) \qquad [9]$$
$$f = 0.040073$$

which means that the forward rate is 4.01%.

Forward Rate Agreement

The contract used to lock in forward rates is traditionally referred to as a Forward Rate Agreement. (Since forward rates only apply to bonds, FRAs implicitly only refer to bonds.) In our example above, the party guaranteeing the one year rate in two years does so through an FRA. Put more formally, an FRA is an agreement for a period of time between two parties that states that a specific interest rate will apply to a certain principal during a specified period of time. Like all securities FRAs can be traded. However, FRAs are not traded on the exchanges, but only in the OTC (Over-the-Counter) market.

Commodities

It is among commodities where you will find most of the publicly traded forward contracts. Typical commodities are raw materials or goods of various sorts: grains (such as corn and wheat), livestock (cattle and pigs), precious metals (gold, platinum, and silver), beverages (cocoa, coffee, and orange juice) or energy related (oil and gas.)

INTRODUCTION TO SWAPS

Swaps exist in a multitude of variations (interest rate swaps, currency swaps, equity swaps, etc), but their basic principle is easy: a swap is an agreement between two parties to exchange cash flows in the future.

Swaps as a Portfolio of Forward Contracts

Before we dive into the specifics of swaps, let's start our discussion on swaps by revisiting the forward contracts we just covered. A forward contract states that someone has to deliver something to you at a certain point in the future. A swap can then be said to be a *portfolio* of forward contracts. Remember that a forward rate agreement is a contract where someone has to deliver a cash flow to you in the future based on an interest rate. With a single FRA, you deal with one single cash flow. Now, suppose you have a contract that says that someone will deliver a cash flow to you at the end of every year for five years. This is in essence the same as having five different FRAs pooled together, where the first FRA is for one year, the second for two years, etc. until the fifth contract for the final year. It is rather cumbersome to have five separate contracts, though, which is why a swap is a handy instrument that handles all five contracts at once. A swap is then a contract with payments at each time period up until maturity, contrasting with the forward contract which only has a cash flow exchange on one future date.

An Interest Rate Swap: Going Long the Swap, Shorting the Swap and the Swap Rate

The words "cash flow exchange" that ended the sentence above are key to understanding swaps. A swap is a contract between two parties to exchange future cash flows, based on an underlying notional principal amount. For the purposes of this note, we will assume that swaps are exclusive to forward interest rates. (Swaps can naturally be used for other derivatives as well. However, the "plain vanilla" interest rate swap is the most common form of a swap.)

Although swaps are sometimes described as difficult instruments to master, they are easy to understand: All that goes on in an interest rate swap is the swapping between two parties of a fixed rate for a floating rate. The rate can refer to any type of underlying, but normally pertain to either bond coupons (swapping fixed rate coupons to floating rate coupons) or cross-currency interest rate swaps (fixed rate in one currency to floating rate in another). Suppose you are involved in a bond interest rate swap with party Y. You are going to give Y a floating rate bond, and Y is going to hand-over a fixed interest rate bond to you. (In trader terms, Y is going long the swap contract and you are shorting the swap.) That's the swap. Going forward, you have promised Y that she will receive payments tied to the floating rate, say the 6-month LIBOR. (The floating rate is also known as the swap rate.) Y in return has promised to give you a fixed set of payments in the future.

Interest Rate Swap Example: Interest Rate Swaps as Swap of Bonds

Let's exemplify. In its simplest form, an interest rate swap exchanges a series of payments calculated by applying a *fixed* rate of interest to a notional principal amount for a stream of payments similarly calculated but using a *floating* rate of interest. This is a fixed-for-floating interest rate swap.

When pricing a swap, it is important to recognize that the price of the floating rate bond is always par (the bond's principal value.) Suppose now that the swap contract between you and your counterparty Y is a three-year agreement with semi-annual payments. Your counterparty Y is receiving floating, and will have to pay a fixed amount to you for the next three years. The question you both ask, though, as you enter into the contract, is what is the fair swap rate?

The easy way to calculate the swap rate is to remember that a swap is an exchange of bonds. The floating rate bond is worth par, say $1000 USD. For the swap to be fair, the fixed rate bond that is handed over from Y to you should also be worth $1000. Nothing wrong with this: you should have a $1000 exchange for a $1000 receiving. Let's also say that the yield curve is as shown in Table A:

TABLE A   Yield Curve (annualized)

Maturity	Yield
6 month	2.0%
1 year	2.5%
1.5 years	3.0%
2 years	3.5%
2.5 years	4.0%
3 years	4.5%

Source: Created by authors.

You now want to find the fixed rate or the swap rate. Let's call it r, so that you can put together an equation to solve for it. The equation is built up on the six semi-annual payments you know you will receive, and you want to set it up so that the present value of these payments matches the $1000 value of the floating rate bond (its par value).

The equation then sums up each payment, discounted by its appropriate yield curve discount rate, and equates that to $1000:

$$\frac{1000 \circ r/2}{(1 + 2\%)^{1/2}} + \frac{1000 \circ r/2}{(1 + 2.5\%)^{1}} + \cdots + \frac{1000 \circ r/2 + 1000}{(1 + 4.5\%)^{3}} = 1000 \qquad [10]$$

$$r = 4.39\%$$

Through iterations in a spreadsheet application, a value for r can be found that meets the criteria of the equation. In this example, the equation can be solved when *r* is 0.0439. The fair swap rate is therefore 4.39%.

PROBLEM SET

Problem 1 Does the forward price equal the expected future spot price?

Problem 2 A stock is expected to pay a dividend of $1 per share in three months. The stock price is $40, and the yield curve is perfectly flat at 3% semi-annual compounded basis. An investor has just taken a short position in a six-month forward contract on the stock.

1. What are the forward price and the initial value of the forward contract?

2. Three months later, the price of the stock is $44 and the yield curve is still perfectly flat at 3%. What are the forward price and the value of the short position in the forward contract?

Problem 3 The following table gives the prices of bonds.

Bond principal ($)	Time to maturity (years)	Semi-Annual Coupon ($)	Bond price ($)
100	0.5	0.00	99.26
100	1.0	0.00	98.04
100	1.5	2.50	102.99
100	2.0	3.00	104.94

What are the forward rates for the periods: 6 months to 12 months, 12 months to 18 months, 18 months to 24 months?

Problem 4 A firm uses gold in its production process. The firm enters into a 2-year commodity swap contract to hedge the price of gold. The current spot price for gold is $382 per ounce. The firm agrees to make payments every six months at a rate of $X per ounce to the swap dealer. The notional principal is 10,000 ounces. The swap dealer agrees to pay the firm the spot price at each payment date. The swap price X is set such that the initial value of the swap is zero. Use the information in the table below, which shows prices of zero coupon debt, to determine the price X. Assume that the convenience yield and costs of carry (except financing costs) are negligible.

Date T (Years)	Treasury Strip Prices[1]
0.5	96.81
1	93.44
1.5	89.47
2	85.64

Note: (1) Zero-coupon securities paying $100 at maturity.

Problem 5   A firm (that is rated AAA) is considering entering into an interest rate swap. Using the spot and forward rate curves implied in the table below, which shows treasury and LIBOR data, determine the swap rate on a 3-year swap (semiannual payments), receiving fixed payments and paying floating payments based on 6-month Libor.

Maturity Dates (Years)	Treasury Strip Yields[1]	Eurodollar Deposit Values[2]	Eurodollar Futures Quotes[3]
0.25	5.02%	98.77	
0.5	5.14%	97.48	
0.75	5.17%	96.29	
1	5.20%	94.92	94.35
1.25	5.21%		94.13
1.5	5.24%		93.81
1.75	5.28%		93.59
2	5.33%		93.3
2.25	5.38%		93.02
2.5	5.43%		92.74
2.75	5.49%		92.61
3	5.54%		92.53

Notes: (1) Annual compounded yields

(2) Deposits that pay no coupon and $100 at maturity.

(3) The price quote for a 3-month Eurodollar futures contract

Problem 6   A year ago, the company in Problem 4 sold a 4-year swap, i.e., it receives fixed and pays floating semiannually, with a swap rate of 6% (bond equivalent yield). That swap currently has a maturity of 3 years. Using the information in the table from Problem 4, determine the market value of the swap today so the company can determine its cash flows if it unwinds the swap. The notional principal is $20 million.

Problem 7   The same company wants to enter into a 3-year basis swap (semiannual payments) to tie its floating-rate liabilities to the 6-month T-bill rate instead of the 6-month Libor. Based on the information in the table from Problem 4, what spread should it expect to pay on the 6-month T-bill rate such that no payments are exchanged at the inception of the basis swap?

15

The Enron Odyssey (A): The Special Purpose of "SPEs"

During April 2001 in Houston, Texas, the atmosphere at Enron Corporation was lively and exciting. The company continued to be touted as one of the best places to work and recommended as a smart investment in both the equity and debt markets.[1] Thanks to the profit-seeking initiatives of its highly motivated and experienced employees, Enron continued to expand its operations into new areas of business.[2] The company accompanied its business expansion with a strong focus on financial innovation that had earned its top management awards for thought leadership.[3] Much of the expansion and innovation had been instigated during a breakthrough strategy meeting held in 1988. At this meeting, the company had decided to make a radical shift away from the commonplace strategies of traditional energy companies and, instead, to create a new company that made money off deregulation and the inefficiencies in various commodity markets.[4]

Professor George Chacko, Professor Bala Dharan of Rice University, and Research Associate Eli Peter Strick prepared this case. While discussions with Enron management proved to be very helpful, this case was prepared from published sources. HBS cases are developed solely as the basis for class discussion. Cases are not intended to serve as endorsements, sources of primary data, or illustrations of effective or ineffective management.

[1] For example, during April 2001, brokerage firms Lehman Brothers and UBS Warburg put out equity research in which they had rated Enron's stock a "strong buy," while Morgan Stanley Dean Witter forecast that Enron would "outperform" as an investment.

[2] See Peter Tufano and Sanjay Bhatnagar, "Enron Gas Services" (HBS Case No. 294-076), for an example of its early expansion activities.

[3] Among the company's accolades, *CFO Magazine* presented Enron's chief financial officer, Andrew Fastow, with the 1999 CFO Excellence Award for "Capital Structure Management." *Fortune* Magazine ranked Enron the Number 1 "Most Innovative Company in America" five years in a row (1996 to 2000). *Fortune* also ranked Enron 22nd on the list of "100 Best Companies to Work for in America" in 2000, up from 24th in 1999.

[4] Malcolm S. Salter, "Innovation Corrupted: The Rise and Fall of Enron Part I," HBS Working Paper No. 03-077, January 14, 2003, p. 5.

The business model of the "new" Enron was complicated and required the expertise of thousands of professionals from a variety of disciplines. As Enron's business model grew more complex, so did its finances. Special purpose entities (SPEs), corporate structures that allowed Enron to move assets off its balance sheet, had been popping up just as quickly as the legal paperwork could be filled out. Recently, some institutional investors and analysts had shown curiosity concerning the growing complexity of Enron's finances and the level of financial disclosure the company provided.

Enron's executive management team tried hard to eliminate organizational obstacles that could stifle their employees' ingenuity and company growth. Still, Enron's board of directors had felt compelled to charge the internal audit division, the Risk Assessment & Control Group (RAC), to review the company's use of SPEs. Specifically, they wished to understand how much risk had been transferred off Enron's balance sheet using SPEs. Ron Tolbert, an analyst in the RAC, was given the responsibility of looking at three of these transactions: Destec, Rhythms, and Fishtail/Bacchus. Tolbert, looking at the project files for these transactions, wondered: 1) Why had Enron chosen to use SPEs in each transaction? 2) Was the risk transfer accomplished successfully? 3) Were there other motivations behind the transactions?

ENRON CORP.: THE COMPANY AND ITS HISTORY

Enron was one of the world's leading integrated energy companies. Following its early financial difficulties in the 1980s, the firm underwent a metamorphosis, changing from a traditional oil and natural gas company into a sophisticated energy services and risk management powerhouse. With its primary business units, Enron Wholesale, Enron Energy Services, Enron Broadband Services, and Enron Transportation Services, the company brought in revenue of $100.8 billion in 2000 based on assets of $65.5 billion. (Exhibits 1a through 1d show Enron's financial statements for the year ending December 31, 2000. Exhibit 2 displays the company's stock price history.)

Enron's Roots

Born from the 1985 merger of natural gas companies InterNorth and Houston Natural Gas, Enron was very much the traditional, "asset-heavy" natural gas company.[5] However, with the installment of Enron's new leadership came the seeds for the company's innovative future. Kenneth Lay, an experienced executive in the energy industry, had been brought over from Exxon to lead InterNorth and, after the merger was completed, became the CEO of Enron. After moving into its Houston headquarters, the company spent the next five years focusing on managing it debt level and capital structure. The merger had given Enron the United State's largest natural gas pipeline system. However, as a result of ongoing deregulation in the gas industry, Enron would no longer have exclusive rights to its pipelines. Such changes in the market were setting the stage for Enron to transform its business model, looking for new ways to make a profit.

Industry Deregulation

Natural gas is a colorless and odorless fuel consisting primarily of methane and ethane. As is oil, natural gas is extracted from the Earth's crust, and then impurities are re-

---

[5] "Asset-heavy" referred to the belief that large amounts of physical assets, along with their associated expenses and financing costs, weighed down a company, making it vulnerable to commodity price and demand changes and limiting its growth.

EXHIBIT 1A

ENRON CORP.'S CONSOLIDATED BALANCE SHEET

In $ Millions	12/31/00	12/31/99	In $ Millions	12/31/00	12/31/99
Current Assets			Current Liabilities		
Cash and cash equivalents	1,374	288	Accounts payable	9,777	2,154
Trade receivables	10,396	3,030	Liabilities from price risk management activities	10,495	1,836
Other receivables	1,874	518	Short-term debt	1,679	1,001
Assets from price risk management activities	12,018	2,205	Customers' deposits	4,277	44
Inventories	953	598	Other	2,178	1,724
Deposits	2,433	81	Total current liabilities	$28,406	$6,759
Other	1,333	535	Long-Term Debt	8,550	7,151
Total current assets	$30,381	$7,255	Deferred Credits and Other Liabilities		
Investments and Other Assets			Deferred income taxes	1,644	1,894
Investments in and advances to unconsolidated equity affiliates	5,294	5,036	Liabilities from price risk management activities	9,423	2,990
Assets from price risk management activities	8,988	2,929	Other	2,692	1,587
Goodwill	3,638	2,799	Total deferred credits and other liabilities	$13,759	$6,471
Other	5,459	4,681	Commitments and Contingencies		
Total investments and other assets	$23,379	$15,445	Minority Interests	2,414	2,430
Property, Plant and Equipment, at cost			Company-Obligated Preferred Securities of Subsidiaries	904	1,000
Natural gas transmission	6,916	6,948	Shareholders' Equity		
Electric generation and distribution	4,766		Second preferred stock	124	130
Fiber-optic network and equipment	839		Mandatorily Convertible Junior Preferred Stock	1,000	1,000
Construction in progress	682	1,120	Common stock	8,348	6,637
Other	2,256	1,913	Retained earnings	3,226	2,698
	$15,459	$13,912	Accumulated other comprehensive income	(1,048)	(741)
Less accumulated depreciation, depletion and amortization	3,716	3,231	Common stock held in treasury	(32)	(49)
Property, plant and equipment, net	$11,743	$10,681	Restricted stock and other	(148)	(105)
Total Assets	65,503	33,381	Total shareholders' equity	$11,470	$9,570
			Total Liabilities and Shareholders' Equity	65,503	33,381

Source: Enron Corp., 2000 10-K.

EXHIBIT 1B

ENRON CORP.'S CONSOLIDATED INCOME STATEMENT

In $ Millions	12/31/00	12/31/99
Revenues		
Natural gas and other products	50,500	19,536
Electricity	33,823	15,238
Metals	9,234	—
Other	7,232	5,338
Total revenues	$100,789	$40,112
Costs and Expenses		
Cost of gas, electricity, metals and other products	94,517	34,761
Operating expenses	3,184	3,045
Depreciation, depletion and amortization	855	870
Taxes, other than income taxes	280	193
Impairment of long-lived assets	—	441
Total costs and expenses	$98,836	$39,310
Operating Income	1,953	802
Other Income and Deductions		
Equity in earnings of unconsolidated equity affiliates	87	309
Gains on sales of non-merchant assets	146	541
Gain on the issuance of stock by TNPC, Inc.	121	—
Interest income	212	162
Other income, net	(37)	181
Income Before Interest, Minority Interests and Income Taxes	$2,482	$1,995
Interest and related charges, net	838	656
Dividends on company-obligated preferred securities of subsidiaries	7776	
Minority interests	154	135
Income tax expense	434	104
Net income before cumulative effect of accounting changes	$979	$1,024
Cumulative effect of accounting changes, net of tax	—	(131)
Net Income	$979	$893
Preferred stock dividends	83	66
Earnings on Common Stock	896	827

Source: Enron Corp., 2000 10-K.

moved in a refining process. As an energy source, it is both easily stored and efficient to transport by pipeline. Cleaner than most traditional fossil fuels, natural gas has gained popularity with producers and consumers alike. The core natural gas industry participants were divided into three broad categories: producers, pipeline companies, and distributors. Producers developed gas reserves and carried out the drilling, refining, and wholesale operations. Pipeline companies used their networks to transport the gas around the country and arranged for the delivery of natural gas according to contracts. Natural gas distributors, or local distribution companies (LDCs), controlled the retail

EXHIBIT 1C

ENRON CORP.'S CONSOLIDATED STATEMENT OF CASH FLOWS

In $ Millions	12/31/00	12/31/99
Cash Flows From Operating Activities		
Reconciliation of net income to net cash provided by operating activities		
Net income	979	893
Cumulative effect of accounting changes	—	131
Depreciation, depletion and amortization	855	870
Impairment of long-lived assets (including equity investments)	326	441
Deferred income taxes	207	21
Gains on sales of non-merchant assets	(146)	(541)
Changes in components of working capital	1,769	(1,000)
Net assets from price risk management activities	(763)	(395)
Merchant assets and investments:		
Realized gains on sales	(104)	(756)
Proceeds from sales	1,838	2,217
Additions and unrealized gains	(1,295)	(827)
Other operating activities	$1,113	$174
Net Cash Provided by Operating Activities	4,779	1,228
Cash Flows From Investing Activities		
Capital expenditures	(2,381)	(2,363)
Equity investments	(933)	(722)
Proceeds from sales of non-merchant assets	494	294
Acquisition of subsidiary stock	(485)	—
Business acquisitions, net of cash acquired	(777)	(311)
Other investing activities	(182)	(405)
Net Cash Used in Investing Activities	$(4,264)	$(3,507)
Cash Flows From Financing Activities		
Issuance of long-term debt	3,994	1,776
Repayment of long-term debt	(2,337)	(1,837)
Net increase (decrease) in short-term borrowings	(1,595)	1,565
Net issuance (redemption) of company-obligated preferred securities of subsidiaries	(96)	—
Issuance of common stock	307	852
Issuance of subsidiary equity	500	568
Dividends paid	(523)	(467)
Net disposition of treasury stock	327	139
Other financing activities	(6)	(140)
Net Cash Provided by Financing Activities	$571	$2,456
Increase (Decrease) in Cash and Cash Equivalents	1,086	177
Cash and Cash Equivalents, Beginning of Year	288	111
Cash and Cash Equivalents, End of Year	1,374	288

Source: Enron Corp., 2000 10-K.

EXHIBIT 1D

ENRON CORP.'S CONSOLIDATED STATEMENT OF CHANGES IN SHAREHOLDERS' EQUITY

$ amounts in millions, share amounts in thousands	2000 Shares	2000 Amount	1999 Shares	1999 Amount
Cumulative Second Preferred Convertible Stock				
Balance, beginning of year	1,296	$130	1,320	$132
Exchange of convertible preferred stock for common stock	−55	($6)	−24	($2)
Balance, end of year	1,241	$124	1,296	$130
Mandatorily Convertible Junior Preferred Stock, Series B				
Balance, beginning of year	250	$1,000	—	$ —
Issuances	—	—	250	$1,000
Balance, end of year	250	$1,000	250	$1,000
Common Stock				
Balance, beginning of year	716,865	$6,637	671,094	$5,117
Exchange of convertible preferred stock for common stock	1,509	$6	465	($1)
Issuances related to benefit and dividend reinvestment plans	28,100	$966	10,054	$258
Sales of common stock	—	—	27,600	$839
Issuances of common stock in business acquisitions	5,731	$409	7,652	$250
Other	—	$330	—	$174
Balance, end of year	752,205	$8,348	716,865	$6,637
Retained Earnings				
Balance, beginning of year		$2,698		$2,226
Net income		$979		$893
Cash dividends				
Common stock		($368)		($355)
Cumulative Second Preferred Convertible Stock		($17)		($17)
Series A and B Preferred Stock		($66)		($49)
Balance, end of year		$3,226		$2,698
Accumulated Other Comprehensive Income				
Balance, beginning of year		($741)		($162)
Translation adjustments and other		($307)		($579)
Balance, end of year		($1,048)		($741)
Treasury Stock				
Balance, beginning of year	−1,338	($49)	−9,334	($195)
Shares acquired	−3,114	($234)	−1,845	($71)
Exchange of convertible preferred stock for common stock			181	$4
Issuances related to benefit and dividend reinvestment plans	3,875	$251	9,660	$213
Balance, end of year	−577	($32)	−1,338	($49)
Restricted Stock and Other				
Balance, beginning of year	—	($105)		($70)
Issuances related to benefit and dividend reinvestment plans		($43)		($35)
Balance, end of year		($148)		($105)
Total Shareholders' Equity		$11,470		$9,570

Source: Enron Corp., 2000 10-K.

EXHIBIT 2

HISTORICAL STOCK PRICE GRAPH FOR ENRON CORP.

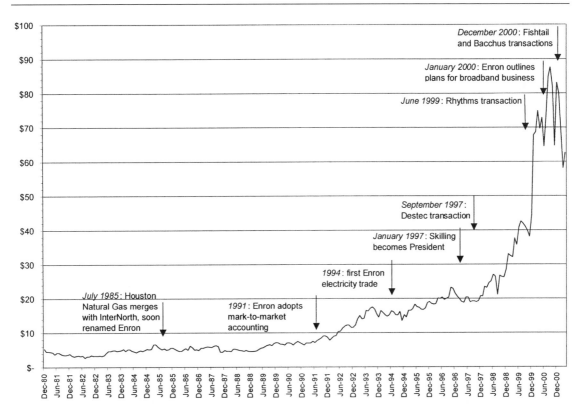

Source: Casewriters' diagram based on Enron Corp. stock price data for December 31, 1980 through April 30, 2001, obtained from Thompson Financial Datastream (accessed June 6, 2003).

operations: they bought natural gas, transported it locally, and sold it to a variety of end users (i.e., residential, commercial, industrial, etc.).[6]

In 1938, through the National Gas Act, the U.S. government had assumed an active role in controlling natural gas prices by regulating the market price charged at each stage of the business (i.e., production, transport, and distribution). However, as the market matured, government regulation proved to be an inefficient means of offering energy consumers the best prices. Therefore, beginning in 1978 with the Natural Gas Policy Act, the federal government began deregulating the industry, allowing gas companies greater freedom and letting market forces play their role. However, deregulation of the natural gas industry led to new levels of price volatility for its commodity.

In the government-regulated market, natural gas producers and suppliers had been restricted to offering their products according to government-stipulated prices. As the government slowly abandoned its regulatory role, the market price for natural gas was

[6] Justin C. McCann, "Natural Gas: Distribution," *Standard & Poor's Industry Surveys*, November 26, 1998. Available from Standard & Poor's NetAdvantage (July 17, 2002).

allowed to fluctuate with shifts in supply and demand. While healthy competition had the propensity to drive prices down in a free market, it did not provide a price ceiling or safety net, exposing end users to the risk of high prices and large price swings. (Nor did deregulation eliminate the occurrence of supply shortages.) While the risk of large price swings may have been in line with the principles of market efficiency, natural gas and energy companies had found themselves in need of new ways to manage the increased risk that had become identifiable with their industry.[7]

New Market Opportunities

Enron was able to leverage its extensive pipeline infrastructure to provide a new set of services to the natural gas industry. Originally engaged in the "physical" roles of the industry (i.e., producer, transporter, marketer, and consumer), the company seized the opportunity to offer the gas companies financial services and risk management tools.[8] Jeff Skilling, a onetime senior partner at the consulting firm of McKinsey & Company, catalyzed the development of Enron's new role in the gas market. After being brought on board to head Enron's trading operation in 1989, Skilling proved his market intermediary model could be effective. The basis of this model was the pooling of energy contracts of different durations from a large number of energy suppliers and using them to service the demand for energy buyers. By pooling contracts from all over the country and taking advantage of its extensive pipeline system, Enron could offer end users long-term fixed-price energy contracts, allowing the buyers to hedge their exposure to the market's volatility.

As a "gas bank," Enron was also capable of using its pool of assets to offer more efficient pricing. That is, if gas prices differed geographically, Enron could exploit price gaps, earning fees by offering buyers lower prices than were obtainable in their local market. Enron increased its risk management portfolio by offering an array of financial products such as futures, swaps, and collars that gave industry participants the ability to hedge their market position or lock in a fixed price for their energy supplies.[9] With buyers and suppliers eager to protect themselves against the volatility in the market, Enron had demand for its services grow consistently from year to year. By 1992, Enron had already become a superpower in the energy industry.[10]

Other Markets

As Enron mastered the natural gas market, the company's management noticed deregulation was going on elsewhere and, as with natural gas before, opportunities were opening up for Enron to earn profits from new trading products and services. The energy

---

[7] For a more in-depth overview of the deregulation of the natural gas industry see Peter Tufano and Sanjay Bhatnagar, "Enron Gas Services," HBS Case No. 294-076 (Boston: Harvard Business School Publishing, 1994).

[8] Tufano and Bhatnagar, p. 4.

[9] Futures, swaps, and collars are types of derivative instruments that allow two parties to contractually exchange payments based upon changes in the value (or price) of an underlying item (e.g., security, commodity, interest rate, index, etc.).

[10] According to Tufano and Bhatnagar, " . . . it [Enron Gas Services] was the largest nonregulated gas merchant in North America, the largest buyer and seller of natural gas in North America, manager of the largest portfolio of fixed-price gas and natural gas derivative contracts in the world, the largest supplier of gas to the electricity-generating industry in North America, and operator of the largest pipeline system in Texas."

giant quickly added electricity to its power-trading services. Other markets that Enron entered into as a trader included broadband capacity, paper and pulp, and weather risk management. Within each of these markets, Enron became an intermediary, or a "middleman," a position from which it could create new efficiencies in how the market dealt with supply and demand. Furthermore, with the advent of the Internet, Enron created a new Internet-based trading platform called Enron Online. As new markets became more standardized, Enron used the Enron Online technology to scale up new business and reach a wider customer audience with its range of products and services

In its Broadband Services business, Enron built the Enron Intelligence Network to serve as a bandwidth intermediary, supplying capacity to telecommunication companies experiencing excess demand and connecting independent networks through its multiple pooling points. As the services for communication capacity became commoditized, Enron planned on driving the market from its network by offering a complete range of services. Built on Enron's investment in its 18,000-mile global fiber network, the company planned on becoming the world's largest marketer of broadband services and provider of commercial content delivery services. By the end of 2000, Enron had already embarked on a new venture to deliver commercial video-on-demand services over its broadband network.

Leveraging its risk management expertise and knowledge of creating markets, Enron had the in-house capability to move into new markets and quickly incorporate them into its business model. An example of this was Enron's Weather unit, which offered risk management products to its growing customer base. Through pooling its different markets, Enron could offer cross-commodity products, such as a financial contract that paid out to its buyer an amount determined by energy prices and precipitation's falling below a predetermined minimum. Such market innovation and flexibility allowed Enron to pitch new services and products that were better customized to customer needs.

THE ENRON STRATEGY: "ASSET LIGHT"

Enron had set its sights on being much more than a successful utility company and energy-trading firm. By hiring the market's most talented professionals and providing them with the autonomy to lead the company into new markets, Enron aimed at becoming the "world's leading company," period.[11] To do this, management felt it was important to stay flexible and mobile; this meant moving away from the physical asset-intensive model most companies of its kind operated on. Once Enron entered into a new market as an intermediary, it did not want to hold a significant net position ("long" or "short") in that market's underlying commodity.[12] Investments in long-term physical assets were fixed by nature, required costly financing, and made the company vulnerable to changes in market prices.[13] The firm's objective was to be a "market maker," creat-

[11] Bala Dharan, "Enron's Accounting Issues: What Can We Learn To Prevent Future Enrons," Written Testimony to House Energy and Commerce Committee Hearing, February 6, 2002, Congressional Records, 107th Congress.

[12] Vince Kaminski and John Martin, "Transforming Enron Corporation: The Value of Active Management," *Journal of Applied Corporate Finance* (Winter 2001): 45.

[13] For example, if Enron bought a power generator, it would have to raise capital to fund the new facility. Debt financing would worsen Enron's leverage ratios and could possibly hurt its credit ratings. Equity financing could dilute shareholder value. As a result of the purchase, Enron would be exposed to changes in the cost (value) of power produced by the generator. Furthermore, such a physical asset is "fixed" (or immobile) by nature and may not be easily sold if the need arises due to market changes.

ing efficiencies where they were not available before, and to be hedged appropriately with respect to market risk. The only long positions Enron was willing to take were those on the strength of its employees and on the benefits available from market deregulation.

The new "asset-light" strategy was the brainchild of Enron's Skilling, and it fit with Lay's belief that grand profits were to be realized from future market deregulation. As Lay had stated, "An imperfect market is preferable to a perfect regulator."[14] Moreover, the company's financial and competitive strength was derived from the mobility of its human capital and not from investments in inefficient physical assets.[15] Hence, instead of investing large sums into new facilities for all the new markets it moved into, Enron developed its expertise in these markets from within. The company believed its knowledge of market economics could be applied to a multitude of situations and should not be limited to energy alone. As markets changed, Enron's personnel changed with them, staying one step ahead.

While Enron had achieved success in the deregulated energy market, it was already in the process of building its presence in such unrelated markets as weather risk, broadband, water, paper/pulp, and metals, among others. Although the company (and its subsidiaries) had made some strategic acquisitions of plants, factories, generators, and other hard assets in these markets, the firm was not focused on becoming a producer of such materials and commodities. Rather, Enron was taking the necessary steps to become a successful service provider and risk manager to those who operated in these "inefficient" markets. The company had to first position itself to understand the way these markets functioned, such as how the prices fluctuated and what the specific needs of suppliers and purchasers were.

At times it was necessary for Enron to invest in certain fixed assets in order to gain market share and build its reputation. For example, in order to provide a quality service, Enron might have first acted as a market supplier in order to gather important data regarding price patterns and volatility and to build reserves in case it needed to fulfill broken contracts. Even where fixed assets were a necessity, Enron's focus remained on innovation and creating services it could provide market participants, making the market more "liquid." As Mercer Management Consulting noted in a report, "the company's [Enron's] commitment to finding ways of adding value for customers continues unabated. Enron does not allow the physical assets it owns to define how it seeks to make money, nor does it assume that a business design that delivers value today will continue to do so indefinitely."[16]

Applying an asset-light strategy to a business in an asset-intensive environment required a great deal of effort, not to mention millions of dollars in legal and other advisory fees. Supporting Enron's trailblazing strategic initiatives was the company's financial and legal expertise, needed to structure the increasingly complex operations. Enron had recruited members from Wall Street's finest institutions to keep the company in the forefront of financial practice. Additionally, the company had formed relationships with top banks and institutional investors around the world, providing it with multiple access points to the capital markets. As the asset-light strategy developed and Enron's business grew, the company came to command a great deal of respect from partners, customers, competitors, and market observers alike. Inside the firm, a few major objectives were constantly on the minds of Enron's personnel: expanding the company's

---

[14] Kaminski and Martin, p. 43.

[15] Kaminski and Martin, p. 46.

[16] Piers Whitehead, Nate Letz, and Jamie Bonomo, "Looking From the Outside In: Achieving Value Growth in Asset-Intensive Industries," a Mercer Management Consulting commentary, p. 8.

role as a market maker, continuing to find new avenues for growing its earnings, and preserving the company's credit quality (without which the rest of the strategy fell apart).

Making Markets

> In the case of Enron, we balance our positions all the time. We're basically making markets, buying and selling, arranging supplies, deliveries. We do not, in fact, speculate on where markets are headed. If we think markets are getting tight, we try not to be somewhat short. We'd rather be somewhat long.
>
> —CEO Lay in a *Frontline* interview on March 27, 2001[17]

As a market maker, Enron could take advantage of new market opportunities as they opened up. In many cases, Enron management would have observed certain business needs of buyers and suppliers in an industry that were not being met. By forming relationships with participants from each side and by gaining a successful understanding of the market's dynamics, Enron could play the role of matchmaker, giving each party what they wanted for a fee. Essentially, by pooling mismatched amounts of supply and demand, Enron would divide contracts and build new ones tailor-fit to each party's specific needs. Enron could break up large supply contracts to provide smaller buyers with units appropriate for their business. At the same time, Enron could pool smaller contracts to meet the greater, long-term demand of their larger clientele.

Once a new market was recognized, Enron could move quickly to develop the expertise it needed to enter as a middleman, generally with minimum investment in fixed assets. The fees Enron earned for its market-making capabilities depended not only on the demand for its services (i.e., the size of the market) but also on the rate at which competitors entered the market-making business. As other firms saw the attractive margins going to Enron in their various commodity markets, some decided it was worth their while to build dealer operations as well. As a result, competitive pricing in market making affected Enron's profits. Since Enron's shareholders believed the company was "focused on earnings," the company needed to stay committed to finding new markets to enter and new inefficiencies to exploit.[18]

As a result of its role in the market, Enron was well positioned to gather a wealth of information on market performance. Since the company witnessed changes in supply and demand firsthand and played an essential part in price setting for the markets it dealt in, it was well equipped for dealing with future fluctuations. As a market leader, the company was also frequently confronted with an assortment of strategic investment opportunities: new energy plants being built, start-up firms looking for funding, expanding infrastructure in a developing country, and so on. In the forefront of innovation, Enron had first-mover's advantage on a variety of deals. Using its proprietary information to analyze investments and its strong relationships with Wall Street and beyond, Enron was able to take on assets as short-term "merchant" investments and later divest them to outside parties. In this fashion, Enron was not only a market maker in commodities but also with investment opportunities. Management felt it could add value by discovering such opportunities and making them available to a broader investor base through the use of specially formed investment vehicles, such as SPEs. Even while it invested its own capital in the beginning, Enron aimed to recover its investment and market the investment opportunity to others for a fee.

[17] "Blackout, Interview: Ken Lay," PBS *Frontline*, at http://www.pbs.org/wgbh/pages/frontline/shows/blackout/interviews/lay.html, accessed June 3, 2003.

[18] Enron Corp. 2000 Annual Report, p. 2.

Credit Quality

Enron's creditworthiness played an essential role in the company's operations. If Enron was at risk of defaulting on its own obligations, it could not provide market participants with the security and confidence they needed to trade and do business. Both buyers and suppliers in the markets that Enron served relied on the company to make good on contracts from both ends. In fact, the credit "enhancement" of contracts was part of the appeal of the services Enron provided. As a market intermediary, it ensured that there would be an adequate supply and proper delivery for each contract, even if a supplier defaulted on its obligations. When customers used Enron to do business, they were paying for the reliability of the "Enron name." Due to its central role in the market, Enron's credit rating (issued by agencies such as Moody's, Standard & Poor's, and Fitch) was watched closely by both the company's customers and its investors.[19]

SPECIAL PURPOSE ENTITIES (SPEs)

Often the most effective route to achieving a goal is not a straight line. Achieving an economic or business objective in the most direct and obvious way may have unpalatable consequences for a company's balance sheet or tax position. By taking advantage of the opportunities offered through innovation in the capital markets, a company can use more subtle approaches to achieving commercial objectives, without compromising shareholder value. The advantage will sometimes come from arbitrage, but not always. Simply opening up an alternative source of funding or risk transfer may reduce costs.[20]

—Stephen Barrett, Head of Capital Markets Practice, Ernst & Young

The term "special purpose entity" applies to certain legal structures that were used to achieve a variety of goals in corporate finance. A special purpose entity (SPE) or, synonymously, a special purpose vehicle (SPV) was a separate legal entity created by a firm to carry out a particular activity, or series of transactions, related to a "special purpose." In other words, an SPE typically had no other purpose than carrying out the set of transactions it was created for. SPEs came in a variety of forms, such as limited partnerships, limited liability companies, trusts, and corporations. They were typically created and operated in "business friendly" jurisdictions (e.g., Delaware and the Cayman Islands) where forming new companies was relatively simple and corporate taxes were advantageous for the SPE's creator and investors.

The majority of SPEs were created to act as counterparties to the companies that formed them. Many times the creator intended to sell a pool of assets or perform a hedging maneuver. By creating a "clean" or "blank" entity, a firm was able to isolate the risks associated with certain assets or hedging transactions inside the SPE. While SPEs might provide some tax and accounting advantages to the companies that created them, the underlying effect of each transaction was a transfer of risk (or set of risks) along with the risk's associated return. While companies isolated risks using SPEs, risk was never erased in the process; it was just repackaged and transferred elsewhere.

---

[19] On March 23, 2000, Moody's Investors Service upgraded all of Enron's long-term debt (from Baa2 to Baa1), affecting approximately $8.2 billion of recognized Enron debt securities.

[20] Stephen Barrett, "Capital Markets, Practical Financing Techniques," a special supplement to *International Tax Review* (June 2000), published in conjunction with Ernst & Young, p. 5.

Who Does What?

Most SPEs had no independent management or employees. In fact, many of these entities were no more than post office box addresses in the Cayman Islands with bank accounts.[21] The major roles associated with maintaining an SPE were the *sponsor* (or *originator*), the *trustee*, the *servicer*, and the SPE's investors. The sponsor was the party that created the SPE, along with the help of its lawyers, bankers, and accountants. The sponsor, also called the originator, was the party that originated the assets (the source of risks and cash flows) that were being transferred to the SPE. (Sometimes, when more than one party had ownership of the assets being transferred, an SPE could have dual or multiple sponsors.) The trustee was an independent third party and was paid a fee for its services. It served as an intermediary between the sponsor and the SPE and acted on behalf of the SPE's investors. The trustee was in charge of the SPE's administrative tasks such as collecting payments from the sponsor and making sure the investor's terms were adhered to. The servicer was in charge of overseeing the performance of an SPE's assets and transferring funds to the SPE. Due to its superior knowledge of the assets, the sponsor typically retained the servicer's role, allowing it to earn a management fee from the SPE. The cost of services (such as salaries) would, however, be reported in the income statement of the SPE.

Asset/Risk Transfer

The assets put into an SPE could be anything from an entire "mature" business unit to a block of equity in a start-up venture to a portfolio of distressed bonds. Any set of assets that potentially generated future cash flows (dividends, sales, interest payments, etc.) at a risk acceptable to investors could be transferred to an SPE as collateral for its investors. To finance the purchase of assets, the SPE had to obtain capital from somewhere. SPEs had similar funding choices to other types of companies; they could borrow (i.e., issue debt securities or take a bank loan), raise equity, or use a combination of the two (as was most often the case). In this manner, the isolated risk in the SPE was transferred to participating investors in the capital markets, possibly gaining a funding advantage for the sponsor and preferential tax and accounting treatment for the sponsor and investors as well. Frequently, the sponsor retained some level of equity exposure to the SPE.[22] This exposure was limited to ensure that a "true sale" of the assets by the originator occurred from a legal point of view.[23] Frequently an SPE had an "investment horizon," after which its assets would be liquidated in the market or, sometimes, sold back to the originator. Once an SPE had paid off its obligations to its lenders, the residual value of the assets would be either distributed to the SPE's shareholders or paid to the sponsor/servicer as part of its management fee contract.

"Bankruptcy Remote"

In order to ensure that the SPE's investors were only exposed to the risks of the transferred assets and not any other credit risks of the originator, it was necessary for an SPE to be structured in a way that it was "bankruptcy remote." In other words, the SPE's

---

[21] The limited nature of SPEs' activities and resources had earned them the description "brain dead."

[22] The level of risk exposure retained by the sponsor was restricted by tax and accounting regulations. These rules are discussed later in the case.

[23] "True sale" is a legal concept used by courts to determine whether a real sale has occurred or whether the transaction is just a form of financing.

assets needed to be protected in the case where the originator defaulted. An SPE investor's main concern was making sure the originator's creditors and investors were not able to lay claim to the SPE's assets and fold the assets back into the originator's balance sheet. To address this concern, transactions involving SPEs were often done in *two steps*.[24] In the *first step*, an SPE was created to handle the initial purchase of the originator's targeted assets. This SPE either had no creditors (i.e., had only investors) or was prohibited by its own corporate charter from filing for bankruptcy (without its investors' consent). This first transaction was designed to be judged a true sale at law, in part by ensuring that the sponsor did not provide excessive credit or yield protection to the SPE.[25] In the *second step*, the initial SPE formed additional SPEs (or other separate entities) to serve as its investors. The funds invested by these separate entities were then applied by the first SPE to the purchase of its assets. These additional structures essentially performed the borrowing function for the first SPE. They sold interests in their investments and could also borrow funds/issue debt. (Exhibit 3 shows a diagram of a generic two-step SPE transaction.) The net effect of this two-step process was that an SPE's investors were taking on the normal business risks of the transferred assets but not the credit risk of the originator.

For an SPE to remain an unconsolidated entity with respect to the originator, it had to meet strict accounting and tax guidelines. These guidelines prohibited companies from creating SPEs to manipulate their earnings, for instance, by selling assets for more than their market value. All transactions taking place between the originator and the SPE had to be judged "at arms length," proving the originator had no control over the SPE and could not manipulate transactions to benefit itself.

Securitization

> Accounting standards mandate that [Enron's] assets and liabilities from its wholesale business be "marked to market"—valued at their market price at a given moment in time. Changes in the valuation are reported in earnings. But these earnings aren't necessarily cash at the instant they are recorded. Skilling says that Enron can convert these contracts [the assets and liabilities mentioned above] to cash anytime it chooses by "securitizing" them, or selling them off to a financial institution. Enron then receives a "servicing fee," but Skilling says that all the risks (for example, changes in the value of the assets and liabilities) are then transferred to the buyer.[26]
>
> —Bethany McLean, *Fortune*

An SPE's investors provided the necessary funds to purchase the targeted assets from the originator. In exchange, the investors had a claim to the future cash flows of assets in the SPE over the life of their investment. The assets serving as the SPE's collateral varied a great deal and, realistically, were only limited by the capability for sophisticated investors to analyze their risks.[27] In the past, financial institutions had sold outstanding loans and mortgages to SPEs, which, in turn, issued securities based on the future interest and principal payments of the obligations. This process was referred to

---

[24] This two-step process was sometimes referred to as the "Norwalk Two Step." For more information see "Heads Up," Deloitte & Touche, April 25, 2001, vol. 8, no. 2.

[25] *Securitization Accounting under FASB 140*, Deloitte & Touche, January 2001.

[26] Bethany McLean, "Is Enron Overpriced," *Fortune*, March 5, 2001.

[27] Since the value of the securities issued by the SPE was closely tied to the value of the assets serving as collateral, the securities were referred to as "asset-backed securities," or ABSes.

EXHIBIT 3

EXAMPLE OF TWO-STEP SPE STRUCTURE

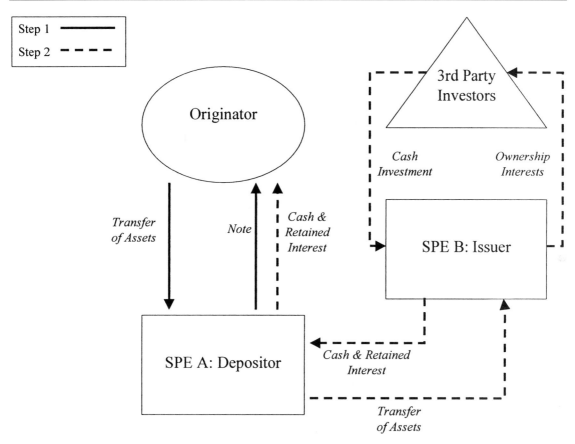

Source: Casewriters' diagram.

as *securitization* because it took assets that were not regularly traded and created new, more liquid assets for a larger market base. By securitizing the loans, financial institutions were able to remove them from their balance sheets and generate funding for more loans or other projects. Other types of companies used SPEs to securitize such receivables as future credit card payments, music royalties, court judgments, Medicare payments, and even movie ticket sales.[28] Some firms would even create "synthetic" risks, using credit derivatives or other secondary sources, to collateralize the SPE's fund-raising.[29] As the market for these types of securities had expanded, the major rating agencies had built models for analyzing securitization deals and issued credit ratings for securitized offerings, and research analysts had started tracking new deals and deals in

[28] Diana B. Henriques, "The Brick Stood Up Before. But Now?" *The New York Times*, March 10, 2002, sec. 3, p. 1, col. 1.

[29] For more information on credit derivatives and synthetic securitization, refer to Chacko et al., "Credit Risk Instruments," HBS Case No. 201-119.

progress. By the turn of the twenty-first century, Wall Street's financial engineers had figured out how to securitize almost anything.

Securitization made markets more efficient by providing investors access to a type of risk they could not get elsewhere. For example, by having access to a larger market, a pool of loans had a greater chance of being funded at a lower cost for the SPE, the originator, and, as a result, the borrower at the other end.[30] Freddie Mac, a government-chartered organization, described the benefits of securitization for providing a liquid mortgage market:

> When Congress created Freddie Mac's charter in 1970, it set a clear mission for us: stabilize the nation's mortgage markets and expand opportunities for homeownership and affordable rental housing. Over the past 30 years, Freddie Mac has accomplished this and more. We have done so not by making individual mortgage loans to consumers, but rather by ensuring that there is a continuous flow of funds to mortgage lenders. As a secondary market for mortgage loans, Freddie Mac purchases mortgages from lenders across the country and packages them into securities that can be sold to investors. Through this securitization process, we ultimately provide low- to middle-income homeowners and renters with lower housing costs and better access to home financing.[31]

In other words, more loans could be made at lower rates by distributing the loans across a wider investor base.

Tax and Accounting Advantages

Companies also used SPEs to take advantage of certain loopholes in tax and accounting regulations. Using modern interpretations of the prevailing accounting standards and tax regulations, SPEs were a convenient way of separating out assets and liabilities for which a company wanted to seek a "blended" treatment, that is, treat them one way for tax purposes and another way for accounting.[32] Companies structured deals with SPEs as counterparties so that different authorities would view the deal differently. Tax and accounting authorities had created rules and tests to decide how a company's assets should be treated. These rules were meant to determine the true ownership of assets and the assignment of responsibility for an asset's risk, return, and public disclosure. Due to the detailed nature of these rules, opportunities existed for companies to operate in a gray area where the rules were unclear. These companies positioned themselves to be granted some ownership responsibilities and not others in an effort to optimize their financial situations. As the different authorities became aware of companies taking advantage of these disparities, they updated their rules to make the regulatory environment more complete.[33] However, with the armies of accountants, bankers, and lawyers that worked around the clock to create new strategies for profiting from such loopholes, it was difficult for authorities to keep up with corporate innovation.

One popular example of using SPEs for tax and accounting purposes was a synthetic lease. Companies used synthetic leases for their office space, factories, and other

---

[30] While a lower cost of funding may have been obtainable through securitization, it was at least partially offset by the cost of organizing the SPE.

[31] "Why Freddie Mac? Our Mission—Our Commitment," copyright Freddie Mac, 2003, at http://www.freddiemac.com/vital_role/, accessed September 15, 2003.

[32] This blended treatment was sometimes referred to as "debt-for-tax/sale-for-accounting."

[33] Such disparities between different types of regulations can be thought of as regulatory "arbitrage" opportunities.

forms of property and equipment. Synthetic leases provided the mechanism to treat the lease as an operating lease for accounting purposes while claiming ownership of the properties for tax purposes. Under an operating lease, a company was able to recognize its payments toward the property as an expense rather than having them show up on its balance sheet as long-term debt (as they would with a capital lease). This made the balance sheet and certain leverage ratios appear more favorable to the common investor. However, in a synthetic lease structure, the company was also able to claim for tax purposes that it was the owner of the property. Therefore, it would be able to deduct its payments for the property as interest payments on debt (rather than a rent expense). According to Donald Weidner, "In short, an investment in a synthetic lease transaction is a high-stakes gamble in the game of form over substance. The bet is that financial accounting standards will honor the transactional form of a lease at the same time that the federal income tax law will perceive that the tenant has made an investment in a depreciable asset with borrowed funds."[34]

In simplified form, a synthetic lease worked as follows: an SPE was created for the sole purpose of borrowing funds, purchasing a new piece of property, and leasing it to a company (the "lessee"). The SPE borrowed from a bank or investors to raise the necessary funds to purchase a property. Its ability to raise capital was based upon the quality of the future lease payments coming from the lessee. Typically, the SPE was able to borrow at a lower rate than the lessee because the financial risk of the SPE was limited to that of the property lease (i.e., the SPE was unable to take on other investments). The lease's terms were kept short (around five years), and the lessee paid the operating costs of the property. The lease payments made to the SPE were set to cover the SPE's obligations to its creditors.

Lawyers carefully structured the terms and covenants of the lease so that the lessee was able to get preferential tax as well as accounting treatments. At the end of the lease, the lessee had the choice of renewing the lease, purchasing the property (for a predetermined price), or selling the property in the market. If the property was sold, the lessee received any gains or losses from changes in the property's value since it had been purchased by the SPE. Given that the lessee received the appreciation or suffered the decline in the value of the property, tax authorities usually recognized the lessee as the virtual owner of the property and allowed depreciation and interest deductions available to owners and borrowers. However, the lease terms were specifically designed to avoid capitalization under the criteria imposed by the Financial Accounting Standards Board (FASB) Statement No. 13 (the accounting standard to be applied to determine whether a lease is an operating lease or a capital lease). In particular, the lease term was less than 75% of the useful life of the asset, and the present value of minimum lease payments was less than 90% of the fair value of the asset. Additionally, there would be no automatic transfer of asset to lessee at the end of the lease or a bargain purchase option given to the lessee. Hence, the property would not be shown on the balance sheet of the lessee, and the lessee would instead report its lease only as an operating expense for accounting purposes.

SPE Accounting Guidelines

On September 29, 2000, the FASB issued Statement No. 140 as a replacement for FASB Statement No. 125. The statement, titled "Accounting for Transfers and Servic-

---

[34] Donald Weidner, "Synthetic Leases: Structured Finance, Financial Accounting and Tax Ownership," *Journal of Corporation Law*, 25(3) (2000): 445–487. Available at http://papers.ssrn.com/sol3/papers.cfm?abstract_id=219588.

ing of Financial Assets and Extinguishments of Liabilities," consolidated and updated many of the accounting guidelines governing the use of SPEs in securitization transactions. According to the summary of FASB 140, the transfer of assets could be accounted for as a sale if the following three conditions were met:

1. The transferred assets had been isolated from the transferor—put presumptively beyond the reach of the transferor and its creditors, even in the bankruptcy or other receivership.

2. Each transferee (or, if the transferee was a qualified SPE, each holder of its beneficial interests) had the right to pledge or exchange the assets (or beneficial interests) it received, and no condition both constrained the transferee (or holder) from taking advantage of its right to pledge or exchange and provided more than trivial benefit to the transferor.

3. The transferor did not maintain effective control over the transferred assets through either (a) an agreement that both entitled and obligated the transferor to repurchase or redeem them before their maturity, or (b) the ability to unilaterally cause the holder to return the specific assets, other than through a cleanup call.[35]

These conditions allowed a company to use an SPE to achieve "off balance sheet" accounting. In other words, if these conditions were met, a company was not required to report the assets and liabilities of the SPE in its financial statements.

While Statement No. 140 and its predecessor, Statement No. 125, were aimed mainly at transfers of financial assets, other accounting rules for SPE accounting and consolidation were created by the FASB as new business uses of SPEs involving the transfer of nonfinancial assets started proliferating during the 1980s. In the 1990s, the FASB's Emerging Issues Task Force (EITF) Issue Number 90-15 added new limitations to companies for them to achieve off balance sheet treatment of SPEs. Among other changes, this EITF "consensus" suggested that a "qualified special purpose entity" (QSPE) needed to have a minimum investment of third-party "outside equity" equal to 3% of the SPE's assets' value.[36] This minimum investment assured that there was an actual transfer of risk taking place and that the residual economics of the assets were held by investors "outside" of the assets' sponsor/transferor. Furthermore, EITF 90-15 specified that an outside party must have a controlling financial interest in the SPE (i.e., 50% or more of the voting interest).

ENRON'S SPEs

> Mr. Fastow [Enron's chief financial officer in 2000] then discussed the Company's [Enron's] private equity strategy and noted that there would be continued significant capital investments by the Company, some of which would not generate cash flow or earning for a number of years. He stated that this would necessitate syndication of capital investments if the Company were to continue to grow. He discussed the Company's current total assets and the total assets when unconsolidated affiliates were included.
>
> —Meeting Minutes, Finance Committee of the Board of Directors,
> Enron Corp., October 6, 2000[37]

---

[35] "Accounting for Transfers and Servicing of Financial Assets and Extinguishments of Liabilities," Financial Accounting Standards Board Statement No. 140, September 2002.

[36] A "QSPE" that met with all the necessary guidelines of the FASB was "qualified" to receive off balance sheet treatment.

[37] From the prepared statement and testimony of Herbert S. Winokur, Jr., in "The Role of the Board of Directors in Enron's Collapse," Hearings by the Permanent Subcommittee on Investigations, U. S. Senate, May 7, 2002, Congressional Records, 107th Congress, p. 141.

Enron engaged in transactions involving hundreds of SPEs. Many of these transactions were used to hedge the risk from various investments Enron had made. Other times, Enron used SPEs in transactions to securitize streams of cash flows. Similarly, the company was able to "monetize" physical investments, moving them off its balance sheet and turning them into cash. The more experienced Enron became with setting up these SPE transactions, the more efficient its personnel became at applying SPE structures to new areas of business. The following transactions show some of the company's many uses for SPEs.

The Destec Transaction[38]

Enron's Destec transaction serves as a good, relatively simple example to illustrate how SPEs are used in business solutions. In the Destec transaction, Enron was able to monetize a stream of incoming royalty payments from certain mining leases it had acquired. As was common with other securitization transactions, Enron was able to transfer its rights to these future royalties in exchange for receiving the present value of these payments.

In the 1970s, Houston Light & Power Company (HL&P) had entered into lease arrangements with The Dow Chemical Company (Dow) for mining coal and lignite, both naturally occurring sources of carbon fuel. The successor to Dow's rights under the leases was Destec Properties Limited Partnership (DPLP). In August of 1997, one month before the Destec transaction, Enron acquired 100% of the general and limited partnership interests of DPLP through its subsidiaries Enron North America (ENA, at the time known as Enron Capital & Trade Resources Corp.) and HGK.[39] At the time of the acquisition, HL&P was committed to buying a minimum of 3.5 million tons of coal and lignite per year, through the year 2016, and paying a fixed price (with the price adjusted upward for inflation during the life of the lease). Under the lease agreement, HL&P was obligated to pay for this amount of coal/lignite regardless of whether it took the commodity from the ground or not (referred to as a "take-or-pay agreement"). This arrangement brought in a fairly fixed stream of cash flows to Enron through its ownership of DPLP. The fixed nature of these cash flows made them suitable for a securitization.

The Destec transaction involved the following steps:

1. DPLP distributed its right to receive the royalty payments to its partners, HGK (i.e., subsidiaries of Enron).

2. HGK assigned the right to receive the royalty payments to ECT Coal Company No. 1 (CoalCo), a subsidiary of Enron formed specifically for the purpose of the Destec transaction. In exchange for the right to these royalties, CoalCo paid HGK $110 million.

3. CoalCo assigned the right to receive the royalty payments to a trust (the Destec Trust), formed by the parties, in exchange for $110 million. The Destec Trust issued notes to investors based on the value of the incoming royalty payments, raising a total of $150 million in proceeds. (There were no equity holders in the Destec Trust.)

---

[38] The primary source of information in this section was Neal Batson, "In re: Enron Corp., et al., Debtors; Chapter 11 Case No. 01-1634, *First Interim Report of Neal Batson*, Court-Appointed Examiner," September 21, 2002, pp. 147–157.

[39] Specifically, the limited partnership interests were held by HGK Enterprises LP, Inc. and general partnership interest was held by HGK Enterprises GP, Inc. (collectively referred to as "HGK" above). Both HGK Enterprises LP, Inc. and HGK Enterprises GP, Inc. were subsidiaries of ENA, at the time called Enron Capital & Trade Resources Corp.

4. The Destec Trust entered into a swap agreement with ENA (a unit of Enron) to hedge interest rate and deflation risk. The Destec Trust made an up-front payment of $40 million in exchange for this swap agreement.

   a. The notes issued by the Destec Trust paid a *floating* interest rate, while it was receiving *fixed* royalty payments. Therefore, in the swap agreement, ENA was obligated to make a floating payment to the Destec Trust covering any accrued and unpaid interest, payable on the notes (i.e., not covered by the royalty payments). Furthermore, ENA was obligated to pay a premium if Enron's credit rating fell below investment grade.

   b. In the deflation component of the swap agreement, ENA was obligated to pay the Destec Trust an amount dependent on the amount of coal and lignite covered by the royalty payments if the inflation-adjusted price set in the take-or-pay agreement fell below a fixed price stated in the swap agreement. Similarly, if the inflation-adjusted price was greater than the fixed price in the swap agreement, the Destec Trust was obligated to com-pensate ENA. This arrangement effectively hedged the Destec Trust against unexpectedly low inflation and against deflation in exchange for ENA credit risk.

5. At the closing of the Destec transaction, Enron guaranteed the payment and performance of all obligations for its subsidiaries and partners in the transaction, including CoalCo, ENA, and DPLP. However, Enron's guaranty did not cover the performance of the notes issued by the Destec Trust or the royalty payments made by HL&P. Therefore, if HL&P's royalty payments were not received as anticipated, the investors in the Destec Trust (i.e., noteholders) would experience a delay in payments or even suffer losses.

Through the Destec transaction, Enron removed the right to receive HL&P royalty payments off its balance sheet, along with the risks associated with that asset, and received $110 million, along with $40 million for entering into a related swap agreement. Since the proceeds from the transaction exceeded the basis of the royalty rights (i.e., their acquisition cost), Enron was able to recognize a gain on the sale of the assets to the Destec Trust. Enron expected to treat the transfer of assets as a true sale for legal and accounting purposes and as a loan transaction for income tax purposes.

Investors in the Destec Trust's "asset-backed" notes took additional steps to protect their investment by receiving documented legal opinions regarding the "fairness" of the true sale and non-consolidation of the Destec Trust's underlying assets. Therefore, if Enron were to go bankrupt, the company's creditors would not be able to lay claim to the assets transferred to the Destec Trust. (Exhibit 4 shows a diagram of the Destec transaction.)

LJM Cayman L.P. and the Rhythms Transaction

Many Enron transactions used an outside entity named LJM Cayman L.P (LJM1). LJM1 was conceived by Enron's CFO as a way for the company to transact quickly and efficiently with a select group of sophisticated investors. In fact, to further expedite these transactions, it was decided that CFO Andrew Fastow would serve as the general partner of LJM1. Fastow's knowledge of Enron's assets and operations gave him a key advantage at identifying investment opportunities with Enron and generating interest from the outside investor community. After convincing Enron's board of directors of the ben-

EXHIBIT 4

ENRON CORP.'S DESTEC TRANSACTION

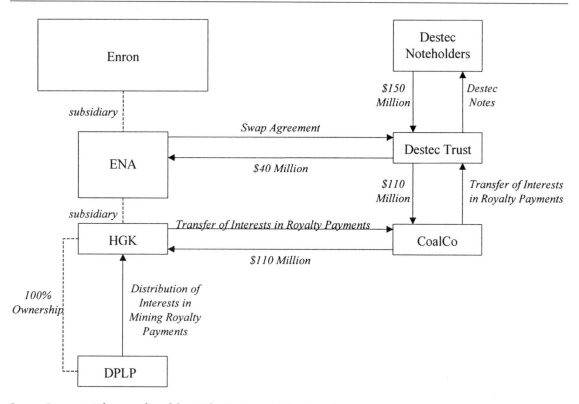

Source: Casewriters' diagram adapted from "The First Examiner's Report."

efits to the company of having Fastow in control of a partnership that existed outside Enron, the new entity was formed in June 1999.

Fastow became the general partner of LJM1 through a chain of new entities: LJM Partners, LLC and LJM Partners L.P. This chain worked by having Fastow as the sole and managing member of LJM Partners, LLC, which was the general partner of LJM Partners L.P., which in turn served as the general partner of LJM1. Fastow invested $1 million of his own capital in LJM1 and successfully raised an additional $15 million from two limited partners. The limited partners, each contributing $7.5 million, were affiliated with major international banking institutions.

In one of the transactions involving LJM1, Enron attempted to hedge its risk exposure to one of its equity investments. In March 1998, Enron had invested $10 million in the stock of Rhythms NetConnections, Inc. (Rhythms), a privately held Internet service provider (ISP) for businesses. Rhythms went public on April 7, 1999; by May 1999, Enron's investment had grown to be worth roughly $300 million. However, due to certain restrictions placed on selling the Rhythms shares before the end of 1999, Enron was unable to sell and lock in the investment's gains. Since Enron included its holdings in Rhythms as part of its merchant portfolio, it marked the investment to market. This meant that changes in the price of Rhythms shares (in the market) were directly reflected in the value of Enron's merchant portfolio and thus in Enron's income statement. Without the ability to sell the shares, Enron had grown concerned that a decline in the price of Rhythms shares could negatively impact Enron's earnings. (Exhibit 5 shows the stock price history of Rhythms.)

Enron's management decided it was important to find a hedge for the Rhythms investment. However, given the size of Enron's stake, the relative illiquidity of Rhythms shares, and the lack of comparable companies trading on the market, it was difficult to identify a proper hedge that was publicly available and not prohibitively expensive to enact. Therefore, through the process of elimination, Enron decided to leverage its own resources to produce a sufficient hedge for its investment.

Corresponding with this effort, Enron's management saw an opportunity to overcome another financial obstacle. Enron had previously entered into forward contracts on its own common stock with an investment bank to hedge the potential dilution in earnings from its employee stock options program. As a result of the growth in Enron's

EXHIBIT 5

HISTORICAL STOCK PRICE GRAPH FOR RHYTHMS NETCONNECTIONS, INC.

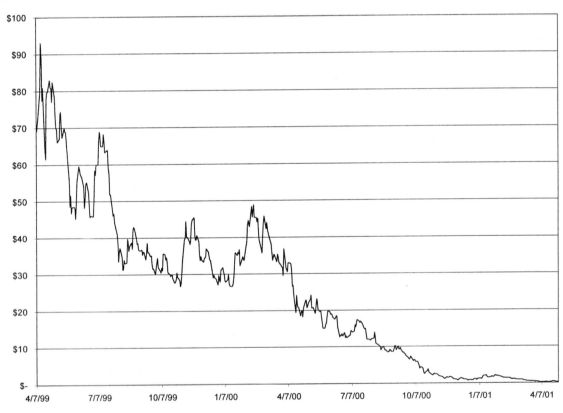

Source: Casewriters' diagram based on Rhythms NetConnections, Inc. price data for April 7, 1999 through April 30, 2001, obtained from Thompson Financial Datastream (accessed June 6, 2003).

stock price, the forward contracts had become considerably more valuable. However, Enron found itself unable to recognize the full value of the forward contracts in its income statement. Accounting principles prohibited a company from recognizing gains resulting from changes in the value of its own common stock (including forward contracts) as income. Therefore, Enron had sought alternatives to release what it deemed as the "trapped value" embedded in these contracts.

CFO Fastow and other members of Enron management envisioned a method of utilizing the value in the forward contracts to hedge the Rhythms investment. The plan required creating an SPE that would be capitalized primarily using the value from the forward contracts and then entering into a hedging agreement with the SPE to lower its exposure to the Rhythms investment. After discussing the strategy with Enron's executive management, the transaction was structured as follows:

1. Enron restructured the forward contracts it had with the investment bank, producing 3.4 million shares of Enron stock.

2. Enron transferred the newly released 3.4 million shares to LJM1.
   a. At the closing price on the date of the transaction (June 30, 1999), the 3.4 million shares were worth $276 million.
   b. A contractual restriction was placed on selling a portion of the Enron shares, precluding their sale or transfer for four years. As a result of this stipulation, the shares were subjected to a so-called marketability discount for valuation purposes and were discounted by 39% of their market value (a discount of about $108 million).
   c. LJM1 provided Enron with a note for $64 million, due on March 31, 2000.

3. LJM1 then transferred 1.6 million Enron shares (estimated market value of $80 million) and $3.75 million in cash to capitalize a newly created SPE (SPE 1). The $3.75 million in cash came from selling an unrestricted portion of the original 3.4 million Enron shares.

4. SPE 1 gave Enron a put option on 5.4 million shares of Rhythms stock. The option, valued at $104 million, had a strike price of $56 per share and was exercisable in June 2004.

5. The put option received by Enron from SPE 1, combined with the $64 million note received from LJM1, was determined to be a fair value in exchange for the restricted Enron stock given to LJM1.

The Rhythms transaction closed at the end of June 1999. The put option gave Enron a payoff opposite that of its Rhythms investment's market value and helped ease the volatility of Enron's merchant portfolio. Furthermore, using the released Enron shares from the restructured forward contracts made the hedge affordable for Enron to pursue.

LJM2 Co-Investment, L.P. and the Fishtail & Bacchus Transactions

After successfully incorporating LJM1 in multiple deals, Enron's management decided to help form another similar outside entity to assist with its business operations. In October of 1999 LJM2 Co-Investment, L.P (LJM2), a Delaware limited partnership, was created to follow in the path of its smaller predecessor, LJM1. LJM2 was, once again, managed by Enron's CFO but would be operated under the oversight of Enron's chief accounting officer and chief risk officer. LJM2 successfully raised over $200 million in capital from institutional private-equity investors. As a private-equity fund, LJM2 could enter into arms-length transactions with Enron, investing in assets that Enron made available. In fact, LJM2's investors were informed that Enron would be the primary source of the fund's investment opportunities. With Fastow at the helm, LJM2 served as a knowledgeable counterparty that could offer Enron quick syndication solutions and financial flexibility for its investment portfolio.

Fishtail

Project Fishtail, established December 19, 2000, was a typical example of how LJM2 became an important element in executing Enron's business strategy. Enron had been considering divesting its paper and pulp trading business. It had been decided that these assets were tying up excessive amounts of Enron's capital and were limiting the new opportunities the company could pursue. More importantly, the paper and pulp trading business had added significant weight to Enron's balance sheet and had not contributed to the earnings growth that was expected of Enron. Moving the paper and pulp assets "off balance sheet" would improve Enron's financial statements by removing the poor-performing assets and their corresponding liabilities from the balance sheet and still allow Enron to retain some presence in the wood-products industry. Therefore, Fishtail was created to achieve the off balance sheet treatment of these assets.

In Fishtail, Enron transferred its targeted paper and pulp assets to a new SPE and created an off balance sheet partnership surrounding these assets with outside private-equity investors. The transaction worked as follows:

1. Enron established the value of its targeted paper and pulp assets and transferred them to a new SPE (SPE 1).
    a. The "hard dollar" assets that made up Enron's paper and pulp-trading operations (e.g., their trading book, inventory of related securities and contracts) had been reported on Enron's balance sheet at a book value of approximately $85 million. These assets were transferred to SPE 1 together with associated "soft assets," including Enron's credit support, management talent, technology platform, Internet experience, and risk management services.
    b. A predominant investment bank, brought in for a third-party valuation, determined the valuation of the total assets (hard-dollar assets and soft assets) transferred from Enron to SPE 1 to be $200 million.
2. A second SPE (SPE 2) was created to invest in SPE 1 and, thus, served as Enron's partner. Enron and SPE 2 respectively held 50% of the voting interests in SPE 1.
3. LJM2 and an outside investment bank (Bank 1) provided $50 million in capital (and capital commitments) to SPE 2.
    a. LJM2 invested $8 million with an investment horizon of six months.
        i. LJM2 was paid a $0.35 million fee by SPE 2.
        ii. LJM2 had an expected return on investment (ROI) of 15%, which was supported through commitments from Enron.
    b. Bank 1 gave SPE 2 a six-month funding commitment for $42 million.
        i. Bank 1 was paid a $0.5 million fee by SPE 2.
        ii. Bank 1 received 15 basis points on any undrawn funds and LIBOR plus 2% on any drawn funds.

4. SPE 2 contributed $50 million in equity to SPE 1.
    a. SPE 2 assigned to SPE 1 the $42 million funding commitment from Bank 1 and contributed $8 million in cash.
    b. Enron's independent auditor permitted the funding commitment of Bank 1 to be counted toward the measurement of equity of SPE 2 in SPE 1, even though it was not actual cash.
5. Enron exchanged certain management services (primarily the management and operation of the paper and pulp-trading platform) with SPE 2 for any residual interests in the partnership (i.e., proceeds left over after Bank 1 and LJM2 were compensated).

The SPE 1 partnership was structured to give Enron the ability to move the paper and pulp assets (the physical assets) off its balance sheet and replace them with a financial asset, namely its investment in SPE 1. According to Enron's independent auditor, Enron needed to transfer a minimum 20% (a 4:1 split) of the economic interest and 50% of the voting interest for the partnership to qualify for off balance sheet treatment under accepted accounting principles. Economic interests are initially measured by the amount of equity contributed by each partner. The SPE needed to acquire the minimum 3% outside equity investment as well. The $8 million in equity from LJM2 was classified as an outside equity investment for this purpose.

Bacchus

Following Fishtail, the Bacchus transaction took place, on December 26, 2000. In Bacchus, Enron sold its partnership investment in Project Fishtail's SPE 1 to a new SPE, treating it as sale of a financial asset under the accounting guidelines for securitizations. The transaction proceeded as follows:

1. Enron transferred its investment in Fishtail to a new SPE (SPE A). In exchange, SPE A gave Enron a note for $200 million. Enron also held "Class A" interest in SPE A, giving it 100% of the voting interest in SPE A along with all of the residual economic interest after the "Class B" interest (see below).
2. SPE A then transferred its Class B interest to another SPE (SPE B). In exchange, SPE B gave SPE A a $200 million note with an 8.36% coupon.
3. SPE B then transferred the Class B interest to SPE C in exchange for $200 million in cash. SPE C was established by Enron and capitalized with a $194 million loan from a large bank (Bank 2) and a $6 million equity investment from another major bank (Bank 3). This $6 million investment covered SPE A's minimum of 3% outside equity.
    a. Bank 2 and Bank 3 entered into a "total return swap," transferring the risk of the $6 million equity investment to Bank 2. This gave Bank 2 the full risk of the $200 million in SPE A. The swap was used once Bank 2 realized holding both the equity and debt in SPE A would not raise regulatory issues.
    b. Enron reduced Bank 2's risk exposure by entering into a total return swap agreement with Bank 2, providing credit support for the $194 million loan. Under this agreement, Enron essentially guaranteed Bank 2's loan by pledging to make the bank whole if the investment's underlying assets were insufficient to pay back the loan. While this swap agreement did not cover the $6 million equity investment, verbal support was given by Enron to ensure repayment of this investment as well.

As a result of Bacchus, Enron booked $200 million in revenue and a $112 million gain in income.

CONCLUSION

As Ron Tolbert of the RAC group reviewed the information on Enron's use of SPEs to offload assets, monetize investments, and mitigate risks, he understood that the board's main concern was whether some of the transactions had left residual risk behind on Enron's balance sheet. The perception that ratings agencies, banks, and shareholders had regarding the risk in Enron's balance sheet greatly impacted Enron's cost of capital. So accurately conveying this information was vital to Enron's ability to carry out business.

DS-1

EQUITY OPTIONS: CONCEPTS

16

Note on Basic Option Properties

Options are contacts that give the right, but not the obligation, to either buy or sell a specific underlying security for a specified price on or before a specific date.

This note takes its cue from this fundamental option definition, to explain the basics of options. It will cover fundamentals such as the payoff schemes of options, parameters that influence their value, the parity between put and call options, and also the upper and lower bounds of options prices. Before we jump into all that, however, let's start with a basic example that shows how options work.

Say that you are interested in owning stock in Acme, Inc. Currently, Acme's shares trade at $100, which you think is low. You believe the stock should be valued more highly and that its price soon will rise. If you bought now and sold it later, you would therefore make money. However, you are not completely sure, so rather than outright buying the stock, you buy an option from someone who does own Acme stock. The option contract gives you the right to buy the stock at $100, no matter what the actual stock price is, before a certain end date that is specified in the contract. Of course, you have to pay an upfront fee to the person that owns the stocks and who might have to part with them. Note that you actually don't own the underlying stock just because you purchased an option. The option derives its value (which is why we call it a derivative instrument) from the stock, but it is not the stock itself. The party that sold you the option contract still holds the stock; what you have is a promise to own the stock later in time, should the share price rise above the level you picked. Your contract also specifies an ending time, after which the option no is longer valid.

In theory, options can be written on almost any type of underlying security. Equity (stock) is the most common but there are also several types of non-equity options, based on securities such as bonds, foreign currency, financial indices, or physical goods like gold or coffee. This note will primarily deal with equity options.

Professors George Chacko and Peter Hecht, Executive Director of the HBS Europe Research Center Vincent Dessain and Research Associate Anders Sjöman prepared this note as the basis for class discussion.

People normally trade in options to speculate in the change in value of the underlying security. For instance, the person who sold you the option on Acme's stock is probably speculating that the stock price will *not* rise above $100. If the price is below $100 by the end of your contract, the seller can then simply pocket the upfront fee—or premium—that you paid. You on the other hand speculate that it will rise.

The person who buys an option is normally called the "buyer" or "holder." Conversely, the seller is known as the "seller" or "writer." Stock option contracts generally represent 100 shares of the underlying stock. Options do not have to be purchased directly from the person or company that either owns the security or wrote the initial options contract—they also trade extensively in the secondary market. Options are traded both in public markets, such as organized exchanges like the Chicago Board Options Exchange and Deutsche Börse's EUREX, and in the so called Over-the-Counter (OTC) market, where financial actors, like investment banks, corporate treasurers and fund managers trade directly with each other over the phone or via inter-connected computer systems. The public markets primarily trade standardized equity options. The OTC market trades all other types of options, plus equity options of large sizes or with unusual characteristics.

CALL AND PUT OPTIONS

The ACME option you just bought gave you the right to purchase stock. In the options industry, this is known as a call option. Conversely, if you owned stock, you could buy the right to *sell* them at a certain price; known as a put option. Let's describe each of these two option types in more detail

Call Options

A call option is the right (but not the obligation) to buy the underlying security at a specific price (known as the exercise or strike price) before a certain date (the expiration or exercise date). If you have the right to exercise the option before the exercise date, it is known as an "American" option; if you can exercise only on the expiration date itself, it is a "European" option. If the call option is on equity, one option normally gives you the right to purchase 100 shares of the underlying stock.

Investors who believe that the value of the underlying will increase before the expiration date usually buy call options. It gives them the possibility of buying stock below future market prices. For instance, let's assume that the ACME option you bought was an "Acme April 100 call option." It gives you the right to buy 100 shares of Acme at any time before the April expiration date. If the price of Acme shares rises to $110 before the expiration date, you could exercise your option and buy the stock. If you then immediately sold the stock, you would realize a profit of $10 per share.

Put Options

A put option is the call options opposite. A put option gives the right, but not the obligation, to sell the underlying security at a specific price on or before the expiration date. A put becomes more valuable if the price of the underlying falls. For example, assume you own 100 Acme shares and that you buy an "Acme April 100 put option." This gives you the right to sell your 100 shares of Acme at a strike price of $100 on or before the April expiration. Say that the Acme shares drop to $80 during the option term. You can then realize a profit of $20 per share by exercising the option, since it guarantees you a price of $100. Just as a call option allows you to speculate in rising stock prices, a put option lets you speculate in falling stock prices.

Note that in this example you speculated against stock that you already owned, known as a "covered option." You can actually trade options for stock that you do not own, known as a "naked option." If you exercise the put option and have to deliver the actual stock, you would have to purchase the stock in a separate transaction.

Option Payoffs: At-the-Money, In-the-Money, or Out-of-the-Money

The payoff pattern for call and put options naturally differ—simply said they are each other's opposites. Figure 1 shows a typical payoff pattern for a call option. Based on our Acme example, the call option does not start to pay off unless the stock price goes above the strike price of $100.

The reverse payoff relationship is true for a put option, as shown in Figure 2. The option has a positive payoff as long as the stock price is below $100. If it hits $100 or more, though, the option becomes valueless to the holder, who will choose not to exercise it since it has zero payoff.

Note that the payoff schemes above are for when you buy options; in trader jargon: holding or going long the options. If you instead short the options (same as writing or selling an option), you have the exact same payoff multiplied by a negative one: for instance, the payoff for a short call is *negative* 10 if the stock price is 110 while the payoff to the holder of the option is *plus* 10.

When traders talk about the payoffs of options, they often discuss whether an option is at-the-money, in-the-money or out-of-the-money. **At-the-money** is the easiest concept to understand: it occurs when the price of the underlying security is equal to the strike price. For both figures above, the at-the-money level is $100.

When an option is **in-the-money**, the option holders gain a profit if they exercise the option. For a call option, in-the-money is when the strike price is less than the market price of the underlying security. In Figure 1 this happens to the right of the $100 level. Conversely, the put option is in-the-money if the strike price is greater than the market price of the underlying security. In Figure 2 this is the area to the left of the $100 level.

Being **out-of-the-money** is when the option holder would *not* gain a profit if the option was exercised. A holder of an option that reaches expiration and is out-of-money simply does not exercise the option. There is no loss associated with not exercising, except the loss of the fee that the holder paid to own the option. Out-of-the-money is the opposite of in-the-money for both option types: a call option is out-of-the-money if the

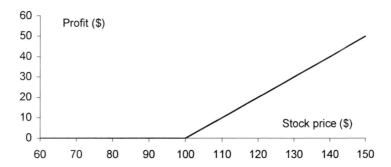

Figure 1 Payoff for a Call Option

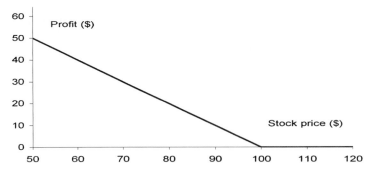

Figure 2 Payoff for a Put Option

strike price is greater than the market price of the underlying security and a put option is out-of-the money if the strike price is less than the market price of the underlying security.

Option Terminology

Since options convey the right but not the obligation to sell or buy, you always have the choice of not exercising your options. Also, instead of exercising an option, you can choose to sell it in the options market, a move normally referred to as "closing a position."

Other terminology you hear in the market is "going long" or "going short" an option. In its most basic form it simply means owning (going long or taking a long position) or selling (going short or shorting) the option. A "short call" means a sale of a call option; a "long call" means a purchase of a call option. Note that you can actually take a short-like position by buying a put option on stock that you don't own. You then potentially make a profit by later buying the stocks at a lower price than you are about to sell them for. The term "short selling" then generally refers to sales of a security that the seller does not own, or any sale that is completed by the delivery of a security borrowed by the seller. The opposite of "selling short" is "going long."

In general, combining long and short positions in various stocks and options is the basis for common trading strategies.

Other common options terms (some of which we have already encountered) are:

- **Underlying interest or security:** The security (such as stock, commodity, or index) on which an option is written and traded.
- **Expiry, expiration or maturity date**: The date that the option expires and the option seller ceases to have an obligation to honor the options contract. (A related expression is expiry cycle which refers to the month or week that the option expires.)
- **Exercise or strike price**: The price at which the underlying security can be bought or sold.
- **Exercise style (American and European options)**: We know that an option holder has the right to exercise the option—but it differs between options exactly when the holder has the right to do so. If the option only can be exercised on the expiration date itself, it is known as a European style option. If it can be exercised any time leading up to the expiry date, it is called an American style option. Most options in developed markets are of the American type.

- **Trading hours**: The days and hours that options are bought and sold. Related is the term "last trading day," which is the last day that your option can be bought or sold.
- **Option Premium**: Another word for the price of the option. It is paid by the buyer to the writer, or seller, of the option. The writer keeps the premium whether or not the option is exercised. You can look at it like this: Since writers lose whenever option buyers find it to their advantage to exercise an option, the writer wants an upfront payment to be compensated for this possible future exposure.

OPTION VALUE SENSITIVITIES

It is common to say that the value of an option, as it is being issued and also as it trades in the secondary market, depends on six important parameters. Since an option is a derivative security—it derives its value from an underlying asset—the price of the underlying asset is naturally a very important influence on the value of the option, but it is not the only one.

Stock Price

For an equity option, the price of the underlying stock is naturally the most important influence on its value. The relationship is easy to understand and is, as always, the opposite for call and put options. We said earlier that call options are in-the-money if the stock price exceeds the strike price. Call options therefore become more valuable as the underlying stock's price increases. Put options, by contrast, become more valuable as the underlying stock price decreases.

Strike Price

The strike price also influences the option value. Referring to Figure 1, assume that the stock price of a call option didn't move—but that its strike price did. If the strike price increased, it would require an increasingly higher stock price for the option to move into-the-money. In other words, the value of the call option decreases as the strike price increased. As always, the opposite holds for the put option: as the strike price increases in value, the put option value increases.

Volatility

Volatility measures how much the value of the underlying is expected to fluctuate (rise and/or fall) over time. Exactly how to calculate volatility is beyond the scope of this note, but in broad terms there are two ways to estimate volatility in the market: historical volatility (based on past price activity) and implied volatility (starts with the option price as a given and works backwards given a pricing model to deduct the volatility.) The more volatile the future is assumed to be, the higher the value for both call and put options. The magnitude and direction of the underlying price movement, however, has differential value impacts for calls and puts. For a call option, large increases in stock prices translate into higher value, whereas large decreases in stock prices only result in a small limited loss (the price of the option itself). For a put option, the opposite is true: large decreases in stock prices result in increased value, whereas large increases only lead to a limited loss.

Time-to-Maturity

Also known as Time-to-Expiration, this is the only parameter of the six that is different for European and American style options. Consider first the American option, which can be exercised at any point up to its expiration date. Its value—both for call and put options—increase as the time to expiration increases. The reason is intuitive: an option with a longer time-to-maturity than an otherwise identical option must have at least the same value—and then a little more.

The European style options behave for the most part in the same way as American, but they have one complication. Take two European call options written on the same underlying stock, one with a two-month time-to-maturity and the other with four months to expiration. Assume now that a large dividend is due in three months. According to normal market behavior, the stock price will decline on the ex-dividend date, which as we know means that a call option becomes less valuable. However, this is only true for the longer-term option. The option with a two-month time to maturity will not be affected by the dividend, so its value is therefore not affected. Consequently, there is no way to generalize the time-to-maturity parameter's impact on European style options.

Interest Rate

Changes in the risk-free interest rate[1] affect the option value in a rather complicated way. If the interest rate increases independently of the other parameters, including stock price, the preset value of a call option (put option) will increase (decrease). However, in practice, when interest rates go up they usually have a negative impact on stock prices. The combined effect is therefore not clear from one time to another.

Dividends

As mentioned for the time-to-maturity parameter, a stock that pays a dividend will drop in value on the ex-dividend date. This means that the dividends expected during the life of the option will make call options lose in value and put options increase in value.

Table A on the following page summarizes the description of the six factors. It shows what happens to the value of an American style option (one that can be exercised at any point up to its expiry) when each factor increases. Note that the table assumes that one factor changes while the others remain fixed; as we discussed for the interest rate factor the connection can be more complicated at times. Furthermore, remember that a European style option will behave almost the same way as an American option. The one exception is that for European type options there is no certain relationship with Time to Maturity. For example, if the maturity date is pushed forward, the extended time-to-maturity might include an extra dividend payment, which in that case would negatively affect a call option.

---

[1] The risk-free interest rate is the rate that you'd get from investing in instruments with no risk. It is a theoretical construct that does not exist in reality. It is however often assumed in practice to be the same as short dated government bonds, such as short term U.S. Treasury Bills or German government treasury bonds (for the Euro zone). These types of bonds are thought to be virtually risk-free since they have close to no default risk (the likelihood these governments would collapse is minimal) and no interest rate risk (since they are of short-term maturities).

TABLE A Impact on Option Prices (American Style Option)

Variable	Call	Put
Stock price	+	−
Strike price	−	+
Volatility	+	+
Time to maturity	+	+
Interest rate	+	−
Dividends	−	+

PAYOFFS FOR STOCKS AND BONDS

Above we showed the payoff for call and put options. For completeness, let's compare these with the payoff for stocks (equity) and risk-free bonds (debt). Figure 3 shows the profit potential that comes from owning stock in a company. As the stock price increases, the payoff increases just as much; if the stock goes up by $50, the profit also increases by $50. The slope of the payoff line is in other words 1.

The payoff for a risk-free bond is different. Figure 4 shows the profit potential of a zero-coupon bond (one that makes no interest payments to the bond holder). As the line shows, no matter how the stock price changes, the bond holder only receives the principal value of the bond when the bond matures (in the figure, the assumed principal amount is $60). Since the stock price has no impact on the bond value, the line is flat.

PUT-CALL PARITY

We have now looked at the payoff schemes for options, stocks and bonds, and we have also covered how the value of an option is affected by parameters such as stock and strike price. Combining these schemes will help illustrate an important option concept known as *put-call parity*. As the word "parity" conveys, there exists a type of equivalence between put and call options; it specifies the relationship between the prices of European call options and European put options of the same class (that is, with the

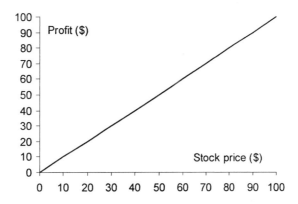

Figure 3 Payoff for stock

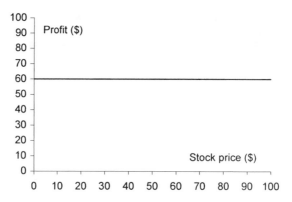

Figure 4   Payoff for bonds

same underlying security, strike price and expiration date). Note that the parity relationship only holds for European options and not for American (which can be exercised before its maturity date).

The parity relationship states that the value of a European call with a certain strike price and maturity can be deduced from the value of a European style put option with the same strike price and maturity (and vice versa). A common way of explaining put-call parity is to compare two portfolios. The first portfolio consists of a stock. The second portfolio consists of a long call option, a short put option,[2] and a zero-coupon bond. The call and the put have the same strike price and maturity, while the bond's maturity matches those of the options and its principal amount equals their strike price. The key observation is that the two portfolios have exactly the same payoff at the maturity of the options/bond. Because they have the same value at maturity no matter what the stock price is at that time, their present values today must then also be the same. This is the put-call parity.

As an alternative way of explaining put-call parity, Figure 5 shows the portfolio replication argument graphically. It combines the payoffs of a long call option, a short put option, and a bond to form the stock payoff. In the graphs, the line crosses the X-axis at the strike price, K. First combining a call option and a short put option gives the straight line of the stock payoff chart. However, relative to the stock payoff, its payoff is everywhere lower by a value of K. If we add the bond payoff, this then brings the whole line back up by K, making the net payoff intersect the x and y axis at the origin (the 0/0 intersection of the two axes).

As the figure shows, combinations of options can create positions that are the same as holding the stock itself—this is the core of financial engineering. By using a call, a put, and a bond we are able to synthetically construct a stock, or put differently assemble a portfolio that replicates the payoff of the stock in the future. Therefore, for no arbitrage[3] opportunities to exist the portfolio's present value today must equal the stock's present value today. So, the value of the call today minus the value of the put today plus the value of the bond today must equal the value of the stock today. This can be expressed as:

---

[2] Remember, a "long call" means buying a call option and a "short put" means selling a put option.

[3] Simply put, an "arbitrage trade" takes advantage of price discrepancies in the market for securities (or portfolios of securities) with identical future payoffs. A long position in the cheap security and a short position in the expensive security lead to a profit today with no possibility of a future liability.

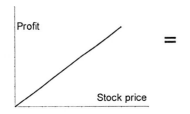

Stock Payoff

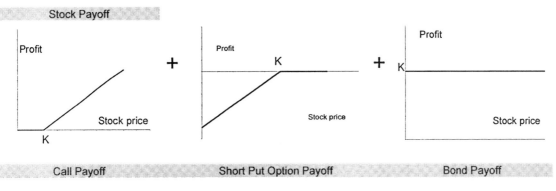

Call Payoff   Short Put Option Payoff   Bond Payoff

Figure 5   Put-Call Parity Explained Graphically

$$S = C(K) - P(K) + PV(K) \qquad [1]$$

where:

S = stock

C = call option

P = put option

PV = present (or discounted) value of the bond (whose payoff at maturity is K)

K = strike price

In other words, if you know the value of three of the parameters, you can deduce the fourth. Suppose you want to know the value of a call option, and you know the value of an equivalent put option, the risk-free interest rate and the stock price. Plug the values into the formula and you receive the value of the call option.

Put-Call Parity in Use

What put-call parity helps us do is to price, for instance, a put option as long as we know the price of a call option on the same underlying and with the same strike price and expiration date. Let's exemplify using the formula above. Suppose that the stock price is $20, the strike price is $20, the price of a European call option is $5, the risk-free interest rate is 5% and that you wanted to know the value of a European put option. Plugging those numbers into [1] gives us:

$$\$20 = \$5 - P(\$20) + PV(\$20) \qquad [2]$$

Present value, *PV*, for $20, assuming a one-year horizon and given the 5% interest rate is $19.05. Now solving for *P* gives us the value of the put option—if no arbitrage possibility exists—at $4.05.

However, what would happen if the parity did *not* hold? What if the put actually traded at $3.50 and not at $4.05? An arbitrage opportunity would present itself, since we know that the payoff of the put should be the same as the call minus the stock plus the present value of the zero-coupon bond. However, despite that their payoff is the same, the price is not. The put is underpriced relative to the combination of the other instruments with the identical net payoff.

The most standard arbitrage strategy is to buy the cheaper instrument and sell the expensive. In this case, this means buying the traded put $3.50 and selling the "synthetic put," or the combination of the other instruments. (Using vocabulary from earlier, you go long the put and short the synthetic put.) This trade results in an up-front payoff of $0.55. There are no further payoff implications since you are both short and long a put at the same time.

UPPER AND LOWER BOUNDS FOR OPTION PRICES

An important feature of options prices is that their value cannot exceed or go below a particular price, given the option's characteristic. For instance, the upper bound is the maximum possible price for a call option or a put option at any point in time. These upper and lower bounds of an option set the price limits that are consistent with no arbitrage opportunities. (If option prices go above the upper bound or below the lower bound, investors have an arbitrage opportunity.) As always, calls and puts differ in their definition of upper bounds. To simplify our description, we'll use European style options based on a non-dividend paying stock.

Call Option: Upper and Lower Bounds for European Calls on Non-Dividend Paying Stock

As we know, a call option gives the holder the right to buy stock. It follows then that the option cannot in any circumstance be worth more than stock price, S. This becomes the upper bound of the European style call option with no dividend payments, C. Its value should be lower or equal to the stock price, expressed as:

$$C \leq S \qquad [3]$$

Conversely, a lower bound for a European call is the stock price minus the present value of the strike price. It can be expressed as:

$$S - PV(K) \leq C \qquad [4]$$

Combine these two bounds and you get the full range for the call option C,

$$S - PV(K) \leq C \leq S \qquad [5]$$

To exemplify, let's pick a situation when one of these bounds actually does *not* hold. Assume you have a stock at $20, a strike price at $15, and a risk-free interest rate at 5%. The price of the call should therefore be greater than or equal to $5.71 (the result of the left hand side of equation [5]).

But suppose now that the call was actually trading at $5.00—which then violates this lower bound. The call is in other words underpriced and an arbitrage opportunity presents itself, where we want to sell (go short) the left-hand side of the equation and buy the call. How this arbitrage trade plays out can be described in tabular form, as done in the table below.

TABLE B   Arbitrage Trade When Lower Bound Does Not Hold

	Today	Future	
		$S > 15$	$S \cdot 15$
Buy call	−5.00	$S − 15$	0
Short sell stock	20.00	$−S$	$−S$
Buy bond	−14.29	15	15
S	0.71	0	15 −

Reading column-by-column, we first look at the value of our trade today. The net upfront gain is $0.71 (we buy a call option at $5.00, we short sell the stock for $20.00, and then buy a bond, whose present value, given a one year time horizon, is $14.29). This is still not an arbitrage—this is what we make today, but we don't know yet what might happen in the future.

In fact, there are two things that could happen in the future: the stock value could be above the strike price of $15, or it could be below. These two states are represented in the table by one column each. To start with, if the stock price goes above $15, then the call will be in-the-money and worth $S − 15$. Short selling the stock results just in the (negative) stock value itself and the bond at maturity is worth $15. All in all, we neither make nor lose money in this state.

However, if the stock price never reaches $15, we do make money. The long call expires worthless, the short stock position has a value of $−S$, and the bond pays off $15. However, since the stock price is below $15, our payoff ends up being the difference between $15 and the stock price. Put differently, $15 − S$ must be positive.

So, in the future, we have no chance of losing money and, in fact, have a chance of making money. Since we make money today and have no possible future liability, this is an arbitrage.

Put Options: Upper and Lower Bound for Non-Dividend Paying European Puts

The upper bound for a European put option is established from the fact that a put gives its holder the right to sell a stock. Given this, no matter how low the stock price becomes, the put option, P, can never be worth more than the strike price, K, at maturity. Thus, the upper bound is simply the option's strike price, K, discounted back to today using the risk-free rate. The value of a put will be lower than or at most equal to the present value of the option strike price, which can be expressed as:

$$P \leq PV(K) \qquad [6]$$

Conversely, a lower bound for a European put is the strike price (discounted using the risk-free interest rate, r) minus the stock price, or:

$$PV(K) − S \leq P \qquad [7]$$

Combine these two bounds and you get the full range for the put option P,

$$PV(K) - S \leq P \leq PV(K) \tag{8}$$

Just as we did for call options, it can be shown that the bounds for put options also have to hold so that there are no arbitrage opportunities.

Effect of Dividends on Put-Call Parity and on Bounds of Call and Put Options

So far, we have only established bounds for European options that pay no dividend. Let's see now what happens when the stock on which these European options are based do hand out dividends. Assume that the present value of dividends, D, during the lifetime of an option can be estimated with reasonable certainty. We then, in the formulas above, will have to substitute stock, S, whenever it appears, with stock minus dividend, $S - D$. For the put-call parity formula used above, this translates into:

$$S - PV(D) = C(K) - P(K) + PV(K) \tag{9}$$

For the call option, this means:

$$S - PV(D) - PV(K) \leq C \leq S - PV(D) \tag{10}$$

And for the put option, the bounds become:

$$PV(K) - S + PV(D) \leq P \leq PV(K) \tag{11}$$

PROBLEM SET

We have now covered the basic properties of options. To conclude, here are some exercises to practice what you have just read. For the problems below refer to the following set of information. As of July 26, the following European options, which expire on August 20, were written on XYZ Corporation. Their prices are:

Exercise Price	Calls	Puts
$35	$4 1/8	$1 3/16
$40	$1 5/16	Not traded
$45	$3/8	Not traded

XYZ pays no cash dividends to its shareholders. A Treasury bill maturing on August 20 that pays $35 at maturity costs $34.94 on July 26.

Problem 1 Could an American call option on a stock ever be worth less than a European call? How does an increase in time-to-maturity affect the value of European calls? American calls?

Problem 2 Suppose the stock on a company is at $150, and the company pays no dividends. Your friend has an American option on the stock with an exercise price of $100, but it is still a few months to expiration. He has decided to lock in his profit and exercise the option. Can you think of a way of arbitraging this situation?

Problem 3   Suppose that XYZ's stock price on July 26 was $50. On that date, what is the very least a $35 call could be worth? The most? What trade would you do if the call was $15?

Problem 4   What price would you expect the $45 put on XYZ above to trade at if the stock were at $37.50? If it traded above this price, what arbitrage opportunity would exist?

Problem 5   Suppose a stock, which pays no dividends, sells for $10 today. Next period, it will either move to $7 or $14. You do not know the probabilities of these two outcomes. Riskless zero-coupon bonds, paying $1.10 in one period, cost $1.00 today.

1. What price would an at-the-money call sell for today?

2. If you wished to synthetically manufacture the at-the-money call option, how many bonds would you buy? How many shares of stock?

3. If the call sold for $3.00, how would you capture arbitrage profits?

4. Now, consider what the stock might do in the second period. If it moves to $14 in the first period, it can either move up to $18 or down to $11 in the second period. If it moves to $7 in the first period, it can either move up to $11 or down to $4 in the second period. Assuming that riskless zero-coupon bonds, paying $1.10 in the second period, cost $1.00 at the end of the first period, what price would an at-the-money call sell for today?

17

Dell Computer Corporation: Share Repurchase Program

Carolyn Evans, a research analyst at LV Technology Fund, looked up from Dell Computer's fiscal 1996 annual report to ponder some news contained therein. Dell Computer, a company in which the fund held a small investment, had recently (February 16, 1996) announced financial results for its fourth quarter, 1996 (quarter ending January 28, 1996). As part of this announcement, Dell had revealed that its board of directors had authorized a stock repurchase program for up to 12 million shares. The announcement also stated that Dell might use equity options as part of the repurchase program.

This statement brought back memories of 1993, Carolyn's first year with the fund. At that time Dell, under attack by securities analysts for its use of foreign exchange options for speculation, had seen its stock price plunge from $49 per share to $16. Now, on March 29, 1996, Carolyn got a glimpse of the types of option transactions that Dell was undertaking. According to the annual report, by late March 1996, Dell had already written 2.8 million put options and bought a similar number of call options on its own stock. Carolyn was trying to understand why Dell was using options and what effect they might have on Dell's stock price.

BACKGROUND

Dell Computer was founded in Austin, Texas in 1984. Initially, Dell was a computer components business, buying excess inventory at cost from IBM dealers and reselling this excess through newspapers and magazines at 10% to 15% below retail costs.[1] By April 1984, Dell was grossing $80,000 per month.[2] Around this time, Dell started build-

---

Professors George Chacko and Luis Viceira prepared this case from published sources as the basis for class discussion rather than to illustrate either effective or ineffective handling of an administrative situation.

[1] At that time, IBM required its dealers to order large monthly quotas of PCs. These quotas almost always exceeded demand, leaving these dealers with excess inventory, which they sold at cost.

[2] Hoover's Online: Company Profile.

ing clones of IBM PCs under the brand PCs Limited. Rather than selling through traditional retail outlets, Dell sold its PCs directly to customers. The elimination of the retail middlemen allowed Dell to sell PCs at around 40% of the price of an IBM PC.

From its founding in 1984, Dell enjoyed enormous growth in revenues and profits. By 1991, revenues had grown to $546 million.[3] However, in 1994 Dell posted its first-ever annual loss. One reason for the loss was Dell's move away from its traditional retail channel of direct marketing to customers. In order to sustain past growth rates, Dell started pushing into alternative sales channels, such as selling PCs through retail stores like CompUSA, Wal-Mart Stores, and Price Club. Unfortunately, these alternative channels took Dell away from its focus and strength: real-time customized manufacturing, which allowed it to meet specific needs of customers while also maintaining low inventory levels and costs relative to competitors.

During the 1992–1994 fiscal years, Dell took losses related to derivatives transactions totaling $62 million. These losses included a $38 million charge related to foreign exchange derivative contracts in the second quarter of fiscal 1993, and a $15 million charge related to interest rate derivative contracts in the first quarter of fiscal 1994. While Dell claimed that these losses were merely from hedging transactions, there was considerable speculation in late 1992 and early 1993 that Dell was, in fact, trading for speculative purposes. These accusations were first brought by a Kidder Peabody analyst, and Dell's stock price dropped more than 10% on the day the accusations were announced.

By 1996, Dell had grown to become one of the largest PC vendors in the world. For its fiscal 1996 year, Dell had revenues of $5.3 billion and net income of $272 million, up about 52% and 82%, respectively, from the previous fiscal year (see Exhibit 1). Approximately 33% of Dell's revenue came from international sales. Dell's product line included desktop computers, notebook computers, workstations, and servers. While the desktop business represented 80% of Dell's current revenues, most analysts expected the notebook and server segments to experience the strongest growth in coming years. This growth in notebooks and servers, with gross margins of 22% and 35%, respectively, compared to a 20% gross margin for desktops, likely meant accelerating growth in earnings for Dell.[4] Furthermore, Dell's operations were becoming even more efficient. Inventory levels, a key metric of Dell's operating performance, were under 30 days of sales. These inventory levels were far below the levels of its main competitors (see Exhibit 2).

Despite the surge in revenues and earnings, Dell's stock price had been falling for the past three months. After seeing a high of nearly $50 per share at the beginning of November 1995, the stock price dropped to almost $25 per share by mid-January 1996. (Exhibit 3 reports stock prices for Dell and its main competitors between January 1994 and March 1996, and Exhibit 4 reports dividend distributions.) As a result, most sell-side analysts had ratings of "Buy" or "Strong Buy" on Dell's stock. For example, Merrill Lynch issued a report on January 16, 1996 stating:[5]

> . . . We believe the fundamentals at Dell are very sound. The company keeps its product cycle continuously fresh, is financially well managed, operates within a low-cost operating model, and is a clear market share gainer . . . we believe the stock represents an attractive value at current levels.

---

[3] *Wall Street Journal*, "Company Profiles."

[4] Dell Computer Corporation: Analyst report by The Chicago Corporation, 1996.

[5] Dell Computer Corporation: Analyst report by Merrill Lynch, Inc., 1996.

EXHIBIT 1

DELL COMPUTER CORP.: QUARTERLY FINANCIAL STATEMENTS (IN MILLIONS)

	Q3-95	Q4-95	Q1-96	Q2-96	Q3-96	Q4-96
Sales	$ 884.6	$1,032.7	$1,135.9	$1,205.6	$1,415.7	$1,538.8
Cost of Goods Sold	694.9	806.0	890.8	933.4	1,116.0	1,250.8
Gross Profit	$ 189.7	$ 226.7	$ 245.2	$ 272.2	$ 299.7	$ 288.0
Selling, General & Administrative Expense	121.9	138.5	148.5	172.0	186.0	183.5
Interest Expense	3.5	4.2	4.0	3.8	3.5	3.7
Income Before Tax	$ 58.1	$ 86.0	$ 86.9	$ 91.7	$ 106.2	$ 98.2
Income Taxes	16.8	25.7	25.2	26.6	30.8	28.4
Net Income	$ 39.2	$ 58.1	$ 50.1	$ 65.0	$ 75.3	$ 69.7
ASSETS						
Cash and Equivalents	$ 400.0	$ 527.2	$ 518.0	$ 569.8	$ 570.8	$ 646.0
Net Receivables	489.3	538.0	588.3	671.8	772.8	726.0
Inventories	274.5	292.9	337.8	382.0	463.6	429.0
Other Current Assets	110.4	112.2	109.0	104.8	135.9	156.0
Total Current Assets	$1,274.0	$1,470.4	$1,553.1	$1,728.4	$1,943.1	$1,957.0
Net Plant, Property and Equipment	110.6	117.0	123.3	145.2	158.5	179.0
Other Noncurrent Assets	5.2	6.7	6.2	11.7	11.3	12.0
Total Assets	$1,389.8	$1,594.0	$1,682.6	$1,885.3	$2,112.9	$2,148.0
LIABILITIES						
Accounts Payable	$ 362.4	$ 447.1	$ 417.7	$ 454.9	$ 531.7	$ 466.0
Debt in Current Liabilities	0.0	0.4	0.0	0.0	48.7	60.0
Other Current Liabilities	252.4	279.0	309.8	410.7	382.8	413.0
Total Current Liabilities	$ 649.4	$ 751.4	$ 772.0	$ 877.5	$ 997.2	$ 939.0
Long-Term Debt	100.0	113.4	113.4	113.4	113.2	113.0
Other Liabilities	58.5	77.4	83.6	91.5	109.2	123.0
Total Equity	581.8	651.7	713.5	802.9	893.3	973.0
Total Liabilities and Equity	$1,389.8	$1,594.0	$1,682.6	$1,885.3	$2,112.9	$2,148.0
Common Shares Outstanding	39.09	39.68	45.07	45.76	93.00	93.45

EMPLOYEE STOCK OPTIONS PLAN

Following the standard practice in the industry, Dell regularly included stock options as part of its executive compensation plan. Incentive awards were not limited exclusively to stock options, however. They could also include stock appreciation rights as well as stock and cash. By granting stock options, Dell sought to motivate and reward executives for maximizing stockholder value and to encourage the long-term employment of key employees.[6] The company's Incentive Plan provided for an aggregate of 17 million shares of common stock to be issued to compensate employees. At the end of fiscal year 1996 (January 28, 1996), 8.48 million shares of common stock remained

---

[6] Dell Computer Corporation: Proxy Statement, 1996.

EXHIBIT 2

COMPARATIVE FINANCIAL STATEMENTS, 1994–1996 ($ MILLIONS)

	Dell Computer Corp.			Compaq Computer Corp.		
	1994	**1995**	**1996**	**1994**	**1995**	**1996**
Sales	$ 2,873.2	$3,475.3	$5,296.0	$10,866.0	$14,755.0	$18,109.0
Cost of Goods Sold	2,339.4	2,704.1	4,191.0	7,971.0	11,153.0	13,651.0
Gross Profit	$ 533.8	$ 771.2	$1,105.0	$ 2,895.0	$ 3,602.0	$ 4,458.0
Selling, General & Administrative Expense	450.7	488.8	690.0	1,461.0	1,864.0	2,319.0
Interest Expense	8.4	12.2	15.0	74.0	106.0	99.0
Income Before Tax	$ (−38.8)	$ 213.0	$ 383.0	$ 1,172.0	$ 1,188.0	$ 1,876.0
Income Taxes	(−2.9)	63.8	111.0	305.0	399.0	563.0
Net Income	$ (−35.8)	$ 149.2	$ 272.0	$ 867.0	$ 789.0	$ 1,313.0
ASSETS						
Cash and Equivalents	$ 337.0	$ 527.2	$ 646.0	$ 471.0	$ 745.0	$ 3,993.0
Net Receivables	410.8	538.0	726.0	2,287.0	3,141.0	3,168.0
Inventories	220.3	292.9	429.0	2,005.0	2,156.0	1,152.0
Other Current Assets	80.3	112.2	156.0	395.0	485.0	856.0
Total Current Assets	$1,048.4	$1,470.4	$1,957.0	$ 5,158.0	$ 6,527.0	$ 9,169.0
Net Property, Plant and Equipment	86.9	117.0	179.0	944.0	1,110.0	1,172.0
Other Noncurrent Assets	5.2	6.7	12.0	64.0	181.0	185.0
Total Assets	$1,140.5	$1,594.0	$2,148.0	$ 6,166.0	$ 7,818.0	$10,526.0
LIABILITIES						
Accounts Payable	$ 282.7	$ 447.1	$ 466.0	$ 888.0	$ 1,379.0	$ 1,962.0
Notes Payable	0.0	0.0	59.0	0.0	0.0	0.0
Long-Term Debt Due in One Year	0.0	0.4	1.0	0.0	0.0	0.0
Other Current Liabilities	471.8	560.9	413.0	1,125.0	1,301.0	$ 1,890.0
Total Current Liabilities	$ 538.0	$ 751.4	$ 939.0	$ 2,013.0	$ 2,680.0	$ 3,852.0
Long-Term Debt	100.0	113.4	113.0	300.0	300.0	300.0
Other Liabilities	31.4	77.4	123.0	179.0	224.0	230.0
Total Shareholders' Equity	471.1	651.7	973.0	3,674.0	4,614.0	6,144.0
Total Liabilities and Equity	$1,140.5	$1,594.0	$2,148.0	$ 6,166.0	$ 7,818.0	$10,526.0

(Continued)

available for future issuance under the Incentive Plan awards. At that time, the company had approximately 93.5 million shares outstanding.

Stock options were usually granted with an exercise price equal to the market value of Dell's common stock at the time the options were issued, and they could not be exercised immediately after issuance. A fraction of the stock options granted in a given year was usually exercisable one year after issuance, with the rest of the options becoming exercisable in subsequent years. At the end of fiscal year 1996, 2,324,451 options on shares were exercisable under the incentive plans. Exhibit 5 shows the number of options, exercise price and expiration date of options granted to Dell's executive

EXHIBIT 2   (Continued)

COMPARATIVE FINANCIAL STATEMENTS, 1994–1996 ($ MILLIONS)

	Gateway Inc.			Hewlett-Packard Corp.		
	1994	**1995**	**1996**	**1994**	**1995**	**1996**
Sales	$2,701.2	$3,676.3	$5,035.2	$38,420.0	$31,519.0	$24,991.0
Cost of Goods Sold	2,325.7	3,022.4	4,009.8	24,202.0	18,875.0	14,484.0
Gross Profit	375.5	$ 653.9	$1,025.4	$14,218.0	$12,644.0	$10,507.0
Selling, General & Administrative Expense	216.5	366.8	607.5	9,195.0	7,937.0	6,952.0
Interest Expense	—	—	—	327.0	206.0	155.0
Income Before Tax	$ 146.1	$ 262.1	$ 382.7	$ 3,694.0	$ 3,632.0	$ 2,423.0
Income Taxes	50.1	89.1	132.0	1,108.0	1,199.0	824.0
Net Income	$ 96.0	$ 173.0	$ 250.7	$ 2,586.0	$ 2,433.0	$ 1,599.0
ASSETS						
Cash and Equivalents	$ 243.9	$ 169.4	$ 516.4	$ 2,478.0	$ 2,616.0	$ 3,327.0
Net Receivables	252.9	405.3	449.7	5028.0	6,735.0	7,126.0
Inventories	120.2	224.9	278.0	4273.0	6,013.0	6,401.0
Other Current Assets	37.1	66.6	74.2	730.0	875.0	1,137.0
Total Current Assets	$ 654.2	$ 866.2	$1,318.3	$12,509.0	$16,239.0	$17,991.0
Net Property, Plant and Equipment	89.3	170.3	242.4	4,328.0	4,711.0	5,536.0
Other Noncurrent Assets	27.1	87.6	112.7	2,730.0	3,477.0	4,172.0
Total Assets	$ 770.6	$1,124.0	$1,673.4	$19,567.0	$24,427.0	$27,699.0
LIABILITIES						
Accounts Payable	$ 183.3	$ 235.1	$ 411.8	$ 1,466.0	$ 2,422.0	$ 2,375.0
Notes Payable	0.0	0.0	0.0	2,469.0	3,214.0	2,040.0
Long-Term Debt Due in One Year	3.8	13.6	15.0	0.0	0.0	85.0
Other Current Liabilities	305.4	509.0	689.0	6,747.0	8,340.0	9,781.0
Total Current Liabilities	$ 348.9	$ 525.3	$ 799.8	$ 8,230.0	$10,944.0	$10,623.0
Long Term Debt	27.1	10.8	7.2	547.0	663.0	2,579.0
Other Liabilities	18.5	32.4	50.9	864.0	981.0	1,059.0
Total Shareholders' Equity	376.0	555.5	$ 815.5	9,926.0	11,839.0	13,438.0
Total Liabilities and Equity	$ 770.6	$1,124.0	$1,673.4	$19,567.0	$24,427.0	$27,699.0

(Continued)

officers in 1995. Exhibit 6 and Exhibit 7 report some information on the number of stock options exercised by Dell's executive officers during fiscal year 1996, as well as information on the unexercised options at the end of fiscal year 1996.

During fiscal year 1996, Dell also offered "discounted stock options" to some of its executives. These options had an exercise price equal to 80% of the market value of Dell's Common Stock on the date of issuance. Participation in this program was voluntary, and participants had to forgo a portion of their pre-tax Incentive Bonus Plan payouts. The number of options granted was calculated by dividing the forgone bonus payment amount by 20% of the fair market value of the common stock on the bonus payment date. These discounted options were subject to a one-year holding period requirement.

EXHIBIT 2   *(Continued)*

COMPARATIVE FINANCIAL STATEMENTS, 1994–1996 ($ MILLIONS)

	International Business Machines Corp.			Micron Electronics Inc.		
	1994	**1995**	**1996**	**1994**	**1995**	**1996**
Sales	$75,947.0	$71,940.0	$64,052.0	$ 266.3	$1,000.0	$1,764.9
Cost of Goods Sold	41,732.0	37,618.0	34,571.0	237.8	803.5	1,481.5
Gross Profit	$34,215.0	$34,322.0	$29,481.0	$ 28.5	$ 196.5	$ 283.4
Selling, General & Administrative Expense	21,508.0	20,448.0	20,279.0	30.2	76.8	156.0
Interest Expense	747.0	748.0	1,247.0	0.0	0.5	0.5
Income Before Tax	$ 8,587.0	$ 7,813.0	$ 5,155.0	$ (−6.3)	$ 108.5	$ 79.6
Income Taxes	3,158.0	3,635.0	2,134.0	0.0	43.4	35.1
Net Income	$ 5,429.0	$ 4,178.0	$ 3,021.0	$ (−6.3)	$ 65.1	$ 44.6
ASSETS						
Cash and Equivalents	$10,554.0	$ 7,701.0	$ 8,137.0	$ 25.3	$ 69.4	$ 115.8
Net Receivables	21,533.0	23,402.0	23,167.0	24.6	92.7	176.5
Inventories	6,334.0	6,323.0	5,870.0	0.0	0.0	0.0
Other Current Assets	2,917.0	3,265.0	3,521.0	0.9	17.9	36.9
Total Current Assets	41,338.0	40,691.0	40,695.0	74.9	308.8	399.1
Net Property, Plant and Equipment	$16,664.0	$16,579.0	$17,407.0	$ 2.1	$ 58.3	$ 129.2
Other Noncurrent Assets	23,089.0	23,022.0	23,030.0	0.6	15.7	1.6
Total Assets	$81,091.0	$80,292.0	$81,132.0	$ 77.6	$ 382.7	$ 529.9
LIABILITIES						
Accounts Payable	$ 3,778.0	$ 4,511.0	$ 4,767.0	$ 43.2	$ 99.1	$ 157.4
Notes Payable	5521.0	8,688.0	10,035.0	0.0	0.0	0.0
Long-Term Debt Due in One Year	4,049.0	2,881.0	2,922.0	0.0	1.0	3.1
Other Current Liabilities	26,510.0	25,033.0	25,883.0	19.5	146.0	168.3
Total Current Liabilities	$29,226.0	$31,648.0	$34,000.0	$ 54.1	$ 202.3	$ 277.4
Long-Term Debt	12,548.0	10,060.0	9,872.0	0.0	5.8	18.2
Other Liabilities	15,904.0	16,161.0	15,632.0	0.0	0.9	5.9
Total Shareholders' Equity	23,413.0	22,423.0	21,628.0	23.5	173.7	228.5
Total Liabilities and Equity	$81,091.0	$80,292.0	$81,332.0	$ 77.6	$ 382.7	$ 529.9

SHARE REPURCHASE PROGRAM

On February 22, 1996, Dell announced that it had been authorized by its board of directors to begin a stock repurchase program that would allow the company to provide shares to employees under the company's long-term incentive, employee stock purchase, and retirement plans. The board of directors authorized Dell to buy up to 12 million shares of its common stock through open market or private transactions. It also authorized Dell to use equity options as part of the repurchase program. The pur-

EXHIBIT 3

COMPARATIVE STOCK PRICES, 1994–1996 (DOLLARS PER SHARE, EXCEPT INDICES)

	Dell Computer	Compaq Computers	Gateway	Hewlett-Packard	IBM	Micron Electronics	S&P 500 Computers (Hardware)— Price Index	S&P 500 Composite— Price Index
Jan-94	11.00	28.67	24.13	85.25	56.50	3.63	111.47	481.61
Feb-94	12.50	32.96	24.00	90.63	52.88	3.00	110.01	467.14
Mar-94	12.63	32.63	20.38	82.13	54.63	3.13	111.02	445.77
Apr-94	11.00	37.00	15.50	80.25	57.50	3.00	110.24	450.99
May-94	14.32	39.42	14.88	78.50	63.00	2.63	118.01	456.50
Jun-94	13.19	32.38	11.13	75.25	58.75	2.50	107.25	444.27
Jul-94	14.00	31.75	14.00	77.63	61.88	3.13	112.95	458.26
Aug-94	16.25	37.25	14.75	90.00	68.50	3.13	127.56	475.49
Sep-94	18.72	32.63	18.63	87.38	69.63	3.25	127.15	462.69
Oct-94	22.25	40.13	23.44	97.88	74.50	4.88	140.93	472.35
Nov-94	21.53	39.13	21.88	97.75	70.75	7.00	135.18	453.69
Dec-94	20.50	39.50	21.63	99.88	73.50	8.38	138.95	459.27
Jan-95	21.32	35.75	20.88	100.50	72.13	10.06	135.96	470.42
Feb-95	20.75	34.50	18.38	115.00	75.25	10.63	139.41	487.39
Mar-95	21.88	34.38	18.75	120.38	82.13	11.81	147.19	500.71
Apr-95	27.38	38.00	18.94	66.13	94.63	14.13	166.72	514.71
May-95	25.19	39.25	17.56	66.00	93.00	14.63	168.06	533.40
Jun-95	30.07	45.25	22.75	74.50	96.00	19.00	176.40	544.75
Jul-95	32.50	50.63	28.88	77.88	108.88	19.13	188.93	562.06
Aug-95	38.50	47.75	26.63	80.00	103.38	18.00	186.31	561.88
Sep-95	42.50	48.38	30.63	83.38	94.50	23.00	180.80	584.41
Oct-95	46.63	55.63	33.38	92.63	97.25	20.75	194.20	581.50
Nov-95	44.25	49.38	27.63	83.00	96.63	14.63	188.52	605.37
Dec-95	34.63	48.00	24.50	83.75	91.38	10.75	183.33	615.93
Jan-96	27.38	47.13	25.88	84.75	108.50	10.25	197.88	636.02
Feb-96	34.38	50.63	29.50	100.75	122.63	10.75	221.16	640.43
Mar-96	33.50	38.63	27.88	94.13	111.25	9.88	197.47	645.50

chases had to be funded from available working capital. When announcing the plan, Thomas J. Meredith, Dell's chief financial officer, had declared that,

> Our direct model has enabled us to generate more than $400 million in cash from operations over the past two years, even while growing revenues at a compound annual rate in excess of 35%. This kind of performance enables us to embark on a stock repurchase program and offset the dilutive effects of our ongoing employee benefit programs."[7]

The Annual Report that Dell filed with the SEC at the end of March 1996 reflected that, as of March 22, 1996, the company had purchased a total of 3.3 million

[7] *PR Newswire*, Thursday February 22, 1996.

EXHIBIT 4

COMPARATIVE DIVIDEND PAYMENTS, 1994–1996 (DOLLARS PER SHARE)

Dell Computer		Compaq Computers		Gateway	
Dividend Rate, US$	**Pay Date**	**Dividend Rate, US$**	**Pay Date**	**Dividend Rate, US$**	**Pay Date**
No Dividends Paid		No Dividends Paid		No Dividends Paid	

Hewlett-Packard		IBM		Micron Electronics	
Dividend Rate, US$	**Pay Date**	**Dividend Rate, US$**	**Pay Date**	**Dividend Rate, US$**	**Pay Date**
$0.25	1/12/94	$0.25	3/10/94		
0.25	4/13/94	0.25	6/10/94		
0.30	7/13/94	0.25	9/10/94		
0.30	10/12/94	0.25	12/10/94		
0.30	1/11/95	0.25	3/10/95	No Dividends Paid	
0.30	4/12/95	0.25	6/10/95		
0.20	7/12/95	0.25	9/9/95		
0.20	10/11/95	0.25	12/9/95		
0.20	1/10/96	0.25	3/9/96		

shares of common stock in open market transactions for $100 million under the repurchase program. In addition, the company had sold 2.8 million put options and had purchased 2.8 million call options on Dell's common stock under the same program. The put exercise prices ranged from $29.36 to $34.62 per share, while the call exercise prices ranged from $32.30 to $38.09 per share. These options were exercisable only at expiration, and the expiration dates ranged from September 3, 1996 to September 20, 1996. Exhibit 8 reports interest rates on government securities on March 29, 1996.

As Carolyn walked to a meeting with the portfolio manager of the fund, she wondered why Dell had chosen to utilize call and put options as part of its share repurchase program. From her basic knowledge on options, she knew options could be effective hedging instruments. But she also knew that they could be regarded simply as levered positions in the underlying equity. Were the options a way for Dell's management to make a strong statement regarding what they felt to be an undervaluation of Dell's shares, or were these options being used to hedge some sort of risk? She didn't know but she would have to come up with a recommendation soon for the fund manager.

EXHIBIT 5

DELL COMPUTER CORP.: INDIVIDUAL GRANTS

Top Managers	Number of Shares Underlying Options Granted	Percentage of Total Options Granted to Employees in Fiscal Year	Exercise Price per Share	Grant Date	Expiration Date	Grant Date Present Value[a]
Michael Dell, CEO	60,000[b]	1.50%	$ 31.41	7-24-95	7-24-05	$ 766,350
Morton Topper, Vice Chairman	50,000[b]	1.25	31.41	7-24-95	7-24-05	638,625
Morton Topper, Vice Chairman	225,000[c]	5.64	35.44	12-22-95	12-22-05	3,376,913
Eric Harslem, Senior VP	37,000[b]	0.93	31.41	7-24-95	7-24-05	472,583
Thomas Meredith, CFO	28,000[b]	0.70	31.41	7-24-95	7-24-05	357,630
Richard Snyder, Senior VP[d]	26,000[e]	0.65	21.19	2-27-95	2-27-05	227,812
	40,000[f]	1.00	31.41	7-24-95	7-24-05	510,900

[a]Calculated using the Black-Scholes model. The material assumptions and adjustments incorporated into the Black-Scholes model in making such calculations include the following: (1) an interest rate representing the interest rate on U.S. Treasury securities with a maturity date corresponding to the option term; (2) volatility determined using daily prices for the Common Stock during the one-year period immediately preceding date of grant; (3) a dividend rate of $0; and (4) in each case, a reduction of 35% to reflect the probability of forfeiture due to termination of employment prior to vesting and the probability of a shortened option term due to termination of employment prior to the option expiration date. The ultimate values of the options will depend on the future market prices of the Common Stock, which cannot be forecast with reasonable accuracy. The actual value, if any, that an optionee will recognize upon exercise of an option will depend on the difference between the market value of the Common Stock on the date the option is exercised and the applicable exercise price.

[b]These options will vest and become exercisable with respect to one-fifth of the underlying shares on each of the first five anniversaries of the date of grant.

[c]These options will vest and become exercisable with respect to one-fourth of the underlying shares on each of the third, fourth, fifth and sixth anniversaries of the date of grant.

[d]Richard Snyder's employment with the Company terminated on March 29, 1996.

[e]These options were granted upon the commencement of Richard Snyder's employment with the Company and were to vest and become exercisable with respect to one-fifth of the underlying shares on each of the first five anniversaries of the date of grant. On February 29, 1996, Snyder exercised the option with respect to 5,200 shares. Snyder's employment with the Company terminated on March 29, 1996, and in connection therewith, Snyder forfeited the remaining options with respect to 20,800 shares.

[f]These options were to vest and become exercisable with respect to one-fifth of the underlying shares on each of the first five anniversaries of the date of grant. Richard Snyder's employment with the Company terminated on March 29, 1996, and in connection therewith, Snyder forfeited all of such options.

Source: Dell Computer Corporation: Proxy Statement, 1996.

EXHIBIT 6

DELL COMPUTER CORP.: AGGREGATE OPTION EXERCISES IN 1996 FISCAL YEAR AND 1996 FISCAL YEAR-END OPTION VALUES

Top Managers	Shares Acquired on Exercise	Value Realized[a]	Number of Shares Underlying Unexercised Options at Fiscal Year-End		Value of Unexercised In-the-Money Options at Fiscal Year-End[b]	
			Exercisable	*Unexercisable*	*Exercisable*	*Unexercisable*
Michael Dell	0	$ 0	0	60,000	$ 0	$ 0
Morton Topper	85,000	2,221,075	15,375	589,625	$220,884	7,235,579
Eric Harslem	50,000	1,274,750	33,343	208,775	526,594	3,854,917
Thomas Meredith	20,000	603,700	75,976	177,042	929,178	3,145,919
Richard Snyder	0	0	0	66,000	0	164,125

[a]Calculated using the difference between (1) the actual sales price of the underlying shares (if the underlying shares were sold immediately upon exercise) or the closing sales price of the Common Stock on the date of exercise (if the underlying shares were not sold immediately upon exercise) and (2) the exercise price.

[b]Amounts were calculated by multiplying the number of unexercised options by the closing sales price of the Common Stock on the last trading day of fiscal 1996 ($27.50) and subtracting the exercise price.

Source: Dell Computer Corporation: Proxy Statement, 1996.

EXHIBIT 7

DELL COMPUTER CORP.: THE STOCK OPTION ACTIVITY UNDER THE INCENTIVE PLANS, 1993–1996

	Price Range	Number of Shares
Outstanding at January 31, 1993	$.005–$18.155	10,087,976
Exercisable at January 31, 1993		1,845,676
For 1993 fiscal year:		
Granted	$.005–$18.155	5,011,180
Canceled	$.005–$15.345	(2,409,628)
Exercised	$.005–$11.830	(1,452,824)
Outstanding at January 30, 1994	$.005–$18.155	11,236,704
Exercisable at January 30, 1994		2,092,426
For 1994 fiscal year:		
Granted	$.005–$23.315	4,322,498
Canceled	$.005–$15.345	(1,641,102)
Exercised	$.005–$18.155	(2,735,054)
Outstanding at January 29, 1995	$.005–$23.315	11,183,046
Exercisable at January 29, 1995		2,837,344
For 1995 fiscal year:		
Granted	$20.125–$48.500	3,987,082
Canceled	$.005–$44.750	(988,967)
Exercised	$.005–$22.095	(2,480,912)
Outstanding at January 28, 1996	$.005–$48.500	11,700,249
Exercisable at January 28, 1996		2,324,451

Source: Dell Computer Corporation: Annual Reports, 1993–1996.

EXHIBIT 8

SELECTED INTEREST RATES ON U.S. TREASURY SECURITIES ON MARCH 29, 1996

Maturity	Interest Rate, %
3 months	5.13
6 months	5.20
1 year	5.41
3 years	5.91
5 years	6.10
10 years	6.34
30 years	6.67

18

Note on Option Valuation

As we know from earlier, options are contracts that give the right, but not the obligation, to either buy or sell a specific underlying security for a specified price on or before a specific date. The option holder has the freedom of action to decide whether to exercise the option or not, depending on market movements. The option writer, by contrast, engages in a liability. For each option, a fair price has to be established; a price that reflects both the risk that the writer takes and the freedom that the holder maintains. How to fairly price options is the topic of this reading note.

A previous note by the same authors, "Basic Option Properties,"[1] covered the fundamentals of options, including their payoff schemes, the parameters that influenced their value (stock price, strike price, volatility, time-to-maturity, interest rate and dividends), the put-call parity, and also bounds of options prices. This note builds on these concepts, applying them to option valuation: How do you price an option, given all we now know about its influencing factors and relationships? We will in this note cover two pricing methods: the binominal tree and the Black-Scholes/Merton formula.

THE BINOMIAL MODEL

Say you want to price an equity-based option. Perhaps you want to sell one that you own; perhaps you are looking to buy one. A common approach is to construct a *binomial tree*, which follows the price of the underlying stock during the lifespan of the option. Figure 1 shows a sample binomial tree.

The binomial model[2] takes the time to expiration for an option and breaks it into a number of time intervals. For all steps between the option's valuation date (today; or the first node to the left in the tree) and its expiration date (the future; or the nodes

Professors George Chacko and Peter Hecht, Executive Director of the HBS Europe Research Center Vincent Dessain and Research Associate Anders Sjöman prepared this note as the basis for class discussion.

[1] See George Chacko, Peter Hecht, Vincent Dessain, and Anders Sjöman, "Note on Basic Option Properties," Harvard Business School Note No. 9-205-105 (Boston: Harvard Business School Publishing, 2005).

[2] The binomial model was first proposed by Cox, J., Ross, S., Rubenstein, M., "Option Pricing: A Simplified Approach," in: Journal of Financial Economics 7, 1979, p. 229–263).

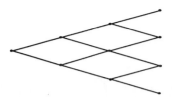

Figure 1   Sample Binomial Tree (With Three Steps)

furthest to the right in the tree), the tree traces what happens to the equity price. For each time interval—a week, a month, a year—it is assumed that the price will move either up or down. For every time step, or node, the stock can have one of two values (higher or lower), hence the name "binomial." The fact that two outcomes are possible at any node gives the tree its branches, resulting in a recombining tree (or binomial distribution) of prices. The tree represents all the possible paths that the price of the underlying stock can take during the life of the option.

The exercise of actually pricing an option based on the stock starts at the final nodes and works backwards, calculating the option value at each node, until the first node at the valuation date. It is the combined calculated result that becomes the option value.[3] An analyst anxious to value an option (or for that matter any other derivative instrument) will take the time to maturity and break it down into 30, 60, 100 or more time steps. However, we will start out easy, using one- and two-step binomial tress, to illustrate how the method works. We'll initially also limit ourselves to working with European options, which cannot be exercised before maturity.

An Example of a One-Period Binomial Tree with Discrete Compounding

Let's begin with a simple situation: how much would you be willing to pay for a three-month European call option on stock in the company Acme, stock that might have one of two values in three months? In such a one-period, two-state setting, the payoff of an option can always be replicated by a portfolio containing some stock and bonds. We want our stock and bond portfolio to give us the same payoff as the option. This can be described as:

$$C = \Delta S + B \qquad\qquad [1]$$

where:

C = the call option

Δ (delta) = amount of stock in the portfolio

S = stock

B = bonds (principal value)

Let's start by looking at the possible payoff schemes of these three variables: the option, its underlying stock, and the bonds. First, the call option will at expiration have one of two values: in-the-money (if the stock goes up) or out-of-money (if the stock

---

[3] A fundamental concept in such an exercise is of course compounding, or computing interest, using the principal plus the previously earned interest. Compounding can be done either continuously (mathematically working with e to the power of r, the interest rate) or in discrete time-separated steps (mathematically using division by $1 + r$). In this note, to simplify the math, we work with discrete compounding.

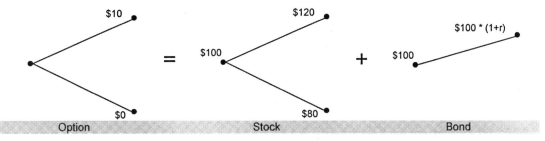

Figure 2   Example of One-Step Binomial Tree

drops). Let's assume that the option will be worth $10 if the stock goes up or $0 if the stock drops. Second, for the stock, assume that it is trading at $100, and that you are confident that within three months it will either go up to $120 or drop to $80. Third, the bond's value does not depend on the stock price, and hence there is no stock-related up or down movement for the bond. Assume just that the bond at the valuation date is worth $100 and that its value grows by the risk-free interest rate,[4] say 10%. Figure 2 graphically shows the relationship between these three variables, organizing the graphics as the variables in equation [1].

Now, since we required identical payoffs between the option and the replicating portfolio, you can plug the numbers you have into equation [1], one for each state of the binominal tree:

$$C_u \text{ (price goes up):} \qquad \$120\Delta + B = 10 \qquad\qquad [2]$$
$$C_d \text{ (price goes down):} \qquad \$80\Delta + B = 0$$

The two equations with two unknowns can be solved by subtracting the bottom equation from the top:

$$(120 - 80)\Delta + (B - B) = (10 - 0) \qquad\qquad [3]$$
$$40\Delta = 10$$
$$\Delta = 0.25$$

You now know that you hold 0.25 shares in your portfolio. With that as a value for Δ, you can solve for B, to find out the face value of the bonds in your portfolio:

$$C_u\text{: } \$120 \degree 0.25 + B = 10 \qquad \rightarrow B = -20 \qquad\qquad [4]$$
$$C_d\text{: } \$80 \degree 0.25 + B = 0 \qquad \rightarrow B = -20$$

There is one thing worth noticing about the bond face value, B. The value is negative, indicating that you are borrowing money (by issuing bonds) rather than investing (by buying bonds). In our example, it means that the portfolio that replicates the call option has $20 of borrowings in face value.

The bond face values you have obtained are for the expiration date of the tree. You want to discount those values back to the present day, the valuation date. Let's assume

---

[4] The risk-free interest rate is the rate that you'd get from investing in instruments with no risk. It is a theoretical construct, but is often assumed in practice to be the same as a short-dated government bond, such as U.S. Treasury bills.

that the annual compounded rate is 10%. Starting with the bonds, valued at $20 at expiration, we can calculate their present day value as:

$$\frac{20}{(1 + 10\%)^{3/12}} = \$19.529 \tag{5}$$

The value of the stock portion of the portfolio is easy to value since we already know its current day value to be $100. To finally find the value of your option, just take the stock price today ($100) times the amount of stocks in your portfolio (0.25). Then detract the present value of the bonds that we just calculated ($19.529), and you end up with a valuation of the call option on Acme's stock:

$$100 \,^\circ\, 0.25 - 19.529 = 5.471 \tag{6}$$

You just calculated the value of the Acme option to be $5.47.

About Probabilities

In the example, notice that we never stated the probabilities for the stock price rising to $120 or dropping to $80. Wouldn't the probabilities associated with future stock price movements influence the option price? As it turns out, actually not. Long arguments can be made as to why; here we just simply state that the probabilities are already incorporated into the stock price at the various nodes. This leaves you free to simply disregard the probabilities when valuing an option using the binominal tree.

A General Formula for the One-Step Binominal Tree

Based on an example like the one we just went through, it can be shown that a generalized approach to calculate Δ and B for the one-step binominal tree can be summarized as:

$$\Delta = \frac{C_u - C_d}{S_u - S_d} \tag{7}$$

$$B = C_u - \Delta S_u \tag{8}$$

where:

B = bonds (principal value)

Δ = amount of stock in the portfolio

S_d = stock price if it goes down

S_u = stock price if it goes up

C_d = call option payoff if stock price goes down

C_u = call option payoff if stock price goes up

Using our example from above, you have $S_d = \$80$, $S_u = \$120$, $C_d = \$0$ and $C_u = \$10$, which gives:

$$\Delta = \frac{10 - 0}{120 - 80} = 0.25 \tag{9}$$

$$B = 10 - 0.25 \degree 120 = -\$20 \qquad [10]$$

As we did before, you would then discount the face value for B, insert the discounted B together with the Δ into the formula, $C = \Delta S + PV(B)$, and receive the option's value.

RISK-NEUTRAL VALUATION AND PROBABILITIES

Remember how we said that you could disregard the probabilities of the two outcomes when evaluating an option using the binomial tree? Although this is all true and well in the case of one-step binominal trees, it does make solving multi-step binomial trees rather cumbersome. You would have to repeat the two-by-two equation calculation we did (see equation [2] above) at every node. Using probabilities simplifies the procedure when you use more than one time step to evaluate an option—which you always do.

However, to be able to use probabilities we need to build on one important principle in option pricing: risk-neutral valuation. Risk-neutral valuation helps us come up with a probability for up- and down-movements that holds for all nodes in our binomial tree. Risk-neutral valuation assumes that we all live in a risk-neutral world; a world where everyone is indifferent to risk and don't have to be enticed by risk premiums to make investments. It means we can use the risk-free interest rate to discount all future expected security payoffs, so that today's price for a derivative security is the discounted value of its future payoff, using the risk-free rate as the discount factor. Risk-neutral valuation also lets us assume that whatever valuation we obtain in our risk-neutral world will also hold in the real, risk-filled world.

Calculating Probabilities

Let's show how risk-neutral valuation helps us find probabilities for up-and down-movements. We'll return to our ongoing example of a call option based on Acme stock, and start with the stock component of our portfolio. (Risk-neutral pricing applies to all securities in the world, including the stock that we have in our portfolio.) Let's define the probability for the price going up as P, and the probability for the price dropping as $1 - P$. Just as earlier, the stock is valued at $100 today, which means that the probability of it being $120 in three months is P, and the probability that it will be $80 is $1 - P$. The expected future stock price then becomes:

$$120P + 80(1 - P) \qquad [11]$$

Discounting this back three months using the risk-free rate, 10%, (which we continue to define as an annual compounded rate) gives us today's stock price, which we know to be $100. We can describe this in a formula as:

$$\$100 = \frac{120P + 80(1 - P)}{(1 + 0.1)^{3/12}} \qquad [12]$$

Solving for P gives us the risk-neutral probability of an upward movement:

$$P = \frac{100(1 + 0.10)^{3/12} - 80}{120 - 80} = 0.5603 \qquad [13]$$

Risk-free valuation thus armed us with the risk-free rate, with which we could figure out the risk-neutral probability of an upward movement at 56.03%, and its sibling, the downward movement, as $1 - P$ or 43.97%.

Equipped with this probability, you can now calculate the option value at every node without having to go through a cumbersome 2×2 matrix equation, but rather using the same probability value at every node. Let's see how you'd do it using the option payoff schedule from Figure 2 above. The figure shows that you expect $10 if the stock increases and $0 if it decreases. We now know that the probability for an upward movement is 56.03% and for a downward swing 43.97% (or $1 - 56.03\%$). Using these values, we calculate the expected value of the option:

$$\$10 \text{ ° } 56.25\% + \$0 \text{ ° } 43.75\% = \$5.603 \tag{14}$$

Discounting three months, using the 10% risk-free rate we have been using all along, gives us

$$\frac{5.603}{(1 + 0.1)^{3/12}} = 5.471 \tag{15}$$

This is the same value we calculated using B and Δ earlier (see equation [6]).

A General Formula for Probabilities

A generalized formula for calculating probabilities can be derived and shown to be:

$$p = \frac{(1 + r) - d}{u - d} \tag{16}$$

where:

p = probability of movement up

d = one plus stock return in the down state ($= S_d/S$)

u = one plus stock return in the up state ($= S_u/S$)

r = risk-free rate

Using our example from above, you have $d = 0.8$, $u = 1.2$ and $r = 0.10$. For r, (which in this note is further defined as a compounded annual rate), we adjust for the interval of 3 months. This gives us:

$$p = \frac{(1 + 0.1)^{3/12} - 0.8}{1.2 - 0.8} = 0.5603 \tag{17}$$

56.03%—the same value as we had earlier.

TWO-PERIOD BINOMIAL TREE, USING RISK-NEUTRAL VALUATION

As we already said, using just one period to value an option is a rather coarse approach. Most professional analysts would want to break the time between the valuation and expiration dates into 30, 60 or more steps. Luckily for them, a key concept in option valuation is that you can add as many steps as you want; the more you add, the more accurate your valuation, but also the more time-consuming your calculations.

The basic process remains the same no matter how many steps you use: first work out the underlying stock prices by working forward from valuation date to expiration date. Then work backwards to calculate the option value at each node, starting with the values at expiration date (the end nodes). Calculate the value for each node by deriving it from the nodes immediately following (to the right in the tree). All along, use the probabilities of the stock price moving up or down and the risk-free rate. In the end, at the left-hand node, you arrive at the value of the option.

Let's try this out, by adding one more step to the example we've been using all along. We extend our tree, continuing to assume that at each node the price may go up or down by 20%, that each time-step is 3 months (meaning that we extend the time-to-maturity to 6 months), and that the annualized risk-free interest rate is 10%. The option we consider has a strike price of $110, which helps us calculate the option payoff (to see when the option is in- or out of the money). The payoff schemes of the stock and option are shown in Figure 3.

The first step is to draw out the stock tree—panel (a) above—and the second step to calculate the option value at each node—panel (b) above—ultimately arriving at node A, the valuation date. The process helps you decide how much you would want to pay for a call option on Acme stock. Panel (b) above shows the actual value; let's now explain how the number was calculated.

As we've done all along, you start by calculating the option's value at the end nodes: At expiry, the option's value is simply its intrinsic exercise value; is it in the money or not? Here, the option is only in the money in node D, which is the only time the stock price is above the call option's strike price. Calculate the value simply by deducting the strike price from the stock price ($144 − $110 = $34). For the two other end nodes, since the stock price is below the strike price, the option would not be exercised (out-of-the-money) and the option payoff would be zero.

We move on to calculate the values of nodes B and C. Starting with C, we can simply establish that its value is 0, since the node leads to nodes E and F, which both are valued at 0. For node B, however, a calculation is required, and this is where the

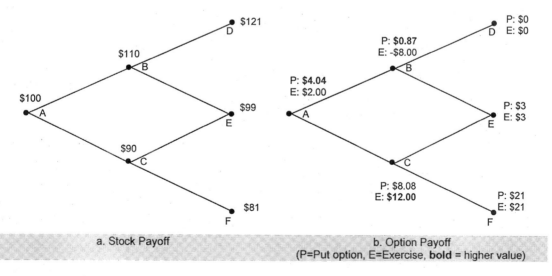

a. Stock Payoff

b. Option Payoff
(P=Put option, E=Exercise, **bold** = higher value)

Figure 3 Example of Two-Step Binomial Tree

probability formula (based on risk-neutral valuation) will come in handy for the first time. Described in words, we calculate the value of node B from the values of nodes D and E, weighting them by their respective probabilities and discounting the result by the risk-free rate.

First, then, we need the probability, based on equation [16]. Since we are reusing the same example, we have already calculated this value for three-month intervals (see equation [17]): 56.03% for an upward movement. Using this value we calculate the expected value at node B, and discount it back. This gives us:

$$\frac{0.5603 \degree 34 + (1 - 0.5603) \degree 0}{(1 + 0.1)^{3/12}} = \frac{19.049}{(1 + 0.1)^{3/12}} = 18.601 \qquad [18]$$

We now repeat the same thing for the last node, A, which is the final—and actual—value we need. We have the values of node B (18.601) and node C (0); we have the risk-neutral probabilities; and use the same formula again:

$$\frac{0.5603 \degree 18.601 + (1 - 0.5603) \degree 0}{(1 + 0.1)^{3/12}} = \frac{10.4219}{(1 + 0.1)^{3/12}} = 10.177 \qquad [19]$$

The value of a call option on this Acme stock over a six-month period, when valued using the binomial model over two periods, is $10.18.

TWO-PERIOD VALUATION OF AN AMERICAN OPTION

So far, we have only concerned ourselves with European options, which cannot be exercised before their maturity date. Our examples have been based on call options, although European puts behave in the same way and can be evaluated using the same method. Let's consider now, however, how to value American options, where the exercise might happen at any point up until the expiration date, changing the value of the option. (Potential dividend payments on the underlying stock also affect the valuation of options, but we are disregarding that for the moment.)

First, it can be shown[5] that American call options behave like European (as long as there is no dividend.) Our focus is therefore on American puts. The basic process remains the same: start drawing the stock tree until the end, then work backwards to get the option value. However, as you work your way backwards, what you do differently is that for each node going left, you take the highest of two values: the discounted value (as we know how to calculate) or the value of the put if it were exercised at that point (calculated as the strike price minus the stock price at that node). Pick the higher of those two values as your value for the node, and continue working back to the beginning, making this choice at every node.

Example of American Put Option

Let's exemplify: You are considering an American put option, strike price of $102, based on Acme stock which today is priced at $100. You assume that for each time step the stock price might move up or down 10%. For the valuation, you will use two time steps, each one of 12 months. The risk-free annual compounded rate is at 4%. This gives you the basis to calculate the risk-neutral probability of an upward movement as:

---

[5] As done by Robert Merton (1973) who showed that a call option always is worth more non-exercised, leaving American and European call options with the same value.

$$p = \frac{(1 + r) - d}{u - d} = \frac{(1 + 0.04) - 0.9}{1.1 - 0.9} = 0.7 \qquad [20]$$

You are now equipped with all the values you need to calculate the option value. The resulting tree (both for the stock and the option) is shown in Figure 4, including the values we'll calculate.

For each node now, you'll want to compare the discounted value of the put option, P, and the payoff from early exercise, E. At the end nodes, they are the same, since they are both the intrinsic exercise value. At node B, calculating the option value, with the 70% probability from above, gives

$$\frac{0.7 \,^\circ\, 0 + (1 - 0.7) \,^\circ\, 3}{1 + 0.04} = 0.865 \qquad [21]$$

The payoff from early exercise is −$8 (strike price $102 − stock price $110 = out of the money) so you choose the option value for node B.

For node C, the option value is

$$\frac{0.7 \,^\circ\, 3 + (1 - 0.7) \,^\circ\, 21}{1 + 0.04} = 8.077 \qquad [22]$$

Here, however, exercising the option would be more beneficial (strike price $102 − stock price $90 = in the money at $12) so you pick the exercise value.

Finally, at the starting node the option value is

$$\frac{0.7 \,^\circ\, 0.865 + (1 - 0.7) \,^\circ\, 12}{1 + 0.04} = 4.044 \qquad [23]$$

Early exercise would bring you $2—so it makes more sense to hold on to the option, which has a higher valuation at $4.04.

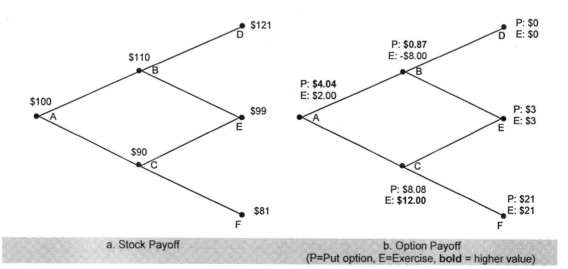

a. Stock Payoff

b. Option Payoff
(P=Put option, E=Exercise, **bold** = higher value)

Figure 4 Example of American Put, Two-Step Binomial Tree

CALIBRATING THE BINOMIAL TREE TO WORK WITH MARKET DATA

The binomial model helps us price options. Or does it really? As all models it is just that—a model of the real world, with limitations in how well it approximates the real market. We have already discussed how some concepts, such as risk-neutral valuation, were vital to efficiently implement the model. However, risk-neutral valuation doesn't tell us how to choose model parameters that best reflect real capital market data. For instance, where do you look in the markets to find the up- and down movements that are needed to calculate the value at each node? Hard to observe, aren't they?

What you have to do is calibrate the model to actual market data. Although the formal proof is beyond the scope of this note, upward and downward stock movements can be approximated using the volatility of the stock price.[6] Requiring that the movements in our binomial tree match the volatility of the stock price gives a formula that is used to calculate the upward movement needed in our option valuation:

$$u = \exp\left[v\sqrt{t}\right] \qquad [24]$$

where:

u = up movement

v = annualized stock price volatility

t = time in between nodes (in years)

Since we want the tree to be recombining (a two step up-down movement will lead to the same node as a down-up movement), it can be shown that the downward movement simply is:

$$d = \frac{1}{u} \qquad [25]$$

With these two variables, you have the needed inputs for the risk-neutral probability formula (which we repeat here for completeness):

$$p = \frac{(1 + r) - d}{u - d} \qquad [26]$$

So, starting with the observed volatility for the stock price helped create the inputs we needed to calibrate the binomial model to best match the real world.

BLACK-SCHOLES/MERTON FORMULA

The reliance on discrete time steps is a key building block of the binomial model. The more time steps you use, the more accurate your valuation. However, the more steps you add, the more complicated and time-consuming the calculations become. Deciding how many time steps to use may actually depend on how much time you have for the analysis. In theory, though, if you made the binomial tree as fine as possible, shrinking the time steps until they were infinitesimally small, you would be getting close to

---

[6] Volatility is typically calculated with the annualized standard deviation of the price or the return of the stock.

using a continuous time approach—which is the underlying assumption behind another valuation approach, the Black-Scholes/Merton analysis[7] (or the Black-Scholes model as it is often called).

The Black-Scholes/Merton approach compensates for the main limitation of the binomial model: its relatively slow calculation speed. To calculate a thousand node points is unwieldy with the binomial model—but the Black-Scholes model can give a result in a second. As we will see, however, the Black-Scholes model has another limitation: it works primarily for European call and put options, with limited use for American calls and none at all for American puts.

Apart from their different approach to time—discrete versus continuous—the two models share many of the assumptions and principles. This is why we could just argue that if we shrink the time intervals in the binomial model, it converges to the Black-Scholes model, producing similar valuation results. Explaining exactly how to derive the Black-Scholes model falls outside the scope of this note. Without a formal proof, we'll just simply state that the model focuses on valuing European call and put options on non-dividend paying stock. (It can be extended to handle dividends, which we will explain later.)

For a European call option, the Black-Scholes formula is:

$$C = SN(d_1) - PV(K)N(d_2) \qquad [27]$$

where $N(d_1)$ and $N(d_2)$ are the cumulative normal distribution functions for d_1 and d_2, defined as:

$$d_1 = \frac{\ln \dfrac{s}{k} + (r + v^2/2)T}{v\sqrt{T}} \qquad [28]$$

$$d_2 = d_1 - v\sqrt{T} \qquad [29]$$

where:

C = call option price

S = stock price

PV = present value

$N(d)$ = cumulative normal distribution function evaluated at d

K = strike price

$\ln$ = natural logarithm

r = continuously compounded risk-free interest rate (annualized)

T = time remaining until expiration (annualized)

v = annual stock price volatility (the standard deviation of the short-term returns over a year)

---

[7] The approach was developed by Fischer Black, Myron Scholes, and Robert Merton. Scholes and Merton received the 1997 Nobel Prize in Economics for their work. (Black passed away in 1995, and the Nobel Prize is not awarded posthumously.) For more information, see their original papers: Black, F. and Scholes, M., "The Pricing of Options and Corporate Liabilities," Journal of Political Economy 81 (May–June 1973); and Merton, R. C., "Theory of Rational Option Pricing," Bell Journal of Economics and Management Science 4 (spring 1973).

Based on put-call parity,[8] the Black-Scholes formula for a European put option, P, can be derived from the European call formula above:

$$P = PV(K)(N-d_2) - SN(-d_1) \qquad [30]$$

The Black-Scholes model was originally devised for European options on non-dividend paying stock. It can however be extended to handle dividend paying stock. The approach is simple: Whenever you see stock price, S, in the formula, replace it by $S - PV(D)$, or stock minus the present value of the dividends.

Comparing Black-Scholes and the Binomial Tree

Remember how we valued an option with the binomial tree? We solved for the stock and bond positions that replicated the option payoffs. Then, we valued the option by referring to the current value of the stock and bond portfolio, leading to the valuation equation:

$$C = \Delta S + PV(B) \qquad [31]$$

After solving the one step binomial model, we then started to add steps to the binomial tree, slowly moving in essence to continuous time as the intervals became infinitesimally small. With more intervals, however, the limits of the binomial model become apparent. The Black-Scholes model adjusts for these—but it is worth noting that the fundamental valuation equation is still the same as for the binomial model. The parameters Δ (for the amount of stock) and the present value of B (for the principal value of the bonds) from the binomial model can in fact be found in the Black-Scholes model, where they are adjusted for continuous-time. The comparison can be made as:

$$C = \underbrace{SN(d_1)}_{\Delta} - \underbrace{PV(K)N(d_2)}_{PV(B)} \qquad [32]$$

The first part—S times the Δ or $N(d_1)$—calculates the value from your long stock position. It turns out that the number of shares held, Δ or $N(d_1)$, can also be shown to represent the change in the call premium with respect to a small change in the underlying stock price. (Another name for this is the option delta.) The second part—the $-PV(B)$ or $-PV(K)N(d_2)$—represents the current value of the short zero coupon bond position. $PV(K)$ is the current value of a zero coupon bond that pays off K at maturity. $N(d_2)$ represents the number of those bonds that are sold short.

Example of Black-Scholes/Merton

Let's return to our original ACME call option to illustrate how to use the Black-Scholes model. We know from earlier that

- S, stock price = $100
- K, strike price = $110

[8] For more information about put-call parity, see George Chacko, Peter Hecht, Vincent Dessain, and Anders Sjöman, "Note on Basic Option Properties," Harvard Business School Note No. 9-205-105 (Boston: Harvard Business School Publishing, 2005).

- *r*, risk-free interest rate = 10% (not continuously compounded, making the continuously compounded rate to be 9.53%, calculated as ln (1 + 0.10))
- *T*, time remaining until expiration = 6 months (6/12 of a year)
- *v*, annual stock price volatility = 20%

Plugging these values into the d_1 and d_2 formulas gives us:

$$d_1 = \frac{\ln \frac{100}{110} + (0.0953 + 0.20^2/2)6/12}{0.20\sqrt{6/12}} = -0.2663 \qquad [33]$$

$$d_2 = d_1 - 0.20\sqrt{6/12} = -0.4077 \qquad [34]$$

We plug these values into the Black-Scholes formula. Using the NORMSDIST function in Excel to calculate $N(d_1)$ and $N(d_2)$, and a continuously compounded interest rate[9] for the present value (calculated as ln (1 + 0.10)), we arrive at:

$$C = 100 \ast N(-0.2663) - PV(110)N(-0.4077) = 3.6585 \qquad [35]$$

$3.66 is then the Black-Scholes value of our ACME call option. Compare that to the value we obtained using a two-step binomial tree (equation [19] on page 296): $10.18. Quite a difference! Our binomial model value would come closer to the Black-Scholes value if we increased the number of time steps in the tree (remember, we only used two steps for a six-month maturity), converging to Black-Scholes in the limit.

Assumptions Underlying Black-Scholes/Merton Approach

For completeness and clarity, let's state the assumptions for the Black-Scholes model. Fundamentally, it is a replication-based result that does not require knowledge of the stock's expected return. However, the price of the option does depend on the volatility of the stock price. In fact, the Black-Scholes model assumes that the volatility of the underlying stock price remains constant over the period of analysis.

The Black-Scholes model shares these basic assumptions with the binomial model. However, it further assumes that the option can be exercised only at expiration; it therefore applies only to European options. It also originally assumes that no dividends are paid (although as we explained above, the model can be adjusted to encompass dividend payments). The model further assumes

- the existence of a complete, efficient and frictionless market, without transactions costs for buying or selling the option or the underlying stock,
- that all options and securities are perfectly divisible (if you want to sell 1/100th of an option, you can),
- that there are no riskless arbitrage opportunities,
- that all market participants can lend and borrow money at the same risk-free interest rate,
- that this risk free rate is known to all and constant during the life of the option,

---

[9] As mentioned earlier, we have used discrete compounded interest rates throughout this note. The Black-Scholes model, however, mandates using a continuously compounded interest rate.

- that security trading is continuous, and
- that the share price evolves over time following a "random walk" or a lognormal distribution.

IMPLIED VOLATILITY: USING THE BLACK-SCHOLES/ MERTON FORMULA PRACTICALLY

The examples of options that we have used throughout this note are considered very simple by traders. In fact, traders never have to value such plain vanilla options, since these options are already traded and have quoted prices. It is for more complicated option structures that an analyst will use the knowledge developed in this note.

In addition to pricing options, the Black-Scholes model can be used to back out the market's assessment of future stock price volatility. All other variables needed by the Black-Scholes model can be observed directly in the markets—but the volatility of an underlying is not listed. One way to obtain an estimate is to solve the Black-Scholes formula for the volatility that equates the model price with the observed market price of options with similar underlyings; hence the term implied volatility.[10] Put generally, implied volatility is the estimated volatility of an option's price, implied by the option's market price based on a theoretical pricing model, such as the Black-Scholes model.

The process is intuitive: Say that you want to price an option for which there is no market price since it is not publicly traded. Find another option that is as close in characteristics as possible (written on the same or comparable stock; close in maturity; similar strike price; etc) but that is publicly traded. For the publicly traded option, calculate the volatility using the Black-Scholes model. This means running the Black-Scholes model in iterations to find the volatility value that makes the result of the Black-Scholes model match the price that the option is trading at. This is the *implied volatility* for the traded option—and a volatility value you then can use to price your other option.

The use of implied volatility is so pervasive in the markets that it is common practice to quote options by their implied volatility rather than their price. To the traders, this quoting practice makes it easier to compare different options. The basic thinking is that since all other parameters affecting an option's price (the strike price, the risk-free rate, the price of the underlying and the expiry) are known, the remaining parameter (the volatility) is the final determinant of the option's price.

Example of Implied Volatility

Suppose you need to price a call option on a non-dividend paying stock with a price of $40. The option has a strike price of $35 and a time-to-maturity of 3 years. The closest call option you can find trading in the markets is one on the same stock with a $35 strike price but with a 6-month maturity. Its price is $6.69. The continuously-compounded risk free rate is at 4%. What you do in this case is use the traded option to calibrate the Black-Scholes model with a 6-month maturity. Then, you will extrapolate from this calibrated model by increasing the maturity on the model to 3 years. The resulting price is your estimate for the price of the 3-year call option.

First, you calibrate the Black-Scholes model such that it prices the traded option. To do this, you have all of the information for the Black-Scholes model except one: the volatility of the stock price. For the volatility, you put in the value that causes the Black-

---

[10] As opposed to looking at the historical volatility of the underlying stock.

Scholes model to match the $6.69 price that we observe the option traded at. (Several software packages are available to simplify the process for you.) This implied volatility turns out to be 29%, or in other words, when the volatility is 29%, the Black-Scholes model outputs a value of $6.69.

Now that you have the model calibrated, you can extrapolate from the model to calculate the value of the 3-year option. Simply extend the value of time-to-maturity to 3 years in the model used to deliver the $6.69 price—and the new price that the model outputs is $12.38.

This would be your best guess for the price of the 3-year option.

PROBLEM SET

Problem 1 In Excel, construct a four-step binomial tree of stock prices to value 1-year call and put options. Use the following information: the initial stock price is $100, and the stock is not expected to pay dividends. $1 invested in a 1-year T-bill (no coupon payments) pays $1.05 at the end of the year. You should calculate the volatility of the stock from this historical, quarterly stock price series: 36, 39, 37, 43, 45. (In order to be technically correct, you should estimate the volatility from the natural logarithm price growth series, $\ln(P_{t+1}/P_t)$. The rationale for this transformation is beyond the scope of this note.) How much would each of the following options be worth?

1. An at-the-money European call option maturing at the end of 1 year?
2. An at-the-money European put option maturing at the end of 1 year?
3. Should put-call parity hold here? Does it?

Problem 2 Consider a five-month American put option on a non-dividend paying stock when the stock price is $50, the strike price is $50, the risk-free rate is 10%, and the stock's volatility is 40%. In Excel, value this option using a binomial model with 1 step per month.

Problem 3 Your friend wants to make a bet with you that the value of Alpha Industries (AHAA), currently trading at $21 with a volatility of 75%, will exceed $40 in one year. If he wins the bet, that is if AHAA's stock price is more than $40 in one year, you have to pay him $50. However, if you win the bet, he pays you $50. How much should you charge him today to make the bet, if the risk-free rate is 5%? Use a 6-step binomial tree for your calculations.

19

Sally Jameson—1999

In the seven years since she graduated from Harvard Business School, Sally Jameson[1] had done quite well. She had left her first job, at Telstar Communications, after working there for six years, and last year became the Director of Marketing for an Internet startup, Everythingsadotcom.Com. While at Telstar, Sally had accumulated 10,200 shares in Telstar stock, from assorted option grants, company-subsidized purchases of shares, and direct investments in the firm. A little after she left the firm, Telstar had been acquired by a larger telecommunications firm, BigBroadBand, Inc. (BBB), a firm with an equity market capitalization of over $15 billion. Her shares in Telstar were exchanged one-for-one for BBB shares, and the rising equity markets, compounded with the extremely attractive performance of BBB, made Sally's BBB investment worth over $800,000, which represented over 70% of her personal portfolio. (Exhibit 1 gives market data on BBB shares and options.) The remainder of her tangible portfolio was composed of her retirement plan, which was invested in an Index Fund whose performance tracked the Standard and Poors Index, and in about a dozen Internet stocks which Sally followed daily. In addition to an annual income of $110,000, she also had been granted 25,000 options on Everythingsadotcom.com, struck at $1.00 per share, but since the firm was at least a year from a possible IPO, she didn't think about them very much.

Sally's fascination with tracking her Internet stocks led her to an investment Web site, *The Motley Fool* (http://www.fool.com), to check prices and read news and chat boards about the stocks nearly every day. She ignored most of the advertisements at the top of the web page, from established firms like Saab, Morningstar or E°Trade, but a series of ads from an obscure firm caught her attention—and struck a sore spot.

This case was prepared as the basis for class discussion rather than to illustrate either effective or ineffective handling of an administrative situation. It was prepared using information from public sources, and First Security Capital declined to review it.

[1] Sally Jameson is a fictitious character as is Telstar, although the First Security Capital (FSC) information is an actual investment offering and the BBB, Inc. data is disguised but actual firm and market data. The material referring to First Security Capital comes from public sources.

EXHIBIT 1A

HISTORY OF BBB STOCK PRICE, 1992–1999

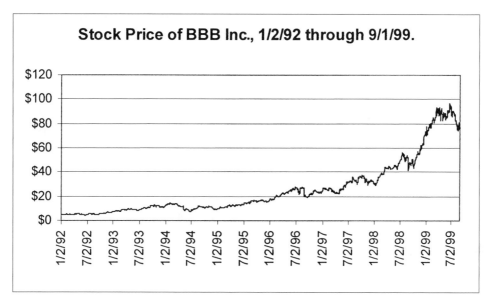

Stock Price of BBB Inc., 1/2/92 through 9/1/99.

Note: Stock price is adjusted for stock splits. While BBB Inc. paid a dividend in 1987, it has not done so since. The firm's Web site listed a set of answers to Frequently Asked Questions. One read: "Will BBB pay a dividend? No. BBB does not pay a dividend to common stockholders." The closing price of BBB, Inc. on September 3, 1999 was $78 1/2.

Source: Datastream International.

Despite holding a substantial stock portfolio, Sally had never bought a home and rented a large and expensive apartment overlooking the Charles River in Boston, Massachusetts. She had intended to buy a home, but with her heavy travel schedule at both Telstar and Everythingsadotcom.com, she had never gotten around to it. With Boston condominium and home prices soaring, and pundits warning of the imminent collapse

---

[2] "Points" refer to the prepayment of interest for a residential loan. Mortgages often allow homeowners to pay "points" in advance and in turn pay a lower periodic interest rate on their mortgage. "Closing costs" refer to the administrative costs of transacting a loan document. The "monthly payments" refers to the monthly payment of principal and interest in a traditional mortgage loan.

HISTORICAL VOLATILITY OF BBB COMMON STOCK RETURNS, 1992–1999

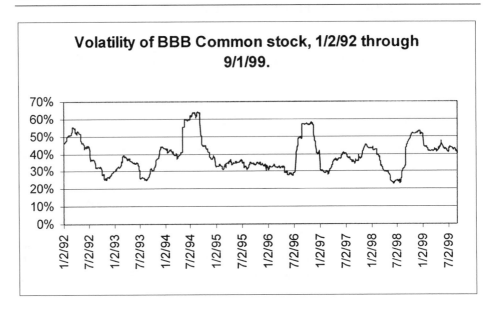

Note: Historical volatility is measured by the annualized standard deviation of daily stock price returns over the prior 90 days. The historical volatility based on the closing price on 9/3/99 was 40%.

Source: Datastream International.

IMPLIED VOLATILITY OF CALLS ON BBB INC. STOCK, 5/95 TO 9/99

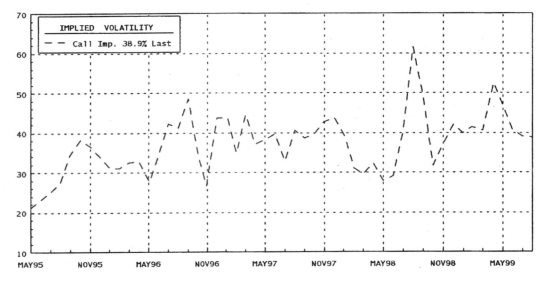

Source: Bloomberg. The data are a weighted-average of the implied volatilities of "at the money" call options traded on BBB Inc. stock.

EXHIBIT 1D

THE IMPLIED VOLATILITIES OF OPTIONS ON BBB INC. STOCK, AS OF 9/3/99

CALLS

| | Expiration Dates: | | | | | |
| | **1999** | | | **2000** | **2001** | **2002** |
Strike Price	**Sept 18th**	**Oct 16th**	**Dec 18th**	**Mar 18th**	**Jan 20th**	**Jan 19th**
65	45%	43%	41%	43%	43%	43%
70	43%	40%	42%	42%	42%	42%
75	37%	39%	41%	41%	41%	42%
80	35%	38%	41%	41%	41%	41%

PUTS

| | Expiration Dates: | | | | | |
| | **1999** | | | **2000** | **2001** | **2002** |
Strike Price	**Sept 18th**	**Oct 16th**	**Dec 18th**	**Mar 18th**	**Jan 20th**	**Jan 19th**
65	45%	43%	41%	41%	41%	40%
70	41%	40%	40%	41%	41%	41%
75	37%	38%	38%	40%	40%	40%
80	36%	37%	38%	39%	39%	39%

Source: Bloomberg, based on the prices of American-style options trading on the Chicago Board Options Exchange (CBOE).

of the equity markets, Sally contemplated moving some of her money from the stock market into real estate, either now or in the coming year.[3] (Exhibit 2 shows the appreciation in the stock market and in real estate prices.) Were she to buy a property now, she anticipated that she might need about $150,000 in equity to fund the downpayment and renovations on a spacious Back Bay condominium she had been admiring. (She planned to borrow the other $600,000 for the 1500 square foot unit.) She couldn't liquidate her retirement plan assets, and she didn't want to sell her Internet stocks quite yet. That left the BBB shares, which she was legally free to dispose of at will.

The good news was that her 10,200 shares or $800,000 stake in BBB shares could easily support her downpayment, and could potentially cover the total cost of the condo. The bad news was that her tax basis in the shares was $26.00 per share. At the current share price of $78.50 per share, if she were to sell her shares, the realized capital gains[4] would be $52.50 per share. Given her tax status, she would owe capital gains taxes of 20% of the gain, or $10.50 per share. Sally's reluctance to pay these taxes led her to continue to hold the BBB shares. Rather than sell the shares, she could borrow against them via a traditional margin loan from her broker. Under the terms of this loan, she could borrow up to 50% against the market value of the shares pledged, and owe in-

---

[3] She thought that if the stock market dropped, perhaps real estate prices would fall as well. In this case, she might prefer to lock in her equity profits now in anticipation of lower real estate prices later.

[4] Capital gains represent the difference between the sale price of her shares and Sally's cost to acquire the shares, or tax basis.

EXHIBIT 2A

THE PERFORMANCE OF EQUITY MARKETS AND BOSTON REAL ESTATE PRICE, 1992–1999

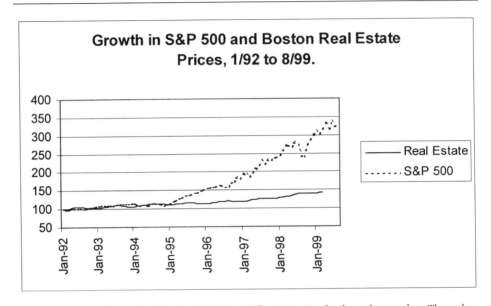

Source: Datastream International for the S&P, Case Shiller Weiss Inc. for the real estate data. The real estate index used is the Case-Shiller Home Price Index of single-family homes over $228K, available up to March 1999. It is a repeat sales index, with current prices compared only to previous transactions for the same properties. Although this index covers 7 counties in Massachusetts and 3 in New Hampshire, Boston accounts for a large part of the transactions recorded. The Standard and Poors (S&P) 500 is a value-weighted index of the 500 largest U.S. stocks.

terest at a rate of 6–7%.[5] (Exhibit 3 reports borrowing and lending rates in the financial markets.) Another alternative would be to borrow BBB shares from her broker, sell these borrowed shares short, collect the proceeds from the short sale and use her existing shares to cover her borrowings. This "short-against-the-box" strategy would provide her with cash flow today. Under the terms of her brokerage agreement, she would get access to 90% of the amount of funds raised through the short sale. Or she could raise cash by selling calls on all or part of her holding.

Sally clicked on the advertisement at the Motley Fool site and her browser came to the First Security Capital Web site (http://www.firstsecuritycapital.com), which described a product called the 90% Stock Loan[SM]. This product promised to provide FSC customers with an unsecured, non-recourse loan equal to 90% of the value of

[5] The limitation of 50% borrowing against securities held on margin was established by Regulation T of the Federal Reserve Board. Sally's broker charged different interest rates depending on the amount of money she borrowed against her securities. Were she to borrow $150,000 against shares worth $300,000, her interest payment would be 6.50% per annum. Were she to borrow $400,000 against the full value of her BBB shares, her interest rate would also be 6.50%. See Exhibit 3.

EXHIBIT 2B

THE P/E RATIO OF THE S&P 500, 1992–1999

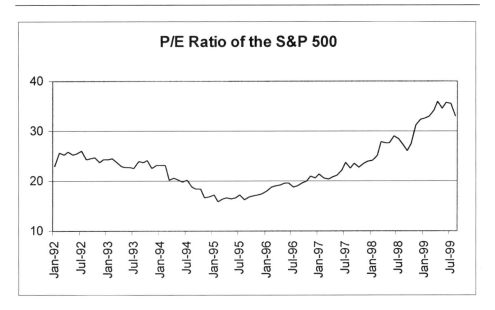

Source: Datastream International. The P/E ratio is the average price divided by the average earnings per share (based on the latest earnings release). Both numerator and denominator are weighted by the number of shares outstanding for each of the S&P's component issues.

their share holdings. At the end of the loan's initial three-year term, the investor could either repay the loan value plus accrued interest[6], in which case they kept their shares, or walk away. If they chose the latter alternative, FSC would keep the shares and the investor would keep the loan amount without paying any penalty. The Web site and other marketing materials sent by FSC provided most of the details about the plan, and Sally got additional information in the mail from FSC. See Exhibit 4. As she initially understood it, the program would allow her to monetize all or a portion of her BBB holdings, effectively lock in 90% of her gains, and defer her capital gain for at least three years.

Sally could find out reasonably little about FSC beyond the information on the Web site. FSC was a small privately-held firm and declined to provide her with financial statements, information about the size of the firm, their customers, trading counterparties or details of their hedging strategy. They stated that this information was proprietary and therefore they would not reveal it. She checked various search engines and databases like Lexis-Nexis and could find virtually no mention of the product or the firm, apart from a few press releases. Curious about the firm, she ordered a credit re-

---

[6] According to FSC's Web page "the interest rate is determined by the market capitalization of the companies for which shares are being submitted as collateral for the loan. The interest rates are somewhat higher than typical broker loan rates to allow FSC to offset the costs incurred in providing the benefits of the 90% Stock Loan[SM]."

EXHIBIT 2C

QUARTERLY DATA FOR BBB SHARE PRICES, THE S&P 500, THE INTER@CTIVE WEEK INTERNET STOCK INDEX AND THE CASE-SHILLER HOME PRICE INDEX

		BBB Inc. ($)	S&P 500	Inter@ctive Week Internet Stock Index[7]	Case-Shiller Home Price Index
1992	Q1	4.92	404.23	n/a	91.02
	Q2	4.83	412.88	n/a	95.14
	Q3	5.58	416.29	n/a	93.39
	Q4	7.48	435.71	n/a	92.69
1993	Q1	8.81	450.30	n/a	94.21
	Q2	8.75	449.02	n/a	97.64
	Q3	12.50	461.29	n/a	97.80
	Q4	12.06	465.44	43.67	95.26
1994	Q1	12.00	445.77	42.76	97.69
	Q2	8.75	446.20	34.96	101.46
	Q3	11.03	461.74	41.03	101.80
	Q4	9.72	459.27	47.31	100.30
1995	Q1	11.69	501.85	52.58	101.07
	Q2	13.50	547.09	60.67	103.35
	Q3	16.06	581.72	71.48	103.20
	Q4	17.63	615.93	77.73	101.84
1996	Q1	23.00	653.73	73.53	103.45
	Q2	27.69	675.88	84.11	106.95
	Q3	21.38	689.08	84.76	107.63
	Q4	26.06	740.74	81.36	106.66
1997	Q1	22.00	759.64	65.39	108.81
	Q2	32.00	891.03	79.46	112.95
	Q3	35.38	955.41	96.27	114.06
	Q4	30.25	970.43	86.75	114.55
1998	Q1	43.06	1108.15	103.72	117.55
	Q2	48.44	1148.56	127.73	123.06
	Q3	48.88	986.39	124.65	125.38
	Q4	71.75	1229.23	213.71	125.44
1999	Q1	88.56	1293.72	305.59	127.55

Source: Datastream International for the BBB Inc. and S&P data, Bloomberg for the Inter@ctive Week Internet Index data, and Case-Shiller-Weiss Inc. for the Case-Shiller Home Price Index.

port on FSC from Dun and Bradstreet, but it provided little new information. It reported that the firm had 11 employees and was founded in 1997, was reasonably current on its phone and other bills, but that the firm had declined to provide more detailed financial information to D&B. She checked with the Better Business Bureau

---

[7] The Inter@ctive Week Internet Index is a value-weighted index of the stocks of 50 firms providing digital interactive services, software or hardware.

EXHIBIT 3

BORROWING AND LENDING RATES, SEPTEMBER 3, 1999

Representative Home Mortgage Rates

Form of Mortgage	APR[8]
1 Year Adjustable Rate Mortgages[9]	7.89%
15 Year Fixed-Rate Mortgages	7.68%
30 Year Fixed-Rate Mortgages	7.99%
30 Year Fixed Jumbo[10], no points	8.42%

Source: www.bankrate.com.

Margin Borrowing Rates

Amount borrowed	Interest Rate
0–$49,999	7.00%
$50,000–$99,999	6.75%
$100,000–$499,999	6.50%
$500,000–$999,999	6.25%
$1,000,000+	6.00%

Source: Rates charged by a major brokerage firm. The appropriate rate applies to the entire margin loan amount.

Credit Card Borrowing Rates

	Variable APR
Standard Card	16.00%

Source: www.bankrate.com.

Other Rates

	Rate
Prime Rate[11]	8.25%
3-month LIBOR[12]	5.53%

Source: Bloomberg.

(Continued)

[8] The annual percentage rate, or APR, is the rate adjusted for origination and discount points, plus any other closing costs charged to the borrower.

[9] An adjustable-rate mortgage has its interest rate set for an initial term, but afterwards the rate varies with market interest rates.

[10] The two mortgage agencies, Fannie Mae and Freddie Mac, set a limit on the size of a loan that can be pooled. Loans larger than this limit, currently around $240,000, are termed "Jumbo" mortgages, and have higher rates of interest.

[11] The Prime Rate is the rate charged by commercial banks to their most credit-worthy customers.

[12] LIBOR, or London Inter-Bank Offered Rate, is the rate at which banks offer to lend to each other in the wholesale money market. The data is collected by the British Bankers Association at 11am each day, based on the rates at which 16 contributor banks (8 banks for some currencies) feel they could borrow funds. The LIBOR fixing is then an arithmetic average of the middle 2 quartiles (i.e. excluding the 4 lowest and 4 highest rates).

EXHIBIT 3   (Continued)

BORROWING AND LENDING RATES, SEPTEMBER 3, 1999

Treasury and Corporate Rates

	1 Year	3 Year	5 Year
U.S. Treasuries	5.20%	5.73%	5.77%
U.S. Treasury Strips[13]	5.51%	5.85%	5.99%
AAA	6.00%	6.34%	6.57%
AA	6.04%	6.37%	6.59%
A	6.20%	6.60%	6.88%
BBB	6.56%	7.01%	7.30%
BB	7.25%	7.85%	8.19%
B	8.19%	8.65%	9.10%

Source: Bloomberg. All yields are quoted on a bond-equivalent basis.

covering the San Francisco area, and found that FSC was a member with a "satisfactory record," but a file on the company had been kept for only 11 months.

Sally decided it was time to figure out what she would do about her BBB shares and her "dream home." Her cherrywood desk was littered with the broker's listing sheet of the condo, as well as printouts of financial data on the markets (Exhibits 1–3), the FSC marketing information (Exhibit 4), and a handwritten summary of her understanding of the relevant parts of the tax code, which she would ask her accountant to review (Exhibit 5).

EXHIBIT 4

FIRST SECURITY CAPITAL MARKETING MATERIAL

Please refer directly to First Security Capital Web site (http://www.firstsecuritycapital.com), in particular the sections titled "90% Stock Loan ^{SM}," "How to Proceed," "Frequently Asked Questions," and "About FSC."

---

[13] STRIPS are zero coupon bonds.

EXHIBIT 5

SALLY'S UNDERSTANDING OF THE TAX CONSEQUENCES OF VARIOUS ALTERNATIVES

First Security Capital's materials recommend that customers consult a tax advisor for advice. Due to the highly complex tax issues raised Sally had an appointment set with her accountant. But, based on the knowledge she picked up in her "Tax Factors" course at HBS, the following summarized her understanding of the tax consequences of various alternatives:

Selling her shares outright: Sally had held her Telstar and successor BBB shares for more than three years, and hence her gains on the shares would be taxed at the long-term capital gains rate. This rate was currently 20%.

Tax status of borrowings: If Sally were to take out a mortgage to purchase her primary residence, the interest on this mortgage would be deductible for Federal income-tax purposes. Sally's Federal marginal tax rate on ordinary income was 31%, given her current salary and investment income. (Mortgage interest was not deductible for Massachusetts State income tax purposes.)

If Sally were to borrow against her BBB shares, in the form of a margin loan, the net interest on this loan would be currently deductible, subject to the limitation that the amount of investment interest deducted for the year could not exceed her investment income. Any investment interest not deductible this year could be carried forward for possible deduction in future years.

90% Stock Loan^{SM} Transactions: At the initiation of the transaction, if the transaction were not deemed an effective sale of the stock, there would be no tax consequences.

During the term of the loan, when the stock loan would be accruing interest but Sally would be paying no cash interest, it is probable that neither she nor FSC would experience an annual interest related tax effect. Instead, upon payment of the interest in cash at the end of the contract, Sally would be entitled to an interest expense deduction, subject to the limitation that annual investment interest deductions can not exceed net investment income. FSC would recognize interest income when it received the cash.

At the end of three years, if Sally were to repay the loan and obtain her shares there would probably be no tax consequences.

At the end of three years, if Sally were to elect to give up her stock to satisfy the balance of the loan, she would be deemed to have sold the stock and realized value equal to the debt she owed and eliminated. From this she would subtract her cost of $26 per share.

Upon maturity, if Sally were to extend the term of the loan there would probably be no tax consequences.

Option transactions: If Sally were to buy options, e.g., put options on BBB stock, the payment of the premium of these options would be treated as the purchase price of the option with no immediate tax effect. Were the options to expire worthless, the transaction probably would be treated as equivalent to sale of the option for zero with a loss being recognized in the amount of the difference between the zero realized and the cost of the option. The capital loss would be long-term or short-term depending on how long the option had been owned. Were the options to be exercised for a positive payoff, its cost would reduce the amount realized upon the sale of the underlying stock.

If Sally were to sell options, e.g. call options on BBB stock, the receipt of the premium for these options would not be immediately taxed. Were the options to expire worthless, the gain would be taxed as a short-term capital gain with the result that it would probably be taxed at ordinary income rates (31%). Were the options to be exercised for a positive payoff and Sally was required to deliver her BBB shares (or the value equivalent to satisfy the option holder's claim), the amount received for the option would probably be treated as an additional sum realized on the stock's sale.

EQUITY OPTIONS: APPLICATIONS

20

Pine Street Capital

Harold Yoon looked up from his workstation at the analysis that he had just printed out. Yoon had come in to work at 4A.M. in the morning today, July 27, 2000, to look over this analysis one more time. As the managing partner for a $32 million equity hedge fund, Yoon was used to coming in early to the partnership's downtown San Francisco office, but this time he had more than the usual monitoring of pre-market news to take care of.

Immediately after the markets closed today, 1P.M. in San Francisco, he and the other partners of the hedge fund would meet to discuss a potential change of hedging strategy. The fund they managed tended to be a market-neutral fund, meaning that the fund hedged out all market risk. In the past, they had hedged this market risk by short-selling, or "shorting," shares of a market index. However, due to the unprecedented volatility (and valuation levels) seen in the markets over the past several months, the partners were now considering hedging this risk by purchasing put options on this market index rather than simply shorting.

Yoon picked up the analysis that an analyst employed by the fund had carried out. Prior to the partners' meeting this afternoon, he needed to have a recommendation ready as to which hedging strategy to pursue.

HEDGE FUNDS

From 1988 to 1998, the number of hedge funds around the globe increased by almost 425%, reaching an estimated 5,830 funds with assets under management. Assets under management during this time period grew from $42 billion to $311 billion.[1] Hedge funds are private group investments that offer equity pooling advantages similar to mutual funds. However, because hedge funds are not publicly owned, they are less regulated than mutual funds and enjoy additional privileges. The lack of regulation gives hedge funds flexibility in investment strategies and risk management that mutual funds do not have. As Exhibit 1a shows, this flexibility seems to translate into higher expected

Research Associate Eli Peter Strick prepared this case under the supervision of Professor George Chacko. HBS cases are developed solely as the basis for class discussion. Cases are not intended to serve as endorsements, sources of primary data, or illustrations of effective or ineffective management.

[1] "Size of Hedge Fund Universe." VAN Hedge Fund Advisors International, Inc. Nashville, TN. 1999.

EXHIBIT 1A

HEDGE FUND VS MUTUAL FUND PERFORMANCE

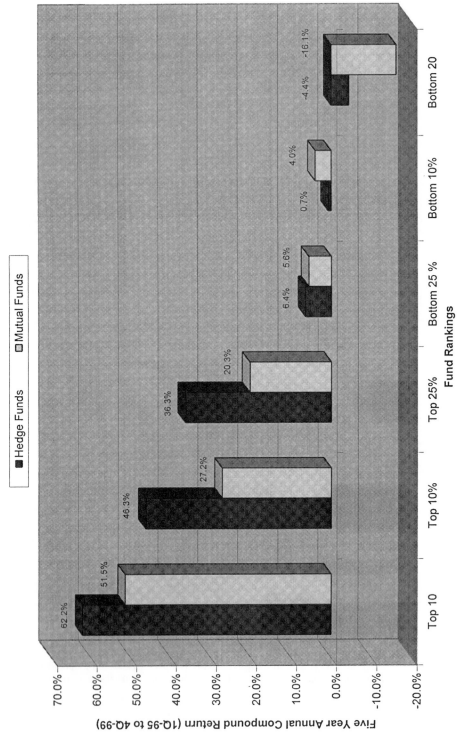

Comparison of Fund Performances

Source: Van Money Manager Research, Inc., Nashville, TN, USA.

HEDGE FUND AND MUTUAL FUND PERFORMANCE DURING QUARTERS WITH NEGATIVE RETURNS FOR THE S&P 500 (1988–1999)

	1Q - 90	3Q - 90	2Q - 91	1Q - 92	1Q - 94	4Q - 94	3Q - 98	3Q - 99	Cumulative Return
S&P 500	−3.0%	−13.7%	−0.2%	−2.5%	−3.8%	−0.02%	−9.9%	−6.2%	−33.8%
VAN U.S. Hedge Fund Index	2.2%	−3.7%	2.3%	5.0%	−0.8%	−1.2%	−6.1%	2.1%	−0.7%
Morningstar Average Equity Mutual Fund	−2.8%	−15.4%	−0.9%	−0.7%	−3.2%	−2.6%	−15.0%	−3.2%	−37.2%
Morningstar Average Taxable Bond Fund	−0.9%	0.6%	1.5%	−1.1%	−2.4%	−0.2%	2.0%	0.3%	−0.3%

Source: Van Money Manager Research, Inc., Nashville, TN, USA.

Leveraged Portfolio (Initial Debt/Equity=1)				Un-leveraged Portfolio			
Today		Tomorrow		Today		Tomorrow	
Assets 100	Debt 50	Assets 200	Debt 50	Assets 50		Assets 100	
	Equity 50		Equity 150		Equity 50		Equity 100
ROE = 200%				ROE =100%			

Figure 1 Balance Sheet Effects of Leverage (ROA = 100%)

returns for hedge funds as compared to mutual funds.[2] Two important ways hedge funds differ from mutual funds are their ability to use leverage and their ability to hedge by shorting or using options.

Leverage

While hedge funds can use leverage, mutual funds, for the most part, cannot. By using debt to finance a portion of the assets in a portfolio, a higher return on the portfolio's equity is possible compared with an all-equity financed portfolio. See Figure 1 for an example of the effect of leverage on a portfolio. The balance sheets of two portfolios, a portfolio that is leveraged and an all-equity portfolio, are shown when assets appreciate 100% (100% ROA). By keeping the initial equity amount ($50) the same in the two portfolios, the impact of leverage can be observed on the portfolio's Return on Equity (ROE).

Of course, if leverage is employed and the assets lose value, then leverage works against the investor, amplifying the loss on equity relative to an all-equity portfolio. Therefore, using leverage increases the risk of an investment. In response, many hedge funds seek arbitrage opportunities in different markets, searching for payoffs with little to no risk. While these opportunities may be overlooked for their marginal size by most investors, hedge funds are able to lever these payoffs to create higher returns.

Leverage doesn't come without a price. Prime brokers, who help finance and execute trades for hedge funds, offer loans to hedge funds and charge the interest. These loans are typically known as margin loans. Prime brokers minimize the credit risk associated with their loans to hedge funds. They do so by diligently monitoring their hedge funds' investments and risks. If the value of a fund's investments, or assets, drops to a level such that little equity remains, the broker can force the fund to put in more equity or the broker can liquidate part or all of the fund's portfolio, quite possibly putting the fund out of business.

Options & Derivatives

A hedge fund's ability to use options gives it another advantage over traditional mutual funds. While some funds use options and other derivative instruments to speculate on risky returns, most hedge funds use options as a hedging tool to limit the overall risk of their investments.

---

[2] This analysis is done with raw returns rather than risk-adjusted returns. However Exhibit 1b illustrates that the higher performance of hedge funds is not simply due to added risk-taking on the part of hedge funds. This exhibit shows that even in times when funds have negative performance, hedge funds continue to outperform mutual funds.

Figure 2 gives an example of using put options to protect a portfolio's value. (Information given: S&P 500 is at 100, S&P volatility = 25%, the portfolio's beta = 1.5, Risk Free Rate = 5%, and the S&P options are two month, at the money puts.) This example shows the balance sheets of two portfolios, an "un-hedged portfolio," only invested in stock, and a "hedged portfolio" that uses put options to minimize changes in the value of the portfolio. At the beginning ("today") both portfolios have equal amounts of equity and assets. In either market outcome, up 5% or down 5%, the Return on Equity (ROE) for the hedged portfolio is more stable than the un-hedged portfolio.

The value of the put options is negatively correlated with the value of the stock in the portfolio. In the example above, put options are held to insure the portfolio against market fluctuations. The ratio of put options to stock needed to perfectly hedge a portfolio is a function of the option and portfolio "deltas." While the hedge position protects the portfolio from the downside of risk, it also limits the potential gains.

Hedge Fund Strategies

One way of categorizing a hedge fund is by its investment strategy. Each fund's particular investment strategy is based on its fund manager's skills and where the fund manager feels he/she has a competitive advantage over other investors in assessing risks. Skilled managers will usually take and, in fact, leverage up those risks that they understand well, while they will hedge away risks where they feel they have no particular comparative advantage. For instance, a manager might feel confident about his ability to value individual companies but have no view on the performance of the entire market. This manager might then adopt what is called a "market-neutral" strategy, where market risk is hedged away while firm-specific risk is kept in the portfolio.

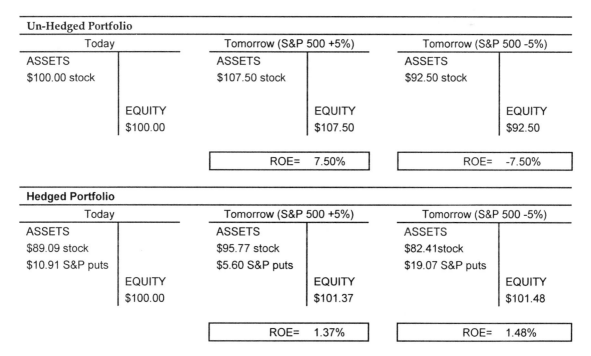

Figure 2   Balance Sheet Effects of Hedging with Put Options

PINE STREET CAPITAL

Pine Street Capital (PSC) was a hedge fund that specialized in the technology sector. Holding undergraduate degrees in engineering/sciences as well as MBAs and/or PhDs specializing in finance, and having worked at an assortment of technology and financial services firms prior to forming PSC in January 1999, the partners of PSC felt their strength to be their ability to evaluate the technology sector and, specifically, to pick out-performing stocks in this sector. They felt less comfortable making bets on the direction of the entire market. PSC's portfolio reflected the partners' strengths, particularly Yoon's.[3]

Up to now, PSC had been using a short-sale strategy to eliminate general market risk from the fund. The short-sale was accomplished in the following way. Using the model:

Expected PSC Portfolio Return = $\alpha + \beta$ ° (Market Return)

and data on PSC's portfolio holdings and market returns, PSC established a relationship between the performance of the market and PSC's portfolio. Beta (**β**) measured how PSC's portfolio responded to changes in the market, while alpha (**α**) was the amount of return in excess of that due to market risk. Thus, beta was a measure of the market risk of PSC's portfolio while alpha measured PSC's expected return if market risk were eliminated from the portfolio. Exhibits 2 and 3 show PSC's current portfolio allocation and historical risk-return characteristics.

Since PSC's goal was to eliminate market risk, this risk was hedged from PSC's portfolio by shorting the market (PSC used the NASDAQ index as its proxy for the market) in proportion to the beta of the assets in the portfolio. Exhibit 4 gives historical price data for the Nasdaq 100 index,[4] while Exhibit 5 shows how PSC's portfolio would have performed on a monthly basis compared to the NASDAQ if the portfolio were completely unhedged.

An example of how short selling the market hedges market risk is given in Figure 3 on page 327. Eliminating market risk from the long portfolio leaves the portfolio with a guaranteed 1% return, which is precisely the alpha of the long positions in the portfolio. Thus, short-selling removes the market return component, and market risk correspondingly, leaving only an alpha return in the portfolio.

Of course, the alpha return that PSC was left with in their portfolio after hedging market risk could have been negative if they picked the wrong investments, but finding positive alpha stocks in the technology sector was exactly what PSC felt to be its comparative advantage. Exhibit 6 shows historical performance of hedge funds in the technology sector, while comparing this performance with funds focusing on other sectors.

Immunizing the portfolio against market fluctuations left much less risk in the portfolio. This allowed PSC to increase the expected return, and corresponding risk, of the portfolio by levering. As a long-run goal, PSC generally maintained a debt ratio of 50% in the fund's capital structure.

---

[3] Yoon held an engineering degree as well as an MBA from MIT. Yoon's work experiences included substantial time spent at a defense/communications firm, a pharmaceutical company, a consulting firm, and an investment bank.

[4] Selling the market portfolio did not require short selling every stock on the NASDAQ; this would be extremely expensive to finance and maintain. Instead, *Exchange Traded Funds* (ETFs) enable investors like PSC to trade single shares that mimic the performance of entire market indices. ETFs can be short sold and, unlike most common stocks, shorted on a downtick. The ticker for the ETF that follows the NASDAQ 100 composite is QQQ.

EXHIBIT 2

PINE STREET CAPITAL'S PORTFOLIO ALLOCATION ON JULY 26, 2000

Ticker	Company Name	Shares	Share Price[1]	Total $	Total Allocation	NASDAQ[2]			S&P 500		
						Beta[3]	Alpha[4]	R-Squared[5]	Beta	Alpha	R-Squared
AMCC	Applied Micro Circuits	24000	162.875	$3,909,000	11.31%	2.15	6.42	0.58	3.06	6.91	0.29
AHAA	Alpha Industries, Inc.	45000	36.1875	$1,628,438	4.71%	1.63	2.14	0.39	2.39	2.16	0.20
ANAD	Anadigics, Inc.	70000	26.8125	$1,876,875	5.43%	1.65	1.22	0.45	2.36	1.24	0.22
CNXT	Conexant Systems Inc.	42500	35.75	$1,519,375	4.40%	1.42	−0.08	0.39	2.24	−0.08	0.24
CY	Cypress Semiconductor	15000	43	$645,000	1.87%	1.07	1.44	0.39	1.64	1.44	0.22
HLIT	Harmonic, Inc.	20000	28.0625	$561,250	1.62%	1.63	−0.81	0.36	2.29	−0.80	0.17
JDSU	JDS Uniphase Corporation	22000	135.9375	$2,990,625	8.65%	1.56	1.08	0.57	2.40	1.13	0.33
LSI	LSI Logic Corporation	12500	32.625	$407,813	1.18%	1.32	2.44	0.48	2.14	2.42	0.31
PWAV	Powerwave Technologies	40500	36.875	$1,493,438	4.32%	1.39	6.23	0.30	1.69	6.38	0.11
QLGC	QLogic Corporation	30000	77.9375	$2,338,125	6.77%	1.87	1.05	0.48	2.19	1.12	0.16
RFMD	RF Micro Devices, Inc.	21000	39.75	$834,750	2.42%	1.62	1.66	0.46	2.45	1.67	0.25
TQNT	TriQuint Semiconductor	25000	48.625	$1,215,625	3.52%	1.74	4.22	0.57	2.34	4.31	0.25
TXCC	TranSwitch Corporation	30000	41.6562	$1,249,686	3.62%	1.64	4.21	0.47	2.35	4.25	0.23
VTSS	Vitesse Semiconductor	20000	65.625	$1,312,500	3.80%	1.65	3.35	0.42	2.42	3.30	0.22
EMLX	Emulex Corporation	30000	55.81	$1,674,300	4.85%	1.86	−0.12	0.40	2.54	−0.10	0.18
PMCS	PMC-Sierra, Inc.	16000	197	$3,152,000	9.12%	1.79	9.99	0.54	2.60	10.07	0.28
SDLI	SDL, Inc.	20000	387.25	$7,745,000	22.41%	1.52	13.53	0.45	2.37	13.52	0.27
PSC	PORTFOLIO			$34,553,799	100.00%	1.65	3.35	0.80	2.41	3.38	0.41

[1] Share prices are adjusted over time to include stock splits and dividends.

[2] Assume there is minimal difference between NASDAQ Betas and QQQ Betas.

[3] Alpha and Beta are calculated using the regression model and appropriate proxy for the market:

Company Return (%) = Alpha (%) + Beta[Market Return (%)] + Error

[4] Alpha is given as an annualized number.

[5] R-Squared measures how much of the underlying data is explained by the regression model.

Source: Company.

EXHIBIT 3

PORTFOLIO STATISTICS FOR DAYS OF POSITIVE AND NEGATIVE MARKET RETURNS

Half Year (1/3/2000 – 7/11/2000)[5]

	Nasdaq Up[1]			Nasdaq Down			S&P 500 Up			S&P 500 Down		
	Beta[2]	Alpha[3]	R-Squared[4]	Beta	Alpha	R-Squared	Beta	Alpha	R-Squared	Beta	Alpha	R-Squared
AMCC	2.53	−0.77	0.32	2.45	208.34	0.50	3.62	−0.55	0.15	3.44	67.61	0.23
AHAA	2.05	−0.60	0.20	0.92	−0.99	0.10	3.14	−0.74	0.12	1.74	−0.51	0.08
ANAD	1.81	−0.63	0.23	1.97	50.07	0.31	2.75	−0.77	0.14	2.86	25.64	0.15
CNXT	1.70	−0.83	0.22	1.08	−0.93	0.13	2.15	0.09	0.09	2.42	0.76	0.15
CY	1.50	−0.90	0.30	0.97	1.03	0.16	1.93	0.08	0.13	1.26	−0.30	0.07
HLIT	1.64	−0.72	0.20	1.37	−0.98	0.11	1.93	0.63	0.08	1.78	−0.98	0.04
JDSU	1.69	0.47	0.27	1.12	−0.95	0.30	3.52	−0.97	0.27	1.97	0.18	0.15
LSI	0.88	87.87	0.11	1.43	3.19	0.32	1.46	23.27	0.07	2.99	51.34	0.30
PWAV	1.81	−0.56	0.16	1.06	−0.16	0.11	1.31	46.17	0.02	1.49	1.15	0.05
QLGC	1.60	7.50	0.18	2.29	54.63	0.34	2.13	1.08	0.07	2.42	4.28	0.09
RFMD	1.78	−0.30	0.25	1.70	6.13	0.25	3.57	−0.95	0.22	1.75	−0.51	0.07
TQNT	2.09	−0.70	0.37	1.77	12.77	0.35	3.42	−0.95	0.21	2.42	21.71	0.15
TXCC	2.27	−0.97	0.30	1.80	62.88	0.36	3.14	−0.66	0.15	1.77	0.10	0.09
VTSS	1.69	1.65	0.15	1.76	11.60	0.34	2.34	3.38	0.08	2.67	10.21	0.15
EMLX	0.80	334.48	0.05	3.23	27706.21	0.43	2.23	−0.82	0.07	5.06	18466.43	0.27
PMCS	1.95	2.19	0.29	1.78	12.76	0.33	3.54	−0.74	0.19	2.36	10.37	0.16
SDLI	1.51	9.17	0.19	1.81	182.00	0.33	2.80	2.63	0.15	1.96	3.27	0.11
PORTFOLIO	1.71	0.89	0.57	1.86	31.15	0.66	2.89	−0.49	0.25	2.49	9.07	0.29

[1] Nasdaq and S&P 500 daily returns were separated into "up" days of positive performance and "down" days of negative performance.

[2] Alpha and Beta are calculated using the regression model and appropriate proxy for the market:

Company Return (%) = Alpha (%) + Beta[Market Return (%)] + Error

[3] Alpha is given as an annualized number.

[4] R-Squared measures how much of the underlying data is explained by the regression model.

[5] The standard deviations for the daily returns of the Nasdaq Composite and the S&P 500 during this half-year period were 3.07% and 1.54% respectively.

Source: Company.

EXHIBIT 4

CUMULATIVE RETURNS[1] OF QQQ (NASDAQ 100) BASED ON HISTORICAL PRICES

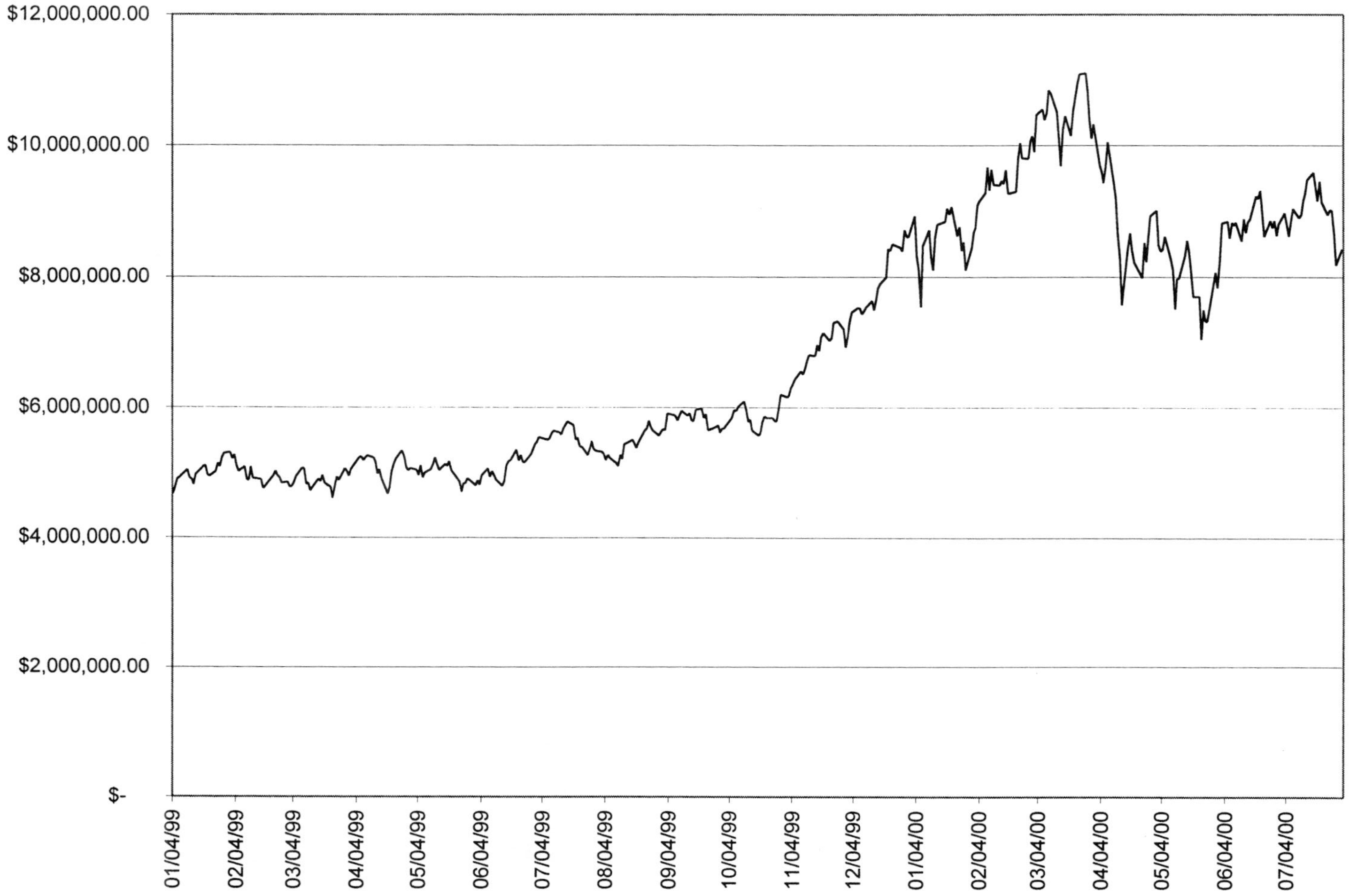

[1]This graph shows the value of equity over time if Pine Street Capital invested their initial equity, $4,663,656.85, in the Nasdaq 100 index.

EXHIBIT 5

PINE STREET CAPITAL'S PORTFOLIO RETURN COMPARED TO THE MARKET RETURN (NASDAQ COMPOSITE)

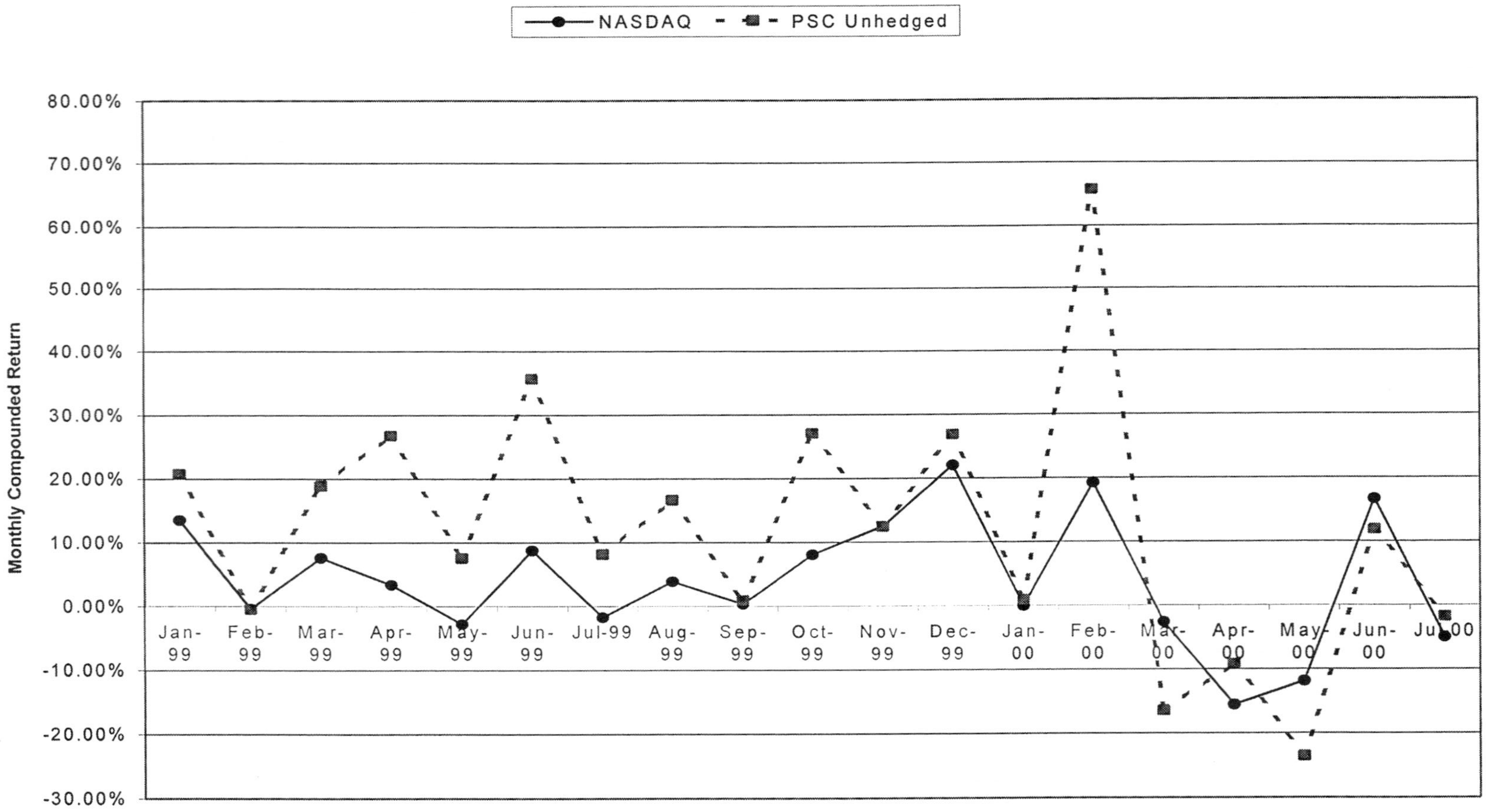

Source: Company.

		Tomorrow's Value	
Today	**Initial Value**	**NASDAQ +10%**	**NASDAQ −10%**
Long Portfolio	$100.00	$116.00	$86.00
Short NASDAQ	$150.00	$135.00	$165.00
TOTAL	$250.00	$251.00	$251.00
	Return on Hedged Portfolio:	1.0%	1.0%

Figure 3   Example of Hedging by Short-Selling[5]

Options-Based Hedging

Over the past year, and particularly over the past four months, the technology sector, as measured by the Nasdaq index, had been extremely volatile. The technology sector, especially any firms connected in any way to the Internet, delivered huge returns during 1999 and the first quarter of 2000. From January of 1999 to March 2000, the Nasdaq appreciated more than 115%. However, from early March 2000 to the end of June 2000, the Nasdaq declined nearly 40%. This enormous volatility exhibited by a fairly broad stock index was unprecedented in the recent history of the U.S. equity markets (Exhibit 7 shows the implied volatility of Nasdaq puts options over the prior $1^1/_2$ years).

While the fund was protected from market movements due to the short-sale hedging strategy it employed, this proved to be only partially effective during the previous few months. Consecutive, large dips in the Nasdaq had resulted in enormous losses for the fund on several days, particularly in March and April of the current year. PSC had been very careful to develop models that would allow it to accurately measure the beta of their portfolio in order to immunize the fund against market fluctuations. However, the volatility of the past few months had not been foreseen and the firm's models appeared to break down somehow, leaving the portfolio under-hedged.

To protect the fund from future periods of high volatility in the market, one of the partners suggested altering PSC's hedging program to use put options on the Nasdaq instead of shorting the Nasdaq. Because put options appeared to be more sensitive to market movements, this partner felt that using put options could better immunize PSC's portfolio to market movements.

To this end, Yoon had one of the analysts in the firm put together some analyses as to how PSC would have done over the previous 1 $^1/_2$ years if the fund had used put options instead of short sales. Exhibit 8 provides a graph comparing how the fund would have performed with an option-based hedging program vs. a short sale-based program vs. no hedging program at all. Additionally, Exhibit 9 shows this comparative performance on the 20 worst-performing days of the Nasdaq over the previous 1 $^1/_2$ years.

CONCLUSION

Yoon looked out the window of his office. The Internet was expanding at a breakneck pace, and he felt this was just the tip of a technological revolution. He could see it occurring all around him, and he wanted PSC to participate in it fully. One way to ensure this would be to use a more conservative investment style by utilizing less leverage, but he felt that this would not be in the best interest of the investors in the fund as it would

---

[5] Assuming an alpha of 1% and a beta of 1.5 for the long portfolio.

EXHIBIT 6

HEDGE FUND PERFORMANCE BY SECTOR

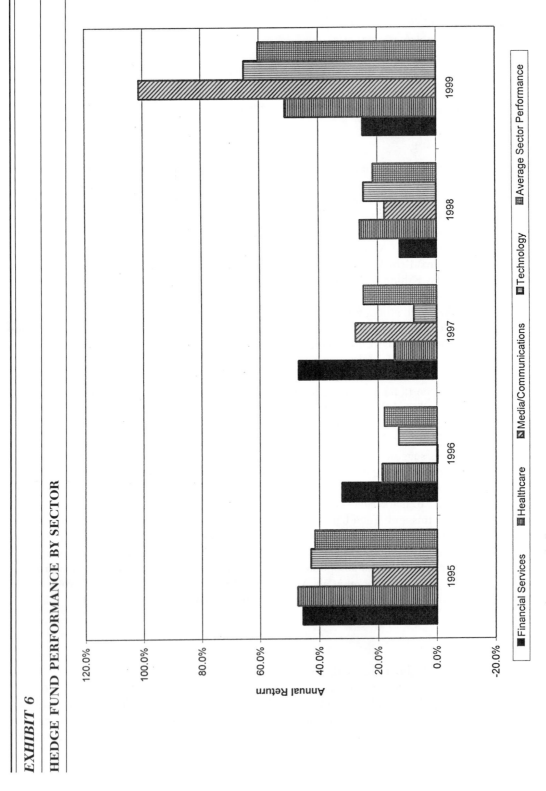

Source: Van Money Manager Research, Inc., Nashville, TN, USA.

EXHIBIT 7

IMPLIED VOLATILITY OF QQQ (NASDAQ) TWO MONTH PUT OPTIONS WITH STRIKE PRICES 20% OUT OF THE MONEY

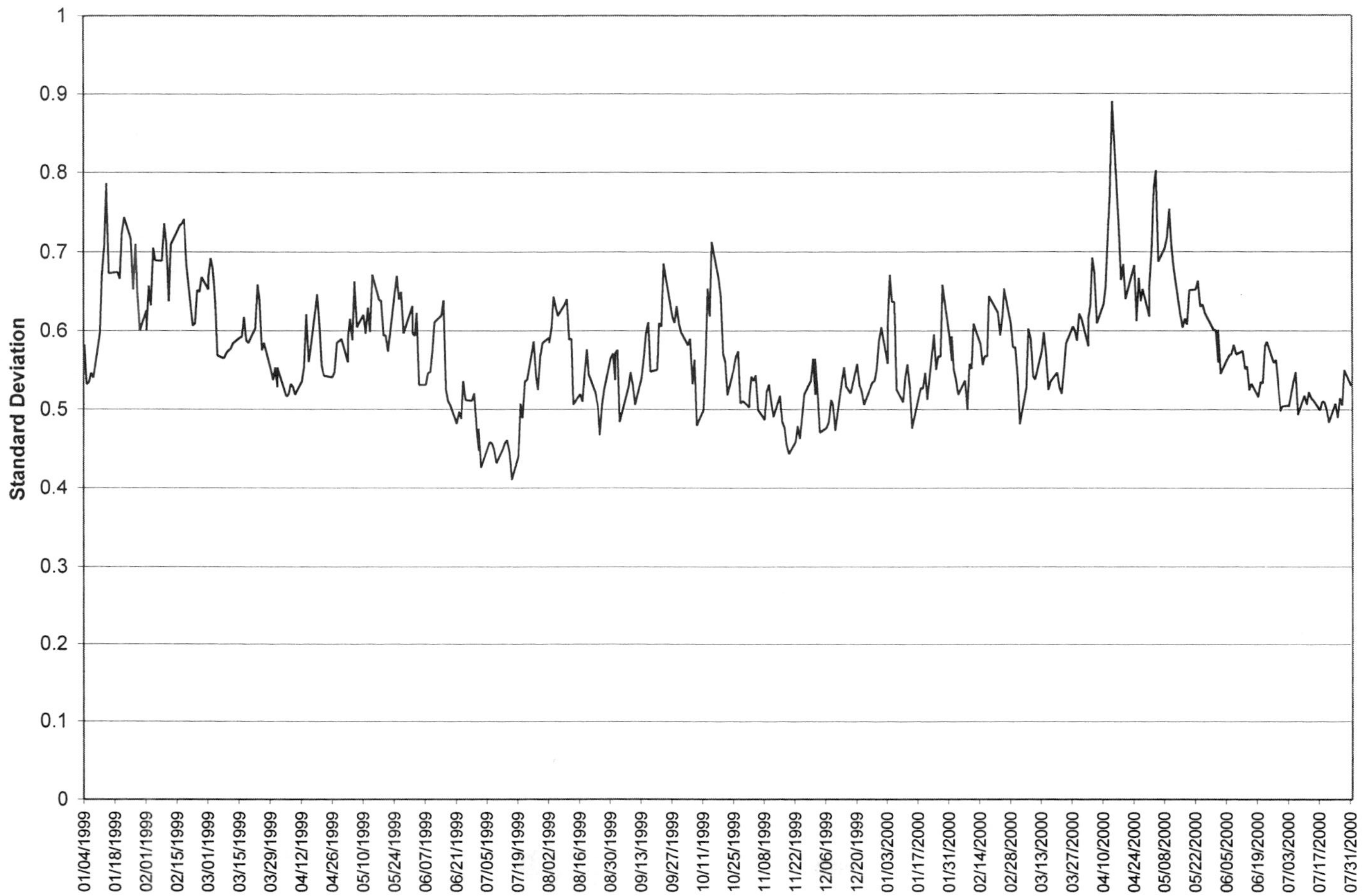

Source: Company.

329

EXHIBIT 8

CHANGES IN EQUITY USING DIFFERENT HEDGE STRATEGIES
(WITH NO TRANSACTION COSTS PURCHASING AND SELLING OPTIONS)

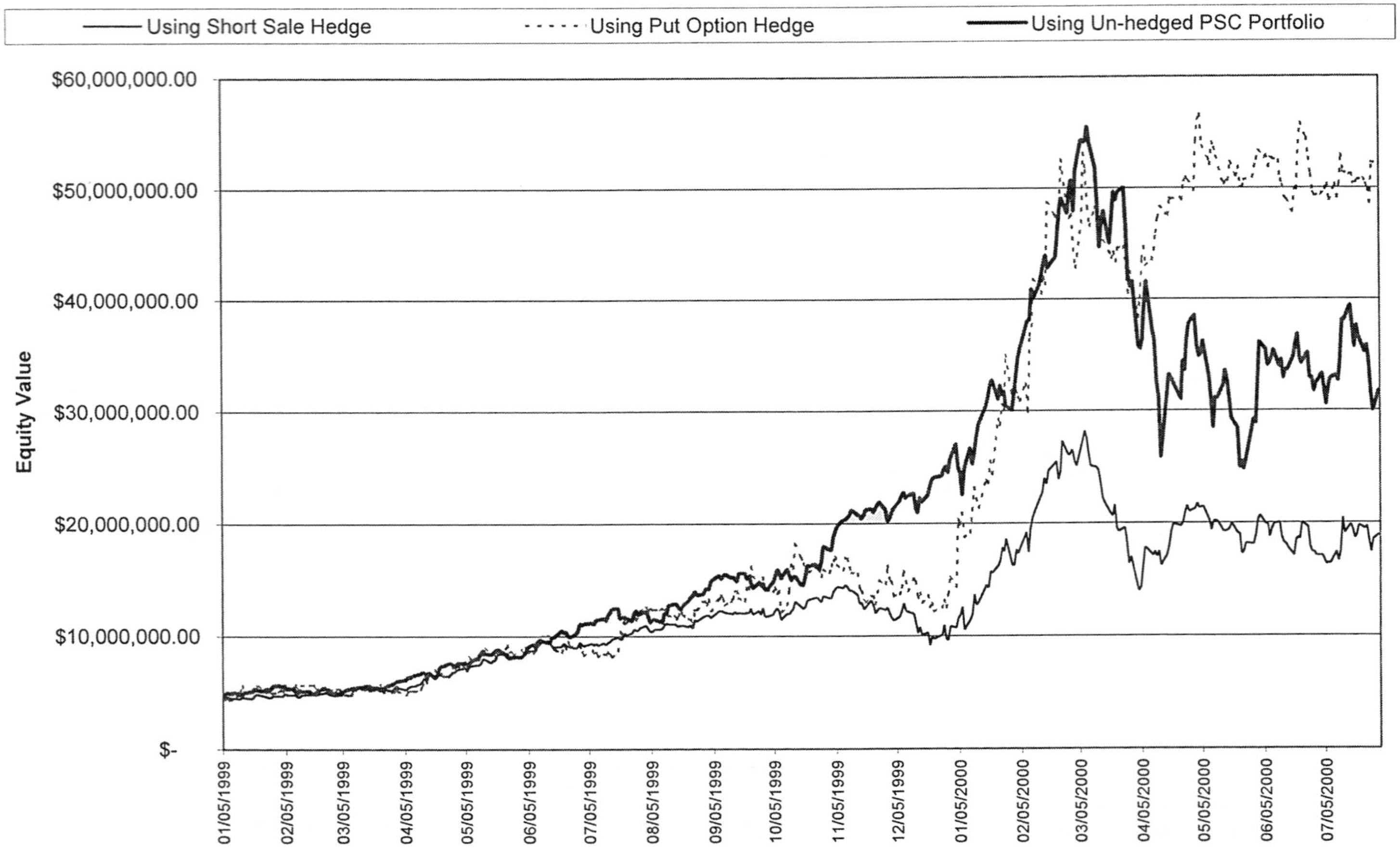

Source: Company.

EXHIBIT 9

PERFORMANCE OF PINE STREET CAPITAL'S HEDGE STRATEGIES DURING NASDAQ WORST 20 DAYS (OVER THE PERIOD 1/04/99 TO 7/26/00)

Date[1]	NASDAQ Return	QQQ Return	Un-hedged PSC Portfolio Return	Short Sale Hedge		Put Option Hedge[3]	
				$ Profit/Loss	ROE[2]	$ Profit/Loss	ROE
14-Apr-00	−9.67%	−8.66%	−16.84%	(1,253,436.86)	−7.18%	935,932.36	1.98%
03-Apr-00	−7.64%	−5.99%	−14.20%	(2,182,183.49)	−13.50%	(3,004,361.57)	−7.27%
12-Apr-00	−7.06%	−5.88%	−9.93%	(437,810.11)	−2.51%	1,599,279.25	3.61%
23-May-00	−5.93%	−8.35%	−12.39%	(27,653.10)	−0.15%	838,441.15	1.64%
10-Apr-00	−5.81%	−6.10%	−10.53%	(615,272.36)	−3.48%	520,987.70	1.21%
10-May-00	−5.59%	−7.27%	−8.25%	751,321.71	3.89%	2,009,996.12	3.86%
19-Apr-99	−5.57%	−4.69%	−6.71%	8,681.20	0.13%	464,170.27	7.09%
04-Jan-00	−5.55%	−6.86%	−7.45%	746,550.20	6.94%	5,963,416.59	41.56%
28-Jul-00	−4.66%	−5.44%	−4.72%	1,082,841.42	6.22%	3,663,503.42	7.54%
24-Apr-00	−4.43%	−2.87%	−4.64%	(140,814.13)	−0.71%	91,294.87	0.19%
02-May-00	−4.36%	−5.75%	−7.21%	484,191.77	2.28%	4,483,090.41	9.01%
19-May-00	−4.19%	−4.74%	−5.53%	444,170.87	2.28%	1,602,169.02	3.16%
14-Mar-00	−4.09%	−3.70%	−6.05%	(287,101.52)	−1.15%	1,417,348.53	2.94%
30-Mar-00	−4.02%	−2.50%	−2.36%	572,243.01	3.49%	1,972,150.27	4.87%
20-Mar-00	−3.92%	−2.82%	−6.11%	(918,421.33)	−4.22%	(1,002,796.54)	−2.22%
29-Mar-00	−3.91%	−4.14%	−10.03%	(1,811,832.73)	−9.95%	(2,382,220.64)	−5.56%
09-Feb-99	−3.91%	−3.91%	−5.23%	26,606.64	0.55%	247,151.80	4.55%
06-Jan-00	−3.88%	−6.87%	−7.56%	646,208.46	5.46%	1,031,268.09	5.19%
08-May-00	−3.86%	−3.90%	−9.09%	(1,214,790.73)	−5.68%	(1,051,204.31)	−1.96%
23-Sep-99	−3.79%	−4.14%	−3.82%	347,743.29	2.88%	963,842.98	13.83%

[1] Days are listed by Nasdaq return (starting with the worst).

[2] ROE is Pine Street's Return on Equity.

[3] Not including transaction costs.

Source: Company.

EXHIBIT 10

QQQ OPTION PRICES AND TREASURY RATES FOR JULY 26TH, 2000

QQQ Share Price $95.63　　　　　　　　**T-bill Rates**[a]　**1 Month:**　5.97%
　　　　　　　　　　　　　　　　　　　　　　　　　　　　　　　　2 Month:　6.13%
　　　　　　　　　　　　　　　　　　　　　　　　　　　　　　　　3 Month:　6.14%

Calls	Bid	Ask	Days to Maturity	Puts	Bid	Ask	Days to Maturity
00 Aug 70	25 1/2	26	23	00 Aug 70	1/16	3/16	23
00 Aug 75	20 5/8	21 1/8	23	00 Aug 75	3/16	5/16	23
00 Aug 80	16	16 3/8	23	00 Aug 80	1/2	11/16	23
00 Aug 85	11 3/4	12 1/8	23	00 Aug 85	1 1/16	1 1/4	23
00 Aug 90	7 7/8	8 1/4	23	00 Aug 90	2 1/8	2 3/8	23
00 Aug 95	4 3/4	5 1/8	23	00 Aug 95	4	4 1/4	23
00 Aug 100	2 1/2	2 3/4	23	00 Aug 100	6 3/4	7 1/8	23
00 Aug 105	1 1/16	1 1/4	23	00 Aug 105	10 1/4	10 5/8	23
00 Aug 110	3/8	1/2	23	00 Aug 110	14 1/2	14 7/8	23
00 Aug 115	1/8	1/4	23	00 Aug 115	19 3/8	19 3/4	23
00 Aug 120	0	1/8	23	00 Aug 120	24 3/8	24 7/8	23
00 Sep 70	26	26 3/4	58	00 Sep 70	1/2	11/16	58
00 Sep 75	21 1/2	22 1/4	58	00 Sep 75	7/8	1 1/16	58
00 Sep 80	17 3/8	17 7/8	58	00 Sep 80	1 9/16	1 3/4	58
00 Sep 85	13 1/2	14	58	00 Sep 85	2 9/16	2 13/16	58
00 Sep 90	10 1/8	10 5/8	58	00 Sep 90	4	4 3/8	58
00 Sep 95	7 1/4	7 5/8	58	00 Sep 95	6	6 3/8	58
00 Sep 100	4 7/8	5 1/4	58	00 Sep 100	8 5/8	9	58
00 Sep 105	3	3 1/4	58	00 Sep 105	11 3/4	12 1/4	58
00 Sep 110	1 11/16	1 7/8	58	00 Sep 110	15 1/2	16	58
00 Sep 115	7/8	1 1/16	58	00 Sep 115	19 3/4	20 1/4	58
00 Sep 120	7/16	9/16	58	00 Sep 120	24 1/4	25	58

[a]Bond equivalent yields

Source: Chicago Board of Exchange.

not be maximizing their equity value.[6] However, given the nature of the technology sector he knew the market could see more volatile times ahead like the past few months, and he didn't want to see the fund liquidated, as it almost was back in April. Could an option-based hedging strategy allow the fund to keep utilizing the leverage it had in the past while also protecting against large, negative fluctuations in the market? Yoon picked up a printout of option prices from the previous day (see Exhibit 10) to recheck his calculations.

[6] PSC's compensation package dictated that 20% of any appreciation in the equity of the fund would be paid to PSC as management fees. So any reduction in returns was directly felt by the partners as well.

21

Tribune Company:
The PHONES Proposal

In early 1999, the Tribune Company began discussions with bankers at Merrill Lynch & Co. about monetizing a portion of its holdings in the Internet company America Online (AOL). The cash raised would be used for general corporate expenditures. An outright sale of the shares was not attractive due to the significant capital gains taxes that Tribune would be forced to pay. Discussions focused instead around a convertible security known as "participating hybrid option note exchangeable securities," or PHONES. Merrill Lynch had suggested that PHONES would enable Tribune to monetize their AOL investment and, at the same time, defer capital gains taxes until the security was converted into cash, which wouldn't occur for thirty years. Tribune's management now had to decide if these securities met their needs and if the valuation suggested by Merrill was reasonable.

TRIBUNE COMPANY

Headquartered in Chicago, Illinois, the Tribune Company was one of the United States' premier media companies, operating in publishing, broadcasting, entertainment, and education. Established in 1847 as a newspaper publisher, the Tribune Company had expanded into almost every aspect of modern media. In 1998, the publishing segment stood for about 50% of the company's total revenues, the combined broadcasting/ entertainment segment for 39%, and the education segment for 11%.[i] Net sales for Tribune were over $2.65 billion. (Exhibit 1 shows historical financial information and stock price data for Tribune; see Exhibit 2 for Historical and Implied Volatility.)

Professor George Chacko and Research Associates Andrew Kuhlman and Eli P. Strick prepared this case. This case was developed from published sources. HBS cases are developed solely as the basis for class discussion. Cases are not intended to serve as endorsements, sources of primary data, or illustrations of effective or ineffective management.

EXHIBIT 1A

TRIBUNE'S BALANCE SHEET ($ MILLION)

	Dec96	Dec97	Dec98
ASSETS			
Cash and Equivalents	274.17	66.62	12.43
Net Receivables	350.77	442.33	555.23
Inventories	80.53	99.49	99.00
Prepaid Expenses	N/A	N/A	N/A
Current Assets - Other	181.25	239.31	278.46
Current Assets - Total	886.72	847.75	945.13
Gross Property, Plant and Equipment	1456.21	1550.90	1664.53
Accumulated Depreciation	813.50	900.45	987.79
Net Property, Plant, and Equipment	642.71	650.45	676.73
Investments at Equity	72.01	58.15	48.60
Other Investments	557.12	423.39	1201.38
Intangibles	1251.47	2503.07	2703.99
Deferred Charges	173.55	162.10	207.76
Other Assets	117.32	132.65	151.98
Total Assets	3700.90	4777.55	5935.57
LIABILITIES			
Long Term Debt Due in One Year	31.07	33.35	29.91
Notes Payable	0.00	0.00	0.00
Accounts Payable	119.61	138.90	157.71
Taxes Payable	83.47	31.37	59.61
Other Current Liabilities	438.96	502.61	580.91
Total Current Liabilities	673.10	706.22	828.13
Long Term Debt	979.75	1521.45	1616.26
Deferred Taxes	189.67	363.19	701.78
Investment Tax Credit	0.00	0.00	0.00
Minority Interest	N/A	N/A	N/A
Other Liabilities	318.87	360.69	432.79
Total Liabilities	2161.39	2951.55	3578.95
EQUITY			
Preferred Stock	101.86	119.68	136.71
Common Stock	1.02	1.02	1.02
Capital Surplus	141.80	197.21	209.47
Retained Earnings	2328.84	2667.93	3450.68
Less: Treasury Stock	1034.01	1159.83	1441.26
Total Equity	1539.51	1826.00	2356.62
Total Liabilities and Equity	3700.90	4777.55	5935.57

Source: Tribune Annual Report 1998, Tribune Annual Report 1997.

EXHIBIT 1B

TIBUNE'S INCOME STATEMENT ($ MILLION)

	Dec96	Dec97	Dec98
Sales	2405.71	2719.78	2980.89
Cost of Goods Sold	1172.66	1254.98	1391.03
Gross Profit	1233.04	1464.80	1589.86
Operating Income Before Depreciation	632.97	814.54	897.86
Depreciation, Depletion & Amortization	142.89	172.51	195.57
Operating Profit	490.08	642.03	702.29
Interest Expense	47.95	86.73	88.45
Non-Operating Income/Expense	32.28	−8.13	−27.87
Special Items	0.00	111.82	119.12
Pretax Income	474.41	659.00	705.09
Total Income Taxes	191.66	265.38	290.82
Income Before Extraordinary Items & Discontinued Operations	282.75	393.63	414.27
Extraordinary Items	0.00	0.00	0.00
Discontinued Operations	89.32	0.00	0.00
Net Income	372.07	393.63	414.27
Dividends Per Share	0.30	0.32	0.34

Source: Tribune Annual Report 1998, Tribune Annual Report 1997.

Publishing Business Line[ii]

Tribune owned four daily newspapers, including south Florida's Sun-Sentinel and The Orlando Sentinel, the Daily Press in Hampton Roads, Virginia, and its flagship the Chicago Tribune, which remained its largest operation. In 1998, daily newspapers made up the lion's share of Tribune's publishing business, accounting for over 93% of the segment's revenues.[iii] In addition to newspapers, the publishing division included Internet publishing and distribution services, cable news programming, and various syndication activities. The acquisition of Premier DataVision, Inc. (PDI) and JDTV in February 1999 expanded Tribune's publishing division to include movie information listings and television advertising services.

In general, a newspaper's revenue mix was derived about 20–25% from circulation revenues and 75–80% from advertising. Of this advertising revenue, 50% of this typically came from retail, 35–40% came from classifieds, and 10% from other sources. Tribune's newspapers held approximately 2.3% of national circulation and were dominant in their respective markets. The Chicago Tribune held a 60/40 readership advantage and a 75/25 advertising advantage over its closest competitor, the Chicago Sun-Times. In southern Florida, The Orlando Sentinel reached 81% of adult consumers in its primary market, and the Sun-Sentinel contained Florida's largest classified section. Even Tribune's smallest newspaper, The Daily Press reached 60% of its primary market. Analysts cited the profitability of Tribune's publishing as exceptionally good relative to industry norms. Exhibit 3 shows historical financial data on the newspaper business of Tribune and its main competitors.

EXHIBIT 1C

TRIBUNE'S CASH FLOW STATEMENT ($ MILLION)

	Dec96	Dec97	Dec98
Indirect Operating Activities			
Income Before Extraordinary Items	282.75	393.63	414.27
Depreciation and Amortization	142.89	172.51	195.57
Extraordinary Items and Disc. Operations	0.00	0.00	0.00
Deferred Taxes	−24.50	−13.96	7.90
Equity in Net Loss (Earnings)	13.28	34.70	33.98
Sale of Property and Investments - Loss (Gain)	0.00	−111.82	−119.12
Funds form Operations	−15.96	−21.45	−12.87
Receivables - Decrease (Increase)	−34.92	−43.96	−49.99
Inventory - Decrease (Increase)	N/A	N/A	N/A
Accounts Payable and Accrued Liabs - Inc (Dec)	N/A	N/A	N/A
Income Taxes - Accrued - Increase (Dec)	−20.30	−46.36	52.51
Other Assets and Liabilities - Net Change	−1.71	20.79	23.61
Operating Activities - Net Cash Flow	341.53	384.08	545.88
Investing Activities			
Investments - Increase	72.13	48.34	40.24
Sale of Investments	83.31	402.47	51.58
Capital Expenditures	93.32	103.85	139.71
Acquisitions	501.38	1239.61	154.71
Investing Activities - Other	432.67	7.01	−64.87
Investing Activities - Net Cash Flow	−150.85	−982.32	−347.95
Financing Activities			
Sale of Common and Preferred Stock	51.26	57.15	46.13
Purchase of Common and Preferred Stock	148.45	140.04	330.15
Cash Dividends	92.42	97.36	101.09
Long-Term Debt - Issuance	470.00	626.38	469.88
Long-Term Debt - Reduction	219.80	55.44	336.89
Current Debt - Changes	N/A	N/A	N/A
Financing Activities - Other	0.00	0.00	0.00
Financing Activities - Net Cash Flow	60.58	390.69	−252.12
Exchange Rate Effect	0.00	0.00	0.00
Cash and Equivalents - Change	251.27	−207.55	−54.19

Source: Tribune Annual Report 1998, Tribune Annual Report 1997.

New electronic mediums were posing a serious threat as an alternative for Tribune's newspapers, especially in regards to the classified section, which by 1998 already had a burgeoning online market. Yet Tribune's strategy had always been the early adoption of new media categories, and by 1998 the online counterpart to their newspaper was the most visited content-based site in Chicago. In addition, Tribune invested an additional $40 million in 1998 to build its Internet business strategy, and established online brand franchises such as the job placement site *careerpath.com* in an effort to corner key markets on a national level. These investments paid off, as Internet revenue grew from just $13 million in 1997 to an estimated $25 million in 1998.[iv]

EXHIBIT 1D

TRIBUNE'S STOCK PRICES HISTORY

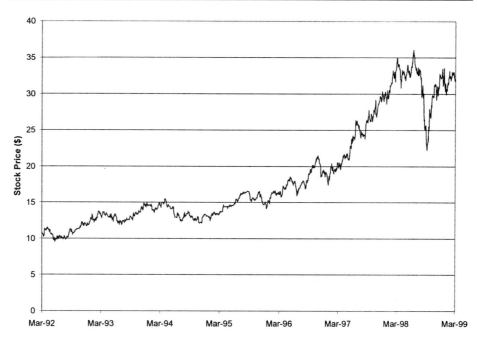

Source: Thomson Datastream, accessed December 2004.

EXHIBIT 2A

TRIBUNE'S HISTORICAL VOLATILITY

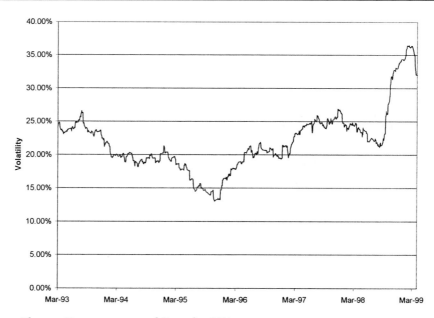

Source: Thomson Datastream, accessed December 2004.

EXHIBIT 2B

TRIBUNE'S IMPLIED VOLATILITIES ON 4/1/99

Option Type	Implied Volatility
Put	34.63
Call	34.77

Note: Implied volatilities for each option category (put and call) are calculated by taking a composite of the three options closest to the at-the-money strike prices with maturity dates closest to 4/1/99, which were about 1 month. The stock price on 4/1/99 was $32.72.

Source: Bloomberg LP, accessed December 2003.

Broadcasting Business Line

Tribune's Broadcasting and Entertainment division included eighteen television stations and four radio stations, as well as the ownership of the Chicago Cubs baseball team. The company's television business accounted for the majority of its broadcasting revenue with 81%, while its radio business accounted for 7%, and its entertainment business (mainly the Chicago Cubs) accounted for 12%.[v] The radio and entertainment businesses served as nice complements to Tribune's television business, and its multiple business lines led to some nice synergies, such as using its Chicago TV and radio stations to broadcast Cubs games.

Advertising was the primary source of revenue in the television sector, and television companies attracted advertising dollars based on the demographic quality and number of viewers watching their stations. Television stations competed directly with other local stations and cable channels for viewers and advertisers, as well as indirectly with newspapers, magazines, and the Internet for consumer's time. Unlike cable channels, which transmitted signals electronically through actual cables, broadcast channels were

EXHIBIT 3

NEWSPAPER PUBLISHING BUSINESS SEGMENT HISTORICAL FINANCIAL DATA FOR TRIBUNE AND ITS MAIN COMPETITORS ($ MILLIONS)

	Tribune Company			New York Times Co			Washington Post Co			Gannett Co		
	1997	1998E	1999E	1997	1998E	1999E	1997	1998E	1999E	1997	1998E	1999E
Revenue	1359	1415	1480	2557	2692	2840	813	850	900	3770.7	4155	4325
Operating Income	368	400	453	442	495	578	163	158	182	1002	1125	1250
Operating Margins	24.7%	25.3%	27.6%	17.3%	18.4%	20.4%	20.0%	18.5%	20.2%	26.6%	27.1%	28.9%

Source: Brown Brothers Harriman & Co., "Newspaper Industry Fourth-Quarter Update," December 18, 1998 via Thomson Research/Investext, accessed December 2003.

transmitted via antennae in the form of waves. The signal from these waves would deteriorate across long distances, and therefore broadcast channels normally served only a specific region. Established broadcasters usually faced little competition from other local broadcasters due to signal constraints (too many signals located in a single area would produce interference), which made broadcasting an ideal medium for advertisers to reach a large audience. Yet cable-based stations were just as apt at targeting specific niche audiences with customized content, and cable channels ate away at a broadcast station's advertising base through these means.[vi]

Many large broadcasting companies formed beneficial affiliations with local stations in order to maximize the size of their audience, giving local station premium programming for free in exchange for access to that local area and a percentage of the advertising revenues. Yet Tribune took a different approach, focusing its broadcasting strategy instead on running independent stations that kept all advertising revenue but provided the costly programming themselves.[vii] Tribune's stations emphasized local programming such as news and sport franchises as key competitive strategies in attracting viewers and advertisers with unique content. Dennis FitzSimons, president of Tribune Broadcasting, was quoted in press, saying:

> Local programming sets us apart from our competitors, including a sea of national cable channels. In each of our markets, we work hard to be the "hometown station," and I think viewers and advertisers appreciate that.[viii]

Tribune's strategy in broadcasting was threefold; to increase its distribution base, to improve its programming mix, and to increase operating margins.[ix] Tribune owned TV stations in 14 of the nation's top 30 markets, making it among the largest broadcast station owners. The company's largest broadcasting stations, located in New York, Chicago, and Los Angeles, comprised nearly 60% of its television operating cash flow, and its Chicago-based WGN station was also transmitted nationally via cable and satellite. In 1998 the company's television stations reached 34% of U.S. television households, and this number jumped to 75% when cable and satellite coverage was included.[x] Tribune also owned 25% of the WB network, a fast growing prime-time network with 88% national coverage. The company's three largest broadcasting stations all increased their market shares in 1998, and the company's Warner Brothers (WB) Network was the only major network to experience a growth in ratings during this same period.[xi] See Exhibit 4 for historical financial data on the television broadcast business of Tribune and its main competitors.

Education Business Line[xii]

Tribune's education division provided core and supplemental educational materials to U.S. schools with students in kindergarten through 12th grade (known as the K-12 range). "Supplemental materials" included everything from classroom textbooks for non-core subjects to consumer educational products. Tribune was one of the largest suppliers of supplemental products and services, a high-margin, fast-growing niche which accounted for one-fourth the overall $6 billion K-12 market. Although the education segment only stood for 11% of Tribune's total revenue, it held a large potential for growth, with annual revenue increasing 46% to 329 million in 1998.[xiii] Education revenue was primary from grades K-8 (63%) but they also derived revenue from high school students (11%) and general consumers (26%). Tribune's education business was divided into five major groups:

EXHIBIT 4

TELEVISION BROADCASTING BUSINESS SEGMENT HISTORICAL FINANCIAL DATA FOR TRIBUNE AND ITS MAIN COMPETITORS ($ MILLIONS)

	Tribune Company			New York Times Company			Washington Post Company			Gannett Company		
	1997	1998E	1999E	1997	1998E	1999E	1997	1998E	1999E	1997	1998E	1999E
Revenue	861	940	1010	145	150	160	338	365	390	703.6	728	760
Operating Income	268	303	338	39	45	48	160	168	184	328.3	345	375
Operating Margins	27.0%	27.5%	28.6%	27.2%	30.0%	30.0%	47.2%	46.0%	47.2%	46.7%	47.4%	49.3%

Source: Brown Brothers Harriman & Co., "Newspaper Industry Fourth-Quarter Update," December 18, 1998, via Thomson Research/Investext, accessed December 2003.

- The Wright Group: Provided traditional schools with language arts and reading material for the elementary grades.
- Everyday Learning/Creative Publications Group: Produced math products for elementary through high school students.
- NTC/Contemporary Publishing Group: Served both school markets and consumer markets. Included foreign language materials, literature, language arts, travel guides, and more.
- Ideal/Instructional Fair Publishing Group: Provided hands on classroom materials, workbooks and teacher resources, and targeted consumer markets through specialty stores.
- Landoll, Inc: A publisher of children's books and educational materials for the home.

Landoll specialized in the large-scale marketing of childrens' books, a market that Tribune estimated was worth over $1.6 billion annually. This strategic acquisition in late 1997 opened the door for Tribune to use this market as a distribution channel for its supplemental education products in the future. In addition, strategic alliances forged with multimedia companies allowed Tribune to continue expanding into the fast-growing interactive learning market through the development of educational software and web-based learning programs.

Competition

Most of Tribune's main competitors were also diversified media companies, with strategic business lines running across multiple synergistic industries. Due to Tribune's many business segments, there were an enormous amount of companies that could be considered competing with Tribune in at least one market category. Some market observers argued that most direct competitors with Tribune's overall business model (given their product lines, which were similar to Tribune's) were the New York Times Company, the Washington Post Company, and Gannett Company.

- The New York Times Company owned the New York Times, the Boston Globe, and 21 regional newspapers. It also owned 8 network affiliated television stations, two New York radio stations, two golf magazines, and numerous electronic properties.

- The Washington Post Company owned numerous newspapers including The Washington Post, as well as six television stations, a cable television company, and Newsweek magazine.

- Gannett Company had the largest U.S. newspaper circulation, with 75 daily newspapers including USA today, the nation's largest selling paper. It also owned and operated 21 television stations.

Exhibit 5 provides historical financial information for some of Tribune's main competitors.

Future of Tribune

In 1998 the company benefited from strong advertising-related revenues and growth in its broadcasting and education divisions, and the strong performance of its secondary business lines set the course for future strategy. Emphasis was to be placed on increasing the size of Tribune's broadcasting division relative to their publishing division, in order to benefit from the greater stability of a more diversified product line, as well as from the higher margins inherent in the broadcasting business.[xiv] In addition, Tribune was focused on pursuing strategic alliances and acquisitions in the education sector, in order to tap into the explosive growth potential of this market.

Finally, an aggressive investment into Internet-based complements to their publication business ensured that Tribune would remain a competitive force in this market as well. One of the Internet companies in which the Tribune held a significant share of stocks was America Online (AOL).

AMERICA ONLINE, INC.

Based in Dulles, Virginia, America Online (AOL) was in 1999 the world's largest online service provider with arguably the strongest brand-name recognition in its industry. Created in 1985, AOL had grown at a tremendous pace, acquiring over 17 million members by April 1999. The company generated revenues from areas such as online services, advertising, and commerce activities. Online service revenues were monthly fees from customers of Internet-provider services, supplied by AOL and the acquired subsidiary, CompuServe Interactive Services. AOL further leveraged these members by generating advertising, commerce, and other revenue through its free online properties. These included AOL.com, the world's most-accessed Web site from home; Digital City, Inc., the number one local content network on the Internet; AOL NetFind, a comprehensive guide to the Internet; and AOL Instant Messenger and ICQ, two online instant communication technologies.[xv] In addition, AOL had recently acquired Netscape Communications Corporation, whose proprietary Internet browsing software and popular Internet portals further should add to AOL's market dominance. By April 1999 AOL's membership base was nearly 10 times larger than that of its nearest competitors.[xvi] Meanwhile, AOL was aggressively expanding its technology infrastructure into cross-platform applications and e-commerce solutions through an alliance in March 1999 with Sun Microsystems, a leading provider of hardware, soft-

EXHIBIT 5A

TRIBUNE COMPETITORS' BALANCE SHEETS ($ MILLION)

	New York Times Co.			Washington Post Co.			Gannett Co.		
	Dec96	Dec97	Dec98	Dec96	Dec97	Dec98	Dec96	Dec97	Dec98
ASSETS									
Cash and Equivalents	39.10	106.82	35.99	102.28	21.12	86.8	731.20	52.78	66.19
Net Receivables	309.16	331.29	331.93	233.06	244.20	271.91	616.95	683.63	717.16
Inventories	33.81	32.13	32.29	24.43	19.21	20.15	73.62	101.08	87.18
Prepaid Expenses	0.00	0.00	0.00	N/A	N/A	N/A	44.84	47. 15	35.86
Current Assets - Other	96.70	145.59	121.76	22.86	23.96	25.95	0.00	0.00	0.00
Current Assets - Total	478.77	615.84	521.98	382.63	308.49	404.88	766 .60	884.63	906.39
Gross Property, Plant, Equipment	2165.15	2235.21	2223.50	1105.56	1231.19	1407.68	3423.40	3754.84	3666.74
Accumulated Depreciation	807.12	868.27	897.30	594.20	577.45	566.62	1429.34	1562.80	1602.96
Net Property, Plant, Equipment	1358.03	1366.93	1326.20	511.36	653.75	841.06	1994.06	2192.04	2063.78
Investments at Equity	137.26	133.05	122.27	199.28	154.79	68.53	0.00	0.00	0.00
Other Investments	0.00	0.00	0.00	N/A	N/A	184.44	N/A	N/A	N/A
Intangibles	1438.51	1384.94	1327.57	544.35	679.71	883.23	3393.93	3584.39	3794.60
Deferred Charges	0.00	0.00	0.00	N/A	N/A	N/A	N/A	N/A	N/A
Other Assets	127.31	138.26	167.09	232.79	280.57	347.52	195.00	229.28	214.71
Total Assets	3539.87	3639.02	3465.11	1870.41	2077.32	2729.66	6349.60	6890.35	6979.48
LIABILITIES									
Long Term Debt Due in One Year	3.36	104.03	1.87	0.00	0.00	0.00	23.30	18.38	7.81
Notes Payable	45.50	0.00	124.10	0.00	296.39	58.36	0.00	0.00	0.00
Accounts Payable	171.85	189.58	163.78	121.49	136.37	170.02	236.56	274.55	282.80
Taxes Payable	0.00	0.00	0.00	5.38	18.35	0.00	46.10	12.89	6.39
Other Current Liabilities	432.98	403.87	338.05	154.77	157.64	160.70	413.04	461.68	430.96
Total Current Liabilities	653.70	697.49	627.80	281.64	608.76	389.08	719.00	767.50	727.97
Long Term Debt	636.63	535.43	597.82	0.00	0.00	395.00	1880.29	1740.53	1306.86
Deferred Taxes	188.56	186.71	165.27	30.15	31.31	83.71	396.17	402.25	442.36
Investment Tax Credit	0.00	N/A	N/A	0.00	0.00	0.00	0.00	0.00	0.00
Minority Interest	N/A	N/A	N/A	N/A	N/A	N/A	0.00	0.00	0.00
Other Liabilities	435.85	491.34	542.75	223.88	241.23	261.90	423.32	500.33	522.47
Total Liabilities	1914.74	1910.96	1933.64	535.66	881.30	1129.68	3418.78	3410.61	2999.66
EQUITY									
Preferred Stock	1.75	0.00	0.00	11.95	11.95	11.87	0.00	0.00	0.00
Common Stock	11.12	11.39	18.66	20.00	20.00	20.00	162.21	324.42	324.42
Capital Surplus	663.01	773.37	0.00	26.45	33.42	46.20	86.13	104.37	126.04
Retained Earnings	1290.90	1488.91	1674.86	2010.18	2230.91	2637.60	3625.09	3967.66	4752.44
Less: Treasury Stock	341.65	545.60	162.05	733.83	1100.25	1115.69	942.61	916.71	1223.08
Total Equity	1625.13	1728.06	1531.47	1334.75	1196.02	1599.98	2930.82	3479.74	3979.82
Total Liabilities and Equity	3539.87	3639.02	3465.11	1870.41	2077.32	2729.66	6349.60	6890.35	6979.48

Source: Compiled by casewriters from company annual reports and Standard & Poor's Compustat® data, accessed Dec 2003.

EXHIBIT 5B

TRIBUNE COMPETITORS' INCOME STATEMENTS ($ MILLION)

	New York Times Co.			Washington Post Co.			Gannett Co.		
	Dec96	Dec97	Dec98	Dec96	Dec97	Dec98	Dec96	Dec97	Dec98
Sales	2615.03	2866.42	2936.71	1853.44	1956.25	2110.36	4421.11	4729.49	5121.29
Cost of Goods Sold	1239.05	1275.34	1326.40	1007.06	1019.87	1139.18	2367.85	2368.57	2593.98
Gross Profit	1375.97	1591.08	1610.30	846.39	936.38	971.18	2053.26	2360.92	2527.31
Operating Income Before Depreciation	408.83	602.13	650.46	432.11	486.39	518.03	1353.78	1617.34	1753.71
Depreciation, Depletion & Amortization	108.79	128.43	135.24	94.94	105.04	139.14	287.37	301.07	310.21
Operating Profit	300.04	473.70	515.22	337.17	381.35	378.90	1066.41	1316.27	1443.50
Interest Expense	50.33	50.43	47.10	1.51	1.25	11.54	139.21	99.87	83.06
Non-Operating Income/Expense	42.13	22.31	24.78	24.56	82.97	−8.90	1.47	−7.42	2.47
Special Items	−93.93	−8.21	12.62	0.00	N/A	309.60	158.00	0.00	306.50
Pretax Income	197.91	437.36	505.52	360.22	463.07	668.06	1 086.67	1208.98	1669.41
Total Income Taxes	113.38	175.06	218.89	139.40	181.50	250.80	462.70	496.30	669.50
Income Before Extraordinary Items & Discontinued Operations	84.53	262.30	286.63	220.82	281.57	417.26	623.97	712.68	999.91
Extraordinary Items	0.00	0.00	−7.72	0.00	0.00	0.00	0.00	0.00	0.00
Discontinued Operations	0.00	0.00	0.00	0.00	0.00	0.00	319.12	0.00	0.00
Net Income	84.53	262.30	278.91	220.82	281.57	417.26	943.09	712.68	999.91
Dividends Per Share	0.28	0.32	0.37	4.60	4.80	5.00	0.71	0.74	0.78

Source: Compiled by casewriters from company annual reports and Standard & Poor's Compustat ® data, accessed Dec 2003.

ware and services. It was also expanding its global reach through its AOL International division, amassing over 2.8 million members outside of the U.S.[xvii] This expansion and market position allowed AOL to consistently outperform consensus estimates for profitability. Net sales for fiscal year 1998 reached $2.6 billion (Exhibit 6 shows selected AOL financial information and stock price data. Exhibit 7 shows historical and implied volatility).

AOL's future looked bright, but it was not without its risks. While it had established itself as the largest Internet company in the world, AOL remained a player in a very volatile market. Providing Internet service to individuals was an extremely competitive and highly fragmented business, with little or no barriers to entry. AOL's size and brand name gave it an industry advantage, but this advantage depended on a continued ag-

EXHIBIT 5C

TRIBUNE COMPETITORS' CASH FLOW STATEMENTS ($ MILLION)

	New York Times Co			Washington Post Co			Gannett Co		
	Dec96	**Dec97**	**Dec98**	**Dec96**	**Dec97**	**Dec98**	**Dec96**	**Dec97**	**Dec98**
Indirect Operating Activities									
Income Before Extraordinary Items	84.53	262.30	286.63	220.82	281.57	417.26	623.97	712.68	999.91
Depreciation and Amortization	147.88	173.90	188.24	94.94	105.04	139.14	287.37	301.07	310.21
Extraordinary Items and Disc. Operations	0.00	0.00	−7.72	0.00	0.00	0.00	0.00	0.00	0.00
Deferred Taxes	−6.01	−26.56	−2.01	−4.27	3.09	26.99	68.25	−14.24	40.10
Equity in Net Loss (Earnings)	−4.76	−1.02	−2.82	−11.10	−7.00	9.15	0.00	0.00	0.00
Sale of Property & Investments-Loss (Gain)	−32.84	−10.39	−12.62	−3.11	−44.56	−314.40	0.00	0.00	N/A
Funds form Operations	126.76	10.10	0.00	10.09	6.78	−43.10	−117.85	−20.17	−360.94
Receivables - Decrease (Increase)	−24.19	−29.22	−0.65	−31.44	−8.44	22.04	−50.05	−41.68	−29.73
Inventory - Decrease (Increase)	9.04	1.15	−0.15	2.34	5.21	−0.94	16.49	−6.34	11.05
Accounts Payable & Accrued Liabs-Inc (Dec)	103.72	22.72	−47.84	26.92	19.64	13.95	N/A	N/A	N/A
Income Taxes - Accrued - Increase (Dec)	N/A	0.00	0.00	1.89	−13.71	−53.75	N/A	N/A	N/A
Other Assets and Liabilities - Net Change	21.89	49.17	50.40	−19.64	−27.54	6.78	−221.31	−50.26	−0.07
Operating Activities - Net Cash Flow	426.03	452.16	451.46	287.43	320.10	223.11	606. 87	881.06	970.53

(Continued)

EXHIBIT 5C (Continued)

TRIBUNE COMPETITORS' CASH FLOW STATEMENTS ($ MILLION)

	New York Times Co			Washington Post Co			Gannett Co		
	Dec96	Dec97	Dec98	Dec96	Dec97	Dec98	Dec96	Dec97	Dec98
Investing Activities									
Investments - Increase	0.00	0.00	0.00	0.00	0.00	164.96	17.51	8.10	16.24
Sale of Investments	0.00	0.00	0.00	12.82	0.00	38.25	3.25	5.39	2.41
Capital Expenditures	211.32	152.67	81.58	79.98	214.57	244.22	260.05	221.25	244.43
Acquisitions	247.76	0.00	0.00	147.47	178.94	320.60	0.00	355.34	369.80
Investing Activities - Other	37.34	33.54	25.41	4.30	117.02	370.48	778.72	40.86	665.00
Investing Activities - Net Cash Flow	-421.74	-119.13	-56.17	-210.33	-276.49	-321.04	504.40	-538.45	36.94
Financing Activities									
Sale of Common and Preferred Stock	0.00	9.93	38.94	11.95	0.00	7.00	26.96	30.42	23.95
Purchase of Common and Preferred Stock	43.27	164.37	480.86	32.30	368.57	20.59	1.44	0.00	328.96
Cash Dividends	55.53	61.87	69.60	51.16	52.59	51.38	197.42	206.56	218.85
Long-Term Debt - Issuance	0.00	0.00	98.43	0.00	0.00	453.36	0.00	0.00	0.00
Long-Term Debt - Reduction	3.38	3.85	177.14	0.00	0.00	296.39	954.92	144.90	470.21
Current Debt - Changes	45.50	-45.50	124.10	-50.21	296.39	N/A	N/A	N/A	N/A
Financing Activities - Other	0.05	0.34	0.00	0.00	0.00	0.00	0.00	0.00	0.00
Financing Activities - Net Cash Flow	-56.63	-265.31	-466.12	-121.73	-124.76	92.00	-1126.82	-321.04	-994.06
Exchange Rate Effect	0.00	0.00	0.00	0.00	0.00	0.00	-0.24	0.00	0.00
Cash and Equivalents - Change	-52.34	67.72	-70.83	-44.62	-81.16	-5.93	-15.78	21.58	13.41

Source: Compiled by casewriters from company annual reports and Standard & Poor's Compustat® data, accessed Dec 2003.

EXHIBIT 6A

AOL'S BALANCE SHEET ($ MILLION)

	Jun96	Jun97	Jun98
ASSETS			
Cash and Equivalents	129.13	124.61	631.00
Net Receivables	72.61	91.40	196.00
Inventories	0.00	0.00	0.00
Current Assets - Other	68.83	107.47	103.00
Current Assets - Total	270.58	323.47	930.00
Gross Property, Plant and Equipment	138.62	289.92	465.00
Accumulated Depreciation	37.35	56.79	102.00
Net Property, Plant, and Equipment	101.28	233.13	363.00
Other Investments	0.00	90.43	471.00
Intangibles	56.64	58.56	381.00
Deferred Charges	314.18	0.00	0.00
Other Assets	216.08	141.09	69.00
Total Assets	958.75	846.69	2214.00
LIABILITIES			
Long Term Debt Due in One Year	2.43	1.45	N/A
Notes Payable	0.00	0.00	0.00
Accounts Payable	105.90	69.70	87.00
Taxes Payable	0.00	0.00	0.00
Accrued Expenses	143.62	317.31	489.00
Other Current Liabilities	181.57	483.31	807.00
Total Current Liabilities	289.91	554.47	894.00
Long Term Debt	19.31	50.00	372.00
Deferred Taxes	135.87	24.41	N/A
Investment Tax Credit	0.00	0.00	0.00
Minority Interest	0.00	2.67	0.00
Other Liabilities	1.17	87.10	350.00
Total Liabilities	446.25	718.65	1616.00
EQUITY			
Preferred Stock	0.00	0.00	0.00
Common Stock	0.93	1.00	2.00
Capital Surplus	519.34	617.22	866.00
Retained Earnings	−7.77	−490.19	−270.00
Less: Treasury Stock	0.00	0.00	0.00
Total Equity	512.50	128.03	598.00
Total Liabilities and Equity	958.75	846.69	2214.00

Source: Compiled by casewriters from company annual reports and Standard & Poor's Compustat ® data, accessed Dec 2003.

EXHIBIT 6B

AOL'S INCOME STATEMENT ($ MILLION)

	Jun96	Jun97	Jun98
Sales	1093.85	1685.23	2600.00
Cost of Goods Sold	608.33	1022.76	1609.00
Gross Profit	485.52	662.47	991.00
Operating Income Before Depreciation	108.34	1.46	292.00
Depreciation, Depletion & Amortization	26.12	24.55	83.00
Operating Profit	82.22	−23.09	209.00
Interest Expense	1.40	1.57	13.00
Non-Operating Income/Expense	7.35	−7.05	21.00
Special Items	−25.83	−482.56	−131.00
Pretax Income	62.34	−514.27	86.00
Total Income Taxes	32.52	0.00	0.00
Income Before Extraordinary Items & Discontinued Operations	29.82	−499.35	92.00
Extraordinary Items	0.00	0.00	0.00
Discontinued Operations	0.00	0.00	0.00
Net Income	29.82	−499.35	92.00
Dividends Per Share	0.00	0.00	0.00

Source: Compiled by casewriters from company annual reports and Standard & Poor's Compustat® data, accessed Dec 2003.

gressive expansion and consolidation policy, which itself carried with it the risks of not being able to integrate or manage new acquisitions properly. Additionally, the forthcoming shift to broadband Internet access, and the dominant positioning of the cable television industry in this market (through the release of high-speed cable-modem technology), provided a genuine threat to the future of AOL's primarily analog modem based service provider business. The company was already taking some significant steps to establish itself in the broadband market, through strategic joint ventures with both Bell Atlantic and SBC Communications, in an effort to provide Digital Subscriber Line (DSL) high-speed Internet access to its customers.[xviii]

TRIBUNE SELLING AOL SHARES: THE PHONES SECURITY

Tribune had made its initial investment in AOL in 1991, and had continued to both buy and sell AOL stock over the coming years. By March 1999 it had realized about $260 million in gross proceeds from various sales of AOL's common stock, and now held approximately 10 million additional shares.[xix] Yet Tribune management believed that these shares were not being appropriately incorporated in investor's valuations of the company, and therefore they remained "hidden" assets, causing Tribune to be undervalued. Analysts picked up on this fact, reporting in March of 1999 that Tribune's stock price did not appropriately reflect the value of its investment portfolio.[xx]

EXHIBIT 6C

AOL'S CASH FLOW STATEMENT ($ MILLION)

	Jun96	Jun97	Jun98
Indirect Operating Activities			
Income Before Extraordinary Items	29.82	−499.35	92.00
Depreciation and Amortization	159.44	123.76	132.00
Extraordinary Items and Disc. Operations	0.00	0.00	0.00
Deferred Taxes	32.52	0.00	0.00
Sale of Property and Investments - Loss (Gain)	0.04	0.00	−17.00
Funds form Operations	16.98	407.70	89.00
Receivables - Decrease (Increase)	−28.73	−14.34	−66.00
Inventory - Decrease (Increase)	0.00	0.00	0.00
Accounts Payable and Accrued Liabs - Inc (Dec)	138.54	N/A	N/A
Income Taxes - Accrued - Increase (Dec)	0.00	0.00	0.00
Other Assets and Liabilities - Net Change	−415.34	105.27	181.00
Operating Activities - Net Cash Flow	−66.73	123.05	411.00
Investing Activities			
Investments - Increase	0.00	0.00	18.00
Sale of Investments	0.00	0.00	24.00
Short-Term Investments - Change	7.96	10.44	N/A
Capital Expenditures	50.26	149.77	297.00
Acquisitions	4.13	0.47	N/A
Investing Activities - Other	−32.63	−56.79	−168.00
Investing Activities - Net Cash Flow	−79.07	−196.59	−459.00
Financing Activities			
Sale of Common and Preferred Stock	217.67	84.51	114.00
Cash Dividends	0.00	0.00	0.00
Long-Term Debt - Issuance	3.00	50.00	441.00
Long-Term Debt - Reduction	2.34	20.04	50.00
Financing Activities - Other	0.00	−35.00	50.00
Financing Activities - Net Cash Flow	218.34	79.46	555.00
Exchange Rate Effect	0.00	0.00	0.00
Cash and Equivalents - Change	72.54	5.92	507.00

Source: Compiled by casewriters from company annual reports and Standard & Poor's Compustat ® data, accessed Dec 2003.

(Exhibits 8 and 9 contain historical financial information on Tribune, while Exhibits 10 and 11 contain the same information for AOL.) Many analysts believed that it was Tribune's plan to monetize a portion of this stock in order to unleash the "hidden value" of these assets, and improve the valuation of Tribune as a result. As reported by Prudential Securities on April 9, 1999:

> The move highlights the underlying value of Tribune's hidden assets . . . and underscores management's commitment to unlocking the value of its remaining off-balance sheet assets.[xxi]

EXHIBIT 6D

AOL STOCK PRICES HISTORY

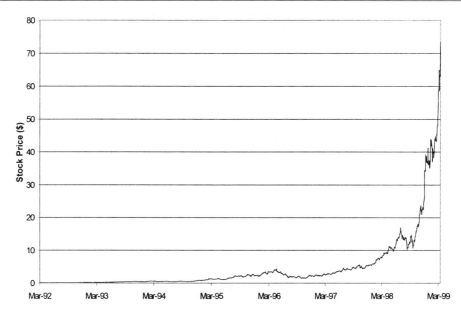

Source: Thomson Datastream, accessed December 2004.

EXHIBIT 7A

AOL HISTORICAL VOLATILITY

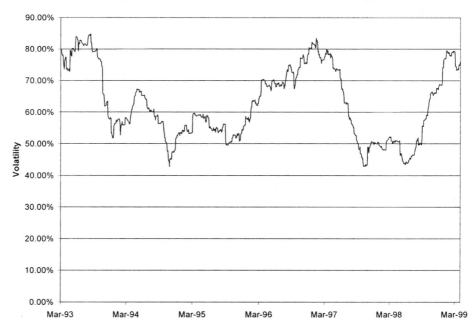

Source: Thomson Datastream, accessed December 2004.

EXHIBIT 7B

AOL TIME WARNER'S IMPLIED VOLATILITIES ON 4/1/99

Option Type	Implied Volatility
Put	70.89
Call	71.17

Note: Implied volatilities for each type (put and call) are calculated by taking a composite of the three options closest to at-the-money strike prices with maturity dates closest to 4/1/99, which were about 1 month. Stock price on that date was $75.00.

Source: Bloomberg LP, accessed December 2003.

EXHIBIT 8A

HISTORICAL RETURNS OF TRIBUNE'S STOCK AND RELATIVE INDUSTRY INDICES

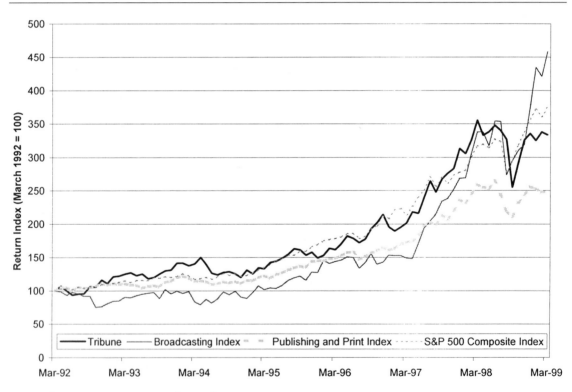

Source: Thomson Datastream, accessed December 2004.

EXHIBIT 8B

BETA OF TRIBUNE VS. RELEVANT INDICES AND THE RETURN ON THESE INDICES

	S&P 500 Composite Index		S&P 500 Publishing and Print Index		S&P 500 Broadcasting and Cable TV Index		Tribune
	Beta	Return(%)	Beta	Return(%)	Beta	Return (%)	Return(%)
3/98 - 3/99	0.91	16.75	1.00	−5.71	0.30	65.00	−7.18
3/97 - 3/99	0.72	69.90	0.99	44.22	0.28	227.57	61.57
3/96 - 3/99	0.81	96.64	1.03	74.30	0.28	168.83	98.67

Note: Beta is a price regression with no adjustments for dividends, etc. It measures the risk of a security relative to the market and is calculated using weekly data. A beta of 1.0 indicates a perfect correlation between the security and the market index. A beta greater than 1.0 indicates that the security is more volatile and riskier than the broad market.

Source: Bloomberg LP, accessed December 2003, and casewriter calculations.

In March of 1999 Tribune sold off 1 million shares of AOL, leaving the company with an estimated 10 million shares remaining. Tribune now sought to sell off an additional eight million shares of AOL, which would generate about $1.3 billion in cash. This cash would be used for capital expenditures, working capital, repayment of long-term and short-term debt, the financing of acquisitions, and share repurchase programs.[xxii] However, an outright sale of the eight million shares would result in a pretax gain of nearly the entire $1.3 billion. Tribune was an early investor in AOL, and its tax basis on the shares was about $0.20 per share.[xxiii] This would have resulted in tax payments of about $400 million, something that the Tribune management did not appreciate.

To explore ways to avoid the tax impact, Tribune management began discussions with Merrill Lynch & Co. The discussions led to the idea of using a convertible security called "participating hybrid option note exchangeable securities," or PHONES.

PHONES[xxiv] were a type of unsecured, subordinated bond that could be issued by Tribune and were only connected to AOL through the value of the reference shares. Each PHONES would be issued in an original principal amount of $157, which represented the closing market price for one share of AOL common stock as reported on the New York Stock Exchange on April 7th, 1999 (see Exhibit 12 for additional company information from around this date, and Exhibit 13 for additional market information from around this date). The minimum amount payable upon redemption or maturity of a PHONES, called the contingent principal amount, would initially be equal to the original principal amount, but would be reduced if AOL began paying a dividend (AOL had never paid a cash dividend on its common stock previously) or made special distributions of cash or assets.

Tribune would pay investors quarterly interest in an amount equal to $.785 per PHONES, or 2% per year of the original principal amount, plus the amount of any cash dividend paid on the AOL shares attributed to each PHONES. Tribune maintained the right to defer these interest payments for up to 20 consecutive quarterly periods. The PHONES would mature thirty years from the date of issuance, at which point an investor would be entitled to receive the greater of the contingent principal amount of

EXHIBIT 9

RELEVANT EARNINGS RATIOS FOR TRIBUNE AND ITS COMPETITORS

	Tribune Co			New York Times Co			Washington Post Co			Gannett Co		
	P/E[1]	P/EBIT[2]	P/EBITDA[3]	P/E	P/EBIT	P/EBITDA	P/E	P/EBIT	P/EBITDA	P/E	P/EBIT	P/EBITDA
1992	28.40	0.04	0.03	73.26	0.15	0.08	19.44	0.99	0.75	22.16	0.04	0.03
1993	25.81	0.04	0.03	77.21	0.10	0.06	20.53	1.07	0.81	21.77	0.04	0.03
1994	17.33	0.03	0.03	15.80	0.05	0.04	17.65	0.88	0.67	17.46	0.03	0.03
1995	17.37	0.04	0.03	20.15	0.06	0.04	16.68	1.04	0.77	18.66	0.04	0.03
1996	19.82	0.04	0.03	56.72	0.06	0.05	17.74	0.99	0.78	21.77	0.04	0.03
1997	22.23	0.05	0.04	27.21	0.07	0.05	20.62	1.28	1.00	22.68	0.05	0.04
1998	20.43	0.05	0.04	23.60	0.07	0.05	13.25	1.53	1.12	18.86	0.04	0.04

Notes: (1) P/E = price over earnings.

(2) P/EBIT = price over earnings before interest and taxes.

(3) P/EBITDA = price over earnings before interest, taxes, depreciation, and amortization.

Source: Compiled by casewriters from companies' annual reports and Standard & Poor's Compustat® data, accessed Dec 2003.

EXHIBIT 10A

HISTORICAL RETURNS OF AOL'S STOCK AND RELATIVE INDUSTRY INDICES

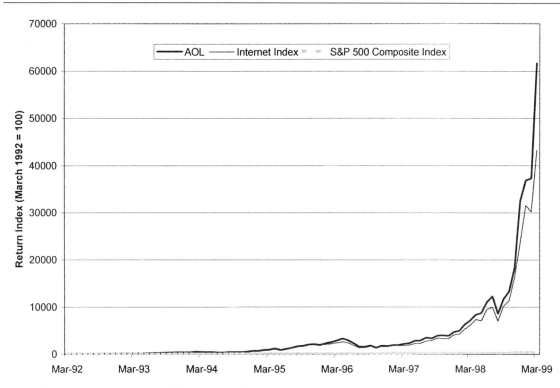

Source: Thomson Datastream, accessed December 2004.

EXHIBIT 10B

BETA OF AOL VS. RELEVANT INDICES AND THE RETURN ON THESE INDICES

	S&P 50 Composite Index		S&P Supercomposite Internet Software and Services Index		Chicago Board of Exchange Internet Index		AOL
	Beta	**Return(%)**	**Beta**	**Return(%)**	**Beta**	**Return (%)**	**Return(%)**
3/98–3/99	2.54	16.75	0.98	754.90	0.93	239.77	760.75
3/97–3/99	1.85	69.90	0.98	2656.33	0.97	511.63	2667.01
3/96–3/99	1.76	96.64	0.98	1985.72	1.02	396.32	2000.00

Note: Beta is a price regression with no adjustments for dividends, etc. It measures the risk of a security relative to the market and is calculated using weekly data. A beta of 1.0 indicates a perfect correlation between the security and the market index. A beta greater than 1.0 indicates that the security is more volatile and riskier than the broad market.

Source: Bloomberg LP, accessed December 2003, and casewriter calculations.

EXHIBIT 11

RELEVANT EARNINGS RATIOS FOR AOL

	Price/Earnings	Price/EBIT	Price/EBITDA
1992	31.40	0.03	0.03
1993	80.44	0.06	0.06
1994	190.00	0.06	0.05
1995	−38.26	0.04	0.03
1996	213.42	0.03	0.03
1997	−11.08	−0.15	2.38
1998	−250.30	0.06	0.05

Source: Compiled by casewriters from company annual reports and Standard & Poor's Compustat® data, accessed Dec 2003.

the PHONES, or the sum of the current market value of the reference shares on the maturity date plus any deferred quarterly payments of interest.

In addition, each PHONES would be exchangeable at any time by the investor for 95% the value of the reference shares. Investors had to be aware that they would not actually be receiving the shares themselves, but merely the return on the shares during a set time period.

The bankers at Merrill Lynch put together a sample prospectus for the Tribune management to review. (See Exhibit 14 for selected excerpts from the PHONES Prospectus, which also explains this security in more detail.) The Tribune now had to decide whether using PHONES actually made sense given their requirements, and if the valuation that Merrill Lynch proposed was reasonable.

EXHIBIT 12A

FINANCIAL AND MARKET INFORMATION FOR THE TRIBUNE COMPANY

	March 1999
Common Shares Outstanding	237.79 Million
Market Value of Equity	$7,787.19 Million
Stock Price as of 3/31/99	$32.72
Market Value of Long-term Debt	$1,624.00 Million
Duration of Long-term Debt	7.3
Senior Debt S&P Rating	A
Subordinate Debt S&P Rating	N/A

Source: Standard & Poor's Compustat® data, accessed Dec 2003, and casewriter calculations.

EXHIBIT 12B

FINANCIAL AND MARKET INFORMATION FOR AOL

	March 1999
Common Shares Outstanding	2,201.79 Million
Market Value of Equity	$136,543.26 Million
Stock Price as of 3/31/99	$73.50
Market Value of Long-term Debt	$346.3 Million
Duration of Long-term Debt	5.8
Senior Debt S&P Rating	BB+
Subordinate Debt S&P Rating	N/A

Source: Standard & Poor's Compustat® data, accessed Dec 2003, and casewriter calculations.

EXHIBIT 13A

US TREASURY YIELDS ON 4/1/99, SEPARATED BY THEIR COUPON PAYMENT ("CPN")

Maturity	US Treasury STRIPS[a]	US Treasury (cpn < 6.75%)	US Treasury (6.75% < cpn < 10.875%)	US Treasury (cpn > 10.875%)
3 Month	4.65%	4.66%	4.60%	4.60%
6 Month	4.76%	4.72%	4.69%	4.69%
1 Year	4.93%	4.91%	4.90%	4.91%
2 Year	5.10%	5.07%	5.07%	5.07%
3 Year	5.20%	5.15%	5.17%	5.20%
4 Year	5.24%	5.25%	5.31%	5.34%
5 Year	5.31%	5.17%	5.28%	5.36%
7 Year	5.49%	5.43%	5.46%	5.51%
8 Year	5.50%	5.42%	5.46%	5.49%
9 Year	5.58%	5.39%	5.42%	5.46%
10 Year	5.69%	5.25%	5.29%	5.30%
15 Year	5.93%	5.77%	5.96%	5.95%
20 Year	6.01%	5.97%	6.00%	6.00%
25 Year	5.96%	5.93%	5.98%	5.97%
30 Year	5.87%	5.73%	5.89%	5.87%

Note: [a]STRIPS = Separate Trading of Registered Interest and Principal of Securities. These are "Zero Coupon" Bond Yields.

Source: Bloomberg LP, accessed December 2003.

EXHIBIT 13B

CREDIT SPREADS (IN BASIS POINTS) ON APRIL 1, 1999, OVER THE US TREASURY STRIPS YIELD FOR INDUSTRIAL COMPANIES OF DIFFERENT CREDIT RATINGS

	US Industrials AAA	US Industrials AA	US Industrials A1	US Industrials A2	US Industrials A3	US Industrials BBB1	US Industrials BBB2	US Industrials BBB3
3 Month	22	28	37	41	49	62	65	72
6 Month	24	30	40	43	51	64	69	79
1 Year	31	36	44	48	56	66	73	84
2 Year	34	39	46	49	66	77	84	97
3 Year	36	41	50	55	72	83	93	114
4 Year	39	47	63	67	77	88	100	127
5 Year	37	48	62	70	81	92	105	138
7 Year	32	41	56	69	82	98	108	148
8 Year	33	42	56	68	83	102	116	151
9 Year	26	35	48	64	78	101	113	143
10 Year	17	23	39	53	67	92	103	131
15 Year	37	38	51	66	85	101	129	148
20 Year	46	54	72	83	99	115	140	160
25 Year	61	70	84	98	113	129	151	172
30 Year	63	73	91	105	123	139	154	178

Source: Bloomberg LP, accessed December 2003.

EXHIBIT 14

EXCERPTS FROM TRIBUNE PHONES PROSPECTUS DATED APRIL 9, 1999

We have summarized below the terms of the debt securities we are offering, which we refer to as the PHONES. For more detail, read "Description of PHONES" in this prospectus supplement.

- **Principal Amount**. Each PHONES is being issued in an original principal amount of $157, the last reported sale price of one share of AOL common stock as reported on the New York Stock Exchange on April 7, 1999. The minimum amount payable upon redemption or maturity of a PHONES, which we call the contingent principal amount, will initially be equal to the original principal amount. The contingent principal amount will be reduced if AOL begins paying a dividend or if there are special distributions on or in respect of the AOL common stock. We refer to AOL common stock and any other publicly traded equity securities that may be distributed on or in respect of the AOL common stock (or into which any of those securities may be converted or exchanged) collectively as the reference shares.

- **Quarterly Interest Payments**. We will pay interest quarterly in an amount equal to $.785 per PHONES, or 2% per year of the original principal amount, plus the amount of any cash dividend paid on the reference shares attributable to each PHONES. As of the date of this prospectus supplement, AOL has never paid a cash dividend on its common stock. We will also distribute to holders of the PHONES, as additional interest, any property or the cash value of any property distributed on or in respect of the reference shares (other than publicly traded equity securities which will themselves become reference shares). We may, at our option, defer the payment of interest, other than additional interest, at any time for periods not to exceed 20 consecutive quarterly periods, although we may defer the payment of interest until maturity or earlier redemption if the reference shares cease to be outstanding. The consequences of a deferral of interest are described in this prospectus supplement. You should read "Certain United States Federal Income Tax Considerations" on page S-21 for a discussion of selected United States federal income tax consequences relevant to the PHONES.

(Continued)

EXHIBIT 14 *(Continued)*

EXCERPTS FROM TRIBUNE PHONES PROSPECTUS DATED APRIL 9, 1999

- **Maturity**. The PHONES will mature on May 15, 2029. At maturity you will be entitled to receive the higher of the contingent principal amount of the PHONES or the sum of the current market value of the reference shares on the maturity date plus any deferred quarterly payments of interest (including any accrued interest thereon), plus, in either case, the final period distribution as we define it in this prospectus supplement.

- **Optional Redemption**. We may redeem the PHONES at any time at prices set forth in this prospectus supplement.

- **Exchangeability**. Each PHONES is exchangeable, at your option, at any time for an amount of cash equal to 95% of the market value of the reference shares attributable to each PHONES.

- **Ranking**. The PHONES are unsecured, subordinated obligations of Tribune and will be subordinate in right of payment to all of Tribune's existing and future senior indebtedness.

Use of Proceeds

We estimate that the net proceeds from the offering will be $1,076,370,000 ($1,230,230,000 if the underwriters exercise their over-allotment option in full). We expect to add substantially all of the net proceeds from this offering to our general funds to be used for general corporate purposes, including capital expenditures, working capital, repayment of long-term and short-term debt, the financing of acquisitions and share repurchase programs. We may invest net proceeds that we do not immediately require in short-term marketable securities.

We will pay all of our expenses, estimated at $650,000, associated with the offer and sales of the PHONES.

Description of PHONES

The following description of the PHONES (referred to as the subordinated debt securities in the accompanying prospectus) supplements and, to the extent inconsistent with, supersedes the general terms of the subordinated debt securities in the accompanying prospectus. The terms of the PHONES include those stated in the indenture dated as of April 1, 1999 executed by Tribune and the trustee under which the PHONES will be issued and those terms made part of that indenture by reference to the Trust Indenture Act of 1939, as amended. We refer to this indenture as the subordinated indenture. The PHONES are subject to those terms, and you should read the subordinated indenture and the Trust Indenture Act for a statement of them. Although we have summarized selected provisions of the subordinated indenture below, this summary is not complete and is qualified in its entirety by reference to the subordinated indenture. A copy of the proposed form of subordinated indenture has been filed as an exhibit to the registration statement we have filed with the SEC that provides for the offering of the subordinated debt securities.

The subordinated indenture does not limit the aggregate principal amount of indebtedness which may be issued under it. The subordinated indenture also provides that subordinated debt securities may be issued from time to time in one or more series. The PHONES constitute a separate series under the subordinated indenture.

The PHONES will be our unsecured, subordinated obligations limited to 7,000,000 PHONES (8,000,000 PHONES if the underwriters exercise their over-allotment option in full) and will mature on May 15, 2029.

Interest   We will make quarterly interest payments in an amount equal to $.785 per PHONES, or 2% per year of the original principal amount, plus the amount of any quarterly cash dividend paid on the reference shares attributable to each PHONES. As of the date of this prospectus supplement, AOL has never paid a cash dividend on its common stock.

Interest on the PHONES will accrue from the date we issue the PHONES. We will pay this interest quarterly in arrears on February 15, May 15, August 15 and November 15 of each year, beginning May 15, 1999, but subject to our right to defer quarterly payments of interest. Our payment on May 15, 1999, will equal $.2791 per PHONES, which is calculated to equal an annual rate of 2% on the original principal amount from the date we issue the PHONES. Holders of the PHONES are not expected to receive interest attributable to any cash dividend on the reference shares for this payment period because AOL has never paid a cash dividend on its common stock.

(Continued)

EXHIBIT 14   *(Continued)*

EXCERPTS FROM TRIBUNE PHONES PROSPECTUS DATED APRIL 9, 1999

We will also distribute, as additional interest on the PHONES, any property, including cash (other than any quarterly cash dividend), distributed on or with respect to the reference shares (other than publicly traded equity securities, which will themselves become reference shares). If the additional interest on the reference shares includes publicly traded securities (other than equity securities), we will distribute those securities to you. We will not, however, distribute fractional units of securities to you. We will pay you cash instead of distributing the fractional units. Otherwise, we will distribute to you the fair market value of any property comprising additional interest as determined in good faith by our board of directors. We will distribute any additional interest to holders of the PHONES on the 20th business day after it is distributed to us. The record date for any distribution of additional interest will be the 10th business day after the date any cash or property is distributed to us.

If quarterly cash dividends on the reference shares are paid, or any additional interest on the PHONES is paid, the contingent principal amount will be reduced on a quarterly basis to the extent necessary so that the yield to the date of computation (including all quarterly interest payments and the fair market value of any additional interest payments) does not exceed 2%. In no event will the contingent principal amount be less than zero. Changes in the contingent principal amount will not affect the amount of the quarterly interest payments.

If interest or additional interest is payable on a date that is not a business day (as defined at the end of this paragraph), payment will be made on the next business day (and without any interest or other payment in respect of this delay). However, if the next business day is in the next calendar year, payment of interest will be made on the preceding business day. A "business day" means each Monday, Tuesday, Wednesday, Thursday and Friday which is not a day on which banking institutions in the City of Chicago or The City of New York are authorized or obligated by law or regulation to close.

Principal, premium, if any, and interest on the PHONES will be payable at the office or agency we maintain for such purpose within the City and State of New York or, at our option, payment of interest may be made by check mailed to the holders of the PHONES at their respective addresses set forth in the register of holders of the PHONES. Until we otherwise designate, our office or agency in New York will be the office of the trustee maintained for that purpose. The PHONES will be issued in denominations of one PHONES and integral multiples thereof.

Principal amount   The original principal amount per PHONES is equal to its initial purchase price, or $157. The minimum amount payable upon redemption or maturity of a PHONES (which we refer to as the contingent principal amount) will initially be equal to the original principal amount. If a quarterly cash dividend is ever paid on the reference shares, or any additional interest on the PHONES is paid, the contingent principal amount will be reduced on a quarterly basis to the extent necessary so that the yield to the date of computation (including all quarterly interest payments and the fair market value of any additional interest payments) does not exceed a 2% annual yield. In no event will the contingent principal amount be less than zero.

If all of the reference shares cease to be outstanding as a result of a tender offer, an exchange offer, a business combination or otherwise, the maturity of the PHONES will not be accelerated and the PHONES will continue to remain outstanding until the maturity date unless earlier redeemed by us.

At maturity you will be entitled to receive the higher of (a) the contingent principal amount of the PHONES or (b) the sum of the current market value (as defined on page S-15) of the reference shares on the maturity date plus any deferred quarterly payments of interest (including any accrued interest thereon), plus, in each case, the final period distribution.

A "final period distribution" means, in respect of (a) the maturity date, a distribution determined in accordance with clauses (2), (3) and (4) below, and (b) the redemption date, a distribution determined in accordance with clauses (1), (2), (3) and (4) below. If the redemption date is in connection with a rollover offering, the distribution determined in accordance with clause (4) shall be all dividends and distributions on or in respect of the reference shares which a holder of reference shares on the pricing date (defined below) would be entitled to receive.

(Continued)

EXHIBIT 14 *(Continued)*

EXCERPTS FROM TRIBUNE PHONES PROSPECTUS DATED APRIL 9, 1999

Exchange option You may at any time or from time to time exchange a PHONES for an amount of cash equal to a percentage of the exchange market value of the reference shares attributable to each PHONES (which we refer to as the early exchange ratio). The early exchange ratio will be equal to (a) 95% of the exchange market value of the reference shares attributable to each PHONES or (b) during a deferral of the quarterly interest payments on the PHONES or, if we so elect, during the pendency of any tender or exchange offer for any of the reference shares, 100% of the exchange market value of the reference shares attributable to each PHONES.

We will pay you the amount due upon exchange as soon as reasonably practicable after you deliver an exchange notice to the trustee, but in no event earlier than three trading days after the date of your notice or later than ten trading days after the date of your notice.

The "exchange market value" means the closing price (as defined below) on the trading day (as defined below) following the date you deliver an exchange notice to the trustee, unless more than 500,000 PHONES have been delivered for exchange on that date. If more than 500,000 PHONES have been delivered for exchange, then the exchange market value shall be the average closing price on the five trading days following that date.

We currently hold approximately 11 million shares of the AOL common stock. We may, but are not required to, hold a number of shares of the AOL common stock equal to the number of the PHONES outstanding until maturity or redemption of the PHONES and sell those shares to raise the proceeds to pay the amount due upon exchange, maturity or redemption of the PHONES. Although we cannot assure you that these sales of the AOL common stock will not adversely affect the market for the AOL common stock or the amount due upon exchange, maturity or redemption, we have no reason to believe that any of these sales will have this effect.

Redemption We may redeem at any time all but not some of the PHONES at a redemption price equal to the sum of (a) the higher of the contingent principal amount of the PHONES or the sum of the current market value of the reference shares plus any deferred quarterly payments of interest, plus, in either case, the final period distribution, and (b) $9.42 per PHONES if we redeem prior to May 15, 2000, $6.28 per PHONES if we redeem prior to May 15, 2001, $3.14 per PHONES if we redeem prior to May 15, 2002, or zero per PHONES if we redeem any time on or after May 15, 2002.

The "current market value" (other than in the case of a rollover offering, which is described below) is defined as the average closing price per reference share on the 20 trading days (which we refer to as the averaging period) immediately prior to (but not including) the fifth business day preceding the redemption date; provided, however, that for purposes of determining the payment required upon redemption in connection with a rollover offering, "current market value" means the closing price per reference share on the trading day immediately preceding the date that the rollover offering is priced (which we refer to as the pricing date) or, if the rollover offering is priced after 4:00 p.m., New York City time, on the pricing date, the closing price per share on the pricing date, except that if there is not a trading day immediately preceding the pricing date or (where pricing occurs after 4:00 p.m., New York City time, on the pricing date) if the pricing date is not a trading day, "current market value" means the market value per reference share as of the redemption date as determined by a nationally recognized independent investment banking firm retained by us.

A "rollover offering" means a refinancing of the PHONES by way of either (a) a sale of the reference shares or (b) a sale of securities that are priced by reference to the reference shares, in either case, by means of a completed public offering or offerings by us and which is expected to yield net proceeds which are sufficient to pay the redemption amount for all of the PHONES. The trustee will notify you if we elect to redeem your PHONES in connection with a rollover offering not less than 30 or more than 60 business days prior to the redemption date. We will also issue a press release prior to 4:00 p.m., New York City time, on the business day immediately before the day on which the closing price of the reference shares is to be measured for the purpose of determining the current market value in connection with a rollover offering. The notice will state we are firmly committed to price the rollover offering, will specify the date on which the rollover offering is to be priced (including whether the rollover offering will be priced during trading on the pricing date or after the close of trading on the pricing date) and consequently, whether the closing price for the reference shares by which the current market value will be measured will be the closing price on the trading date immediately preceding the pricing date or the closing price on the pricing date. We will provide that press release to DTC for dissemination through the DTC broadcast facility.

(Continued)

EXHIBIT 14 (Continued)

EXCERPTS FROM TRIBUNE PHONES PROSPECTUS DATED APRIL 9, 1999

The "closing price" of any security on any date of determination means the closing sale price (or, if no closing sale price is reported, the last reported sale price) of that security (regular way) on the NYSE on that date or, if that security is not listed for trading on the NYSE on that date, as reported in the composite transactions for the principal United States securities exchange on which that security is so listed, or if that security is not so listed on a United States national or regional securities exchange, as reported by the Nasdaq National Market, or if that security is not so reported, the last quoted bid price for that security in the over-the-counter market as reported by the National Quotation Bureau or similar organization. In the event that no such quotation is available for any day, our board of directors will be entitled to determine the closing price on the basis of those quotations that it in good faith considers appropriate.

A "trading day" is defined as a day on which the security, the closing price of which is being determined, (a) is not suspended from trading on any national or regional securities exchange or association or over-the-counter market at the close of business and (b) has traded at least once on the national or regional securities exchange or association or over-the-counter market that is the primary market for the trading of that security.

Subordination   The PHONES are unsecured and junior in right of payment to all senior indebtedness (as we define below). This means that no payment on the PHONES may be made if:

- any senior indebtedness is not paid when due, any applicable grace period with respect to any default for non-payment has ended and that default has not been cured or waived or ceased to exist; or
- the maturity of any senior indebtedness has been accelerated because of an event of default and that acceleration has not been rescinded.

On any distribution of our assets to creditors upon any dissolution, winding-up or liquidation whether voluntary or involuntary or in bankruptcy, insolvency, receivership, reorganization or other similar proceedings, all principal of, premium, if any, interest and any other amounts due or to become due on, all senior indebtedness must be paid in full before the holders of the PHONES are entitled to receive or retain any payment. Upon payment in full of the senior indebtedness, the holders of the PHONES will assume rights similar to the holders of senior indebtedness to receive payments or distributions applicable to senior indebtedness until all amounts owing on the PHONES are paid in full. The PHONES are intended to rank equally with all other general obligations of Tribune.

"Senior indebtedness" means:

- principal, premium, if any, and interest on and other amounts due in connection with:
  - indebtedness for money borrowed by us; or
  - indebtedness evidenced by notes, bonds, debentures or similar evidences of indebtedness Issued by us;
  - all of our capital lease obligations;
- all of our indebtedness for the deferred purchase price of property or services (other than on normal trade terms); and
- all obligations of the type referred to above of other persons for the payment of which we are responsible or liable as obligor or guarantor.

Senior indebtedness does not include:

- any indebtedness that is by its terms junior to or equal with the subordinated debt securities;
- any series of subordinated debt securities under the subordinated indenture;
- trade accounts payable arising in the ordinary course of business; and
- indebtedness to any of our subsidiaries.

The PHONES do not limit our ability or that of our subsidiaries to incur additional indebtedness, including indebtedness that ranks senior in priority of payment to the PHONES. As of April 7, 1999, we had approximately $1.6 billion of senior indebtedness.

(Continued)

EXHIBIT 14   (Continued)

EXCERPTS FROM TRIBUNE PHONES PROSPECTUS DATED APRIL 9, 1999

Amount payable upon bankruptcy   Upon dissolution, winding-up, liquidation or reorganization, whether voluntary or involuntary or in bankruptcy, insolvency, receivership or other similar proceedings in respect of Tribune, holders of the PHONES should be entitled to a claim against us in an amount equal to the higher of (a) the contingent principal amount of the PHONES or (b) the sum of the current market value (without giving effect to the provisions relating to rollover offerings) of the reference shares plus any deferred quarterly payments of interest (including any accrued interest thereon), plus, in either case, the final period distribution determined as if the date of such event was the maturity date of the PHONES.

Tribune is a holding company and our subsidiaries hold a substantial portion of our assets. Our right and the rights of our creditors, including the holders of the PHONES, to participate in the assets of any subsidiary upon its liquidation or recapitalization would be subject to the prior claims of that subsidiary's creditors, except to the extent that we may ourselves be a creditor with recognized claims against that subsidiary. There is no restriction in the subordinated indenture against our subsidiaries incurring unsecured indebtedness.

Dilution adjustment   For purposes of this prospectus supplement, "reference company" means AOL and any other issuer of a reference share. A "reference share" means, collectively one share of the AOL common stock. A "reference share offer" means any tender offer or exchange offer made for all or a portion of a class of reference shares of a reference company.

If a reference share offer is made, we may, at our option, either:

- during the pendency of the offer, increase the early exchange ratio to 100%; or
- make a reference share offer adjustment.

A "reference share offer adjustment" means each share of publicly traded equity securities, if any, deemed to be distributed on or in respect of a reference share as average transaction consideration less the reference share proportionate reduction (as defined below).

The average transaction consideration deemed to be received by a holder of one reference share in a reference share offer will be equal to (a) the aggregate consideration actually paid or distributed to all holders of reference shares in the reference share offer, divided by (b) the total number of reference shares outstanding immediately prior to the expiration of the reference share offer and entitled to participate in that reference share offer.

The "reference share proportionate reduction" means a proportionate reduction in the number of reference shares which are the subject of the applicable reference share offer and attributable to one PHONES calculated in accordance with the following formula:

$$R = X/N$$

where:

   R = the fraction by which the number of reference shares of the class of reference shares subject to the reference share offer and attributable to one PHONES will be reduced.

   X = the aggregate number of reference shares of the class of reference shares subject to the reference share offer accepted in the reference share offer.

   N = the aggregate number of reference shares of the class of reference shares subject to the reference share offer outstanding immediately prior to the expiration of the reference share offer.

If we elect to make a reference share offer adjustment, we will distribute as additional interest on each PHONES the average transaction consideration deemed to be received on the reference shares of the class subject to the reference share offer and attributable to each PHONES immediately prior to giving effect to the reference share proportionate reduction relating to that reference share offer (other than average transaction consideration that is publicly traded equity securities which will themselves become reference shares as a result of a reference share offer adjustment).

EXHIBIT 14 *(Continued)*

EXCERPTS FROM TRIBUNE PHONES PROSPECTUS DATED APRIL 9, 1999

If we elect to make a reference share offer adjustment, and during the pendency of the reference share offer another reference share offer is commenced in relation to the reference shares the subject of the then existing reference share offer, we can change our original election by electing to increase the early exchange ratio to 100% during the pendency of the new reference share offer, or we can continue to elect to make a reference share offer adjustment. We will similarly be entitled to change our election for each further reference share offer made during the pendency of any reference share offer for the same class of reference shares. For the purposes of these adjustments, a material change to the terms of an existing reference share offer will be deemed to be a new reference share offer.

If we elect to increase the early exchange ratio to 100% in connection with a reference share offer, no reference share offer adjustment will be made and we cannot change our election if any further reference share offer is made.

We will give the trustee notice of our election in the event of any reference share offer. We will also prepare a press release and provide it to DTC for dissemination through the DTC broadcast facility. We will give this notice no later than 10 business days before the scheduled expiration of the reference share offer.

Note: Substantial portions of this prospectus have been omitted by the casewriter.

Source: Tribune PHONES Prospectus, April 9, 1999. Available from ⟨www.sec.gov⟩.

END NOTES

i. Tribune Co., SalomonSmithBarney; Company Report, February 3, 1999. Available from ⟨www.investext.com⟩.

ii. This section draws on "Tribune Company, Inc." by Barrington Research Associates, Inc.; Economic and Investment Research, August 10, 1998. Available from ⟨www.investext.com⟩.

iii. Tribune Company: 1998 Annual Report.

iv. Tribune Co., CIBC Oppenheimer Equity Research, October 6, 1998. Available from ⟨www.investext.com⟩.

v. Ibid.

vi. Ibid.

vii. Tribune Company, Inc.; Barrington Research Associates, Inc; Economic and Investment Research; August 10, 1998.

viii. Dennis FitzSimons, Tribune Broadcasting president. Tribune Company: 1998 Annual Report. Available from ⟨www.globalaccess.com⟩.

ix. Tribune Co., CIBC Oppenheimer Equity Research, October 6, 1998.

x. Tribune Company: 1998 Annual Report..

xi. Tribune Co., CIBC Oppenheimer Equity Research, October 6, 1998.

xii. This section draws on Tribune Co., CIBC Oppenheimer Equity Research, October 6, 1998.

xiii. Tribune Company: 1998 Annual Report.

xiv. In Depth Review, Company Report: Tribune Company. Bear, Stearns & Co. Inc., May 17, 1999. Available from ⟨www.investext.com⟩.

xv. America Online, Inc.: Still Master of the Internet Universe, ING Baring Furman Selz LLC Global Research, March 22, 1999. Available from ⟨www.investext.com⟩.

xvi. America Online Inc./S&P –2: Ratings Outlook Stable)AOL. Dow Jones News Service, April 15, 1999. Available from ⟨www.factiva.com⟩.

xvii. America Online, Inc.: Still Master of the Internet Universe.

xviii. Ibid.

xix.   Tribune Co., Credit Suisse First Boston Corporation, Equity Research, April 16, 1999. Available from ⟨www.investext.com⟩.

xx.   Tribune: Monetizing AOL Investment Reveals Portfolio Values and Boosts Share Price, Wasserstein Perella Securities, Inc.; Equity Research, April 8, 1999. Available from ⟨www. investext.com⟩.

xxi.   Tribune Company, Prudential Securities, April 9, 1999. Available from ⟨www.investext.com⟩.

xxii. Tribune PHONES Prospectus, April 9, 1999. Available from ⟨www.sec.gov⟩.

xxiii. Tribune Co., Credit Suisse First Boston Corporation, Equity Research, April 16, 1999.

xxiv. This section draws on the Tribune PHONES Prospectus, April 9, 1999. Available from ⟨www.sec.gov⟩.

22

Cox Communications, Inc., 1999

Summer in Atlanta, Georgia, home of Cox Communications, Inc., (Cox) was usually quite warm, but the summer of 1999 was especially hot for Dallas Clement, Cox's 34-year-old treasurer. At the beginning of 1999, Clement and his team (Susan Coker and Mark Major, co-assistant treasurers) anticipated that Cox would be making several major acquisitions over the next three to five years, probably spending $7–$8 billion in the process. However, unexpectedly aggressive competition by rivals seeking to lock up valuable cable systems had brought a number of important properties into play sooner than expected. From a strategic viewpoint, Cox could not afford to lose these cable properties, especially those that could be combined with its existing systems to yield substantial market presence and attendant cost savings. By the beginning of July, the firm had already committed to over $7 billion in acquisitions to be completed by the end of the year, which would add over 1.6 million new subscribers in eight states. These deals would put stress on the firm's complicated balance sheet, requiring Clement's team to scramble to fund several years' of acquisitions in little more than six months.

Then, in mid-July, Cox learned that Gannett Co. would put its cable properties up for sale. Cox's parent, Cox Enterprises, Inc. ("CEI"), and Gannett were both approximately 100-year-old newspaper companies that had branched out into other communications businesses, including television and radio broadcasting, print media, production and cable. There had been little indication that Gannett would sell its cable system, but the high prices being paid for cable subscribers apparently convinced Gannett to part with its cable assets. The Cox team estimated that, based on comparable recent transactions, Cox would need to bid about $2.7 billion to win the right to serve Gannett's 522,000 customers. With this acquisition and the others to which it had recently committed, Cox's subscriber base would grow 60% from the levels at the beginning of the year. This newest acquisition, however, would put even more pressure on the firm's funding ability, and Clement's team had to recommend how to fund it.

Clement's team had to figure out how much debt, equity or equity-linked securities to issue, or how many of its appreciated non-strategic assets to sell, to fund these acquisitions. Their recommendation for funding the Gannett acquisition had to be

Professors George Chacko and Peter Tufano and Research Associates Matthew Bailey and Joshua Musher prepared this case. HBS cases are developed solely as the basis for class discussion. Cases are not intended to serve as endorsements, sources of primary data, or illustrations of effective or ineffective management.

consistent with the firm's long-run capacity to fund future activities. Specifically, they had to be mindful of the impact of their actions on the firm's investment-grade bond rating, which its board was keen to protect. At the same time, their recommendation had to respect the preferences of the Cox family, who owned more than two-thirds of Cox through their ownership of the privately held CEI, and who sought to maintain their super-majority ownership of Cox. The heat outside the Cox headquarters was nowhere as blistering as the heat within Clement's organization as his team worked late into the night.

COX COMMUNICATIONS, INC. AND THE CABLE/BROADBAND INDUSTRY

Since its establishment in 1898 until 1962, Cox Enterprise's main business had been newspapers. The firm first entered the cable television business in 1962 with the purchase of cable systems in California, Oregon, Pennsylvania, and Washington. These cable systems carried television signals to homes via coaxial landlines, offering subscribers clear reception and new programming choices. By 1977, Cox's cable division operated in nine states and served 500,000 subscribers. By 1990, it served 1.5 million subscribers and by the beginning of 1999, it was serving almost 3.7 million subscribers. In 1995, the cable business was partially spun off by CEI in the form of Cox Communications (Cox), with majority control and economic ownership retained by CEI.

Technological innovations, including the Internet, fiber optics, and wireless communications, as well as deregulation, made the late 1990s a period of tremendous change for cable operators. Cable operators spent billions of dollars replacing coaxial cables with fiber optic bundles, which provided 1000 times more capacity. This extra capacity allowed cable companies—now labeled "broadband" companies reflecting the breadth of services they offered—to provide consumers with pay-per-view and digital cable television services, high-speed Internet access, and digital telephony. Cable operators anticipated these and other new services (video-on-demand, Interactive TV, video gaming, etc.) would drive much of the profit growth for at least the next several years. Increasing the breadth of services brought broadband companies into competition with a wider range of rivals, including satellite systems, telephone companies, and wireless companies, as part of the telecommunications convergence. Deregulation, in the form of the Telecommunications Reform Act of 1996 made this convergence possible by allowing cable operators and telephone companies to enter each other's businesses. While the traditional part of the cable industry was quite regulated, the growth of the broadband industry—and the competitive battles that would ensue—would take place in less-regulated territory.

Cox prided itself on delivering high-quality technology and services and was very aggressive in upgrading its network and introducing new services. By mid-1999, close to 60% of Cox's cable systems had been upgraded to 750 megahertz[1] (MHz) of capacity. Since analog video services took up only 550 MHz of capacity, this upgrade allowed Cox to offer high-speed Internet access to its cable television customers through Cox@Home, telephone service under the Cox Digital Telephone brand, and advanced

---

[1] Megahertz (MHz) in this context is a measure of bandwidth for high-speed digital data transfer. The bandwidth of a cable line is the maximum data speed that the line can transmit. Generally, the higher the bandwidth, the higher the maximum data transfer speed of the cable line. A 750 MHz line can transmit data at a rate of 750 million bits per second, where a bit is a 1 or a 0, representing one piece of information.

digital television programming under the Cox Digital TV brand. Digital video was expected to drive the growth of Cox's core video revenues, which were otherwise anticipated to grow at an annual rate of 6%–8% for the next five years. This growth came from expected rate increases of 3%–5% and natural growth of the subscriber base. Revenues from high-speed Internet access and digital telephony, however, were anticipated to grow at significantly higher rates. (See Table A.) On an aggregate basis, these additional services were expected to raise operating cash flow growth from 8% to 15% annually. Not included in these estimates were additional services, such as Home Security Monitoring, that were still in the concept stage. Total capital expenditures, including those for network upgrades and expansion of services, were expected to be $1.3 billion in 2000 and close to $1.1 billion in 2001.

TABLE A   Gross Margins and Growth Rates for Cable Services

	Monthly Cash Flow	Gross Margin[a]	Current Subscriber Penetration[b]	Target Penetration[c]
Analog TV	$30	75%	67%	67%
Digital TV	16–18	55	2	30
High-speed Internet	35–40	30	2	25
Digital telephony	55–60	55	1	25

[a] Gross margin is defined as revenue minus direct costs of the service.

[b] As a percentage of homes passed.

[c] Cox expected to reach these target levels within eight years.

Source: Casewriter estimates and Cox Communications, Inc.

Cable operators realized that they had to expand to spread the fixed costs of their operations and networks over as large a number of customers as possible. High *local* market share through consolidation led to tangible cost savings in the form of local scale economies, such as sharing the same cables and fleets of service technicians and vans. On a *national* scale, consolidation provided bargaining power when dealing with content providers, such as firms like HBO or Fox, that produced and distributed programming. Expansion also allowed cable operators to realize increasing returns by bundling services to more households.

As a result, Cox, as well as its competitors, rapidly expanded their customer bases via acquisitions. (See Exhibit 1 for some recent cable mergers and acquisitions, and Exhibit 2 for data on the largest operators that resulted.) For example, in 1995 Cox acquired Times Mirror Cable Television, which increased Cox's subscriber base by 1.3 million customers. In the first half of 1999 alone, Cox announced its intentions to purchase cable systems from Media General (April), merge with TCA Cable (May), and acquire certain AT&T cable properties. These acquisitions were expected to close by the end of 1999, but were by no means guaranteed to occur. They were contingent on regulatory approval, and the transfer of franchise rights by local communities. Obtaining the necessary approvals could take 3 to 15 months. These acquisitions would bring Cox's customer base to 5.5 million in 18 different states, making Cox the fifth-largest cable operator in the United States.

Competition among cable companies for customers had driven up the cost of new customers. Some analysts felt that the race became heated when Charter, owned by Paul Allen of Microsoft, purchased Marcus Cable in April 1998. As a result, while cable firms had paid approximately $2,000 per subscriber to expand their cable operations through-

EXHIBIT 1

COST PER CUSTOMER OF CABLE ACQUISITIONS, 1994–1999

Announcement Date	Acquirer	Seller	Total Value of Acquisition	Price Paid per Cable Customer
June 94	Comcast	Maclean Hunter	$1.27 billion	$2,300
October 95	Comcast	E. W. Scripps Co.	$1.49 billion	$1,900
April 98	Paul Allen	Marcus Cable	$2.78 billion	$2,200
June 98	Cox	TCI	$250.2 million	$2,176
June 98	AT&T	TCI	$59.4 billion	$2,700
July 98	Paul Allen	Charter	$4.5 billion	$3,750
October 98	Cox	Prime South Diversified[a]	$1.325 billion	$3,329
February 99	Adelphia	FrontierVision	$2.0 billion	$2,900
March 99	Adelphia	Century	$5.7 billion	$3,600
March 99	Adelphia	Harron Communications	$1.2 billion	$4,100
April 99	AT&T	Media One[b]	$62.5 billion	$4,700
April 99	Cox	Media General[c]	$1.4 billion	$5,380
May 99	Charter	Avalon Cable	$845 million	$3,250
May 99	Charter	Falcon	$3.6 billion	$2,250
May 99	Comcast	AT&T[d]	$3.4 billion	$4,500
May 99	Cox	TCA Cable TV[e]	$4.1 billion	$4,600
June 99	Comcast	Greater Media	$292 million	$3,700
June 99	Charter	Bresnan	$3.1 billion	$4,500
July 99	Cox	AT&T[f]	$2.15 billion	$4,350

[a]This deal included access to 105,000 hotels, together with interests in various nonconsolidated operations, and thus is not directly comparable to wholly residential transactions.

[b]Agreed to a swap of cable subscribers with MediaOne, including payment of cash.

[c]Agreed to buy cable systems covering 260,000 customers from Media General for $1.4 billion.

[d]As part of the deal Comcast also had an option to acquire from AT&T, in three years, additional cable systems covering between 1.0 million and 1.4 million subscribers for $4.8 billion to $6.7 billion. Comcast also agreed to supply AT&T-branded telephony in its cable systems, provided AT&T concluded telephony deals with two other non-AT&T cable companies.

[e]Merger with TCA Cable TV, serving 883,000 customers. TCA stock either converted into $62.50 cash, 0.7418 Cox shares plus $31.25 in cash, or 1.4836 Cox shares. Cox paid $4.1 billion.

[f]Cox and AT&T agreed that Cox would exchange its holding in AT&T for stock in AT&T subsidiaries that own cable TV systems. The swap consisted of 50.3 million AT&T shares (worth $2.8 billion), for which Cox acquired subsidiaries with approximately 495,000 customers and $750 million cash and other assets.

Source: Assorted Bloomberg News stories.

out most of the 1990s and as recently as 1998, this figure had risen to well over $4,000 per subscriber by 1999. With the number of available cable assets rapidly shrinking, incumbents in the industry had no choice but to pay these prices or face the prospect of becoming second-tier competitors.[2] Forrester Research estimated that the top five cable companies would serve 70% of subscribers in four years, up from around 56%.[3]

[2] Some of the recent acquisitions were swaps of subscribers being served by competing companies. The main reason for this was that there were economies associated with having clustered subscribers.

[3] T. Rhinelander, C. Mines, and K. Kopikis, "Cable's Multiservice Future." Forrester Research, February 1999.

EXHIBIT 2

COMPARATIVE FINANCIAL DATA FOR MAJOR CABLE OPERATORS, 1998 (IN MILLIONS OF DOLLARS, EXCEPT RATIOS)

	AT&T	Cox	MediaOne	Time Warner	Comcast	Charter
Total assets	59,550	12,878	28,192	31,640	14,817	4,335
Equity market value[a] (7/99)	178,390	20,436	45,111	90,571	26,839	NA
Debt book value	6,727	3,920	5,422	10,944	5,577	NA
Operating cash flow	10,309	666	5,517	1,845	1,078	30
Cable subscriber base[b]	15.5	6.0	NA	12.9	8.0	6.2
Net income/ total assets	0.11	0.14	1.48	0.01	0.07	NM
ROE	26.0%	33.3%	235.3%	−6.0%	43.4%	NA
ROA	8.7%	13.1%	5.2%	0.5%	7.7%	−1.0%
Total liabilities/total assets	0.57	0.58	0.47	0.70	0.68	0.50
Debt-to-equity[c]	0.26	0.74	0.38	1.24	1.42	NA
Total debt/EBITDA[d]	0.6	5.1e	5.7	4.1	3.7	87.6
EBITDA interest coverage[f]	19.4	3.0	1.9	2.3	3.1	1.2
Bond rating	AA-/Aa3	A-/Baa2	BBB/Ba1	BBB/Baa3	BBB-/Baa3	NA
Equity Beta	0.61	0.68	1.08	0.87	0.88	NA

[a]As of August 1999, Charter had not yet sold shares to the public.

[b]As of July 1999, the data for AT&T included the MediaOne subscriber base.

[c]As measured by the ratio of the book value of long-term debt to book value of shareholders' equity.

[d]Ratio of Total Debt to Earnings Before Interest, Taxes, Depreciation and Amortization. This is a commonly used ratio for analysis of debt capacity.

[e]As reported by Cox on pro forma basis to credit agencies.

[f]EBITDA divided by the interest expense (for the same period) is a common ratio used for debt analysis. It approximates ability to repay on the basis of cash availability.

Source: Bloomberg Financial Analysis and Global Access.

Achieving scale was expensive. The deals Cox announced in the first half of 1999, if consummated, would require nearly $7.6 billion in gross funding. Media General would cost $1.4 billion in cash, TCA would cost $4.1 billion ($2.0 billion in cash, $1.9 billion in Cox common equity, and $190 million in assumed debt), and AT&T would cost $2.1 billion (paid for with 50.3 million shares of AT&T. Cox, through subsidiaries, would acquire cable systems and other assets, including $750 million cash).

The possible acquisition of Gannett's cable properties would make 1999 an extraordinary year for Cox. Gannett Co., founded in 1906 by Frank E. Gannett, was a diversified media company. Its 75 newspapers (including *USA Today*, the largest-selling daily newspaper in the United States) made it the nation's largest newspaper group, and its 21 television stations reached 17% of the United States. In 1995, the company had purchased Multimedia Inc., which gave Gannett cable systems in Indiana, Illinois, Kansas, North Carolina and Oklahoma, and in 1999 reached about 522,000 subscriber households. Gannett's properties were attractive to Cox not only because of the number of subscribers, but also because they fit in well with its own strategy of concentrating subscribers in geographical areas to achieve economies of scale and scope. The Gannett systems, however, would not be cheap. Gannett would sell its cable properties by auction and Cox estimated that it would have to pay $2.7 billion, or over $5000 per subscriber, to win.

FINANCING COX'S GROWTH AND THE GANNETT ACQUISITION

James Kennedy, the chairman of Cox's Board, and James Robbins, the firm's president and CEO, wrote in the annual report, "We constantly review potential growth opportunities and weigh them against a very clear litmus test: Will they create significant shareholder value? . . . Cox has the flexibility to [pursue these growth opportunities] in part because of our strong balance sheet." A key issue for Clement and his team to consider as they struggled with the current financing decision was how to retain sufficient financial flexibility to continue to fund planned and unexpected business opportunities.

Surely, funding the acquisitions would affect Cox's balance sheet. Even without the Gannett acquisition, internal cash flow would not be sufficient to fund the acquisitions that had been announced to date. Cox had financed its capital expenditures for network upgrades, acquisitions, capital investments, and new products through $1.9 billion from internal cash flow in conjunction with $1.9 billion of net issuance of debt, $370 million of equity (including its IPO in 1995) and $900 million from sales of non-strategic assets. The funding and asset sale choices were complicated by a variety of factors that Clement, Coker, and Major had to consider. In particular, the team was acutely aware of changing market conditions that could materially affect their ability to execute the transactions needed to fund the Gannett acquisition. (See Exhibits 3 and 4 for financial information about Cox and debt issuances.)

Issuing Common Shares

Cox could issue shares to the public for all or part of the required amount of funding. The firm's first and only share issuance had been almost four years earlier, in June 1995, when it raised a little under $400 million through public and private placements of equity. Any recommendation, however, to sell equity had to be mindful of the firm's unique ownership structure. CCI had two classes of common stock outstanding: class A shares were entitled to one vote each, and class C shares had supervoting privileges with 10 votes each. Neither class of common equity paid dividends. Through CEI, the Cox family owned 379.2 million out of 533.8 million class A shares, and all of the 27.6 million class C shares outstanding. After the anticipated issuance of 38.3 million shares as part of the TCA transaction in the next fiscal quarter, CEI would own 67.3% of Cox's common shares and would control 76.8% of Cox's voting stock.[4] The chairman and CEO of CEI, James Kennedy, was also the chairman of the board of Cox and was the grandson of CEI's founder.

Cox had a number of financial objectives. The first was to double the size of the company every five years. The second was to preserve the family's economic ownership of Cox. The firm's initial public offering of Cox's equity in 1995 had allowed Cox to expand via acquisitions, but CEI did not want its ownership interests further diluted. To ensure that their interests as management were consistently aligned with those of the

---

[4] The number of shares was calculated on a fully diluted basis, assuming that 6.1 million outstanding stock options were exercised and that 5 million outstanding convertible preferred shares were converted. The convertible preferred shares had voting privileges, and did not receive dividends.

EXHIBIT 3

FINANCIAL SUMMARY FOR COX COMMUNICATIONS
(IN MILLIONS OF DOLLARS UNLESS NOTED)

	1996	1997	1998	99Q1	99Q2
Revenue	1,460	1,610	1,717	499	510
Cost of goods sold	468	496	540	168	159
Selling, general and administrative	436	505	518	142	156
EBITDA	557	610	659	189	196
Depreciation and amortization	335	405	458	123	159
Nonoperating income (expense)	(104)	(193)	2,115	384	890
Interest expense	146	202	223	54	69
Income tax expense (refund)	23	(54)	883	144	352
Net income (loss)	(52)	(137)	1,271	251	506
Cash and marketable securities	42	28	31	90	23
Total current assets	165	377	197	265	210
Total assets	5,785	6,557	12,878	14,727	16,169
Current liabilities	250	245	336	334	362
Deferred taxes	294	722	2,887	3,668	4,152
Long-term debt	2,824	3,149	3,920	3,383	3,587
Other liabilities	155	84	359	485	439
Total liabilities	3,523	4,199	7,502	7,870	8,539
Total shareholders equity	2,261	2,357	5,377	6,857	7,629
Capital expenditures	(579)	(708)	(809)	(225)	(277)
Cash flow from operations	309	555	666	176	18
Cash flow from investing activity	(552)	(1,108)	(1,600)	515	(292)
Cash flow from financing activity	246	539	937	(631)	207
Shares outstanding (all classes, millions)	540	541	545	555	555
Long-term debt / EBITDA[a]	5.1 x	5.2 x	5.9 x	4.5 x	4.6 x
EBITDA interest coverage	3.8 x	3.0 x	3.0 x	3.5 x	2.9 x
Free cash flow/long-term debt	−9.6%	−4.9%	−3.7%	−1.4%	−7.2%
Long-term debt/(long-term debt + equity)	55.5%	57.2%	42.2%	33.0%	32.0%
ROE (%)	−2.3%	−5.8%	23.6%	3.7%	6.6%
Price/book	2.76 x	4.61 x	3.64 x	3.11 x	2.72 x
Debt-to-equity[b] (book value)	1.25 x	1.34 x	0.73 x	0.49 x	0.47 x
Debt-to-equity (market value)	0.45 x	0.29 x	0.20 x	0.16 x	0.17 x

[a]Source: Cox Communications. As reported pro forma numbers that include EBITDA of new acquisitions when debt is already on the balance sheet.

[b]As measured by the ratio of long-term debt to shareholders' equity.

Source: Bloomberg Financial Analysis and Global Access.

other shareholders, the family considered it appropriate to maintain a supermajority stake in conjunction with their control of the firm. This preference constrained the amount of equity financing Cox could undertake, as any equity issuance would have reduced the percentage ownership of CEI. Finally, there was a reluctance to increase the leverage of the firm, as discussed below.

EXHIBIT 4A

MONTHLY ISSUANCE OF NONCONVERTIBLE DEBT BY CREDIT RATING, JULY 1988–JULY 1999

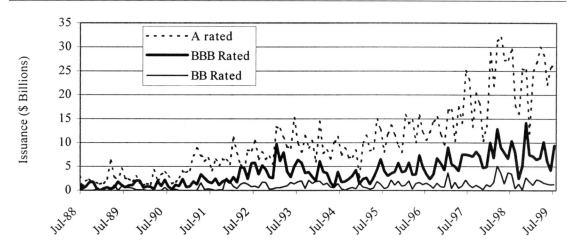

Source: Securities Data Corporation. Represents the face value of public offerings of nonconvertible debt. For example, the dark line represents the monthly issuance volume of bonds rated BBB.

Also on Clement's mind was his tactical ability to place a large block of Cox equity in the market. Charter Communications was expected to make its initial public offering in the fall. Because Charter and Cox appealed to similar investors, Clement was concerned that these investors would have less of an appetite for Cox shares after the Charter deal had been placed. Were he to issue equity, he might want to do so before

EXHIBIT 4B

CREDIT SPREADS FOR LONG-MATURITY BONDS, JULY 1992–JULY 1999

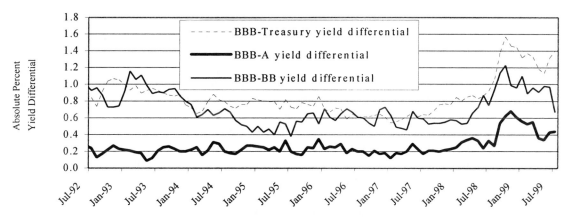

Source: Securities Data Corporation. Represents the face value of public offerings of nonconvertible debt. For example, the dark line represents the monthly issuance volume of bonds rated BBB.

EXHIBIT 4C

SUPPLEMENTARY MONTHLY STATISTICS FOR EXHIBITS 4A AND 4B, JULY 1992–JULY 1999

	A Issuance ($ MM)	BBB Issuance ($ MM)	BB Issuance ($ MM)	BBB − Treasury Spread (%)	BBB − A Spread (%)	BB − BBB Spread (%)
Minimum	2,628	791	100	0.54	0.09	0.38
Average	14,503	5,248	1,299	0.85	0.26	0.71
Maximum	32,007	14,149	5,126	1.57	0.68	1.23
Standard deviation	7,279	2,638	919	0.23	0.12	0.20
Standard deviation/Average	50%	50%	71%	44%	28%	27%

Source: Securities Data Corporation.

Charter's IPO. Clement also had to consider overall market condition. The equity markets had enjoyed, for almost a decade, a long period of high returns as part of a prolonged economic expansion in the United States, but many pundits warned of an imminent correction in the markets. (See Exhibit 5.)

A minor consideration was the direct costs of an equity issue, including underwriting fees and expenses, which would likely be between 2%–3% of the amount raised. In addition, there might be some "market impact" of a large equity issue, as the market typically greeted new shares by reducing the price of the firm's outstanding equity (and thereby the price at which the new shares could be offered). Academic studies suggested that this response usually amounted to an additional 3%–4% reduction in the price of a firm's stock, although this discount varied across firms and over time.[5]

Issuing Debt or Borrowing

Alternatively, Cox could issue debt to fund the Gannett cable acquisition, whether in the form of a public debt issue or bank borrowing. The structure of the debt could take many forms determined by the source of the debt, the maturity structure, the level of cash coupons, and various options (such as the right to redeem or call the debt at par). Since 1995, Cox had raised $1.9 billion in debt. This debt had maturities ranging from 5 to 30 years, with yields ranging from 65 to 115 basis points above the yields on U.S. Treasury obligations of similar maturity.

The Cox executives, however, were concerned about increasing financial leverage. The Cox family was very conservative about the use of debt. Cox already had the highest level of debt financing of all the CEI subsidiaries. Furthermore, Cox had a publicly articulated goal of maintaining a high debt rating. Cox executives had stated, "We want to get the right balance of debt and equity. We obviously are continuing to be investment grade and that's important." Maintaining that rating required careful monitoring of several financial variables, the most important of which being Debt/EBITDA. Cur-

---

[5] See Grinblatt, Mark and S. Titman, "Financial Markets and Corporate Strategy," Irwin/McGraw-Hill, 1998, pp. 15–16 and the references therein for more information regarding the direct and indirect costs of issuing equity.

EXHIBIT 5A

SHARE PRICE OF COX COMMUNICATIONS' COMMON STOCK, JANUARY 1995–JULY 1999

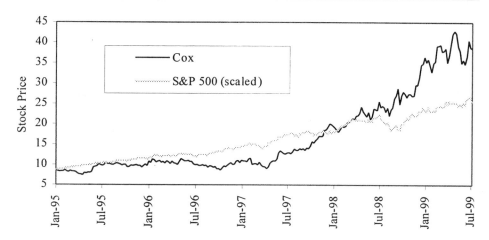

Note: These prices are corrected for stock splits. The price of Cox Communication Common stock as of 8/9/99 was $34.6875.

Source: Datastream International.

EXHIBIT 5B

HISTORICAL VOLATILITY OF COX COMMUNICATIONS' COMMON STOCK, JUNE 1995–JULY 1999

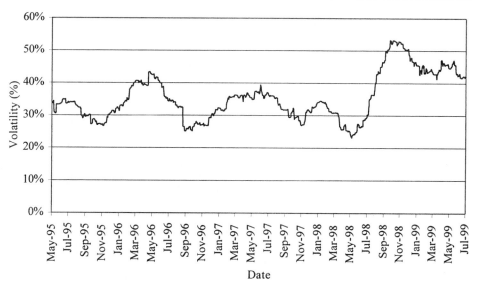

Note: The historical volatility is measured by the annualized standard deviation of the log of daily stock price returns over the previous 90 days. The historical volatility as of 8/9/99 was 42%. Implied volatilities on options on Cox Communications were about 47% as of 8/9/99.

Source: Bloomberg Financial Markets.

EXHIBIT 6

YIELDS FOR GOVERNMENT AND CORPORATE BONDS FOR JULY 15, 1999

	1 Year	2 Year	3 Year	5 Year	10 Year
Treasury bonds	5.38	5.64	5.70	5.83	5.83
U.S. Treasury strips	5.38	5.66	5.71	5.88	6.16
A-rated industrial bonds	5.99	6.33	6.44	6.70	6.93
BBB-rated industrial bonds	6.30	6.62	6.81	7.05	7.37
BB-rated industrial bonds	6.84	7.51	7.71	8.00	8.80

Note: All yields quoted on a semi-annual basis.

Source: Bloomberg.

rently, Cox was targeting a Debt/EBITDA ratio of no greater than 5 going forward, the maximum that senior management felt would retain an investment-grade rating. Externally, the debt markets for companies rated investment grade seemed larger and more stable than for noninvestment grade firms.[6] Noninvestment grade firms could find it difficult to obtain access to credit at times, as had happened in the late 1980s when Drexel, Burnham, Lambert, the premier underwriter of noninvestment grade debt went out of business, and more recently during the Asian currency and Russian debt crises in 1998. Additionally, sub-investment grade debt cost more, as indicated by the BBB-to-BB yield spread versus the BBB-to-A spread. Such circumstances could severely limit future flexibility.

In addition to the risk that credit spreads might widen in the fall, Clement had to consider the fact that the 30-year Treasury yield had increased more than half a percent over the past six months. (See Exhibit 6 for current interest rates.)

The direct and indirect costs of a debt issuance would be less than that for issuing equity. Clement anticipated that the transaction costs would be less than 2%. Academic studies estimated the market impact of issuing debt (on Cox's stock price) to be around 1%–2%.[7]

Hybrid Security Issuance

Another possibility was to issue hybrid securities, which had characteristics of both debt and equity. The most common examples of this class are preferred stock or convertible bonds.[8] A more recent innovation in the hybrid market were "mandatory convertible" structures and "trust preferred" products, that sought to combine the best features of

[6] An investment-grade rating was one of the four top ratings awarded by the national debt rating agencies.

[7] See Grinblatt, Mark and S. Titman, "Financial Markets and Corporate Strategy," Irwin/McGraw-Hill, 1998, pp. 15–16 and the references therein for more information regarding the direct and indirect costs of issuing debt.

[8] A preferred stock pays a fixed dividend and has seniority between that of common equity and junior debt. Failure to pay dividends on preferred stock does not trigger bankruptcy, but sometimes leads to actions such as giving the preferred shareholders seats on the firm's board. A convertible bond is debt where the investor has the right to use the debt to purchase equity at a fixed price. In contrast, in mandatory convertible securities, the investor has the obligation to purchase equity in the future, although the price may not be set in advance.

both debt and equity. Many investment banks offered these products, but one particular variety that had recently been proposed to Clement was an equity-linked hybrid product developed by Merrill Lynch called FELINE Income PRIDES.[9]

This security had elements of both debt and equity. Each Income PRIDES was a unit consisting of (i) an obligation by the investor to purchase a fixed dollar amount of Cox's Class A Common Stock in three years, and (ii) preferred equity. Payments made by Cox to the preferred equity component of the Income PRIDES would be essentially deductible for tax purposes, but the security was treated like equity for financial reporting purposes due to the obligation of the holder to purchase equity in the future.

The legal structure that delivered this treatment was somewhat complicated.[10] Essentially, Cox would establish a legal entity (a Trust) that would issue preferred equity and common equity. Cox would purchase all the common equity and exercise full control of the Trust. The preferred equity of the Trust was bundled together with the purchase obligation described above and sold to investors as Income PRIDES.[11] For example, an investor would pay $50 for an Income PRIDES unit and receive a 7% preferred dividend yield for three years, on a principal amount of $50. At the end of three years, the investor could satisfy the purchase obligation detailed above (to purchase the Class A Common Stock) by (a) exchanging the preferred equity for shares or (b) exchanging cash for shares. In either case, the number of shares Cox delivered to the Income PRIDES holder for this $50 varied depending on the market value of Cox's common shares at maturity. Generally, the higher the stock price in three years, the smaller the number of shares that the Income PRIDES holder would receive. (See Exhibit 7.)

After issuing the preferred equity, the Trust would use the proceeds to purchase new Cox debt. The 7% interest on this debt matched the payment terms of the preferred equity, so the Trust effectively served to pass through payments from Cox to the holders of the preferred equity. In effect, therefore, Cox would sell its debt to the Trust, which in turn would sell its preferred equity to investors. Cox would own the residual portion of the Trust through the Trust's common equity.

The financial reporting advantage of this structure to Cox was that its debt would not appear on the balance sheet as debt. Because Cox owned the Trust, Cox would have effectively issued debt to itself, which cancelled out when the two balance sheets were rolled up. Instead all that would appear on Cox's financial statements would be a line item for "Minority Shareholder Interest" reflecting the preferred equity issuance. This account would appear between debt and shareholders' equity on the balance sheet. For tax purposes, however, Cox would be able to deduct the interest payments it made on the debt issued to the Trust. Thus, for financial reporting purposes the FELINE Income PRIDES would appear to be equity, but for tax purposes the payments on the back-to-back debt would be treated like ordinary interest payments. Furthermore, ratings agencies would give equity credit to the debt due to the contractual obligation of

---

[9] The description provided in this section of the FELINE PRIDES product issued by Cox and its associated structure has been greatly simplified, and at times deviates from the actual product, for pedagogical reasons. As with most hybrid products, there was a great deal of detail, critical to the accounting and tax treatment of the transaction, which this thumbnail description does not capture.

[10] This trust structure had been introduced first in an earlier set of products in the early to mid-1990s. These products went by many banks' acronym-labeled servicemarks such as MIPS, QUIPS and TOPrS.

[11] Simultaneously with the issuance of the Income PRIDES, Cox issued FELINE Growth PRIDES and Capital Securities independent of the Income Prides. Growth PRIDES are similar to Income PRIDES except that instead of bundling the purchase obligation with a Capital Security, the purchase obligation is bundled with U.S. Treasury zero-coupon securities of the same maturity. There were also a few other contractual differences between Growth and Income PRIDES in terms of obligations/options retained by Cox and the holders of these securities.

EXHIBIT 7

FELINE PRIDES STRUCTURE: INCOME PRIDES

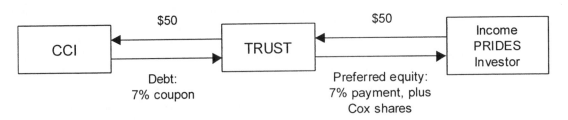

Under the Income PRIDES structure, the holders would receive a 7% cash payment for three years. At the end of the three years they were required to purchase a certain number of Cox's shares in exchange, at their option, for cash or their preferred equity in the Trust. The number of shares would be determined by Cox's share price in three years (S), as shown in the first column. The second column shows the number of shares delivered to the holder of a Feline PRIDE in three years and the third column shows the value of the shares delivered in three years.

Simultaneous with the Income PRIDES offering, the Trust would buy the debt that Cox issued. The Cox debt would pay a 7% coupon per year.

Cox Share Price in 3 years	Number of Cox Shares Delivered	Value of Cox Shares Delivered
$S \leq \$34.6875$	1.4414	$1.4414 \degree S$
$\$34.6875 < S < \$41.7984$	50/S	$50
$S \geq \$41.7984$	1.1962	$1.1962 \degree S$

Source: Cox Communications, Inc.

investors in FELINE Income PRIDES to purchase Cox common stock in the future. Thus, the FELINE Income PRIDES allowed Cox to simultaneously issue debt and receive the tax benefits of deducting the interest payments, while receiving equity credit from ratings agencies and for accounting purposes.

Asset Sales

Cox could also sell, swap or monetize some of the firm's non-strategic equity investments, as was anticipated with the AT&T transaction. For example, Cox held equity in Sprint PCS worth approximately $4.1 billion. Similarly, Cox held substantial equity investments in Discovery Communications ($2.5 billion), @Home ($1.5 billion), and Flextech ($300 million), along with smaller stakes in other firms. Simply selling these investments into the public markets would have meant a considerable tax burden for Cox.[12] Monetizing, or obtaining equivalent cash to, some of the non-strategic investments in a tax-efficient manner was an ongoing effort within the Cox Treasury.

Clement could sell some of these equity investments directly into the public market and use the proceeds to pay for some or all of the Gannett properties. One disad-

---

[12] Cox faced a marginal tax rate of 35% on its gain on the sale of assets. The gain is the difference between the sale price of the assets and Cox's "tax basis," roughly the amount it had paid to acquire the assets less accumulated depreciation. The respective taxable bases were $0, $34 million, $7 million, and $48 million. Cox's shares in AT&T had a tax basis of zero.

vantage of an outright sale was that Cox would have to pay taxes on the capital gains. Tax efficient disposals of these appreciated assets were also possible, such as in the AT&T transaction, where Cox had effectively swapped its AT&T shares for shares in AT&T subsidiaries that owned cable assets without triggering a taxable event. Through other types of monetizations, Cox might be able to receive the cash equivalent in value in these assets, yet defer the capital gains taxes from any sale for a number of years.[13] There were a number of practical limitations, however. The Sprint PCS investment could not be sold or hedged until November. Additionally, the stakes in Sprint, @Home, and Flextech were large relative to average daily trading volumes in those stocks. Hence, actually trading these positions would be difficult.

Market Conditions

Apart from the policy issues surrounding the firm's capital structure choices, there were substantial execution concerns as well. As mentioned above, the team was worried that an IPO by its rival might make it harder for Cox to issue equity. More generally, there was considerable anxiety about the outlook for the markets in the fall. In the fall of 1998, the capital markets had almost melted down when Russia defaulted on part of its debt. The Dow Jones Industrial Average, a barometer equity market index, fell more than 10% in the following two weeks. Credit spreads (the difference between a corporate bond yield and an equivalent-maturity Treasury yield) roughly doubled over the next five months. For A-rated borrowers, spreads rose from 56 basis points to a high of 135 basis points, while for BBB-rated issuers, spreads increased from 95 basis points to 181 basis points.[14]

This had led to a dearth of debt issues in late 1998. While the markets recovered somewhat in the first part of 1999, more recent weakness in the bond markets had already led to the cancellation of some previously announced deals. For example, on May 21, Great Lakes Power Inc., a Canadian utility rated Baa3/BBB-, had postponed a $200 million 10-year issue, and further postponements of more than $1 billion of issuance had followed. Hardest hit were noninvestment grade issuers, and Internet and telecommunications companies.

The other major concern for the fall was the potential impact of Year 2000 issues. Many feared that computer systems that used two digits for tracking years would malfunction when the year 2000 began. While the risks for catastrophe seemed exaggerated, there was a real possibility that the markets would be inhospitable to new issues until some of the risks had been resolved.

THE RECOMMENDATION

Regardless of whether Cox completed the acquisition of Gannett's cable operations, the other acquisitions of 1999 would materially change Cox's balance sheet. Any action Clement took would have to take into account ownership dilution on the one hand and the reaction of ratings agencies on the other. Additionally, Clement's team needed to evaluate the appropriate long-term financial policy for Cox and the specific financing of the potential Gannett acquisition and the other acquisitions Cox had recently announced in the context of this policy. Exhibit 8 shows various pro forma financial statements under different financing policies, with and without the Gannett purchase.

---

[13] See the case "Times Mirror Company PEPS Proposal Review" (Harvard Business School Case No. 296-089), written by Peter Tufano and Cameron Poetzscher, for more on the issue of equity monetizations.
[14] Source: Bloomberg.

PRO FORMA CASH FLOWS[a] FOR COX COMMUNICATIONS IF IT DID NOT PURCHASE GANNETT, BUT IF OTHER PROPOSED ACQUISITIONS WERE UNDERTAKEN (FIGURES ARE IN MILLIONS OF DOLLARS)

	1999 E	2000 E	2001 E	2002 E	2003 E
OPERATING ACTIVITIES					
EBITDA Cox + Acquisitions	878	1,344	1,490	1,697	1,913
EBITDA Gannett	0	0	0	0	0
Interest Expense	(312)	(540)	(443)	(472)	(432)
TOTAL CASH FROM OPERATIONS[b]	566	804	1,047	1,225	1,481
INVESTING ACTIVITIES					
Acquisitions[c]	(2,673)	0	0	0	0
Gannett Acquisition	0	0	0	0	0
CapEx	(983)	(1,304)	(1,078)	(822)	(734)
Total Other	(122)	48	34	10	10
TOTAL CASH FROM INVESTMENTS	(3,778)	(1,256)	(1,044)	(812)	(724)
FINANCING ACTIVITIES					
Equity Issued	0	0	0	0	0
Monetization[d]	1,243	1,500	0	0	0
Beginning Debt	4,091	6,249	5,202	5,198	4,786
Maturing Debt		(431)	(341)	(200)	(277)
New Debt Financed (Retired)[e]	1,968	(617)	337	(212)	(480)
Ending Total Debt	6,249	5,202	5,198	4,786	4,029
TOTAL CASH FROM FINANCING	3,401	452	(4)	(412)	(757)
CONDENSED INCOME STATEMENT					
EBITDA	878	1,344	1,490	1,697	1,913
Depreciation	(197)	(261)	(216)	(164)	(147)
Interest	(312)	(540)	(443)	(472)	(432)
Taxes	(85)	30	10	10	10
Net Income	285	573	842	1,070	1,344
DEBT RATIOS					
Pro Forma Annualized EBITDA[f]	1,201	1,344	1,490	1,697	1,913
Leverage Ratio[g]	5.2 x	3.9 x	3.5 x	2.8 x	2.1 x
EQUITY INTEREST					
Cox Family Economic Equity[h]	67.3%	67.3%	67.3%	67.3%	67.3%
Cox Family Voting Equity[i]	76.8%	76.8%	76.8%	76.8%	76.8%

[a]Assumes that planned monetizations of $500 million in 1999Q3 and $1.5 billion in 2000Q1 are implemented.

[b]As a result of significant accumulated tax losses to carry forward, Cox did not anticipate paying any cash taxes for the years shown here.

[c]This figure included $2.023 billion for cash portion of TCA merger, $1.4 billion for Media General acquisition, less $750 million in cash and other assets Cox was supposed to receive as part of the AT&T transaction.

[d]Monetization included $743 million raised in the first quarter, and $500 million scheduled for the third quarter of 1999. Both of these transactions were independent of the Gannett transaction. Cox also planned to raise $1.5 billion in 2000Q1 by monetizing a portion of the Sprint PCS position.

[e]Debt was treated as a plug, or balancing figure in this pro forma.

[f]Pro forma Annualized EBITDA is 4 x the Quarterly EBITDA results.

[g]Leverage ratio defined as the Ending Total Debt divided by the Pro Forma Annualized EBITDA.

[h]Economic equity was the percentage of the firm owned by the Cox family. Were the firm to be sold, they would receive this percentage of the proceeds. Calculation assumes maximum dilution from FELINE PRIDE conversion.

[i]Voting equity was the percentage of the firm controlled by the Cox family. They cast this percentage of the votes in any question that came before the shareholders.

Source: Cox Communications, Inc.

EXHIBIT 8B

PRO FORMA CASH FLOWS FOR COX COMMUNICATIONS IF IT PURCHASES GANNETT BY ISSUING DEBT (FIGURES ARE IN MILLIONS OF DOLLARS)

	1999 E	2000 E	2001 E	2002 E	2003 E
OPERATING ACTIVITIES					
EBITDA Cox + Acquisitions	878	1,344	1,490	1,697	1,913
EBITDA Gannett	0	151	163	176	190
Interest Expense	(312)	(540)	(657)	(667)	(640)
TOTAL CASH FROM OPERATIONS	566	955	996	1,207	1,463
INVESTING ACTIVITIES					
Acquisitions	(2,673)	0	0	0	0
Gannett Acquisition	0	(2,700)	0	0	0
CapEx	(983)	(1,334)	(1,103)	(847)	(759)
Total Other	(122)	48	34	10	10
TOTAL CASH FROM INVESTMENTS	(3,778)	(3,986)	(1,069)	(837)	(749)
FINANCING ACTIVITIES					
Equity Issued	0	0	0	0	0
Monetization	1,243	1,500	0	0	0
Beginning Debt	4,091	6,249	7,781	7,854	7,484
Maturing Debt		(431)	(341)	(200)	(277)
New Debt Financed (Retired)	1,968	1,962	414	(169)	(437)
Ending Total Debt	6,249	7,781	7,854	7,484	6,770
TOTAL CASH FROM FINANCING	3,401	3,031	73	(369)	(714)
CONDENSED INCOME STATEMENT					
EBITDA	878	1,495	1,653	1,873	2,103
Depreciation	(197)	(267)	(221)	(169)	(152)
Interest	(312)	(540)	(657)	(667)	(640)
Taxes	(85)	30	10	10	10
Net Income	285	718	785	1,047	1,322
DEBT RATIOS					
Pro Forma Annualized EBITDA	1,201	1,495	1,653	1,873	2,103
Leverage Ratio	5.2 x	5.2 x	4.8 x	4.0 x	3.2 x
EQUITY INTEREST					
Cox Family Economic Equity	67.3%	67.3%	67.3%	67.3%	67.3%
Cox Family Voting Equity	76.8%	76.8%	76.8%	76.8%	76.8%

Source: Cox Communications, Inc.

EXHIBIT 8C

PRO FORMA CASH FLOWS FOR COX COMMUNICATIONS IF IT PURCHASES GANNETT BY ISSUING EQUITY (FIGURES ARE IN MILLIONS OF DOLLARS)

	1999 E	2000 E	2001 E	2002 E	2003 E
OPERATING ACTIVITIES					
EBITDA Cox + Acquisitions	878	1,344	1,490	1,697	1,913
EBITDA Gannett	0	151	163	176	190
Interest Expense	(258)	(310)	(413)	(420)	(377)
TOTAL CASH FROM OPERATIONS	620	1,185	1,240	1,453	1,726
INVESTING ACTIVITIES					
Acquisitions	(2,673)	0	0	0	0
Gannett Acquisition	0	(2,700)	0	0	0
CapEx	(983)	(1,334)	(1,103)	(847)	(759)
Total Other	(122)	48	34	10	10
TOTAL CASH FROM INVESTMENTS	(3,778)	(3,986)	(1,069)	(837)	(749)
FINANCING ACTIVITIES					
Equity Issued	2,700	0	0	0	0
Monetization	1,243	1,500	0	0	0
Beginning Debt	4,091	3,495	4,797	4,625	4,010
Maturing Debt		(431)	(341)	(200)	(277)
New Debt Financed (Retired)	(785)	1,732	170	(415)	(700)
Ending Total Debt	3,495	4,797	4,625	4,010	3,033
TOTAL CASH FROM FINANCING	3,348	2,801	(171)	(615)	(977)
CONDENSED INCOME STATEMENT					
EBITDA	878	1,495	1,653	1,873	2,103
Depreciation	(197)	(267)	(221)	(169)	(152)
Interest	(258)	(310)	(413)	(420)	(377)
Taxes	(85)	30	10	10	10
Net Income	339	948	1,029	1,293	1,584
DEBT RATIOS					
Pro Forma Annualized EBITDA	1,201	1,495	1,653	1,873	2,103
Leverage Ratio	2.9 x	3.2 x	2.8 x	2.1 x	1.4 x
EQUITY INTEREST					
Cox Family Economic Equity	59.0%	59.0%	59.0%	59.0%	59.0%
Cox Family Voting Equity	69.9%	69.9%	69.9%	69.9%	69.9%

Source: Cox Communications, Inc.

EXHIBIT 8D

PRO FORMA CASH FLOWS FOR COX COMMUNICATIONS IF IT PURCHASED GANNETT WITH A COMBINATION OF DEBT, EQUITY ($680 MILLION) AND PRIDES ($720 MILLION) (FIGURES ARE IN MILLIONS OF DOLLARS)

	1999 E	2000 E	2001 E	2002 E	2003 E
OPERATING ACTIVITIES					
EBITDA Cox + Acquisitions	878	1,344	1,490	1,697	1,913
EBITDA Gannett	0	151	163	176	190
Interest Expense	(310)	(473)	(580)	(591)	(521)
TOTAL CASH FROM OPERATIONS	568	1,022	1,074	1,283	1,582
INVESTING ACTIVITIES					
Acquisitions	(2,673)	0	0	0	0
Gannett Acquisition	0	(2,700)	0	0	0
CapEx	(983)	(1,334)	(1,103)	(847)	(759)
Total Other	(122)	48	34	10	10
TOTAL CASH FROM INVESTMENTS	(3,778)	(3,986)	(1,069)	(837)	(749)
FINANCING ACTIVITIES					
Equity Issued	1,400	0	0	0	0
Monetization	1,243	1,500	0	0	0
Beginning Debt	4,091	4,847	6,311	6,306	5,861
Maturing Debt		(431)	(341)	(200)	(277)
New Debt Financed (Retired)	566	1,895	336	(245)	(556)
Ending Total Debt	4,847	6,311	6,306	5,861	5,028
TOTAL CASH FROM FINANCING	3,399	2,964	(5)	(445)	(833)
CONDENSED INCOME STATEMENT					
EBITDA	878	1,495	1,653	1,873	2,103
Depreciation	(197)	(267)	(221)	(169)	(152)
Interest	(310)	(473)	(580)	(591)	(521)
Taxes	(85)	30	10	10	10
Net Income	287	786	863	1,123	1,440
DEBT RATIOS					
Pro Forma Annualized EBITDA	1,201	1,495	1,653	1,873	2,103
Leverage Ratio	4.0 x	4.2 x	3.8 x	3.1 x	2.4 x
EQUITY INTEREST					
Cox Family Economic Equity	65.1%	65.1%	65.1%	63.0%	63.0%
Cox Family Voting Equity	75.0%	75.0%	75.0%	73.3%	73.3%

Source: Cox Communications, Inc.

23

DigaMem Inc.

At the end of the day on January 15, 1998, Brad Simpson, the president and CEO of DigaMem Inc., sat in his office at the corporate headquarters in San Jose, California. On his mind was the $27.3 million his company needed to continue its research and production. On his desk was a pile of messages, the returned calls and e-mails from various bankers and large-scale investors. The collective message of the stack had a grim theme and had confirmed Simpson's suspicion: DigaMem was, once again, in a financial crisis. Fortunately, Simpson had seen DigaMem through hard times before. With the future of the company's semiconductors looking brighter than ever, he felt confident that this situation was only another bump on the road to stable profitability. Factories overseas were preparing to produce millions of DigaMem's chips to serve as memory components for devices ranging from air-bag controllers to Smart Cards. Companies were quickly developing new products to take advantage of DigaMem's promising technology. On the other hand, the company's loans were approaching maturity, and market conditions for new financing were worsening. Traditional sources of funding for the company were drying up. The company needed an influx of capital fast and, in this extreme environment, it would have to bend to meet investors' terms.

THE SEMICONDUCTOR INDUSTRY[1]

Types of Chips

Semiconductor chips were electronic components made of materials that shared insulating and conductive electrical properties. These chips could be split into two major categories: *analog* and *digital*. Analog semiconductor chips processed signals of light, heat, and other natural forms. They were used in applications such as amplifying voltage, regulating voltage, transferring signals, and converting signals from analog to

---

Professor George Chacko, Research Associates Eli Strick and Andrew Kuhlman, and Chris Smith, MBA '01, prepared this case. Certain details have been disguised. HBS cases are developed solely as the basis for class discussion. Cases are not intended to serve as endorsements, sources of primary data, or illustrations of effective or ineffective management.

[1] The primary source for this section was Stephen Madonna, "Semiconductors," Standard & Poor's Industry Surveys, July 31, 1997.

digital. Digital semiconductor chips processed information in binary form, as a series of zeros and ones. The digital semiconductor chip industry was divided into three segments: *microprocessors*, *memory chips*, and *logic chips*. (Exhibit 1 shows each group of semiconductors' proportion of the world's market [as a percentage of 1996 sales].)

Microprocessors

These semiconductor chips, including the popular Pentium chip series produced by Intel, were used as the central processing units (CPUs) for computers. However, these chips were also used as the "brains" for many other electronic devices such as clock radios and car fuel-injection systems. The role of these chips was twofold: to execute instructions/commands from memory sources and to perform calculations and logical operations. Microprocessors differed from one another mostly in their "bandwidth" and "clock speed." Bandwidth described the amount of information, measured in "bits," that could be transferred in a single instruction. Clock speed referred to the number of instructions a processor could execute per second and was usually measured in megahertz (MHz). Greater bandwidth and greater clock speed both increased the power of a microprocessor.

Memory Chips

These chips were used to store information and instructions. Different types of memory, including dynamic random access memory (DRAM), static random access memory (SRAM), and flash/read only memory (ROM), had different advantages and disadvantages. Some chips had "volatile" memory, which required power to store data, while other chips had "nonvolatile" memory and were able to retain stored data when their source of power was interrupted. Memory chips also differed in their ability to transfer data (the speed at which they could be "read" and "written" to) and their capacity for storing data or their amount of memory (usually measured in megabytes: 16, 64, 256 MB, etc.). The amount of memory available in a computer controlled the amount of programs it could run simultaneously and the amount of data a program could readily use.

EXHIBIT 1

PERCENTAGE OF 1996 WORLD SALES BY TYPE OF SEMICONDUCTOR

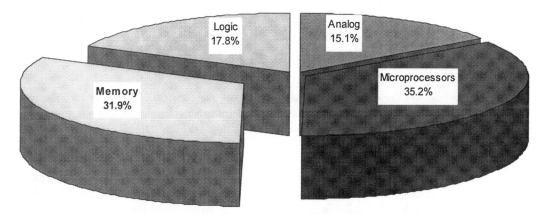

Source: Data adapted from Stephen Madonna, "Semiconductors," Standard & Poor's Industry Surveys, July 31, 1997.

Logic Chips

Logic devices were used for managing the interchanging of signals within a digital system. They were programmed to perform a series of complex functions based upon "logical" values and conditions. Some of these chips were made for custom applications, while others were standard and used for more common applications. The variety of logic chips used by product designers was large relative to their microprocessor and memory needs.

Industry Characteristics

Product Design and Customer Relations

Semiconductors were sold to a wide range of original equipment manufacturers (OEMs) for use in the production of a variety of electronic devices. When an OEM selected a company's chip to use in the design of a new product, it was called a "design win." This achievement gave the chip manufacturer an advantage in getting its chip used if the final product reached mass production. The close relationship between chip companies and OEMs allowed for product designs to quickly incorporate technological advances in semiconductor research. Consequently, semiconductor companies strived to design chips that would allow OEMs to make smaller, faster, more powerful, and sometimes cheaper electronic products.

Capital vs. Competition

While the capital intensity (physical capital and intellectual capital) of the industry caused large obstacles for those looking to enter the market, the industry was highly competitive for its participants. In an effort to become less capital intensive and to focus on their core competencies (research and development), some semiconductor companies had chosen to outsource their chip manufacturing to contractors. The rapid rate of technological change in the semiconductor chip industry added to the competition. Since chip prices decreased soon after they had been introduced to the market, even successful chip designers and manufacturers had to continue to hustle and develop the next profitable innovation. Furthermore, competition stemmed from the global nature of the industry. Many companies had foreign counterparts and had to compete for foreign business. (Exhibit 2a shows the percentage of total semiconductor consumption [as a percentage of sales] by geographic region for 1996, and Exhibit 2b shows geographic market share for total semiconductor sales.)

Cyclicity and Growth

While semiconductors had a wide variety of uses, over half of the industry's revenues had come from computing applications in 1996. Since the production of personal computers (PCs) used multiple types of semiconductor chips, strong PC demand contributed to a strong semiconductor chip industry across its segments. Furthermore, since investment in new computers and other "nonessential" end products that used these chips decreased during times of economic turmoil, the semiconductor market had exhibited high correlation with the overall economy. (Exhibit 3 compares real gross domestic product growth with total semiconductor sales growth.) According to world semiconductor trade statistics, industry revenues were supposed to increase 20% in 1998, 1999, and 2000, with worldwide industry revenues forecasted at $245.7 billion in 2000.

EXHIBIT 2A

PERCENTAGE OF TOTAL 1996 SEMICONDUCTOR CONSUMPTION BY REGION

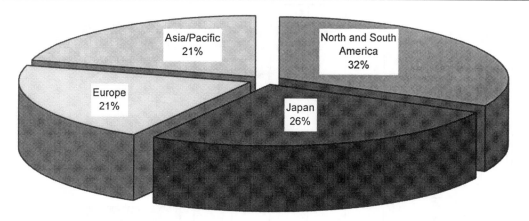

Source: Data adapted from Stephen Madonna, "Semiconductors," Standard & Poor's Industry Surveys, July 31, 1997.

BUSINESS DESCRIPTION

DigaMem Inc.

DigaMem Inc. was founded as a research and development (R&D) company to develop technology for use in semiconductor memory chips. Like other memory chip companies, DigaMem's technology was designed to store data for electrical devices such as cell phones and computers and enable them to do everything from retrieve a phone number to back up an encyclopedia. However, at the time DigaMem was founded, the two best-selling types of semiconductor memory chips had limitations to their usage. Random access memory (RAM) was fast and efficient at storing and retrieving data but lost its information when the power went out and therefore required constant battery backup. Read only memory (ROM) retained its information when the power went out but was much slower than RAM at storing and retrieving data and eventually wore out and could not be used again. DigaMem planned to create high-performance memory semiconductors using chromatic crystals for the memory storage capacitor. The chromatic crystals were fast and efficient at storing and retrieving data, retained information even when the power was lost, and could be used indefinitely. They essentially combined the best features of RAM and ROM to create an ideal memory device. This device was called crystal random access memory, or CRAM, and it was heralded in the industry as a major leap forward in computing. At the end of 1997 CRAM products and licensing fees accounted for 50% of DigaMem's revenues. DigaMem's management expected revenues from CRAM to increase once the market became more comfortable with the technology and as more products were developed to take advantage of its applications. According to the company, revenue from CRAM was expected to grow at an annual rate of roughly 50% for the next five years. (See Exhibits 4a, 4b, and 4c for DigaMem's financial history. Exhibit 5 lists DigaMem's major stakeholders, and Exhibit 6 gives information on DigaMem's competitors in the semiconductor industry.)

EXHIBIT 2B

GEOGRAPHIC MARKET SHARE FOR THE WORLD SEMICONDUCTOR MARKET

World Semiconductor Market Share by Geographic Region

Legend: ▨ Americas ■ Japan ☐ Other

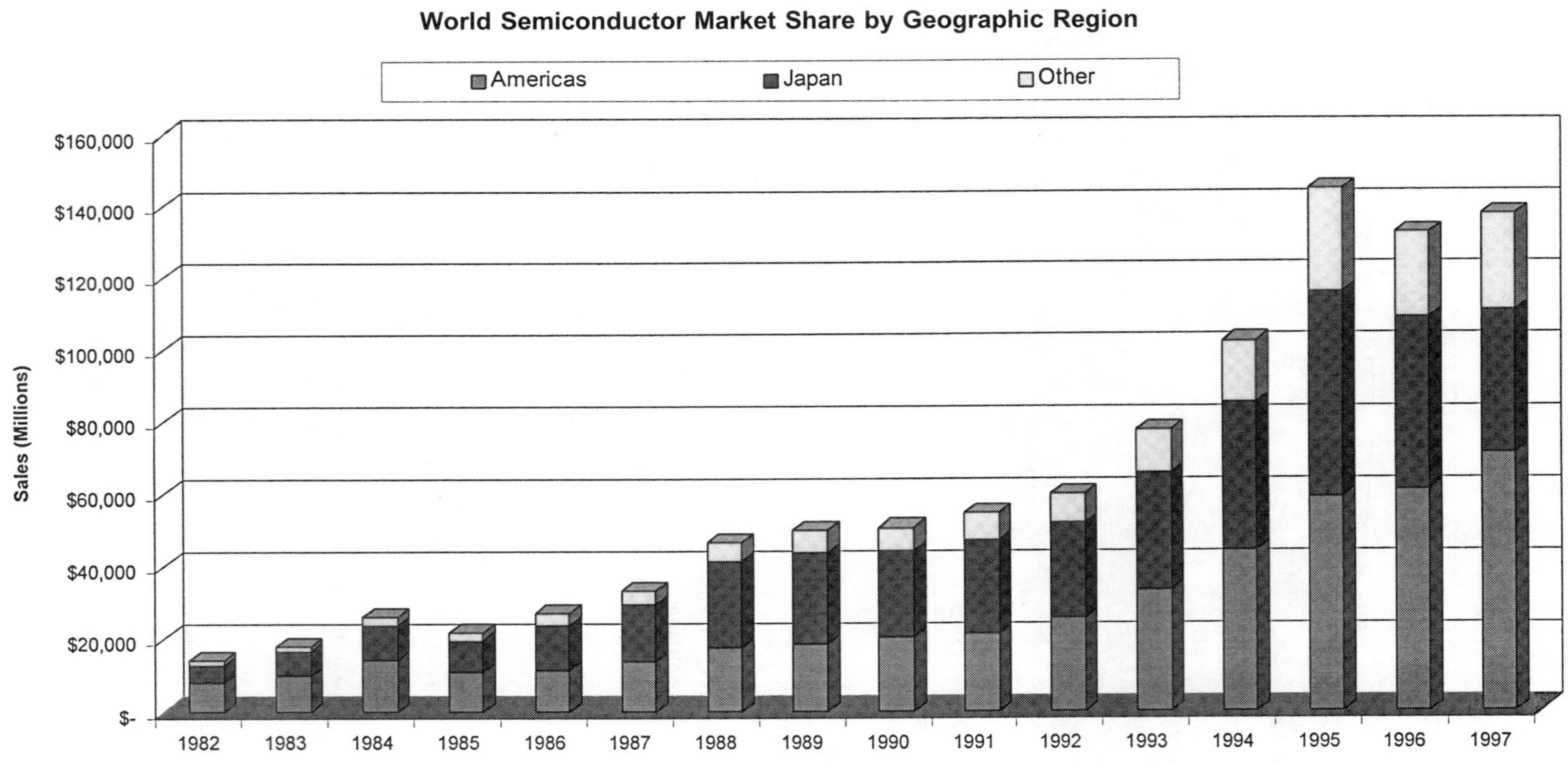

Source: Data adapted from "Industry Statistics," Semiconductor Industry Association Web page, ⟨http://www.sia-online.org/pre_statistics.cfm⟩, accessed March 21, 2002.

EXHIBIT 3

TOTAL SEMICONDUCTOR SALES GROWTH COMPARED WITH REAL GDP GROWTH

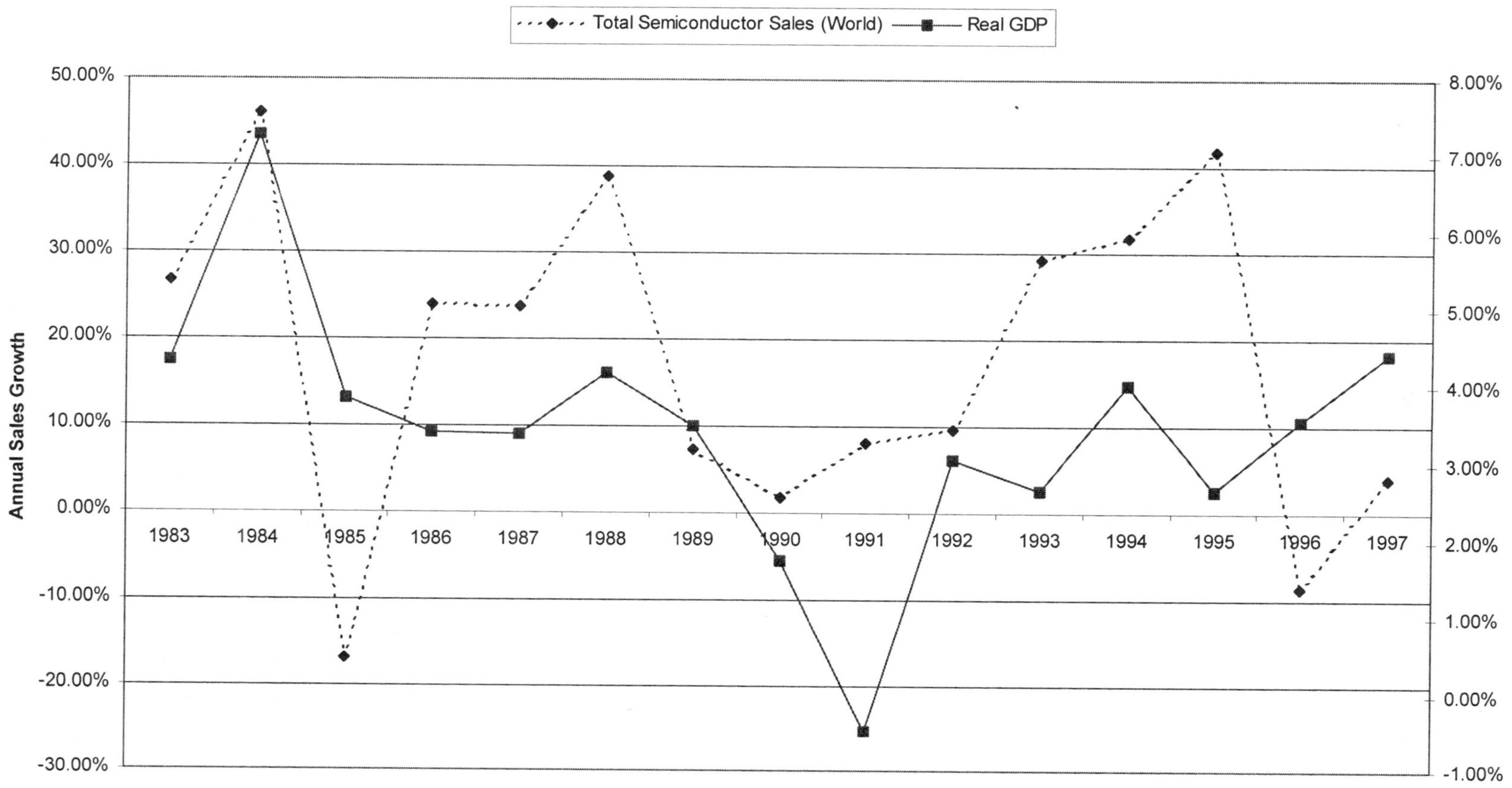

Source: Data adapted from "Industry Statistics," Semiconductor Industry Association Web page, ⟨http://www.sia-online.org/ pre_statistics.cfm⟩, accessed March 21, 2002; and "National Accounts Data," Bureau of Economic Analysis Web page, ⟨http:// www.bea.doc.gov/bea/dn1.htm⟩, accessed March 21, 2002.

EXHIBIT 4A

DIGAMEM'S CONDENSED FINANCIAL HISTORY

Annual Assets (000s)

Fiscal Year Ending December 31,	1997	1996	1995	1994	1993
Cash	$ 9,728	$ 4,998	$ 9,869	$ 284	$ 26,474
Receivables	7,480	10,697	4,082	5,663	3,723
Inventories	11,226	11,533	8,721	17,598	23,706
Other current assets	369	930	10,056	204	60
Total current assets	28,804	28,158	32,729	23,749	53,963
Prop., Plant, & Equip.	12,604	13,661	15,973	19,893	21,881
Intangibles	7,372	8,039	8,690	5,187	4,392
Deposits and other assets	NA	33	33	1,210	2,598
Total Assets	**$48,780**	**$49,892**	**$57,425**	**$ 50,038**	**$82,834**

Annual Liabilities (000s)

Fiscal Year Ending December 31,	1997	1996	1995	1994	1993
Accounts payable	$ 4,739	$ 3,129	$ 5,257	$ 9,627	$ 15,529
Accrued expenses	3,061	2,849	2,741	10,273	5,399
Other current liabs.	13,433	3,083	4,789	32,208	917
Total current liabs.	21,233	9,062	12,788	52,108	21,845
Other long-term liabs.	NA	5,845	6,211	NA	31,944
Total Liabilities	**$21,234**	**$14,907**	**$18,999**	**$ 52,108**	**$53,823**
Preferred stock	NA	NA	NA	52	52
Common stock, net	595	581	572	280	225
Capital surplus	244,977	238,494	232,933	188,778	188,563
Retained earnings	−218,027	−204,090	−195,079	−191,180	−159,829
Shareholder Equity	**27,545**	**34,985**	**38,426**	**−2,070**	**29,011**
Tot Liabs. & Net Worth	**$48,780**	**$49,892**	**$57,425**	**$ 50,038**	**$82,834**

Source: Casewriter.

Advanced Memory Products, Inc.

Advanced Memory Products, Inc. was founded as a separate corporate entity to deal exclusively with the sale and service of advanced dynamic random access memory (ADRAM). ADRAM was based on an advanced DRAM technology developed by DigaMem utilizing its foundry supplier, NMB Semiconductor (NMBS). It enabled conventional memory chips to work at enhanced speeds. At the end of 1997, ADRAM accounted for 50% of DigaMem's sales and, according to management, revenue from ADRAM was supposed to increase 20% annually.

DigaMem K.K.

DigaMem K.K. was established as a Japan-based subsidiary to establish a liaison with partners in a growing Japanese market. DigaMem K.K. established a number of re-

EXHIBIT 4B

DIGAMEM'S CONDENSED FINANCIAL HISTORY

Annual Income (000s)

Fiscal Year Ending December 31,	1997	1996	1995	1994	1993
Net sales	$ 32,193	$ 49,309	$ 45,374	$ 32,121	$ 10,941
Cost of goods	16,886	22,323	16,487	20,764	5,479
Gross profit	15,307	26,986	28,887	11,357	5,462
R&D expenditures	17,029	20,303	18,047	26,686	30,753
Sell. gen. & admin. exp.	12,617	14,901	13,719	13,792	12,174
Inc. before dep. & amort.	−14,338	−8,217	−2,879	−29,121	−37,465
Nonoperating inc.	1032	−297	2,091	1268	258
Interest expense	606	498	3,110	3,498	4,491
Income before tax	−13,913	−9,012	−3,899	−31,352	−41,698
Net inc. before exp. items	−13,913	−9,012	−3,899	−31,352	−41,698
Net Income	**$−13,913**	**$−9,012**	**$−3,899**	**$−31,352**	**$−41,698**
Outstanding Shares	**59,569**	**58,115**	**57,157**	**27,948**	**22,478**

Source: Casewriter.

EXHIBIT 4C

DIGAMEM'S CONDENSED FINANCIAL HISTORY

Cash Flow Provided by Operating Activity (000s)

Fiscal Year Ending December 31,	1997	1996	1995	1994	1993
Net income (loss)	$ −13,913	$ −9,012	$ −3,899	$ −31,352	$ −41,698
Depreciation/amortization	4,079	4,492	4,744	4,651	4,174
Net incr. (decr.) assets/liabs.	6,731	−1,665	−320	−1,071	−6,905
Other adjustments, net	NA	1,945	1,533	−851	1,242
Net Cash Prov. (Used) by Oper.	**$ −3,102**	**$ −4,240**	**$ 2,058**	**$ −28,623**	**$ −43,187**

Cash Flow Provided by Investing Activity (000s)

Fiscal Year Ending December 31,	1997	1996	1995	1994	1993
Incr. (decr.) in prop., plant	$ −2,366	$ 1,696	$ −861	$ −2,620	$ −4,466
Incr. (decr.) in securities inv.	NA	NA	−24	−123	−72
Other cash inflow (outflow)	8	302	2,945	1,308	53
Net Cash Prov. (Used) by Inv.	**$ −2,358**	**$ −1395**	**$ 2,061**	**$ −1434**	**$ −4,485**

Cash Flow Provided by Financing Activity (000s)

Fiscal Year Ending December 31,	1997	1996	1995	1994	1993
Issue (purchase) of equity	$ 6,498	$ 763	$ 1,937	$ 270	$ 41,002
Incr. (decr.) In borrowing	3,691	NA	3,530	3,597	31,334
Net cash prov. (used) by finan.	10,190	763	5,466	3,867	72,337
Net Change in Cash or Equiv.	**4,730**	**−4,871**	**9,585**	**−26,190**	**24,665**
Cash or equiv. at Year Start	4,998	9,869	284	26,474	1,810
Cash or Equiv. at Year End	**$ 9,728**	**$ 4,998**	**$ 9,869**	**$ 284**	**$ 26,474**

Source: Casewriter.

EXHIBIT 5

DIGAMEM STAKEHOLDERS AND PARTIES OF INTEREST AT MARCH 15, 1997

Name	Number of Shares (000s)	Total Ownership
Southern Labor Benefit Fund	12,534,661	30.3%
Brian Lewis (Debtor-in-Possession)	9,634,859	24.1%
ITR Associates, Inc.	6,162,342	16.7%
All current directors and executive and officers as a group (10 people)	700,298	1.9%

Source: Casewriter.

---

search and licensing agreements with Japanese corporations, including Hitachi and Toshiba. In addition, DigaMem shifted production of CRAM to facilities provided by Rohm, Inc. of Kyoto, Japan in order to increase efficiency and decrease costs.

COMPANY HISTORY

Chromatic crystal research began at San Jose State University. It took DigaMem, founded in 1984, eight years to firmly grasp the science behind this new technology, and as with all R&D companies, DigaMem required steady funding to sustain itself during this period of development sans revenue. For this capital, DigaMem turned in 1986 to an Australian firm, Ventech Capital. Ventech took a 55% interest in DigaMem with the intent of financing and managing its development in order to produce licensing agreements with large corporations. DigaMem unveiled its first memory prototype in 1988 and, within a year, the firm secured several potential multimillion dollar licensing and manufacturing contracts. In the late 1980s, the market for CRAM was forecast to reach $6.37 billion by 1995. Many technology companies were trying to develop similar technologies to get a piece of the marketplace.

Yet chromatic crystal technology proved much more difficult and expensive to develop than company officials had predicted. By the end of 1991 the company had spent over $50 million on research and accumulated losses of over $48 million. None of the joint venture deals had yielded any commercial production, and the company had yet to receive any commercial orders. DigaMem was burning cash at a rate of over $1 million per month, and transferring its technology from the laboratory to mass production would still require more time and millions in additional funding.

DigaMem had found two main investors to temporarily alleviate its cash flow problem. The first was Brian Lewis, a California investor who had made a fortune through oil drilling, refining, and financing. By 1992, Lewis had over $25 million invested in the company. Since the founding of the company he had provided financing through credit lines and equity investments, as well as arranging leasing assistance. DigaMem's other major U.S. shareholder was the Texas-based Southern Labor Benefit Fund (SLBF) pension plan. The SLBF had invested a total of $32.5 million in the company by 1992.

EXHIBIT 6

YEAR-END 1997 INFORMATION FOR DIGAMEM INC. AND OTHER COMPETITORS IN THE SEMICONDUCTOR AND RELATED DEVICES INDUSTRY (SIC 3674) (NUMBERS IN $ MILLIONS EXCEPT BETA AND ROE)

Company Name	Sales	R&D[a]	Net Income	Total Assets	Total Debt	Long-Term Debt	ROE[b]	Market Value	Beta[c]
ALLIANCE SEMICONDUCTOR CORP.	118.400	15.254	-5.737	248.265	2.739	1.276	-2.840	303.375	1.977
ATMEL CORP.	958.282	122.896	1.801	1,822.040	638.911	571.389	0.229	1,851.060	2.137
CYPRESS SEMICONDUCTOR CORP.	539.856	93.842	18.419	956.270	175.000	175.000	2.862	759.478	0.859
INTEGRATED DEVICE TECH. INC.	587.136	121.449	8.247	968.955	208.422	203.325	1.509	1,144.200	1.422
MAXIM INTEGRATED PRODUCTS	433.710	51.264	136.974	556.386	0.000	0.000	29.421	3,624.590	1.572
MICRON TECHNOLOGY INC.	3,515.500	208.900	332.2	4,851.300	951.600	762.300	11.522	9,402.850	1.415
DIGAMEM INC.	32.193	17.029	-13.913	48.780	10.284	0.000	-50.508	331.325	-0.723
STMICROELECTRONICS N V	4,019.150	610.847	406.554	5,445.740	780.965	356.407	12.292	8,495.680	1.426
XICOR INC.	122.453	18.475	-2.531	115.261	25.511	18.974	-4.511	57.276	0.725

[a]R&D expense.
[b]Return on equity.
[c]Beta calculated using the S&P 500 for the market return.

Source: Data compiled from Compustat.

In 1992 DigaMem abandoned its Australian operations and consolidated in the U.S. market through a capital-restructuring plan. The U.S. market was more developed than the Australian market, and its investors were more knowledgeable about DigaMem's technology. This allowed DigaMem to raise more money to expand its development operations. In the same year the company began mass production of ADRAM at NMBS, a product that carried a high demand. Within a year DigaMem was receiving contracts in the millions of dollars, and ADRAM was providing the bulk of the company's revenue. Finally, Simpson, a technology industry veteran with a knack for managing fast-growing companies, was brought in to serve as president and chief operating officer (COO) for DigaMem.

Over the course of the next three years DigaMem continued to grow its market share in the memory industry through new licensing agreements. In addition, DigaMem continued to fund its growth through issuing $35 million of preferred stock. Lewis and SLBF remained proactive and further invested millions of dollars into the company through loans and convertible debt. In 1994 Lewis assumed the position above Simpson as chairman and CEO in order to focus more personal attention on the company's growth and development.

In August of 1994 DigaMem shifted its manufacturing operations to industry giant Hitachi of Japan through a licensing agreement in order to cut costs and increase efficiency. Production at these facilities was expected to begin the following year. In addition, DigaMem penned a $100 million purchase agreement to sell almost all of its current capacity of ADRAM to Hong Kong-based Ocean Office Automation Ltd. Finally, DigaMem established a separate corporate entity, Advanced Memory Products, Inc., to deal with the large orders of ADRAM it was receiving. Confident that DigaMem was back on track, Simpson felt it was time to move on to other endeavors and resigned his post as president and COO.

Simpson's resignation would not last long. In February of 1995, Lewis filed for bankruptcy and resigned as chairman and CEO of DigaMem. Lewis's share of the company was to be liquidated and distributed to his creditors. Millions of shares of DigaMem stock were placed in liquidating trusts and would eventually hit the market with the capability of driving the stock price downwards. News of the investor's financial difficulties sent DigaMem's stock plummeting. Lewis canceled a $22.7 million debt-to-equity conversion, and it was rumored that the financial pressure on DigaMem could cause the stock to be delisted from the NASDAQ. After the company's largest investor pulled out, DigaMem was left with only $181,000 in the bank. The company quickly secured a $3 million line of credit from the SLBF, yet this amount was insufficient to alleviate its financial problems and served only as a temporary fix. (Exhibit 7 shows the historic performance of DigaMem's common stock in comparison to the NASDAQ Index. Exhibits 8a, 8b, and 8c show volatility measurements [historical and implied] for DigaMem's stock and different indices.)

Simpson was brought back to the company as chairman and CEO to fill the management void. He said then:

> I am excited about the opportunity to finish the job I started in 1992. Among my top priorities at DigaMem will be to guide the company to profitability through our alliance program. The key to DigaMem's near-term success resides in our ability to lower product costs through our strategic foundry partnerships. Our relationships with Hitachi and Rohm continue to make excellent progress, and we expect to add new partners as chromatic crystal technology continues to gain momentum in the industry.

EXHIBIT 7

DIGAMEM'S HISTORICAL STOCK RETURNS

DigaMem's Company Stock Performance Compared with Market and Industry Performance

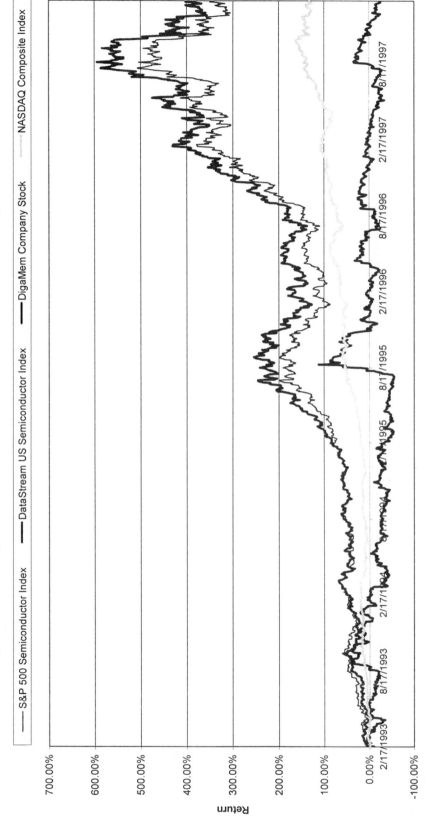

Source: Data compiled from DataStream.

393

DIGAMEM'S HISTORICAL STOCK RETURN VOLATILITY

DigaMem Daily Stock Return Volatility vs. NASDAQ (Measured Over a 6 Month Period)

Source: Data compiled from DataStream.

AVERAGE HISTORICAL IMPLIED VOLATILITIES FOR "AT-THE-MONEY" S&P 100 (CBOE VIX INDEX) AND NASDAQ 100 (CBOE VNX INDEX) PUT AND CALL OPTIONS WITH 30 DAYS TO MATURITY

Historical Values for Chicago Board Of Option Exchange's (CBOE) VIX and VNX Indices

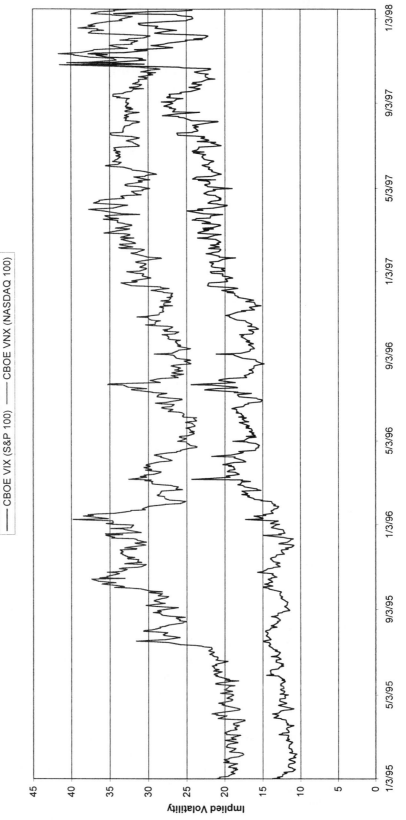

Source: Adapted from the Chicago Board of Options Exchange, (www.cboe.com/Mktdata/vix.asp).

EXHIBIT 8C

DIGAMEM'S ANNUALIZED HISTORICAL STOCK RETURN VOLATILITY

Period	Historical
1 Month	84.31%
3 Month	71.85%
6 Month	73.61%
9 Month	70.99%
1 Year	66.56%
2 Year	67.86%
3 Year	80.61%
4 Year	84.12%

Source: Casewriter.

Simpson made good on his promise by forming an ADRAM manufacturing agreement with IBM in May of 1995, showing the company's technology was still viable. At the same time DigaMem sold off its 50% stake in a design company to co-owner NMBS to raise working capital. With the support of IBM and a more focused business, DigaMem was able to leverage an agreement with Lewis's creditors and the SLBF (assisted by ITR Associates, a California investment firm). Through this deal the company would retire $24.3 million in debt through the issuance of approximately 7.9 million shares of common stock. This would place DigaMem's shareholder equity at a net positive $19 million. As part of this deal, the SLBF agreed to provide a $12 million credit facility for working capital secured by DigaMem's assets. This put DigaMem back on solid financial ground for the time being. In the middle of 1995, DigaMem licensed to Toshiba its CRAM technology, which provided additional funding to help support the company.

Simpson continued to produce for DigaMem. In 1996, the company signed a valuable licensing pact with Fujitsu and developed a new high-density CRAM chip through its research facilities at Hitachi. In addition, DigaMem K.K. was established that same year.

Yet despite DigaMem's research successes and aggressive expansion, the company could not turn a profit on its CRAM chips without its new manufacturing facilities being built by Rohm. Originally set to begin in 1995, production in these facilities had been delayed until 1997. During this time old technology and poor equipment had made for exorbitant in-house manufacturing costs that DigaMem had to bear. In addition, market demand for CRAM had remained low, as companies were just beginning to develop products that could take advantage of its advanced features. While DigaMem's advanced memory division was earning modest profits, the company's CRAM division continued to incur losses upwards of $9 million annually, with an accumulated net loss of over $100 million by the end of 1997. In addition, a $7 million loan from the SLBF was approaching its deadline, and DigaMem did not have the capital to repay it.

Simpson nevertheless remained optimistic about his company. For 14 years DigaMem had survived the ups and downs of technological, manufacturing, and financial crises as it attempted to create a profitable business. However, at this point, the heralded CRAM was finally in production, and it was only a matter of time before the industry caught up to the technology DigaMem was producing. "What's different today is we see a path," Simpson said. "Our new agreements with production facilities are a path to start making some money. . . . For the first time in our history, DigaMem will be able to sell its chip technology for more money than it costs to make it. . . . This is going to enable us to make a real business out of this product."

FINANCING DECISIONS

The technology that DigaMem had pioneered was looking promising and, with the help of Rohm and Fujitsu, management saw the opportunity to cut production costs and finally turn a profit. Simpson was confident that CRAM would be well received by the market based on overall industry feedback and a healthy backlog of orders. However, DigaMem needed approximately $27.3 million in order to help finance operations while it transferred its technology to its production partners. It was the common opinion of DigaMem's bankers and advisors that the company's best strategy for reaching investors would be through a private placement offering. Working within that framework, the firm could pursue financing in three basic ways: it could issue equity, it could borrow, or it could issue a preferred security. In addition, some bankers were recommending a more innovative method. (Exhibits 9a, 9b, and 9c show historical trends in new-security issuances in DigaMem's industry.)

Equity Issuance

Simpson felt unsure that he would be able to issue equity capital on acceptable terms. The firm's current financial situation made it difficult to attract additional equity investment. The firm had nearly $7 million in debt from a lender who refused to refinance the debt any longer, and the firm's existing large shareholders were unable to invest any further due to the bankruptcy. With nearly 9.2 million of the firm's 38 million shares at the time in a liquidating trust, any new investor would run the risk of a massive block of shares reaching the market at the same time. However, several large investors (primarily hedge funds) had offered to invest in the firm at a 30%-plus discount to the current market price. On January 15, 1998, DigaMem's common stock closed trading at a price of $8.15.

Debt Issuance

Simpson did not think DigaMem would be able to raise enough cash through a straight debt financing. Due to the recent Asian monetary crisis, firms that sold their products in Asia were finding it difficult to issue debt. The market was acting particularly shy toward semiconductor companies, and DigaMem's "exotic" technology and lack of profitability did not help its situation. Unfortunately, the firm's tangible assets were already being used as collateral for the original $7 million investment made to begin prototyping. Secured debt was ruled out without additional assets to use as collateral. (Exhibit 10 shows U.S. Treasury yields for different maturities. Exhibit 11 shows historical yields for 10-year corporate debt by credit rating. Exhibit 12a shows recent debt-security issuances in DigaMem's industry.) If investors for a DigaMem debt issuance could be found, Simpson expected the company to have to offer a yield upwards of 11% for a five-year offering.

NEW ISSUANCES IN DIGAMEM'S INDUSTRY (SIC 3572 AND 3674) BY TYPE OF FINANCING

Historic Fund Raising in DigaMem's Industry (SIC 3572 and 3674)

Source: Data compiled from SDC database.

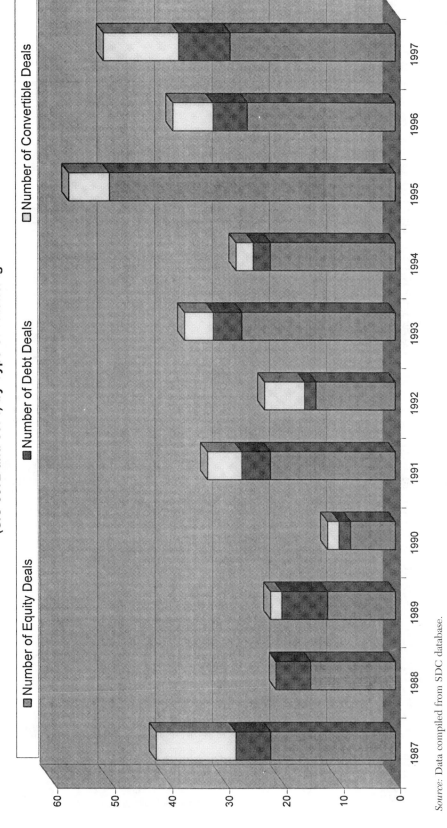

Number of Fund Raising Deals in DigaMem's Industry (SIC 3572 and 3674) by Type of Financing

Legend: Number of Equity Deals — Number of Debt Deals — Number of Convertible Deals

Source: Data compiled from SDC database.

DOLLAR VOLUME OF NEW ISSUANCES FOR THE COMPUTER STORAGE DEVICES INDUSTRY (SIC CODE 3572) AND SEMICONDUCTOR AND RELATED DEVICES INDUSTRY (SIC CODE 3674) BY YEAR

Dollar Volume of Deals for DigaMem's Industry

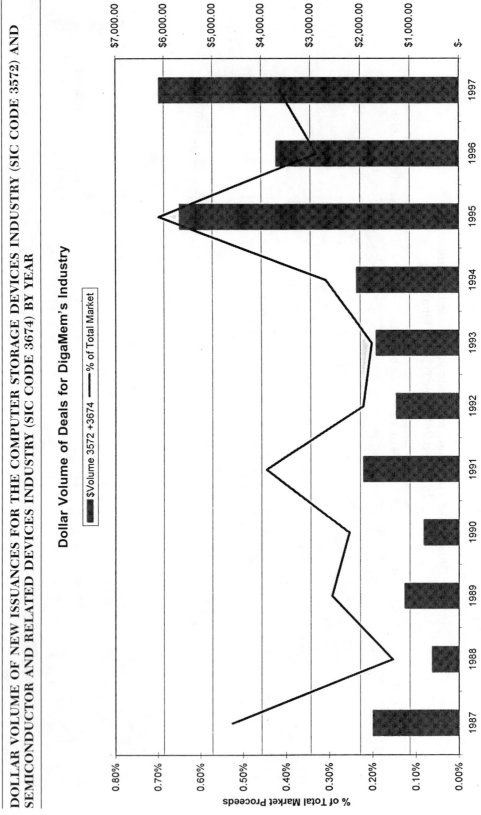

Source: Data compiled from SDC database.

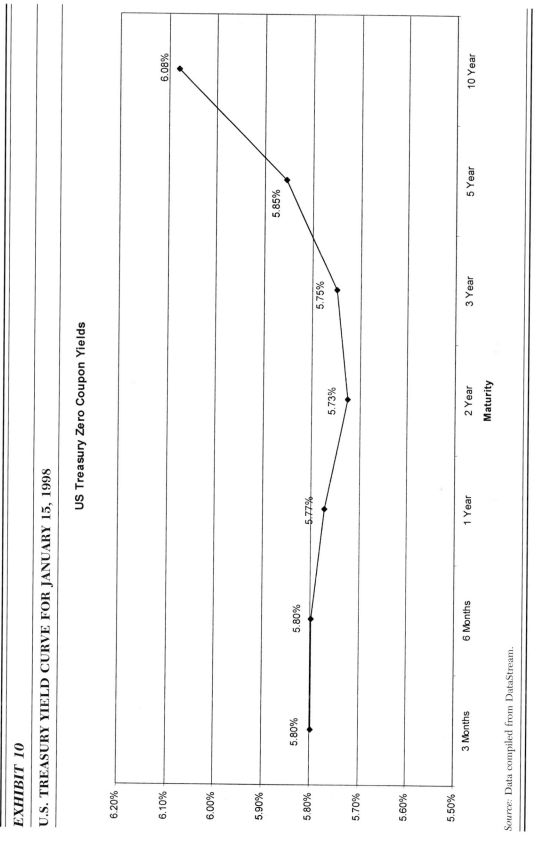

EXHIBIT 10

U.S. TREASURY YIELD CURVE FOR JANUARY 15, 1998

US Treasury Zero Coupon Yields

Source: Data compiled from DataStream.

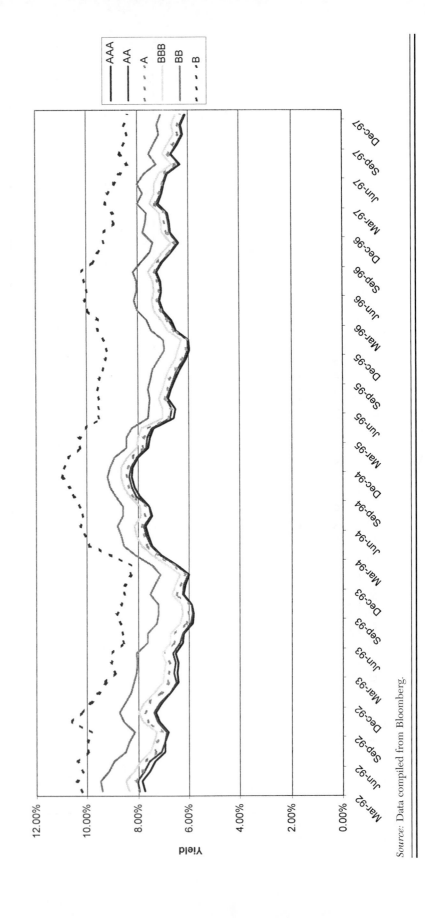

EXHIBIT 11

HISTORICAL CORPORATE DEBT YIELDS BY RATING

Historic Corporate Debt 10-Year Yields by Rating

Source: Data compiled from Bloomberg.

EXHIBIT 12A

RECENT DEBT DEALS IN DIGAMEM'S INDUSTRY

Date	Issuer	Principal ($ mil)	Proceeds ($ mil)	Offer Price	Description	Coupon (%)	Offer Yield to Maturity (%)	Spread to Treasury	Moody Rating	Standard & Poor's Rating
07/07/97	Gradiente Eletronica SA	15.0	14.8	98.900	9.625% Notes due '05	9.625	9.701		NR	NR
05/15/97	Hyundai Semiconductor	200.0	198.8	99.387	8.250% Notes due '04	8.250	8.367	172	Ba1	B+
05/15/97	Hyundai Semiconductor	200.0	199.4	99.700	8.625% Notes due '07	8.625	8.670	197	Baa3	BBB−
03/06/97	Fairchild Semiconductor Corp.	300.0	300.0	100.000	10.125% Sr Sub Notes due '07	10.125	10.125		B2	B
02/27/97	Seagate Technology Inc.	200.0	200.0	100.000	7.450% Debentures due '37	7.450	7.450	88	Baa3	BBB
02/27/97	Seagate Technology Inc.	100.0	99.9	99.85	7.875% Debentures due '17	7.875	7.890	105	Baa3	BBB
02/27/97	Seagate Technology Inc.	200.0	200.0	100.000	7.370% Notes due '07	7.370	7.370	80	Baa3	BBB
02/27/97	Seagate Technology Inc.	200.0	199.7	99.825	7.125% Notes due '04	7.125	7.157	65	Baa3	BBB

Source: Data compiled from SDC database.

EXHIBIT 12B

RECENT CONVERTIBLE DEALS IN DIGAMEM'S INDUSTRY

Date	Issuer	Proceeds ($ mil)	Offer Price	Description	Coupon (%)	Conversion Price	Conversion Premium (%)	Moody Rating	Standard & Poor's Rating
10/01/97	Advanced Semiconductor	200.0	100.000	Zero Cpn Cvt Bonds due '02	Zero			NA	NA
08/22/97	Level One Communications Inc.	100.0	100.000	4.000% Cvt Subord Nts due '04	4.000			NA	NA
08/20/97	Read-Rite Corp.	300.0	100.000	6.500% Cvt Subord Nts due '04	6.500	40.24	45.01	Ba3	BB−
08/19/97	Lam Research Corp.	310.0	100.000	5.000% Cvt Subord Nts due '02	5.000			NA	NA
07/29/97	Quantum Corp.	250.0	100.000	7.000% Cvt Subord Nts due '04	7.000	46.33	70.00	Ba2	NR
06/19/97	Micron Technology Inc.	435.0	100.000	7.000% Cvt Subord Nts due '04	7.000	67.44	64.99	Ba2	BB
05/22/97	Photronics Inc.	90.0	100.000	6.000% Cvt Subord Nts due '04	6.000	55.94	25.01	B2	B
03/06/97	EMC Corp.	450.0	100.000	3.250% Convertible Nts due '02	3.250			Ba3	BB−

Source: Data compiled from SDC database.

Convertible Debt

Convertible debt[2] securities gave a company's investors the right to exchange their debt for a fixed amount of shares of common stock. The security's exchange rate was called the *conversion ratio*. The convertible security had been referred to as a "hybrid" security because it provided investors with some upside potential (like equity) along with some downside protection (like debt). For example, if a convertible security had a principal of $1,000 and had a conversion ratio of 10:1, an investor would have the right to convert security into 10 shares of common stock. At conversion the investor would essentially be paying the fixed price of $100 per share ($1,000/10). The $100 was referred to as the *conversion price*. Therefore, following this example further, if the common stock later traded at $150, the investor could convert his or her $1,000 security into $1,500 of stock (10 shares times $150). In this example, if the common stock traded above the fixed conversion price, it was profitable for the investor to convert the bond into stock. On the other hand, if the company's stock traded below the conversion price, the investor would be better off holding the bond.

While adding a convertible feature would add some incentive to investors, Simpson was skeptical that it would be enough to raise the $27.3 million DigaMem needed. Although it was difficult to get an accurate quote, Simpson estimated a 6% coupon and a 15% conversion premium to be the minimum terms to get enough subscribers for a five-year convertible.[3] (Exhibit 12b shows recent convertible issuances in DigaMem's industry.)

Future-Priced Convertibles

Simpson had been recently approached by a group of investment bankers who believed it would be possible to raise the necessary funds using a specially constructed convertible preferred security. Essentially, the security would be designed to give the investor protection by ensuring conversion at a prespecified value instead of at a specified number of shares. Since the conversion ratio of a traditional convertible dictated its specific conversion price, this specialized security was referred to as a "future-priced" convertible due to the delayed determination of its conversion price. The delayed or *floating* conversion price prevented fluctuations in the price of the common stock from influencing the value of the security at conversion.

The floating conversion price was especially important because the security had a mandatory conversion policy. Instead of being redeemable in cash, both the preferred share dividend and principal were paid in common shares (with only fractional shares paid in cash). For example, if a $1,000 future-priced security was converted when company common shares were trading at $50, the investor would receive 20 common shares. But, if the stock price climbed to $75 instead, the investor would receive 13.333 shares. In both cases the investor would receive $1,000 worth of stock but, at the lower stock price, the investor would own a greater percentage of the company. A maximum conversion price placed a lower limit on the amount of shares that could be issued to the investor. For example, if the maximum conversion price of a $1,000 future-priced se-

---

[2] Convertible debt, in this case, covers convertible bonds as well as convertible preferred stock.

[3] The term "conversion premium" refers to the amount that the conversion price (or "strike price") of a bond is greater than the trading price of the convertible bond's associated stock. As a conversion premium increases, the conversion option of a convertible bond becomes further "underwater" as less valuable. The conversion premium is usually stated as a percentage.

curity was $100 and the issuer's common stock was trading at $120, the investor would still receive 10 shares of stock (not 8.333 shares). Thus, investors experienced additional upside from share appreciation beyond a certain point, as with other convertible securities. (Exhibit 13 gives some of the important details for the prospective future-priced security offering. Exhibit 14 gives recent option data for DigaMem's common stock.)

EXHIBIT 13

EXPECTED FUTURE-PRICED SECURITY OFFERING DETAILS

Security	Series A Preferred Convertible Stock
Offering	Private Placement
Issuance Date	February 25, 1998
Maturity Date	February 25, 2003
Proceeds	$27.3 million
Use of Proceeds	Working capital and research and development
Principal	$1,000 per share
Dividend Rate	6% per annum ($60)
Dividend Payment Method	Dividend accrual with payment in kind (additional preferred convertible shares)
Liquidation Preference	Shareholders are entitled to $1,000 per share plus any accrued, unpaid dividends before any other series of capital stock in the case of the company's default.
Convertibility	• The Series A preferred convertible stock is convertible into the company common stock. • The preferred shares become convertible 3 months after the date of issuance. • Each preferred share (and fraction thereof)[a] is convertible into a certain number of shares of common stock using the following formula: $1,000 / "conversion price."
Conversion Price	• Until September 1, 1998, the conversion price will be $10. • After September 1, 1998, the conversion price will be equal to the lowest trading price of the issuing company's common stock for the 22 trading days preceding conversion.
Conversion Price Discount	The conversion price (above) is reduced by the appropriate percentage according to the following schedule: • 7% starting on the first day of the 7th calendar month after closing • 8% starting on the first day of the 8th calendar month after closing • 9% starting on the first day of the 9th calendar month after closing • 10% starting on the first day of the 10th calendar month after closing • 11% starting on the first day of the 11th calendar month after closing • 12% starting on the first day of the 12th calendar month after closing • 13% starting on the first day of the 13th calendar month after closing • 14% starting on the first day of the 14th calendar month after closing • 15% starting on the first day of the 15th calendar month after closing
Maximum Conversion Price	• The conversion price will be capped at $20.
Mandatory Conversion	Every preferred convertible share is converted into common stock at the end of its five-year maturity.

[a]Fractional amounts of preferred shares, obtained through dividend payments, are also convertible into common stock. However, fractional shares of common stock will not be issued at conversion; instead, fractional common shares will be paid in cash.

Source: Casewriter.

EXHIBIT 14

DIGAMEM TRADED OPTION DATA

	Date	Closing Stock Price	Maturity	Strike	Open	High	Low	Close	Volume	Open Interest
Call	1/13/98	7.85	Apr-98	12.00	0.460	0.460	0.460	0.460	22	1,404
Put	1/13/98	7.85	Apr-98	12.00	4.221	4.316	4.221	4.316	200	278

Source: Casewriter.

CONCLUSION

DigaMem's options for raising funds were not enviable, but Simpson kept reminding himself that success was just around the corner. The normal approaches of issuing debt were very expensive at the moment. While the future-priced security seemed to have enough downside protection and upside potential packed in to lure investors away from their capital, the instrument was fairly new and unproven in the market. Most importantly, with deadlines approaching and creditors calling, the time to make a financing decision was running out.

24

ALZA and Bio-Electro Systems (A): Technological and Financial Innovation

In September 1988, Martin Gerstel, co-chairman and chief executive officer of ALZA Corporation, reread the draft prospectus for the rights offering that would create Bio-Electro Systems, Inc. (BES). This new organizational entity and the drug delivery technologies it would develop would play a key role in the future of ALZA. This very uncertain and risky venture resembled ALZA in its early days, when Gerstel joined the firm in 1968 as its chief financial officer with a newly minted MBA degree from Stanford University. In 1968, ALZA had just been founded, had no products, and was years from earning profits. Two decades later, ALZA was a recognized leader in drug delivery technologies. A few of the products it had developed were among the most successful in the industry, and still many others were under development. ALZA held 342 U.S. patents, generated positive profits and operating cash flow, and was regarded by Wall Street analysts as a relatively low-risk yet high-profit player in the growing pharmaceutical segment.

Mr. Gerstel realized that ALZA's success had spurred its rivals to accelerate their drug delivery development efforts, and that new technologies could significantly affect the company's future. ALZA's continued growth, profitability, technical preeminence, and ability to attract and retain its unique staff depended upon advancing these new drug delivery technologies. Mr. Gerstel and the board of directors of ALZA accepted this imperative but still had to address how to organize and pay for a $40 million new development effort. Months of discussions between him and David Hoffmann, ALZA's vice president and treasurer, had led to the complicated proposal to create BES as a new type of R&D offshoot of ALZA.

The proposal was unique. (Selected excerpts from its 53-page prospectus are given in Exhibit 1.) ALZA would sell common shares in an entity, Bio-Electro Systems, Inc.,

Professors Joshua Lerner and Peter Tufano prepared this case as the basis for class discussion rather than to illustrate either effective or ineffective handling of an administrative situation.

EXHIBIT 1

EXCERPTS FROM BES OFFERING STATEMENT

$45,416,943

BIO-ELECTRO SYSTEMS, INC.
ALZA CORPORATION

4,128,813 Units

Each Unit Consisting of One Share of Class A Common Stock of Bio-Electro Systems, Inc. and One Warrant to Purchase One Share of Class A Common Stock of ALZA Corporation

THESE SECURITIES ARE SPECULATIVE AND INVOLVE A HIGH DEGREE OF RISK. SEE "RISK FACTORS."

Transferable rights ("Rights") to subscribe for units ("Units") consisting of one share of callable Class A Common Stock of Bio-Electro Systems, Inc.("BES") and one Warrant ("Warrant") to purchase one share of Class A Common Stock of ALZA Corporation ("ALZA") are being distributed (the "Subscription Offering") to the holders of ALZA Class A Common Stock and ALZA Class B Common Stock of record on November 18, 1988 (the "Record Date"). Eight Rights are required to subscribe for one Unit, and the subscription price of each Unit (the "Subscription Price") is $11, subject to possible reduction as described under "The Offering—Subscription Offering—Subscription Price Reduction." Each ALZA stockholder of record on the Record Date will receive one Right for each share of ALZA Class A Common Stock held, and one Right for each share of ALZA Class A Common Stock into which each share of ALZA Class B Common Stock held is convertible. Persons exercising Rights are also entitled to subscribe for any additional Units ("Additional Units") which may be available as a result of Rights expiring without exercise. Ciba-Geigy Corporation, the sole holder of ALZA's Class B Common Stock, Dr. Alejandro Zaffaroni, the founder and Co-chairman of the Board of ALZA, and ALZA's Employee Stock Ownership Plan have indicated their intention to exercise all their Rights (to subscribe for approximately 699,000 Units in the aggregate) and have agreed not to subscribe for Additional Units.

The Units have been approved for listing on the American Stock Exchange upon official notice of issuance. The callable BES Class A Common Stock and the Warrants comprising the Units will be traded only as units until two years after the closing of the offering or such earlier day on which ALZA's Purchase Option (as defined below) is exercised (the "Separation Date"). After the Separation Date, it is expected that the Warrants will be listed on the American Stock Exchange but that the callable BES Class A Common Stock will not be eligible for listing on the American Stock Exchange or any other national securities exchange or for quotation on the NASDAQ National Market System. The Warrants may not be exercised before December 13, 1990 and expire five years after the closing of this offering. The exercise price of the Warrants is $30 per share. See "The Warrants."

The Rights are evidenced by divisible, transferable certificates and expire at 5:00 p.m., Eastern Standard Time, on December 12, 1988, if not exercised at or before that time. The Rights will trade on the American Stock Exchange under the symbol AZA.RT until 4:00 p.m., Eastern Standard Time, on December 9, 1988.

Beginning on the earlier of (i) February 1, 1991 and (ii) the day BES provides ALZA with quarterly financial statements of BES showing stockholders' equity of less than $4 million, and ending on the earlier of (i) January 31, 1995 and (ii) the 90th day after BES provides ALZA with quarterly financial statements of BES showing stockholders' equity of less than $4 million, ALZA will have an option (the "Purchase Option") to purchase all (but not less than all) of the shares of callable BES Class A Common Stock at a substantial premium over the Subscription Price. See "The Agreements and the Purchase Option—Purchase Option."

If the aggregate proceeds of all Units subscribed for in the Subscription Offering are less than $30 million, BES and ALZA will either (i) withdraw the Subscription Offering or (ii) attempt to raise additional proceeds through an underwritten offering of Units (the "Underwritten Offering"); if, however, such Underwritten Offering is undertaken and the aggregate proceeds of the Subscription Offering and the Underwritten Offering are less than $30 million, BES and ALZA will withdraw the Subscription Offering by December 31, 1988. In the event of any such withdrawal, all subscription payments will be refunded (together with interest earned thereon), and an additional $.25 per Unit (excluding Additional Units) subscribed for will be paid to subscribers. In the event of such withdrawal, purchasers of Rights in the market or through the subscription agent for the offering will not recover the consideration paid for such Rights. See "The Offering."

THESE SECURITIES HAVE NOT BEEN APPROVED OR DISAPPROVED BY THE SECURITIES AND EXCHANGE COMMISSION NOR HAS THE COMMISSION PASSED UPON THE ACCURACY OR ADEQUACY OF THIS PROSPECTUS. ANY REPRESENTATION TO THE CONTRARY IS A CRIMINAL OFFENSE.

	Subscription Price (1)	Financial Advisory Fee (2)	Proceeds to BES (2) (3)
Per Unit	$11.00	$.352	$10.648
Total Offering	Minimum $30,000,000 Maximum $45,416,943	Minimum $960,000 Maximum $1,453,342	Minimum $29,040,000 Maximum $43,963,601

(See footnotes on following page)

The date of this Prospectus is November 21, 1988.

(Continued)

EXHIBIT 1 *(Continued)*

EXCERPTS FROM BES OFFERING STATEMENT

(Footnotes from preceding page)

(1) The Subscription Price is subject to reduction if there is an Underwritten Offering of Units at a lower price to the public. See "The Offering—Subscription Price Reduction."

(2) Assumes that the Units are sold in the Subscription Offering. To the extent that any Units are sold in the Underwritten Offering, the proceeds to BES will be lower. See "The Offering—Potential Underwritten Offering of Unsubscribed Units."

(3) Before deducting expenses, estimated at $1.0 million, payable by BES. ALZA will not receive any of the proceeds of this offering.

AVAILABLE INFORMATION

ALZA is subject to the information requirements of the Securities Exchange Act of 1934, as amended (the "Exchange Act") and, in accordance therewith, files reports, proxy statements and other information with the Securities and Exchange Commission (the "Commission"). Such reports, proxy statements and other information can be inspected and copied at the public reference facilities maintained by the Commission at 450 Fifth Street, N.W., Judiciary Plaza, Washington, D.C. 20549, and at the regional offices of the Commission, Everett McKinley Dirksen Building, 219 South Dearborn Street, Room 1204, Chicago, Illinois 60604, 26 Federal Plaza, Room 1028, New York, New York 10278, and 5757 Wilshire Boulevard, Suite 500 East, Los Angeles, California 90036. Copies of such material can also be obtained at prescribed rates from the Public Reference Section of the Commission, 450 Fifth Street, N.W., Washington, D.C. 20549. ALZA Class A Common Stock is traded on the American Stock Exchange and copies of all reports and proxy materials filed with the Commission and other information concerning ALZA can be inspected at such Exchange.

BES will be required to file reports and other information with the Commission pursuant to the Exchange Act. Holders of BES Class A Common Stock will receive annual reports containing financial information including the report of certified public accountants as to the financial statements of BES.

ALZA and BES have filed with the Commission a Registration Statement under the Securities Act of 1933, as amended (the "Act"), with respect to the securities offered by this Prospectus. This Prospectus does not contain all of the information set forth or incorporated by reference in the Registration Statement and the exhibits thereto. For further information with respect to ALZA, BES and the securities offered hereby, reference is hereby made to such Registration Statement and exhibits, which may be obtained from the Public Reference Section of the Commission, 450 Fifth Street, N.W., Washington, D.C. 20549, upon payment of the fees prescribed by the Commission.

DOCUMENTS INCORPORATED BY REFERENCE

ALZA hereby incorporates by reference in this Prospectus the following documents filed by ALZA with the Commission:

(a) ALZA's Annual Report on Form 10-K for the fiscal year ended December 31, 1987 filed pursuant to the Exchange Act, which report incorporates, by reference to ALZA's 1987 Annual Report, ALZA's consolidated financial statements for such fiscal year.

(b) ALZA's Quarterly Reports on Form 10-Q for the quarters ended March 31, June 30 and September 30, 1988.

(c) All other reports filed by ALZA pursuant to Sections 13 or 15(d) of the Exchange Act since December 31, 1987.

(d) ALZA's definitive proxy statement (the "Proxy Statement") filed pursuant to Section 14 of the Exchange Act in connection with ALZA's 1988 annual meeting of stockholders.

All documents subsequently filed by ALZA pursuant to Sections 13, 14, or 15(d) of the Exchange Act prior to the termination of the offering made hereby will be deemed to be incorporated by reference in this Prospectus and to be a part hereof from the date of filing of such documents.

Any statement contained in a document incorporated by reference herein shall be deemed to be modified or superseded for purposes of this Prospectus to the extent that a statement contained herein or therein or in any other subsequently filed document which also is incorporated by reference herein modifies or supersedes such statement. Any such statement so modified or superseded shall not be deemed, except as so modified or superseded, to constitute a part of this Prospectus.

Upon written or oral request directed to Corporate Public Relations, ALZA Corporation, 950 Page Mill Road, P.O. Box 10950, Palo Alto, California 94303-0802 (telephone: (415) 494-5222), ALZA will provide, without charge, to any person to whom this Prospectus is delivered, a copy of any document incorporated by reference in this Prospectus (not including exhibits to any such document except to the extent any such exhibits are specifically incorporated by reference in the information incorporated in this Prospectus).

(Continued)

EXHIBIT 1   *(Continued)*

EXCERPTS FROM BES OFFERING STATEMENT

PROSPECTUS SUMMARY

The information set forth below should be read in conjunction with, and is qualified in its entirety by, the information appearing elsewhere in this Prospectus and incorporated herein by reference, including "Risk Factors."

The Subscription Offering:	In the Subscription Offering, transferable Rights to subscribe for Units are being distributed to the holders of ALZA Class A Common Stock, $.01 par value ("ALZA Class A Common Stock"), and ALZA Class B Common Stock, $.01 par value ("ALZA Class B Common Stock"), of record at the close of business on November 18, 1988 (the "Record Date"). Each Unit consists of one share of BES Class A Common Stock, $.01 par value ("BES Callable Class A Common Stock"), and one Warrant to purchase one share of ALZA Class A Common Stock. Eight Rights are required to subscribe for one Unit at a Subscription Price of $11 per Unit, subject to possible reduction as described under "The Offering—Subscription Offering—Subscription Price Reduction." Each ALZA stockholder of record on the Record Date will receive one Right for each share of ALZA Class A Common Stock held, and one Right for each share of ALZA Class A Common Stock into which each share of ALZA Class B Common Stock held is convertible. Rights also entitle holders to subscribe for Additional Units. Subscriptions for Units (including Additional Units) must be accompanied by payment of the total Subscription Price therefor. See "The Offering." The Chase Manhattan Bank, N.A. is acting as the Subscription Agent (the "Subscription Agent") for the Subscription Offering.

Ciba-Geigy Corporation, the sole holder of ALZA's Class B Common Stock, Dr. Alejandro Zaffaroni, the founder and Co-chairman of the Board of ALZA, and ALZA's Employee Stock Ownership Plan (the "ESOP") have indicated their intention to exercise all their Rights (to subscribe for approximately 699,000 Units in the aggregate) and have agreed not to subscribe for Additional Units. Ciba-Geigy Corporation, Dr. Zaffaroni and the ESOP have agreed not to sell Units until at least 90 days after the closing of this offering.

If the aggregate proceeds of all Units subscribed for in the Subscription Offering are less than $30 million, BES and ALZA will either (i) withdraw the Subscription Offering or (ii) attempt to raise additional proceeds through an Underwritten Offering; if, however, such Underwritten Offering is undertaken and the aggregate proceeds of the Subscription Offering and the Underwritten Offering are less than $30 million, BES and ALZA will withdraw the Subscription Offering by December 31 1988. In the event of any such withdrawal, all subscription payments will be refunded (together with interest earned thereon), and an additional $.25 per Unit (excluding Additional Units) subscribed for will be paid to subscribers. In the event of such withdrawal, purchasers of Rights in the market or through the Subscription Agent will not recover the consideration paid for such Rights. See "The Offering."

Potential Underwritten Offering:	If fewer than all of the Units are subscribed for in the Subscription Offering, BES and ALZA may attempt to arrange for an Underwritten Offering of all or some portion of the unsubscribed Units through Merrill Lynch Capital Markets ("Merrill Lynch"), which has acted as financial advisor to BES and ALZA in respect of the Subscription Offering. The ability of BES and ALZA to arrange for such an Underwritten Offering will depend, among other things, upon market conditions, the aggregate number of Units subscribed for in the Subscription Offering, and the ability of BES and ALZA to reach agreement with Merrill Lynch as to pricing and other terms of the Underwritten Offering.

If an Underwritten Offering were to occur, the closing of the Subscription Offering and the Underwritten Offering would be simultaneous and the

(Continued)

EXHIBIT 1   (Continued)

EXCERPTS FROM BES OFFERING STATEMENT

	price paid by subscribers in the Subscription Offering and by purchasers in the Underwritten Offering would be the same. There can be no assurance that the Underwritten Offering will occur. See "The Offering—Potential Underwritten Offering of Unsubscribed Units."
American Stock Exchange Information:	The Rights will trade on the American Stock Exchange under the symbol AZA.RT until 4:00 p.m. Eastern Standard Time, on December 9, 1988. The Units have been approved for listing on the American Stock Exchange upon official notice of issuance, to trade under the symbol AZA.U. The BES Callable Class A Common Stock and the Warrants will trade only as units until the Separation Date. After the Separation Date, it is expected that the Warrants will be listed on the American Stock Exchange, but that the BES Callable Class A Common Stock will not be eligible for listing on the American Stock Exchange or any other national securities exchange or for quotation on the NASDAQ National Market System.
ALZA:	ALZA is the recognized leader in the development of advanced pharmaceutical products incorporating drugs in therapeutic systems that control not only the quantity, but also the rate and duration, of drug release. ALZA's therapeutic systems are designed to improve the medical value of drugs by reducing many of their harmful or undesirable side effects while preserving or enhancing their beneficial action. In addition, these therapeutic systems are designed to simplify therapy and make it more convenient by reducing the number of times medication needs to be administered. The majority of ALZA's research and development activities are, and for the past five years have been, directed toward development of products incorporating specific drug compounds into various ALZA delivery systems. These systems include oral, rectal and implantable systems based on osmotic technology, diffusional systems for transdermal and site specific delivery and elastomeric intravenous infusors. Research and development activities are undertaken through joint arrangements with client companies, including two research and development partnerships, which arrangements generally provide for the client companies to reimburse ALZA for its fully burdened costs. In 1987, worldwide sales by ALZA and its client companies of ALZA-developed products were estimated to be $350 million. ALZA currently has approximately 40 products in various stages of development, including nine products currently awaiting United States Food and Drug Administration ("FDA") marketing approval.
Bio-Electro Systems:	BES was formed in October 1988 to develop drug delivery systems incorporating ALZA's proprietary ALZAMER® Bioerodible Polymer ("ALZAMER Polymers") and electrotransport ("Electrotransport") drug delivery technologies (together, the "Technologies") and to commercialize, most likely through licensing, products utilizing such systems for use in the prevention, treatment or cure of human illness, disease or other medical condition (the "Field"). BES has conducted no business to date. Building upon and expanding ALZA's research, BES intends to develop various systems utilizing the Technologies, which systems could provide the basis for commercial products. BES anticipates that it also will commence product development of selected products and that, if the maximum net proceeds are realized, up to three ALZAMER Polymer products and up to three Electrotransport products will enter final product development. It is also anticipated that additional funds will be required from third parties to complete the development of products, including those on which development work is performed by ALZA for BES, and to develop other products. See "Bio-Electro Systems—ALZAMER Bioerodible Polymers—Development Budget" and "Bio-Electro Systems—Electrotransport—Development Budget."

(Continued)

EXHIBIT 1 *(Continued)*

EXCERPTS FROM BES OFFERING STATEMENT

Reasons for BES and Benefits to ALZA:	While a significant amount of basic research on the Technologies has been done by ALZA, the Technologies are at an earlier stage of development than certain of ALZA's other technologies, which have been or are soon expected to be incorporated in commercial products. The development of new delivery systems and products based on the Technologies will involve significantly increased risks compared to ALZA's development activities based on its currently available systems. Funding of BES as contemplated in this Prospectus allows ALZA stockholders to choose whether or not they wish to participate in these higher risk development projects and, if such projects are successful, to obtain the potential rewards associated with them.
	The licensing of the Technologies to BES, and the subsequent funding by BES of systems development of the Technologies, will allow ALZA to more effectively utilize its funds in product development and commercialization activities on its other technologies. If the systems development work on the Technologies is successful, ALZA could exercise the Purchase Option and thus regain the exclusive right to use the Technologies.
The Technologies:	*ALZAMER® Bioerodible Polymers.* The ALZAMER Polymers comprise a family of polyorthoester bioerodible polymers patented by ALZA which can be used for the controlled delivery of many compounds. In the presence of moisture, an ALZAMER Polymer will erode, thereby permitting a drug compound formulated within the ALZAMER Polymer matrix to be released at a controlled rate over an extended period of time. The erosion rate of the ALZAMER Polymers, and therefore the rate of drug release, can be carefully controlled. In addition, since the ALZAMER Polymers can be processed to have physical properties ranging from free-flowing or slow-flowing viscous liquids to glassy or elastic solids, they offer many potential product opportunities. Possible uses of the ALZAMER Polymers include wound care products, topical dosage forms, injectables, tissue repair products, periodontal products and surgical "leave behind" products. Under agreements with third parties, two potential ALZAMER Polymer products are in the early stages of product development.
	Electrotransport. ALZA's Electrotransport involves the delivery of drug compounds across the skin, nails or mucosal membranes under the influence of an extremely low electric current. Electrotransport systems can be used to deliver drug compounds that cannot be delivered through the skin from passive transdermal systems. For example, polypeptides from the biotechnology field are candidates for Electrotransport because these molecules are too large to transport across skin by the process of passive diffusion. Electrotransport systems also can be used to deliver compounds in precise patterns or on an as-needed basis by the patient. BES expects initially to develop three basic Electrotransport systems—a zero order system (delivering a continuous steady amount of drug), a patterned delivery system (for example, providing periodic high doses with intervening small doses) and a patient controlled system. ALZA is evaluating various forms of these systems, and has fabricated and is testing in pilot clinical studies a prototype of a zero order system.
Development Contract:	BES has entered into a development contract with ALZA (the "Development Contract") under which ALZA will use diligent efforts to conduct systems research and development and to commence product development. ALZA has the right, subject to certain dollar limitations, to designate drugs for screening and has the right to designate one ALZAMER Polymer product and one Electrotransport product to be under development. Payment to ALZA under the Development Contract will be the full amount of all Development Costs (as defined in the Development Contract) incurred by ALZA beginning on January 1, 1988 in performing these activities

(Continued)

EXHIBIT 1   (Continued)

EXCERPTS FROM BES OFFERING STATEMENT

	(approximately $2.6 million through September 30, 1988). Development Costs will be charged on the same basis as ALZA generally charges its client companies. ALZA will provide appropriate scientific and technical personnel, necessary laboratories and equipment, and administration of research and development operations. BES is required to pay to ALZA under the Development Contract substantially all of the proceeds of this offering, any interest earned thereon, and any revenues received by BES under any agreements with ALZA. It is anticipated that such amounts will be expended under the Development Contract by the end of 1993. The Development Contract terminates at the earlier of January 31, 1995 or expenditure of all available funds thereunder. See "The Agreements and the Purchase Option—Development Contract."
License Option:	BES has granted ALZA an option to acquire a license to use the Technologies on a product by product basis (the "License Option"). The License Option is exercisable with respect to any product at any time after a screening evaluation has been completed for that product and remains exercisable until 90 days after approval to market the product has been received from the FDA, but in no event after the earlier of January 31, 1995 or 60 days after termination of the Development Contract. If the License Option is exercised as to any product, ALZA will acquire a worldwide license, with the right to sublicense, to make, have made, use and sell the product. ALZA's license for each product will be exclusive until seven years after FDA marketing approval of the product and nonexclusive thereafter. ALZA will make the following payments to BES with respect to each licensed product:

(a) if the product is sold by ALZA or an ALZA affiliate, base royalties of 3% of net sales of the product and additional royalties of up to 3% of such net sales, the exact amount of additional royalties to be determined based upon the portion of the total research and development costs with respect to such product paid by BES;

(b) if the product is sold by a third party, base sublicensing fees of 25% of (i) any royalties or percentage of sales payments received by ALZA or an ALZA affiliate, and (ii) any "front-end" distribution fees, prepaid royalties or similar one-time, infrequent or special payments received by ALZA or an ALZA affiliate, and additional sublicensing fees of up to 25% of such payments, the exact amount of such additional sublicensing fees to be determined based upon the portion of the total research and development costs with respect to such product paid by BES; and

(c) 10% of certain amounts paid by any third party to ALZA or an ALZA affiliate, before January 1, 1999 for research and development activities relating to products utilizing the Technologies in the Field.

The payments under (a) and (b) above will continue on a country by country basis until the expiration in such country of the last to expire of any patents covering the licensed product or, if there never are any patents in such country, until December 31, 2007. If the License Option is not exercised with respect to any product developed under the Development Contract, the rights to such product will remain in BES and BES will need to find other methods of commercially exploiting the product.

ALZA has the right to develop products utilizing the Technologies in the Field for its own account and for third parties in addition to the activities funded by BES under the Development Contract. In such cases (i) no BES funds will be used for product development, (ii) BES will have an exclusive license to the technology developed (other than technology relating to a third party's proprietary compound) and any products will be subject to ALZA's License Option, (iii) if the License Option is exercised for any

(Continued)

EXHIBIT 1 (Continued)

EXCERPTS FROM BES OFFERING STATEMENT

	product, BES will receive royalties and sublicensing fees as described above and (iv) BES will receive the payments described in (c) above, whether or not the License Option is exercised. See "The Agreements and the Purchase Option—License Option."
Purchase Option:	ALZA has the right to purchase all of the BES Callable Class A Common Stock (the "Purchase Option"). The Purchase Option will be exercisable by notice given at any time beginning on the earlier of (i) February 1, 1991 and (ii) the day BES provides ALZA with quarterly financial statements of BES showing stockholders' equity of less than $4 million, and ending on the earlier of (i) January 31, 1995 and (ii) the 90th day after BES provides ALZA with quarterly financial statements of BES showing stockholders' equity of less than $4 million. If the Purchase Option is exercised, the purchase price calculated on a per share basis (the "Purchase Option Exercise Price") will be as follows:

If the Purchase Option Is Exercised	Purchase Option Exercise Price(1)
At any time before February 1, 1991(2)	$23
On or after February 1, 1991 and on or before January 31, 1992.....	$23
On or after February 1, 1992 and on or before January 31, 1993.....	$31
On or after February 1, 1993 and on or before January 31, 1994.....	$42
On or after February 1, 1994 and on or before January 31, 1995.....	$57

(1) If the Subscription Price is reduced as a result of the sale of Units to the public in the Underwritten Offering at a lower price (see "The Offering—Subscription Offering—Subscription Price Reduction"), the Purchase Option Exercise Price will be reduced by the same percentage.

(2) The Purchase Option may be exercised before February 1, 1991 only if, prior to that date, BES provides ALZA with quarterly financial statements of BES showing stockholders' equity of less than $4 million. It is not expected that this will occur before that date, even if the minimum proceeds are realized. See "Use of Proceeds."

	The Purchase Option Exercise Price may be paid in cash, in ALZA Class A Common Stock or in any combination of cash and ALZA Class A Common Stock, at ALZA's sole discretion. See "Federal Income Tax Consequences."
	Under its Restated Certificate of Incorporation, BES will be prohibited from taking or permitting any action inconsistent with ALZA's rights under the Purchase Option. In addition, until the expiration of the Purchase Option, BES will not be able, without the consent of ALZA, as the holder of the BES Class B Common Stock, to issue additional capital stock, merge, liquidate, sell all or substantially all of its assets, or amend its Restated Certificate of Incorporation to alter the Purchase Option or the rights of the Class B Common Stock. See "BES Capital Stock."
Services Agreement:	BES has entered into a services agreement (the "Services Agreement") with ALZA pursuant to which ALZA has agreed to provide management and administrative services to BES on a fully burdened cost reimbursement basis. The Services Agreement has a one-year term and may be renewed for successive one-year terms during the term of the Development Contract at the option of BES. In addition, BES may terminate the Services Agreement at any time upon 60 days' notice. Under the Services Agreement, ALZA will be reimbursed for its expenses associated with this offering.
The Warrants:	Each Unit includes a Warrant to purchase one share of ALZA Class A Common Stock. The Warrants will be exercisable from December 13, 1990 until the date that is five years after the closing of the offering (the "Warrant Expiration Date") at $30 per share (the "Exercise Price"). The

(Continued)

EXHIBIT 1 *(Continued)*

EXCERPTS FROM BES OFFERING STATEMENT

	Warrants will trade separately from the BES Callable Class A Common Stock beginning on the Separation Date. See "The Warrants."
Federal Income Tax Consequences:	Material federal income tax consequences applicable to the receipt of Rights, the purchase of Units in the Subscription Offering or in the Underwritten Offering and the sale of Rights, Warrants and BES Callable Class A Common Stock by purchasers in such offerings are discussed under "Federal Income Tax Consequences."
Use of Proceeds:	The estimated net proceeds of this offering will be at least $28 million and at most $43 million. BES will receive all of the net proceeds of the offering. BES expects to use substantially all of such proceeds to undertake systems research and development, screening evaluations and, to the extent funds are available, product development under the Development Contract. BES expects that during the term of the Development Contract it will be engaged solely in research and development of the Technologies and will have very limited sources of revenue other than the net proceeds of this offering, plus interest earned thereon. See "Use of Proceeds."

ALZA Summary Financial Data (in thousands, except per share data)

	Years Ended December 31,					Nine Months Ended September 30,	
	1983	1984	1985	1986	1987	1987	1988
						(unaudited)	
Statement of Income Data:							
Total Revenue	$22,454	$30,484	$45,547	$57,799	$70,812	$51,544	$62,052
Income Before Extraordinary Item(1)	732	2,968	5,055	9,005	13,984	9,947	12,623
Net Income	1,320	5,938	9,707	16,753	13,984	9,947	12,623
Income Before Extraordinary Item Per Share(1)	.03	.12	.19	.28	.42	.30	.38
Net Income Per Share	.05	.24	.36	.52	.42	.30	.38
Balance Sheet Data:							
Working Capital	$16,909	$19,713	$ 81,797	$ 84,610	$148,614	$152,848	$146,109
Total Assets	39,572	44,871	160,444	137,306	243,479	229,116	248,105
Convertible Debentures	25,000	25,000	22,575	—	75,000	75,000	75,000
Other Long Term Liabilities	3,067	3,095	2,894	2,686	6,090	5,599	7,780
Stockholders' Equity	3,415	10,007	79,042	121,219	138,985	133,434	153,169

(1) The extraordinary item for 1983 to 1986 relates primarily to the use of United States federal income tax net operating loss carryforwards.

which would have virtually no employees. BES would contract with ALZA to research and develop the new technologies. ALZA retained the right to license any products developed, and it held the option to buy out the BES shareholders at a preset schedule of prices. In addition, purchasers of BES shares would receive a warrant allowing them to purchase shares of ALZA common stock for $30 in the next 5 years.

Mr. Gerstel had to determine whether this proposal was the best for ALZA or whether another plan might work better. Should he commit ALZA to an untested financing strategy, or would it be better to fund the initiative from internal resources? Would ALZA shareholders understand this proposal? What was a fair price for the BES share plus warrant package?

THE ROOTS OF ALZA: SYNTEX

ALZA's early history was closely linked with the Syntex Corporation, from which the firm drew its founder and much of its initial credibility.[1] In the 1930s, Dr. Russell Marker, a chemistry professor at Pennsylvania State University and a leading researcher in the synthesis of human hormones, discovered a family of Mexican plants that could be used to produce human hormones easily and cheaply. At the time, steroids and hormones were distilled from animal carcasses and body fluids through a time-consuming and costly process. Dr. Marker's discovery held the promise of making the therapeutic use of human hormones less restricted and costly.

While Dr. Marker was an adept researcher, with over 75 patents and over 160 published articles, he was a less able businessman. Unable to interest any pharmaceutical firm in funding his work, he began his own enterprise in 1943. Within two years, he resigned his university position, moved to Mexico, single-handedly produced a supply of the human hormone progesterone equal to the world's annual production, formed a Mexico City-based company with two European refugees, fought with those partners, and resigned. Rather than buy the rights back from his partners, he set up a competing firm, which soon failed.

Dr. Marker's former partners continued the product development effort by recruiting George Rosenkranz, a Hungarian chemist who had fled to Cuba from Nazi Germany. Mr. Rosenkranz assembled a team of European refugees, Mexican scientists trained in the United States and Mexico, and (increasingly in the 1950s) U.S. academic scientists. From its Mexico City base, Syntex emerged as a center of research in the production of human hormones from plants. In the years after World War II, Syntex produced human hormones at a fraction of the price of animal-derived products.

Syntex's laboratories blossomed, but its business operations were less healthy. During the 1950s the firm derived almost all its revenues from bulk sales of hormones to the major pharmaceutical manufacturers, which then resold them for many times the price they paid Syntex. The conflict between the innovative research and conservative marketing strategy led to a rift between Mr. Rosenkranz and the firm's owners. The conflict was resolved in 1956 when New York investor Charles Allen bought out the firm and installed Mr. Rosenkranz as Syntex's president.

Mr. Allen, founder of the investment bank Allen and Company, had a reputation as one of the most savvy investors in emerging companies. In 1958 he distributed

---

[1] This discussion of Syntex's history is drawn from "Mexican Hormones," *Fortune*, May 1951, pp. 86–90, 161–68; "Syntex Doesn't Want to Rely on the Pill," *Business Week*, May 20, 1972; Syntex Corporation, *A Corporation and a Molecule: The Story of Research at Syntex*, Palo Alto, Syntex, 1966; and discussions with ALZA management.

Syntex shares to his investors, thereby turning the firm into a public company. The company sold $2.2 million of additional shares to the public in 1960, and with the capital began building its own marketing force. The firm renegotiated its contracts with the major pharmaceutical houses so that the prices for raw materials were tied to eventual product revenues, in a royalty-like arrangement. By 1963 the firm was profitable and seemed poised for boundless growth as a major supplier of hormones for birth-control pills. Syntex's valuation soared: In late November 1963 the firm commanded a market capitalization of $855 million, even though annual sales and assets were only $16 million each.

Syntex emerged as the first major pharmaceutical firm to be established after World War II. Sales grew steadily, not only of hormones for birth-control pills but also of steroid-based products for treating inflammation and of animal growth hormones. Investors also paid attention to Syntex's creative research organization, which had the capacity for producing a wide variety of products. While its pharmaceutical competitors turned inward, Syntex built relationships with the academic research community by constructing a major research center near Stanford University, encouraging its researchers to publish in scientific journals, and aggressively recruiting recent Ph.D. graduates. Much of the credit was given to Dr. Alejandro Zaffaroni, a Uruguay-born biochemist who joined Syntex in 1951. After receiving medical training in Uruguay, Dr. Zaffaroni specialized in steroidal chemistry while obtaining his Ph.D. degree at the University of Rochester. He served as Syntex's executive vice president and directed the firm's research from 1956 to 1968. During the 1960s, Dr. Zaffaroni focused on structuring innovative collaborative research and marketing deals for new products.

THE POTENTIAL OF DRUG DELIVERY SYSTEMS

In the 1960s, Dr. Zaffaroni became fascinated by the medical and economic potential of new drug delivery systems. Until the 1930s pharmaceutical companies manufactured the active ingredients in drugs, while pharmacists converted these into final products, using traditional drug delivery systems of pills, ointments, or liquids. Over the succeeding decades, drug manufacturers vertically integrated, manufacturing the drug delivery vehicles. Dr. Zaffaroni felt that drug companies had neglected research into the mechanisms through which active ingredients were directed into the body in favor of the more glamorous discovery research. He was fond of pointing out that the most common drug delivery mechanism, the pill, had changed little since its invention by the ancient Egyptians in the fifteenth century BC.

Pills have several medical disadvantages. First, they are rapidly absorbed into the blood stream through the stomach. Thus, a pill administers its dose in a single jolt—an initial overdosage followed by a period of underdosage—when a continuous series of small doses usually is preferable. Consequently, many drugs that would work effectively within a narrow dosage range would be rejected in clinical trials. Improved drug delivery systems could release drugs into the body in a slow and controlled manner.

Second, pills commonly deliver many times the needed dosage because only a small portion of the therapeutic agent reaches the desired part of the body. The remainder of the agent goes elsewhere in the body, causing unfortunate side effects in other body organs. Improved delivery systems could limit the probability of side effects by ensuring that the drug was absorbed mainly by the part of the body where it was needed.

Improved delivery systems promised both economic and medical advantages. Firms developing new drugs applied for patent protection, which typically enabled them to market the product for 10–15 years without competition. Once the patent expired, generic competitors frequently entered the market. Existing products about to go "off-patent" could be repackaged with advanced drug delivery systems to improve their safety, efficacy, or convenience. The "new and improved" version of the drug might allow a firm to maintain attractive sales, even in the face of generic competitors to the drug in its original form.

Dr. Zaffaroni tried to persuade Syntex to make a major development push into drug delivery systems. The firm resisted the suggestion, arguing it would be too great a distraction from its efforts to develop new chemical entities, which was the primary focus for all major pharmaceutical companies and seen as the only important way to create new pharmaceutical products. Moreover, it argued that it was unclear how great the reward from drug delivery systems would be. Advanced drug delivery systems might be expensive to develop and to manufacture, while pills and other traditional delivery systems were already available at a negligible cost. Doctors and patients might not see the benefits of these novel delivery systems as justifying any added expense. Finally, the scientific understanding of drug delivery was still rudimentary. Unpleasant surprises might await: for instance, patients might develop a tolerance to a drug more quickly when it was continuously delivered in small doses.

THE BIRTH AND CRISIS OF ALZA

Failing to persuade Syntex to invest in drug delivery technologies, Alejandro Zaffaroni left Syntex in 1968 to begin his own firm.[2] He named the new firm ALZA (after the first two letters of his first and last names). ALZA was capitalized with $3 million of Dr. Zaffaroni's own money. Its only other assets were Syntex's patents and research personnel in the area of drug delivery. As part of the disengagement agreements between Dr. Zaffaroni and Syntex, Syntex acquired 25% of ALZA's equity at a nominal cost. Syntex distributed its ALZA shares to its shareholders in 1970, transforming ALZA into a publicly traded start-up just as Syntex had been.

Despite ALZA's weak capitalization as well as the anticipated long delays and large capital demands until the firm reached profitability, there was a tremendous interest in the financial community regarding the future potential of the company. Within a few days of the distribution to Syntex's shareholders, ALZA (trading on the Pacific Stock Exchange) had a market capitalization exceeding $100 million. In 1969 and 1970, ALZA raised funds through private placements from successful entrepreneurs, including the presidents of Marion Laboratories and Memorex. Priced at between $10 and $15 per share (the higher priced offerings also included a warrant), the private placements raised nearly $19 million. In 1971, ALZA also raised $12 million in a rights offering to existing shareholders managed by Allen and Company, in which a share and a warrant were sold for $15.

One of Dr. Zaffaroni's first priorities was to build a blue-chip panel of scientific advisors and a board of directors, including Nobel laureates, noted academics, and business leaders. Dr. Zaffaroni had known many of the scientists while at Syntex; others were attracted by his reputation as a leading researcher-turned-entrepreneur. Based on his experience at Syntex, he took care to develop a research-oriented culture at ALZA. After recruiting a former M.I.T. professor specializing in membrane technology to lead

---

[2] This discussion of ALZA's history is drawn from Gene Bylinsky, "Visionary on a Golden Shoestring," *Fortune*, June 1973, pp. 150–53, 226–30; Ignatius Chithelen, "Drug Extender," *Forbes*, July 10, 1989, pp. 95–96; Yves Doz, "Technology Partnerships Between Larger and Smaller Firms: Some Critical Issues," *International Studies of Management and Organization*, 17, 1988, pp. 31–57; David A. Loehwing, "ALZA to Zoecon," *Barron's*, October 14, 1974, pp. 3, 8, 13, 18; analysts' reports; and discussions with ALZA management.

the research effort, Dr. Zaffaroni focused on recruiting researchers in their twenties and thirties. Researchers were drawn from many disciplines rarely seen in pharmaceutical firms, including physicists, polymer chemists, and mechanical engineers. He cultivated an informal atmosphere with few administrative structures. Scientific project leaders often bypassed the firm's formal organizational structure and spoke directly to Dr. Zaffaroni on key issues. As he noted in one interview, "There isn't a company outside the Metropolitan Opera that functions this way."[3] Neither base pay nor bonuses were high, but stock options were made widely available. The Palo Alto facility was located next to that of another Syntex spin-off, Zoecon, and informal contact between the researchers was encouraged.

ALZA's initial development focus was on two products: the Ocusert and Progestasert. Glaucoma, a chronic condition in which excessive pressure builds up in the eyeball, could cause blindness unless treated by the drug pilocarpine. The traditional drug delivery method, eye-drops applied four times a day, resulted in blurred vision for up to an hour after each administration. ALZA developed a tiny polymer pouch (Ocusert), to be inserted under the eyelid. Each pouch, which lasted for a week, slowly released pilocarpine into the eye. With the steady doses of the drug from the Ocusert, the debilitating vision-blurring did not occur. ALZA's second product, the Progestasert, provided birth control for an entire year without replacement. An intrauterine device that released small amounts of the same hormone used in birth-control pills, it prevented conception while eliminating the potentially serious side effects of the pills.

ALZA also pursued long-range development projects in a variety of other areas. These projects advanced basic science and worked to perfect therapeutic systems, or alternative technologies to deliver drugs to the body. The two most promising therapeutic systems were membrane-coated capsules that released drugs only very slowly, which the firm dubbed the oral osmotic (OROS) system, and transdermal patches placed like adhesive bandages on the skin that allowed drugs to be very gradually absorbed into the body. Once the therapeutic systems were developed, they could be combined with a wide variety of different drugs to produce an almost endless number of different products.

By 1974, ALZA had filed for marketing approval for its first two products. In anticipation of commercialization, the firm had established a substantial manufacturing facility and had begun building up a sales force. This significantly increased the expenditures of ALZA. The firm met its financing needs by selling 1.25 million common shares at $12.50 per share and arranging a $20 million line of credit from a group of banks led by Chase Manhattan. The financial planning was based on the expectation that sales of the first two products would reach at least $20–$30 million within the first few years of marketing and that at this sales level ALZA could achieve profitability.

By 1976 the Food and Drug Administration (FDA) had approved ALZA's first two products, and they had been introduced into the marketplace. Unfortunately, sales in fiscal year 1976 were just over $2 million; in 1977, only $7 million. More ominously, by mid-1977 it was apparent that these products would not reach the necessary volumes for ALZA to report positive profits. Both products encountered market resistance, exacerbated by unfortunate external events. Elderly glaucoma patients, reluctant to insert Ocusert pouches under their eye-lids, chose to remain with eyedrops, which had the added benefit of costing about $1 a day less than ALZA's new product. At about the same time, Merck introduced an improved eye-drop medication for glaucoma, which sharply reduced the blurring of vision. Meanwhile, patients resisted trying the new Progestasert device. One reason was that the initial expenditure was much higher than

[3] Bylinsky, p.219.

either birth-control pills or competing intrauterine devices. In addition, another company's intratuerine device, the Dalkon Shield sold by A.H. Robbins, was at this time the focus of intense negative publicity and litigation. Doctors were reluctant to recommend the new Progestasert, or any other intrauterine device, because of concerns about product safety and litigation.

As monthly sales fell in early 1977, ALZA faced a major financial crisis. Marketing and R&D operations each consumed $2 million a month. The firm had little more than $1 million in cash on hand, its bank line of credit was rapidly being drawn down, and it was in violation of several bank covenants. Apart from its dwindling sales, its only other source of revenues was a small amount of contract research it did for major pharmaceutical houses. As ALZA's share price fell, the firm was criticized in the financial community for its inflated promises. Dr. Zaffaroni realized that in this environment another public equity issue would be impossible. Instead, he sought an equity investment by a major U.S. pharmaceutical or, less satisfactorily, chemical firm. Failing to interest U.S. firms, he looked overseas.

ALZA AND CIBA-GEIGY

During 1977 and 1978, Dr. Zaffaroni convinced Ciba-Geigy, a multinational chemical and pharmaceutical firm based in Basel, Switzerland, with 75,000 employees and sales of $1.2 billion, to invest in ALZA. Ciba-Geigy laboratories had been relatively active in exploring pharmaceutical delivery systems, recently developing a slow-release capsule. ALZA began negotiating with Ciba-Geigy in April 1977, and the two firms continued to negotiate for most of the year. In January 1978, Ciba-Geigy's U.S. subsidiary purchased $30 million of a new class of convertible preferred stock in ALZA, and Ciba-Geigy agreed to commission at least $15 million of contract research from ALZA over a 5-year period, thus allowing ALZA to continue its corporate life.

In return, Ciba-Geigy gained control over ALZA's corporate affairs. Ciba-Geigy was granted 80% of the voting rights and eight of eleven ALZA board seats.[4] ALZA's research projects (with the exception of a small amount of discretionary research) needed to be approved by a joint review board of ALZA and Ciba-Geigy representatives. In view of its 80% voting rights, Ciba-Geigy could consolidate ALZA's financial statements with its own for tax purposes. Hence the Swiss firm could enjoy the accumulated tax losses of ALZA, which included not only an operating loss carryforward of $30.4 million but also $32.2 million of deferred research costs and $2.9 million of deferred patent costs to be amortized over future periods.[5] Ciba-Geigy had the exclusive right to license virtually all of ALZA's existing and future technology for at least a decade, by paying ALZA royalties of 5% of sales for most products and 10% for a few products already under development by ALZA and nearing commercialization. ALZA was allowed to license its technologies to third parties, but only with the approval of Ciba-Geigy. Ciba-Geigy was allowed to treat the $15 million payments for contract research as the first $20 million in paid-in royalties. Thus, ALZA would not receive any royalties until Ciba-Geigy had sold between $200 and $400 million of ALZA-derived products. Finally, Ciba-Geigy was granted the right to take over the manufacture of any product being produced by ALZA, if it felt significant cost savings could be achieved.

[4] Ciba-Geigy purchased a new class of preferred stock. If it converted the preferred shares into common stock, it would hold 53% of the equity in ALZA.

[5] ALZA Corporation, *Proxy Statement*, December 23, 1977, p. 25. These two benefits were expected to yield savings to Ciba-Geigy of at least $27 million over a 5-year period ["Advanced Drug Delivery Systems: ALZA and Ciba-Geigy (B)," unpublished INSEAD case, 1988].

From January 1977 to the end of 1978, ALZA's staff fell from 700 to just under 400 as marketing and production were dramatically cut back. The R&D effort was left untouched. The implementation of this agreement encountered difficulties. ALZA's managers perceived Ciba-Geigy's research personnel as lacking interest in ALZA technologies and its sales force as indifferent to the promotion of ALZA products. Delays in processing ALZA's requests to undertake collaborations with third parties were another source of frustration. Meanwhile, Ciba-Geigy management was frustrated by ALZA's increasing losses and its constant requests to develop products with other pharmaceutical companies. The reported financial losses resulted from the sluggish sales of ALZA's two existing products. At the time the agreement was signed, these sales had been projected to be $43 million in the years 1978–1980, but actual sales in this period totaled $8 million. Additional tensions were introduced by the conflict between the highly informal, nonhierarchical approach of ALZA and Ciba-Geigy's more restrained corporate culture.

Rather than renew the agreement in 1981, Ciba-Geigy determined to give up control of ALZA through a series of complex agreements. Ciba-Geigy's licenses to ALZA technologies were converted into nonexclusive licenses, giving ALZA the freedom to offer these technologies to others. In view of the fact that ALZA was losing money in 1981 and had no obvious sources of capital, Ciba-Geigy provided ALZA with $10 million. Ciba-Geigy exchanged its preferred shares for non-voting class B common shares, representing approximately 40% of the equity of ALZA.[6] In addition, Ciba-Geigy obtained nonvoting "series 1982" convertible preferred shares that ALZA would redeem and thereby repay Ciba-Geigy $10 million plus interest. Ciba-Geigy surrendered its board seats, and the marketing and production agreements were canceled. In turn, ALZA gave up all claims to royalties from Ciba-Geigy on its existing technologies, with the exception of two skin patches expected to reach the market in 1983 for which Ciba-Geigy was to pay a 5% royalty (reduced from 10% in the original agreement).

ALZA was once again an independent entity, but it was thinly capitalized and faced a skeptical capital market. The total market value of the firm's equity was under $20 million. The company was not profitable and still owed approximately $10 million to the banking syndicate that had provided the loans to commercialize its first products.

THE REBIRTH OF ALZA

Several favorable events in 1983 helped boost ALZA's chances for survival as an independent company. First, Ciba-Geigy's first skin patch (developed by ALZA and for which ALZA received a royalty of 5%), which delivered nitroglycerine to angina sufferers, proved an unqualified success. While nitroglycerine drugs had previously been applied in ointments, the skin patch was easier and more effective. Ciba-Geigy's sales of the skin patch soon exceeded the cumulative sales of all other nitroglycerine-based drugs. Another patch product introduced at about the same time that dispensed the drug scopolamine (which prevents motion sickness) also proved successful.

ALZA discovered that the drug industry's interest in alternative delivery systems had increased dramatically since 1977, in part because of the publicity associated with the firm's ties with Ciba-Geigy and the success of the first two transdermal products. Freed from the oversight of Ciba-Geigy, ALZA quickly signed licensing agreements with other firms, including Eli Lilly, Glaxo, Pfizer, and Schering-Plough. ALZA confined its efforts to R&D in delivery systems, leaving the discovery of new drug entities and the marketing of the resulting pharmaceutical products to other firms. It would

---

[6] Common stock held by other entities was renamed class A common. At the same time, a substantial employee stock ownership plan was established for all ALZA employees, using class C common shares.

profit by allowing pharmaceutical firms to license its technology, in return for which they would pay ALZA royalties.

Soon ALZA was able to approach the capital markets again. In 1983 it raised money three times. First, ALZA issued a $17 million public offering for an R&D limited partnership to develop products based on its transdermal technologies, placed by Merrill Lynch White Weld. Second, it sold $25 million of convertible subordinated debentures, again managed by Merrill Lynch White Weld, which was used to buy back Ciba-Geigy's preferred shares. Finally, ALZA undertook a $31 million private placement for an R&D limited partnership to develop products based on its OROS technologies.

The firm's strategy proved increasingly successful as the 1980s progressed. Not only did the firm's market capitalization climb steadily, but new offerings were well received. In 1985, ALZA raised $93 million through the sale of 3 million shares of class A common stock, underwritten by Merrill Lynch Capital Markets. With the proceeds, it repurchased half the class B shares held by Ciba-Geigy for $43 million (these were convertible into 2.9 million class A shares). In 1986 its rising stock price allowed it to call its convertible debt issue. A year later ALZA raised $75 million, through the sale of convertible Eurobonds, co-managed by Merrill Lynch Capital Markets, Credit Suisse First Boston, and Smith Barney.

By 1988 ALZA had signed contracts with over a dozen major pharmaceutical firms and had over 40 products in development that would deliver existing drugs through its delivery systems, nine of which were awaiting final marketing approval by the FDA. In these agreements, ALZA's partner incurred all costs of developing the product, and ALZA would receive a revenue stream in the form of royalties on net sales if it succeeded.[7] Both the skin-patch technology and the controlled-release OROS system proved highly successful, able to accommodate the release of a wide variety of drugs. ALZA owned 342 U.S. patents and had another 104 U.S. patents pending. Although by the late 1980s a number of other companies were attempting to develop drug-delivery technology, ALZA continued to be recognized as the worldwide leader in its field. ALZA's product pipeline in 1988 is shown in Exhibit 2, and its financial history is summarized in Exhibit 3.

Based on its successes to date in developing and licensing its drug delivery technologies to established pharmaceutical firms, ALZA had created an enviable royalty stream. Many Wall Street analysts, projecting ALZA's future revenues (see Exhibit 4), were optimistic about the company:

> The translation of ALZA's technology base to practicable systems defined the high-risk phase both for the company and for investors. That has passed. At this stage, applying ALZA's systems to product development provides leverage that is inherently lower risk and lower cost than traditional pharmaceutical developments. Indeed, multiple product marketing opportunities emerge, limited only by the imagination of ALZA and its pharmaceutical company clients.[8]

Another analyst dubbed ALZA "the ultimate royalty trust"[9] in that its shareholders were the residual claimants to the large stream of royalties the firm enjoyed from

---

[7] Among the companies funding R&D at ALZA in 1987 were American Home Products, Baxter, Boehringer-Ingelhiem, Bristol-Myers, Ciba-Geigy, Cyanimid, Du Pont, Glaxo, Hoffman-LaRoche, Johnson and Johnson, Merck, Merrell-Dow, Monsanto, Pfizer, Recordati, Sandoz, and Schering-Plough. ALZA also continued to sell its own drugs, but its sale of the three products—the Ocusert, the Progestasert, and the Alzet, a slow release tablet for animal studies—totaled only $7 million.

[8] A.M. Haley et al., "ALZA Corp.—Company Report," analyst's report, Alex. Brown & Sons, October 17, 1988.

[9] Royalty trusts were first pioneered in the mid-1980s by Mesa Petroleum to spin off oil and gas reserves to a trust, thereby avoiding corporate taxation of the earnings on these revenue streams. ALZA's structure was not a royalty trust in the same fashion, in that as a corporation its revenues were subject to corporate taxation.

EXHIBIT 2

ALZA PROJECT PORTFOLIO, JANUARY 1988

Sold Under License

Name	Sold By	Disease/Use	Royalties on Net Sales	1987 Gross Sales ($ mil.)
Transdermal Systems				
Transderm-Nitro	Ciba-Geigy	Angina	5%	234
Transderm-Scop	Ciba-Geigy	Motion sickness	5	17
Estraderm	Ciba-Geigy	Female hormone	1[a]	20
Catapres-TTS	Boehringer	Hypertension	7.5	30
OROS Osmotic and Related Technologies				
Acutrim	Ciba-Geigy	Appetite suppression	0%	—
Acusystem C	American Health	Vitamin C	5–10	1
Volmax	Glaxo	Asthma	5–10	3
Tranvenol-Infuser	Baxter	Cancer patients	5–10	16

Selected New Drug Applications Filed by ALZA or its Licensees

Name	New Drug Application Filed	Sponsor	Use
Transdermal Systems			
TTS-testosterone	Sept. 1987	ALZA TTS	Male hormone
TTS-fentanyl	Dec. 1987	ALZA TTS	Analgesic
Oral Osmotic Systems			
Procardia-GITS (nifedipine)	Jan. 1987	Pfizer	Angina/hypertension
Minipress-GITS (prazosin)	Sept. 1987	Pfizer	Hypertension
OROS-albuterol (Volmax)	June 1986	Glaxo	Asthma
Pseudoephedrine/ brompheniramine	Dec. 1986	ALZA OROS	Decongestant/ antihistamine
Chlorpheniramine	Sept. 1987	ALZA OROS	Allergy remedy
Potassium chloride	Sept. 1987	ALZA OROS	Hypertension
Veterinary Osmotic System			
RUTS-selenium[b]	Sept. 1987	Schering-Plough	Cattle supplement

ALZA OROS = ALZA OROS Products Limited Partnership; ALZA TTS Research Partners Ltd.

a. Estraderm was royalty-free under Ciba-Geigy's termination agreement, but Ciba-Geigy subsequently provided a 1% royalty to ALZA in exchange for its cooperation in completing product development.

b. Food Additive Petition pending.

Source: Compiled from analyst reports.

licensing its drug delivery technologies to other firms. As of mid-1988, nearly half of ALZA's common stock was held by institutions (mutual funds, pension plan advisors, bank trust departments, and insurance firms); Mr. Gerstel sensed that a material proportion of these investors held ALZA because it allowed them to participate in a high-growth product segment via a relatively low-risk firm with lower fixed costs and more stable cash flows than many of its rivals.

EXHIBIT 3

ALZA CORPORATION FINANCIAL STATEMENTS, 1968–1987 (MILLIONS OF DOLLARS)

	Fiscal Year Ending June 30								Fiscal Year Ending December 31										
	1970[a]	1971	1972	1973	1974	1975	1976	1977	1977	1978	1979	1980	1981	1982	1983	1984	1985	1986	1987
Income Statement Data																			
Revenues:																			
Own sales[b]	$0.0	$0.0	$0.0	$0.0	$0.0	$0.0	$2.4	$6.7	$4.5	$3.7	$2.6	$2.8	$4.6	$4.8	$4.8	$5.8	$15.1	$15.8	$19.4
Research revenues	0.0	0.0	0.0	0.0	0.0	0.0	0.4	1.1	1.7	5.0	7.9	7.6	6.6	9.1	12.5	15.6	19.1	22.8	25.9
Other noninterest revenues[c]	0.0	0.0	0.0	0.0	0.0	0.0	0.0	0.0	0.0	0.0	0.6	1.1	0.8	1.8	5.2	9.1	11.3	19.4	25.5
Expenses																			
Research and development	1.9	2.4	4.2	6.7	8.1	9.0	8.4	8.1	7.6	8.0	8.4	8.2	8.4	10.1	10.0	11.8	14.5	19.4	23.0
Cost of goods sold	0.0	0.0	0.0	0.0	0.8	0.7	2.2	3.7	4.0	3.8	3.4	3.0	4.6	4.0	4.5	4.8	12.5	11.7	13.8
General and administrative	0.7	1.1	1.3	1.7	3.7	7.1	8.4	9.1	8.1	3.7	3.4	3.0	3.3	4.3	4.8	4.6	5.8	7.7	8.6
Depreciation	0.1	0.1	0.3	0.2	0.6	0.9	0.9	0.9	1.0	1.0	0.8	0.4	1.0	0.5	1.2	1.1	1.6	1.8	3.4
Income taxes	0.0	0.0	0.0	0.0	0.0	0.0	0.0	0.0	0.0	0.0	0.0	0.0	0.0	0.1	0.0	0.1	1.0	1.5	9.4
Net Income	(2.0)	(3.5)	(4.4)	(7.0)	(10.3)	(15.0)	(16.3)	(16.2)	(17.5)	(9.0)	(7.1)	(2.9)[d]	(6.6)	9.7[e]	1.3	6.1	9.7	16.8	14.0
Assets																			
Cash and short-term investments	$4.1	$25.8	$21.0	$19.8	$18.9	$10.1	$4.5	$1.6	$0.9	$4.2	$3.4	$5.1	$1.1	$6.7	$17.5	$15.8	$77.8	$81.2	$142.8
Other current assets minus current liabilities[f]	(0.2)	(0.3)	(0.1)	(0.2)	(0.8)	3.3	1.8	(9.6)	(17.0)	2.4	1.6	1.1	2.8	4.2	(0.4)	4.1	4.2	3.6	6.0
Gross plant, property and equipment	3.5	3.9	6.0	7.6	11.9	16.3	18.2	18.9	19.0	19.0	20.6	17.4[d]	19.1	19.8	21.3	26.6	32.9	50.7	83.2
Total assets	9.6	30.6	27.0	22.4	32.0	30.6	23.5	23.3	21.3	23.1	22.2	21.0	18.5	26.7	39.6	44.9	160.4	137.3	243.5

(Continued)

425

EXHIBIT 3 *(Continued)*

ALZA CORPORATION FINANCIAL STATEMENTS, 1968–1987 (MILLIONS OF DOLLARS)

	Fiscal Year Ending June 30								Fiscal Year Ending December 31										
	1970[a]	1971	1972	1973	1974	1975	1976	1977	1977	1978	1979	1980	1981	1982	1983	1984	1985	1986	1987
Capital structure																			
Long-term debt	$0.4	$5.0	$0.0	$0.0	$0.0	$6.1	$2.8	$1.7	$1.7	$21.7	$22.5	$16.8	$14.4	$10.2	$3.1	$3.1	$2.9	$2.7	$6.0
5½% convertible debt	—	—	—	—	—	—	—	—	—	—	—	—	—	—	—	—	—	—	75.0
8% convertible debt	—	—	—	—	—	—	—	—	—	—	—	—	—	—	25.0	25.0	22.6	—	—
Series 1982 preferred stock	—	—	—	—	—	—	—	—	—	—	—	—	—	11.4	—	—	—	—	—
6% preferred stock	—	—	—	—	—	—	—	—	—	10.5	16.1	21.7	29.0	—	—	—	—	—	—
Class A common[g]	—	—	—	—	—	—	—	—	—	—	—	—	—	81.9	82.1	86.6	152.3	177.7	0.30[h]
Class B common[g]	—	—	—	—	—	—	—	—	—	—	—	—	—	18.7	18.7	18.7	9.3	9.3	0.01[a]
Class C common[g]	—	—	—	—	—	—	—	—	—	—	—	—	—	0.9	0.9	—	—	—	—
Common stock[g]	3.0	5.0	5.0	5.1	6.1	6.2	7.6	7.8	7.8	7.8	7.8	7.8	7.8	—	—	—	—	—	—
Paid-in capital	5.6	30.8	34.6	37.3	50.8	55.6	71.8	73.7	73.7	73.7	73.7	73.7	73.7	—	—	—	—	—	190.5[h]
Deficit	2.0	5.5	10.0	16.9	27.2	42.3	58.6	74.8	83.6	92.5	99.7	102.6	109.2	99.4	98.2	92.2	82.5	65.8	51.8
Market value of equity at fiscal year end	99[i]	74[i]	138[i]	99[i]	121[i]	161	128	55	42	48	55	67	69	230	200	235	446	601	837

a. 1970 income statement includes period from inception (June 1968 through June 30, 1970).

b. Own sales include sales of manufactured products to other pharmaceutical firms, which then resell them under license.

c. Other revenues are primarily royalties and fees.

d. 1980 net income includes $4.3 million from the sale of a major ALZA facility.

e. 1982 net income includes a one-time payment of $10 million from Ciba-Geigy.

f. Defined as all current assets except cash and short-term investments minus current liabilities (excluding current portion of long-term debt).

g. ALZA: common stock had never paid a dividend.

h. ALZA reincorporated in 1987 in Delaware, leading to a change in the accounting treatment of equity.

i. These calculations are based on the mid-point of the share price range in the second quarter of the calendar year.

Source: Compiled from corporate documents, Compustat, and Daily Stock Price Guide.

EXHIBIT 4

ALZA CORPORATION FINANCIAL STATEMENTS, DECEMBER 31, 1987, AND ANALYSTS' ESTIMATES, OCTOBER 1988–1992 (MILLIONS OF DOLLARS EXCEPT PER SHARE DATA)

	Actual 1987	Estimates[a] 1988	1989	1990	1991	1992
Income Statement Data						
Royalties and fees	$17.1	$20.5	$46.5	$80.0	$138.5	$205.0
Net sales	19.4	24.5	37.0	60.0	100.0	170.0
Research revenues[b]	25.9	29.0	32.6	37.5	42.0	48.0
Other, primarily interest income	8.4	9.1	8.5	8.0	10.5	13.5
	70.8	83.1	124.6	185.5	291.0	436.5
Cost of goods shipped	13.8	15.0	25.2	40.2	66.0	108.8
R&D	23.0	28.5	36.0	46.5	60.0	75.0
General, administrative, and marketing	8.6	10.9	13.0	16.0	20.5	25.0
Interest expense	2.0	3.4	3.8	2.0	.5	.5
	47.4	57.8	78.0	104.7	147.0	209.3
Net income before taxes & extraordinary items	23.4	25.3	46.6	80.8	144.0	227.2
Taxes	9.4	8.0	16.8	29.1	51.8	81.8
Net income	14.0	17.2	29.9	51.7	92.2	145.4
Shares outstanding (millions)[c]	33.6	33.6	33.6	34.5	35.4	35.5
Earnings per share	$.42	$.51	$.89	$1.5	$2.6	$4.1
Statement of Cash Flows						
Cash flow from operating activities						
Net income	$14.0	$17.2	$29.9	$51.7	$92.2	$145.4
Depreciation	3.6	3.7	4.9	6.0	7.2	.5
Change in working capital and deferred taxes	(1.2)	(1.3)	(5.5)	(7.8)	(12.9)	(17.3)
	$16.4	$19.6	$29.3	$49.9	$86.5	$136.6
Cash flow from investment activities						
Capital expenditures[d]	(32.5)	(25.0)	(22.5)	(25.0)	(27.5)	(24.0)
Purchase of OROS[e]	—	(5.0)	(2.0)	(3.0)	(3.0)	(3.0)
Other	(8.9)	—	—	—	—	—
	($41.4)	($30.0)	($27.5)	($28.0)	($30.5)	($27.0)
Planned cash flows from financing activities[f]						
Sale of 5.5% convertible subordinate debentures	$72.8	—	—	—	—	—
Principal payments on debt	(0.2)	(0.2)	(0.1)	(0.1)	(0.1)	(0.1)
Issuance of stock[c]	3.8	1.5	1.8	2.5	2.5	2.5
	$76.4	$1.3	$1.7	$2.4	$2.4	$2.4

(Continued)

EXHIBIT 4   (Continued)

ALZA CORPORATION FINANCIAL STATEMENTS, DECEMBER 31, 1987, AND ANALYSTS' ESTIMATES, OCTOBER 1988–1992 (MILLIONS OF DOLLARS EXCEPT PER SHARE DATA)

Balance Sheet 12/31/87

Cash and investments	$142.8
Receivables	19.6
Inventories	6.0
Other current assets	3.6
Current assets	172.0
Net property plant & equipment	67.3
Other assets	4.2
Total assets	$243.5
Current liabilities[a]	$23.4
5.5% convertible subordinated debentures	75.0
Other liabilities	6.1
Total liabilities	104.5
Class A common stock[h]	0.3
Class B common stock[i]	0.01
Additional paid-in capital	190.5
Accumulated deficit	(51.8)
Stockholders' equity	139.0
Total liabilities and stockholders' equity	$243.5

a. Analysts' estimates, October 1988. These numbers do not reflect the impact of BES on ALZA's financial statements.

b. In 1987, ALZA received $5.9 million in research revenues from its two R&D limited partnerships.

c. Analyst has included additional shares due to projected exercise of stock options.

d. For facilities expansion, additional R&D campus, and new commercial manufacturing facilities.

e. Represents payments to holders of OROS R&D Limited Partnership.

f. ALZA paid no cash dividends at any point through 1988.

g. Includes $0.2 million of current portion of long-term debt.

h. 29.7 million shares outstanding; pays no dividends.

i. 1.45 million Class B shares outstanding granted to Ciba-Geigy in conjunction with 1982 restructuring agreement. These shares are non voting and are not listed. Otherwise, these shares are equivalent to Class A shares. Convertible at Ciba-Geigy's option into two shares of ALZA Class A shares. These shares pay no dividends.

Source: ALZA 1987 annual report for actual numbers. Estimates from analysts' reports published in July–October 1988.

OPPORTUNITIES AND CHALLENGES OF INNOVATION

Just as new technologies had led to ALZA's current success, they posed challenges and opportunities for ALZA's future. As the firm's success had been increasingly recognized, several competitors accelerated their drug delivery development efforts. These included both established pharmaceutical firms and venture capital-financed startup firms. Several of the new firms explicitly noted their intention to become "the next ALZA" in their promotional material. Recent advances in materials science and biotechnology suggested that the fundamental technologies of drug delivery were likely to change dramatically in the years to come.

Advances in materials, electronics, and the understanding of the human body had made possible an array of new delivery mechanisms. ALZA management considered two technologies to be especially critical to their long-run success. The first was bio-erodible polymer technologies. ALZA was experimenting with a variety of advanced materials, which released drugs slowly and then degraded. These "Alzamer" materials combined features of fabric and plastics. Such advanced polymer technologies had been important to ALZA since its initial formation, but the extent to which the rate and duration of drug delivery could be controlled had increased vastly. Their potential was enormous. For instance, pouches of drugs could be surgically implanted into the human body and remain active for up to six months, accelerating the healing of broken bones or damaged tissues. After the drug was delivered, the packet containing the drug would erode. Similarly, chemical implants could be placed next to cancerous tumors, avoiding most of the debilitating side effects of chemotherapy.

A second emerging technology for drug delivery was electrotransport. ALZA's skin patches had been based on passive diffusion: the drug crossed the skin barrier on its own accord and entered the blood stream. By running a low electric current through the drug reservoir, the rate of transport and the types of drugs that could be transmitted both increased. For instance, complex molecules like proteins, which would not move through the skin on their own accord, could be delivered through electrotransport. This technology also permitted much more control over the drug delivery process. For instance, a patient facing chronic pain might adjust the flow of a drug as needed. In other cases, electronic monitors could assess the patient's condition and adjust the drug delivery rate.

Individual products incorporating these therapeutic systems were not likely to reach the marketplace until at least the mid-1990s. The two new technologies had the potential, however, to open up the field of drug delivery to many applications that would otherwise not be possible with the company's OROS and transdermal drug delivery technologies. Mr. Gerstel was aware that several competitors had targeted these new technologies as well and had launched their own R&D programs. Wall Street observers felt that many of these competing products might infringe on ALZA's patents, but it would take protracted litigation to resolve this issue. Exhibit 5 summarizes some of these competitors and their key products in 1988.

The strategic future of the firm demanded investments in polymer and electrotransport drug delivery. From an operational and organizational perspective, the research to bring these technologies to fruition would best be done by ALZA scientists in ALZA laboratories. The research team and the informal open environment that Dr. Zaffaroni had put in place and that Mr. Gerstel and Dr. Jane Shaw (ALZA's president and chief operating officer) had cultivated were ideally suited for work on these two newest technologies. In addition, ALZA's two decades of experience negotiating with large pharmaceutical firms gave its executives the skills and contacts to profitably license any products the technologies might produce without surrendering substantial benefits to their much larger partners. Stripping the necessary people from ALZA to staff a stand-alone entity would damage the base business, and trying to reconstruct the research environment using outsiders would be costly and risky. Therefore, the technologies would need to be developed in ALZA laboratories and commercialized by ALZA executives dealing with ALZA customers.

EXHIBIT 5

KEY COMPETITORS OF ALZA CORPORATION, 1988

Company	Product	Status	Type of Firm
Transdermal Delivery			
Key Pharmaceuticals	Nitroglycerine patches	Manufacturing product	Subsidiary of U.S. firm traded on New York Stock Exchange
G.D. Searle	Nitroglycerine patches	Manufacturing product	Subsidiary of U.S. firm traded on New York Stock Exchange
Health-Chem	Nitroglycerine patches	Manufacturing product	U.S. firm traded on American Stock Exchange
Health-Chem	Other patch products	Product trials	U.S. firm traded on American Stock Exchange
Elan Corporation	Nicotine patch	Early stage research	Irish firm, publicly traded
Forest Laboratories	Nitroglycerine patches	Early stage research	U.S. firm traded on American Stock Exchange
Moleculon	Several patch products	Early stage research	U.S. firm traded on NASDAQ
Cygnus Research	Several patch products	Product trials	U.S. firm, privately-held and venture-financed
Several Japanese firms	Nitroglycerine patches	Product trials	Japanese firms, publicly-traded
Oral Drug Delivery			
PennWalt	Ion-exchange mechanisms	Product trials	U.S. firm traded on New York Stock Exchange
KV Pharmaceutical	Various technologies	Product trials	U.S. firm traded on American Stock Exchange
Elan Corporation	Liquid suspensions	Product trials	Irish firm, publicly traded
Elan Corporation	Slow-release tablets	Product trials	Irish firm, publicly traded
Forest Laboratories	Controlled release tablets	Manufacturing product	U.S. firm traded on American Stock Exchange
Gacell Laboratories	Slow-release tablets	Manufacturing product	Subsidiary of major Swedish firm
Astra	Slow-release tablets	Product trials	Major Swedish firm

(Continued)

EXHIBIT 5 (Continued)

KEY COMPETITORS OF ALZA CORPORATION, 1988

Company	Product	Status	Type of Firm
Drug Delivery to Eye			
Merck	Eye injections	Early stage research	U.S. firm traded on New York Stock Exchange
Diversified Tech, Inc.	Eye pouch insert	Early stage research	U.S. firm traded on NASDAQ
Bausch and Lomb	Corneal shield	Early stage research	U.S. firm traded on New York Stock Exchange
Intrauterine Devices			
Gynopharm	Various technologies	Early stage research	U.S. firm, privately-held
Electrotransport			
Motion Control	Anaesthesia delivery in surgery	Product being marketed	U.S. firm, privately-held
	Hypertension drug delivery		
Medtronic	Polypeptide drug delivery	Early stage research	U.S. firm traded on New York Stock Exchange
Drug Delivery Systems	Polypeptide drug delivery	Early stage research	U.S. firm, privately-held
MacroChem	Antibiotic delivery	Early stage research	U.S. firm traded on NASDAQ
Lectec	Delivery of various drugs	Early stage research	U.S. firm, privately-held and venture-financed
Cygnus Research		Early stage research	U.S. firm, privately-held and venture-financed
Advanced Polymers			
INTERX	Delivery of various drugs	Early stage research	Subsidiary of U.S. firm traded on New York Stock Exchange
Nova Pharmaceutical	Delivery of cancer drugs	Early stage research	U.S. firm traded on NASDAQ
Eli Lilly	Delivery of insulin	Early stage research	U.S. firm traded on New York or American Stock Exchange
Enzytech	Delivery of various drugs	Early stage research	U.S. firm, privately-held and venture-financed

Source: Compiled from analyst reports, *Corporate Technology Directory, Moody's Industrial Directory, Moody's OTC Directory, BioScan,* and other directories.

FINANCING ALTERNATIVES

Funding the new technologies would not be inexpensive, as shown in Exhibit 6. Bringing the therapeutic systems to the point where they could incorporate products and their continued development could be underwritten by potential licensees would cost more than $40 million over the coming 5 years. Mr. Gerstel could identify at least three broad alternatives for financing the new technologies: (1) using ALZA's money, whether internally generated funds or new securities issued by the firm, and organizing the new venture inside ALZA, (2) establishing a joint venture with a major pharmaceutical company, or (3) setting up a partly ALZA-owned R&D organization funded by ALZA and equity investors in the subsidiary.

While the first choice was feasible, it had unattractive financial implications. Even though the $40 million was arguably a long-term investment in the future like an investment in property or plant, FASB rules insisted that these R&D costs be expensed each year. Thus, a current direct investment in these technologies, if funded either through internally generated funds or by external funds raised directly by the firm, would substantially depress ALZA's reported earnings. Mr. Gerstel worried about the effect this might have on ALZA's stock price.

Most important, funding these newer, riskier products through ALZA would subject its shareholders to much higher risk than present in its traditional product development and licensing business. Mr. Gerstel publicly stated his concerns about existing shareholders:

> ALZA is an extremely low-risk pharmaceutical company . . . (but) in addition to just developing products for today, we want to continue to be a world leader in new technology. This involves much higher risk. ALZA shareholders have waited a long time for us to be as successful as we are today. If we're going to develop higher-risk technology, we want to give our shareholders a choice in whether they want to participate.[10]

ALZA's second alternative was to enter into a joint venture agreement with a cash-rich large pharmaceutical firm. This arrangement could be structured to have much less effect on ALZA's reported earnings, but to the degree that ALZA had an ownership interest, it would need to report losses. A large pharmaceutical partner might be able to contribute skills and expertise to the projects, but ALZA's experience with Ciba-Geigy demonstrated the potential problems of managing these relationships. Furthermore, negotiating with a pharmaceutical firm from the outset meant that ALZA's shareholders would surrender much of the upside of the new technologies. In exchange for providing the financing, ALZA's potential corporate partner almost surely would demand unrestricted rights to use the technology and perhaps even the right to sublicense it to others. Mr. Gerstel guessed that bringing in a large pharmaceutical partner would reduce ALZA's potential profits from the technologies by 50% or more.

A third alternative to fund the new technologies was for ALZA to sell equity in an off balance sheet R&D subsidiary to several investors. If the Tax Reform Act of 1986 had not been enacted, Mr. Gerstel could have funded the work on polymers and electrotransport using a vehicle called an R&D limited partnership (RDLP). This financing structure is diagrammed in Exhibit 7, using as an example one of ALZA's RDLPs. ALZA had funded the development of products incorporating its two main delivery

---

[10] Comments by Martin Gerstel, reported in Stuart Weiss, "Beating SWORDs into Stock Shares," *CFO Magazine*, August 1990, p. 46.

EXHIBIT 6

BIO-ELECTRO SYSTEMS PROJECTED FINANCIAL STATEMENTS, 1988–1993 (MILLIONS OF DOLLARS)

	1988	1989	1990	1991	1992	1993	Total
Cash Flow Assuming Maximum Net Proceeds Raised From Offering							
Beginning cash balance	—	$39.7	$35.2	$27.9	$19.5	$9.8	—
Net offering proceeds	43.0	—	—	—	—	—	43.0
Interest income[a]	.3	2.4	2.0	1.5	.9	.3	7.4
Total	43.3	42.1	37.2	29.4	20.4	10.1	50.4
Development contract payments[b]							
"Alzamer" polymers	1.8	2.7	4.5	5.1	5.8	5.2	25.1
Electrotransport	1.7	3.7	4.2	4.2	4.2	4.3	22.3
General and administrative expenses[c]	0.1	0.5	0.6	0.6	0.6	0.6	3.0
Total	3.6	6.9	9.3	9.9	10.6	10.1	50.4
Ending cash balance[d,e]	$39.7	$35.2	$27.9	$19.5	$9.8	—	—
Cash Flow Assuming Minimum Net Proceeds Raised From Offering							
Beginning cash balance	—	$24.5	$19.2	$12.7	$6.9	$3.3	—
Net offering proceeds	$28.0	—	—	—	—	—	$28.0
Interest income[a]	0.1	1.4	1.0	0.6	0.2	0.1	3.4
Total	28.1	25.9	20.2	13.3	7.1	3.4	31.4
Development contract payments[a]							
"Alzamer" polymers	1.8	2.5	3.0	2.5	0.9	0.6	11.3
Electrotransport	1.7	3.7	3.9	3.3	2.3	2.2	17.1
General and administrative expenses[c]	0.1	0.5	0.6	0.6	0.6	0.6	3.0
Total	3.6	6.7	7.5	6.4	3.8	3.4	31.4
Ending Cash Balance[d,e]	24.5	19.2	12.7	6.9	3.3	—	—

a. BES was not projected to earn any revenues, other than interest income, over this period. The ultimate revenue potential of products incorporating BES's therapeutic systems was thought to be in the "hundreds of millions of dollars," although it was impossible to estimate a more exact value.

b. These payments will be made from BES to ALZA and recognized as revenue by ALZA.

c. These charges include virtually no non-cash charges like depreciation or amortization.

d. BES's stockholders' equity in each year would be calculated as its capital raised from the offering less cumulative *pre-tax* losses.

e. While BES's cumulative losses would generate substantial net operating losses for financial reporting purposes, they would not generate large net operating losses for tax purposes.

Source: BES Prospectus.

technologies, the transdermal and OROS delivery systems, through off balance sheet RDLPs in 1983.

In an RDLP the sponsoring corporation sets up the partnership, licenses the rights to a technology to the partnership for specific uses, and obtains a general partner's interest in the partnership. As general partner, the sponsoring corporation acts as manager of the partnership, making operating decisions for the partnership. Limited partners, who do not manage the day-to-day operations of the venture, invest money in the project, but their personal liability is limited to the amount of their capital contributions. In a standard RDLP the sponsoring corporation retained the right to buy out the

EXHIBIT 7

EXAMPLE OF AN R&D LIMITED PARTNERSHIP: ALZA TTS RESEARCH PARTNERS, LTD.

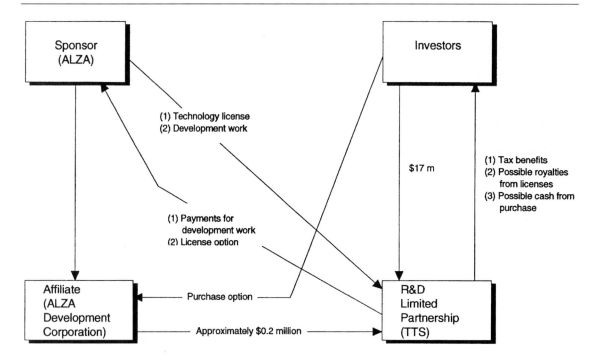

In February 1983, a R&D limited partnership, ALZA TTS Research Partners Ltd. (TTS), was set up to develop three to six products in certain specified therapeutic categories. ALZA gave TTS a non-exclusive, royalty-free license to use ALZA's technology for the specific products identified. ALZA's wholly owned subsidiary, ALZA Development Corporation, as the general partner of ALZA TTS, contributed 1% of the cash capital to the partnership. TTS entered into a development contract with ALZA by which ALZA would use its best efforts to complete development of the products.

An offer of 3,200 units of the Class A limited partnership interests were offered to investors for $5,000 per unit, raising about $17 million. (Class B partnership units were also privately placed.) Effectively, 99% of the tax losses generated by TTS were passed along to the Class A limited partners, while ALZA Development Corporation received 1% of the tax losses.

While TTS "owned" the products it developed, as part of the agreement setting up the RDLP, it granted ALZA Development Corporation certain rights. ALZA Development Corporation retained the right, but not the obligation, to acquire the interests of the limited partners by paying a lump sum equal to $60 million, $90 million, or $120 million if it bought them out in 1987, 1988, or 1989 and beyond, respectively. ALZA also retained the right to continue development of products once TTS ran out of funds, and to license individual products, paying predetermined royalty fees.

TTS ran out of funds in 1987, and as of November 1988, ALZA Development Corporation had not exercised its purchase option. However, in 1987, ALZA did exercise its option to continue product development for two of the partnership's products and entered into a marketing agreement with a partner for one of these products.

limited partners and obtain exclusive right to use or license the technology through purchase or license options.

One clear appeal of RDLPs in the early 1980s was their tax advantages. The R&D ventures funded typically produced large losses in their early years, given that moneys spent on R&D were expensed and not capitalized. These losses were passed through to the limited partners, who were then able to use them to reduce their personal income taxes. Therefore, RDLP investors were typically individuals with high marginal tax rates. In contrast, sponsoring corporations generally faced lower marginal tax rates, and with net operating loss carry forwards, would have had to effectively defer the use of these taxable losses for many years. Many of the investors in ALZA's RDLPs were thought to be highly taxed individuals also holding ALZA common stock.

A second appeal of RDLPs was their accounting treatment from the sponsoring firm's perspective. The partnership contracted with the sponsoring corporation to conduct the actual R&D and paid development fees to the sponsoring corporation. Thus, the sponsoring corporation could effectively convert its R&D activities from expenses to revenues.

Mr. Gerstel was reluctant to use an RDLP to fund the polymer and electrotransport drug delivery research. The Tax Reform Act (TRA) of 1986 significantly diminished the attractiveness of RDLPs. Not only did the TRA lower the top marginal tax rate on households from 50% to 28% and raise the tax on capital gains relative to ordinary income, it also severely limited the deductions individuals could take from investments like RDLPs, which were termed passive activities. As a result, the RDLPs were out-of-fashion and hard to sell.

The proposal on Mr. Gerstel's desk to form Bio-Electro Systems, Inc. had many similarities to the earlier RDLPs. As in an RDLP, ALZA would contribute certain technologies to the new firm, would contract to conduct BES's R&D, and would retain the right to obtain exclusive licenses to the technology and ultimately to purchase the common stock of BES along a predetermined schedule. Yet the proposal to create BES had some striking differences from a typical RDLP. First, it would be funding therapeutics systems research much further from commercialization than the product development in a typical RDLP. Second, it would create an exchange-listed investment vehicle, as compared with illiquid, nontradable limited partnership interests. Unlike RDLPs sold to high net worth individuals, the investment would likely be targeted to the normal buyers of initial public offerings, i.e., institutional investors like mutual funds, pension plans, and individual shareholders. Finally, it would give BES shareholders a warrant to buy ALZA shares.

If the BES proposal was sensible, Mr. Gerstel still had to worry about its execution. His initial reaction, reflected in the offering document, was to distribute the BES units through a nonunderwritten rights offering. In a rights offering, existing shareholders are given an opportunity (or right) to purchase a new security by paying a subscription price. Shareholders who do not wish to subscribe can either let their right expire or sell the right to others who choose to exercise it, pay the subscription price, and receive the new security. In contrast to a rights offering, a public offering would have been made to all interested parties regardless of whether they currently held shares. While rights offerings were typically less costly than public offerings, they were uncommon because of their greater complexity. Whether a security is offered narrowly through a rights offering or broadly through a public offering, the issuer must decide whether to have the offering underwritten. If an offering is underwritten, an investment bank commits to purchase the unsold or unsubscribed portion of the deal at an agreed-upon price. While virtually all public offerings by major firms were underwritten, not all rights offerings were.

If he went forward with a nonunderwritten rights offering, Mr. Gerstel would have to price the units to be attractive to ALZA shareholders, so that they could sell their rights if they chose not to subscribe. Setting the price of the novel BES units was a challenge. There were few publicly-traded companies to compare to BES. Several start-ups were specializing in advanced drug delivery systems but remained privately held; other, more established firms were developing such systems as part of a range of R&D activities. None of these utilized the financial innovation embodied in the BES proposal. Data that Mr. Gerstel and his team would use to set the price of the offering are included in Exhibits 8 and 9.

By structuring the offering as a pure rights offering, Mr. Gerstel would not have an investment bank's sales force to sell the novel deal to his shareholders. To the extent practical and allowed by the Securities and Exchange Commission, Mr. Gerstel would meet with groups of ALZA investors to explain the plan. In addition, ALZA retained Merrill Lynch to serve as financial advisor, for which it would be paid 3.2% of the gross proceeds raised. Merrill Lynch had helped prepare the financing plan and would assist in presenting the deal to ALZA shareholders and in pricing the BES units.

While Mr. Gerstel was confident that ALZA needed to move forward on the polymer and electrotransport research, how it would be financed was not a trivial decision. ALZA's future dictated that the firm find $40 million to fund new high-risk businesses that would be advanced inside the firm. Yet for accounting reasons and based on his reading of his shareholders, Mr. Gerstel would prefer that these new research efforts reside outside the firm or off its balance sheet. As he reviewed the proposed plan, he wondered whether it made sense, how he would sell it to his shareholders, and what price he should charge them for the right to participate in BES.

EXHIBIT 8

CAPITAL MARKETS DATA, NOVEMBER 18, 1988

ALZA Class A common	$23\frac{1}{8}$
Interest Rates[a]	
Treasury Securities	
1-Month	6.86%
6-Month	8.36
1-Year	8.57
3-Year	8.83
5-Year	8.91
10-Year	9.03
Long-term corporate bonds by credit rating[b]	
AAA	9.70%
AA	10.08
A	10.53
BBB	10.86
BB	11.78
B	12.25

a. Expressed on a bond equivalent yield basis.

b. ALZA senior debt was rated Ba or BB at this time.

Source: Interactive Data Corporation (IDC).

EXHIBIT 9

ALZA CORPORATION COMMON STOCK PRICE DATA

ALZA Class A Common Stock Price, 1983 - November 18, 1988[a]

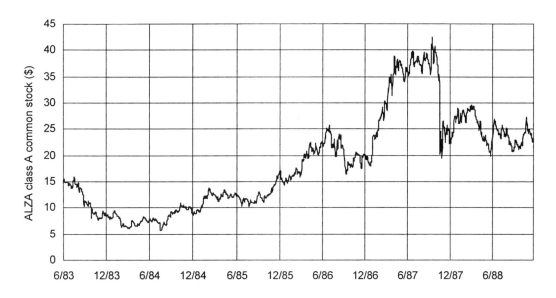

Annualized Volatility of ALZA Class A Common Stock, 1983 - November 18, 1988[b]

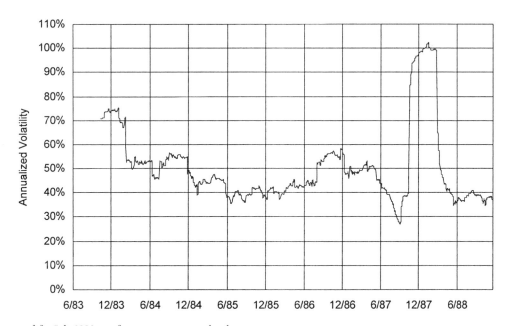

a. Corrected for July 1986 two-for-one common stock split.

b. Calculated on the basis of past three months' data. ALZA's common stock beta: 2.0 (calculated on basis of prior sixty month's data by Value Line).

Source: IDC (stock price data) and casewriters' analysis (volatility).

DS-3

CREDIT DERIVATIVES

25

Note on Credit Derivatives

A derivative is a contingent contract that derives its value from changes in the specified risk of an underlying, which could be a particular asset or a reference index. In contrast to cash instruments, derivatives are primarily used to transfer risk rather than value. As such, they are meaningful contracts even when their value is zero.

Derivatives are typically identified by the type of risk that causes changes in their value. Interest rate derivatives (such as interest-rate swaps) fluctuate with the changes in interest rate, equity derivatives (for instance stock options) with equity prices, and commodity derivatives (such as commodity futures) with commodity prices. Some derivatives embody more than one type of risk, such as cross-currency swaps, which simultaneously transfer both exchange rate risk and interest rate risk, or basis swaps, which trade one type of risk for another. A credit derivative is a contingent agreement that subjects the timing and amount of its settlement cash flows, and consequently its value as well, to the changes in the designated underlying's credit risk.

CREDIT RISK

Simply put, credit risk is the risk that a borrower (the obligor) won't pay back the lender. When pricing credit derivatives, this risk is most visibly shown in the spread between the promised yield on a defaultable bond or loan and the yield on the default-free U.S. Treasury bond of the same maturity. This is known as the yield spread. The following formula shows the two parts that make up the yield spread.

$$\text{Yield Spread}^1 = \text{Default Probability} \times \text{Loss Given Default} + \text{Credit Risk Premium}$$

The first part concerns the uncertainty of the obligor's ability to make contractual payments. It expresses in percentage terms the potential loss to the creditor due to the obligor's default. Default probability measures the probability that the obligor will be unable to make payments on time. Loss given default (LGD) equals loss, total obliga-

Professors George Chacko and Peter Hecht, Research Associate Anders Sjöman of the HBS Europe Research Center and Kate Hao (MBA 04) prepared this note as the basis for class discussion.

[1] The formula is often presented as "Yield Spread = Probability of Default × Loss Given Default." The probability of default is then under the special risk-neutral measure, which assumes that the expected yield equals the risk free rate.

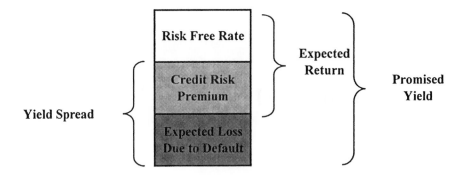

Figure A   Decomposing the Promised Yield on a Defaultable Obligation

Source: Authors.

tion reduced by the amount that cannot be recovered, as a percentage of the total obligation. The second part, credit risk premium, reflects the market's risk aversion toward defaults in general. When the market has low tolerance for default risk exposure, the credit risk premium is large. Figure A above summarizes the relationship.

Defaulting is rare but can inflict significant damages. The typical firm has an average per annum default probability of 2%.[2] Credit ratings issued by agencies, such as Moody's and S&P, reflect estimates of an entity's default probability, which due to cross default clauses pervades all the entity's obligations. (See Exhibit 1 for an example of a credit rating system.) Corporations of the same rating share similar assessment of their probabilities to default. Empirical evidence shows that the probability of default increases exponentially with descending credit rating. On average, two out of 10,000 AAA-rated companies as compared to four of every 100 CCC rated firms default in a year.

LGD depends on the terms of the individual obligation, including seniority of claim,[3] value of underlying collateral, and timing of cash flows. For instance, one empirical study shows that LGD ranges from 49% for senior secured bonds, 69% for subordinated bonds, to 81% for zero coupon bonds.[4]

Credit risk premium is the difference between expected return and risk free rate. It can be calculated from the Capital Asset Pricing Model (CAPM)[5] as the product of market risk premium and the beta of the obligation.[6] The more systematic risk the obligation conveys, the greater is the credit risk premium's influence on the expected return of the obligation and consequently the promised yield. High yield debts typically have higher beta. Unsurprisingly, their yields are sensitive to changes in market risk premium. By contrast, investment grade debts have much smaller beta and more stable yields.

In summary, credit risk encompasses default risk of the obligor and an adverse change in credit risk premium. Default risk broadly includes both the risk of the obligor actually defaulting and the risk of credit agencies' downgrading the obligor's credit rating. (The risk of credit rating changes is usually referred to as credit migration risk.)

---

[2] P. Crosbie, J. Bohn, "Modeling Default Risk," Moody's KMV working paper, Dec. 18, 2003.

[3] Corporate bonds are normally issued with a ranking against previously issued bonds by the same corporation. The ranking, or seniority, shows which bond will be repaid first, in case of a default.

[4] P. Crosbie, J. Bohn, "Modeling Default Risk," Moody's KMV working paper, Dec. 18, 2003.

[5] As a model, the CAPM describes the pricing of all assets, including derivatives.

[6] "Beta" is a measurement of an asset's risk in relation to the market.

EXHIBIT 1

EXAMPLE OF RATING SYSTEM: STANDARD & POOR'S CREDIT RATING SYSTEM

Rating	Description
AAA	Best credit quality—Extremely reliable with regard to financial obligations.
AA	Very good credit quality—Very reliable.
A	More susceptible to economic conditions—still good credit quality.
BBB	Lowest rating in investment grade.
BB	Caution is necessary—Best sub-investment credit quality.
B	Vulnerable to changes in economic conditions—Currently showing ability to meet financial obligations.
CCC	Currently vulnerable to nonpayment—Dependent on favorable economic conditions.
CC	Highly vulnerable to a payment default.
C	Close to or already bankrupt—payment on the obligation currently continued.
D	Payment default on some financial obligation has actually occurred.

Source: Compiled by case author from Standard and Poor's website, www.standardandpoors.com, and from Riskglossary, http://www.riskglossary.com/articles/credit_risk.htm. (Both sites accessed April 2005.)

CREDIT DERIVATIVES

Credit risk permeates the market—it resides in every private contract. Before settlement, the buyer risks the seller's failure to deliver, and the seller risks the buyers' failure to pay. Naturally, credit protection of various shapes and forms has existed as long as there has been exchange of goods. In capital markets, credit insurance and loan guarantees have been the most widely applied credit protection. Structured securities that incorporate credit as a risk factor also have enjoyed a reasonably long history. Options on corporate bonds have been traded since the 1970s. Total rate of return swaps (TRORS) on mortgage-backed securities were introduced in the 1980s.[7]

Derivative instruments that trade on isolated credit risk, thus named "credit derivatives," first entered the market in 1992,[8] when Wall Street bankers attempted to engineer new contracts that would strip out credit risk from market risk[9] and trade it independently. The innovation was instigated by demand from two client groups: commercial banks and securities dealers. Commercial banks when faced with clients' requests for additional loans often were caught between the conflicting goals of preserving customer relationship and limiting credit risk concentration. In the derivatives market, customers' preference for strong counterparty credit worthiness drove disproportionately large amount of business to a small circle of highly rated dealers. Also wary of counterparty risk, the handful of dealers frequently transacted among themselves to offload the risks attained from writing derivative contracts with their customers. As the size of the risk in each contract grew, the capacity of the inner circle to digest risk constrained dealers from scaling up their derivatives business. When the investment bankers found credit derivatives to solve these problems, little did they know they were inau-

---

[7] J. Tavakoli, *Credit Derviatives & Synthetic Structures.* John Wiley & Sons, 2001, pg. 10–11.

[8] Jonathan Isaac, "Credit derivatives make tentative start in London," Reuter News, 26 May 1993.

[9] See Sanjiv Das and Stephen Lynagh, "Overview of Credit Derivatives," Harvard Business School Note No. 297-086 (Boston: Harvard Business School Publishing, 1997).

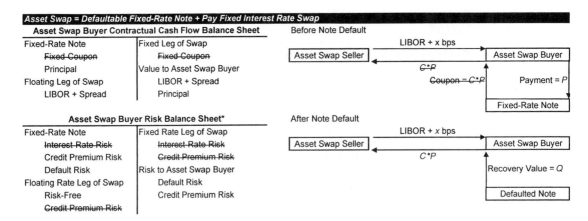

Figure B   Asset Swap

Note: Assume no counterparty risk, and that the interest-rate risk on the credit spread is negligible.
C = Fixed Rate Note Coupon Rate   Q = Recovery Value of Note after Default
x = Credit Spread at Inception   P = Principal/Par Value of Fixed Rate Note
Source: Authors.

gurating a new breed of structured credit products that would fundamentally change the securities market.

The distinguishing feature of credit derivatives from earlier structured credit products is that the later generation detaches risk from capital and delineates credit risk from the other risk factors.[10] We will now introduce three major types of credit derivatives—let's think of them as building blocks for credit derivatives—by decomposing them into more elementary security types. The examples used are plain vanilla structures and the mechanics are simplified for illustration purposes.

The Ancestor—Asset Swaps

Credit derivatives trace their lineage to asset swaps. A plain vanilla asset swap is a bilateral contract combining a fixed-rate note and a fixed-to-floating interest-rate swap. The cash flows from the fixed leg of the swap and from the coupon payments on the fixed-rate note are opposite in direction but identical in amount and timing, thereby completely offsetting each other. An asset swap is effectively a floating rate note (FRN) with coupon rate equal to LIBOR plus a spread that reflects the credit risk in the fixed rate note. Almost all of the interest-rate risk[11] is hedged out. The residual risk is primarily the credit risk of the fixed-rate note, born by the asset swap buyer. If the note defaults, the owner of the asset swap will sustain a loss on the loan and continue to pay the fixed-leg of the swap. If the credit spread on the note widens, either due to an increase in credit risk premium or a rating downgrade of the note, the asset swap will also decline in value. In the following sections we will show how an asset swap turns into the most basic credit derivative structures with some minor makeovers.

Figure B above shows a typical Asset Swap. Please note that in the figure (as well as in other figures in this note), we will use the following notation:

[10] An exception is Total Rate of Return Swaps, which also incorporate interest rate risk.

[11] The floating leg is not a pure floater because in most cases the underlying note of the asset swap is below AA, the equivalent rating of LIBOR, the most common reference floating rate. The spread added to the floating leg has non-zero duration.

- Elements that cancel each other out are stricken out
- *MTM* = Mark to Market Note Value
- *Q* = Recovery Value of Note after Default
- *W* = Put Option Premium
- *C* = Fixed Rate Note Coupon Rate
- *P* = Principal Amount or Par Value of Fixed Rate Note
- *x* = Credit Spread at Inception
- *y* = Credit Spread at Termination

Building Block Structure I—Credit Default Swaps

Imagine the above asset swap buyer financed her purchase with a pure floater. Before the fixed-rate note defaults, she receives the asset swap rate, which equals LIBOR plus the credit spread, and pays LIBOR on the pure floater. Her net periodic cash inflow as a percentage on the principal equals the yield spread. At maturity, the principal on her asset swap and the principal from the pure floater, if paid in full, will cancel each other out. However, if the fixed-rate note defaults, the asset swap buyer is still obligated to pay the par amount on the pure floater, although her asset swap package has devalued due to the default. At this point, the recovery value of the asset swap, to the extent it is insufficient to repay the pure floater principal, results in a loss to the investor.

A credit default swap (CDS) can be thought of as an asset swap and a short pure floater (FRN with coupon rate set at LIBOR). The protection seller in a CDS takes a very similar position to that of an asset swap buyer financed by a pure floater. She receives a periodic payment approximating the yield spread on the underlying, a fixed-rate note in this example. In exchange, she is liable to make the protection buyer whole if the underlying defaults. In a CDS contract that requires physical delivery, the defaulted note is presented to the protection seller for par.

However, there are a couple of important differences in the above two transactions. First, a default terminates contractual cash flows in a CDS but does not cancel the interest swap agreement in an asset swap. Thus, the asset swap buyer remains exposed to interest rate risk on the swap. Secondly, a CDS does not cover the risk of credit risk premium widening. If the underlying depreciates without actually defaulting, the CDS protection seller is free from any obligation, yet the asset swap holder will suffer a loss.

Figure C shows both a floating rate note (which has been financed by a pure floater) and a credit default swap.

Building Block Structure II—Total Rate of Return Swaps

In introducing an asset swap, we separated it into a defaultable fixed-rate note and a pay-fixed interest-rate swap. Likewise, the position taken by the total return receiver in a total rate of return swap (TRORS) can be decomposed into a long defaultable fixed-rate note and a short pure floater. Suppose an investor financed her purchase of a fixed-rate defaultable bond with a pure floater that matures before the note. When the floater is outstanding, the investor receives the cash flows from the note while paying LIBOR on her debt. When the floater matures, the investor has to pay back the principal out of her asset, the fixed-rate note at market value.

The total return receiver in a TRORS gets all the cash flows from a reference asset, including the coupon income and the marked-to-market value of the asset at ter-

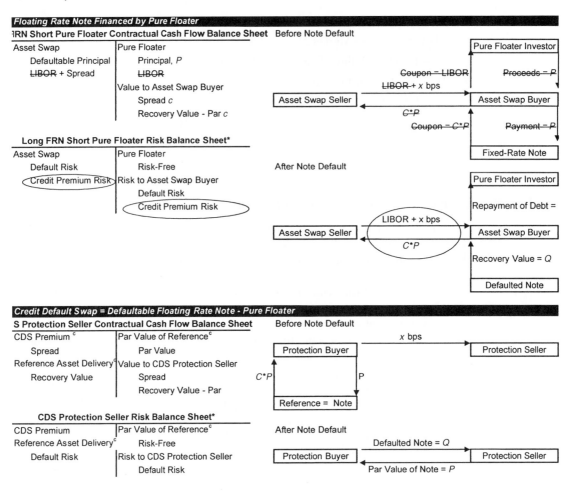

Figure C Floating Rate Note (Financed by Pure Floater) and Credit Default Swap

Note: [c]Contingent upon reference default.
Assume no counterparty risk, and that the interest-rate risk on the credit spread is negligible.
C = Fixed Rate Note Coupon Rate Q = Recovery Value of Note after Default
x = Credit Spread at Inception P = Principal/Par Value of Fixed Rate Note
Source: Authors.

mination of the agreement. Parallel to these benefits, she pays a LIBOR based fee before termination and surrenders the par value of the reference asset at termination. In our example diagram below, we set both the interest on the pure floater financing and the fee to the TRORS total return payer at LIBOR. In practice, the rate is usually greater by a spread commensurate with the credit risk of the investor.[12] One should note that compared to CDS and asset swaps, TRORS do not delineate credit risk from market risk. Figure D shows a fixed rate defaultable note (financed by a pure floater) and a total rate of return swap.

Now let's return to the earlier challenges presented to the investment bankers in the 1990s. A loan TRORS would solve the commercial banks' problem by allowing banks to exchange exposures without moving the loans on their balance sheet, thereby re-

---

[12] The spread is called a "haircut."

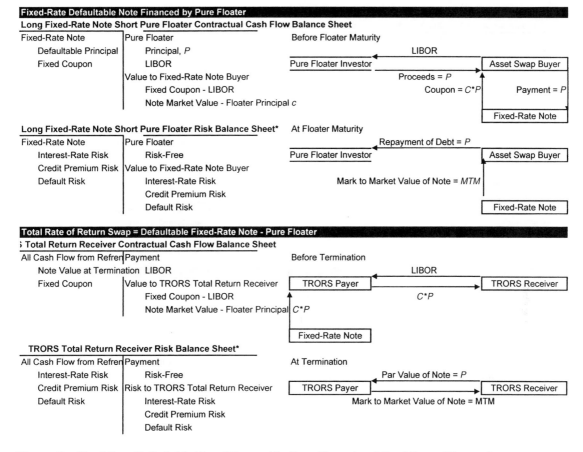

Figure D Fixed Rate Defaultable Note (Financed by Pure Floater) and Total Rate of Return Swap

Note: Assume no counterparty risk, and that the interest-rate risk on the credit spread is negligible.
C = Fixed Rate Note Coupon Rate MTM = Mark to Market Note Value
P = Principal of Floater/Par Value of Fixed Rate Note/Notional of Reference
Source: Authors.

ducing both parties' credit risk concentration. With such arrangements, banks can de-
vote more time and resources to customer relationship building and marketing. A CDS
could solve the securities dealers' problem. Signing a CDS with a third party, which
could be of a lower credit rating, to protect themselves from counterparty risk, the securities dealers could add a large number of lower credit quality institutions to the ros-
ter of partners to offload risk. Thus risks in derivatives market can be diffused through
a much wider realm.

Building Block Structure III—Credit Spread Options

The other credit derivatives structure that completes the building blocks is credit spread
options. They are essentially options on asset swaps. Suppose a one-year put option is
purchased on a newly issued five-year asset swap with strike set at the original asset
swap spread. At the end of one year, if the current spread on a four-year asset swap is
wider than the strike, the put option is in the money, and the owner can exercise the

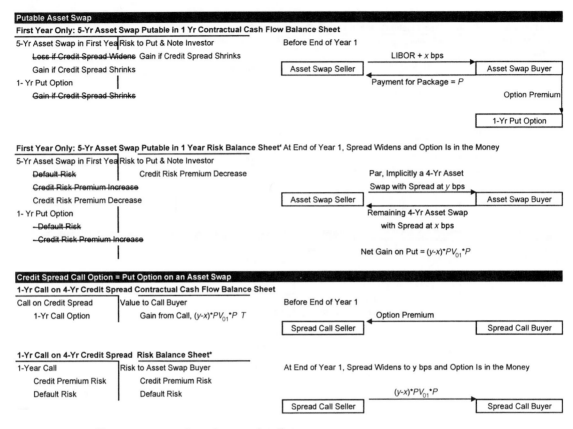

Figure E   Puttable Asset Swap and Credit Spread Call Option

Note: T Credit spread does not widen and option expires without being exercised.
$x = $ 5-Yr Asset Swap Spread at Inception
$y = $ 4-Yr Asset Swap Spread at Y/E
$PV_{01} = $ present value of a 1 bps, 4-Yr maturity annuity note priced off issuers' curve
$P = $ Principal of Note in Asset Swap/Notional of Credit Spread Option
Source: Authors.

put by surrendering the remaining four-year asset swap for par, which is effectively the value of a four-year asset swap at the present market spread.[13] A credit spread call option works exactly like the put option on an asset swap.

A one-year call option on the next year's four-year credit spread, with strike set at the asset swap spread at inception, produces the same payoff as does the put option. If credit spread widens in a year, the payoff on the credit spread call is the notional multiplied by the increment in credit premium and the percentage value change in the underlying bond due to a one basis point change in the interest rate. If the credit spread narrows or stays unchanged, the option expires.

Options on credit spread express views on the spread and encompass both default risk and risk of changes in credit risk premium. Therefore, the premium for a credit spread call should be at least as much as the premium for a CDS.

Figure E above shows a puttable asset swap and a credit spread call option.

___
[13] All asset swaps at prevailing market spread are valued at par.

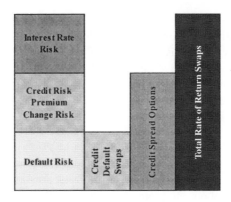

Figure F The Building Blocks of Interest Rate and the Credit Instruments to Deal with Them

Source: Authors.

Comparison of the Building Block Structures

The three different building block structures all contain credit risk or part of it. Credit default swaps cover the default risk portion only. Credit spread options include both the credit risk premium and the default risk as their risk factors. Total rate of return swaps represent all key risk factors in a fixed-income security—both the full credit risk and interest rate risk. Figure F above summarizes this relationship.

MORE COMPLEX STRUCTURES

Financial innovation follows a spiral of customization—standardization—and further customization. The evolution of the credit derivatives market exemplifies this process. Originated to address individual customers' concerns, credit derivatives' function to decouple and transfer credit risk without the actual transfer of any assets appealed to many customers. Credit derivatives experienced major market expansion after the International Security Dealers' Association (ISDA) unified key definitions and standardized the basic structures. When the basic structures traded to adequately high volume and low margin, customer-tailored and more complex credit products blossomed. (See Exhibit 2

EXHIBIT 2

MARKET SHARE OF CREDIT DERIVATIVES PRODUCTS (%)

	1996	1997	1999	2002 (est.)
Credit Default Swaps	35	52	38	37
Credit Spread Products	15	16	5	6
Total Return Products	17	14	11	10
Credit-linked Notes	27	13	10	11
Repackaged Notes / Hybrids	6	5	6	7
Portfolio / CLO	NA	NA	18	18
Asset Swaps	NA	NA	12	11

Source: British Bankers' Association Credit Derivative Report 2000. Reproduced with permission.
© BBA Enterprises Ltd. 2000.

for numbers on how the credit derivatives market grew between 1996 and 2002.) A myriad of structured credit products have been formed by incorporating the three building blocks discussed earlier. With improving standards and soaring market size, the number of novel structures will only continue to proliferate. Here we will present only a few widely recognized structures.

Funded Structures

One key advantage of credit derivatives (or any derivative instrument) is to transfer risk without a cash instrument. Certain investors, however, are not authorized to hold derivatives. Also, some potential protection buyers shun credit derivatives because of doubts about the protection sellers' ability to honor their liability for a sudden and large contingent payment in the future. Funded structures assuage both concerns by embedding credit derivatives in generic cash instruments. The most common form is a Credit Linked Note (CLN); an example is shown below in Figure G.

From the investor's perspective, a CLN is a combination of a long position in a generic corporate note and a long position on the credit risk of a separate entity through a credit derivative. While any of the aforementioned derivative building blocks may be found in a CLN, CDSs are the most popular. In a typical structure, the investor simultaneously buys the package of a note and becomes the protection seller on a CDS, which is linked to an unrelated entity. The investor pays upfront the par of the note and receives in return interest payments at LIBOR plus a spread. The spread is the sum of two spreads: one to compensate for the credit risk on the note, one for the CDS premium. If the credit event in the CDS is triggered, the investor will receive the recovery value of the underlying asset in the CDS and lose her claim over the note principal.

Repackaging Vehicles

Repackaging vehicles refer to structured credit products issued through securitization. While their cash flow mechanics are standard, their legal structure brings a number of

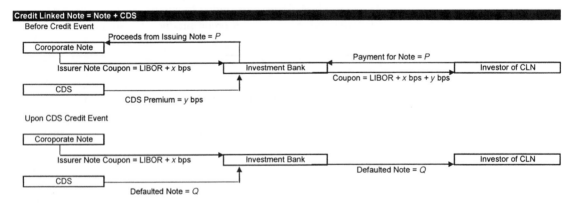

Figure G   Credit Linked Note

Note: P = Principal of Issuer note and notional amount of embedded CDS
Q = Value of Reference after default
x = credit spread on Issuer's Note
y = CDS premium on CDS reference asset
Source: Authors.

advantages. Hold everything constant in the CLN transaction in the above example, except that a Special Purpose Vehicle (SPV) substitutes the investment bank—and we get a repackaging vehicle. The SPV is a legal trust established to shield investors from the transaction sponsor's (the investment bank in the previous case) credit risk. The trust purchases and holds the notes as collateral and simultaneously enters into a CDS as protection seller. Shares of the SPV's total assets are sold to investors. Before a credit event is triggered, the SPV parses out the coupon on the notes as well as the premium on the CDS to investors. After a credit event is triggered, the SPV will liquidate the notes first to indemnify the CDS protection buyer and then to distribute the remainder to the shareholders. In addition to eliminating the sponsor's credit risk, the key benefits of repackaging vehicles are liquidity and flexibility. While the example CLN in the last section requires a tri-party agreement (issuer of note, investment bank sponsor, and the investor), a SPV utilizes market traded securities and caters solely to the interest of investors. Further, SPV issued shares can be rated and listed on an Exchange.

Portfolio/Multi-Name Products

A. First to Default CDS Baskets

Individual credit derivatives are pooled to generate portfolio products mainly for two purposes—diversification or creation of nonexistent risk profiles.

With the same expected return, diversification dampens default risk. To illustrate this, we take as an example two portfolios, A and B, each of which contains five bonds (see Figure H below). Bonds in A are diversified and have default correlation of zero. Bonds in B are identical or perfectly correlated. All of the bonds have the same face value (100), probability of default (10%), and recovery value (0). The panel below shows the payoff of each portfolio. There are six probable outcomes for the end value of Portfolio A—no default, one default, two defaults, three defaults, four defaults, and all five defaults. There are only two probable outcomes for the end value of Portfolio B—no default or all defaults. While the expected end portfolio values are the same (450), the

Portfolio A					Portfolio B				
# of Defaults	Probability	End Value	Loss	Probability Weighted Value	# of Defaults	Probability	End Value	Loss	Probability Weighted Value
0	59%	500	0	295.25	0	90%	500	0	450.00
1	33%	400	100	131.22	5	10%	0	500	
2	7%	300	200	21.87					
3	1%	200	300	1.62					
4	0%	100	400	0.05					
5	0%	0	500	—					
		Expected Value:		450.00			Expected Value:		450.00
		Variance:		4,500			Variance:		22,500
		Standard Deviation:		67			Standard Deviation:		150

Source: Authors.

Figure H   Portfolio Comparison

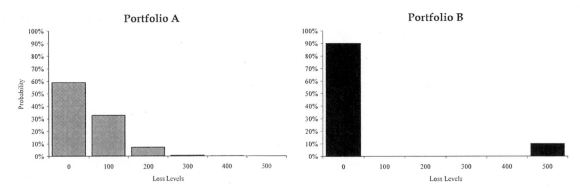

Figure I   Portfolio Comparison, Continued

Source: Authors.

standard deviation of the end value for the diversified portfolio A (67) is much lower than the standard deviation of the undiversified B (150).

Investors seeking diversified credits can purchase ready-made portfolios at reduced transaction costs than accumulating the securities one-by-one. For investors already exposed to diverse credit risk, Basket Credit Default Swaps are cost-effective hedging instruments. They are typically diversified portfolios of 30–40, equal-notional, high-grade CDS and often structured as first-to-default or second-to-default baskets. A first-to-default basket requires the protection seller to compensate for the loss of the first CDS in the basket to default during the specified term, provided there is any. The rest of the mechanics works like a single-name CDS.

While pricing is beyond the scope of this note, the somewhat counterintuitive pricing of basket products merits mentioning here. The perplexity arises because diversification works in opposite directions on the two contributing factors to default risk—the probability of default and the loss given default. The probability of default is compounded when the credits are not correlated. Suppose we have two bonds, X and Y. Each has a 10% probability of default. If their defaults are completely independent, then the probability of default for a portfolio made of equal positions in the two is 19%.[14] If their defaults are perfectly correlated, the probability of default for the portfolio remains 10%.

But we have shown earlier that diversification reduces the default risk of a portfolio. That is because the magnitude of LGD more than reverses the impact of higher probability of default. Going back to Portfolios A and B, Figure I above shows the probability distribution of losses for the 5-bond portfolios. The LGD is moderate and gradual for the diversified portfolio but massive and sudden for the concentrated portfolio. Since a first-to-default swap concerns only the first, albeit undetermined CDS, the probability of default is more important than the potential loss in pricing the basket. In fact, the premium of a first-to-default basket ranges within a bound. The more diversified the underlying portfolio is, the closer is the first-to-default CDS' premium priced to the maximum, set by the sum of the premiums of all CDS. The more concentrated the portfolio is, the closer is the premium priced to the minimum, set by the premium of the riskiest CDS in the basket.

---

[14] The probability of no default is 90% × 90% × 81%. The probability of both default is 10% × 10% = 1%. The probability of one default is 90% × 10% × 2 = 18%.

B. Synthetic CDOs

Some portfolio products are used to transform less marketable securities to more sought-after structures through securitization. In the cash market, fixed-income securities are collected to form portfolios, which are then sliced into different tranches by cash flow priority. Collateralized Debt Obligations (CDO), as one such example, has been an important credit risk cash instrument. (See Figure J for an example of a CDO.) An SPV is formed to hold relatively lower rated uncallable corporate bonds in combination with an interest rate swap to get rid of the interest rate risk. The floating rate portfolio is then separated into tranches. The top tranche gets paid first, the bottom tranche last. The timing and amount of the cash flows, primarily of the lower tranches, are determined by the credit risk of the bonds in the portfolio.

Synthetic Collateralized Debt Obligations apply this technology to credit derivatives. For instance, a CDS and government bonds are combined to substitute corporate loans as the assets in the SPV. The premium from the CDS and the interest earned on the risk-free securities are paid to investors. The asset is reduced when a CDS is triggered. The lower tranches' payoff depends on the amortizing rate of the assets, which is determined by the number of CDS triggered.

MAJOR CREDIT DERIVATIVES END USERS

According to a survey by the British Bankers Association, users of credit derivatives concentrate in the financial sector. (Exhibit 3 gives an overview of the major users.) Banks dominate both as protection sellers and protection buyers, but are on the balance net protection buyers. Earlier, we discussed how TRORS can help banks diversify their loan portfolio. Another major motivation for banks to trade in TRORS and CDS is funding cost arbitrage. Banks of different credit ratings are charged different interest rates, when they borrow. Thus, when offering the same product, their costs can be quite different. As shown in the diagram below, letting the higher rating bank issue a loan and swapping the credit risk to a bank of lesser credit quality provides superior risk/return opportunities to both banks than letting the lower credit quality bank issue the loan directly. Additionally, first-to-default basket of credits provides a low cost way for banks to manage the credit risks of their loan portfolio.

Securities firms maintain a relatively balanced profile on both sides of the transactions. We mentioned that securities firms were early adopters of credit derivatives to manage counterparty risks in their derivatives business. Credit derivatives are a deft tool

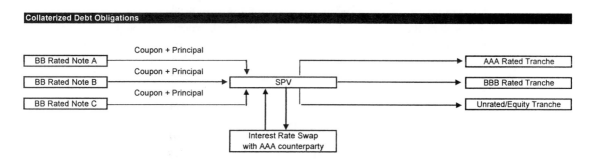

Figure J   Collateralized Debt Obligation (CDO)

Source: Authors.

EXHIBIT 3

MARKET SHARE OF CREDIT DERIVATIVES PRODUCTS (%)

Counterparty	Protection Buyer (%)	Protection Seller (%)
Banks	63	47
Securities Firms	18	16
Insurance Companies	7	23
Corporations	6	3
Hedge Funds	3	5
Mutual Funds	1	2
Pension Funds	1	3
Government/Export Credit Agencies	1	1

Source: British Bankers' Association Credit Derivative Report 2000. Reproduced with permission. © BBA Enterprises Ltd. 2000.

---

to relieve regulatory capital as well. The Bank for International Settlement (BIS) in Basel establishes guidance on capital reserve requirements for international banks. Assets are assigned different risk weight. A minimum capital reserve of 8% of the risk weighted asset value must be kept as the cushion to risk. Debt to OECD banks receives 20% weighting, and risky debts 100%. Regarding long positions hedged by credit derivatives, the current regulation permits the hedger to choose between the weighting of the derivative counterparty and the reference assets. An investment bank looking to release the regulatory capital tied up in the risky and illiquid bonds that it was unable to sell could purchase a short maturity TRORS from an OECD international bank, thereby moving the regulatory capital related to the bonds from 8% to 1.6%—an 80% reduction.

Insurance companies and hedge funds happily pick up the credit risk sold off by banks and securities firms. Traditionally, loans were not traded except after securitization. Now, loan TRORS and Synthetic CLOs open the door to more active participation in loans with greater liquidity and flexibility. Bond TRORS are usually cheaper and definitely more liquid than traded bonds for the same exposure. Moreover, the features of credit derivatives inherently mimic the business models of insurance companies and hedge funds. Some reinsurance companies are selling protection on certain tranches of basket credit products as an alternative to writing credit insurances. Also, credit derivatives allow the protection sellers to gain credit risk exposure through implicit leverage without taking a view on interest rate movements—a structure reflecting the investment philosophy of many hedge funds. Besides the implicit leverage, credit derivatives also have multiplied the ways through which hedge fund managers could make bets in the fixed income market.

Asset managers are currently a small force in the market but promise great potential. Credit derivatives can bring exposures that are unavailable in the cash market. To circumvent the limitations imposed on the use of derivatives, investment banks have created Credit Linked Notes (the mechanics of which were described earlier). The default contingency in a CLN can be based on a variety of underlying assets, including a specific corporate loan or bond, a portfolio of loans or securities, sovereign debt instruments, a bond or emerging markets index, or even on a first-to-default basket or a credit spread option. Fund managers can use these tools to diversify the risk or to enhance the yield of their portfolio.

CHALLENGES AHEAD

Credit derivatives enjoyed explosive growth throughout the 1990s. From 1992 to 1993, their worldwide transactions counted to only over 100. At the end of 1996, the estimated global size of the credit derivatives market measured by notional amount outstanding reached $100 billion to $200 billion. The Asian crisis in 1997 and Russian default in 1998 drew more attention to credit management products, which at the time were still mainly structured through private negotiations. By 1998, the ISDA had developed fairly standardized definitions describing the key aspects of credit derivative contracts. In the mean time, high demand had prompted every major investment house to dedicate a desk to credit derivatives. The turbulence in corporate credit markets buffeted by telecom implosions and several high profile corporate bankruptcies such as Enron and Parmalat further boosted the demand for credit derivatives in the new Millennia. As of mid-2003, the total notional amount stood at $2.7 trillion. Many expect the strong momentum to continue as credit derivatives still have a long way to catch up with their interest rate and currency brethren.

Despite their stunning growth, a few issues have deterred more capital market participants from embracing credit derivatives. One concern is the leaking firewall between the credit sales & trading unit and the loan origination unit at major banks. Fund managers and insurance companies have complained that the lending officers could tip off their colleagues on the credit derivatives trading desk about their loan customers' pending problems before the information went public. While investment banks have denied any wrongdoing, they also realize that the perceived information asymmetry can retard the sale of credit products. Another concern is the challenge to broaden the market beyond financial institutions and hedge funds. After the fall of Enron, corporations have been visibly missing from the credit derivatives market. In its hay days, Enron managed to sell protection on its own credit. The subsequent disillusionment might have snuffed corporate treasurers' interest in credit derivatives. Managed properly, credit derivatives can be of great value for prudent corporate risk management. They could buy protection to remove the credit risk in receivables, buy protection to neutralize an existing guarantee written for a risky affiliate, or buy broad credit protection to hedge against credit spread widening risk at refinancing.

26

First American Bank: Credit Default Swaps

It was approaching 8 p.m. on a Wednesday in April 2002 when Chris Kittal received an urgent call from a contact at Charles Bank International (CBI). Kittal was a managing director in First American Bank's credit derivatives unit in New York City. CBI, a medium-sized U.S. commercial bank based on the East Coast, had recently been approached by one of its corporate clients in need of additional funding. The client, CapEx Unlimited (CEU), a rapidly growing telecommunications company, had been a loyal banking customer with CBI for over five years and had used the bank in some lucrative transactions during that time. CEU was in the middle of an industry shakeout and required $50 million to finance the expansion of its network. The company had already accumulated $100 million in previous loans from CBI and was depending on their relationship with the bank for the additional funding. While reasonable by itself, the new loan, when added to CBI's existing loans to CEU, would put CBI over its credit exposure limit with respect to a single client. In compliance with its internal lending statutes, CBI was unable to extend the additional loan to CEU and faced the possibility of damaging their banking relationship. Taking steps to prevent this, CBI's management called on Kittal to see if CBI could use credit derivatives to their advantage. Kittal envisioned helping CBI mitigate the credit risk exposure to the additional loan using a single-name credit default swap.

FIRST AMERICAN BANK

First American Bank was one of the largest financial services firms in the United States. With more than 7,500 employees and over $50 billion in assets as of December 31, 2001, the bank served more than 10 million customers in more than 50 countries. (See Exhibits 1, 2, and 3 for First American Bank's financial statements.) First American

Research Associate Eli Peter Strick prepared this case under the supervision of Professor George Chacko using published sources. Certain details are fictional. HBS cases are developed solely as the basis for class discussion. Cases are not intended to serve as endorsements, sources of primary data, or illustrations of effective or ineffective management.

EXHIBIT 1

FIRST AMERICAN BANK'S BALANCE SHEET

In $ Millions for Period Ended December 31, 2001	12/31/01	12/31/00
Cash and due from banks	1,662	1,763
Deposits with banks	937	613
Federal funds sold and securities purchased under resale agreements	4,686	5,108
Securities borrowed	2,690	2,380
Trading assets:		
Debt and equity instruments	8,695	10,239
Derivative receivables	5,232	5,616
Securities:		
Available-for-sale	4,359	5,375
Held-to-maturity	35	43
Loans	15,656	15,617
Private equity investments	676	840
Accrued interest and accounts receivable	1,088	1,516
Premises and equipment	463	521
Goodwill and other intangibles	1129	1165
Other assets	3,692	1,804
Total assets	$51,000	$52,600
Total deposits	21,592	20,542
Federal funds purchased and securities sold under repurchase agreements	9,445	9,687
Commercial paper	1,361	1,827
Other borrowed funds	797	1,459
Debt and equity instruments	3,896	3,835
Derivative payables	4,122	5,626
Accounts payable, accrued expenses and other liabilities	3,516	2,997
Long-term debt	2,881	3,184
Firm's junior subordinated deferrable interest debentures	326	290
Total liabilities	$47,936	$49,447
Preferred stock of subsidiary	40	40
Preferred stock	76	111
Common stock	147	143
Capital surplus	919	853
Retained earnings	1,985	2,066
Accumulated other comprehensive income (loss)	(33)	(18)
Treasury stock, at cost	(70)	(42)
Total stockholders' equity	3,064	3,153
Total liabilities, preferred stock of subsidiary and stockholders' equity	$51,000	$52,600

Source: Created by casewriter.

Credit Derivatives (FACD) was an independent business unit housed within First American's structured products branch. This group's business model was essentially to utilize First American Banks's capital base and expertise in risk management and financial engineering to provide clients with risk management and investment products. First American Bank's efforts in the area of credit derivatives had been recognized in the banking community and given FACD a reputation as an emerging leader in its field.

EXHIBIT 2

FIRST AMERICAN BANK'S INCOME STATEMENT

In $ Millions Except Per Share Amounts for Period Ended December 31, 2001	12/31/01	12/31/00	12/31/99
Revenue			
Investment banking fees	266	321	259
Trading revenue	362	463	386
Fees and commissions	677	679	579
Private equity—realized gains	48	151	124
Private equity—unrealized gains (losses)	(139)	(76)	107
Securities gains (losses)	64	17	(14)
Other revenue	65	168	77
Total noninterest revenue	$1,342	$1,722	$1,518
Interest income	2,366	2,694	2,295
Interest expense	1,572	1,995	1,538
Net interest income	$ 794	$ 699	$ 756
Revenue before provision for loan losses	2,136	2,421	2,274
Provision for loan losses	234	101	106
Total net revenue	$1,902	$2,320	$2,168
Expense			
Compensation expense	878	937	775
Occupancy expense	99	95	88
Technology and communications expense	194	180	160
Merger and restructuring costs	186	105	2
Amortization of intangibles	54	39	24
Other expense	303	321	275
Total noninterest expense	$1,713	$1,678	$1,323
Income before income tax expense and effect of accounting change	189	642	845
Income tax expense	62	221	293
Income before effect of accounting change	126	421	552
Net effect of change in accounting principle	(2)	0	0
Net income	$ 125	$ 421	$ 552
Net income applicable to common stock	$ 120	$ 414	$ 544

Source: Created by casewriter.

CAPEX UNLIMITED

CapEx Unlimited was formed in 1996. The company focused primarily on the communication needs in less competitive markets of Northeast and Midwest United States. Originally established as a voice-only provider, CapEx had continuously upgraded and expanded its infrastructure in order to keep pace with the growing customer demand for new features and services. In 2001, its services included high-speed Internet access, Web hosting, data networking, voice communication, and video-/tele-conferencing. As a full-facility long-distance provider, CapEx possessed over 15,000 miles of fiber and over 20 advanced switching systems (for rerouting information). The company had over

EXHIBIT 3

FIRST AMERICAN BANK'S CASH FLOW STATEMENT

In $ Millions for Period Ended December 31, 2001	12/31/01	12/31/00	12/31/99
Operating activities			
Net income	125	421	552
Provision for loan losses	234	101	106
Merger and restructuring costs	186	105	2
Depreciation and amortization	213	187	143
Private equity unrealized losses (gains) and write-offs	139	76	(107)
Trading-related assets	1,928	(2,556)	(641)
Securities borrowed	(310)	232	(289)
Accrued interest and accounts receivable	428	(5)	(193)
Other assets	(1,967)	(302)	(500)
Trading-related liabilities	(1,481)	712	722
Accounts payable and other liabilities	279	23	209
Net cash (used in) provided by operating activities	$ (226)	$ (1,006)	$ 4
Investing activities			
Deposits with banks	(324)	1,624	(1,533)
Federal funds sold and securities purchased under resale agreements	423	(772)	(698)
Loans due to sales and securitizations	5,116	2,431	3,008
Other loans, net	(5,053)	(3,668)	(3,595)
Proceeds from maturities	595	714	1,294
Proceeds from sales	13,722	7,779	8,733
Purchases	(13,573)	(8,180)	(8,718)
Net cash provided by (used in) investing activities	$ 906	$ (72)	$ (1,509)
Financing activities			
Domestic deposits	2,141	779	(565)
Foreign deposits	(1,091)	(1,345)	2,000
Federal funds purchased and securities sold under repurchase agreements	(242)	1,610	346
Commercial paper and other borrowed funds	(1,128)	656	51
Other, net	(7)	(32)	225
Proceeds from the issuance of long-term debt and capital securities	661	1,093	764
Repayments of long-term debt	(925)	(1,062)	(850)
Proceeds from the issuance of stock and stock-related awards	67	161	196
Treasury stock purchased	(64)	(217)	(477)
Cash dividends paid	(198)	(168)	(157)
Net cash (used in) provided by financing activities	$ (786)	$ 1,475	$ 1,533
Effect of exchange rate changes on cash and due from banks	5	(9)	3
Net (decrease) increase in cash and due from banks	(101)	388	31
Cash and due from banks at the beginning of the year	1,763	1,375	1,344
Cash and due from banks at the end of the year	$ 1,662	$ 1,763	$ 1,375
Cash interest paid	1,690	2,001	1,462
Taxes paid	35	250	139

Source: Created by casewriter.

100 co-location and interconnecting agreements with all the major carriers. (Exhibits 4, 5, and 6 show CEU's financial statements while Exhibit 7 gives the company's historic stock performance.)

APPLYING CREDIT DEFAULT SWAPS TO THE SITUATION

Kittal knew he was in a position to help CBI. In this particular situation, he thought it best to use a credit default swap. A credit default swap was appealing because it made the credit risk accessible to a broad range of investors in a way that was simple and, more importantly, confidential. The default swap added flexibility to the situation be-

---

EXHIBIT 4

CAPEX UNLIMITED'S BALANCE SHEET

In $ Millions for Period Ended December 31, 2001	12/31/01
Cash and cash equivalents	554
Accounts receivable, net	726
Finance receivables, net	1,622
Inventories, net	615
Equipment on operating leases, net	230
Deferred taxes and other current assets	397
Total current assets	$4,145
Finance receivables due after one year, net	2,533
Land, buildings and equipment, net	794
Investments in affiliates, at equity	434
Intangible and other assets, net	974
Goodwill, net	502
Total assets	$9,382
Short-term debt and current portion of long-term debt	857
Accounts payable	329
Accrued compensation and benefits costs	211
Unearned income	80
Other current liabilities	519
Total current liabilities	$1,996
Long-term debt	4,903
Postretirement medical benefits	381
Deferred taxes and other liabilities	597
Deferred ESOP benefits	(70)
Minorities' interests in equity of subsidiaries	45
Obligation for equity put options	10
Company-obligated, mandatorily redeemable preferred securities of subsidiary trust holding solely subordinated debentures of the Company	203
Preferred stock	206
Common shareholders' equity	1,112
Total liabilities and equity	$9,383

Source: Created by casewriter.

EXHIBIT 5

CAPEX UNLIMITED'S INCOME STATEMENT

In $ Millions Except Per Share Amounts for Period Ended December 31, 2001	12/31/01	12/31/00	12/31/99
Revenues			
Sales	3,202	3,323	3,396
Service, outsourcing, and rentals	2,457	2,561	2,477
Finance income	294	344	364
Total revenues	$5,953	$6,228	$6,237
Costs and expenses			
Cost of sales	1,973	1,892	1,872
Inventory charges	29	—	36
Cost of service, outsourcing, and rentals	1,532	1,464	1,376
Equipment financing interest	193	174	181
Research and development expenses	332	316	329
Selling, administrative and general expenses	1,798	1,684	1,701
Restructuring charge and asset impairments	172	—	487
Gain on affiliate's sale of stock	(7)	—	—
Purchased in-process research and development	9	—	—
Gain on sale of China operations	(64)	—	—
Other, net	109	91	70
Total costs and expenses	$6,075	$5,621	$6,052
Income (loss) from continuing operations before income taxes (benefits) equity income and minorities' interests	(122)	607	184
Income taxes (benefits)	(35)	187	46
Income (loss) from continuing operations after income taxes (benefits) before equity income and minorities' interests	(88)	420	138
Equity in net income of unconsolidated affiliates	19	22	24
Minorities' interests in earnings of subsidiaries	14	16	14
Income (loss) from continuing operations	(82)	426	147
Discontinued operations	—	—	(60)
Net income (loss)	$ (82)	$ 426	$ 87

Source: Created by casewriter.

cause it could also be combined with another risk transfer mechanism, such as loan syndication, to separate the loan into different portions.

Using a credit default swap, CBI would make a periodic fee payment to First American in exchange for receiving credit protection. First American would assume the credit risk of the additional loan to CEU by guaranteeing a payment to CBI if CEU defaulted on its debt. Even though a credit default swap was unfunded (meaning that it was unsecured by collateral), the counterparty risk for CBI was low. The low counterparty risk was a result of First American Bank being a highly rated entity and the low probability of First American defaulting at the same time as CEU.

Using the credit default swap, CBI could preserve its banking relationship with CEU without violating its internal credit limits. From the client's perspective, CBI would

EXHIBIT 6

CAPEX UNLIMITED'S CASH FLOW STATEMENT

In $ Millions for Period Ended December 31, 2001	12/31/01	12/31/00	12/31/99
Cash flows from operating activities			
Income (loss) from continuing operations	(82)	426	147
Adjustments required to reconcile income (loss) from continuing operations to cash flows from operating activities, net of effects of acquisitions:			
Depreciation and amortization	302	248	231
Provision for doubtful accounts	206	129	96
Restructuring and other charges	206	—	523
Gains on sales of businesses and assets	(94)	(31)	(11)
Cash payments for restructurings	(118)	(139)	(106)
Minorities' interests in earnings of subsidiaries	14	16	14
Undistributed equity in income of affiliated companies	(6)	(22)	(9)
Decrease (increase) in inventories	89	21	(178)
Increase in on-lease equipment	(165)	(76)	(123)
Increase in finance receivables	(337)	(590)	(629)
Proceeds from securitization of finance receivables	—	476	—
Increase in accounts receivable	(86)	(127)	(190)
Proceeds from securitization of accounts receivable	104	92	18
(Decrease) increase in accounts payable and accrued compensation and benefit costs	(1)	(30)	40
Net change in current and deferred income taxes	(170)	74	(81)
Change in other current and non-current liabilities	7	40	32
Other, net	(79)	(96)	(81)
Net cash (used in) provided by operating activities	$ (211)	$ 412	$(304)
Cash flows from investing activities			
Cost of additions to land, buildings and equipment	(144)	(189)	(180)
Proceeds from sales of land, buildings and equipment	14	32	24
Proceeds from sale of China operations	175	—	—
Proceeds from sales of other businesses	29	21	—
Acquisitions, net of cash acquired	(272)	(34)	(121)
Other, net	(6)	(8)	2
Net cash used in investing activities	$ (205)	$(179)	$(276)
Cash flows from financing activities			
Net change in debt	1,137	(58)	776
Dividends on common and preferred stock	(187)	(187)	(169)
Proceeds from sales of common stock	—	41	40
Settlements of equity put options, net	(22)	(2)	—
Repurchase of preferred and common stock	—	—	(55)
Dividends to minority shareholders	(2)	(10)	(1)
Net cash provided by (used in) financing activities	$ 927	$(215)	$ 591
Effect of exchange rate changes on cash and cash equivalents	4	(3)	(9)
Increase in cash and cash equivalents	514	15	1
Cash and cash equivalents at beginning of year	40	25	24
Cash and cash equivalents at end of year	$ 554	$ 40	$ 25

Source: Created by casewriter.

EXHIBIT 7

CAPEX UNLIMITED'S HISTORICAL STOCK PRICES

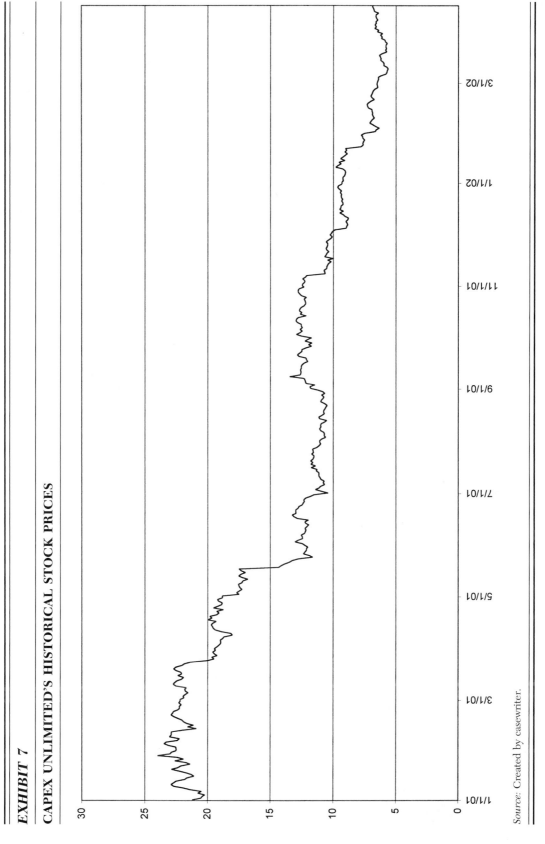

Source: Created by casewriter.

just be lending its client money in a normal manner. However, without the client's knowledge, CBI would have passed the credit risk of the loan on to First American Bank.[1] Essentially, CBI would be acting as an intermediary between CEU and First American. (See Exhibit 8 for yields on U.S. Treasury STRIPS. Exhibit 9 shows credit spreads for bonds of firms in the telecommunications industry, and Exhibits 10a and 10b show historic default rates for certain industries and credit ratings.)

CREDIT DEFAULT SWAP OVERVIEW

The market for credit default swaps was the most liquid credit derivatives market. Through a single name credit default swap,[2] a party could have bought protection from another party with respect to various predefined credit events occurring to a certain reference entity/obligation. The party buying the protection (equivalently going short the credit) was called the "protection buyer." The party selling the protection (or equivalently going long the credit event risk) was called the "protection seller."

In exchange for receiving credit protection, the protection buyer paid a periodic fee to the protection seller until the contract expired *or* a credit event occurred. The credit protection consisted of a payment made by the protection seller to the protection buyer, *contingent* on the occurrence of one or more predetermined credit events. In exchange for the contingent payment, the protection seller either received the underlying asset ("physical settlement") or the determined market value of the asset in cash ("cash settlement"), which netted out against the contingent payment.

The two swap counterparties could have defined the credit event(s) as they saw fit. However, in 1999, the International Swaps and Derivatives Association (ISDA) developed standard definitions and documentation to simplify the use of these instruments. Standardization allowed for faster execution of deals and minimized "documentation risk" by promoting a common understanding of the precise definitions of standard credit events. As a result, the standardization of credit default swap contracts facilitated the netting of contracts and resulted in enhanced liquidity in the market.

In simple terms, the credit default swap contract was written for the event that the entity defaulted on its obligations. Therefore, an investor could have assumed an entity's default risk, among other defined risks, without having taken on the other risks of the debt itself (i.e., interest rate risk). Moreover, on an ongoing basis throughout the life of the contract, the value of a credit default swap reflected the market credit spread of the entity. Thus, through a credit default swap, an investor could have gained exposure to (or hedge) an entity's credit spread risk, as well as default risk.

The flexibility in specifying the length of the life of the swap contract meant that an investor could have specified the desirable maturity exposure to the entity. It was possible that no other market could have provided the investor with this preferred maturity exposure to the particular entity. For example, an investor may have wished to take on five-year exposure to a company that did not have a five-year bond outstanding. However, by selling five-year protection on the company, the investor could have achieved the credit exposure he desired. (Exhibits 11a and 11b show the historic growth of the interest rate swap and credit derivative markets, and Exhibit 12 shows the primary protection buyers and protection sellers of protection through credit default swaps.)

---

[1] The actual loan stays on CBI's accounting books, but may receive different treatment under regulations due to the risk hedge.

[2] Single name refers to a contract written on a single entity/debtor rather than a group or portfolio.

EXHIBIT 8

TREASURY STRIP YIELDS

Maturity	STRIP Yield	Maturity	STRIP Yield	Maturity	STRIP Yield
3 Month	1.40%	4 Year	4.22%	10 Year	5.42%
6 Month	1.47%	5 Year	4.51%	15 Year	5.73%
1 Year	2.14%	7 Year	4.96%	20 Year	5.80%
2 Year	3.20%	8 Year	5.17%	25 Year	5.79%
3 Year	3.89%	9 Year	5.23%	30 Year	5.70%

Source: Prepared by casewriter using data from Bloomberg.

EXHIBIT 9

CREDIT SPREAD (IN BASIS POINTS OVER THE U.S. TREASURY STRIP YIELD) BY RATING AND MATURITY FOR THE TELECOMMUNICATIONS INDUSTRY

Maturity	AA3	A1	A2	BBB1
3 Month	104	143	156	236
6 Month	114	152	164	248
1 Year	74	114	151	239
2 Year	76	120	156	260
3 Year	72	119	150	232
4 Year	94	140	163	254
5 Year	101	131	161	256
7 Year	119	147	169	263
8 Year	121	141	172	256
9 Year	130	148	176	264
10 Year	125	143	169	263
15 Year	107	128	149	244
20 Year	110	131	149	245
25 Year	116	143	162	252
30 Year	142	163	177	273

Source: Prepared by casewriter using data from Bloomberg.

EXHIBIT 10A

HISTORIC DEFAULT RATES

	2000	1970–2000 Average
Industrial	4.73%	1.37%
Banking	0.15%	0.46%
Consumer Products	5.51%	1.34%
Energy	0.00%	1.47%
Financial (Non-Bank)	0.76%	0.81%
Hotel, Gaming, Leisure	4.68%	3.16%
Media	2.37%	1.92%
Other	3.33%	0.86%
Retail	4.22%	2.44%
Tech	2.50%	1.24%
Transport	3.63%	2.15%
Utilities	0.00%	0.10%

Source: David Hamilton, Greg Gupton, and Alexandra Berthault, "Default and Recovery Rates of Corporate Bond Issuers: 2000," *Moody's Investors Service: Global Credit Research* (February 2001).

ISOLATING CREDIT RISK

To properly transfer the credit risk from CBI to First American Bank, a model was needed to isolate and value the credit portion of CEU's risky debt. It was necessary to decompose the risky debt into different elements, value them separately and then decide how much the protection seller should be compensated for in the form of a swap premium.

Kittal gathered the information he needed to complete the deal. CEU would receive the additional loan from CBI for $50 million, bringing their total long-term debt to approximately $5 billion; however, CBI was only looking for credit protection for the additional $50 million in principle. CEU's publicly traded debt was already below investment grade (with a B2 rating from Moody's) and the additional loans were not expected to have much impact on the market value of the existing debt. The terms of this new loan included a coupon rate of approximately 9.8% and a maturity of two years. CEU's existing debt had an average maturity of five years, with an average semi-annual coupon of $130 million. This debt had a total market value of approximately $4.1 billion, representing an average yield of 9.6%. At the time of the deal, the five-year risk-free rate was approximately 4.5%. An analyst presented Kittal with information on traded long-term options on a comparable firm with no debt.[3] (See Exhibit 13 for the comparable's option data.) CEU's equity had a current market value of $6.8 billion (the firm had recently announced the cessation of all dividend payments on all of its stock) and, using statistics from a Moody's report, Kittal could project the dollar amount CBI would recover from its loan if CEU were to enter default. (Exhibit 14 shows Moody's average defaulted values, and Exhibit 15 shows market share of credit derivative products.) In

---

[3] Long-term Equity AnticiPation Securities (LEAPS) typically have maturities from two to three years.

AVERAGE CUMULATIVE DEFAULT RATES FROM 1 TO 10 YEARS, 1983–2000[a]

	1	2	3	4	5	6	7	8	9	10
Aaa	0.00%	0.00%	0.00%	0.06%	0.18%	0.25%	0.34%	0.43%	0.43%	0.43%
Aa1	0.00%	0.00%	0.00%	0.21%	0.21%	0.35%	0.35%	0.35%	0.35%	0.35%
Aa2	0.00%	0.00%	0.06%	0.18%	0.41%	0.49%	0.59%	0.71%	0.85%	1.01%
Aa3	0.06%	0.09%	0.17%	0.26%	0.37%	0.49%	0.49%	0.49%	0.49%	0.49%
A1	0.00%	0.03%	0.30%	0.47%	0.59%	0.73%	0.79%	0.86%	0.86%	0.96%
A2	0.00%	0.02%	0.16%	0.41%	0.62%	0.84%	0.99%	1.35%	1.63%	1.71%
A3	0.00%	0.12%	0.22%	0.30%	0.35%	0.47%	0.68%	0.77%	0.97%	1.09%
Baa1	0.07%	0.30%	0.53%	0.86%	1.19%	1.43%	1.82%	2.05%	2.20%	2.20%
Baa2	0.06%	0.29%	0.61%	1.22%	1.89%	2.54%	2.93%	3.17%	3.46%	3.81%
Baa3	0.39%	1.05%	1.62%	2.47%	3.15%	4.09%	4.99%	5.95%	6.54%	7.03%
Ba1	0.64%	2.10%	3.81%	6.15%	8.12%	10.09%	11.43%	12.75%	13.35%	14.08%
Ba2	0.54%	2.44%	4.95%	7.32%	9.27%	10.88%	12.59%	13.60%	14.27%	14.71%
Ba3	2.47%	6.82%	11.68%	16.18%	20.63%	24.74%	28.39%	32.28%	35.83%	38.22%
B1	3.48%	9.71%	15.59%	20.56%	25.62%	30.78%	36.15%	40.30%	44.16%	48.01%
B2	6.23%	13.70%	20.03%	24.63%	28.24%	31.14%	32.73%	34.33%	35.03%	35.90%
B3	11.88%	20.18%	26.71%	31.95%	36.68%	39.89%	42.81%	46.80%	51.42%	53.53%
Caa1-C	18.85%	28.29%	34.51%	40.23%	43.42%	46.48%	46.48%	49.73%	53.92%	59.04%
Investment-grade	0.05%	0.17%	0.35%	0.60%	0.84%	1.08%	1.28%	1.47%	1.62%	1.73%
Speculative-grade	3.69%	8.39%	12.87%	16.80%	20.39%	23.61%	26.44%	29.04%	31.22%	32.89%
All corporates	1.21%	2.72%	4.12%	5.34%	6.39%	7.30%	8.05%	8.71%	9.23%	9.61%

[a]Describes the percentage of issuers with a specific initial credit rating that defaulted over different subsequent lengths of time. For example, according to the exhibit, 0.18% of Aaa issuers defaulted within five years during the period 1983–2000.

Source: David Hamilton, Greg Gupton, and Alexandra Berthault, "Default and Recovery Rates of Corporate Bond Issuers: 2000," *Moody's Investors Service: Global Credit Research* (February 2001).

EXHIBIT 11A

HISTORIC GROWTH IN THE INTEREST RATE SWAP MARKET

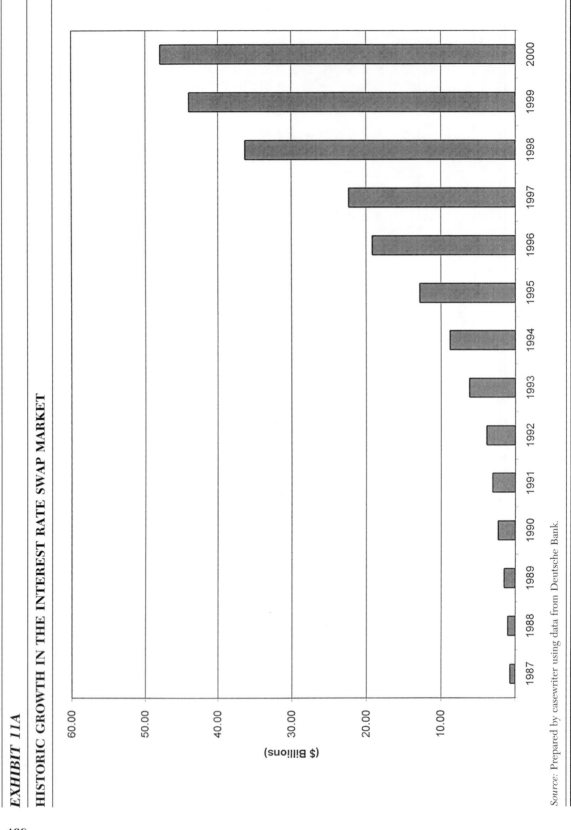

Source: Prepared by casewriter using data from Deutsche Bank.

HISTORIC GROWTH IN THE CREDIT DERIVATIVES MARKET

Source: Prepared by casewriter using data from Deutsche Bank.

EXHIBIT 12

MARKET SHARE OF CONTRACTS TO BUY AND SELL PROTECTION (%)

	Buy			Sell		
	1997	1999	2002 (est.)	1997	1999	2002 (est.)
Banks	64	63	51	54	47	38
Insurance companies	5	7	11	10	23	26
Securities firms	18	18	15	22	16	16
Hedge funds	0	3	4	4	5	5
Pension funds	1	1	3	2	3	5
Corporations	7	6	10	3	3	5
Mutual funds	1	1	3	4	2	4
Government agencies	4	1	3	1	1	1

Source: Prepared by casewriter using data from Deutsche Bank.

EXHIBIT 13

LEAP QUOTES AND SUPPLEMENTAL INFORMATION FOR "DEBT-FREE" CEU COMPARABLE

Calls[a]	Last Sale	Bid	Ask	Volume	Implied Volatility[b]
04 Jan 10.00	15.90	14.50	15.00	0	0.63
04 Jan 12.50	15.50	12.70	13.20	0	0.61
04 Jan 15.00	12.40	11.00	11.50	0	0.59
04 Jan 17.50	11.30	9.50	10.00	0	0.57
04 Jan 20.00	8.30	8.20	8.70	4	0.56
04 Jan 25.00	5.80	6.00	6.50	42	0.54
04 Jan 30.00	4.30	4.40	4.80	149	0.53
04 Jan 35.00	3.10	3.10	3.50	40	0.51
04 Jan 40.00	2.45	2.25	2.55	41	0.50
04 Jan 45.00	1.70	1.65	1.85	1	0.49
04 Jan 50.00	1.40	1.20	1.35	0	0.49
04 Jan 55.00	1.70	0.90	1.05	0	0.49
04 Jan 60.00	1.10	0.65	0.80	0	0.49
04 Jan 65.00	0.90	0.50	0.65	0	0.49
04 Jan 70.00	0.60	0.35	0.50	0	0.48

[a]The underlying stock price was $23.45.

[b]Implied volatility was calculated using the average of the Bid and Ask call prices.

Source: Prepared by casewriter.

EXHIBIT 14

AVERAGE DEFAULTED RECOVERY VALUES (PER $100 PAR AMOUNT), BY SECURITY AND RATING, 2000 VS. HISTORICAL

| | 1981–1999 | | | | | 2000 | | | | | Grand |
	B	Caa	Ca	C	Total	B	Caa	Ca	C	Total	Total
Bank loan/senior unsecured	82.0	60.3			69.0		58.9			60. 3	64.3
Bond/senior secured	61.7	57.2	50.7		55.3					38.8	53.9
Bond/senior unsecured	53.4	44.5	46.1		51.1		29.3	32.1		29.8	47.4
Bond/senior subordinated	42.3	37.3	32.3	16.2	36.0		28.7	13.9		20.5	33.3
Bond/subordinated	41.2	31.9	24.3		32.5						32.3
Preferred stock	24.1	16.6	8.6	—	18.9	—	—	—	—	—	18.4
Total	44.1	38.7	30.0	15.8	40.0	35.6	40.5	25.5	15.8	33.2	39.1

Source: David Hamilton, Greg Gupton, and Alexandra Berthault, "Default and Recovery Rates of Corporate Bond Issuers: 2000," *Moody's Investors Service: Global Credit Research* (February 2001).

exchange for protection against a CEU credit event, CBI would make semiannual swap fee payments to First American Bank that coincided with the interest payments it received on the CEU loan.

CREDIT RISK SEEKERS

Once CBI agreed to the swap premium and credit event definitions stated in the contract, the bank would have the protection it needed to make the loan while observing internal credit rules. On the other hand, Kittal knew he would have only completed half the transaction from First American Bank's perspective. Before the CBI transaction had been completed, Kittal would be on the phone to potential investors, gauging their risk appetites. Unless First American wanted to keep the risk "in-house," Kittal would have

EXHIBIT 15

MARKET SHARE OF CREDIT DERIVATIVE PRODUCTS (%)

	1996	1997	1999	2002 (est.)
Credit default swaps	35	52	38	37
Credit spread products	15	16	5	6
Total return products	17	14	11	10
Credit-linked notes	27	13	10	11
Repackaged notes/hybrids	6	5	6	7
Portfolio/CLO	NA	NA	18	18
Asset swaps	NA	NA	12	11

Source: Prepared by casewriter using data from Deutsche Bank.

to find investors interested in taking on CEU credit risk. Instead of investing in the credit risk itself, First American would make a fee by acting as an intermediary and passing the credit risk from its source to the appropriate investors, or perhaps by hedging the credit risk using some set of market transactions.

In the back of his mind, Kittal already had a list of prospective investors to contact. Kittal thought the most likely investors would be two relatively low-rated banks and a hedge fund and, as a result, he was aware that a credit default swap would probably not work for the back end of the deal.

CREDIT DEFAULT SWAP BOUNDARIES

A default swap was not feasible as a mechanism for transferring the CEU credit risk to the potential investors since a credit default swap was an unfunded contract and these protection sellers presented high counterparty risk for First American Bank, the protection buyer. The low credit quality of these entities meant that they might default during the life of the contract and not be able to make contingent payments if a CEU credit event took place. In addition, there was a considerable risk that both these protection sellers would default at the same time.

In order for First American to protect itself from losses, it would have to require the protection sellers to post large amounts of collateral. These potential investors would be forced to tie up significant portions of their capital as collateral and have to forego other investment opportunities. Since collateral earned a low return, it would significantly lower each firm's overall return on capital. This made an unfunded structure unattractive for them. In other words, the size of collateral that First American required resulted in high opportunity costs for their investors, which would make the default swap structure prohibitively "expensive" for these investors.

Therefore, Kittal needed to find a funded solution that would be attractive to a broader investor group. One possibility was to use a credit-linked note. By repackaging the risk in note form it could be marketed to investment managers and other investors as a product competitive to other bonds and asset-backed securities with similar characteristics.

Kittal had two tasks left. First and foremost, he had to determine the semi-annual fee to be charged to CBI for the default swap. Second, Kittal needed to ensure that First American Bank could hedge its end of the default swap by selling off the credit exposure in the form of another default swap or through another means.

27

Morgan Stanley and TRAC-X: The Battle for the CDS Indexes Market

It was April 2004 and Lisa Watkinson faced a strategic challenge. As Executive Director for Credit Default Swaps (CDS) at Morgan Stanley's Fixed Income Division, Watkinson had been instrumental in developing TRAC-X (pronounced *tracks*), a credit derivatives index made up of individual CDSs, similar to the S&P 500 index for stocks. Launched a year earlier, TRAC-X had grown in trading volume for direct client transactions from about $5 billion to $15-20 billion per week.[1] However, TRAC-X now faced a serious challenger in the form of competing index iBoxx, launched a few months earlier by a rival consortium.

At the time of its launch in April 2003, TRAC-X was praised as an innovative solution to trading credit as a separate asset class. However, dealers soon voiced complaints about what they saw as an arbitrary selection of which corporate credits were included in the index. Furthermore, they took offense to the fact that they had to receive permission from J.P. Morgan and Morgan Stanley, the index's joint owners, if they wanted to tailor new structures based on TRAC-X, a troublesome process by which they potentially had to share proprietary trading information.

A competing CDS index, known as iBoxx, had positioned itself as a response to these concerns. iBoxx let its member banks set rules and allowed full freedom in index-adapted product innovation. iBoxx promised to surpass TRAC-X in transparency, flexibility and ultimately liquidity—and quickly gathered a large following. As a response, J.P. Morgan and Morgan Stanley had transferred the management of TRAC-X to index company Dow Jones. Dow Jones now had final sign-off on the index composition and

Professor George Chacko, Executive Director of the HBS Europe Research Center Vincent Dessain, Research Associate Anders Sjöman, Léonie Maruani (MPA, KSG 04) and Kate Hao (MBA 04) prepared this case. HBS cases are developed solely as the basis for class discussion. Cases are not intended to serve as endorsements, sources of primary data, or illustrations of effective or ineffective management.

[1] Charles Batchelor, "A good barney piques interest in the arcane science of CDSs," Financial Times, 13 March 2004, page 20.

handled licensing to market makers to produce adapted products. The two Morgan banks, however, retained the ownership of the index, now named Dow Jones TRAC-X.

A few months later, it was clear to Watkinson, however, that despite TRAC-X's move to Dow Jones, iBoxx had attracted many of the same large credit derivatives players. Opinions in the market still diverged as to which index would surpass the other. More importantly, thought Watkinson, was that the rivalry left many investors confused as to which index to follow. Many clients hedged their bets, transacting in both indexes, which affected liquidity. Others, Watkinson assumed, were simply staying away from the market until the situation stabilized, as they preferred to deal with a single platform with concentrated trading volume.

Watkinson knew that the current circumstances were to the benefit of no one. TRAC-X had been the first mover and was the market reference, but now faced a standards war with iBoxx. What could Watkinson and Morgan Stanley do to resolve this value destructing war—while still staying true to Morgan Stanley's interests? What were the options available, with what timing and at what risk?

THE DEVELOPMENT OF CDS INDEXES

Historically, investing in credit instruments such as corporate bonds had not reached the same levels as investing in government bonds and equities, primarily because of the lack of standardization. The creation of credit derivatives—instruments which transferred credit risk from one party to another—had, however, helped develop the credit market. The most common credit derivative was the credit default swap, where one party agreed to make a payment to another party should a specified credit event, such as a default on a debt, occur. In return, the counterparty had to pay a fixed periodic fee. CDSs were traded in the Over-the-Counter (OTC) market, and like most credit instruments, they referenced the credit of individual companies.

In 2002, the credit derivatives market was valued at slightly over US$2 trillion notional outstanding. Some analysts expected it to exceed US$7 trillion by 2006. (See Exhibit 1 for details on corporate debt in the U.S. and Exhibit 2 for historical and

EXHIBIT 1

ESTIMATED U.S. CORPORATE DEBT OUTSTANDING (IG AND HY) IN USD BILLION

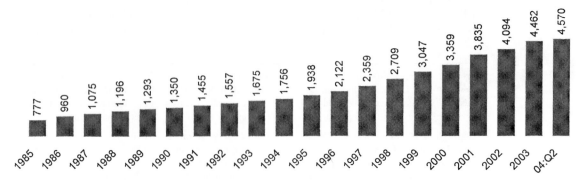

Note: IG = Investment Grade, HY = High Yield.

Source: Adapted by case writer from Morgan Stanley data, based on Bond Market Association estimates.

EXHIBIT 2

ESTIMATED GLOBAL CREDIT DEFAULT SWAPS MARKET SIZE (IN USD BILLION)

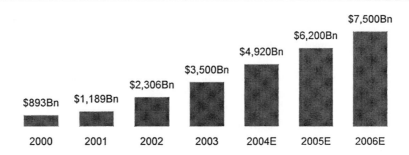

	2000	2001	2002	2003	2004E	2005E	2006E
	$893Bn	$1,189Bn	$2,306Bn	$3,500Bn	$4,920Bn	$6,200Bn	$7,500Bn

Source: Morgan Stanley, based on Celent Communication estimates.

projected market size numbers for the CDS market.) Even if credit derivatives only accounted for about 1% of the market for derivative contracts, the segment grew nearly 16 times between 1997 and 2003, compared with less than three times for the overall derivatives market.[2] Some believed that credit derivatives could grow to match the interest rate derivatives market used by government bond investors, which was 30–50 times as big.[3] Furthermore, increased liquidity in the credit derivatives market was believed to also boost overall investment in corporate bonds.

The promise held by the credit derivatives market had attracted many participants. Some banks began to develop CDS indexes as a new instrument for investors. Morgan Stanley was one of them, as it launched Cash TRACERS in 2001 and Synthetic TRACERS in 2002. Both types of TRACERS were tradable baskets of credit, structured to be easy-to-understand for investors. Other financial firms, such as fellow banker J.P. Morgan, also developed similar CDS products.

Launching TRAC-X

In early 2003, Morgan Stanley and J.P. Morgan decided to merge their CDS indexes, bringing J.P. Morgan's high-yield index together with Morgan Stanley's investment grade (IG) index. The new joint product suite was named TRAC-X and provided current pricing information for widely traded CDSs, quoted as their average premium. As a product, TRAC-X allowed investors not only to buy and sell insurance against default on bonds or loans that they held, but also to take broad views on the credit markets, in both directions. TRAC-X launched in Europe and North America on April 1, 2003 and immediately drew a crowd. Observers estimated a trading volume of $2.4 billion on the first day.[4] Over the following months, several new TRAC-X products were added, such

[2] Michael Mackenzie, "Exchange-Listed Credit Derivatives Index Crucial," Dow Jones Newswires, 24 February 2004.

[3] Alex Skorecki, "Potential exists for further growth in trading of credit default swaps," Financial Times, 2 July 2004.

[4] Natasha de Teran, "New swaps attract strong demand on first trading day," eFinancialNews, 13 June 2003.

as TRAC-X Japan, TRAC-X Australia, TRAC-X EM (Emerging Markets) and TRAC-X Asia. (See Exhibit 3 for a list of all TRAC-X products by April 2004.) According to Morgan Stanley, by November 2003 over $150 billion linked to the TRAC-X indexes had been traded and 13 indexes and various offshoot products such as options and tranches had been added to the TRAC-X index family.

The main driver for Morgan Stanley and J.P. Morgan in developing TRAC-X was the potential of creating derivative products of the indexes, once these indexes had developed sufficient liquidity. However, the benefits of owning an industry standard index went beyond the success of the index itself. Ingenuity was generally valued highly as a characteristic of servicing brokerage firms and the ascendance of TRAC-X brought recognition to the two investment houses. (J.P. Morgan won the 2003 Derivative House of the Year Award from Banker Magazine, and Morgan Stanley won an identical prize in 2004 from Risk Magazine as well as from Euromoney.) Also valuable to the index owners was the access to first hand deal flow information, an edge treasured highly by traders.

Rumble Among the Traders

Morgan Stanley and JP Morgan followed a three-step approach when determining which reference entities to include in the index. Their first criterion was liquidity. Both banks created its own shortlist of 200 CDS entities for the previous six months, ranked by vol-

---

EXHIBIT 3

DOW JONES TRAC-X PRODUCTS (APRIL 2004)

Product Name

North America
DJ TRAC-X North America
DJ TRAC-X NA Hi-Vol
Tranched DJ TRAC-X NA
Options on DJ TRAC-X NA
DJ TRAC-X NA funded notes
DJ TRAC-X North America High Yield

Europe
DJ TRAC-X Europe Series
Tranched DJ TRAC-X Europe
Options on DJ TRAC-X Europe
DJ TRAC-X Europe funded notes
DJ TRAC-X Europe High Yield

Asia
DJ TRAC-X Asia
DJ TRAC-X Australia
DJ TRAC-X Japan

Emerging Markets
DJ TRAC-X Emerging Markets
DJ TRAC-X EM funded notes
Options on DJ TRAC-X EM

Source: Morgan Stanley.

---

ume. They then merged their two lists and only kept names that appeared on both lists. Secondly, they eliminated entities with poor credit quality from the list. Finally, they took away entities that would cause counterparty conflict, which occurred when a potential entity was a company likely to trade the product.

Based on this approach, Morgan Stanley and JP Morgan had outlined a strict set of rules governing the composition of the list. The rules were published for the investor base to see and understand. Watkinson soon realized, though, that the banks could have been better in communicating the rules, since the perception in the dealer community became that selection and removal of entities were at the discretion of the Morgan banks. The perception spread to industry media, which grumbled about a lack of independence and transparency in the management of TRAC-X. The complaints grew in force when JP Morgan and Morgan Stanley were accused of changing the composition of the index without warning at one point in September 2003.

Traders also complained about restrictions on launching new products, limitations that meant that banks had to seek permission with the Morgan banks if they wanted to tailor new structures employing TRAC-X. It implied giving out proprietary trading information up front and therefore losing a major edge when launching new products.

Competition Appears: iBoxx

In what seemed to be a response to the criticism of TRAC-X, eleven dealers formed a consortium in October 2003 and launched a competing CDS index suite, known as iBoxx. (See Exhibit 4 for a list of iBoxx dealers.) In contrast to TRAC-X, iBoxx followed

---

EXHIBIT 4

CONSORTIUM BANKS IN IBOXX (COVERING THE U.S. MARKET)

iBoxx

ABN AMRO

Barclays

Bear Stearns

Citigroup

Credit Suisse First Boston

Deutsche Bank

Goldman Sachs

HSBC

Lehman Brothers

Merrill Lynch

UBS

Note: The banks were active in the U.S. market. Some additional banks were active in the European or Asian markets only.

Source: Compiled by casewriters from public sources (primarily http://www.dowjones.com/Pressroom/PressReleases/Other/US/2004/ 0428_US_DowJonesIndexes_9673.htm, http://www.epn-magazine.com/ news/categoryfront.php/id/97/29_March_2004_(Issue_149).html; IBOXX website, www.indexco.com (all accessed January 2005).

rules agreed upon by *all* member banks in determining the index composition and allowed full freedom in index-adapted product innovation. iBoxx was also quick to announce that it would soon offer traders a chance to trade sub-sectors of the index: industrial, consumer, energy, financial and telecom/media/technology.

The launch of the iBoxx index caused immediate friction. The Morgan banks resented iBoxx for copying their idea and their product and also for damaging the liquidity of the market. iBoxx criticized the Morgan banks for their lack of independence and argued that their product was better-designed and responded to market needs. The entrance of a competitor did however not seem to please all CDS index customers, since some actually preferred to have just one index suite. They preferred a single platform with concentrated trading volume and believed that the still nascent CDS index market lacked sufficient liquidity to sustain two competing standards and that a second index fragmented overall liquidity.

TRAC-X Moves to Dow Jones

Almost immediately following iBoxx's launch, JP Morgan and Morgan Stanley responded by introducing two changes in the operation of TRAC-X. First, as an answer to the five sub-sectors traded in the iBoxx, TRAC-X started offering two sub-sectors for the U.S. market (financial and telecom/media/technology) in October 2003. The second announcement was even more radical: the two banks transferred the management of TRAC-X to index and publishing company Dow Jones. From October 2003, Dow Jones was from now on responsible for licensing, product development, branding, marketing and public relations. Dow Jones maintained and marketed the indexes, which were renamed Dow Jones (DJ) TRAC-X. However, Morgan Stanley and J.P. Morgan retained ownership of the indexes.

The key change to Dow Jones TRAC-X after the move was that Dow Jones, and not the owners, would make the final decision on the composition of the index. The Morgan banks still put together suggestions for which entities to include, but Dow Jones now had to sign off on these. Dow Jones also provided a license contract granting market makers liberty to produce adapted products after consultation[5] with all the market makers. Said Lee McGinty, head of credit derivatives index strategy at J.P. Morgan in London,

> The most obvious difference people will see is when the indices roll, Dow Jones will manage the process of deciding the composition of the new version of the product. And given their expertise in index creation, we are confident they will do so in an efficient and timely fashion.[6]

Competition Intensifies

In early 2004, according to one market analyst, the global trading volume on both index platforms combined was estimated at around $10 billion a day. The competitive outlook regarding which product group would win was getting murkier. Some market observers expected DJ TRAC-X to emerge with all the liquidity, since it had more global coverage, was further along in getting listed on an exchange and had attracted greater volumes. (Exhibits 5 through 7 detail notional outstanding DJ TRAC-X products, and

[5] The decision would be made in consultation with a governance committee of credit derivative professionals, which the company would assemble to give advice on the development of the indexes.

[6] Lee McGinty, as quoted in "Dow Jones set to manage Trac-x," Creditflux Issue 27, 3 November 2003.

EXHIBIT 5

DOW JONES TRAC-X AND TRACERS NOTIONAL OUTSTANDING (MARKET ESTIMATE) IN USD BILLION

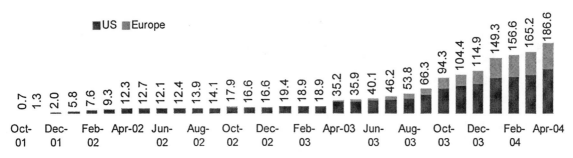

Source: Adapted by casewriters from Morgan Stanley.

Exhibits 8 and 9 show daily DJ TRAC-X trading volumes. Exhibit 10 shows characteristics for a specific CDS instrument.) However, others argued that iBoxx would win, giving as an example that BNP Paribas, a long-term supporter of DJ TRAC-X, had begun working with iBoxx indexes in January 2004. iBoxx was grabbing significant ground in the U.S., although DJ TRAC-X held a substantial position internationally.

Competition grew even fiercer throughout the spring, as first the new iBoxx Diversified Index was unveiled (with 14 changes to the old index) and then when iBoxx recruited another three European market makers, bringing the number of iBoxx consortium participants to 14 in Europe (the number remained 11 for the U.S.). However, while iBoxx had more banks in its league than TRAC-X, a number of those banks, like Bear Stearns, Credit Suisse First Boston, HSBC, Lehman Brothers, Merrill Lynch and UBS, were hedging their bets and making markets in both indexes.

In general, however, market participants found it difficult to make a good apples-to-apples comparison of the two indexes and even to calculate market shares. In fact,

EXHIBIT 6

DOW JONES TRAC-X TRANCHED NOTIONAL OUTSTANDING (MARKET ESTIMATE) IN USD BILLION

Legend: Dark color: U.S. Investment Grade
Light color: Europe Investment Grade

Source: Adapted by casewriters from Morgan Stanley.

EXHIBIT 7

OPTIONS ON DOW JONES TRAC-X NA AND EUROPE NOTIONAL OUTSTANDING (MARKET ESTIMATE) IN USD BILLION

Legend: Dark color: U.S.
Light color: Europe

Source: Adapted by casewriters from Morgan Stanley.

---

iBoxx did in general not publish notional outstanding data or volume data. The few numbers that were published, which at first glance appeared comparable, differed in whether or not they included inter-dealer transaction (so called "street flow") or just used client transactions (so called "customer flow") in their sales volume reports. (In general, iBoxx included street flow transactions in each sales report, whereas Dow Jones TRAC-X chose not to do it.)

Looking for an Exchange Listing

The two indexes were also competing in getting listed on an exchange. So far, the indexes had been traded purely on the OTC market. However, security exchanges around the world, from London to Frankfurt and from Singapore to New York, were getting ready to join the race. Exchanges had long sought listed futures and options that tied to

---

EXHIBIT 8

DOW JONES TRAC-X AND TRACERS DAILY U.S. TRADING VOLUMES ($BN, MARKET ESTIMATE)

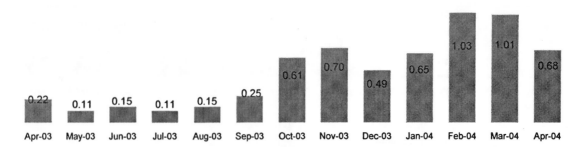

Note: Exhibit depicts daily volumes **on a monthly basis** for all index products.

Source: Adapted by casewriters from Morgan Stanley.

EXHIBIT 9

INVESTMENT GRADE MARKET DAILY TRADING VOLUME (5-DAY ROLLING AVERAGE) FOR CASH BONDS IN USD BILLION

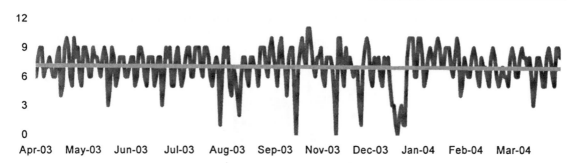

Source: Adapted by casewriters from Morgan Stanley, based on TRACE, reported via MarketAxess.

EXHIBIT 10

SAMPLE PORTFOLIO CHARACTERISTICS: DOW JONES TRAC-X NA HY SERIES 2

a. Industry Distribution (Dow Jones Classification, October 2004)

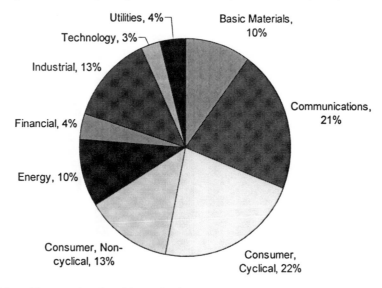

Source: Adapted by casewriters from Morgan Stanley.

(Continued)

EXHIBIT 10 **(Continued)**

**SAMPLE PORTFOLIO CHARACTERISTICS:
DOW JONES TRAC-X NA HY SERIES 2**

---

b. Sample Portfolio Distribution by Moody's Rating, October 2004

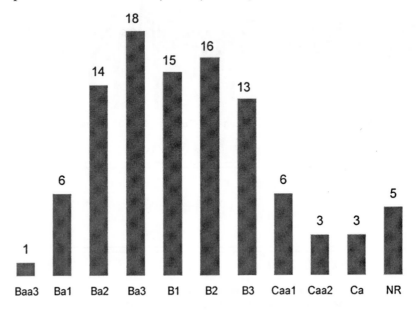

Source: Adapted by casewriters from Morgan Stanley.

c. Sample Portfolio Distribution by S&P Rating, October 2004

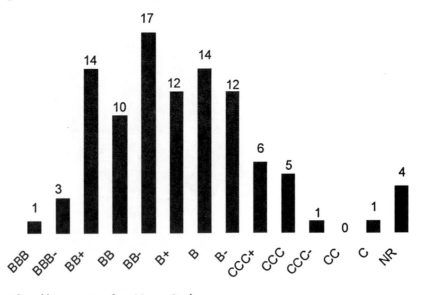

Source: Adapted by casewriters from Morgan Stanley.

indexes of cash-traded corporate bonds. Twenty years earlier, the Chicago Mercantile Exchange had failed in introducing credit futures since they could not attract sufficient liquidity. Now, however, with the arrival of independently managed CDS indexes that were highly standardized and already claiming sizable volume, exchanges believed they were close to an ideal prototype for exchange traded credit derivative products.

Nonetheless, to successfully launch futures products required a significantly higher degree of standardization and even broader appeal to general investors. Both CDS index groups were racing to hammer out the last details related to settlement and clearing with the prospective exchanges. Exchange listing could mean a giant leap forward in liquidity and cost-efficiency. The index group that first realized this goal would likely be assured the winning title in the competition war. In a press release, Dow Jones actually announced that DJ TRAC-X had an agreement with the Singapore exchange. IBoxx was quick to respond by saying that they had an agreement in the works with an undisclosed European exchange.

Market Pushes for an Index Merger

By the beginning of 2004, some banks started pushing for a merger between the two competing indexes. Some market observers believed that the liquidity of the joint index would be even greater than the sum of the liquidity in the two families. A rumor even circulated that a group of six banks had written to J.P. Morgan (DJ TRAC-X) and Deutsche Bank (iBoxx) to press them to reach an agreement. Farid Ammellal, global head of credit derivatives at BNP Paribas, explained the market's perspective,

> The ideal would be to establish one index, and then everyone, from customers to dealers, will be happy. It is detrimental to the market that some big players cannot agree on a common strategy on developing an index. It would be much healthier to have one index per region and sector. Having two indices that offer the same thing does nothing but split liquidity.[7]

Unlike many industries where cooperation among competitors was seen as illegal collusion, market observers argued that declaring an early truce via a merger could benefit consumers as well as vendors. The alliance would be perfectly acceptable, since it was crucial for market growth. Analysts argued that there was scope for considerable growth, since only 30%–40% of all potential users were using index products. Merging Dow Jones TRAC-X and iBoxx would boost development and innovation for example in the area of second generation credit default products such as futures, options and tranches on the CDS indexes. These developments would certainly allow reaching out to more traditional bond fund managers on top of the predominant hedge fund clients.

However, some voices argued against a merger, saying the market was big enough for two and that competition was always valuable. Having more than one index gave the market additional benchmarks for creating structured products.

Beginning Merger Discussions—And Finding Obstacles

Pushed by the market, the two index groups began preliminary discussions in early 2004. Watkinson at Morgan Stanley knew however that even if the market thought it made strategic sense to merge the indexes, there were several serious obstacles to overcome.

---

[7] Farid Ammellal, as quoted in Natasha de Teran, "Credit products to lead growth," Financial news, 4 January 2004.

To start with, the two parties had for a while now waged an intense index war, leaving both sides with good measures of mistrust, misunderstanding and pride. The first discussions were highly charged, and a March deadline for an agreement was missed. The parties found themselves locked into their positions, unable to make a first move. Volumes were however starting to shift in iBoxx's favor as it now had 15 dealers. At the same time, though, J.P. Morgan and Morgan Stanley knew that iBoxx could not become the benchmark without their participation, given the Morgan banks' strong presence in the credit derivatives market.

Another stumbling block to the negotiations was the name of a merged index. Both groups wanted to keep their name for branding reasons. Additionally there was the issue of how to manage the merged index. For instance, under which rules would companies be added or removed from the index? Another point of contention was that some traders saw little benefit in employing a media company, Dow Jones, with limited track record in credit indexing to promote the indexes. However, DJ TRAC-X wanted to keep Dow Jones since they believed their presence facilitated a merger between two equals. Some media added that TRAC-X would have to pay a substantial breach-of-contract fee should they leave Dow Jones. However, iBoxx did not want to keep Dow Jones because it would then look as if iBoxx had joined DJ TRAC-X.

WATKINSON'S DECISION

As the merger discussions came to an impasse, Watkinson knew it was high time to take action. Analyzing the situation, she weighed four options.

The first option was to continue the discussions and eventually merge with iBoxx. Although it was the outcome most welcomed by constituents, negotiations had already proved difficult, to say the least. Watkinson's second option was to fight back. After all, Morgan Stanley was the original designer and still held significant market share. It could prove a costly strategy, though. A third option was to cancel any further investment in Dow Jones TRAC-X and simply join iBoxx. Patrons of iBoxx included several large global credit derivative dealers and market makers. However, the success of Dow Jones TRAC-X had brought a great deal of recognition to the firm. To give in to a copycat product would be hurtful to everyone involved in taking the product to success. Finally, a fourth option was to form a duopoly with iBoxx where each group would specialize in different segments of the market.

Watkinson feared that the battle would be costly no matter which option she chose. The pressure to negotiate a truce was great but Watkinson had to assess carefully what were her key assets if she chose to wage a standards war. Some of the obvious ones were an existing user base, first mover's advantage, brand name and reputation, ability to innovate, rights and licensing, and distribution capabilities.

It was not the first time Watkinson had to make a tough decision. In a similar situation with the first index product, TRACERS, Morgan Stanley had stayed the track alone and their fast innovation had starved off competition. However, this time, Watkinson was up against pretty much the rest of the industry combined. Did Morgan Stanley and J.P. Morgan have adequate resources to fight it out?

It had been little over a year since Dow Jones TRAC-X was unveiled. (Exhibit 11 shows Dow Jones TRAC-X development over time.) Was it already time to retreat? Or should she continue to wage battle, when there seemed to be very little space for coalition building? The only thing Watkinson knew for sure was that the longer she waited, the more difficult it would be to find a solution.

EXHIBIT 11

THE EVOLUTION OF DOW JONES TRAC-X

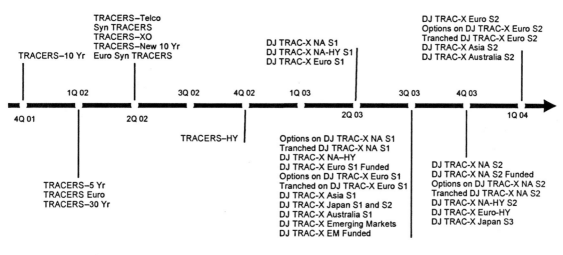

Source: Morgan Stanley.

DS-4

INTEREST RATE DERIVATIVES

28

Introduction to Interest Rate Options

Like all financial derivatives, interest rate options derive their value from an underlying security. In their case, the underlying is normally a reference interest rate or an interest rate index. Just like equity options, interest rate options can be said to provide protection against adverse market moves, while still allowing the holder to benefit from favorable market shifts. In the case of equity options, these shifts would be changes in stock prices or the value of the underlying asset. For interest rate options, the moves would be in the overall interest rate. Thus, this instrument helps companies manage their interest rate exposure.

This note gives a very brief introduction to interest rate options, looking at three basic structures: interest rate caps, interest rate floors, and swaptions.

PAYOFF SCHEMES FOR CALL AND PUT INTEREST RATE OPTIONS

Before getting into caps, floors and swaptions, however, we'll start with a more basic construction: call and put options on an interest rate. The payoff diagrams of interest rate calls and puts look very much like those of equity calls and puts, with which you should be familiar.[1]

INTEREST RATE CALL OPTION

We'll start with the payoff of an interest rate call option. Let's say that Acme Corporation has issued $100 million bonds, and that the bonds' coupon is not a fixed payment, but based on a floating rate. Acme set its floating rate debt to be an annual payment of LIBOR[2] + 3%, no matter what the LIBOR rate happens to be. However, Acme also

---

Professor George Chacko and Research Associate Anders Sjöman of the HBS Europe Research Center prepared this note as the basis for class discussion.

[1] See for instance George Chacko, Peter Hecht, Vincent Dessain, and Anders Sjöman, "Note on Basic Option Properties," Harvard Business School Note No. 9-205-105 (Boston: Harvard Business School Publishing, 2005).

[2] LIBOR (London Inter Bank Offered Rate) is the interest paid for dollars and euros at international markets in inter bank borrowings. The LIBOR rate is fixed daily by the British Bankers' Association (BBA). It is similar to the U.S. Federal Reserve rate, in that it is used as a reference rate for other short term interest rates.

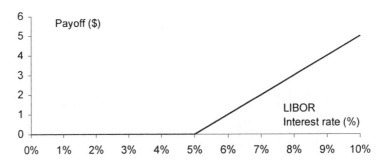

Figure 1   Payoff for an Interest Rate Call Option

wanted to protect itself from very sharp spikes in interest rate levels. The level at which Acme would like to cover itself is 8% total, or put differently, LIBOR at 5%.

To gain this protection, Acme buys an interest rate call option, which gives them the right (but not the obligation) to receive payments if the LIBOR rate rises above 5%. The option contract has to include a so called notional amount (you'll soon see why), in this case let's assume $100 million, which matches Acme's issued debt. The option contract also has a strike rate: 5% LIBOR, which is the level at which Acme wants its hedge to go into action, and it has a maturity date, at which point the call option expires.

Now, assume that the LIBOR rate does rise: it goes to 6%. Consequently, Acme owes its bondholders LIBOR + 3% = 9%. This is above the 8% maximum level they had set for themselves. Luckily, the call option is now in-the-money, and the option issuer (which normally is an investment bank) will have to pay an amount to Acme. The actual amount is determined as the difference between the interest rate and the strike level, times the notional amount, or:

$$\text{Call Option Payoff} = (\text{Interest Rate Level} - \text{Strike Level}) * \text{Notional Amount}$$

In this example, the payment then becomes (6% − 5%) * $100 million = $1 million. Practically, Acme has to pay out 9% of their $100 million issue, or $9 million. They receive, however, $1 million from their call option, so their total payment stays at $8 million. The call option helps Acme never pay more than 8% on their floating rate debt issue. They will of course benefit if interest rates start to drop, at which point they would pay out less than 8%.

The payoff pattern for the interest rate call option we just described is shown in Figure 1 above.

Interest Rate Put Options

Let's now look at an interest rate put option. We'll take the same bond issue as above (Acme's $100 million floating rate debt at LIBOR + 3%), but let's now assume that you are an investor that is investing in Acme's bonds. You want to receive the bond coupons which could grow quite nicely, if LIBOR increases—but you also want to protect yourself against drops in the LIBOR level. If interest rates drop very low, the coupon payments that you receive could theoretically become as low as 3%. You want to protect yourself in case the coupon rate drops below, say, 8%, or in other words, against the LIBOR dropping below 5%.

The solution for you is to buy an interest rate put option. Just as the call option, the put option contract specifies a notional amount, the strike rate and the expiration date of the contract. In your case, the notional amount is again set to $100 million and the strike rate at 5%, as we just explained.

Now, suppose that LIBOR drops to 3%. Your put option is in-the-money, and you will receive a payment from the option issuer. The payment is calculated as the difference between the strike rate and the interest rate level, times the notional amount, or:

$$\text{Put Option Payoff} = (\text{Strike Level} - \text{Interest Rate Level}) \degree \text{Notional Amount}$$

In your example, this results in (5% − 3%) ° $100 million = $2 million. Practically, you as the bond investor will receive $6 million from Acme (LIBOR + 3% times $100 million) and then an additional $2 million on the put option, so that you receive your minimum required level of 8%. Naturally, you (as well as Acme in the call option example above) would have to pay a fee for your options in order to compensate the option issuer for providing you protection.

The payoff pattern for the interest rate put option we just described is shown in Figure 2 below.

Caplets and Floorlets

Now that we know what the payoff schemes for interest rate options look like, let's call these options by their proper name: The call option is generally known as a "**caplet**" and the put option as a "**floorlet**." Summarizing what we know will help you understand why. In general, these types of contracts are used as protection against adverse movements in interest rate levels. For corporations with floating rate debt, we have shown how a caplet will protect against large increases in interest rates, by setting a limit—a cap—on outgoing payments. And we have also shown how an investor can use a floorlet as protection against *drops* in the interest rate level, setting a minimum guaranteed payment level, a floor.

INTEREST RATE CAPS AND FLOORS

In our example so far, Acme Company and you as an investor both wanted to protect yourselves over time. Let's say that Acme's bond issue is a 10-year bond. Let's also assume the two of you want to protect yourselves for the same length of time, 10 years. For each time period in those ten years (which we, for the sake of simplicity, assume is one year), Acme and you, the investor, will receive a payment whenever a caplet or floorlet is in the money. From Acme's side, there will be a caplet that matures in one year, another in two years, a

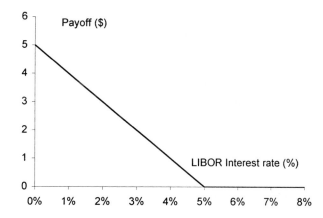

Figure 2 Payoff for an Interest Rate Put Option

third in three years, etc. until ten years. For the investor, the situation is similar: there is a floorlet with an expiration date of one year, a second of two years, a third of three years, etc. Now, to simplify for companies and investors, who prefer not to buy all these instruments separately, they can be bundled together into one product. Such a product for caplets is called an "**interest rate cap**" and for floorlets an "**interest rate floor**."

Interest rate caps and floors then become a series of options on interest rates, where all options have the same strike rate, but different maturities. In the U.S., where bonds normally have semi-annual payments (and not annual as in our example above), caplets and floorlets within a cap and a floor will typically mature on a semi-annual basis.

Let's state what we know about caps and floors a bit more formally. An interest rate cap protects its holder against rising short-term interest rates by having the cap issuer make a payment to the holder if the underlying interest rate exceeds a specific rate ceiling. An interest rate floor is the opposite of an interest rate cap: it protects the holder from the underlying interest rate falling below a certain strike rate. The payment for a cap is calculated as the difference between the reference rate and the strike rate, times the notional amount in the option contract. The payment for a floor is defined as the difference between the strike rate and the reference rate, times the notional amount. Payments are typically made in regular intervals during the lifespan of the contract; each individual payment can be seen as a caplet or floorlet.

It should also be noted that caps and floors are always traded on the Over-the-Counter (OTC) market, between an investment bank and an individual, and not on organized exchanges.

Interest Rate Option Put-Call Parity

To illustrate an important concept known as interest rate option put-call parity (which should be familiar to anyone who remembers equity option put-call parity), let us add one more payoff diagram to the ones we just did for caplets and floorlets.

Here's now the payoff diagram for a bond. It is seen from the point of view of an investor (who has *not* taken out a floorlet protection). Continuing with our example from above, the investor will at the very least receive 3% on this bond, since its coupon is by the issuer Acme as LIBOR + 3%. From that starting level, the payoffs increase by $1 million for every 1% that LIBOR increases (which is the same as 1% times the issued debt of $100 million). Figure 3 on the next page shows the payoff, and note that this is the payoff for a single payment of the bond.

Now, what happens to the payoff diagram when the investor buys the floorlet we described above (5% strike price, $100 million notional) and which was graphically shown in Figure 2? Combining Figure 2 and Figure 3 gives us the payoff for an investor with a floorlet (Figure 4 on the next page).

Now, let's take the same bond and look at its payoff from Acme's point of view. They have not yet invested in a caplet, so as they issue the bond and have to pay out coupons, the payoff is naturally negative, as shown in Figure 5.

Now Acme buys a caplet, whose payoff we've already shown in Figure 1. Combining that payoff with the payoff diagram above gives us the combined payoff for caplet protected Acme (Figure 6 on page 494).

Notice how we have used diagrams to help us understand how caplets and floorlets work, instead of reverting to mathematical formulas? Let's continue that approach as we now expand our discussion to a concept known as **interest rate option put-call parity**. We will now look at the payoff schedules (or payment streams) if you as an investor bought a caplet and sold a floorlet, both at the same time. In investor jargon, you

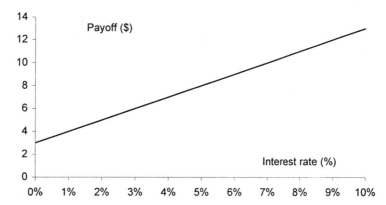

Figure 3 Payoff for bond

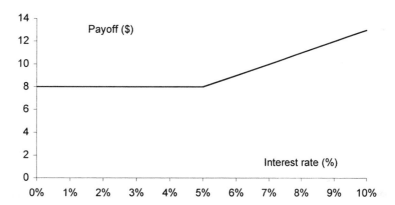

Figure 4 Payoff for investor with a floorlet

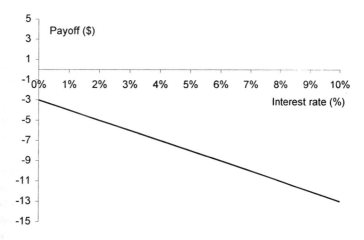

Figure 5 Payoff for bond for ACME

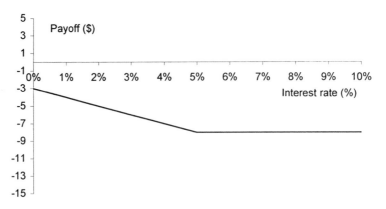

Figure 6 Payoff for bond for ACME with caplet protection

went long the caplet and you shorted the floorlet. This would give you two opposing payment streams. The payoff for your long caplet is shown in Figure 7 (and you should of course notice that is the same payoff as in Figure 1).

The figure shows that as interest rate levels are below 5%, you receive nothing. However, when interest rate levels rise above your strike price of 5%, the option is in-the-money and you start receiving payments. Similarly, the payoff for your short floorlet is shown in Figure 8.

Here, the opposite holds true: you receive payments up until the point that interest rate levels reach the strike rate of 5%.

Now, let's take the two payoff streams and combine them into one graph: Figure 9 on the next page.

The combined graph gives us the payment stream of your dual investment—and if you look closely at the graph, you might recognize it from your readings about interest rate swap contracts.[3] The graph actually shows the single payment from the payment schedule of a plain vanilla interest rate swap contract. Let's call such a single payment a swaplet (just as we think of caplets and floorlets as individual payments in a pooled group). Of course, if a single caplet together with a single floorlet forms a single swaplet, then a portfolio of caplets—a cap—combined with floorlets—a floor—becomes a portfolio of swaplets, or a swap. This gives us a put-call parity between caps, floors and swaps, which traditionally is expressed as:

$$\text{Cap}(R\%) - \text{Floor}(R\%) = \text{Swap}(\text{Swap Rate} = R\%)$$

where R is the strike rate in the fixed payment rate.

Remember that a swap is about exchanging fixed payments for floating rate payments, or vice versa? Concerning Figure 9, given the way the example is set up, you should note that the investor receives the floating end and pays the fixed. But how much is the fixed? The graph shows that when interest rates are at 5%, the investor breaks even. At break-even, since the investor receives floating and pays fixed, she must be receiving and paying just as much—and we already know that she is receiving 5%. The fixed payment then is 5% as well. What we then have here is a swaplet where the investor receives floating and pays fixed 5%.

---

[3] See George Chacko, Peter Hecht, Vincent Dessain, and Anders Sjöman, "Note on Forward Contracts and Swaps," Harvard Business School Note (Boston: Harvard Business School Publishing, 2005).

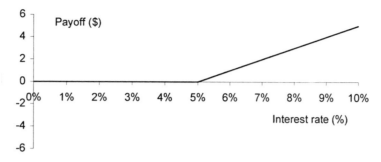

Figure 7   Long Caplet

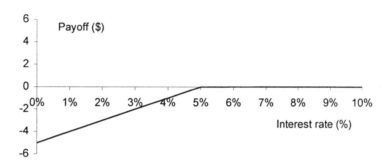

Figure 8   Short Floorlet

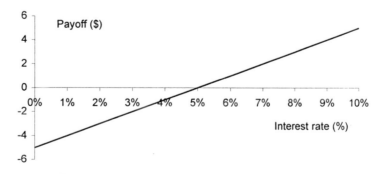

Figure 9   Combined Long Caplet with Short Floorlet

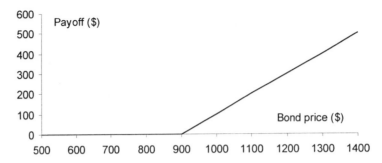

Figure 10   Call Option on a Bond

SWAPTIONS

Put simply, swaptions are options on a swap. Before we define these further, however, let's introduce another structure: options on bond.

Payoffs for Bond Options

So far we have talked about options on an interest-rate (and in a previous note about options on equity). You can, however, also buy an option on a bond. Say there is a corporate bond that is issued with a $1000 principal value. An option contract on that bond could be constructed, based on the price of the bond in the market, with a strike price of, say, $900. Figure 10 shows what a call option on such a bond would look like.

Similarly, Figure 11 shows what a put option on such a bond would look like, using the same strike price of $900.

Swaptions

We are now ready to discuss swaptions, which, again, are options on a swap. As a holder of a swaption, you have the option of entering into a swap contract at a predetermined fixed rate. A one-year swaption, for example, gives you the right to purchase a swap within the next year, where you receive a floating rate and pay a fixed rate (or vice versa). At the end of this year, you can then decide whether you want to enter into this swap contract or not.

As always with options, there are calls and puts. A call swaption gives you the right to enter a swap contract where you pay fixed and receive floating. Remember from the note on swaps that if you are receiving floating and paying fixed that is the equivalent

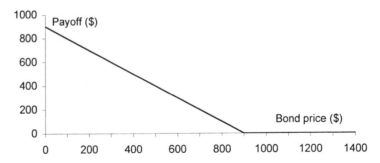

Figure 11   Put Option on a Bond

of being long a floating rate bond and short a fixed rate bond (which we incidentally also showed in Figure 9 where we went long a caplet and short a floorlet). A call swaption then is the same as having to right to receive a floating rate bond and sell a fixed rate bond (where the fixed rate is predefined by the terms of the swaption).

Continuing with the example we have been using throughout this note, a call swaption would then give you the right to receive a floating rate bond and sell a fixed rate bond at 5%. But we know from previous readings that the value of any floating rate bond is par, since the bond coupon always adjusts to keep the bond price the same, i.e. its par or principal value. With this in mind, you should see that your call swaption is the same as having the right to sell a fixed-rate bond at 5% and to receive the par (principal) value of the underlying bond, let's say $1000. That is the same as a contract where you have a put option on the fixed rate bond with a strike price of par. Such an option, when exercised, means that you give someone the fixed rate bond and they give you back the strike price of par. In this way, we have just demonstrated that a call swaption at 5% is equivalent to simply owning a put option on a fixed rate 5% bond with a strike price of par.

A put swaption similarly is nothing more than a call option on a fixed rate bond, where the strike price is par. Using our running example, a put swaption gives you the right to sell a floating rate bond and receive a fixed rate bond at 5%. And since we still know that the value of any floating rate bond is its principal value, this, in effect, is the same as selling the par value of the underlying bond and receiving the 5%—which then is the same as holding a call option on a fixed rate bond, where the strike price is par.

This means that the payoff diagrams for call and put swaptions are simply the payoff diagrams given above in the bond section: Figure 10 for a call swaption and Figure 11 for a put swaption.

PROBLEM SET

This note has gone through three interest rate instruments: caps, floors and swaptions. All are instruments that hedge against unfavorable movements in interest rates. Here are a few problems to practice what you have just learned. The problems refer to data in Exhibits 1 and 2 on the next page.

Problem 1   The U.S. Treasury is considering issuing a 4-year Treasury note (with a 5% annual coupon and $1000 principal amount) with a rate reset feature: in two years (immediately after the second coupon payment for that year is made), the U.S. Treasury has the right to reset the coupon rate on the bond to the yield-to-maturity of a two-year, coupon-paying T-Note without a reset feature. What is the cost of this reset feature, i.e., how much additional yield-to-maturity will the U.S. Treasury have to pay investors to obtain this feature? Use the interest rate tree given in Exhibit 1.

Problem 2   The value of a 3-year floor on 6-month Libor (making semi-annual payments) with a strike price of 5.5% and a notional amount of $1 million is $1,023. Using the information in Exhibit 2 (this is the same set of rates used in the previous problem set), calculate the value of a 3-year cap on Libor (making semi-annual payments) with a strike price of 5.5% and a $1 million notional.

Problem 3   Using the interest rate tree given in Exhibit 1, value a 3-year interest rate cap (making annual payments) with a cap rate of 5%. The cap has a notional amount of $10M.

Problem 4   With interest rates declining, an insurance company is worried about the possibility of its callable corporate bond holdings being called away by the issuing firms. It is therefore considering the purchase of a 1-year call swaption (struck at 4%)

EXHIBIT 1

NON-RECOMBINING INTEREST RATE TREE (UP-DOWN PROBABILITIES = 0.5)

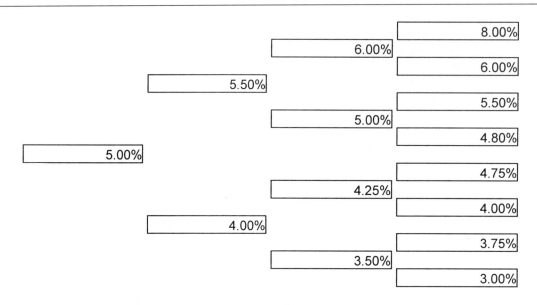

Source: Authors.

on a 3-year fixed-floating swap ($1000 notional; semi-annual payments) to protect its investments. Suppose a 1-year call option (exercise price of $1000) on a 4-year coupon paying bond ($1000 principal, 4% coupon price of $1000) has a value of $31.54. The 6-month and 1-year spot rates are 5 and 5.2% respectively. The 4-year bond has a current market price of $970. Find the value of the swaption.

EXHIBIT 2

PRICES OF ZERO COUPON DEBT PAYING $100 AT MATURITY

Payment Dates (Years)	Treasury Bill Prices	Eurodollar Deposit Values
0.5	97.72	97.48
1.0	95.39	94.92
1.5	93.02	92.27
2.0	90.63	89.60
2.5	88.21	86.87
3.0	85.78	84.13
3.5	83.35	81.36
4.0	80.93	78.57
4.5	78.51	75.77
5.0	76.11	73.02

Source: Authors.

29

Advising on Currency Risk at ICICI Bank

In March 2003, Shilpa Kumar, Joint General Manager of the Markets Advisory Group at ICICI Bank, India's second largest bank, had to come up with a recommendation. One of ICICI Bank's customers, the Power Finance Corporation Ltd (PFC), had asked ICICI Bank's advice on its currency exposure. PFC worked with the Indian power sector and especially with India's various State Electricity Boards (SEB) to finance their operations. PFC's loans to the boards were primarily in Indian rupees (INR) but the loans that PFC had to take itself were often denominated in other currencies. PFC therefore found itself regularly with large foreign exchange exposures.

At her last meeting in New Delhi with PFC's Deputy General Manager, Rajeev Mehrotra, Kumar had learned that PFC's current exposure was running close to INR 1,300 crore[1] (about $300 million USD), mostly in U.S. Dollars and Japanese Yen (JPY). Out of this exposure, Mehrotra was especially interested in hedging a Japanese Yen loan, equivalent to $100 million, with a five-year tenor. Back at ICICI Bank's headquarters in Bombay, Kumar now had to come up with recommendations for how PFC should handle this JPY exposure. Mehrotra had made it clear that he wasn't interested in hearing about a full hedge for the entire exposure, but that he hoped that ICICI Bank could present alternative strategies that potentially were more profitable to PFC.

Whatever the recommendation, Kumar's team would have to take a view of the development of interest rates and also exchange rates for the dollar and yen. This would help decide what should be hedged of interest rate risk and exchange risk—and how much of them? Kumar's recommendation would have to take all these aspects into consideration.

Professor George Chacko, Professor Marti G. Subrahmanyam of the Stern School of Business at New York University, Executive Director Vincent Dessain and Research Associate Anders Sjöman of the HBS Europe Research Center prepared this case. HBS cases are developed solely as the basis for class discussion. Cases are not intended to serve as endorsements, sources of primary data, or illustrations of effective or ineffective management.

[1] It was common in India to use units from a traditional numbers system: A crore was 10 million and a lakh 100,000. In terms of currency, a crore in 2003 fluctuated between $200,000 and $250,000 USD.

ICICI BANK LIMITED

Headquartered in Mumbai on India's western coast, ICICI Bank was India's second largest bank after the State Bank of India. ICICI Bank boasted total assets of INR 106,811 crore (about $22.5 billion) and profit after tax of INR 1,206 crore (about $254 million) for the fiscal year ending March 31, 2003. (For ICICI Bank's financials, see Exhibit 1.) ICICI Bank operated about 450 branches and 1,700 ATMs across India. Its commercial banking activities operations serviced corporate customers with lending and deposit services, and individual retail customers with deposit accounts, loans, and credit cards. ICICI Bank also ran investment banking activities, such as treasury operations for handling the bank's investment portfolio, and offered Internet banking services, on-line bill paying, and debit cards. Life and other insurance products were offered through joint ventures with Prudential and Lombard Canada.

The origins of ICICI Bank were found in ICICI (Industrial Credit and Investment Corporation of India) Limited, an Indian financial institution, formed in 1955 at the initiative of the World Bank, the Indian Government and Indian industry. At the time, ICICI Limited's objective was to offer medium- to long-term project financing to Indian businesses. Over the years, ICICI Limited transformed its business to a diversified financial services group, offering a wide variety of products and services. It began with venture capital financing in 1988, asset management and investment banking in 1993, and commercial banking through its subsidiary ICICI Bank in 1994. After selling off equity in its subsidiary, ICICI Limited only kept a 46% in ICICI Bank.

In 1999, ICICI Limited was the first Indian company to be listed on the New York Stock Exchange (NYSE), through American Depository Receipts (ADRs). Then, in October 2001, driven by a realization that the key success factors in the Indian banking industry were a large capital base and considerable size and scale of operations, ICICI Limited reverse merged with ICICI Bank and formed one company. The current day ICICI Bank was born. In 2002, ICICI Bank set up an international banking group to service clients with cross border needs, and to offer its products internationally. By 2003, the bank was running subsidiaries in the U.K. and Canada, with branches in Singapore and Bahrain, and offices in the U.S., China, United Arab Emirates and Bangladesh.

In 2004, the bank's shares were traded on the Mumbai Stock Exchange and the National Stock Exchange of India and ADRs on the NYSE. ADR holders held 21% shares of the bank.

Advising on Market Risk: ICICI Bank's Markets Advisory Group

Risk was inherent to ICICI Bank's business as a financial institution. The bank both managed its own risk and provided risk management activities for its corporate customers. These activities addressed credit risk (the possibility of loss due to changes in the quality of counterparties), operational risk (the potential for loss arising from breakdowns in policies and controls, human error, contracts, systems and facilities) and market risk. Especially for market risk, ICICI Bank ran a Markets Advisory Group, headed by Shilpa Kumar. Market risk was the risk of loss from changes in interest rates, foreign currency exchange rates, equity prices and commodity prices. ICICI Bank's own exposure to market risk came from its trading, its asset and liability management activities and its role in customer-related transactions. In their work with external clients, the Markets Advisory Group that Kumar headed consulted clients on how to manage their market risks. When meeting clients, Kumar and her colleagues most often met with the client's treasury departments. In those meetings, their baseline presentation

EXHIBIT 1

ICICI BANK FINANCIALS (IN INDIAN RUPEE, INR, THOUSANDS)

Balance Sheet	March 31, 2003	March 31, 2002
BALANCE SHEET		
Capital and Liabilities		
Capital	9,626,600	9,625,472
Reserves and Surplus	63,206,538	56,324,080
Deposits	481,693,063	320,851,111
Borrowings	343,024,203	492,186,592
Other liabilities and provisions	170,569,258	162,075,756
TOTAL	1,068,119,662	1,041,063,011
Assets		
Cash and balance with Reserve Bank of India	48,861,445	17,744,682
Balances with banks and money at call and short notice	16,028,581	110,118,817
Investments	354,623,002	358,910,797
Advances	532,794,144	470,348,661
Fixed Assets	40,607,274	42,393,443
Other Assets	75,205,216	41,546,611
TOTAL	1,068,119,662	1,041,063,011
PROFIT AND LOSS ACCOUNT		
Income		
Interest earned	93,680,561	21,519,297
Other income	19,677,741	5,746,598
Profit on sale of shares	11,910,517	—
TOTAL	125,268,819	27,265,895
Expenditure		
Interest expended	79,439,989	15,589,235
Operating expenses	20,116,900	6,225,770
Provisions and contingencies	13,650,139	2,867,900
TOTAL	113,207,028	24,682,905
Profit/Loss		
Net profit for the year	12,061,791	2,582,990
Profit brought forward	195,614	8,294
TOTAL	12,257,405	2,591,284
Appropriations/Transfers		
Statutory Reserve	3,020,000	650,000
Transfer from Debenture Redemption Reserve	−100,000	—
Capital Reserves	2,000,000	—
Investment Fluctuation Reserve	1,000,000	160,000
Special Reserve	500,000	140,000
Revenue and other Reserves	600,000	960,000
Proposed equity share Dividend	4,597,758	—
Proposed preference share Dividend	35	—
Interim dividend paid	—	440,717
Corporate dividend tax	589,092	44,953
Balance carried over to Balance Sheet	50,520	195,614
TOTAL	12,257,405	2,591,284

Source: ICICI Bank, Annual Report 2003.

covered areas such as "What drives corporate value?" and "Philosophy for a treasury policy." In addition to such enterprise-wide considerations, the group also often then included other strategic topics such as "Foreign Exchange (FX) Risk Management Policies."

In the Corporate Value-section of a presentation, the group discussed drivers of corporate value, and how earnings volatility affected P/E multiples,[2] which in turn impacted corporate value. They discussed market risks hiding in both the balance sheet (in the form of interest rate risks for cash or long term debt) and the income statement (as exchange rate and commodity risk for sales and cost of sales, and just exchange rate risk for selling, general and administrative expenses).

In the presentation's Treasury-part, ICICI Bank argued that a company's treasury should manage the cost of debt as well the cost of equity, which came from the volatility of income streams. The discussion often turned to how much of market risk a treasury should hedge. Was there an ideal balance between being fully hedged and not hedged at all? Further, ICICI Bank argued that division treasuries should not be allowed to take a view on the markets. This should be left for the central corporate treasury. Instead, individual treasuries should completely hedge exposures as they arose. This would help secure earnings by providing low volatility.

Finally, in the FX Risk Management-part, the group went into quite some detail about the origins of FX risk. They outlined how a company's functional currency could be different from its local currency and how the operating income itself could have a net FX-risk due to inter-market linkages. ICICI Bank also believed that—with increasingly global customers, competitors and shareholders—merging strategic intent with the overall risk management was increasingly important. This meant that a centralized treasury should monitor the financial risk as well as the currency risk embedded in the business. The presentation normally ended with a few comments on how management could define the company's risk strategy, combining FX composition (fixed or floating hedges of various durations) with a view on how independent the treasury could operate, and also setting an exposure limit that matched the company's size and business.

In addition to broad risk consideration, the group would also offer advice on specific transaction strategies for corporates to tackle market exposure on their balance sheet or income statement. Depending on the company's objective, the focus of any client meeting could therefore be either strategic, transactional or a mixture of both. Presentations normally also varied in focus depending on whether the client was a private or public company. Private companies were generally seeking more enterprise-wide advice, whereas public companies liked to spend more time on the specific risk hedging, as it was more focused on risks that company would like to fix. Explained Kumar,

> Public sector companies in India are subject to the regulations and supervision of the auditor general of India, in addition to internal and statutory audits. There is greater focus on volatility/risk reducing structures rather than cost minimization strategies.

Mehrotra at PFC clarified,

> India's central bank, the Reserve Bank of India, does however permit all customers and users of foreign exchange to access risk management products, almost at par with such opportunities to companies in other developing countries.

---

[2] The P/E ratio (the share price to its per-share earnings) was a measurement of the value that the market placed on a stock. In general, companies expected to grow and have higher earnings in the future had a higher P/E than those in decline.

POWER FINANCE CORPORATION (PFC) OF INDIA

One of the public companies that Kumar and her group had as a client was the state-owned financing institute Power Finance Corporation (PFC) Ltd. of India. PFC had been founded by the Indian Government in July 1986 to provide finances to India's power sector, primarily the various State Electricity Boards. The Government of India was PFC's sole shareholder with a share capital of about $233 million.

India's Power Sector[3]

On the production side, India was in 2003 the world's third-largest producer of coal, and also had substantial resources in gas as well as untapped hydro potential. Combined, this allowed India to import only about 20% of its energy needs from abroad. On the consumption side, India was the world's sixth largest energy consumer. Electricity usage was divided primarily between industry (33%), agriculture (30%) and households (18%). However, the country had one of the lowest per capita electricity consumption levels in Asia. Bringing electricity to all of India had always been difficult, given the country's large and mostly rural population. In 2003, the power sector still struggled to meet demand and only managed to provide half of the country's 1.1 billion inhabitants with electricity. The sector was also burdened with chronic and widespread electricity shortages.

The Indian power sector was split into three areas: the central sector, with government-owned utility companies, the state sector, primarily engaged through the states' own State Electricity Boards (SEBs) and the private sector. The central sector handled both generation and transmission of power through its various utility companies. On the state level, SEBs handled some transmission and almost all of the country's distribution. (India's electricity market was divided into 5 regions and 29 states.)

The energy sector was for many years funded and run by the states, which however ran it consistently at a loss. Several reasons explained this pattern, such as the prevalent policy of subsidizing electricity for the needy, their weakness in following up regulatory regimes, and above all the federal mandate to electrify rural India. (The electrification program helped India become self-sufficient in food and crops.) The worsening power shortages brought the situation to a head in the 1970s, and the central government decided to become more directly involved. It founded a number of companies, called Central Public Sector Utilities (CPSUs), in the power generation and transmission segments. Through the CPSUs, the Indian government started large energy infrastructure investments. Among the CPSUs were also two lending institutions, PFC and Rural Electrification Corp. (See Exhibit 2 for a list of CPSUs. Exhibit 3 presents India's power sector in 2003.)

In 1991, the government continued the reforms and opened the sector to private investors. Private investment remained scarce, though. On the plus side, the Indian market provided a very compelling demand story, with increasing need for electricity across the country (which still outgrew supply and lead to continued electricity shortages; see Exhibit 4 for more details). On the minus side, investors worried about the industry's problems in billings and collection, system dependability, counterparty risk and regulatory protection. Events in 2001 made investors even more hesitant, as they saw state utilities go through a financial crisis. At the source of the crisis was the states' ongoing practice to give large electricity subsidies to farmers and residents. These were

---

[3] This section draws on the work of Fitch Ratings Corporate Finance, "Back to the Basics—The Indian Power Sector," by analysts Charles Chang and Manish Makhan, 24 September 2003, and on interviews with PFC and ICICI.

EXHIBIT 2

CENTRAL POWER SECTOR UTILITIES (CPSU)

	Initial	MW produced	%
National Thermal Power Corp	NTPC	21,249	65
National Hydroelectric Power Corp	NHPC	2,149	7
Bhakra Beas Management Board	BBMB	2,794	9
Damodar Valley Corporation	DVC	2,535	8
North Eastern Electric Power Corp.	NEEPCO	1,015	3
Nuclear Power Corp. of India Ltd	NPCIL	2,720	8
Powergrid Corp. of India	PGCIL		
		32,462	**100**

Note: CPSU listed above cover power generation, transmission and distribution. CPSU also include the lending institutions Power Finance Corporation and Rural Electrification Corporation.

Source: Fitch Ratings Corporate Finance, "Back to the Basics—The Indian Power Sector," by analysts Charles Chang and Manish Makhan, 24 September 2003, page 5.

mostly given in the form of flat rates, and priced much lower than the actual cost. Since flat rates did not require checking at the individual consumer level, the system of metering consumption slowly disintegrated. By 2001, only 51% of all electricity generated was actually billed, and only 41% paid. The SEBs felt the revenue loss. By year end 2001, all SEBs operated at a loss (compared to nine out of 29 in 1996.) Unable to pay their bills, the SEBs built up large debts to the CPSUs: By March 2001, the SEBs owed the CPSUs INR 414.7 billion (37% of which was accrued penalty and interest).

The crisis at the state level caused the Government of India to intervene again. It renegotiated the SEB loans, and worked out payment schedules with the Reserve Bank of India. Then, to help restore the sector, including investor faith, the government focused on what it saw as fundamentals. Against a goal of providing reliable and afford-

EXHIBIT 3

INDIA'S REGIONAL POWER MARKETS, 2003

	GDP INRbn	% India	Cap. GW	% Total	% Capacity share of			% Capacity Share of						
					State	Private	Central	Hydro	Coal	Gas	Dsl	Thrml	Wind	Nucl
North	4,638	27.4	28.4	26.4	59.7	0.3	40.0	30.0	54.6	11.2	0.1	65.8	0.1	4.2
West	4,720	27.9	31.6	29.4	60.0	19.4	20.6	14.2	65.9	15.6	0.1	81.5	1.9	2.4
South	4,504	26.6	28.5	26.5	63.9	13.6	22.5	35.2	46.3	8.8	3.3	58.5	3.6	2.7
East	2,560	15.1	16.7	15.5	47.4	8.6	44.0	14.7	84.0	1.1	0.1	85.3	0.0	0.0
Northeast	488	2.9	2.4	2.2	47.5	1.5	51.1	47.0	16.3	29.3	7.3	53.0	0.0	0.0

Source: Fitch Ratings Corporate Finance, "Back to the Basics—The Indian Power Sector," by analysts Charles Chang and Manish Makhan, 24 September 2003, page 6.

EXHIBIT 4

POWER SHORTFALL (FISCAL YEAR 2003)

Region	Energy Gap (%)	Peaking Gap (%)
Western	12.6	20.3
Southern	7.2	8.9
Northern	3.1	7.7
North-Eastern	2.4	6.1
Eastern	2.7	5.0

Source: India Ministry of Power, as quoted in Fitch Ratings Corporate Finance, "Back to the Basics—The Indian Power Sector," by analysts Charles Chang and Manish Makhan, 24 September 2003, page 5.

able power supply for the entire country by 2012, the government set up programs focused on giving financial assistance to states for plant modernization, upgrading Transmission & Distribution (T&D) networks, addressing the issues of poor metering, low collection and subsidized rates, and restoring the SEBs to financial soundness. Notable programs included the Electricity Regulatory Commissions Act 1998, the Accelerated Power Development Program (APDP) in 2002, the Accelerated Power Development and Reform Program (APDRP) and Electricity Act in 2003.

The PFC played an important role in that last objective, helping to finance a sustainable Indian power sector and providing financial incentives to states to achieve SEB profitability.

PFC Activities: "Funding For a Brighter Tomorrow"

As a financial institution under the Ministry of Power, PFC was charged with providing financial assistance for the power sector. With the slogan "Funding for a Brighter Tomorrow," PFC helped state power utilities meet their funds requirements for power projects. Based in New Delhi, PFC not only provided financial services (such as Term Loans, Equipment Leasing, and Buyers Line of Credit), but also technological and managerial services.

Explained Mehrotra,

> PFC developed as a lean team with about 130 highly skilled professionals in finance, thermal and hydrogenation, transmission and distribution, consulting services and institutional reforms. It has been growing at an annual rate of about 30% in sanctions and disbursements and enjoys the highest credit ratings from domestic rating agencies, and rates at par with the sovereign rating for India from Standards & Poor and Moody.

As an organization, PFC had three main objectives. First, to raise financial resources from international and domestic sources, and lend these to power projects in India. Second, to help bring institutional, managerial, operational and financial improvement to the state power utilities. Third, to assist the states in carrying out reforms and to support the state power sector during transitional periods of reforms.

Practically, PFC was actively persuading state governments to reform their power sectors and make them commercially viable. To help in this, PFC provided financial assistance under relaxed lending criteria as well as assisted SEBs in creating restructuring programs. The programs normally focused on the difficulties states faced in high transmission and distribution losses, low efficiency and low tariffs. Commonly, PFC loans were conditioned on the state setting up an Operational and Financial Action Plan, which PFC would help the state develop. PFC was available as a resource also for private sector initiatives.[4] In total, PFC had about 35 state level customers in 2003.

By 2003, 23 states had set up regulatory commissions and 18 states had committed to power sector reforms with financial and technical assistance by PFC. Mehrotra was happy to report that "for its consistently high performance, PFC has been awarded by the President of India as one of the top ten performing Indian Government companies for the last seven years running."

PFC's Funds—and Its Currency Exposure

In the fiscal year ending March 31, 2003, PFC reported a net profit of INR 11.71 billion (about $249 million), up from INR 7.78 billion the year before. Total income was up 24% and reached INR 25.98 billion. During the year, PFC had sanctioned a record number of loans, reaching INR 140.01 billion and beating their target by 86.7%. Actual loan disbursements also reached a high of INR 73.38 billion (63.1% over target.)[5] To meet these financing needs, PFC had raised INR 70.02 billion, 167% over the target and 59.2% higher than the previous year. PFC's interest expenses as a percentage of operating income had fallen to 44.6% from 50% the preceding year. The recovery rate of loans had grown to 99%, a number impressive to industry observers. (See Exhibit 5 for PFC financials.)

Kumar's team at ICICI Bank estimated PFC's annual borrowing need to run in the neighborhood of INR 5,000–8,000 crore (roughly $1.5 billion–$2 billion USD). PFC's lending needs were largely rupee based, since they provided funds to SEBs who needed national currency. PFC's own funds came from a variety of sources (see Exhibit 6 for details), most of which were domestic. However, the Indian debt market was not large enough to cover all of PFC's financing needs at a reasonable cost, and PFC often had to turn to off-shore markets to borrow. PFC's international lenders included World Bank, Asian Development Bank, Overseas Development Administration of UK, kfW of Germany, Credit Lyonnais, Credit National and others.

Mehrotra explained, "PFC has done almost one international borrowing every year since 1997 of about USD 100 million through different instruments, such as USD bond issues—fixed and floating, or syndicated bank loans." As an example, PFC raised $100 million in 2002 through a syndicated loan facility, denominated in Japanese Yen (JPY). The loan was of JPY Libor[6] + 50 basis points for the first two years, and JPY Libor + 85 basis points thereafter with 5 years maturity before full reimbursement had to be made.

In 2003, little over 10% of PFC's lending was done in foreign currencies. The goal was to increase that number to 30% over the next three years. In rough numbers, about

---

[4] In addition to the SEBs and private investors, PFC also serviced State Power Utilities, State Electricity/Power Departments, other State Departments engaged in the development of power projects, Central Power Utilities, and Municipal Bodies.

[5] Between the time that PFC accepted to finance a project—sanctioned it—and the time it actually paid out the loan—disbursement—there was normally a 3–6 month time lag.

[6] LIBOR (London Inter Bank Offered Rate) was an interest rate fixed daily by the British Bankers' Association (BBA). Similar to the U.S. Federal Reserve rate, it was used as a reference rate for other short term interest rates.

EXHIBIT 5

OVERVIEW PFC FINANCIALS (INDIAN RUPEES, INR, IN CRORE)

	1988–89	1999–2000	2000–01	2001–02	2002–03
Resources (at year end)					
Equity Capital	1030.45	1030.45	1030.45	1030.45	1030.45
Interest Subsidy Fund	505.86	732.29	896.22	1093.44	1128.54
Reserves and Surplus	1871.33	2355.61	2779.14	3367.63	4301.57
Borrowings					
PFC Bonds	2008.85	2508.57	3637.06	5027.09	6281.40
Foreign Loans	1810.74	2281.96	2241.48	2134.71	2482.14
Rupee Loan Govt. of India	1531.13	1529.13	1513.60		
Term Loans from Banks	700.00	1425.00	1925.00	3515.00	5364.00
Commercial Paper				135.00	100.00
Cash-credit from Banks				170.00	136.56
Financing Operations					
No of loans	79	93	155	145	251
Loans Sanctioned	3339	6490	7706	8506	14001
Loans Disbursed	2467	3404	3230	5150	7338
Repayment by Borrowers	698	993	1416	1992	2811
Working Results					
Administrative Expenses	19.79	28.39	30.79	27.63	38.34
Profit before Tax	660.03	738.57	745.97	950.38	1367.95
Provision for Tax	118.67	116.10	141.83	172.05	196.06
Profit after Tax	541.36	622.47	604.13	778.33	1171.89
No. of Employees	271	272	268	268	272

Note: A crore was a traditional Indian expression for ten million.

Source: PFC Annual Report 2003.

half the foreign loans were in USD, a third in Japanese Yen, and about 10% in Euros. PFC main objective in managing the exchange risk that followed these foreign currency loans was to fix the cost of the loan liabilities. Mehrotra explained further,

> In essence, PFC faces long duration assets that are cyclical with the economy. Economies are associated with the interest rate level in the inverse manner—so to hedge against that, we put on floating rate liabilities. We use a mix of short-term, medium-term and long-term loans with a basket of floating and fixed rates.

In addition to currency risk, PFC also faced the normal risks of financing operations, such as credit risk, liquidity risk and interest rate risk. One of the credit risks PFC faced was actually tied to currency fluctuations. It came from the fact that the SEBs did not exclusively deal in rupees. They bought some of their energy and fuel for the power stations from foreign providers, paying them primarily in dollars or other G4 currencies.[7] This left the SEBs with a dollar exposure, and if the dollar appreciated

[7] "G4 currencies" was a common term for a group of strong currencies: the U.S. Dollar (USD), Euroland's Euro (EUR), the Japanese Yen (JPY) and the Chinese Yuan (CNY).

EXHIBIT 6

**PFC COMPOSITION OF RESOURCES
(AS OF 31 MARCH 2002)**

	Indian Rupees (INR) billions
Paid-up Capital	10.30
Reserves and Surplus	33.68
Bonds	50.27
Term Loans	36.50
Line of Credit	1.70
Foreign Currency Loans	21.35
Interest Subsidy Fund from Government of India	10.93
TOTAL	**164.73**

Source: PFC website, www.pfcindia.com, accessed 13 December 2004.

vis-à-vis the rupee, the SEBs would now have its margins impacted. They would be in a worse situation to pay off their loans to PFC—and so, a currency fluctuation could translate into a credit risk for PFC.

PFC was wholly-owned by the Indian government and was under strict government control. Its CEO and board members were appointed by the Indian government. PFC had however recently obtained a so called Mini-Ratna Status. By Indian law, a public service utility with a Mini-Ratna Status had a certain amount of autonomy versus the government with regard to capital expenditure, establishing joint venture companies, entering into Transfer of Technology agreements and implementing human resources management schemes. Still, the Government, through the Auditor General, kept a close eye on the company.

PFC'S EXPOSURE AND ICICI BANK'S RECOMMENDATION

Over the years, Kumar had been in touch several times with Mehrotra at PFC, discussing PFC's overall risk management. However, in March 2003, she received a phone call from Mehrotra about a specific transaction for which he wanted to discuss possible hedging tactics. Mehrotra explained,

> PFC will take a loan of 12 billion Japanese Yen, or about 100 million USD, from a group of eight foreign banks spread over Europe and Asia-Pacific. The loan will have a five-year maturity. We want to convert this loan into rupees. Now, the way we look at it, we have two issues: the yen/dollar and the rupee/dollar movement. All in all, three currencies are involved. We also need to consider how interest rates might develop.

Customers in India had to trade through the USD for all other currencies. As such, any cross rate between USD and Yen would also affect the liabilities of Yen borrowers in India. Therefore, in this case also, ultimately the Yen/Rupee exchange rate would be decided by the Dollar/Yen and Dollar/Rupee rates.

PFC wanted ICICI Bank's help in devising a sound strategy to hedge the currency exposure resulting out of its JPY liability. Kumar remembered her initial reaction to Mehrotra's request,

> One side of the issue was in terms of drawdown, or when to actually take the loan. What do they do with the size that they carry in yen to rupee, in terms of when they should draw down the money? Secondly, at what point should they actually convert this into rupee funding? If all they looked for was a complete hedge, it would be an open and shut case. PFC should lend out as soon as they took the loan and convert the whole sum at that point in time into rupees.

A full currency swap would ensure interest rate risk hedging as well as exchange rate risk hedging. However, Mehrotra made it clear that he wasn't interested in a full hedge. Instead, he was open to hedging the exchange and interest rate risks separately, using structured instruments such as Interest Rate Swaps (IRS) and Principle-Only Swaps (POS). He said,

> We have seen in the past that doing a complete hedge is very costly. We have of course considered it now too, and I have in fact already an offer from another large Mumbai bank to do a complete Yen to rupee hedge. They will charge me a 6.3% fixed rate per annum for this. What I hope ICICI Bank will do, though, is to give me ideas on what else I could do to optimize the hedge of this exposure—and that would be cheaper than 6.3%.

The benchmark that PFC set for ICICI Bank was 6.0%. PFC had arrived at this number by taking the lending rate that PFC charged the electricity boards and its other borrowers (9.25%) minus an average annualized cost of this lending (1%) and minus the return on capital that PFC wanted to earn (2.25%).

Mehrotra wanted the 6.0% to be enough to cover costs needed to hedge three risks: appreciation of yen against dollar, depreciation of rupee against dollar and appreciation in Yen LIBOR. To come up with a recommendation, Kumar and her team, which included economists and market analysts, discussed fundamental economic outlook in each of the three countries involved (Japan, U.S., and India). Their final view and recommendation had to consider the currency development and interest rates development. Exhibit 7 shows currency rates for March 2003. (Interestingly, Kumar thought, for the first time in Indian history, the rupee was actually appreciating vis-à-vis the U.S. dollar.) Exhibit 8 then shows the interest rate swap rates and zero coupon rates for indian rupees, Exhibit 9 the same for U.S. dollar, and Exhibit 10 for Japanese Yen, all of them for the month of March 2003.

Based on the economic information, Kumar and her team could picture several recommendations. The target cost of 6% was achieved with a mix of following: a dollar/rupee hedge for the principal of the loan, a similar dollar/rupee hedge for the interest or coupon part of the loan, a yen/dollar cross currency swap, and finally a yen-IRS (Interest Rate Swap).

In addition to this, Kumar's team also put together some possible currency structures to hedge the JPY exposure. Exhibit 11 presents these structures in detail.

Kumar now had to evaluate the possible solutions, consider if there were any other combination of interest rate instruments that would meet PFC's requirements, and finally arrive at a recommendation to give PFC.

EXHIBIT 7

CURRENCY RATES VS. USD (ASK-PRICE) FOR MARCH 2003

Date	Indian Rupee	Japanese Yen
3 March 2003	47.68	117.59
4 March 2003	47.80	117.88
5 March 2003	47.80	117.32
6 March 2003	47.63	117.43
7 March 2003	47.80	117.11
10 March 2003	47.70	116.89
11 March 2003	47.64	117.13
12 March 2003	47.65	117.33
13 March 2003	47.66	118.68
14 March 2003	47.66	118.28
17 March 2003	47.68	118.57
18 March 2003	47.68	118.89
19 March 2003	47.70	120.51
20 March 2003	47.75	120.29
21 March 2003	47.66	121.49
24 March 2003	47.70	120.81
25 March 2003	47.64	120.19
26 March 2003	47.60	120.04
27 March 2003	47.60	120.01
28 March 2003	47.55	119.83
31 March 2003	47.53	117.98

Source: Compiled by case authors based on Reuters.

EXHIBIT 8

INDIAN RUPEE INTEREST RATE SWAPS AND ZERO COUPON RATE FOR VARIOUS MATURITIES

a. IRS

Date	0.5 year	1 year	2 year	3 year	5 year	7 year	10 year
31-Mar-03	4.40%	4.50%	4.83%	5.45%	5.30%	5.75%	5.95%
28-Mar-03	4.43%	4.70%	4.93%	5.20%	5.35%	5.63%	5.95%
27-Mar-03	4.52%	4.75%	4.86%	4.96%	5.29%	5.65%	5.95%
26-Mar-03	4.78%	4.90%	5.05%	5.19%	5.49%	5.75%	6.05%
25-Mar-03	4.87%	4.95%	5.05%	5.15%	5.47%	5.80%	6.10%
24-Mar-03	4.86%	4.85%	5.15%	5.27%	5.59%	5.90%	6.20%
21-Mar-03	4.81%	4.85%	5.05%	5.17%	5.53%	5.85%	6.20%
20-Mar-03	4.98%	5.05%	5.23%	5.37%	5.73%	6.05%	6.35%
19-Mar-03	4.94%	5.00%	5.20%	5.40%	5.70%	6.00%	6.30%
17-Mar-03	4.90%	4.75%	5.20%	5.35%	5.67%	6.00%	6.35%
13-Mar-03	4.80%	4.80%	5.05%	5.20%	5.50%	5.75%	6.10%
12-Mar-03	4.82%	4.85%	5.10%	5.20%	5.51%	6.05%	6.35%
11-Mar-03	4.82%	4.95%	5.17%	5.33%	5.65%	5.95%	6.30%
10-Mar-03	4.95%	5.10%	5.30%	5.40%	5.80%	6.13%	6.45%
7-Mar-03	4.91%	4.90%	5.32%	5.42%	5.77%	6.10%	6.40%
6-Mar-03	4.77%	4.85%	5.16%	5.30%	5.63%	5.93%	6.25%
5-Mar-03	4.78%	4.90%	5.30%	5.42%	5.75%	6.05%	6.35%
4-Mar-03	4.76%	4.90%	5.25%	5.40%	5.70%	5.95%	6.20%
3-Mar-03	4.74%	5.00%	5.22%	5.37%	5.66%	5.95%	6.25%

(Continued)

EXHIBIT 8 (Continued)

INDIAN RUPEE INTEREST RATE SWAPS AND ZERO COUPON RATE FOR VARIOUS MATURITIES

b. Zero Coupon Rate

Date	0.5Y	1Y	1.5Y	2Y	2.5Y	3Y	3.5Y	4Y	4.5Y	5Y	5.5Y	6Y	6.5Y	7Y	7.5Y	8Y	8.5Y	9Y	9.5Y	10Y
31-Mar-03	4.31%	4.40%	4.56%	4.72%	5.03%	5.35%	5.30%	5.26%	5.22%	5.17%	5.30%	5.42%	5.54%	5.67%	5.70%	5.74%	5.78%	5.81%	5.85%	5.88%
28-Mar-03	4.33%	4.59%	4.71%	4.82%	4.95%	5.09%	5.12%	5.16%	5.20%	5.24%	5.31%	5.39%	5.46%	5.54%	5.60%	5.66%	5.72%	5.78%	5.84%	5.90%
27-Mar-03	4.42%	4.64%	4.69%	4.75%	4.80%	4.85%	4.93%	5.01%	5.10%	5.18%	5.28%	5.38%	5.48%	5.58%	5.63%	5.69%	5.74%	5.80%	5.86%	5.91%
26-Mar-03	4.67%	4.78%	4.86%	4.93%	5.00%	5.07%	5.15%	5.22%	5.30%	5.38%	5.45%	5.52%	5.59%	5.66%	5.71%	5.77%	5.83%	5.88%	5.94%	6.00%
25-Mar-03	4.76%	4.83%	4.88%	4.93%	4.98%	5.03%	5.11%	5.19%	5.28%	5.36%	5.45%	5.54%	5.63%	5.71%	5.77%	5.83%	5.88%	5.94%	6.00%	6.05%
24-Mar-03	4.75%	4.74%	4.88%	5.03%	5.09%	5.15%	5.23%	5.31%	5.39%	5.48%	5.56%	5.64%	5.73%	5.81%	5.87%	5.92%	5.98%	6.04%	6.09%	6.15%
21-Mar-03	4.70%	4.74%	4.83%	4.93%	4.99%	5.05%	5.14%	5.24%	5.33%	5.42%	5.51%	5.59%	5.68%	5.76%	5.83%	5.90%	5.96%	6.03%	6.10%	6.16%
20-Mar-03	4.86%	4.93%	5.01%	5.10%	5.17%	5.24%	5.33%	5.43%	5.52%	5.61%	5.70%	5.78%	5.87%	5.96%	6.01%	6.07%	6.13%	6.18%	6.24%	6.30%
19-Mar-03	4.82%	4.88%	4.98%	5.07%	5.17%	5.27%	5.35%	5.42%	5.50%	5.58%	5.66%	5.74%	5.82%	5.90%	5.96%	6.02%	6.07%	6.13%	6.19%	6.24%
17-Mar-03	4.78%	4.64%	4.86%	5.08%	5.15%	5.23%	5.31%	5.39%	5.47%	5.55%	5.64%	5.73%	5.82%	5.91%	5.98%	6.04%	6.11%	6.18%	6.24%	6.31%
13-Mar-03	4.69%	4.69%	4.81%	4.93%	5.01%	5.08%	5.16%	5.23%	5.31%	5.39%	5.45%	5.52%	5.59%	5.65%	5.72%	5.79%	5.86%	5.92%	5.99%	6.06%
12-Mar-03	4.71%	4.74%	4.86%	4.98%	5.03%	5.08%	5.16%	5.24%	5.32%	5.40%	5.54%	5.69%	5.84%	5.99%	6.04%	6.10%	6.16%	6.21%	6.27%	6.32%
11-Mar-03	4.71%	4.83%	4.94%	5.05%	5.13%	5.20%	5.29%	5.37%	5.45%	5.53%	5.61%	5.69%	5.77%	5.86%	5.92%	5.99%	6.06%	6.12%	6.19%	6.26%
10-Mar-03	4.83%	4.97%	5.07%	5.17%	5.22%	5.27%	5.37%	5.47%	5.58%	5.68%	5.77%	5.86%	5.94%	6.03%	6.09%	6.15%	6.22%	6.28%	6.34%	6.40%
7-Mar-03	4.79%	4.78%	4.99%	5.19%	5.24%	5.29%	5.38%	5.47%	5.56%	5.65%	5.74%	5.83%	5.92%	6.01%	6.06%	6.12%	6.18%	6.23%	6.29%	6.35%
6-Mar-03	4.66%	4.74%	4.89%	5.04%	5.11%	5.18%	5.26%	5.35%	5.43%	5.51%	5.59%	5.67%	5.75%	5.83%	5.89%	5.96%	6.02%	6.08%	6.14%	6.20%
5-Mar-03	4.67%	4.78%	4.98%	5.17%	5.23%	5.29%	5.38%	5.46%	5.55%	5.63%	5.71%	5.79%	5.87%	5.95%	6.01%	6.07%	6.12%	6.18%	6.24%	6.29%
4-Mar-03	4.65%	4.78%	4.95%	5.13%	5.20%	5.27%	5.35%	5.43%	5.50%	5.58%	5.65%	5.71%	5.78%	5.84%	5.89%	5.94%	5.99%	6.03%	6.08%	6.13%
3-Mar-03	4.63%	4.88%	4.99%	5.09%	5.17%	5.24%	5.32%	5.39%	5.47%	5.54%	5.62%	5.70%	5.77%	5.85%	5.91%	5.97%	6.02%	6.08%	6.14%	6.19%

Note: In reality, Indian inter-bank borrowing is liquid up to the 1-day period. A derived measure, MIFOR or Mumbai Interbank Forward Offer Rate, is used as an approximation for longer maturities. The table above is based on the MIFOR measure. However, for the sake of case simplification, assume here that MIFOR exactly equals the Indian Rupee interest rate.

Source: Compiled by case authors based on Reuters.

EXHIBIT 9

U.S. DOLLAR INTEREST RATE SWAPS AND ZERO COUPON RATE FOR VARIOUS MATURITIES

a. IRS

Date	0.5	1	2	3	4	5	6	7	8	9	10
03-Mar-03	1.34%	1.34%	1.80%	2.32%	2.74%	3.01%	3.37%	3.61%	3.78%	3.92%	4.11%
04-Mar-03	1.33%	1.32%	1.72%	2.29%	2.71%	3.05%	3.33%	3.57%	3.77%	3.93%	4.07%
05-Mar-03	1.32%	1.29%	1.74%	2.16%	2.58%	2.98%	3.23%	3.54%	3.69%	3.87%	4.03%
06-Mar-03	1.31%	1.29%	1.76%	2.19%	2.63%	3.03%	3.29%	3.56%	3.74%	3.92%	4.09%
07-Mar-03	1.31%	1.23%	1.70%	2.18%	2.60%	3.01%	3.30%	3.51%	3.72%	3.89%	4.07%
10-Mar-03	1.21%	1.17%	1.58%	2.08%	2.52%	2.92%	3.18%	3.46%	3.64%	3.82%	3.98%
11-Mar-03	1.17%	1.19%	1.67%	2.19%	2.61%	2.94%	3.21%	3.46%	3.66%	3.84%	3.99%
12-Mar-03	1.18%	1.23%	1.73%	2.24%	2.66%	2.99%	3.24%	3.51%	3.68%	3.85%	3.99%
13-Mar-03	1.23%	1.37%	1.82%	2.36%	2.79%	3.15%	3.44%	3.67%	3.86%	4.02%	4.16%
17-Mar-03	1.22%	1.37%	1.90%	2.44%	2.88%	3.25%	3.54%	3.77%	3.97%	4.13%	4.28%
19-Mar-03	1.27%	1.38%	2.02%	2.57%	3.03%	3.43%	3.70%	3.94%	4.12%	4.27%	4.42%
20-Mar-03	1.28%	1.37%	1.95%	2.51%	2.98%	3.37%	3.66%	3.89%	4.08%	4.25%	4.41%
21-Mar-03	1.28%	1.45%	2.08%	2.67%	3.15%	3.54%	3.83%	4.05%	4.24%	4.40%	4.53%
24-Mar-03	1.28%	1.37%	1.97%	2.54%	3.00%	3.38%	3.67%	3.90%	4.10%	4.26%	4.40%
25-Mar-03	1.28%	1.38%	1.93%	2.50%	2.96%	3.34%	3.63%	3.87%	4.06%	4.23%	4.38%
26-Mar-03	1.28%	1.35%	1.88%	2.46%	2.93%	3.31%	3.60%	3.84%	4.04%	4.20%	4.35%
27-Mar-03	1.27%	1.33%	1.85%	2.42%	2.89%	3.28%	3.58%	3.82%	4.03%	4.20%	4.35%
28-Mar-03	1.26%	1.30%	1.79%	2.39%	2.84%	3.23%	3.54%	3.79%	4.00%	4.17%	4.33%
31-Mar-03	1.23%	1.26%	1.75%	2.32%	2.81%	3.22%	3.43%	3.69%	3.89%	4.07%	4.22%

(Continued)

EXHIBIT 9 (Continued)

U.S. DOLLAR INTEREST RATE SWAPS AND ZERO COUPON RATE FOR VARIOUS MATURITIES

b. Zero Coupon Rate

Date	0.5	1	1.5	2	2.5	3	3.5	4	4.5	5	5.5	6	6.5	7	7.5	8	8.5	9	9.5	10
03-Mar-03	1.33%	1.33%	1.56%	1.79%	2.05%	2.31%	2.52%	2.73%	2.87%	3.00%	3.14%	3.28%	3.42%	3.56%	3.71%	3.85%	4.00%	4.15%	4.30%	4.46%
04-Mar-03	1.32%	1.31%	1.51%	1.71%	1.99%	2.28%	2.49%	2.71%	2.88%	3.05%	3.23%	3.41%	3.59%	3.78%	3.96%	4.15%	4.35%	4.54%	4.74%	4.95%
05-Mar-03	1.31%	1.28%	1.51%	1.73%	1.94%	2.14%	2.36%	2.58%	2.78%	2.99%	3.20%	3.41%	3.63%	3.84%	4.07%	4.29%	4.52%	4.75%	5.00%	5.24%
06-Mar-03	1.31%	1.28%	1.52%	1.75%	1.97%	2.18%	2.40%	2.62%	2.83%	3.03%	3.24%	3.45%	3.66%	3.87%	4.10%	4.32%	4.55%	4.78%	5.02%	5.26%
07-Mar-03	1.30%	1.22%	1.46%	1.69%	1.93%	2.17%	2.38%	2.59%	2.80%	3.02%	3.24%	3.45%	3.68%	3.90%	4.13%	4.37%	4.61%	4.85%	5.10%	5.36%
10-Mar-03	1.21%	1.16%	1.37%	1.57%	1.82%	2.07%	2.29%	2.51%	2.72%	2.93%	3.14%	3.35%	3.57%	3.79%	4.02%	4.24%	4.48%	4.71%	4.96%	5.20%
11-Mar-03	1.16%	1.18%	1.42%	1.66%	1.92%	2.18%	2.39%	2.61%	2.78%	2.95%	3.12%	3.30%	3.48%	3.66%	3.84%	4.03%	4.22%	4.41%	4.61%	4.81%
12-Mar-03	1.17%	1.22%	1.47%	1.72%	1.97%	2.23%	2.44%	2.66%	2.82%	2.99%	3.17%	3.34%	3.52%	3.69%	3.87%	4.06%	4.25%	4.43%	4.63%	4.83%
13-Mar-03	1.22%	1.36%	1.58%	1.81%	2.08%	2.35%	2.57%	2.78%	2.97%	3.16%	3.34%	3.53%	3.73%	3.92%	4.12%	4.32%	4.53%	4.74%	4.96%	5.18%
17-Mar-03	1.21%	1.36%	1.62%	1.89%	2.16%	2.43%	2.65%	2.87%	3.06%	3.26%	3.45%	3.65%	3.85%	4.06%	4.26%	4.47%	4.69%	4.91%	5.14%	5.37%
19-Mar-03	1.26%	1.37%	1.69%	2.01%	2.28%	2.56%	2.79%	3.02%	3.23%	3.44%	3.65%	3.86%	4.08%	4.30%	4.53%	4.75%	4.99%	5.23%	5.48%	5.73%
20-Mar-03	1.27%	1.36%	1.65%	1.94%	2.22%	2.50%	2.74%	2.97%	3.18%	3.38%	3.58%	3.79%	4.00%	4.21%	4.43%	4.65%	4.88%	5.10%	5.34%	5.58%
21-Mar-03	1.27%	1.44%	1.75%	2.07%	2.36%	2.66%	2.90%	3.14%	3.34%	3.55%	3.75%	3.96%	4.17%	4.38%	4.60%	4.82%	5.05%	5.28%	5.52%	5.76%
24-Mar-03	1.27%	1.36%	1.66%	1.96%	2.24%	2.52%	2.76%	2.99%	3.19%	3.38%	3.58%	3.78%	3.99%	4.19%	4.41%	4.62%	4.84%	5.06%	5.30%	5.53%
25-Mar-03	1.27%	1.37%	1.64%	1.91%	2.20%	2.48%	2.72%	2.96%	3.15%	3.34%	3.54%	3.74%	3.94%	4.15%	4.36%	4.57%	4.79%	5.01%	5.24%	5.47%
26-Mar-03	1.27%	1.34%	1.61%	1.87%	2.16%	2.45%	2.68%	2.92%	3.12%	3.31%	3.51%	3.71%	3.91%	4.12%	4.33%	4.54%	4.76%	4.98%	5.21%	5.44%
27-Mar-03	1.26%	1.32%	1.58%	1.84%	2.13%	2.41%	2.65%	2.89%	3.09%	3.29%	3.49%	3.70%	3.91%	4.12%	4.33%	4.55%	4.78%	5.00%	5.24%	5.48%
28-Mar-03	1.25%	1.29%	1.53%	1.77%	2.08%	2.38%	2.61%	2.84%	3.04%	3.24%	3.45%	3.65%	3.86%	4.07%	4.29%	4.51%	4.74%	4.96%	5.20%	5.44%
31-Mar-03	1.22%	1.25%	1.50%	1.74%	2.02%	2.31%	2.56%	2.81%	3.02%	3.23%	3.45%	3.66%	3.88%	4.11%	4.34%	4.57%	4.81%	5.05%	5.30%	5.55%

Source: Compiled by case authors based on Reuters.

EXHIBIT 10

JAPANESE YEN INTEREST RATE SWAPS—ASK PRICES FOR VARIOUS MATURITIES IN MARCH 2003

Date	2 Year	3 Year	4 Year	5 Year	6 Year	7 Year	8 Year	9 Year
3-Mar-03	0.117	0.167	0.227	0.298	0.372	0.459	0.562	0.668
4-Mar-03	0.117	0.167	0.227	0.29	0.362	0.447	0.542	0.642
5-Mar-03	0.119	0.169	0.227	0.29	0.362	0.447	0.542	0.64
6-Mar-03	0.12	0.168	0.225	0.287	0.359	0.442	0.535	0.632
7-Mar-03	0.118	0.165	0.223	0.285	0.354	0.435	0.529	0.625
10-Mar-03	0.115	0.163	0.22	0.28	0.35	0.43	0.522	0.62
11-Mar-03	0.113	0.155	0.208	0.271	0.336	0.411	0.503	0.598
12-Mar-03	0.11	0.15	0.2	0.26	0.325	0.4	0.488	0.58
13-Mar-03	0.113	0.155	0.205	0.266	0.331	0.409	0.501	0.596
14-Mar-03	0.117	0.157	0.208	0.264	0.331	0.411	0.503	0.599
17-Mar-03	0.111	0.151	0.196	0.254	0.317	0.394	0.484	0.577
18-Mar-03	0.112	0.149	0.197	0.253	0.318	0.395	0.485	0.575
19-Mar-03	0.114	0.152	0.197	0.25	0.313	0.388	0.473	0.563
20-Mar-03	0.12	0.16	0.21	0.268	0.336	0.416	0.506	0.596
21-Mar-03	0.12	0.16	0.21	0.27	0.337	0.417	0.507	0.597
24-Mar-03	0.123	0.165	0.215	0.271	0.339	0.416	0.504	0.594
25-Mar-03	0.122	0.165	0.213	0.273	0.336	0.413	0.501	0.589
26-Mar-03	0.126	0.17	0.218	0.278	0.341	0.418	0.504	0.591
27-Mar-03	0.125	0.172	0.225	0.285	0.353	0.433	0.518	0.605
28-Mar-03	0.125	0.173	0.228	0.285	0.353	0.435	0.523	0.613
31-Mar-03	0.123	0.168	0.22	0.276	0.338	0.413	0.498	0.586

Source: Compiled by case authors based on Reuters.

EXHIBIT 11

CURRENCY OPTIONS STRUCTURES SUGGESTED BY KUMAR'S TEAM

Structure

Structure 1	Action	Buy USD Put/JPY Call at Strike 95.00
		Sell USD Call/JPY Put at Strike 108.0
	Tenor	5 years
	Cost	Zero
	Pay off on Maturity	Best case: 1.40%
		Worst case: −1.20%
Structure 2	Action	Buy USD Put/JPY Call at Strike 95.00
		PFC to pay 2.90% of Face Value when 125.00 is traded
		PFC to pay 5.20% of Face Value when 135.00 is traded
		PFC to pay 12.50% of Face Value when 145.00 is traded
	Tenor	5 years
	Cost	No up-front payment of premium
	Pay off on Maturity	Best case: Unlimited
		Worst case: −1.20%
Structure 3	Action	Buy USD Put/JPY Call at Strike 95.00
		Sell USD Call/JPY Put at Strike 101.00 for 70% of the Face Value
	Tenor	5 years
	Cost	Zero
	Pay off on Maturity	Best case: Unlimited
		Worst case: −1.20%
Structure 4	Action	Buy USD Put/JPY Call at Strike 101.25
		Sell USD Call/JPY Put at Strike 101.25, K.I. 135.00
		Sell USD Put/JPY Call at Strike 88.00
	Tenor	5 years
	Cost	Zero
	Pay off on Maturity	Best case: 6.74% if 135 is not seen
		Worst case: 0.60% if 35 and 88 is not seen

Source: ICICI Bank.

DS-5

EQUITY AND OPTIONS EXCHANGES

30

Deutsche Börse

Since Werner Seifert had been appointed its CEO in 1993, Deutsche Börse had become the world's largest securities trading and related technology powerhouse, as measured by its revenue, profit, or market capitalization. Under his leadership, Deutsche Börse had successfully automated its cash market operations and created the largest fully electronic derivatives exchange in the world. Furthermore, by leveraging its technology and market know-how, Deutsche Börse had established a chain of related businesses offering superior information and operative systems to securities market participants.[1] As a result, the company could no longer be considered a mere stock exchange. Instead, Deutsche Börse had become a "transaction engine" providing turnkey services to the full range of market participants.[2] Seifert had long argued that Deutsche Börse would not support a market system in which exchanges were to become over-regulated utilities. Rather, he had promoted a landscape in which exchanges could compete based on the merits of their ability to offer new services and products and use technology to support and fuel innovation. Now, in May of 2002, Seifert found himself at a crossroads; faced with deciding the proper investments for Deutsche Börse to retain its competitive edge.

Deutsche Börse's holdings included a 50% stake in Clearstream International. Clearstream was one of two existing International Central Securities Depositories (ICSD) in Europe specializing in clearing, settlement and custody of securities across borders.[3] While Clearstream controlled the clearing and settlement process for securi-

---

Professor George Chacko and Executive Director of the European Research Center, Vincent Dessain and Research Associates Eli Peter Strick and Jose-Abel Defina prepared this case. HBS cases are developed solely as the basis for class discussion. Cases are not intended to serve as endorsements, sources of primary data, or illustrations of effective or ineffective management.

[1] Deutsche Börse designed and operated market technology tools for its own needs, as well as those of third parties.

[2] As a "transaction engine," Deutsche Börse went beyond the function of a marketplace by providing services spanning the full transaction value chain: informing investors through its proprietary information products, receiving trades through Deutsche Börse's terminals, processing trades over its exchange network, and clearing and settling trades in the back office.

[3] Clearstream was created in 1999 as a merger of equals from Deutsche Börse Clearing, a subsidiary of Deutsche Börse in charge of clearing, settlement, and custody in Germany, and Cedel, an international securities depository located in Luxembourg offering cross-border clearing, settlement, and custody services. This deal was struck at a time when mergers and alliances in the stock exchange industry were still determined by the politics of national infrastructure providers rather than by the economics of publicly listed companies.

ties trading in Germany and Luxembourg, its most important competitor, the user-owned ICSD Euroclear, cleared and settled operations in France and the Netherlands.[4] With sufficient cash at his disposal from Deutsche Börse's February, 2001 IPO, Seifert was considering acquiring full control of Clearstream. Meanwhile, as Seifert probed the market, Euroclear re-launched the idea of a merging with Clearstream.[5] This proposition was backed by a powerful group of international banks, which, at the same time, played an important role as the shareholders and customers of Clearstream. While it was clear that the future of Clearstream could not be decided against Deutsche Börse, a continued fundamental disagreement between Clearstream shareholders on its strategy would create unsustainable frictions for the company. Seifert had to quickly decide which direction to take for Deutsche Börse's investment in Clearstream.

MARKET OVERVIEW

Global equity markets had expanded significantly during the last thirty years. Starting at less than $1.0 trillion in 1974, capitalization of equity markets grew to reach over $27.0 trillion by the end of 2001. The United States represented about 51% of the global equity markets capitalization at $13.8 trillion, while the European Union accounted for $7.5 trillion.[6] While this created significant cost pressure on market participants due to decreasing asset management fees, commissions and a virtual ebbing of the IPO activities, the impact on stock exchanges was less severe as total trading volumes (including stock and derivatives markets) did not decline as strongly as market prices.

Financial integration in Europe was leading to profound changes in the structure and operation of the financial services sector throughout the continent. A more open and effective European financial market benefited both consumers and the corporate sector. Investors benefited from higher risk-adjusted returns through enhanced opportunities for portfolio diversification and more liquid and competitive capital markets. Meanwhile, the corporate sector benefited from easier access to financing.

Growth in equity markets had been coupled with significant changes as to how trading activities were performed in financial markets. Securities trading in general, and equities trading in particular could be divided into "front office" and "back office" activities. Front office trading activities involved the issuance and capture of orders from investors (institutional and individual), and the trading processes within market venues. Back office activities dealt with the clearing and settlement of trades, as well as custody services for securities.

In the front office, investors and intermediaries' ease of access to trading venues had surged fueled by the success of on-line discount brokers and proprietary Electronic

---

[4] Euronext, a large competitor of Deutsche Börse, owned 3% of Euroclear.

[5] At the time of the Clearstream merger, a merger between Cedel and Euroclear had been discussed as an alternative.

[6] Europe also trailed behind the U.S. in terms of capital markets integration despite the process of economic convergence and the introduction of a common currency. Starting with the Single Act and later with the Maastricht Treaty, the European Union had envisioned the creation of a common capital markets system. The European Round Table for Financial Services calculated that integrated financial markets would lower the cost of capital, and, as a result, add half of a percentage point to Europe's annual GDP growth rate. The introduction of the Euro eliminated exchange risk within Europe Union and created incentives for financial integration in the form of lower transactions costs, higher integration of the investor base, and opportunities for investment in a wider range of instruments across borders than ever before. However, this process of financial integration still had a long way to go, and many of the trading rules/regulations had yet to be written.

Communication Networks (ECNs). In the United States, ECNs like Instinet, Island and Archipelago had challenged the dominant position of traditional exchanges, like the New York Stock Exchange (NYSE) and Nasdaq.[7] However, in the case of the European Union, high competition among the largest traditional exchanges (e.g. the London Stock Exchange, Euronext, and Deutsche Börse) spurred innovation across European Capital Markets.[8] European exchanges had introduced highly efficient electronic trading platforms and more efficient market models, and consequently preempted the surge of proprietary ECNs.

Contributing to the growth in equity markets, and in a league of their own, derivatives markets had expanded from 1.7 billion contracts in 1995 to more than 4.5 billion in 2001. Derivatives trading had become a highly dynamic sector and, although the U.S. derivative market venues remained on top in terms of market turnover, European exchanges were highly competitive as measured by their share of number of the contracts traded worldwide. Exhibit 1 shows yearly trading volumes (in contracts) for major international derivative exchanges.

As for the back office, the industry was focused on developing efficient clearing, settlement and custody systems, capable of providing low-risk, fast and reliably automated straight through processing (STP) from the point of trade to the final exchange of securities and cash. While traders benefited from the highly efficient electronic markets in Europe by way of lower liquidity-costs, they were still faced with greater settlement costs in Europe compared to U.S markets.[9] Some of this disadvantage resulted from higher transaction volumes in the U.S., bringing economies of scale to the mostly fixed costs of the back office business. However, clearing and settlement across European borders introduced additional expenses to transactions. Even within the EU, European countries remained fragmented by their differences in market practices, tax and legal policy, and technological deployment. Such market frictions made handling "cross-border" trades more complicated and expensive. For example, a cross-border wholesale trade (e.g. buying 200,000 in Nokia stock) in Europe costs traders an estimated 3.8 basis points in additional settlement fees.[10]

FRONT-OFFICE TRADING ACTIVITY

Trading in equities required investors—both individuals and institutions—to use the services of "brokers" that routed orders to the different market venues where a stock is traded.[11] In most European markets including Germany, the order had to be sent to a domestic regulated exchange unless an investor specified a market of preference. With the consent of investors, brokers could direct orders to a regulated securities exchange

---

[7] Off-exchange trading, initially conceived for non-listed stocks, had moved aggressively into exchange listed securities posing a threat to traditional exchanges as a result of more efficient communication networks and trade processing technologies available.

[8] Euronext was the result of the merger of Paris, Amsterdam and Brussels Securities Exchanges with operations in the cash and derivative markets.

[9] "Liquidity costs" refers to the difference in "bid" and "ask" prices and any impact a trade has on the available market price.

[10] Clearstream International, "Cross-Border Equity Trading, Clearing & Settlement in Europe," White Paper Order No. 1010-1335, April 2002, p. 22.

[11] Investors issue orders to buy or sell securities under different pricing and matching strategies. The two basic types of orders are market and limit orders. When an investor issues a limit order, he or she must set a price at which the trade must be executed. A market order does not indicate a price and is carried out at the best price available in the market.

EXHIBIT 1

TRADING VOLUMES FOR MAJOR DERIVATIVES EXCHANGES FOR 2000 THROUGH 2002

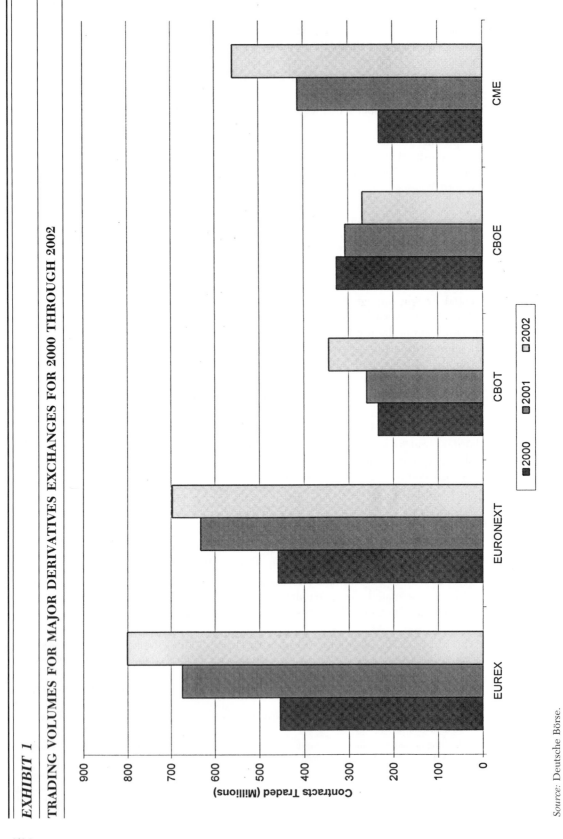

Source: Deutsche Börse.

listing the stock, another exchange, a dealer (a market participant trading on his or her own account), or to an alternative trading platform, such as an ECN (e.g. Instinet and Archipelago).

In any case, brokers were bound by their duty of "best execution" when handling investors' orders. However, the best execution rule did not guarantee the best price for an investor (i.e. lowest price for buying, highest price for selling) because it also factored in other characteristics of the trade such as speed and security. The brokers' choice of trading venue depended upon the characteristics of the markets for the specific security, the size of the order, and the brokers' relations with the markets of choice.

In the U.S., the Internet had provided fertile ground for the expansion of electronic securities trading, especially with "discount" brokerage houses like E°trade and Ameritrade. Traditional "full service" brokers charged higher commissions in exchange for packaging research services and other benefits in with their brokerage services. In contrast, discount brokers focused their services on trading and, due to their reduced overhead costs, offered lower commission rates to individual investors. For the larger institutional investor community, there were also some more sophisticated communication networks, linked to intermediaries, ECNs and dealer markets, offering convenience, privacy, and speed.

Trading With Dealers

In terms of dollars, the largest financial markets were dealer markets. Corporate bonds, swaps, foreign exchange and block trades of securities were mostly and equities were partly traded "over the counter," i.e. outside of a regulated exchange and, more specifically, via telephone. Dealers stood ready to accept investors' orders and trade using their own portfolio. They competed with other dealers by quoting and negotiating buy and sell prices for specific securities and profited from their ability to make small margins between the prices at which they sold and bought.[12] Dealers also traded on exchanges and inter-dealer markets in order to "build" and "unwind" their security inventories. Some dealers also carried out brokers' functions by routing orders for their own investors or for other brokers' investors.

Ideally, a broker sent an order to a specific dealer to take advantage of the best execution opportunity (transaction cost and speed of execution, etc.) available for that order. However, it had become common practice for brokers to route orders to a dealer or marketplace that paid for order flow (pay-for-flow). This practice was considered to be potentially harmful as it could prevent brokers from seeking best execution, as well as increase market fragmentation.[13]

Trading On Electronic Communication Networks

ECNs were trading platforms capturing order flow through electronic means from brokers, dealers and institutional investors, and matching buy and sell orders directly

---

[12] The price margin of a security, the difference between the bid price and the ask price, is referred to as the "bid-ask spread," or just "spread."

[13] Under rule 11Ac1-6, broker/dealers that route customer orders in equity and option securities are required to make publicly available quarterly reports that, among other things, identify the venues to which customer orders are routed for execution. In addition, broker/dealers are required to disclose to customers, on request, the venues to which their individual orders were routed. By making visible the execution quality of the securities markets, the rules are intended to spur more vigorous competition among market participants to provide the best possible prices for investor orders.

through computerized systems. Similar to the practice of dealers, a broker might decide to route orders to a particular ECN that pays the broker for order flow. One of the main ways a proprietary ECN differed from a security exchange was its non-existent or lower quality regulation. While some ECNs traded highly liquid securities and relied on the liquidity provided by their links to other ECNs and regulated exchanges (in particular in equities), others had dealers who quoted bid and ask orders on their systems, thereby providing liquidity for less liquid securities such as bonds. ECNs did not perform the primary market responsibilities carried out by regulated exchanges.

In the United States, ECNs represent about 4% of the volume traded in U.S. listed stock and 30% of all Nasdaq securities—Island, alone, claimed to perform one of every five transactions in Nasdaq listed securities. The Securities and Exchange Commission (SEC) reported that Nasdaq securities represented about 96% of the total U.S. securities volume traded on ECNs.

The SEC regulated the activities of ECNs in the U.S. An ECN could act as a broker-dealer, following the appropriate rules and regulations, or become an exchange, assuming the listing and self-regulating responsibilities. ECNs as broker-dealers were responsible for disclosing information about quality of execution. They were also required to post quotes through the NASDAQ quotation and trading system, or some other regional exchange, so that other investors were able to trade within the ECN's order book.

In Germany and other continental European markets, trading in the domestic markets was mainly concentrated on the regulated exchanges provided by organizations like Deutsche Börse and Euronext, with little participation of ECNs. In the case of London, however, most of the trading took place "over the counter."[14] While ECNs had been able to offer new levels of efficiency in the U.S., European exchanges had been quicker and more innovative at adopting electronic trading platforms. As a result, ECNs had not been successful in entering Europe.

Trading on Securities Exchanges

While U.S. exchanges had lost a significant share of trading volume to ECNs, domestic trading in equities in Europe still took place on regulated traditional exchanges. Exchanges listed securities that met previously set financial accountability standards and organized the market that provided liquidity for trading on these securities. Exchange trading mechanisms varied widely but were based, for the most part, on some combination of order driven and quote driven markets. Specialists or market makers quoted prices on certain listed securities that they were willing to trade at. While some security exchanges in Europe and the U.S. were still only physical exchanges (i.e. venues where people interacted and trading occurred "on the floor"), most exchanges had established electronic trading platforms to supplement, or even replace conventional floor trading.

In order to trade on securities exchanges, brokers, dealers and financial institutions either had to be members of the exchange or direct their orders to a member of the exchange. Exchanges' trading platforms generated revenues in the form of membership subscriptions paid by market participants and fees for their listing, trading, clearing, and settlement activities. Providing information products, such as quote/trade data and company news, and information technology services to financial intermediaries and institutional investors was becoming an increasingly important other revenue stream for exchanges.

---

[14] "Over the counter" (OTC) refers to a market where no securities exchange/venue is involved and, instead, broker-dealers negotiate directly with each other by phone or through an electronic network.

The main exchanges for equities in the U.S. were the New York Stock Exchange and the National Securities Dealers Automated Quotation System (NASDAQ).[15] Other regulated stock exchanges in the U.S. were the American Stock Exchange (AMEX), the Chicago Stock Exchange and the Pacific Stock Exchange, among others. With the exception of AMEX and the NYSE, all the other exchanges not only traded their own listed securities, but also the most liquid stocks listings on other exchanges.[16] The United States also established the Intermarket Trading System (ITS), which linked price quotations for equities in all the exchanges. Therefore, a specialist from the NYSE had to check the prices on other exchanges before letting a trade on NYSE get executed.

Within the European Union, the expected integration of financial markets was a complicated process that involved dealing with 15 different jurisdictions and some more than 20 stock markets across the Union. Among the large number of securities exchanges, the most important, in terms of market capitalization and turnover volumes were the London Stock Exchange (LSE), Euronext and Deutsche Börse. The three main exchanges constituted decisive players in the process of European integration. After the merger of the Paris, Amsterdam, Brussels and Lisbon exchanges that created Euronext, the failed merger talks between the LSE and Deutsche Börse in 2000 offered a prominent example of the conflicts arising from integrating European financial markets. The deal between the LSE and Deutsche Börse would have created the second largest stock exchange in the world (by market capitalization of traded companies) but collapsed under the pressure of local brokers, who felt that the envisaged merger did not adequately protect their interests.

BACK OFFICE TRADING ACTIVITIES

Clearing, settlement, and custodian activities followed trade execution as the necessary steps for buyers to acquire ownership of securities, sellers to receive cash payments, securities to be efficiently safeguarded, and trades to be tracked and recorded. Brokers communicated with investors throughout the process in order to secure delivery of securities and cash. However, as qualified trading intermediaries, brokers were directly responsible for the post-trade operations and fulfilling the back office obligations that originated from a trade. Exhibit 2 offers a diagram of front and back office activities.

Clearing Services

During clearing, trade details were automatically sent from the exchanges, or ECNs, to a designated central clearinghouse. The clearinghouse communicated with the counterparties in order to confirm and reconcile the terms of the trade (security identity, price, quantity, settlement date, cash correspondent bank, and settlement agent, etc.) and

---

[15] The largest securities exchange in the world was the New York Stock Exchange. The NYSE executed trades for around 307 billion shares with a total value of 10 Trillion dollars in 2001, up 17% from the previous year. In dollars terms, stock trading on the NYSE represented 35% of total turnover in the U.S. and was almost equal to the total value of stock trading within the European Union, including the United Kingdom.

[16] Securities listed in one U.S. exchange can be traded in any of the other national exchanges. In 1936, the U.S. Congress established "unlisted trading privileges" for all exchanges. Under the current system, NYSE-listed stocks can be traded on the Nasdaq InterMarket, regional stock exchanges like the Boston, Chicago and Cincinatti, and ECNs. However, the NYSE and the American Stock Exchange (AMEX) trade only equities listed on their own exchanges.

EXHIBIT 2

DIAGRAM OF "FRONT OFFICE" AND "BACK OFFICE" OPERATIONS

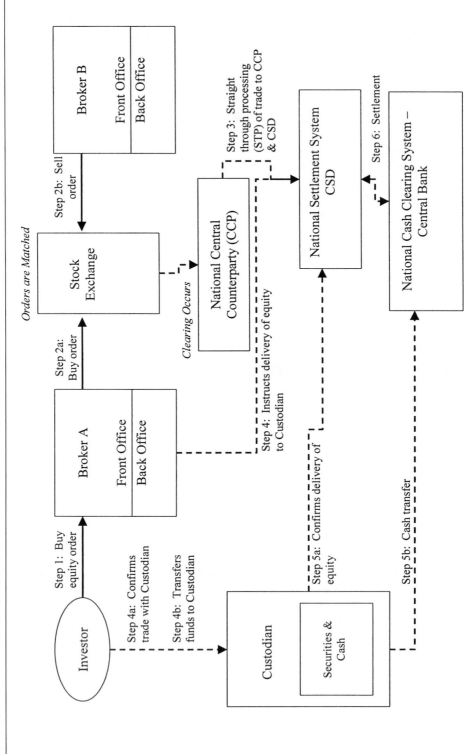

Source: Adapted from Deutsche Börse, "Vision + Money," July 2002, Page 31 ⟨http://deutsche-boerse.com/INTERNET/EXCHANGE/index_e.htm⟩, accessed March 24, 2003.

determined each party's obligations.[17] Clearing could be accomplished on a gross or a net basis. Gross clearance occurred when obligation were established for each trade individually. For clearance on a net basis, all buy and sell trades from a party, during a given day, were grouped together and allowed to offset each other in order to establish a net positive or negative balance of securities and cash to be settled.[18] Clearance on a net basis legally required that the clearinghouse would be a Central Counter Party (CCP) that broke trades into two separate transactions for which it assumed each party's obligation with respect to the other. The presence of a CCP further benefited market participants by assuming counter-party default risk and also providing increased anonymity for trading parties. The combined effect of these benefits made trading both less risky and more efficient for all parties involved. Through increasing traders' confidence in the market and their willingness to trade, a CCP helped to increase a market's liquidity.

Settlement Services

Once each party's obligations to a trade became firm, the clearinghouse sent the details of the trade to the designated CSD to manage the settlement process. Settlement involved the delivery of securities from the seller to the buyer and the reciprocal transfer of cash. Trading parties instructed their respective custodians to deliver and receive cash and securities on their account. CSDs were in charge of managing the settlement process for a particular market. Accordingly, CSDs held securities in custody and maintained records of its members' holdings. Although CSDs mostly handled securities for the domestic market in which they settled trades, CSDs could also offer custodial services across markets by holding accounts in other CSDs.

ICSDs (International Central Securities Depository) were specifically established to provide clearing, settlement and custody services for a broad range of securities across the different international markets. Clearstream and Euroclear both served as ICSDs in Europe. Clearstream was also the CSD for the security markets in Germany and Luxembourg while Euroclear acted also as the CSD for France, Belgium, and the Netherlands.

The market rules for the time for a trade to be processed, from the moment a security was traded on an exchange to its final delivery, varied from one market to another. In the U.S. and the U.K., the rule was 3 days from the time of the trade (T + 3). While T + 3 was virtually the standard European settlement period Germany operated under T + 2 settlement for quite some time already due to a high level of automation.

In the U.S., the Depository Trust and Clearing Corporation (DTCC) was the designated clearing and settlement management facility for all trades executed on securities exchanges and other recognized market venues across the country.[19] In the year 2001, DTCC's clearing system processed over 3.5 billion transactions worth more than $89.0 trillion. DTCC's settlement capacity executed book entries for more than $120.0 trillion. The DTCC transferred ownership of securities within its domain through a sin-

---

[17] Brokers were required to become members of the clearinghouse or clear transactions through brokers who were members. Dealers trading directly on their own account had the choice of clearing securities transactions in-house or outsourcing the services of a clearinghouse.

[18] Net clearing reduced overall costs, including the required provision of collateral, disposable assets and subsequent settlement costs, but it could also create higher systemic risk than gross clearing when parties failed to fulfill their obligations.

[19] DTCC post-trade activities span over a wide range of securities traded in the United States, which includes equities, corporate and municipal debt, money market instruments, American depository receipts, emerging markets sovereign and quasi-sovereign debt and exchange traded funds among other securities.

gle book-entry on its computers. Eliminating the need to move physical paper stock certificates allowed the DTCC to substantially reduce costs. The DTCC set up a CCP for trades in the U.S. and cleared positions on a net basis.

The DTCC also acted as the CSD for the U.S. markets, holding securities for financial institutions' and their customers' accounts. The DTCC stored most of the physical stocks and bonds in the United States, while custodians kept track of investors' portfolio holdings. As a depository, the total value of securities deposited at the DTCC amounted to more than $23.0 trillion.

In Europe, cross-border clearing and settlement had become critical to the integration of capital markets within the European Union. National markets in Europe had been built around national securities depositories and settlement systems that were intimately connected to their national payment infrastructures. Consequently, cross-border transactions were affected by the rigidity of domestic systems. The number of organizations involved in a single trade added significant expenses to cross border trading. In some cases tax law made cross-border investment expensive. In other cases regulation and national laws regarding the status of CSDs and the offering of settlement and custody services created cross-border barriers. Differing rules for payment systems from one country to another also complicated the efficient integration process of CSDs across Europe. Finally, two major currencies, the Euro and the Pound Sterling, created exchange risk and conversion costs for cross-border activities between the United Kingdom and continental Europe.

Custodian Services

Custodians provided investors with safe deposit, record keeping, and reporting services for cash and securities trusted to them. Custodians settled trades, collected income from securities, and facilitated participation in corporate actions such as the exercise of corporate rights (e.g. voting rights). Additionally, the range of services offered by custodians had expanded to include the management of collateral for trading purposes and the lending of securities and cash to settle trades, among others. Whereas local custodians limited their services to domestic markets, global custodians provided access across different markets worldwide through subsidiaries or relationships with independent local custodians. Global custodian networks allowed investors to establish one single access channel for settlement of trades in different markets, and to benefit from economies of scale.

Banks were the main suppliers of custodian services to investors and financial intermediaries. Investors had the choice of establishing their own custody accounts or using brokerage houses, which had accounts for their own portfolio and their clients under custody within specialized banks. Institutional investors, due to the size of their portfolios, usually found it cheaper to establish their own custody accounts within banks than retained the services of a broker.

Custodians either carried securities in book-entry form or in very rare cases physically. When using book-entry form securities were either immobilized (i.e. securities certificates were deposited with the CSD which recorded transfers in such securities via book-entry in their clients' accounts) or dematerialized (i.e. securities which were even initially not evidenced by physical certificates but only recorded in an electronic securities register). CSDs carried the advantage of being the designated settlement center for trades within their domestic exchanges, and therefore offered a convenient place to immobilize or dematerialize securities and take on custodian responsibilities in the name of financial intermediaries. As ICSDs, both Clearstream and Euroclear were able to provide custodian services at an international level, competing with global custodians in particular for bond settlement and custody services.

DEUTSCHE BÖRSE

Deutsche Börse had been established in 1992 with the Frankfurt Stock Exchange, the German cash market floor exchange, at the center of its business operations. The Frankfurt Stock Exchange dated back to the end of the 16th century as a marketplace that specialized in bills of exchange. In the 19th century, the exchange began trading shares of joint-stock banks. Later, railway construction and industrialization brought high securities issuing activity and increased trading turnover on the exchange. Over time, the Frankfurt Stock Exchange established a preeminent position over the other German Exchanges. Finally, it became part of Deutsche Börse, which had embarked in a journey of expansion to become one of the main providers of trading solutions for the financial markets. By the end of 2001, Deutsche Börse operated trading platforms that accounted for approximately 21% of the total trading volume on the European stock exchanges. Through its Eurex division, Deutsche Börse also claimed the highest trading volume of any international derivatives exchange, boasting 674 million contracts traded in 2001.

No longer restricted to its trading floor, Deutsche Börse leveraged its market expertise to take on building new trading systems, operating systems for third parties, and loading different markets with transactions and useful content. Exhibit 3 shows a diagram of Deutsche Börse's "build, operate, and load" business model. In fact, trading fees and other income from Deutsche Börse's cash and derivatives markets only

---

EXHIBIT 3

DEUTSCHE BÖRSE'S BUSINESS MODEL

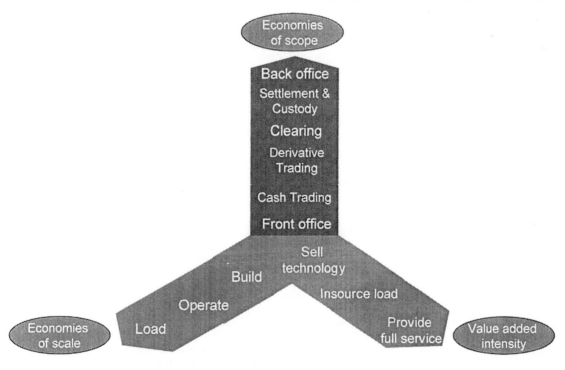

Source: Deutsche Börse.

amounted to 33% of Deutsche Börse's total revenues in 2001. Other businesses, such as trading systems ("Systems"), information products, and clearing and settlement activities amounted to nearly 60% of Deutsche Börse's sales. Through the seamless integration of its different divisions, Deutsche Börse was able to optimize the services it provided the capital markets. Exhibits 4a, 4b, and 4c show the consolidated financial statements for the Deutsche Börse. Exhibit 5 shows the financial performance of Deutsche Börse's different business divisions. Deutsche Börse, like the other main exchanges in Europe, had gone through the process of demutualization, becoming a publicly traded company in February 2001. Its 2001 IPO had been oversubscribed by a factor of 23 and the stock had climbed from its initial share price of EUR 37 to EUR 43 in less than a year, giving the exchange a market capitalization of EUR 4.44 billion. Demutualization allowed Deutsche Börse to act more independently from its market members and to raise capital through public offerings.

Xetra

Within the cash markets, Deutsche Börse operated the Frankfurt Stock Exchange and the electronic market, Xetra. Together, Xetra and the Frankfurt Stock Exchange captured 86% of the average 17 million cash market transactions each month going through German exchanges. Xetra had been successful in taking away businesses from other German exchanges and even cannibalized from the Frankfurt Stock Exchange. Transactions on Xetra increased 27.4% in 2001, reaching 49.7 million. However, due to declining performance in equity markets, revenue from the Xetra division fell in 2001 to

---

EXHIBIT 4A

DEUTSCHE BÖRSE'S CONSOLIDATED INCOME STATEMENT

For year ending Dec 31 (€ Millions)	2000	2001
Net sales	702.3	760.3
Own expenses capitalized	31.0	62.6
Other operating income	95.7	77.3
Total sales	**829.0**	**900.2**
Staff Expenses	(105.0)	(112.0)
Depreciation and amortisation	(83.1)	(83.3)
Total other operating expenses	(487.9)	(471.6)
Income from equity investments	73.2	58.0
Write-downs on long-term investments	(9.7)	(13.2)
Earning before interest and taxes (EBIT)	**216.5**	**278.1**
Net interest income	2.2	41.1
Profit before tax from ordinary activities	**218.7**	**319.2**
Extraordinary gains	74.2	0.0
Total taxes	(72.6)	(116.2)
Net profit for the period	**220.5**	**203.0**

Source: Deutsche Börse, 2001 Annual Report, ⟨http://deutsche-boerse.com/ir/index.php?lang=en&ir=ef5bdbc575bdb0170736e2ba02099b1d⟩, accessed May 16, 2003.

EXHIBIT 4B

DEUTSCHE BÖRSE'S CONSOLIDATED BALANCE SHEET

For year ending Dec 31 (€ Millions)	2000	2001
Noncurrent assets		
Intangible assets		
Software	153.9	207.7
Goodwill	0.0	51.3
Payments on account	20.1	0.8
	174.0	**259.8**
Plant and equipment		
Leasehold improvements	15.4	15.2
Computer hardware, operating and office equipment	49.1	41.7
Payments on account of construction in progress	0.0	0.4
	64.5	**57.3**
Long-term investments		
Investments in subsidiaries	1.1	1.2
Investments in associates	341.9	382.8
Other equity investments	2.5	2.5
Noncurrent financial investments	34.8	32.1
Other long-term loans	1.5	1.5
	381.8	**420.1**
Total noncurrent assets	**620.3**	**737.2**
Current assets		
Receivables and other assets		
Trade recievables	116.8	112.7
Receivables from banking business	0.0	6.9
Intragroup receivables	1.1	0.8
Associate receivables	8.4	2.2
Receivables from other investors	0.0	2.9
Other assets	25.5	41.4
	151.8	**166.9**
Current financial investments	0.0	302.9
Cash and bank balances	140.6	916.9
Total current assets	**292.4**	**1,386.7**
Defferred tax assets	10.0	11.2
Total assets	**922.7**	**2,135.1**

For year ending Dec 31 (€ Millions)	2000	2001
Shareholders' equity		
Subscribed capital	18.8	102.8
Share premium	44.8	945.5
Legal reserve	0.2	0.3
Other retained earnings	306.4	5.7
Revaluation surplus	7.8	446.0
Unappropriated surplus	41.8	60.0
	419.8	**1,560.3**
Minority interests	**4.3**	**10.6**
Provisions and liabilities		
Long-term provisions		
Provisions for pensions and other employee benefits	24.5	31.2
Deferred tax liabilities	28.7	47.6
Other long-term provisions	31.1	26.3
	84.3	**105.1**
Short-term provisions		
Tax provisions	58.0	26.9
Other short-term provisions	8.7	25.4
	66.7	**52.3**
Noncurrent liabilities		
Interest-bearing liabilities	90.0	0.0
Other noncurrent liabilities	0.0	11.1
	90.0	**11.1**
Current Liabilities		
Bank loans and overdrafts	34.5	90.0
Trade payables	71.1	70.2
Payables to other investors	13.4	12.6
Cash deposits by Eurex participants	71.1	164.7
Other current liabilities	67.5	58.2
	257.6	**395.7**
Total provisions and liabilities	**498.6**	**564.2**
Total shareholder's equity and liabilities	**922.7**	**2,135.1**

Source: Deutsche Börse, 2001 Annual Report, ⟨http://deutsche-boerse.com/ir/index.php?lang=en&ir=ef5bdbc575bdb0170736e2ba02099b1d⟩, accessed May 16, 2003.

EXHIBIT 4C

DEUTSCHE BÖRSE'S CONSOLIDATED STATEMENT OF CASH FLOWS

For year ending Dec 31 (€ Millions)	2000	2001
Net Profit for the period	220.5	203.0
Depreciation and amortization expense	92.8	96.5
Decrease in long-term provisions	(38.9)	(0.7)
Deferred tax expense/income	(6.7)	19.8
Other non-cash income and expense	(132.1)	(36.0)
DVFA/SG cash flow	**135.6**	**282.6**
Change in working capital, net of non-cash items:		
Decrease/(increase) in receivables and other assets	(43.5)	4.7
Increase/(decrease) in short-term provisions	(5.5)	13.3
Increase in noncurrent liabilities	0.0	1.5
(Decrease)/increase in current liabilities	13.2	(21.3)
Adjustments for interest and taxes contained in net profit for the period	75.8	55.3
Interest received and income from other noncurrent financial investments and long-term loans	8.5	48.4
Interest paid	(0.7)	(7.3)
Income tax paid	(86.6)	(128.9)
Net loss on disposal of plant and equipment	4.7	0.5
Cash flows from operating activities	**101.5**	**248.8**
Investments in noncurrent assetts	(253.2)	(113.0)
Investments in subsidiaries	0.0	(48.9)
Proceeds from disposal of noncurrent assets	0.9	1.2
Cash flows from investing activities	**(252.3)**	**(160.7)**
Net IPO proceeds	0.0	961.8
Dividends paid	(58.7)	(30.8)
Proceeds from long-term financing	100.0	0.0
Repayment of long-term borrowings	0.0	(10.0)
Cash flows from financing activities	**41.3**	**921.0**
Net change in cash and cash equivalents	(109.5)	1,009.1
Cash and cash equivalents at beginning of period		
(excl. Eurex participants' cash deposits)	227.1	45.0
Deconsolidation of receivables and liabilities from banking business		
(included in cash and cash equivalents in previos year)	(72.6)	0.0
Cash contributed by first-time consolidation of subsidiaries	0.0	7.9
Cash and cash equivalents at end of period		
(excl. Eurex participants' cash deposits)	**45.0**	**1,062.0**

Source: Deutsche Börse, 2001 Annual Report, ⟨http://deutsche-boerse.com/ir/index.
php?lang=en&ir=ef5bdbc575bdb0170736e2ba02099b1d⟩, accessed May 16, 2003.

243.1 million Euros. As the focus of securities trading shifted from floor exchanges to efficient electronic trading, the main driver of Deutsche Börse's growth in the cash markets came from Xetra. Deutsche Börse was committed to offering the most modern and cost-efficient trading systems available. Maintaining the low trading costs, along with a wide product offering for investors to choose from, were essential to Deutsche Börse's competitiveness in the exchange arena.

EXHIBIT 5

FINANCIAL BREAKDOWN OF DEUTSCHE BÖRSE BY BUSINESS SEGMENT

	Xetra		Eurex		Information Products		Xlaunch		Systems		Licence fees Passed-Through		Corporate Services		Settlement		Total for All Segments	
	2001	2000	2001	2000	2001	2000	2001	2000	2001	2000	2001	2000	2001	2000	2001	2000	2001	2000
Employees	194.0	174.0	116.0	86.0	84.0	72.0	8.0	2.0	536.0	494.0			185.0	173.0			1,123.0	1,001.0
Assets (€m)	138.3	143.1	295.3	181.6	63.1	49.6	0.4	2.8	150.1	111.2			1,052.3	64.6	370.2	319.2	2,069.7	872.1
Net Assets (€m)	106.9	103.9	86.7	65.5	42.6	34.4	0.0	2.4	66.3	25.8			1,006.8	14.3	274.7	213.8	1,584.0	460.1
External Sales Revenue (€m)	243.1	277.8	268.8	160.4	109.9	82.5	2.4	0.0	136.1	116.2		65.4					760.3	702.3
Net Income/(Loss) from Equity Investments (€m)	(0.4)	(2.4)	(9.8)	3.3	(0.6)	(1.2)	0.0	0.0	0.0	0.0		0.0	(0.6)	2.3	56.2	61.5	44.8	63.5
Total Expenses (€m)	(233.3)	(232.5)	(252.6)	(220.2)	(109.6)	(92.5)	(8.3)	(2.4)	(288.5)	(311.6)		(65.4)	(132.9)	(142.0)			(1,025.2)	(1,066.6)
EBIT (€m)	38.4	82.5	99.3	10.4	17.0	6.8	(5.9)	(2.4)	93.4	73.8		0.0	(20.3)	(16.1)	56.2	61.5	278.1	216.5

Note: Totals may differ from those reported in Deutsche Börse's consolidated statements due to reconciliation of inter-company sales and expenses.

Source: Adapted from Deutsche Boerse, 2001 Annual Report, ⟨http://deutsche-boerse.com/ir/index.php?lang=en&ir=ef5bdbc575bdb017073 6e2ba02099b1d⟩, accessed May 16, 2003.

EXHIBIT 6A

HISTORICAL TRADING VOLUME ON EUREX BY TYPE OF PRODUCT (IN EUR MILLION)

	Index Products	Equity Products	Money Market Products	Capital Market Products	Total
1997	2,270,843	299,482	723,924	8,328,626	11,633,841
1998	3,093,409	447,499	650,795	19,575,729	23,768,082
1999	3,396,874	402,617	3,135,750	28,040,011	34,975,252
2000	4,759,859	558,660	1,179,316	29,961,474	36,459,308
2001	5,860,395	710,773	638,804	43,727,188	50,937,159

Source: Data taken from Eurex Web site, "Market Information, Monthly Statistics," ⟨http://www.eurexchange.com/index2.html?mp&2&marketplace/market_marketstatistics_en. html⟩, accessed March 21, 2003.

Eurex

Eurex, established in 1998, is a joint venture between Deutsche Börse and the Swiss Exchange to create an electronic trading and clearing platform for options, futures and other derivative contracts. As the world's largest derivatives market in 2001, Eurex served global 427 members and handled 30.7 million trades for over 674 million contracts (worth 50.9 trillion).[20] Roughly 60% of the Eurex's contract volume was in "capital markets products" with 20% coming from both "index products" and "equity products."[21] However, while trading capital markets products had increased 65% from 1999 to 2001, trading rose 100% in both index products and equity products.[22] Exhibits 6a and 6b show historical trading volumes for Eurex by product type.

[20] These 427 members included banks, brokerages, and financial service providers in 17 countries.

[21] Less than 1% of Eurex trading volume came from "money market products."

[22] Deutsche Börse, "Roadshow Presentation," PowerPoint presentation, April 2002, Deutsche Börse, Frankfurt, Germany.

EXHIBIT 6B

HISTORICAL NUMBER OF CONTRACTS TRADED ON EUREX BY TYPE OF PRODUCT

	Index Products	Equity Products	Money Market Products	Capital Market Products	Total
1997	44,455,743	42,695,173	1,131,032	63,450,369	151,983,100
1998	45,455,822	60,958,770	831,328	140,962,300	248,222,487
1999	65,608,952	64,805,177	3,104,457	245,630,053	379,148,639
2000	75,794,263	89,237,816	1,227,113	287,812,314	454,071,506
2001	131,988,426	132,543,515	663,980	408,961,942	674,157,863

Source: Data taken from Eurex Web site, "Market Information, Monthly Statistics," ⟨http://www.eurexchange.com/index2.html?mp&2&marketplace/market_marketstatistics_en. html⟩, accessed March 21, 2003.

EXHIBIT 7

COSTS PER TRADE FOR DEUTSCHE BÖRSE'S TRADING PLATFORMS, INDEXED TO 1997 AND 1998 FOR EUREX AND XETRA, RESPECTIVELY

Year	Eurex Transactions (millions)	Eurex Costs Per Trade	Xetra Transaction (millions)	Xetra Costs Per Trade
1997	152.0	100%		—
1998	248.2	75%	7.1	100%
1999	379.2	54%	15.8	70%
2000	454.1	44%	39.0	46%
2001	674.2	35%	49.7	30%

Souce: Deutsche Börse.

Deutsche Börse's integrated business model for controlling trading, processing, clearing and settlement, allowed the company to implement new products much faster, with less glitches, and at a lower cost than other exchanges. Its ability to innovate in a complex market environment combined with its speed of implementation strengthened Eurex's position as a derivatives trading platform. Between 1998 and 2001, Eurex had successfully introduced 98 new products. These new products accounted for approximately 34% of the exchange's trading volume in 2001.[23] Revenue-wise, the continuous revamping of Eurex's product mix allowed Deutsche Börse to capture higher fees as new higher value contracts became available (e.g. index and equity products).

Eurex not only generated more revenue than the cash market, but it was also more profitable. The derivatives business contributed 268 million to Deutsche Börse's revenues in 2001 compared to 290 million generated by the cash trading business. Additionally, Eurex's EBIT margins were 36.9% of total sales versus 15.8% for the Xetra division.

Systems

As electronic trading platforms became the norm across the world, Deutsche Börse had moved aggressively to expand its role as a technology service provider. Xetra and Eurex provided Deutsche Börse with two of the most successful electronic trading platforms in the world. By pooling its technology expertise in its Systems division, Deutsche Börse was able to provide financial service companies and other exchanges with a full range of information technology (IT) services. Through its different business areas, the Systems division designed complex IT solutions for trading activities, operated trading systems and applications for other international exchanges, and offered components for other systems operators. It systems "solutions" covered all aspects of trading, from order routing and order matching to clearing, settlement, and distribution of trade information. By the end of 2001, the Systems division supported 19 different exchanges using Xetra and Eurex technology.[24] While the Systems division was also responsible for the day-to-day operation of Deutsche Börse's exchanges, the division increased its external revenue (i.e. sales to third parties) 17% to 136.1 million in 2001. By expanding the use of Eurex and Xetra, Deutsche Börse was able to benefit from economies of scale. Exhibit 7 shows a

[23] Ibid.

[24] These exchanges included the Chicago Board of Trade, the Irish Stock Exchange, and the Vienna Stock Exchange.

decrease in trading costs for Eurex and Xetra as a result of user expansion and higher transaction volumes.

Information Products

The Information Products (IP) division collected "raw data" from Deutsche Börse's various markets and processed the data to create useful information for its members and other market participants. Tapping into Xetra and Eurex, along with other data sources, Deutsche Börse was able to accumulate a valuable pool of information. Creating greater transparency in the marketplace, Deutsche Börse used its proprietary price and turnover data to derive a range of ratios, indices, and other helpful statistics for investors. Serving both data vendors (e.g. Reuters, Bloomberg, etc.) and information end users (e.g. banks, brokerages, etc), the IP division had increased its customer base from 95 customers in 1997 to 427 customers in 2001. IP revenues increased 33% in 2001 to 109 million, accounting for about 9% of Deutsche Börse's total sales. Contributing to Deutsche Börse's innovation, the IP division introduced new information products to satisfy investors' demands. New products, introduced by IP in 2000 and 2001, contributed to 40% of the division's increase in sales revenue in 2001.

Clearing and Settlement

Through its participation in clearing and settlement operations, Deutsche Börse was able to provide its customers with integrated front and back office operations. Deutsche Börse had an interest in Eurex Clearing through its participation in the Eurex venture. Eurex Clearing served as a clearinghouse with CCP functionality for the Deutsche Börse's derivatives market. In addition, Deutsche Börse had a 50% interest in Clearstream. Clearstream operated clearing and settlement in Germany and Luxembourg, which included Deutsche Börse's trading platforms, as well as provided custody services for equities and international bonds. In 2001, Clearstream served 2,500 customers from 94 countries, holding securities worth 7.5 trillion in custody and settling transactions for 119 million securities. Deutsche Börse received 56.2 million in 2001 from its investment in Clearstream.

Deutsche Börse's Competitors

Due to the diversity of its businesses, Deutsche Börse competed with large players from across the financial markets. Competition had increased as a result of the economic-integration taking place in the European Union. Deutsche Börse's securities exchanges wrestled with the London Stock Exchange and Euronext in the cash markets and with Euronext's LIFFE in the derivative markets. For back office services, Euroclear and Crest (the United Kingdom's CSD and settlement house) contested Clearstream in the clearing and settlement business. Deutsche Börse's information technology business was faced with a large number of competitors, some being other exchange operators, like Euronext and OM.[25] Exhibit 8 compares the different revenue stream of Deutsche Börse and its competitors.

---

[25] In the case of OM, its IT systems business was much more competitive than its trading business, as owner of the Stockholm Stock Exchange.

EXHIBIT 8

COMPARISON OF REVENUE STREAMS FOR THE DEUTSCHE BÖRSE, EURONEXT, LSE, AND OM

Source: Adapted from company annual reports, accessed on company Web sites.

COMPETITIVE ENVIRONMENT

London Stock Exchange

The LSE was the largest exchange in Europe in terms of capitalization and turnover volume. Globally, the LSE's market capitalization was only second to that of the NYSE. However, the LSE had been slower and less successful than its European competitors (i.e. Deutsche Börse and Euronext) at increasing its scope of operations and acting in accordance with the wave of technological change, industry globalization, and consolidation. Recent major setbacks experienced by the LSE included the failed merger negotiations with Deutsche Börse. Had the deal gone to fruition, it would have created a giant stock exchange, only comparable to the NYSE. Another strategic failure of the LSE was losing LIFFE, the London derivatives exchange, to Euronext. This loss cost the LSE the ability to tap into the high growth area of derivatives trading.

The LSE's revenues revolved around its information services and cash trading operations. The Information Service division was a large and important source of revenues for the LSE, bringing in 44% of total revenues in 2001, compared to 50% revenue coming from cash trading fees. About 20% of all exchange fees originated from off-exchange transactions.[26] Major investment banks had internalized large parts of the trading in the UK market, especially by catering to retail investors. The loss of retail investor orderflow translated into lower revenues for the LSE, given the exchange's fee structure. However, the increase in hedge fund transactions had compensated in part for the shortfall in retail trading. In 1997, the LSE introduced the SETS trading system. SETS was the LSE's electronic central order book. Two hundred of the most liquid UK stocks were listed for trading on the electronic platform. By October 2001, the SETS platform had taken over 57% of all trading volume on the LSE.[27] Exhibits 9a, 9b, and 9c show the consolidated financial statements for the London Stock Exchange.

Euronext

Euronext is one of the largest European equity markets in terms of capitalization and turnover, second only to the LSE. The exchange was formed in September 2000 through the merger of the Paris, Amsterdam and Brussels national exchanges. Since its creation, Euronext had been successful at acquiring one of the most important derivatives markets in Europe (LIFFE), and merging with the Lisbon Stock Exchange (BVLP). Euronext's main objective was to create a fully functional cross-border European stock exchange. Such an exchange would have multiple entry points for members and list equity securities for French, Dutch, and Belgian companies on a single trading platform. Euronext would provide Europe with one CCP offering consolidated netting activities between countries and specialized clearing and settlement for cross-border trades.

In addition to its trading business, Euronext operated a clearinghouse, Clearnet, which cleared the French derivative markets and Euronext's cash equities markets with CCP functionality. Different from Deutsche Börse, Euronext did not own the domestic CSDs which were controlled by Euroclear.

[26] Members of the LSE were required to report off-exchange transactions either to the LSE or any other foreign exchange. Members were charged 1 pound sterling for each off-exchange trade.
[27] Although higher fees were charged for trading SETS, it had lowered overall transaction costs from an average of 60 points to 25 basis points (mostly due to the system's positive effects on spreads).

EXHIBIT 9A

LONDON STOCK EXCHANGE CONSOLIDATED STATEMENT OF PROFIT AND LOSS

For year ending Dec 31 (£ Millions)	2000	2001
Turnover		
Group and share of joint venture		
Continuing operations	164.0	193.4
Discontinued operations	11.7	1.2
Gross turnover	**175.7**	**194.6**
Less: share of joint venture's turnover -		
Continuing operations	(4.5)	(6.2)
Net turnover	**171.2**	**188.4**
Administative expenses		
Operating Costs	(124.2)	(129.7)
Exceptional items	(5.1)	(18.9)
	(129.3)	(148.6)
Operating profit		
Continuing operations		
Before exceptional items	41.8	57.9
After exceptional items	36.7	39.0
Discontinued operations	5.2	0.8
	41.9	**39.8**
Share of operating profits of joint venture and income from other fixed asset investments	0.3	0.3
Net interest receivable/(payable)		
Before exceptional item	6.3	7.9
Exceptional item	—	(17.6)
	6.3	**(9.7)**
Profit on ordinary activities before taxation	**48.5**	**30.4**
Taxation on profit on ordinary activities	(16.4)	(15.2)
Profit for the financial year	**32.1**	**15.2**
Dividend	—	**(9.5)**
Retained profit for the financial year	**32.1**	**5.7**

Source: London Stock Exchange, 2001 Annual Report, ⟨http://www.londonstockexchange.com/ annualreport2001/business_financial_highlights.asp⟩, accessed May 16, 2003.

The Euronext's electronic order book system for cash markets was called NSC. The NSC allowed for continuous trading of equities and that had proven successful in the French market. Euronext had swiftly dismantled the floor-trading operations in Amsterdam and Brussels as it had accomplished in Paris before the merger. The success of Euronext's NSC system was emphasized by the licensing agreements formed for its technology with 14 other exchanges around the world. The list of clients eager to benefit from the NSC included exchanges in Warsaw, Singapore, Montreal and Mexico. However, further improvement of Euronext's margins could not be expected to origi-

EXHIBIT 9B

LONDON STOCK EXCHANGE CONSOLIDATED BALANCE SHEET

For year ending Dec 31 (£ Millions)	2000	2001
Fixed assets		
Tangible assets	114.4	117.1
Investments		
Investments in joint venture:		
Share of gross assets	5.8	7.1
Share of gross liabilities	(3.7)	(4.8)
	2.1	**2.3**
Other investments	0.4	10.1
	2.5	**12.4**
Total fixed assets	**116.9**	**129.5**
Current assets		
Debtors		
Debtors – amounts falling due within one year	35.7	37.3
Deferred tax – amounts falling due after more than one year	12.2	10.7
	47.9	**48.0**
Investments – term deposits	196.0	143.0
Cash at bank	4.4	4.9
Total current assets	**248.3**	**195.9**
Creditors – amounts falling due within one year	59.1	58.8
Net current assets	**189.2**	**137.1**
Total assets less current liabilities	**306.1**	**266.6**
Creditors – amounts falling due after more than one year	30.0	—
Provisions for liabilities and charges	31.0	24.6
Net assets	**245.1**	**242.0**
Capital and reserves		
Called up share capital	—	1.5
Reserves		
Revaluation reserve	49.6	47.7
Capital redemption reserve	8.8	—
Trade and compensation reserve	15.0	—
Profit and loss account	171.7	192.8
Total shareholders' funds	**245.1**	**242.0**

Source: London Stock Exchange, 2001 Annual Report, ⟨http://www.londonstockexchange.com/annualreport2001/business_financial_highlights.asp⟩, accessed May 16, 2003.

nate from the use of the NSC system because the bulk of the exchange trading was already going through the central order book.

LIFFE had aided Euronext in catching up to Deutsche Börse in derivatives trading volumes. Post-acquisition, Euronext integrated its existing derivatives trading operations with the LIFFE Connect trading system. Still, Euronext's derivative business

EXHIBIT 9C

LONDON STOCK EXCHANGE CONSOLIDATED STATEMENT OF CASH FLOWS

For year ending Dec 31 (£ Millions)	2000	2001
Net cash inflow/(outflow) from:		
Ongoing operating activities	46.4	74.5
Exceptional items	(1.4)	(22.4)
Net cash inflow from operating activities	**45.0**	**52.1**
Returns on investments and servicing of finance		
Interest received	10.6	12.1
Interest paid	(3.0)	(4.1)
Premium on redemption of debenture	—	(17.6)
Dividends received	0.1	0.1
Net cash inflow/(outflow) from returns on investments and servicing of finance	**7.7**	**(9.5)**
Taxation		
Corporation tax paid	(12.1)	(20.6)
Capital expenditure and financial investments		
Payments to acquire tangible fixed assets	(14.7)	(22.7)
Payments to acquire own shares	—	(10.0)
Receipts from sale of fixed asset investments	1.2	—
Net cash outflow from capital expenditure and financial investments	**0.1**	**(32.7)**
Equity dividends paid	—	(3.0)
Acquisitions and disposals		
Payments to acquire shares in joint venture	(1.5)	—
Net cash inflow/(outflow) before use of liquid resources and financing	**25.7**	**(13.7)**
Management of liquid resources		
Decrease/(increase) in term deposits	(2.0)	53.0
Financing		
Redemption of mortgage debenture	—	(30.0)
Redemption of 'A' shares	(25.8)	(8.8)
Increase/(decrease) in cash in the year	**(2.1)**	**0.5**

Source: London Stock Exchange, 2001 Annual Report, ⟨http://www.londonstockexchange.com/annualreport2001/business_financial_highlights.asp⟩, accessed May 16, 2003.

lagged 276 million contracts behind Eurex in 2001. Euronext's revenue from derivatives trading increased 165% from 2000 to 2001. This growth helped to reduce Euronext's dependency on the cash trading business. LIFFE's product offering concentrated on interest rate derivatives and the development of new products (e.g. single stock futures, swap notes, and weather futures).[28] Exhibits 10a, 10b, and 10c show the consolidated financial statements for Euronext.

[28] Other influential derivative exchanges included the MATIF market in Paris, offering interest rate derivatives, and the Amsterdam derivatives markets dedicated to equity options.

EXHIBIT 10A

EURONEXT CONSOLIDATED INCOME STATEMENT

For year ending Dec 31 (€ Thousands)	2000	Pro forma Unaudited 2000	2001
Revenues:			
Cash trading	140,641	188,845	177,376
Listing fees	48,682	59,758	49,686
Derivatives trading	31,697	82,253	84,326
Clearing	134,569	169,012	172,771
Settlement and custody	9,263	31,526	33,254
Information services	45,019	68,704	64,268
Sales of developed software/solutions	76,770	76,770	101,639
Other income	6,685	15,320	14,579
Total revenues	**493,326**	**692,188**	**697,899**
Costs and expenses:			
Salaries and employee benefits	116,884	166,108	199,007
Depreciation	19,537	38,434	36,719
Other expenses	246,934	326,251	344,124
Total expenses	**383,355**	**530,793**	**579,850**
Profit from operations before goodwill amortisation	**109,971**	**161,395**	**118,049**
Goodwill amortisation	6,245	18,865	19,048
Profit from operations after goodwill amortisation	**103,726**	**142,530**	**99,001**
Net financing income	4,579	9,042	81,609
Gain on sale of associates/subsidiaries	56,489	56,489	33,846
Income from associates/joint ventures	3,441	3,475	5,518
Total	**64,509**	**69,006**	**120,973**
Profit before tax	**168,235**	**211,536**	**219,974**
Income tax expense	58,549	80,001	85,926
Profit after tax	**109,686**	**131,535**	**134,048**
Minority interests	−4,402	−4,508	−6,719
Net profit	**105,284**	**127,027**	**127,329**
Result before goodwill amortisation	111,529	145,892	146,377

	(€) 2000	Pro forma Unaudited 2000	2001
Basic earnings per share	1.55	1.31	1.20
Basic earnings per share before amortisation of goodwill	1.65	1.50	1.38
Diluted earnings per share	1.51	1.28	1.19
Diluted earnings per share before amortisation of goodwill	1.60	1.47	1.37

Source: Euronext, 2001 Annual Report, ⟨http://actionnaires.euronext.com/vgb/frame.html?page=ifi-RESA2001.html⟩, accessed May 16, 2003.

EXHIBIT 10B

EURONEXT CONSOLIDATED BALANCE SHEET

(€) Thousands	Dec 31 2000	Dec 31 2001	(€) Thousands	Dec 31 2000	Dec 31 2001
Assets			**Equity and liabilities**		
Property and equipment	69,603	57,296	Issued capital	97,937	116,132
Intangible assets	361,491	324,054	Share premium	777,481	1,077,720
Investments in associates/			Revaluation reserve	26,380	—
joint ventures	21,817	25,258	Reserve own shares	−7,447	−8,647
Other investments	35,328	128,973	Other reserves	902	—
Other receivables	2,255	15,737	Retained earnings	2,899	129,936
Deferred tax assets	20,422	24,202	**Total capital and reserves**	**898,152**	**1,315,141**
Total non-current assets	**510,916**	**575,520**	**Minority interests**	**13,728**	**16,526**
Investments	1,510,390	2,272,564	**Liabilities**		
Income tax receivable	14,193	18,335	Interest-bearing loans and		
Receivables re clearing			borrowings	7,629	5,624
activities	306,374	520,882	Employee benefits	9,986	37,685
Other receivables	180,266	205,432	Provisions	17,295	16,061
Cash	836,774	950,857	Deferred tax liabilities	19,758	22,774
Total current assets	**2,847,997**	**3,968,070**	**Total non-current liabilities**	**54,668**	**82,144**
Total assets	**3,358,913**	**4,543,590**	Bank overdraft	2,972	—
			Interest-bearing loans		
			and borrowings	6,433	1,090
			Income tax payable	59,758	23,509
			Clearing deposits	1,615,603	2,130,871
			Payables re clearing activities	362,624	596,037
			Other payables	276,962	364,030
			Provisions	68,013	14,242
			Total current liabilities	**2,392,365**	**3,129,779**
			Total equity and liabilities	**3,358,913**	**4,543,590**

Source: Euronext, 2001 Annual Report, ⟨http://actionnaires.euronext.com/vgb/frame.html?page=ifi-RESA2001.html⟩, accessed May 16, 2003.

CLEARSTREAM

Clearstream had been formed at the end of 1999 by the merger of Deutsche Börse's German CSD (Deutsche Börse Clearing) and Cedel. Cedel had been established in the 1960s to facilitate cross-border exchange of bonds within Europe and provide depository and custody services to its members. Deutsche Börse, on the other hand, had consolidated the different German securities depositories over time and, through its efforts, had gained control over clearing and settlement for all the German markets. After the merger, Deutsche Börse had a 50% participation in Clearstream while the other 50% was held by a financial holding company, owned by over 90 banks. As a result of the split ownership, neither Deutsche Börse nor the holding company had control over

EXHIBIT 10C

EURONEXT CONSOLIDATED STATEMENT OF CASH FLOWS

For year ending Dec 31 (€ Thousands)	2000	2001
Cash flows from operating activities		
Net profit	105,284	127,329
Income tax	58,459	85,926
Depreciation	19,537	36,719
Goodwill amortisation	6,245	19,048
Other non cash expenses	72,063	30,036
Realisation of revaluation reserve	—	(26,380)
IPO costs (charged to income)	—	16,064
Gain on sale of associates/subsidiaries	(56,489)	(33,846)
Total cash flow from operations before changes in working capital	**205,099**	**254,896**
Changes in working capital		
(Increase)/decrease in non-current receivables	(797)	(13,482)
(Increase)/decrease in other receivables	16,565	(25,166)
Increase in short-term payables	6,187	19,406
Income tax paid	(31,906)	(119,481)
Other movements	3,467	—
Net cash flows from operating activities	**198,615**	**116,173**
Cash flows from investing activities		
Disinvestments in tangible assets	(6,045)	(1,704)
Disinvestments in intangible assets	(43,396)	(4,319)
Consolidation of AEX/BXS	164,707	—
Disposal of activities	—	36,718
Other investing activities (net)	10,469	(39,066)
Net cash flows from investing activities	**125,735**	**(8,371)**
Cash flows from financing and clearing activities		
Net effect of clearing	(2,691,471)	534,173
Issued capital	—	412,043
Total IPO costs	—	(46,022)
Dividends paid on ordinary shares	(36,704)	(72,152)
Net cash flows from financing and clearing activities	**(2,728,175)**	**828,042**
Total cash flow over period	**(2,403,825)**	**935,844**
Net (decrease)/increase in cash and cash equivalents		
Beginning of period	4,638,364	2,234,539
End of period	2,234,539	3,170,383
Net (decrease)/increase in cash and cash equivalents	**(2,403,825)**	**935,844**
Cash	836,774	950,857
Current investments	1,397,765	2,219,526
Total cash and cash equivalents	**2,234,539**	**3,170,383**
Of which resulting from clearing activities	1,671,853	2,206,026
Own cash and cash equivalents	562,686	964,357

Source: Euronext, 2001 Annual Report, ⟨http://actionnaires.euronext.com/vgb/frame.html?page=ifi-RESA2001.html⟩, accessed May 16, 2003.

Clearstream.[29] This ownership structure provided Clearstream's management the ability to act somewhat independently from the company's shareholders.

Clearstream became one of two international settlement and custody houses in Europe. Its main competitor, Euroclear, settled transactions for Euronext. It acted as CSD within Germany and Luxembourg and also provided custody services across Europe, acting as a settlement agent for investors and financial intermediaries, through its linkages to other CSDs. Clearstream's revenue could be divided into three main categories: clearing & settlement income, interest income, and custody income. Clearing & settlement income covered all fees paid for handling clearing and settlement for a transaction (e.g. 0.40 per transaction settled for a standard domestic German trade). Interest income was received based on the interest margin earned on the cash balances deposited by Clearstream's customers (i.e. interest earned by Clearstream on customer deposits minus the interest paid to customers for their deposits). Custody income covers the fees on customers' deposits for safeguarding securities (e.g. 1.55 basis points charged for the first $500 million of European securities deposited). Clearsteam's revenue from clearing services was relatively marginal compared to its revenues from custodian and settlement services. It had 7.5 trillion in assets under custody and provided value added services to its clients, such as securities lending. As a settlement processor, Clearstream settled around 500,000 transactions per day, dealing with over 200 thousand securities. Exhibits 11a, 11b, and 11c show the consolidated financial statements for Clearstream.

Given its close business relationship to Clearstream, Deutsche Börse had considered acquiring full control of the Clearstream. Clearstream already managed clearing and settlement for Deutsche Börse's cash trading markets. However, the system did not provide exchange customers with a CCP or the benefits of netting transactions, the way Euronext's link to Clearnet and Euroclear had already provided to their clients. A successful acquisition of Clearstream (from 50% to 100% ownership) by Deutsche Börse would provide the company with a fully integrated and controlled value chain from trading to clearing, settlement and custody services. Exhibit 12 shows the overlap of Clearstream's customers with customers of Xetra and Eurex. As part of the vertical integration process, Deutsche Börse and Eurex Clearing could create a CCP for equity trading, which had been a non-existent feature on the German stock exchanges. The Equity Central Counter-party (ECCP) would eliminate transaction risks between buyers and sellers, lower settlement costs through the netting of transactions, and increase anonymity for market participants.[30]

The envisaged synergies created through the integration of Clearstream calculated that cost synergies alone would at least generate savings of 20 million in 2002, 41 million in 2003, and 50 to 80 million per annum, starting in 2004. In order to take full advantage of these synergies, Seifert expected restructuring Clearstream to cost 35 million in 2002 and 15 million in 2003. Deutsche Börse's bankers had estimated the company's cost of capital using an equity Beta of 1.15 and a market risk premium of roughly 6.0%.[31] Based on these expectations and the projections for Clearstream's future

---

[29] For various reasons the DBC/Cedel was implemented as an asset swap which involved the creation of a new company "Clearstream" to which both partners contributed their business operations. As a consequence Cedel continued to exist as a financial holding company with its former shareholders and virtually only a single asset, namely its 50% in Clearstream.

[30] The introduction of central counterparties implied that settlement of trades would take place between the ECCP and the market participants instead of the traditional system in which buyers and sellers settled trades with one another.

[31] The risk free rate used in these calculations was roughly 4.6%. Deutsche Börse used these inputs to calculate a range to discount rates to suggest a distribution of prices for the acquisition of Clearstream.

CLEARSTREAM CONSOLIDATED BALANCE SHEET

Assets (amount in €000s)	31-Dec 2001	31-Dec 2000
Cash and balances with the central banks and post-office banks	25,886	91,193
Placement with, and loans and advances to other banks: repayable on demand	4,447,702	2,208,882
other loans and advances	1,394,880	1,976,304
	5,842,582	4,185,186
Derivative assets used for hedging	22,491	—
Other money market placements	864,774	413,421
Loans and advances to customers	135,814	60,956
Investment securities	395,877	321,749
Tax assets	10,176	7,251
Deferred tax assets	2,020	2,311
Other assets	77,336	59,428
Prepayments and accrued income	112,954	114,461
Intangible assets	234,572	188,415
Property and equipment	168,996	84,095
Investment property	10,667	—
Total assets	**7,904,145**	**5,528,466**

Liabilities and Equity (amount in €000s)	31-Dec 2001	31-Dec 2000
Deposits from banks:		
repayable on demand	5,945,936	3,678,340
with agreed maturity dates or periods of notice	28,839	156,004
	5,974,775	3,834,344
Amounts owed to other depositors: other debts:		
repayable on demand	505,142	344,037
with agreed maturity dates or periods of notice	14,026	2,462
	519,168	346,499
Derivative liabilities used for hedging	6,049	—
Commercial paper	245,186	286,714
Tax liabilities	110,359	117,246
Deferred tax liabilities	33,760	10,365
Retirement obligations	40,530	34,312
Other liabilities	49,302	51,465
Accruals and deferred income	151,655	176,834
Total liabilities	**7,130,784**	**4,857,779**
Minority interests	**32,975**	**32,413**
Issued capital	150,000	150,000
Share premium	245,879	245,879
Consolidated reserves	137,508	117,035
Accumulated profits	206,999	125,360
Total shareholders' equity	**740,386**	**638,274**
Total liabilities and equity	**7,904,145**	**5,528,466**

Source: Clearstream International, 2001 Annual Report, p. 36, ⟨http://www.clearstream.com/c_co_annrep.htm⟩, accessed May 17, 2003.

EXHIBIT 11B

CLEARSTREAM CONSOLIDATED STATEMENT OF INCOME

For the year ended December 31, 2000 (amount in € 000s)	2001	2000
Interest and similar income	320,343	342,198
of which: that arising from debt securities and other fixed income securities	66,014	33,058
Fee and commission income	659,206	679,052
Gross operating income	**979,549**	**1,021,250**
Interest and similar expense	(138,631)	(142,011)
Fee and commission expense	(200,443)	(192,670)
Net interest and commission income	**640,475**	**686,569**
Dividend income	215	389
Net gains arising from investment securities	10,909	1,644
Net loss on financial operations	48	(6,258)
Other operating income	3,471	8,523
Own work Capitalized	87,401	71,048
Staff costs	(173,427)	(165,351)
Other administrative expenses	(309,349)	(297,776)
Total general and administrative expenses	**(482,776)**	**(463,127)**
Depreciation and amortisation expense	(79,439)	(74,321)
Other operating expense	14,225	(10,055)
Profit on ordinary activities before tax	**166,079**	**214,412**
Tax on profit on ordinary activities	(49,842)	(84,164)
Profit on ordinary activities after tax	**116,237**	**130,248**
Other taxes	(2,087)	127,596
Profit (loss) after tax	**114,150**	**(2,652)**
Minority interest	(782)	(2,232)
Net profit (loss) for the year/period	**113,368**	**125,364**

Source: Clearstream International, 2001 Annual Report, p. 38, ⟨http://www.clearstream.com/c_co_annrep.htm⟩, accessed May 17, 2003.

performance, Seifert went about calculating the proper acquisition price for the rest of Clearstream. Exhibit 13 shows the projected future cash flows for Clearstream through 2005 if it remained an independent entity, i.e., if Deutsche Börse did not acquire it.

CONCLUSION

At the time Clearstream was formed, Deutsche Börse had envisioned creating a large platform of back office services capable of absorbing the wealth of local clearing and settlement facilities spread across Europe. However the aspirations for expanding cross-border trading had been high and, after almost two years since Clearstream's inception, clearing and settlement across Europe had remained highly fragmented. The acquisition offer from Euroclear had necessitated Seifert to re-ask the question: how was Clearstream contributing to Deutsche Börse's strategic growth?

EXHIBIT 11C

CLEARSTREAM CONSOLIDATED STATEMENT OF CASH FLOWS

For the year ended December 31, 2000 (amount in € 000s)	2001	2000
Cash flows from operating activities:		
Profit after tax	114,150	127,596
Adjustments to reconcile net income with Net cash provided by operating activities:		
Depreciation and amortisation	79,439	74,321
Change in other assets and liabilities	(31,547)	(79,494)
Gain from sale of investments	(9,203)	(1,597)
Foreign currency translation difference	(4,775)	(1,372)
Cash from operating activities	**148,064**	**119,454**
Cash flows from investing activities:		
Net cash outflow arising on business combination	—	(660,702)
Acquisition of new subsidiaries	(97,878)	—
Acquisition of fixed-income securities	(235,402)	(109,056)
Proceeds from sale and redemption of fixed-income securities	207,632	77,235
Acquisition of equity investments	(26,637)	(26,120)
Proceeds from sale of equity investments	10,233	33,379
Acquisition of participating interest	(20,171)	(229)
Proceeds from sale of participating interest	13,910	826
Movements in other investments over 3 months:		
other money market placements	(201,252)	853,028
loans and advances to banks and customers	(44,932)	(558,423)
Acquisitions of tangible and intangible assets	(119,325)	(130,157)
Net cash used in investing activities	**(513,822)**	**(520,219)**
Cash flows from financing activities:		
Movements in amounts owed to credit institutions over 3 months	(1,931)	10,747
Movements in commercial paper over 3 months	(10,000)	(165,418)
Reimbursement of share premium	—	(17,505)
Dividends paid	(28,995)	—
Dividends paid - minority interest	(1,071)	(120)
Purchase of shares - minority interest	(2,468)	—
Issuance of shares - minority interest	2,183	1,685
Capital increase in cash	—	102,753
Net cash used in financing activities	**(42,282)**	**(67,858)**
Net decrease in cash and cash equivalents	**(408,040)**	**(468,623)**
Cash and cash equivalents at the beginning of the year	(468,498)	125
Cash and cash equivalents at the end of the year	**(876,538)**	**(468,498)**
Cash flows include:		
Interest received	317,423	312,451
Interest paid	(142,946)	(119,046)
Dividend received	215	389
Income tax paid	(46,656)	(45,489)

Source: Clearstream International, 2001 Annual Report, p. 40, ⟨http://www.clearstream.com/c_co_annrep.htm⟩, accessed May 17, 2003.

EXHIBIT 12

CUSTOMER OVERLAP OF DEUTSCHE BÖRSE AND CLEARSTREAM

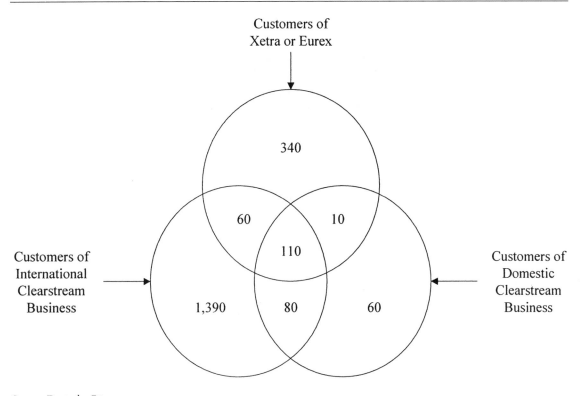

Source: Deutsche Börse.

EXHIBIT 13

PROJECTED CASH FLOWS FOR CLEARSTREAM

Amounts in € millions	2002	2003	2004	2005
Interest Revenues	161	142	160	163
Custody Revenues	307	332	375	430
Clearing & Settlement Revenues	162	195	141	150
Other Comission Revenues	66	63	62	68
Other operative Income	60	56	57	62
Staff Costs	186	177	173	175
Other Administrative Costs	202	196	187	186
Depreciation	105	121	116	93

Clearstream Revenue Terminal Growth Rate   2.5%
Deutsche Börse's Annual Tax Rate   32%

Source: Deutsche Börse.

31

The Chicago Board Options Exchange (CBOE)

On a late afternoon in June 2004, William Brodsky, Chairman and CEO of the Chicago Board Options Exchange (CBOE) and Richard DuFour, Executive Vice President for Corporate Strategy, looked down from the visitor's gallery onto the CBOE's 45,000 square foot trading floor and considered what was about to happen.

The floor had changed substantially during Brodsky's thirty-six years in the industry and DuFour's twenty-four. The introduction of technology into the open outcry marketplace had transformed the pits into a massive trading arcade. Only ten years earlier, traders would have been wading ankle deep in paper by this time of day. Now, very little clutter covered the green tiled floor. Members, who previously would have yelled their bids and offers and gestured in the Chicago method of hand signals, were now glued to the screens of their laptops and handheld computers. Connected to the CBOE's main trading engine, they adjusted their positions and risk parameters with the click of a mouse and traded, sometimes all day, in near silence.

Introducing electronic trading to the CBOE, in large part through the exchange's Hybrid market model, had been but one step in the CBOE's competitive-driven evolution. Overall though, the growth of electronic trading in the options market had reached a critical point for the floor-based CBOE. Now, with Brodsky leading the charge, the exchange was about to take its next step with Hybrid 2.0, a step that the many local Chicago members had sought to avoid.

Founded in 1973, CBOE had pioneered the market for listed options, starting as an open-outcry marketplace like its Chicago derivative exchange siblings, the Chicago Mercantile Exchange (CME) and the Chicago Board of Trade (CBOT). From 1975 to 2000, CBOE dominated the listed options market that it shared with four other floor-based options exchanges. Starting in 1999, however, the options industry began to undergo significant changes, including the multiple listing of all equity options, the deci-

---

Professor George Chacko, Research Associates Anders Sjöman and Daniela Beyersdorfer of the HBS Europe Research Center and George Robert Nelson (MBA 04) prepared this case. HBS cases are developed solely as the basis for class discussion. Cases are not intended to serve as endorsements, sources of primary data, or illustrations of effective or ineffective management.

malization of prices, a bear market, and, most importantly, the entry of the first fully electronic options exchange in 2000, the International Securities Exchange (ISE).

Within four short years, the ISE had risen to rival CBOE in total options market share. Its model of competing electronic quotes, a fully screen-based market governed by only a few large, institutional members had proven very adept at seizing market share from the traditional exchanges. Further, it seemed able to respond more swiftly to competitive pressures. ISE had to deal with only 17 firms, which owned all of the memberships on the exchange. By contrast, Brodsky and DuFour reflected, CBOE could at times show a relative slowness given its governance structure which comprised hundreds of individual members and made it difficult to quickly alter the exchange's direction. The fact that CBOE maintained a narrow lead in total market share was generally attributed to its dominance in heavily traded index options, for which CBOE had certain exclusive listing rights. Nevertheless, ISE's growth led the existing floor exchanges to develop their own electronic trading models, including CBOE's launch of Hybrid, a system that in a novel way blended screen-based and open-outcry trading. Despite early successes, CBOE recognized by the fall of 2003 that Hybrid needed to expand. A recent growth in trading volume had given all exchanges some breathing room, but new competitors—like the second all-electronic exchange, the Boston Options Exchange (BOX)—were just around the corner. With that, Hybrid 2.0 was conceived and put into development.

Now, with version 2.0 launching in less than a month, Brodsky and DuFour held daily discussions. A recurring theme was how CBOE's membership (the over 1,200 individual traders, brokers and member firms that actually owned the exchange) would react. They had already agreed to the introduction of Hybrid 2.0, but their continued support was dependent upon it delivering some beneficial results. More practically, Brodsky and DuFour had three main questions. First, was the timing right for 2.0 and would it deliver on its expectations? Second, did the new version contain all the necessary functionality or should they have gone directly for a more ambitious launch, a "Hybrid 3.0" that would most certainly have been met with significant resistance by the membership? Third, and most important, would Hybrid 2.0 be enough to gain back market share and keep CBOE as the leading options marketplace?

CBOE AND TRADITIONAL OPTIONS TRADING (1973–1999)

About Options

When it first opened on April 26, 1973, CBOE was the first organized market for standardized options. While stocks had traded on centralized, listed exchanges for over two hundred years, options had always been an esoteric (some observers even said arcane) marketplace. In layman's terms, an option provided its holder with the right to buy or sell shares of an underlying security, such as an equity, for a predetermined price (the strike price) on or before a given date (the expiration date). Options were part of a class of financial instruments called derivatives, since their value was determined by—or "derived" from—the value of some other underlying asset, such as securities, interest rates, or indexes. There were two basic kinds of options: call options (which granted the right to buy) and put options (which granted the right to sell). As an example, for options written on equity for company X, a call gave the purchaser the right to buy stock of company X, at a certain price and on or before a certain date, while a put gave the purchaser the right to sell stock of company X, at a certain price and on or before a certain date.

From an investor's perspective, options were used both to manage risk and to speculate on future market direction. The individual that purchased an option, whether a call or put, was the option "buyer" or "holder." Conversely, the person who sold an option, whether a call or put, was the option "seller" or "writer." In the listed options industry, options were generally standardized to equal 100 shares of stock, or a level of 100 times an index or other instrument. As such, one equity call option normally represented the right to buy 100 shares of the underlying stock, whereas an equity put option represented the right to sell 100 shares. The price of an option was referred to as its "premium." The ask price was the price at which a seller or writer offered to sell an option or stock. The bid price was the price at which a buyer was willing to buy an option or stock. (Exhibit 1 summarizes the option terms.)

Options exchanges listed standardized options, called contracts, for trading, meaning that key terms such as strike price and expiration date were preset by the Exchange. The expiration date could be up to nine months from the date the options were first listed and up to three years if the exchange allowed for longer-term contracts, called LEAPS (Long-term, Equity Anticipation Securities). So called "American-style" contracts could be exercised at any time before the expiration date. Others—known as "European-style" options—could only be exercised on the day of expiration. The last full day of trading for most exchange traded options was the 3rd Friday of each month, often referred to as expiration Friday.

Unlike stock, options did not originate from the company on which they were based. Options exchanges were permitted to list contracts on any security (equity, index or other such product) that met their rules. The company identified by the underlying—for example IBM—could not approve nor disapprove of the listing, and had no involvement in the issuance, trading or settlement of these contracts. Since multiple parties were able to write options on the same stock with different contract terms, many options existed for the same underlying stock. Options for a specific stock were called an "options class," and were separated into multiple options "series," each with its own strike price and maturity date. By 2004, there were over 2,400 options classes, covering more than 100,000 different options series, trading in the marketplace. (This made the U.S. options market the single largest generator of price and quote information in the global financial industry, a distinction not lost on the data vendors who disseminated this data around the world.) The majority of options trading were however in a concentrated set of classes. In 2004, 87.5% of the total average daily industry volume took place in the top 400 classes, with over 50% in the top 100 classes. That year, CBOE had the largest number of listings of any exchange, over 1,600 different classes. Competing exchange ISE, by contrast, had the fewest—targeting only the top 600 classes.

Several participants were active in the options market, such as individual and institutional investors, their respective brokers, and the multiple classes of members on

---

EXHIBIT 1

OPTION SPEAK TRANSLATED

Option Speak:	Holder	→	Bids	→	Premium	→	for 1 option
English:	Buyer	→	Pays	→	Price	→	for right to buy 100 shares

Source: Casewriters.

the exchanges. There were liquidity providers, comprised of market makers, Designated Primary Market Makers, Lead Market Makers and specialists, and, on the physical exchanges, there were also Floor Brokers, who acted as agents for customer orders. About 90% of the exchange members were market makers of some type, a testament to the industry's need for liquidity. Options investors and their brokers tended to be more sophisticated than the average stock market customer, due to the mathematical complexities of options. The exchanges all cleared their transactions through a common entity, the Options Clearing Corporation (OCC). The only central counterparty in the world to have an 'AAA' credit rating from Standard & Poor's, the OCC guaranteed the performance of every options contract, meaning it insured that even if a writer went bust, the contract to buy or sell would be honored. So far, there had never been a default on any listed options contract cleared by the OCC. Owned equally by the exchanges and managed by the industry's member firms, the OCC was a very profitable enterprise. And although it distributed all excess revenues it collected back to its member firms or invested it in capital projects, it was sometimes viewed with envy by the executives of the highly competitive exchanges. The CBOE had started the OCC but had been forced to divest of it by the Securities and Exchange Commission (SEC) when other exchanges entered the business. This event triggered the onset of "fungibility," whereby contracts entered into on one market could be closed out in another. As such, the business that the CBOE had built in its early years instantly became available to new entrants as they joined the options marketplace.

The CBOE

Located in a 10-story building on the south end of Chicago's business district (the "Loop"), the CBOE stood in the shadow of the Chicago Board of Trade, the marketplace that had been its parent. Begun and spun off by the CBOT in its early days, the CBOE building's population would swell to over 3,000 people during the trading day, with 1,300 plus members, over a thousand clerks and trading firm staff, 700 exchange employees and countless other visitors, reporters, contractors and such. The building itself was windowless below the fifth floor and built of solid granite; with hardened technology facilities and dual diesel generators, it was meant to keep trading no matter what happened outside. The initial members of CBOE paid $10,000 each for a "seat" on the new exchange, and the first contract traded on the world's first standardized options market were the "XEROX July 160 calls." That first day, CBOE traded 911 contracts; by December 2004, the daily average was 1.3 million.

Standardized options quickly gained popularity following the launch of CBOE primarily due to two factors: first, the establishment of the standardized marketplace and, second, the work of Myron Scholes, Fischer Black (two Chicago economists) and Robert Merton in developing the first widely accepted model for pricing options, the Black-Scholes Theorem. The three had published this formula in a seminal paper in 1973 in the Journal of Political Economy.[1] As demand in options took off, the number of listed options classes grew rapidly. After initially trading only call options, puts were introduced in 1977. Competitors soon arrived, starting with the American Stock Exchange

---

[1] Earlier attempts to have the paper published had failed because, according to Scholes, they were told "options were too narrowly focused and didn't have wide application in the field of economics." (Source: Dow Jones News Service, 05/01/2003, Kopin Tan on the occasion of the CBOE's thirtieth anniversary.) In 1997, Scholes and Merton were awarded the Nobel Prize in economics for their groundbreaking option-pricing theory.

(AMEX) and the Philadelphia Stock Exchange (PHLX) in 1975 and the Pacific Stock Exchange (PCX) in 1976. Much later, in 1986, the New York Stock Exchange (NYSE) joined the crowd, along with, for a very brief time, the NASD. When the ISE came along in 2000, it was not only the first new options exchange in almost 15 years, it was the first new securities exchange in the U.S. in over 25 years.

From 1973 to 1999, CBOE's annual volume grew to 254.3 million contracts from 1.1 million contracts, with the exchange's market share consistently exceeding 40%. CBOE focused on product innovation, introducing for instance LEAPs, FLEX options and the VIX, a market volatility index. Its most important innovation, after equity options, was the creation, in 1983, of options on broad-based indexes. Index options allowed investors to buy options that tracked major market segments or the market as a whole. For instance, an investor could buy an option on the S&P 500, thus benefiting from movements in the broad market represented by the index. Through licensing arrangements, the CBOE became the exclusive market for index options on the S&P 100, S&P 500, DJIA and Russell 2000. (Exhibit 2 summarizes CBOE innovations.)

Starting in the 1980s, CBOE began automating many of its operations, as the growing number of option classes made manual trade processing unwieldy. Most of CBOE's innovations were rapidly copied by the other options exchanges. DuFour commented, "For a long time, our competitors' best weapon was the Xerox-Machine. All they did was to read CBOE's SEC rule filings and then copy them."

EXHIBIT 2

CBOE PRODUCT DEVELOPMENT

Date	Product(s) Introduced
1973	• Call options began trading
1975	• Black-Scholes model was adopted for pricing options
1977	• Put options began trading
1983	• Introduces options on broad-based stock indexes: S&P 100 Index (OEX), S&P 500 Index (SPX)
1985	• Options on NASDAQ stocks are listed
1989	• Options on interest rate products began trading
1990	• Creates LEAPS®, long-term options that provide investors with great flexibility in using options in their portfolios
1992	• Sector indexes begin trading
1993	• Introduces FLEX options, which allow investors to create certain specifications on options contracts.
	• Introduces VIX, a market volatility index that gauges investor sentiment, widely referred to as the "fear gauge"
1997	• Introduces options on the DOW index
2001	• Develops the VXN volatility index, based on the NASDAQ 100
2003	• Introduce BXM, a buy/write index that tracks the total return of a consistent buy/write strategy
2004	• Introduces futures on the S&P 500 Volatility Index

Source: CBOE.

Governing and Managing the CBOE

The CBOE was a non-stock membership corporation, regulated by the U.S. Securities and Exchange Commission (SEC). CBOE was owned by its 931 members or seat owners. Owning a seat gave the member the right to trade—the "seat" itself—and also an equity stake in CBOE's assets. Moreover, given the historical link between CBOE and its founder CBOT, the 1,402 seat owners on the CBOT were *also* granted a perpetual "exercise right," with which they could trade on the CBOE floor and vote on CBOE matters. Several hundred CBOT members commonly exercised that right, causing the membership to expand and contract. Having averaged for a long time around 500, the number of CBOT members trading on the CBOE floor had recently fallen to around 385.

The Chairman and CEO of CBOE since 1997 had been William Brodsky. Brodsky had brought with him extensive experience as Executive Vice President of the American Stock Exchange and as CEO of the Chicago Mercantile Exchange. As had been the practice at CBOE since 1979, Brodsky was hired from the outside, but he was flanked by the CBOE Vice Chairman, a member selected by the membership to represent their interests with the Board and Management. The Chairman answered to a board of directors with 23 members, 11 of whom were independent public directors. However, unlike stakeholders in traditional stock companies, the CBOE members themselves actively participated in the management. They were active through the Exchange's advisory committee system, and through their right to vote on any important exchange related matter. Said DuFour, "In a way, it is like a country club with the members representing different constituencies."

Brodsky called the active involvement of members the "Chicago dimension," since all the Chicago exchanges were marked by this characteristic. Even times of huge competition did not stop the members from interfering, often slowing down decision processes. Management always had to keep in mind that many CBOE seat owners leased out their trading rights and had no active presence on the trading floor. In some cases they might not even have any knowledge of the options trading business. The population on the trading floor therefore brought together traders with and without an ownership stake, and with or without a long-term financial interest in the exchange—all these differing motivations left ample ground for conflicting interests and drawn-out discussions. DuFour illustrated,

> Any member can call for a member vote on any exchange rule by gathering 150 signatures on a petition. Although we may have only one or two actual petitions a year, the notion of them hangs like the Damocles sword over management decisions. It makes rapid change very difficult.

Most major decisions did however not follow the petition path. Instead they were introduced for debate and arguments using the exchange's committee system. In total, the CBOE had 27 different committees. DuFour explained how decisions were normally made,

> Issues related to trading and procedures are referred to committees, which bring valuable expertise to the decision making process. However, as the business has become more complex, the committees have come to reflect a diversity of interests that can often be at cross-purposes. Often the recommendation that comes out of a committee reflects a compromise rather than the path that best serves the Exchange's interests. And then, let's not forget that once we all agree, any major business decision still has to be approved by the SEC—which gives all our competitors about 90 days notice of any new initiative. There are very few surprises left in the industry.

Clients and Products

Externally, CBOE customers can be divided into retail users and professional (institutional) users. Retail users accessed CBOE through brokerage firms, such as Charles Schwab or Merrill Lynch. They were responsible for the majority of the exchange's daily transactions, though not of the actual contract volume since they mostly traded in small lots of 20 options or less. As customers, their main concerns were the best price, fast execution and efficient order processing.

The second customer group—the professional users—was further divided into three categories: individual professionals, buy-side institutions and sell-side institutions. Individual professionals were brokers/dealers (in some cases former members) that used considerable technological resources to trade for their own accounts. They took advantage of the multiple listing of options and often engaged in arbitrage trading, seeking out profitable price differentials on like products at different exchanges. Buy-side institutional users were firms (large and small) that used options professionally for market speculation, hedging and income enhancement. They could be mutual funds, pension funds, hedge funds or large financial institutions such as Goldman Sachs. Sell-side institutional users were usually large firms that acted as brokers or intermediaries for large institutional customers. They represented a small share of CBOE's transactions but a large share of the volume, since they traded in large quantities.

The CBOE of 2004 offered four main product lines for trading: options on individual equities (with over 1400 different stocks listed), options on equity indexes (with 40 broad-based and narrow-based indexes), options on exchange traded funds and options on interest rates. For its June 30, 2003 fiscal year end, the CBOE generated $163.8 million in revenue and $7.4 million in net income. The largest part of the revenues ($104.8 million) came from transaction and trade related fees that CBOE charged market makers. In 2003, CBOE had a volume of 283.9 million options contracts, equal to a 31.3% market share over other options exchanges in the U.S. 110.9 million or 39% of those contracts were on index options (53.7% market share). Exhibit 3 shows 2003 financials, and Exhibit 4 shows historical transaction revenues.

The Open-Outcry System and the Specialist Market Maker Model

The "heart" of CBOE was the trading floor with its pits, where traders still shouted orders to each other despite considerable automation. CBOE's market model incorporated members who acted as market makers and provided liquidity by trading for their own account. Market makers quoted prices at which they would buy and sell options (the "bid" and "ask" prices.) Historically, it was the difference—the "bid-ask" spread—that allowed market makers to earn a fee for providing liquidity. By 2004, spreads had narrowed and most market makers earned a return by putting on positions and then managing the risk. For example, a market maker might sell options and then try to lock in a portion of the premium by hedging the risks. Market makers normally attempted to minimize the amount of capital they had at risk through various hedging techniques. The floor brokers, another major category of participants, did not trade for their own account. Their sole purpose was to represent and execute customer orders.

In 1999, the CBOE implemented a floor-wide Designated Primary Market Maker (DPM) system for all its equity option classes. Said DuFour, "We wanted specialists to serve as a point of accountability for the member firms who bring customer orders to

EXHIBIT 3

CBOE 2003 FINANCIAL STATEMENTS

a. Income Statement

Year ending June 30 ($ in thousands)	2003	2002
Revenues:		
Transaction fees	104,827	89,436
Other member fees	26,642	24,641
Options Price Reporting Authority Income	15,614	18,884
Regulatory fees	10,800	11,231
Interest	368	459
Equity in income of CSE	1,867	141
Other	3,674	4,031
Total Revenues	**163,792**	**148,823**
Expenses:		
Employee costs	64,094	63,920
Depreciation and amortization	29,252	29,709
Data processing	17,771	17,492
Outside services	11,794	13,458
Royalty fees	11,028	8,989
Travel and promotional expenses	4,853	5,428
Facilities costs	4,240	4,351
Equity in loss of OneChicago	4,165	1,483
Other	2,583	2,195
Communications	621	727
Severance expense		4,499
Total Expenses	**150,401**	**152,251**
Income (Loss) Before Income Taxes	**13,391**	**(3,428)**
Provision (Benefit) for Income Taxes:		
Current	5,201	(3,102)
Deferred	798	5,294
Total Provision (Benefit) for Income Taxes	**5,999**	**2,192**
Net Income (Loss)	**7,392**	**(5.620)**
Retained Earnings at Beginning of Year	**103,670**	**109,290**
Retained Earnings at End of Year	**111,062**	**103,670**

Source: CBOE Annual Report 2003.

(Continued)

the Exchange and to have an interest in building a business trading his assigned classes." Selected by the exchange, the DPMs had certain rights and obligations in order to incent and enable them to perform these functions. The DPM—or "specialist"—had to assume the responsibility of maintaining fair and orderly markets for a specific series of options, by continuously quoting both bid and ask prices. Other market makers could then join the quotes at the determined price or offer their on bids and offers. Figure A on page 561 summarizes the traditional options trade on the CBOE.

EXHIBIT 3   *(Continued)*

CBOE 2003 FINANCIAL STATEMENTS

---

b. Balance Sheet

Year ending June 30 ($ in thousands)	2003	2002
Assets		
Current Assets:		
Cash and cash equivalents	20,558	6,861
Accounts receivable	18,473	17,207
Income taxes receivable	1,519	4,361
Prepaid medical benefits	1,777	1,028
Other prepaid expenses	4,464	4,406
Other current assets	912	673
Total Current Assets	**47,703**	**34,536**
Investments in Affiliates	**14,976**	**13,861**
Land	**4,914**	**4,914**
Property and Equipment		
Building	57,609	57,609
Furniture and equipment	110,006	170,152
Less accumulated depreciation and amortization	(104,577)	(157,621)
Total Property and Equipment-Net	**63,038**	**70,140**
Other Assets:		
Goodwill	1,388	1,388
Software development work in progress	5,440	6,455
Data processing software and other assets		
(less accumulated amortization-2003, $31,854; 2002, $28,334)	38,325	34,412
Total Other Assets-Net	**45,153**	**42,255**
Total	**175,784**	**165,706**
Liabilities and Member's Equity		
Current Liabilities:		
Accounts payable and accrued expenses	15,173	14,436
Marketing fee payable	687	1,079
Unearned income	1,500	1,250
Membership transfer deposits	200	657
Total Current Liabilities	**17,560**	**17,422**
Long-term Liabilities		
Unearned income	2,000	250
Deferred income taxes	24,228	23,430
Total Long-term Liabilities	**26,228**	**23,680**
Total Liabilities	**43,788**	**41,102**
Members Equity		
Memberships	20,934	20,934
Retained Earnings	111,062	103,670
Total Members Equity	**131,996**	**124,604**
Total	**175,784**	**165,706**

Source: CBOE Annual Report 2003.

(Continued)

EXHIBIT 3   (Continued)

CBOE 2003 FINANCIAL STATEMENTS

c. Statements of Cash Flows

Year ending June 30 ($ in thousands)	2003	2002
Cash Flows from Operating Activities:		
Net Income (Loss)	7,392	(5,620)
Adjustments to reconcile net income to net cash flows from operating activities:		
Depreciation and amortization	29,252	29,709
Long-term settlement obligations		(5,333)
Deferred income taxes	798	5,294
Equity in income of CSE	(1,867)	(141)
Equity in loss of OneChicago	4,165	1,483)
Gain on disposition of property		**(277)**
Changes in assets and liabilities:		
Accounts receivable	(1,266)	5,005
Income taxes	2,842	(1.048)
Prepaid medical benefits	(749)	(101)
Other prepaid expenses	(58)	(220)
Other current assets	(239)	(119)
Accounts payable and accrued expenses	737	793
Marketing fee payable	(392)	(8,095)
Unearned income	2,000	1,396
Membership transfer deposits	(457)	657
Other deposits		(416)
Net Cash Flows from Operating Activities	**42,158**	**22,967**
Cash Flows from Investing Activities		
Capital and other assets expenditures	(23,047)	(21,871)
OneChicago investment	(3,414)	(4,388)
Proceeds from disposition of property		413
Net Cash Flows from Investing Activities	**(28,461)**	**(25,846)**
Net Increase (Decrease) in Cash and Cash Equivalents	**13,697**	**(2,879)**
Cash and Cash Equivalents at Beginning of Year	**6,861**	**9,740**
Cash and Cash Equivalents at End of Year	**20,558**	**6,861**
Supplemental Disclosure of Cash Flow Information		
Cash paid for income taxes	3,875	0

Source: CBOE Annual Report 2003.

Options Exchange Competition Before 1999

CBOE had long served as a model for the other options exchanges, which included the AMEX, the PHLX, the PCX and, later, the NYSE. They all had trading floors; all used the open outcry system; and all had comparable participants, such as market makers, floor brokers and specialists. Like CBOE, all of them derived the majority of their revenue from transaction fees. Historically, CBOE had been the market share leader, followed by the AMEX, PHLX, PCX and the NYSE. In 1997, CBOE acquired the op-

EXHIBIT 4

CBOE HISTORICAL TRANSACTION REVENUES

Year	Year End Revenue
2003	104,827,000
2002	89,436,000
2001	96,091,800
2000	114,460,300
1999	96,469,900
1998	84,639,200
1997	74,986,000
1996	71,925,800
1995	78,834,000
1994	68,205,500
1993	54,321,700
1992	48,275,000
1991	54,178,100
1990	51,536,900
1989	52,036,500
1988	62,525,200
1987	81,227,700
1986	77,141,000
1985	57,177,800
1984	42,625,900
1983	37,336,200
1982	26,406,100
1981	26,625,100
1980	19,159,600
1979	11,324,200
1978	9,611,394
1977	7,557,995
1976	7,261,744
1975	3,883,833
1974	1,308,575
1973	NM

Note: CBOE operates under fiscal year beginning in July.

Source: CBOE Annual Reports, 1973 through 2003.

tions business of the New York Stock Exchange. (Exhibit 5 shows historical exchange volumes.)

Up until 1999, competition between the exchanges was limited. For most of the history of options multiple listing was prohibited by the SEC. The regulators started to phase this out in the late 1980's but multiple listing in many of the most attractive equity option classes was not allowed until the early 1990's. Even then, the exchanges avoided listing option classes that were listed on another exchange. All market participants were charged transactions fees, with the highest fees paid by retail customers.

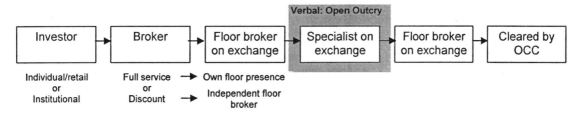

Figure A An Option Trade with an Open-Outcry Model and Market Maker Specialists

Source: Casewriters.

A CHANGING MARKET PLACE AND THE ARRIVAL OF ELECTRONIC TRADING (1999–2004)

1999 turned out to be a year filled with changes for the options exchange industry. Most importantly, exchanges started to list one another's option classes. In fact, the SEC had allowed multiple listings of options for several years. However, the exchanges had not been aggressive in listing one another's products. DuFour explained,

> Even after options on NASDAQ stocks began to trade, and all stocks progressively moved to multiple listings, the incentive for the options exchanges to multiply list the "big names" was simply not strong enough. From a business standpoint it was not clear that the additional business gained would offset the combination of business lost and lower margins.

In the end, the Justice Department had launched a probe into the listing practices, looking for an agreement among the exchanges to not list one another's classes or any evidence of pressure being put on an exchange to not multiply list. At the same time, the new all-electronic exchange ISE announced that it would list the 600 most popular stock options, regardless of whether they were traded somewhere else. Effectively, these pressures prompted multiple listings. The CBOE started the listing war in August 1999 when it listed Dell options, until then the most active issue on the Philadelphia Exchange. The AMEX quickly joined in trading Dell options. The Philadelphia exchange countered by trading AMEX's Apple options, as well as CBOE's IBM, Coca-Cola and Johnson & Johnson options. As multiple listing became widespread, the SEC required that the exchanges linked their markets so that an investor could access the best price on any of the exchanges. (This effort of inter-market linkage was eventually completed in 2003.) Seeing that competition would increase, CBOE also changed its fee schedule in 1999, shifting the balance of costs from the external user of the exchange onto the trading floor members and market making firms.

A second major development affecting the options markets was the 2001 change in the securities industry from fractional pricing to pricing in decimals, so called decimalization. In the case of options the minimum price increment went from one-sixteenth ($0.0625) to nickel and dimes ($0.05–$0.10).

The result of decimalization, combined with the intense competition brought on by multiple listing, was a further narrowing of spreads. According to the SEC, the industry average bid-ask spread decreased substantially, falling 38%, from $.29 to $.18, during 2000. As an outcome, many smaller market making firms that depended on the bid-ask spread left the industry.

The global economic downturn that began in 2001 did not help market participants either, and in 2002, option-volume growth slowed for the first time since 1990. The

EXHIBIT 5

U.S. OPTIONS EXCHANGES COMPARISON 1973–2004, Q1

a. Options Volume

	CBOE	AMEX	PHLX	PCX	ISE	BOX	NY SE	MSE	NASD	Total
Q12004	94,591,726	55,380,996	42,916,446	28,837,665	92,081,629	1,165,949				314,974,411
2003	283,946,495	179,756,014	112,574,473	86,246,572	245,121,837					907,858,655
2002	267,616,496	185,693,079	88,945,424	85,824,532	152,143,489					780,223,020
2001	306,667,851	205,043,075	101,841,724	102,637,138	65,353,969					781,543,757
2000	326,359,531	207,726,689	76,549,892	108,541,840	7,565,684					726,743,636
1999	254,331,851	129,662,189	48,125,415	75,801,209						507,920,664
1998	206,865,991	97,661,673	42,844,295	58,971,239						406,343,198
1997	187,243,741	88,107,842	30,364,035	46,686,240			1,421,260			353,823,118
1996	173,944,877	61,591,891	21,938,865	33,881,762			3,438,990			294,796,385
1995	178,533,465	52,391,899	22,000,030	30,905,131			2,885,698			286,716,223
1994	183,934,483	48,505,380	25,704,131	20,929,869			2,300,700			281,374,563
1993	140,348,955	47,883,957	25,699,888	16,364,744			2,052,965			232,350,509
1992	121,467,604	42,314,942	22,947,867	13,066,618			2,177,041			201,974,072
1991	121,689,918	38,805,589	22,365,110	13,852,604			2,059,969			198,773,190
1990	129,500,018	40,914,962	22,808,688	13,881,269			2,817,811			209,922,748
1989	126,765,253	49,873,264	27,970,765	18,091,434			4,315,944			227,016,660
1988	111,784,045	45,022,497	23,165,112	13,349,148			2,627,789			195,948,591
1987	182,112,636	70,988,990	29,155,308	19,410,875			3,499,095			305,166,904
1986	180,357,774	65,440,500	24,467,468	14,075,872			4,823,782		45,239	289,210,635
1985	148,889,091	48,559,122	18,134,575	12,793,451			4,426,855		107,453	232,910,547
1984	123,273,736	40,104,605	16,109,050	11,366,056			4,093,816			194,947,263
1983	82,468,750	38,967,725	16,808,125	11,155,906			656,480			150,056,986

(Continued)

EXHIBIT 5 *(Continued)*

U.S. OPTIONS EXCHANGES COMPARISON 1973–2004, Q1

	CBOE	AMEX	PHLX	PCX	ISE	BOX	NY SE	MSE	NASD	Total
1982	75,735,739	38,790,852	13,466,652	9,309,563					137,302,806	
1981	57,584,175	34,859,475	10,009,565	6,952,567					109,405,782	
1980	52,916,921	29,048,323	7,758,101	5,486,590				1,518,611		96,728,546
1979	35,379,600	17,467,018	4,952,737	3,856,344				2,609,164		64,264,863
1978	34,277,350	14,380,959	3,270,378	3,289,968				2,012,363		57,231,018
1977	24,838,632	10,077,578	2,195,307	1,925,031				600,780		39,637,328
1976	21,498,027	9,035,767	1,274,702	550,194				15,237		32,373,927
1975	14,431,023									18,102,569
1974	5,682,907	3,530,564	140,982							5,682,907
1973	1,119,177									1,119,177

Legend: CBOE   Chicago Board Options Exchange
AMEX   American Stock Exchange
PHLX   Philadelphia Stock Exchange
PCX   Pacific Stock Exchange
ISE   International Securities Exchange
BOX   Boston Options Exchange
NYSE   New York Stock Exchange
MSE   Montreal Stock Exchange
NASD   NASDAQ

Source: CBOE.

(Continued)

EXHIBIT 5   (Continued)

U.S. OPTIONS EXCHANGES COMPARISON 1973–2004, Q1

b. Percentage of Options Volume

	CBOE	AMEX	PHLX	PCX	ISE	BOX	NY SE	MSE	NASD	Total
Q1 2004	30.0%	17.6%	13.6%	9.2%	29.2%	0.4%				100.0%
2003	31.3%	19.8%	12.4%	9.5%	27.0%					100.0%
2002	34.3%	23.8%	11.4%	11.0%	19.5%					100.0%
2001	39.2%	26.2%	13.0%	13.1%	8.4%					100.0%
2000	44.9%	28.6%	10.5%	14.9%	1.0%					100.0%
1999	50.1%	25.5%	9.5%	14.9%						100.0%
1998	50.9%	24.0%	10.5%	14.5%						100.0%
1997	52.9%	24.9%	8.6%	13.2%			0.4%			100.0%
1996	59.0%	20.9%	7.4%	11.5%			1.2%			100.0%
1995	62.3%	18.3%	7.7%	10.8%			1.0%			100.0%
1994	65.4%	17.2%	9.1%	7.4%			0.8%			100.0%
1993	60.4%	20.6%	11.1%	7.0%			0.9%			100.0%
1992	60.1%	21.0%	11.4%	6.5%			1.1%			100.0%
1991	61.2%	19.5%	11.3%	7.0%			1.0%			100.0%
1990	61.7%	19.5%	10.9%	6.6%			1.3%			100.0%
1989	55.8%	22.0%	12.3%	8.0%			1.9%			100.0%
1988	57.0%	23.0%	11.8%	6.8%			1.3%			100.0%
1987	59.7%	23.3%	9.6%	6.4%			1.1%			100.0%
1986	62.4%	22.6%	8.5%	4.9%			1.7%		0.0%	100.0%
1985	63.9%	20.8%	7.8%	5.5%			1.9%		0.0%	100.0%
1984	63.2%	20.6%	8.3%	5.8%			2.1%			100.0%
1983	55.0%	26.0%	11.2%	7.4%			0.4%			100.0%
1982	55.2%	28.3%	9.8%	6.8%						100.0%
1981	52.6%	31.9%	9.1%	6.4%						100.0%
1980	54.7%	30.0%	8.0%	5.7%				1.6%		100.0%
1979	55.1%	27.2%	7.7%	6.0%				4.1%		100.0%
1978	59.9%	25.1%	5.7%	5.7%				3.5%		100.0%
1977	62.7%	25.4%	5.5%	4.9%				1.5%		100.0%
1976	66.4%	27.9%	3.9%	1.7%				0.0%		100.0%
1975	79.7%	19.5%	0.8%							100.0%
1974	100.0%									100.0%
1973	100.0%									100.0%

Legend: CBOE   Chicago Board Options Exchange
       AMEX   American Stock Exchange
       PHLX   Philadelphia Stock Exchange
       PCX   Pacific Stock Exchange
       ISE   International Securities Exchange
       BOX   Boston Options Exchange
       NYSE   New York Stock Exchange
       MSE   Montreal Stock Exchange
       NASD   NASDAQ

Source: CBOE.

options exchanges and market participants continued to compete aggressively for the remaining business. With no exclusivity on listings, exchanges and their liquidity providers had to find other ways to attract order flow. Controversial competitive practices became more commonplace, including payment for order flow and the internalization of customer orders.

Payment for Order Flow

Payment for order flow referred to brokerage firms that sought compensation from exchange market makers for sending customer orders to them and not to another exchange. Critics believed the practice amounted to a kickback, and that brokerage firms should send orders to the exchange offering the best price for the client and not to the specialist who offered the greatest payment. CBOE did not offer payment for order flow, but it allowed its market making firms to follow such practice. In CBOE's view, the fight for order flow shifted from the exchanges to the liquidity providers, who were now in more direct contact with order flow providers.

Internalization

The second debated practice was internalization. Internalization occurred when a brokerage firm took a client's order and sent it to another division of the broker's firm, thereby "internalizing" the order. The brokerage firm acted as both principal and agent by taking the opposite side of its customers' orders. The broker made money on any difference between the purchase and sale prices. Critics questioned whether the brokerage firm could do this fairly.

The International Securities Exchange (ISE) and All-Electronic Trading

In 1999, the options exchange industry also saw the arrival of the first "floorless" all-electronic options exchange, International Securities Exchange (ISE). Located in New York, ISE was the first new securities exchange approved by U.S. regulators in 27 years. ISE claimed that it would bring greater liquidity, reduced costs, and transaction efficiency to the equity options market through state-of-the-art technology and a new market model built on lower overhead costs.

ISE opened with just three option classes (on Alcoa, LSI Logic Corp and SBC Communications) and saw very slow growth in its first months. Some CBOE members, along with those from other exchanges, quickly discounted ISE—only to be surprised when ISE's business began to pick up speed. By the end of 2002, the ISE had become the third largest options exchange with 19.5% market share, and 152.1 million contracts traded that year. At the end of the first quarter in 2004, ISE had become the market leader in non-index options, with 33.6% of that market. Including index-options (for which CBOE held close to a monopoly), ISE was a close second with an overall 29.2% market share to CBOE's 30%.

Several important features distinguished ISE from the traditional floor-based exchanges. Instead of face-to-face floor trading, brokers and the market makers could now interact wholly electronically and anonymously. In the electronic model, members directed their orders to the central order book. The trades were then allocated following exchange specific rules depending on the quote's size and number of members participating. Proponents for electronic trading emphasized the speed with which trades could be executed. A popular claim was that an order that would take floor specialists up to 30 seconds to handle would take the electronic systems 3 seconds.

ISE was the first exchange to allow multiple market makers to send in competing electronic quotes. This real time electronic updating of quotes produced a narrower composite bid/ask spread than the traditional consensus quote disseminated by specialists. ISE operated with a concept called Primary Market Makers (PMMs), for each option class with up to 16 Competing Market Makers trading in these same classes. ISE also allowed for an unlimited number of member firms to send orders to the exchange electronically, for a yearly fee.

Originally founded as a limited liability partnership, the ISE converted in 2002 into a for-profit stock corporation. Trading rights were separated from ownership, which was represented by equity shares. ISE's announced intention to float an initial public offering by the end of 2004 had recently been pushed off until sometime in 2005. Although still impressive, ISE's growth had started to slow down in early 2004, as electronic trading solutions began to spread within the industry.

The Boston Options Exchange (BOX)

A tangible sign of how electronic trading solutions progressed were new market entrants. In February 2004, the Boston Options Exchange (BOX) became America's sixth options exchange, and its second full-electronic exchange. Founded by the Boston Stock Exchange, the Montreal Exchange and the electronic brokerage firm Interactive Brokers, and with various Wall Street firms as minority investors (including Credit Suisse First Boston, J.P. Morgan Chase, Citigroup and UBS), the new exchange achieved a 1.1% market share in its first quarter. This share was greater than the ISE's share after its first two months. BOX rolled out over 200 option classes in its first three months, for a planned final total of 700.

The BOX model was novel in four key ways. First, BOX had no specialists; instead, liquidity was supplied by a pool of market makers responsible for maintaining two-sided quotes in a number of option classes. Second, because BOX was owned by firms and not individual members, there were no seat owners and no limit to the numbers of participants or market makers.[2]

Third, trading rules allowed brokers to internalize their customers' orders. To counter the criticisms of this feature, BOX used a price-improvement process (PIP) mechanism, which allowed brokers to trade against their own orders if they improved the National Best Buy Bid or Offer (NBBO) by at least one cent.[3] The system worked such that the broker had to expose the trade to the market for 3 seconds in an electronic "mini-auction" to allow other traders the chance to better the price. Some voices argued that 3 seconds was not long enough and that internalization should be prohibited all-together by the SEC. BOX itself leaned heavily on their PIP feature, claiming in ads that it would save users $2 per contract.

Fourth, the BOX PIP was conducted in penny increments, as opposed to the trading on existing exchanges in nickel and dime increments. With nickels, the bid-ask spread effectively had a 5 cent-floor; with penny increments, the floor narrowed to 1 cent. BOX argued that penny increments reduced the bid-ask spread to the benefit of investors. However, critics (mostly other exchanges and market makers) contended that penny increments would overload the quoting system, provide a disincentive for market makers

---

[2] BOX charged a transaction fee that varied by volume, operating on a "pay as you trade" basis with a flat $0.20 per contract fee.

[3] The NBBO was established by comparing the bids and offers at the five other U.S. options exchanges at any given point in time.

to quote aggressively (since they could preemptively step in front of the best bid or offer by going just a penny better) and ultimately reduce liquidity. "When stocks were quoted in pennies, we saw reduced liquidity and I believe this will be the same in options," said a market maker. Nevertheless, in order to compete, the other exchanges filed for SEC approval to adopt similar measures. By mid-2004 the SEC was still refusing to allow any of the exchanges to quote in penny increments.

Industry observers generally thought it too soon to predict whether BOX would succeed or not.

Potential Foreign Competitors

Over recent years, several foreign competitors had entered the U.S. market. Recently, in February 2004, the Swiss-German derivatives exchange Eurex attacked the futures market by launching Eurex US, a Chicago-based all-electronic U.S. futures exchange. Their main target was CBOT's monopoly on trading U.S. Treasury bond and note futures. Future development could include offering options as well.

Eurex was the world's biggest derivatives market in 2004. It offered mainly U.S. and European fixed income and index derivatives (futures and options). Like the BOX, it utilized a "flat-and-open" access market model. Eurex had been created in December 1996 through the merger of the Deutsche Terminbörse (DTB) and the Swiss Options and Financial Futures Exchange (SOFFEX). Eurex was owned by the Swiss Exchange and the German stock exchange operator Deutsche Börse AG, a public company with vast financial resources that far exceeded those of any U.S. options exchange. DuFour believed, however, that Eurex might be too late in attacking the U.S. market. He said,

> They probably missed the window. By now, their all-electronic niche is already taken by ISE and BOX. It seems like they started late, and that they also underestimated the regulatory problem of operating in a multi-exchange environment under the SEC.

According to DuFour another potential competitor could be Eurex's European rival Euronext.Liffe. The London-based exchange had also been trying to wrestle market share away from CME and CBOT in key U.S. financial futures products, for instance by launching electronically traded Eurodollar contracts.

THE OPTIONS TRADING INDUSTRY IN 2004— AND CBOE'S PLACE IN IT

By 2004, electronic trading represented the majority of all options trades. Most orders on U.S. markets were already sent to the exchanges electronically and a significant portion of them were being filled in automatic execution systems. After the success of ISE, all the traditional exchanges were adopting varying forms of electronic trading. CBOE had introduced the first parts of its own Hybrid Trading System in 2001 and by 2003, 59% of all contracts were electronically executed. Some market participants believed that as much as two-thirds of volume could be executed electronically within five years.

In a parallel development, firms acting as designated market specialist (whether called DPMs at CBOE, PMMs at ISE or something else) were exiting the business because of increased costs and competition and less financial rewards (as seen in much tighter spreads). The CBOE saw their number of specialist firms fall from 42 in 2001 to 24 in 2003. (On the smaller Pacific Exchange, there were in 2003 only eight specialist firms versus 44 in 1998.) To CBOE it was clear that the previous sharp distinction between the liquidity providing specialists and the order flow providers had been removed, as the latter could now on ISE trade as market makers on their own orders. Many of the exiting specialist firms, finding that their obligations as specialists now outweighed the privileges, appeared to become competing market makers instead. Said DuFour, "It often appears that the privileges of being a market maker no longer compensate for the obligations and many participants feel that they have a better advantage by being a price taker than a price maker." Some market veterans feared that the market's liquidity would be hurt by the concentration of specialists firms.

Many analysts believed six options exchanges are more than the market needed. Consolidation rumors were frequent, but so far no acquisitions had taken place. While consolidation seemed to make sense, the large number of seat owners with often disparate interests made completing transactions difficult. The CBOE management knew that before looking into acquisitions they would almost certainly have to consider demutualization[4] and how to separate trading rights from equity and convert the exchange to a stock corporation. A shareholder structure would make acquisitions easier to carry out and open the door for equity partnerships, bond issuance or even a public stock offering. The neighboring Chicago Mercantile Exchange had in 2002 completed one of the year's most successful initial public offerings. Other options exchanges had also started the process, with PHLX and PCX eliminating seats in exchange for shares of exchange stock. However, because its membership structure was intertwined with the CBOT, any demutualization for the CBOE would be especially difficult.

The intensified competition had benefited investors and contributed to the growing popularity of options. Most option spreads now ranged from $0.10 to $0.20. (See Exhibit 6 for the most active options and their spreads on 27 April 2004.) Also, intermarket linkage had created greater transparency, and arguably greater liquidity. The recent world events and high market volatility had caused investors to diversify their investment portfolios, including options and other investment classes. As a result, options volume ended at record levels in 2003 and was up another 67% in the first quarter of 2004.

Nevertheless, from their position as a market leader, CBOE had by 2004 lived through some difficult years. Fiscal year 2002 had been especially tough, with a rare $5.6 million loss, and with transaction revenue per trade decreasing to $.30—a close to 50% reduction from its historical ranges of $.40 to $.45.[5] CBOE quickly pared its staff positions by 160, to 720, and omitted bonuses for fiscal year 2002. These cost saving moves helped the exchange regain profitability in 2003.

Through the last few years, only an increase in index options trading had helped CBOE maintain its leading position in the market, over the new number two, ISE. Overall, index options represented the fastest growing segment of the options market. In 2003, for instance, the overall market for index options grew 20.1% with the CBOE's index volume growing 17.5%. (Exhibit 7 gives market data on index options.) The CBOE maintained its exclusive licensing arrangement with the S&P, DOW and Russell 2000, obliging investors to trade options based on these indexes on CBOE. Competing exchanges estimated that this exclusivity resulted in $13.1 million of uncontested transaction fees. Highly contested by other exchanges, the agreement was challenged by ISE,

---

[4] A term for changing the structure of an organization from a membership structure to a corporate form with share holders.

[5] Transaction fees per contract, which were charged by the exchange, should not be confused with the bid/ask spread, which was charged by market makers.

EXHIBIT 6

THE MOST ACTIVE OPTIONS AND THEIR SPREADS ON 27 APRIL 2004

Symbol	Name	Volume 27 April 2004	Average Option Spread
GNTA	GENTA INC	243,974	$ 0.21
FON	SPRINT CORP	113,618	$ 0.13
EBAY	EBAY INC	111,711	$ 0.26
MSFT	MICROSOFT CORP	80,828	$ 0.12
IMCL	IMCLONE SYSTEMS	74,190	$ 0.28
MOT	MOTOROLA INC	69,765	$ 0.12
X	UNITED STATES STEEL CORP	66,475	$ 0.16
INTC	INTEL CORP	62,094	$ 0.12
YHOO	YAHOO! INC	61,484	$ 0.17
LU	LUCENT TECHNOLOGIES INC	56,895	$ 0.12
TWX	TIME WARNER INC	55,618	$ 0.11
OSIP	OSI PHARMACEUTICALS INC	47,754	$ 0.73
ELN	ELAN CORP PLC - SPONS ADR	44,877	$ 0.16
DELL	DELL INC	44,029	$ 0.12
F	FORD MOTOR CO	40,757	$ 0.13
CMCSA	COMCAST CORP-CL A	39,775	$ 0.12
DNA	GENENTECH INC	35,890	$ 0.37
AMZN	AMAZON.COM INC	34,518	$ 0.22
NT	NORTEL NETWORKS CORP	31,329	$ 0.09
AMAT	APPLIED MATERIALS INC	31,231	$ 0.12

Source: CBOE.

which went to the SEC, claiming unfair monopoly advantages. CBOE management had vowed to protect its option licenses. Brodsky told the options industry's annual conference in April 2003,

> The last time I checked, there is still a law in the United States that if you make a contract that relates to exclusivity, you have rights to it. We'll vigorously protect these contract rights, whether it is with the SEC or the Supreme Court of the United States.

In the end, CBOE felt confident in its position and maintained its exclusive index offerings, since, as DuFour put it,

> Despite massive lobbying by the other exchanges nothing happened. There is a clear distinction between securities regulation and property rights. And the index providers, themselves, are not likely to discontinue exclusive contracts as these contracts are a significant source of revenue for them.

CBOE continued to introduce new products, launching several each year. In 2002, the exchange added, for instance, options on DIAMONDS, which were shares in an

EXHIBIT 7

MARKET DATA ON INDEX OPTIONS (IN MILLIONS UNLESS OTHERWISE NOTED)

| | Volume of Index Options | | | | | | | | Growth over last year | | CBOE | Index % |
	CBOE	AMEX	PHLX	PCX	ISE	NYSE	NASD	Total	Market	CBOE	Share	of Options
2003	110.9	37.9	23.4	15.0	19.2			206.4	20.1%	17.5%	53.7%	22.7%
2002	94.4	40.8	10.5	14.1	12.1			171.8	55.0%	81.4%	54.9%	22.0%
2001	52.0	37.3	8.4	7.0	6.2			110.8	65.5%	9.7%	46.9%	14.2%
2000	47.4	15.7	3.9	0.0	—			67.0	7.5%	15.7%	70.8%	9.2%
1999	56.2	2.8	3.2	0.0				62.3	−16.8%	−17.7%	90.3%	12.3%
1998	68.3	3.3	3.1	0.0				74.8	−4.3%	−4.0%	91.3%	18.4%
1997	71.1	4.2	2.8	0.1		0.0		78.2	−15.4%	−16.7%	91.0%	22.1%
1996	85.4	4.5	2.5	0.0		0.0		92.4	−14.2%	−15.8%	92.4%	31.4%
1995	101.4	3.5	2.8	0.1		0.0		107.8	−11.0%	−11.6%	94.1%	37.6%
1994	114.7	3.7	2.5	0.1		0.0		121.1	38.5%	40.6%	94.8%	43.0%
1993	81.6	4.5	1.2	0.2		0.0		87.4	5.1%	6.8%	93.3%	37.6%
1992	76.4	6.2	0.4	0.1		0.1		83.2	−0.5%	0.1%	91.8%	41.2%
1991	76.4	6.0	0.4	0.7		0.2		83.7	−5.1%	−5.6%	91.3%	42.1%
1990	80.9	6.6	0.2	0.1		0.3		88.2	19.3%	25.2%	91.8%	42.0%
1989	64.6	8.3	0.2	0.2		0.6		73.9	4.1%	3.8%	87.5%	32.6%
1988	62.3	7.5	0.2	0.3		0.7		71.0	−45.3%	−42.5%	87.7%	36.2%
1987	108.4	18.2	0.5	0.5		2.2		129.7	−6.3%	−5.6%	83.5%	42.5%
1986	114.8	18.3	1.4	0.1		3.8	0.0	138.5	25.8%	26.4%	82.9%	47.9%
1985	90.8	12.4	2.3	0.1		4.3	0.1	110.0	45.3%	41.1%	82.5%	47.2%
1984	64.4	7.0	0.1	0.2		4.1		75.8	440.5%	503.6%	85.0%	38.9%
1983	10.7	2.7	0.0	—		0.7		14.0			76.1%	9.3%

Source: Compiled by casewriters from CBOE data.

exchange-traded fund that tracked the performance of the Dow Jones Industrial Average. Diamond options became one of the CBOE's top five actively traded index products. (See Exhibit 8 for CBOE's product line.) In November 2002, CBOE joined CBOT and CME in creating "One Chicago" to trade single stock futures. CBOE took further steps in the futures arena, launching its own all-electronic futures exchange, the CBOE Futures Exchange (CFE), in March 2004, that offered trading in proprietary futures products, including futures on the CBOE S&P 500 Volatility Index (VIX).

In 2004 CBOE had resumed the administration of a payment for order flow plan on behalf of its members. Despite its strong opposition to the practice, the Board concluded that payment was a commercial reality that the Exchange could not ignore. In a written statement, Brodsky clarified that the exchange remained opposed to payments, but they were "often the deciding factor for brokerage firms routing orders. CBOE is compelled to assist its members in implementing a payment for order flow plan in order to remain competitive." Still, CBOE continued to petition the SEC to outlaw payment for order flows, as well as the practice of internalization. Commented DuFour,

EXHIBIT 8

CBOE PRODUCT LINE

Products by Product Groups

Equity Options
Equity Options
Equity LEAPS

Broad Based Index Options
DJX - Dow Jones Industrial Average
Dow Jones Industrial Average LEAPS
OEX® - American-style S&P 100® Index
OEX® - American-style S&P100® Index LEAPS
XEO® - European-style S&P 100® Index
XEO® - European-style S&P 100® LEAPS
SPX - S&P 500® Index
SPX - (Reduced-value) LEAPS
SPL - S&P Long-Dated
SML - S&P® SmallCap 600 Index
NDX - Nasdaq-100® Index
MNXSM - CBOE Mini-NDX Index
MML - CBOE Mini-NDX Long-Dated

Dow Jones Index Options
DTX - Dow Jones Transportation Average
Dow Jones Transportation Average LEAPS
DUX - Dow Jones Utility Average
DJR - Dow Jones Equity REIT Index
MUT - Dow 10 Index
ECM - Dow Jones Internet Commerce Index

Options on ETFs
AGG - Options on iShares® Lehman Aggregate
    Bond Fund
DGT - streetTRACKS®-DJ Global Titans
    Index Fund
DIA - Options on DIAMONDS®
EFA - Options on iShares MSCI EAFE®
IBB - iShares® Nasdaq® Biotechnology
IDU - iShares DJ® US Utilities Sector
IEF - iShares Lehman 7-10 Year Treasury Bond Fund
IGM - iShares Goldman Sachs® Technology Index
IGN - iShares® Goldman Sachs Netwg Index Fund
IGV - iShares Goldman Sachs Softwar Index Fund
IGW - iShares Goldman Sachs Semicon Index Fund
IWB - iShares Russell 1000® Index Fund
IWD - iShares Russell 1000 Value Index Fund
IWF - iShares Russell 1000 Growth Index Fund
IWM - iShares Russell 2000® Index Fund
IWN - iShares Russell 2000 Value Index Fund
IWO - iShares Russell 2000 Growth Index Fund
IWP - iShares Russell Midcap® Grwth Index Fund
IWR - iShares Russell Midcap Index Fund
IWS - iShares Russell Midcap Value Index Fund
IVV - iShares Russell 3000® Index Fund
IWW - iShares Russell 3000 Value Index Fund
IWZ - iShares Russell 3000 Growth Index Fund
IYE - iShares Trust - DJ US Energy Index Fund

CBOE's Options on HOLDRs
BDH - Broadband HOLDRs Trust
HHH - Internet HOLDRs Trust
IAH - Internet Architect HOLDRs Trust OIH -
    Oil Services HOLDRs Trust
PPH - Pharmaceutical HOLDRs Trust
RKH - Regional Bank HOLDRs Trust
RTH - Retail HOLDRs Trust
SMH - Semiconductor HOLDRs Trust
SWH - Software HOLDRs Trust
TTH - Telecom HOLDRs Trust
UTH - Utilities HOLDRs Trust
WMH - Wireless HOLDRs Trust

Interest Rate Options
IRX - 13 Week Treasury Bill
FVX - 5 Year Treasury Note
TNX - 10 Year Treasury Note
TYX - 30-Year Treasury Bond

Structured Products
DSB - S. S. Barney Hold Inc. DJIASM Index
    Equity Linked Notes
NSB - S.S. Barney Holdings Inc. S&P 500®
    Callable Equity Linked Notes
KSB - Salomon Smith Barney Holdings Inc.
    S&P 500® Equity Linked Notes

(Continued)

571

EXHIBIT 8 (Continued)

CBOE PRODUCT LINE

Products by Product Groups

Russell Index Options

RUI - Russell 1000® Index
RLG - Russell 1000® Growth Index
RLV - Russell 1000® Value Index
RUT - Russell 2000® Index
RUO - Russell 2000® Growth Index
RUJ - Russell 2000® Value Index
RUA - Russell 3000® Index
RAG - Russell 3000® Growth Index

IYH - iShares Trust-DJ US Healthcare Index Fund
LQD - iShares GS$ InvesTop Corp. Bond Fund
OEF - Options on iShares® S&P 100® Index Fund
QQQ - Nasdaq-100® Index Tracking Stock
SHY - iShares Lehman 1-3 Year Treas Bond Fund
TLT - iShares Lehman 20+ Year Treas Bond Fund
XLB - Materials Select Sector SPDR
XLE - Energy Select Sector SPDR
XLF - Financial Select Sector SPDR
XLI - Industrial Select Sector SPDR
XLK - Technology Select Sector SPDR
XLP - Consumer Staples
Select Sector SPDR
XLU - Utilities Select Sector SPDR
XLV - Health Care Select Sector SPDR
XLY - Consumer Discretionary Select Sector SPDR

Goldman Sachs Technology Index Options

GHA - GSTI™ Hardware Index
GIN - GSTI™ Internet Index
GIP - GSTI™ Multimedia Networking Index
GSM - GSTI™ Semiconductor Index
GSO - GSTI™ Software Index
GSV - GSTI™ Services Index
GTC - GSTI™ Composite Index

Morgan Stanley Index Options

MVR - Morgan Stanley Retail Index
MVB - Morgan Stanley Biotech Index
MGO - Morgan Stanley Oil Services
NFT - Morgan Stanley Multinational Company Index

Source: CBOE.

I'd be very interested in seeing what would happen to our new competitors if the SEC started to address some of the new strategies being used to attract order flow; ISE being the biggest payment for order flow provider and BOX being based on internalization.

In April 2004, CBOE members had (by a margin of 408 against 346 voices) approved management's proposal to initiate a repurchase offer for a significant number of CBOT exercise rights. Although the change still needed SEC's approval, Brodsky explained,

Our membership's approval is an investment in the future of CBOE. Today, when our respective marketplaces demand the utmost in agility and flexibility, this offer is an important step toward increasing the autonomy of both institutions.

CBOE'S ELECTRONIC TRADING INITIATIVE: THE HYBRID TRADING SYSTEM (HyTS)

Of all the strategic actions CBOE had taken recently, launching its own electronic trading model was the most crucial. "Maybe imitation is the sincerest form of flattery," said Brodsky to the press. "The ISE took the best of the existing system, the specialists and market makers, and created a business model that changed the way options are traded. Now we're taking a page from their book."[6] CBOE's Hybrid Trading System was still a unique offering, as it integrated the open outcry forum, aiming at combining the advantages of both types of marketplaces. It gave CBOE customers "point-and-click" access to CBOE's order book and electronic execution against displayed quotes. At the same time the customer or firm could also electronically route their order to the trading floor. CBOE also made available a universal terminal (HyTS) that provided a user other options, futures and stock exchanges, all on a single screen.

Hybrid 1.0

The development of the electronic trading platform had started early. Explained DuFour,

Back in 1999, even before ISE was launched, we knew that we had to reposition CBOE. The membership voted on whether to go all-electronic, stay with the floor based model or adopt a hybrid model. Most members believed at the time that electronic trading would not work for options due to their complexity. However, they did green-light a hybrid model. The most logical decision as a business would probably have been to go directly to screen-based trading, but this would have been inconsistent with the business models of our seat owners and traders. Therefore, the decision was made to move toward a hybrid model allowing owners, traders and management to learn and adjust as we went.

Brodsky added, "You have to understand that people are making their living on the trading floor and fear that electronic trading will put them out of the business. Owners, some of whom are retired traders, often retain a romantic vision of the floor and are adverse to any changes at all."

After the vote, a CBOE member committee was put in charge of defining the screen-based trading platform, named CBOE*direct*. Launched in early 2002, the platform was first used for extended hours trading. It was then augmented in May 2002

---

[6] Dow Jones News Service, 4/30/2003.

with an electronic quoting system, called "Dynamic Quotes with Size," that allowed investors to see real-time prices and sizes for all CBOE options series. In July, more functionality was added with the Large Order Utility (LOU) module, a point-and-click trading application that allowed customers to execute large size orders immediately. (Previously, only smaller orders of less than 50 contracts could be executed instantaneously.) A year later, in June 2003, Hybrid 1.0 was completed with a module that allowed traders to shop an order on the floor to obtain the best price.

Hybrids 1.0 now allowed all market makers at CBOE to "stream" or electronically update their quotes into the trade engine. Customers were able to access the market via the CBOE Order Routing System (ORS) with incoming orders electronically directed for display and execution. Depending on the order and the parameters set by the member firms, orders could be routed to CBOE's Hybrid Trading System, an automatic execution system, a human floor broker or the electronic order book. Exhibit 9 provides a graphical depiction of the trading model.

By January 2004, CBOE's top 600 option classes were traded on the Hybrid platform and about 80% of CBOE's trades in these classes were electronically executed.

EXHIBIT 9

CBOE HYBRID TRADING SYSTEM (HYTS) MODEL, VERSION 1.0

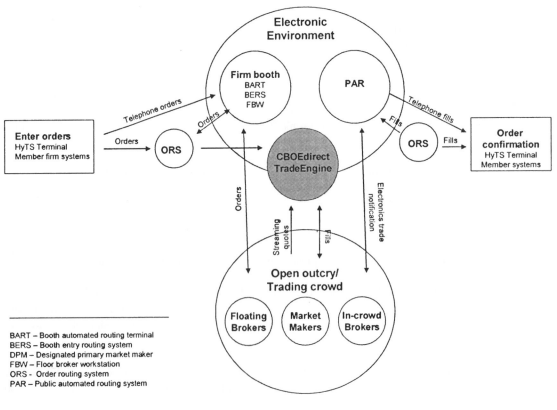

BART – Booth automated routing terminal
BERS – Booth entry routing system
DPM – Designated primary market maker
FBW – Floor broker workstation
ORS - Order routing system
PAR – Public automated routing system

Source: CBOE Annual Report 2003.

Prior to hybrid, about 49% of CBOE's quotes within the top 500 were at the National Bid Best Offer (NBBO) level versus 70% for the ISE. Now, 72% of the quotes were at NBBO. (NBBO was used as a benchmark of the price competitiveness of the exchanges.) The CBOE intended to implement Hybrid in all equity classes by the end of 2004.

DuFour was keen to point out that large and complex orders were still directed to the floor. These larger orders represented 46% of CBOE's total contract volume. Du-Four commented,

> It seems that the floor brokers still have their role to play as they can negotiate with the crowd and shop the order around to test the market. It turns out to be a real advantage to have kept the floor component of the hybrid model.

The Hybrid 2.0 Launch

Even with Hybrid 1.0 in place, there remained several key differences with the new all electronic marketplaces that had to be addressed if CBOE wanted to retain its members and customers. A new version of Hybrid had to be implemented—and CBOE management announced that it would launch Hybrid 2.0 on July 21, 2004, pending a green light from the SEC.

Hybrid 2.0 would include four major changes. First, CBOE would expand its community through the creation of a new class of CBOE members, called Remote Market Makers (RMMs). RMMs would be required to own or lease a CBOE seat, but would be allowed to stream quotes to the CBOE without being present on the trading floor. This new category of market maker was expected to draw additional electronically oriented firms to the CBOE and to enhance the liquidity base and market depth provided by the floor market makers. This would also allow existing floor members to stream quotes while they were away from the trading floor, previously a key difference with the ISE.

Second, the concept of DPMs or specialists would be expanded by creating electronic Designated Primary Market Makers (eDPMs). eDPMs would operate in parallel with the DPM. They would be able to stream quotes into the CBOE remotely in addition to quotes provided by CBOE's on-floor DPMs. In return for fulfilling market-making obligations similar to the DPM's, eDPMs would share in the DPM participation rights and would be offered fee inducements related to volume. CBOE had limited eDPM assignments to no more than four in any given class, and had already selected the first seven firms to be designated as eDPMs. Hybrid 2.0 consolidated e-DPM and RMM quotes and liquidity with that of floor-based market participants. The two new types of members meant that CBOE changed its single specialist model to one of competing specialists. "A huge change, by any measurement," said DuFour.

Third, CBOE would streamline its procedures to allow firms sending orders to the Exchange to designate a particular DPM or eDPM to receive the order. When this designation occurred, the recipient was entitled to a higher participation right. An order-sending firm could also designate orders in which it would like to participate and be assured of a certain percentage of the order. Fourth and final, Hybrid 2.0 revised CBOE's transaction fee structure to provide incentives for members and member firms to bring substantial additional liquidity and business to the CBOE.

A key module of the Hybrid Trading System was the matching algorithm used to distribute trades to market makers and the DPM complex. Called the Ultimate Matching Algorithm (UMA), it allocated orders to competing market makers based on the total number of market makers for a given option and the size of each respective market maker's quote in an option. UMA followed the CBOE practice of giving priority to public customer orders over brokerage orders. UMA was conceived to ensure auto-execution priority and to reward market participants who provided the most competitive price and size. Currently, the DPMs were entitled to 30% of any order (as long as they were at the best price and of sufficient size when the order came in). With Hybrid 2.0, the DPM's participation right was limited to 15% of all orders, the other 15% being shared by the eDPMs. The remaining 70% of an order was available to market makers that were on the market when the order arrived.

CBOE management held several hopes for Hybrid 2.0. The new version should increase competition by introducing competing eDPMs. This should build liquidity and the likelihood that the best option prices would be available on CBOE. Hybrid 2.0 should also make CBOE more attractive for specialist firms acting on other exchanges. For example, a specialist firm that had been the primary market maker in option "X" on PHLX could now choose to leave PHLX and become an eDPM on CBOE. With the continued consolidation and margin pressures on specialist firms, the chance to reduce costs by rationalizing floor presence should be attractive. DuFour said,

> Part of our strategy is to have the largest players concentrate on CBOE. Until now, to be a specialist in the most important classes, the big firms had to spread out over the different exchanges as franchises were limited and it would be impossible to be appointed the specialist in everything. Maintaining operations on multiple exchanges is expensive for the firms and as a result a number of firms encourage consolidation among the exchanges. Putting exchanges together is extremely difficult. When mergers did not happen, specialist firms asked CBOE to provide some sort of a franchise that would justify concentrating more of their business here. Now, with Hybrid 2.0 they can become an eDPM on CBOE and minimize their cost of operating by making markets from a remote location.

Management believed that Hybrid 2.0 would make electronic trading at CBOE very similar to ISE. They also believed that it was important to keep the open outcry method, since it still added value for institutional investors. Although 80% of CBOE's transactions were executed electronically, only about half of the trading volume came from electronic trading. According to CBOE management this was due to the fact that value still existed in physically negotiating large or complex trades, and that adequate functionality simply did not yet exist to do this electronically. Hybrid 2.0 was therefore constructed to supplement and complement the floor, but not replace it. Order-entry firms could still send larger orders directly to the floor to seek price improvement in the crowd. With Hybrid 2.0, CBOE also hoped to draw more business from the Over the Counter (OTC) markets as well, where the biggest and most complex trades often happened.

GOING FORWARD

As Brodsky and DuFour overlooked the CBOE trading floor in June 2004, they took stock of CBOE. Benefiting from a rise in options demand, CBOE had completed an outstanding May with a total of 27,906,821 contracts traded, a 22% increase over its May 2003 volume. May was the ninth consecutive month in which CBOE registered volume gains over year-ago levels. Volumes in equities had risen 6% while index options rose 4%, with options on the S&P 500 Index (SPX) being the most actively traded index options at CBOE with over 4 million contracts.

However, the battle among the exchanges was as fierce as ever. Marketwise, CBOE and ISE were neck-and-neck with a market share of 31.2% versus 30.8% when all types of options where considered. In an apple-to-apple comparison that stripped out index

EXHIBIT 10

ANALYSIS OF 2003 MARKET SHARE: THE EFFECT OF THE EXCLUSIVE LISTING OF INDEXES

	CBOE	AMEX	PHLX	PCX	ISE	Total
Total Options Volume	283,946,495	179,756,014	112,574,473	86,246,572	245,12 1,837	907,858,655
Share	31%	20%	12%	10%	27%	
Index Volume	110,882,000	37,890,000	23,400,000	15,030,000	19,150,0 00	206,352,000
Share	54%	18%	11%	7%	9%	
Options Volume without Index Volume	173,064,495	141,866,014	89,174,473	71,216,572	225,971 ,837	701,506,655
Share	25%	20%	13%	10%	32%	

Source: Compiled and calculated by casewriters based on CBOE data and market data.

options, ISE led with 34% over 25.4%. AMEX was ranking third with a market share of 17.7%, PHLX with 11.4%, PCX with 7.8% and BOX posted 1.16%—a new high in its fourth month of trading. (The situation was similar in 2003, as shown in Exhibit 10.)

To Brodsky and DuFour's relief, the decline in market share seemed to have come to a halt around 30%. They were happy that CBOE would soon launch Hybrid 2.0. They still worried however that they might not be fast enough. The other traditional floor competitors were not sitting still, launching their own electronic platforms, changing their business model and fees, and expanding their product offering. European multi-product competitors were also threatening to start to compete on similar contracts. The electronic trading model had proved its efficiency and it was clear to Brodsky and DuFour that CBOE should continue its development of electronic trading systems. They did wonder, however, whether Hybrid 2.0 had all the required features to make the impact they wanted in the market place. Was there functionality they could and should have included?

There were other issues to consider as well. Assuming that Hybrid 2.0 did fulfill their expectations, was it enough to help CBOE keep its leadership? Would CBOE's outcry function remain a competitive advantage or would an increasingly quiet floor just become too costly? (Already now, on quiet days, traders were joking that the space would make an excellent bowling alley.) Would technology finally be able to handle even the more complex trades or would some investors still prefer the personal interaction of the open outcry auction model? In addition, would CBOE be able to maintain its exclusive index franchises? With the continued shift to electronics and the continued pressure on spreads, what in the end would differentiate the exchanges? And, finally, given the decreasing trade revenue and increasing technology and surveillance costs, should they consider an alliance with any of the other existing or potential competitors?

Any new strategic move or change of CBOE's market or business model would also have to be accepted by their membership and approved by the SEC. This meant that it had to be in line the diverging interests of the over 1,200 individual traders, brokers and member firms but also that it would take a considerable amount of time and briefing to prepare the move. Should they try and simplify this structure and would they have a chance in doing it even if they wanted?

Brodsky and DuFour paused and looked down at the trading floor once more.

32

The International Securities Exchange: New Ground in Options Markets

On Monday, September 23, 2002, David Krell and Gary Katz sat down for a lunch meeting. As the CEO and chief operating officer (COO), respectively, of the International Securities Exchange (ISE), the two executives had a great deal to discuss. First, however, they took a moment to congratulate each other on the exchange's progress. According to a report by The Options Clearing Corporation (OCC), month to date the ISE had 26.03% of the market for trading options on the 506 issues it listed. The ISE had traded a total of 7,361,341 options contracts from September 3, 2002 to September 20, 2002. Its share of trading ISE-listed options put the exchange in first place for September, ahead of the Chicago Board Options Exchange (CBOE), the industry's long-time champion.[1] Feeling somewhat vindicated by the exchange's recent success, Krell and Katz thought back to the ISE's early days.

The ISE's creators had known that, for a market to be successful, it had to attract enough participants to act as buyers and sellers. On the other hand, nothing attracted buyers and sellers more than a successful market. You had to build the egg, but you could not ignore the chicken either. Krell and Katz had begun investigating the prospects for building the ISE, an all-electronic options exchange, in 1997. No mysterious voice had whispered to them, "If you build it, they will come." Rather, there had been a collective plea from the discount broker community for Krell and Katz to put their expertise to use and bring greater efficiency to the options market. Even with such strong support from the retail side, the idea of a new, "floorless" options exchange had been met with a great deal of skepticism. Would the ISE be able to attract enough partici-

Professor George Chacko and Research Associate Eli Peter Strick prepared this case. Professor Chacko would like to thank Bruce Goldberg, Senior Vice President of Marketing at the ISE, for his valuable contributions during the casewriting process. HBS cases are developed solely as the basis for class discussion. Cases are not intended to serve as endorsements, sources of primary data, or illustrations of effective or ineffective management.

[1] The ISE had 23.00% of all trading equity options during the same period, making it third overall behind the CBOE (27.50%) and the American Stock Exchange (AMEX) (25.00%).

pants to offer the liquidity investors demanded? Was the technology for such a demanding venture actually available? There had not even been a new exchange approved by the Securities and Exchange Commission (SEC) since the CBOE in 1973. Even as the benefits of a completely electronic exchange had become clearer, many professionals in the industry thought the ISE would be lucky if it captured 5% of the market's trading volume away from the four already-established floor exchanges in the United States.

Krell and Katz understood where the uncertainty had come from. Still, the recent accomplishments of the ISE did not surprise them. They had succeeded in designing an innovative approach to trading options, and the market had responded as expected. Then again, Krell and Katz knew there was further room for change in the options market, and they planned on remaining pioneers in the industry. For instance, on the menu for their lunch meeting was a discussion of quote sizes (the number of contracts available at a "quoted" price). Right now, the number of contracts available for an exchange member to trade depended on the characterization of the customer. This had many people in the industry debating how "firm" market quotes should be. Should the same size be available for all types of customers?

THE INTERNATIONAL SECURITIES EXCHANGE: COMPANY DESCRIPTION

In May of 2000, after receiving the green light from the SEC, the ISE became the first entirely electronic securities exchange for trading equity options in the United States. The ISE's mission was to bring greater liquidity, cost reduction, and transaction efficiency to the equity options market by implementing its state-of-the-art technology and unique market model. By eliminating the high overhead costs associated with the traditional floor exchange model, the ISE was able to pass those cost savings to its clients. Additionally, by automating many market functions electronically, the exchange was able to reduce trading fees even more.

For the ISE's greatly anticipated opening on May 26, 2000, its management intentionally restricted its trading to options on three stocks, each with only a modest average daily trading volume.[2] Once the exchange had proven its technology worthy of further activity, it steadily increased its trading capacity, adding roughly 25 new names to its list every month. By the end of 2000, the exchange listed the 178 most actively traded equity options on the market. The ISE had grown to 81 employees and generated over $8 million in revenue with assets of $23 million. (Exhibit 1 shows the number of options listed on the ISE increasing over time. Exhibits 2a and 2b give the ISE's balance sheet and income statement, respectively, for the year ending 2001. Exhibits 3a, 3b, and 3c show the financial statements for the CBOE.)

Forming the ISE

The roots of the ISE traced back to 1996 when William A. Porter, the founder and then-chairman of the online brokerage house E*Trade, and his colleague Marty Averbuch began researching the possibilities for making equity options more affordable to trade for retail investors. At the time, options markets were characterized by limited competition, high transaction costs for trading, and, as a result, only mediocre liquidity. Porter and Averbuch had first tried to work with the existing options exchanges to

---

[2] The first three options traded by the ISE were SBC, LSI, and AA, with first-day trading volumes of 2,371, 1,649, and 1,282, respectively.

EXHIBIT 1

NUMBER OF EQUITY OPTIONS LISTED ON THE ISE

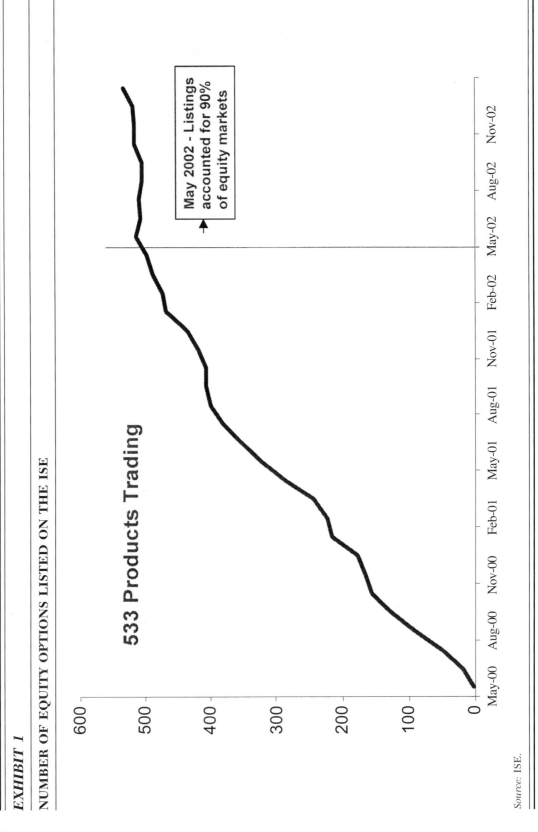

Source: ISE.

EXHIBIT 2A

ISE FINANCIAL HIGHLIGHTS: BALANCE SHEET

Year Ending December 31 ($ in 000s)	2001
Assets:	
Current Assets	$27,035
Investments	$2,965
Fixed and Other Assets	$6,131
Total Assets	$36,131
Liabilities and Members' Equity:	
Liabilities	$26,093
Members' Equity	$10,038
Total Liabilities and Members' Equity	$36,131

Source: ISE 2001 Annual Report.

see what could be accomplished through them. However, due to the monopolistic structure and environment of the options market at that time, the exchanges were unwilling to lower their fees for executing options orders. The lack of assistance from the options exchanges available coupled with the combined entrepreneurial expertise of Porter and Averbuch set the stage for the creation of the ISE.

Porter and Averbuch had not been alone in their desire to see the expense of options trading lowered. Other major players in the broker/dealer community voiced similar concerns and had pledged their support. Combined, these firms provided a significant portion of the retail order flow to the options exchanges. While it would have been less costly to trade with one another through their own accounts, circumventing the

EXHIBIT 2B

ISE FINANCIAL HIGHLIGHTS: STATEMENT OF OPERATIONS

Year Ending December 31 ($ in 000s)	2001
Revenue:	
Transaction Fees	$29,403
Software & Access	$12,201
Other	$1,404
Total Revenue	$43,008
Expenses:	
Compensation and Benefits	$16,479
Technology and Communications	$25,397
Other Expenses	$9,536
Total Expenses	$51,412

Source: ISE 2001 Annual Report.

EXHIBIT 3A

THE CHICAGO BOARD OPTIONS EXCHANGE FINANCIAL STATEMENTS: INCOME STATEMENT

	2001	2000
Revenues:		
Transaction fees	$96,091,800	$114,460,300
Other member fees	$24,612,500	$23,263,000
Communications fees	$21,538,600	$22,580,700
Regulatory fees	$10,835,500	$8,095,400
Interest	$1,347,800	$1,890,900
Equity in income of CSE[a]	$716,700	$415,900
Other	$2,670,800	$4,635,100
Total Revenues	$157,813,700	$175,341,300
Expenses:		
Employee costs	$67,411,600	$69,003,700
Outside services	$17,451,300	$17,351,600
Facilities costs	$3,993,000	$3,914,300
Communications	$879,600	$781,000
Data processing	$15,263,700	$12,118,600
Travel and promotional expenses	$6,452,100	$6,279,900
Depreciation and amortization	$24,634,200	$21,985,200
Settlement expense	$0	$16,000,000
Royalty fees	$7,396,600	$6,430,400
Other	$2,421,000	$2,665,500
Total Expenses	$145,903,100	$156,530,200
Income Before Income Taxes	$11,910,600	$18,811,100
Provision (Benefit) for Income Taxes:		
Current	($2,943,000)	$8,401,600
Deferred	$7,717,700	($446,900)
Total Provision (Benefit) for Income Taxes	$4,774,700	$7,954,700
Net Income	$7,135,900	$10,856,400
Retained Earnings at Beginning of Year	$102,154,500	$91,298,100
Retained Earnings at End of Year	$109,290,400	$102,154,500

[a]Cincinnati Stock Exchange (CSE).

Source: CBOE Annual Report, ⟨http://www.cboe.com/AboutCBOE/AnnualReport2001/financialsummary.asp⟩.

---

exchanges, creating a "third market" was not a feasible plan for options as it had been with trading stock.[3]

Since the counterparty/transaction risk of options contracts is separate from the underlying company, "standardized" options are subject to a formal clearing procedure. While the contracts originate on exchanges, all standardized options are issued and

---

[3] Porter had previously been successful creating efficiencies in the stock market through his work with electronic communication networks (ECNs) and, specifically, E°Trade. The strong relationships he had formed with members of the broker/dealer community supported his conquest of the options market.

EXHIBIT 3B

THE CHICAGO BOARD OPTIONS EXCHANGE FINANCIAL STATEMENTS: BALANCE SHEET

Assets	2001	2000
Current Assets:		
Cash and cash equivalents	$9,740,200	$2,200,800
Investments available-for-sale	$0	$20,132,800
Accounts receivable	$22,212,200	$17,451,200
Income taxes receivable	$3,313,400	$3,328,600
Prepaid medical benefits	$926,700	$16,400
Other prepaid expenses	$4,185,500	$4,913,600
Other current assets	$554,400	$515,500
Total Current Assets	$40,932,400	$48,558,900
Investments in Affiliates	$10,848,700	$10,165,400
Land	$4,914,300	$4,914,300
Property and Equipment:		
Building	$57,608,500	$57,608,500
Furniture and equipment	$159,011,700	$138,297,000
Software development work in progress	$26,219,600	$17,447,700
Less accumulated depreciation and amortization	($139,434,000)	($121,472,500)
Total Property and Equipment-Net	$103,405,800	$91,880,700
Other Assets:		
Goodwill[a]	$2,145,300	$2,902,500
Data processing software and other assets[b]	$14,783,000	$12,489,100
Total Other Assets-Net	$16,928,300	$15,391,600
Total	$177,029,500	$170,910,900

Liabilities and Members' Equity	2001	2000
Current Liabilities:		
Accounts payable and accrued expenses	$13,746,800	$19,560,200
Settlement payable	$0	$5,333,300
Marketing fee payable	$9,173,400	$0
Membership transfer deposits	$0	$1,465,500
Other deposits	$416,000	$378,800
Total Current Liabilities	$23,336,200	$26,737,800
Long-term Liabilities:		
Long-term settlement obligations	$5,333,300	$10,666,700
Deferred income taxes	$18,136,000	$10,418,300
Total Long-term Liabilities	$23,469,300	$21,085,000
Total Liabilities	$46,805,500	$47,822,800
Members' Equity:		
Memberships	$20,933,600	$20,933,600
Retained earnings	$109,290,400	$102,154,500
Total Members' Equity	$130,224,000	$123,088,100
Total	$177,029,500	$170,910,900

[a]Less accumulated amortization—2001, $3,130,200; 2000, $2,373,000.

[b]Less accumulated amortization—2001, $21,762,600; 2000, $15,881,200.

EXHIBIT 3C

THE CHICAGO BOARD OPTIONS EXCHANGE FINANCIAL STATEMENTS: STATEMENT OF CASH FLOWS

	2001	2000
Cash Flows from Operating Activities:		
Net income	$7,135,900	$10,856,400
Adjustments to reconcile net income to net cash flows from operating activities:		
Depreciation and amortization	$24,634,200	$21,985,200
Long-term settlement obligations	($5,333,400)	$10,666,700
Deferred income taxes	$7,717,700	($446,900)
Equity in income of CSE[a]	($716,700)	($415,900)
Changes in current assets and liabilities:		
Accounts receivable	($4,761,000)	$515,300
Income taxes	$15,200	($3,468,900)
Prepaid medical benefits	($910,300)	$747,400
Other prepaid expenses	$728,100	($994,900)
Other current assets	($38,900)	($88,300)
Accounts payable and accrued expenses	($5,813,400)	($2,545,500)
Settlement payable	($5,333,300)	$5,333,300
Marketing fee payable	$9,173,400	$0
Membership transfer deposits	($1,465,500)	($1,195,500)
Other deposits	$37,200	($34,900)
Net Cash Flows from Operating Activities	$25,069,200	$40,913,500
Cash Flows from Investing Activities:		
Capital and other assets expenditures	($37,662,600)	($39,803,700)
Investments available-for-sale:		
Proceeds from maturities	$115,751,800	$187,285,300
Purchases	($95,619,000)	($196,807,700)
Net Cash Flows from Investing Activities	($17,529,800)	($49,326,100)
Net Increase (Decrease) in Cash and Cash Equivalents	$7,539,400	($8,412,600)
Cash and Cash Equivalents at Beginning of Year	$2,200,800	$10,613,400
Cash and Cash Equivalents at End of Year	$9,740,200	$2,200,800

[a]Cincinnati Stock Exchange (CSE).

Source: CBOE Annual Report, ⟨http://www.cboe.com/AboutCBOE/AnnualReport2001/financialsummary.asp⟩.

guaranteed by OCC. This property allows for the contracts to be fungible (i.e., purchased on one exchange but tradable on other recognized options exchanges). As a result, for standardized options contracts to be universally tradable, they had to originate on a national securities exchange that was a member of OCC. Therefore, Porter, Averbuch, and their consortium of broker/dealers discovered it would be necessary to create an actual registered securities exchange if they were to successfully impact the market.

Krell and Katz had been managers of the options division at the New York Stock Exchange (NYSE). After leaving the NYSE in May 1997, they had founded K-Squared Research, a specialized organization that offered education, training, and consulting on derivatives and structured products and services to the broker/dealer community. Having found the industry expertise they needed to proceed, Porter and Averbuch hired

K-Squared Research to investigate the possibilities for a new exchange. Upon joining the project, Krell and Katz examined many of the modern exchanges around the world and met with a broad selection of exchange software and hardware providers. They became increasingly convinced that an all-electronic exchange would be the best avenue for the group to pursue. With the conclusion of their research efforts, the ISE was founded in September 1997 with Porter as the chairman, Krell as the CEO, and Katz as senior vice president of marketing and business development.[4]

During their extensive research on the technological demands of an electronic options exchange, Krell and Katz entered into negotiations with OM, a Swedish company based in Stockholm that specialized in market-transaction technology. Since 1985, OM had been working with a variety of marketplaces and financial exchanges to develop their operating software. Serving as a partner to its clients, the company took an active role in the operation and management of the systems it created. In 1998, the ISE officially selected OM to provide the trading technology for the first floorless options exchange in the United States. The OM CLICK® exchange system was chosen for its combination of reliability, security, and efficiency. Furthermore, the CLICK® system was flexible enough so that it could grow and change along with the ISE's operations and business strategy.

In accordance with the creation of the ISE, Adirondack Trading Partners (ATP) was formed to fund the design, development, and implementation of the new exchange. Averbuch took on the lead role as president and CEO of ATP. ATP was a syndicate of firms that purchased all the memberships in order to provide ISE with the initial capital necessary for the expenditures associated with establishing an exchange, such as developing a trading system, purchasing hardware, creating a regulatory structure, and hiring staff. ATP then sold the memberships to firms that would become the market makers on the exchange.[5]

THE OPTIONS MARKET

In securities markets, an option provides its investor with the right to buy or sell a specific security for a specified price during a certain period. The name "option" is appropriate because option holders are not obligated to buy or sell a security but, rather, have the choice or option to do so.[6] Options are also referred to as derivative instruments because their value is determined by, or "derived" from, the value of some other security, interest rate, index, and so on (referred to as "the underlying"). Most options are classified as either call options (calls) or put options (puts). For options "written" on equity securities, a call gives the right to buy stock, while a put gives the right to sell stock.[7] For example, a standardized "American" call option written on Microsoft with a "strike price" of $100 and an expiration date in three months gives its holder the right to purchase 100 shares of Microsoft at $100 (per share) at any time during the next three months.[8] Likewise, a put option with the same terms gives its holder the right to sell shares of Microsoft for $100 (per share) anytime during the next three months.

---

[4] Katz became COO of the ISE in February 2001.

[5] These memberships allowed firms to become ISE primary market makers (PMMs) and competitive market makers (CMMs). The different roles and responsibilities of these ISE market makers are described later in the case.

[6] "Holders" buy options, while "writers" sell options.

[7] In U.S. markets, one options contract provides the right to buy or sell 100 shares of stock.

[8] An "American option" allows an investor to exercise the option before its expiration date, while a "European option" can only be exercised at maturity.

EXHIBIT 4

EXAMPLE OF BID AND ASK PRICES FOR EQUITY OPTIONS TRADING ON XYZ COMPANY STOCK

Calls	Bid	Ask	Volume	Puts	Bid	Ask	Volume
XYZ 02 OCT 70	6.40	6.50	200	XYZ 02 OCT 70	0.25	0.30	140
XYZ 02 OCT 75	2.65	2.75	123	XYZ 02 OCT 75	1.50	1.60	165
XYZ 02 OCT 80	0.70	0.80	190	XYZ 02 OCT 80	4.50	4.70	110
XYZ 02 NOV 60	16.40	16.50	130	XYZ 02 NOV 60	0.15	0.25	273
XYZ 02 NOV 65	11.70	11.90	200	XYZ 02 NOV 65	0.65	0.70	220
XYZ 02 NOV 70	7.90	8.00	178	XYZ 02 NOV 70	1.75	1.85	160
XYZ 02 NOV 75	4.90	5.00	100	XYZ 02 NOV 75	3.60	3.75	165
XYZ 02 NOV 80	3.00	3.20	250	XYZ 02 NOV 80	6.50	6.60	180

Source: Casewriter.

Unlike stocks, standardized options do not originate from the company on which their value is based.[9] In fact, most of the time options are bought and sold on a company's stock without the company having any involvement. Hence, the amount of options trading on a particular company is a result of the market's interest and not the company's capital needs.

Since multiple parties are able to write options on the same stock and the contractual terms of options contracts vary, many different options often exist for the same underlying stock name. Options with the same underlying company stock are separated into "series," groups of options with the different strike prices and maturity dates. For example, one series might be the "January $50 Dell calls," or all calls written on Dell with a strike price of $50 and a January expiration date.[10] (Exhibit 4 shows hypothetical bid and ask prices of different options series for company XYZ as they might appear on an exchange.)

A number of different parties are involved in the options market, including individual investors ("retail investors"), financial institutions, market makers, and the exchanges. Each party plays a particular role as part of the market and, as a result, deals with options differently in their operations.

Options Investors: Retail versus Institutional

Options investors were generally placed into one of two categories: "retail" or "institutional." Retail investors, or individual investors, made up the largest portion of the investor base in the options market. Able to execute orders through relationships with a variety of brokerages, retail investors used equity options as part of their investment strategies. With the creation and expansion of online brokerage accounts, retail investors were able to trade options with greater ease using the Internet. (Exhibits 5a, 5b, and 5c

---

[9] Exchange-traded "standardized" options are different from, and should not be mistaken for, employee stock options, which are issued by companies to their employees as a form of compensation.

[10] The expiration year usually does not need to be specified because most options have expiration dates of less than a year.

EXHIBIT 5A

EXCHANGE TRADE VOLUME IN 2000 (DATA STARTING MAY 26)

2000 (from May 26th) Exchange Trade Volume Separated By Trade Type

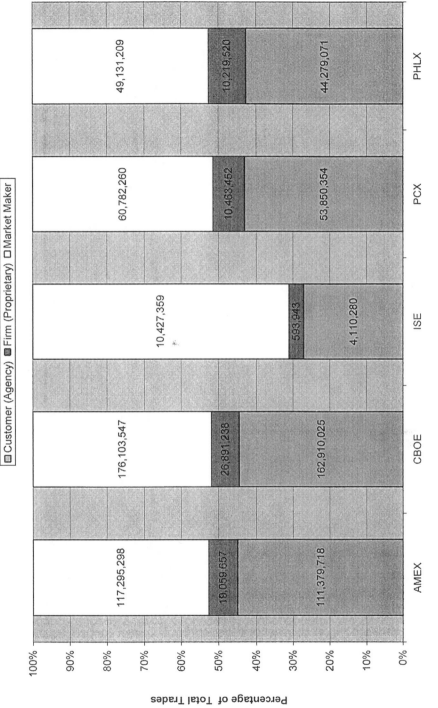

Source: ISE.

EXHIBIT 5B

EXCHANGE TRADE VOLUME IN 2001

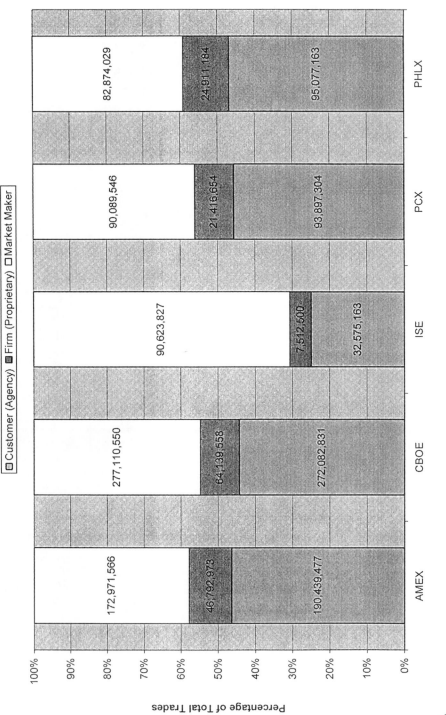

2001 Exchange Trade Volume Separated By Trade Type

Customer (Agency) Firm (Proprietary) Market Maker

Percentage of Total Trades

	AMEX	CBOE	ISE	PCX	PHLX
Customer (Agency)	172,971,566	277,110,550	90,623,827	90,089,546	82,874,029
Firm (Proprietary)	46,792,973	64,139,558	7,512,500	21,416,654	24,911,184
Market Maker	190,439,477	272,082,831	32,575,163	93,897,304	95,077,163

Source: ISE.

EXCHANGE TRADE VOLUME IN 2002 (DATA THROUGH SEPTEMBER 30)

2002 (through September 30th) Exchange Trade Volume Separated By Trade Type

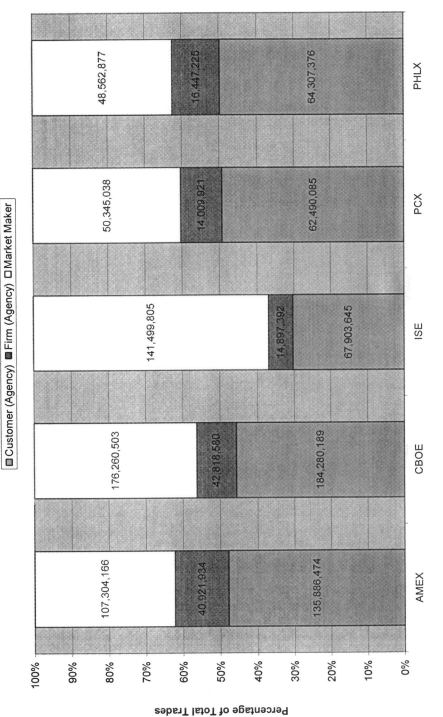

Source: ISE.

589

show the number of contracts traded on behalf of customers [i.e., individual and institutional investors], firms [e.g., broker/dealer proprietary accounts], and market makers on each of the major options exchanges by year.)

Options had gained the reputation from their early years as high-risk investments where an investor could lose his shirt. This reputation had inhibited the growth of options investing among retail investors. Options were touted as securities meant for only wealthy and sophisticated investors who could afford to take such risks with their funds. As the greater population of investors became more educated on the use of options and their fundamental qualities became better understood, the retail market for these securities started expanding. Options no longer were isolated at the high end of the risk spectrum and became a popular method of managing losses or buying insurance on a stock's performance.

Institutional investors in the options market were professional investment companies and included banks, mutual funds, hedge funds, pension funds, and insurance companies. This type of investor was usually in charge of large portfolios of various financial instruments. While these firms differed greatly in the services they provided and the investments they made, most of them were very concerned with how their investments performed in comparison to the overall market (e.g., the S&P 500). This relative performance served as one measure for judging their ability at managing investments. Consequently, standardized options contracts written on market indices (e.g., the Nasdaq 100) proved to be popular products with institutional investors as ways for them to manage their market risk.

Many investors from both categories found options trading to be prohibitively expensive. Brokers typically charged higher rates for the ability to trade options and also tacked on high transaction fees for each contract traded. Furthermore, the bid-ask differential for options was noticeably higher than with stocks. This large cut, consumed by market makers, made trading even more expensive.

Options Exchanges

Before the existence of organized options exchanges, options existed in various forms and were usually investment contracts with the terms tailored according to the parties involved. As a result of their inconsistent contractual terms, the market for specific contracts offered little liquidity. Furthermore, without a central market where these securities could be traded in an organized fashion, it was difficult to determine who was interested in buying (or selling) a contract. Even if another investor was identified, the lack of historical trade information and the unconformity of contracts made arriving at a market price challenging. Plus, the counterparty risk associated with nonstandardized options made the credit quality of the parties involved very important.

Standardized options contracts on equity securities began trading in the United States in 1973 with the creation of the CBOE. The CBOE, established by the Chicago Board of Trade, was designed to eliminate many of the early problems plaguing options trading. The SEC approved the CBOE at the beginning of February 1973 to register as a national securities exchange. The new exchange was to act as a test for trading standardized options on common stock. Initially, the CBOE only traded call options on 16 companies' stocks. Put options were introduced on the exchange in 1977. The options traded on the exchange were referred to as "listed options" and had their contractual terms (i.e., strike price, expiration date, number of shares, etc.) made uniform for easier trading. On its first day of trading, the CBOE had a trading volume of

911 contracts. By the end of 1974, the average daily trading volume was over 200,000 contracts.[11]

As the market for trading options continued to skyrocket, other securities exchanges decided they wanted a piece of the business. The American Stock Exchange (AMEX), the Pacific Stock Exchange (PCX), the Philadelphia Stock Exchange (PHLX), and, eventually, the ISE joined the CBOE as exchanges where trading of standardized equity options occurred.[12] (Exhibit 6 shows the historical growth in the options market, and Exhibit 7 shows the market share of the different options exchanges.)

Until the ISE, all of the exchanges used the familiar "floor exchange" model for trading options. With floor exchanges, brokers and market makers interacted face-to-face to execute orders for different options. The floor exchanges were physical facilities where members met to conduct their business. While advances in information technology had led to changes in the way people communicated on floor exchanges, the underlying fundamentals for the floor exchange model had remained unchanged. Unfortunately, the floor model, with all its benefits, experienced difficulties dealing with various practicalities of options trading. There was an overwhelming lack of trust among traders and a sentiment that some traders had more information than others. There was no formal "customer service" available with floor exchanges, making it challenging for broker/dealers to address these trading difficulties. The combined reaction of these floor exchange "disabilities" was to inhibit all parties' willingness to trade. Still, until the creation of the totally electronic ISE, most options professionals had refused to challenge the role of personal interaction, as done on trading floors, in providing liquid markets.

At the beginning, as new exchanges joined the industry, the different exchanges did not trade one another's names. This was pursuant to a process that the SEC condoned. For instance, if PCX had options trading on Microsoft, the other exchanges would abstain from listing options for that underlying stock. This allowed an exchange to corner the demand for certain major names without having to compete with the other exchanges. While it was arguably efficient to have a single destination specialized in trading certain options, the SEC had voiced concerns regarding the lack of competition between the exchanges and its effect on the cost of trading. In 1990, the SEC formally abolished the process of listing options on only one exchange. Still, the exchanges did not compete with one another in the high-volume options. Catalyzing the SEC's efforts, the ISE announced on November 11, 1998 that it planned on eventually listing the 600 most frequently traded options across all the exchanges.[13] As a result of the ISE's aggressive entry into the market, the cross-listing of options became a reality.

In the summer of 1999, the existing exchanges caved in on their long-standing practice, and a listing war commenced. Chicago started trading Dell options, the bread and butter of Philadelphia. The AMEX followed suit, also listing options on Dell. The PHLX then counterattacked by listing options on IBM, Coca-Cola, and Johnson & Johnson, the gems of the CBOE, and Apple, which had traditionally been traded on the AMEX.

---

[11] "Learning Options—The Options Players," Taking Care of Business Web site, ⟨http://www.1010wallstreet.com/education/options/history/options_03.asp⟩, accessed December 3, 2002.

[12] The NYSE entered the options market in 1985. Abandoning the options business in 1996, the stock exchange never gained more than a 2% share in the options market.

[13] The ISE was committed to listing options on names that made up 90% of the total equity options market's trading volume; this was estimated to be roughly 600 names.

EXHIBIT 6

AVERAGE DAILY TRADING VOLUME OF THE EQUITY OPTIONS MARKET

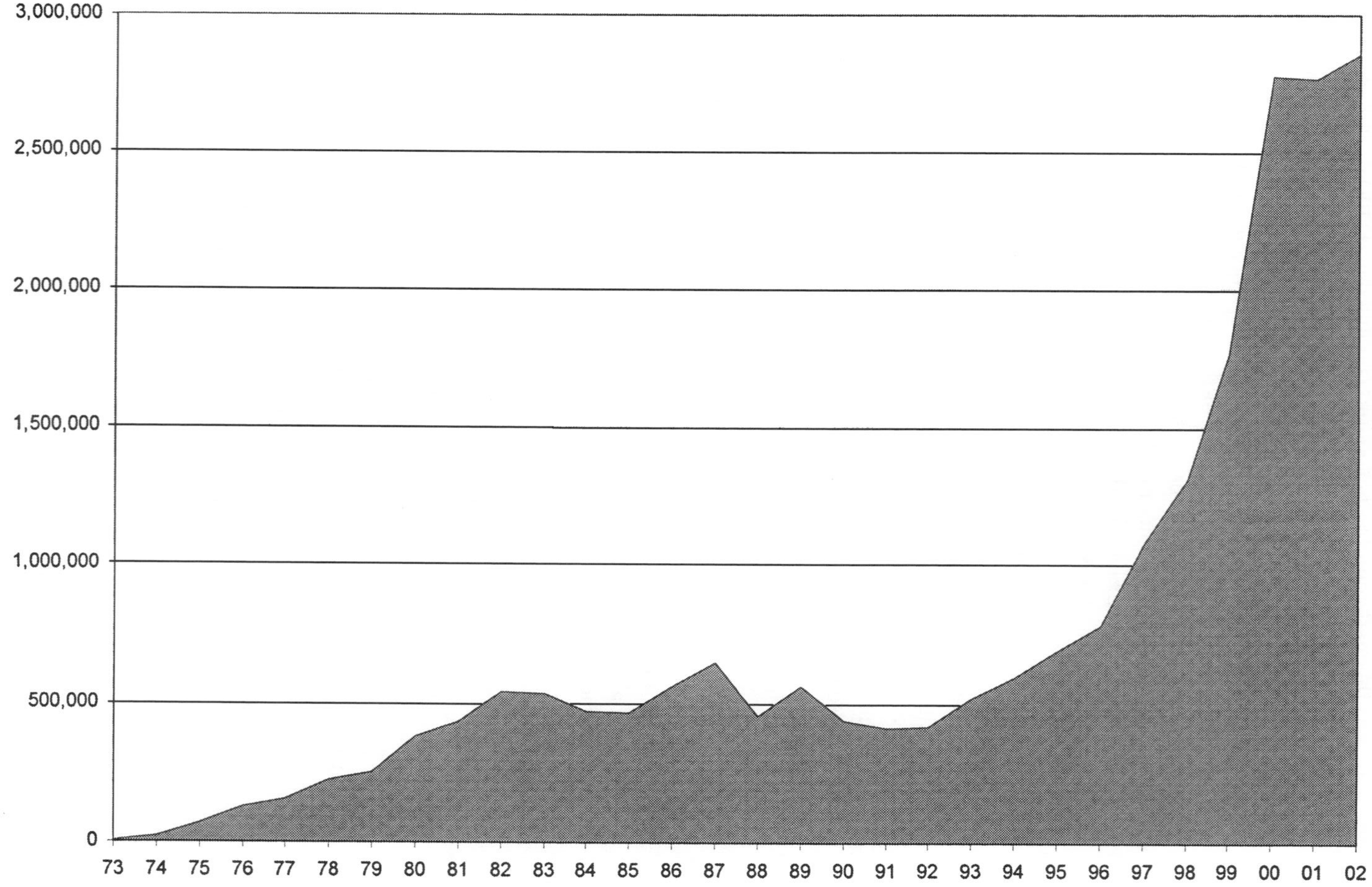

Source: ISE.

EXHIBIT 7

EXCHANGE MARKET SHARE BY TRADING VOLUME

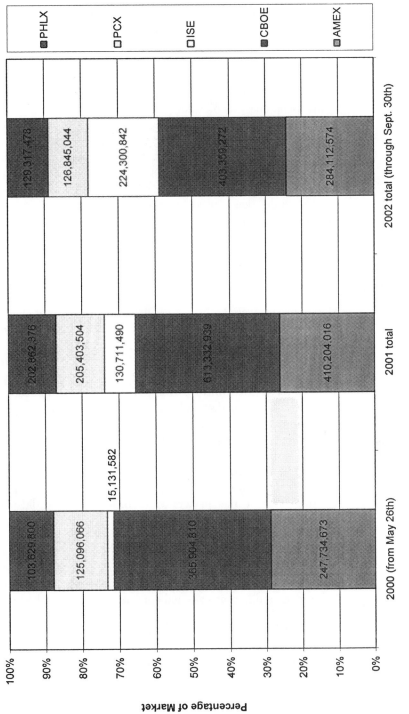

Exchange Market Share By Contracts Traded

Source: ISE.

According to a report by the SEC, the percentage of options classes trading on more than one exchange increased from 32% in August 1999 to 45% in September 2000.[14] Virtually 100% of options were cross-listed on multiple exchanges by the end of 2001.

As exchanges lost market share on their best names, they gained volume from the other exchanges' star options. While the competition seemed beneficial for the consumer, it also created a "best price" dilemma. With the same options existing on multiple exchanges, investors were at risk of having their orders executed at prices inferior to those from other exchanges. The new choice available in the market had introduced some operational complexities.

As the competition in the options market increased, the exchanges started offering commissions to broker/dealers for them to route options orders to their exchanges instead of the others. This trend was termed "payment for order flow" and became an accepted practice across the industry. It was expected that such payments would be collected by broker/dealers and used to reduce the trading fees of their customers. Payment for order flow caused some controversy. The SEC was concerned that such payments might result in investors' orders going to an exchange that did not offer the best market price. The best price available in the market was referred to as the "national best bid and offer" (NBBO).

Market Makers

Market makers were exchange members that were essential to providing liquidity in the market. As their name suggests, these exchange participants created continuous markets for their designated options names. Market makers were responsible for quoting prices at which they were willing to buy and sell options.[15] The prices a market maker would buy and sell at were the "bid" price and "ask" price, respectively. The difference between these prices was referred to as the "bid-ask spread," or the "bid-ask differential," and allowed market makers to scalp a fee for their liquidity services. For example, if a market maker quoted a bid price of $9.50 and an ask price of $10.00 for a certain option (e.g., Company X, call or put, $50.00 strike price, expiring in December) and two simultaneous orders came in to buy and sell 100 contracts (one order to buy 100 contracts and the other order to sell 100 contracts), the market maker would earn $5,000.00 (100 contracts × 100 multiplier × $0.50 bid-ask spread).

In general, market makers were not investors and did not care to hold large unhedged positions in the names they traded. Rather, they tried to earn proceeds from frequent buying and selling, receiving the bid-ask spread, and not leaving their capital at risk. Ideally, a market maker received matching buy and sell orders for the same number of options contracts, but usually this was not the case. More frequently, in order to stay "risk neutral," market makers had to adopt various trading strategies to deal with orders of different sizes and contracts with unmatched maturity and strike prices.

Floor exchanges usually assigned one primary market maker to handle the trading for a specific series of options. This market maker was known as the "lead market maker" or the "specialist" for that specific name. In the "open outcry" system customary to floor exchanges, specialists, in their assigned trading pits, verbally auctioned off options con-

---

[14] "Special Study: Payment for Order Flow and Internalization in the Options Markets," SEC Web site, ⟨http://0-www.sec.gov.library.csuhayward.edu/news/studies/ordpay.htm⟩, accessed December 3, 2002.

[15] Market makers were charged low fees per contract traded by exchanges relative to the fees imposed on customer trades. In this way, exchanges helped subsidize the market makers' trading activities, which provided the essential liquidity for exchanges. Floor exchange fees for customer orders were roughly $0.36 per contract, while fees for market makers were around $0.06 per contract.

tracts to floor brokers.[16,17] The floor exchange specialist was in charge of setting "two-sided quotes" (or "two-sided markets") in its options, quoting both bid and ask prices. Other market makers were allowed to join the quote, offering to buy and/or sell at the prices determined by the specialist. The ISE was the first U.S. options exchange to allow multiple market makers to quote competitively in two-sided markets for every option.

The Trading Process

Investors usually accessed the options market through a broker. Brokers usually fell into one of two camps: "full-service" broker/dealers, and "discount" broker/dealers. Full-service broker/dealers usually offered both trading and research services to their customers. Most full-service firms also employed their own floor brokers to handle their trades. Discount broker/dealers, on the other hand, limited their services to order taking and routing. As a result of their more limited service selection and lower overhead costs, discount broker/dealers were able to offer their customers reduced commissions on their trades compared with those of their full-service competitors. Instead of employing their own floor brokers on exchanges, discount brokers often used independent floor brokers, known as "two-dollar brokers," to execute their options orders.

While full-service broker/dealers had the ability to send their clients' orders directly to exchanges, many discount brokers used separate broker/dealers, called "consolidating" brokers, to route orders to exchanges. Consolidating broker/dealers maintained trading staff on each of the options exchanges and used a variety of systems to route customer orders efficiently. Sometimes the consolidating broker decided where to send options orders, while other times this decision was handled by the initiating broker/dealer. Firms generally had their trading systems configured to send all option orders in the same class to one exchange.

Together, these broker/dealers essentially introduced investors' options orders to the market. If routed to a floor exchange, the order was sent to a floor broker to trade with the appropriate specialist. Smaller retail orders (fewer than 50 contracts) were usually executed using an automated trading system, while a floor broker typically handled larger orders personally, manually entering the trading crowd in a floor pit.

Once an option was traded, a member of OCC had to clear the trade. Each of the options exchanges was a partial owner of OCC. Through its clearing members, OCC provided financial integrity to the options marketplace. If a broker/dealer was not a member of OCC, it had to arrange to clear its trades with a firm that was a member. OCC helped prevent investors from defaulting on the obligations of options contracts. Investors who purchased options had to pay for the contracts up front in full. Investors selling (or "writing") contracts were required to maintain margin accounts with their brokers (OCC members). In this account, the investor kept a certain percentage of the outstanding market value of the options he or she had sold. Accordingly, broker/dealers also had to maintain margin accounts with OCC covering their customers' contracts. This chain of margin accounts protected the options market from investors defaulting when the contracts they sold were exercised.

When an investor decided to exercise an option, she then notified her broker. The broker, in turn, contacted OCC with the exercise order. In response, OCC randomly selected another member with an outstanding short position in the same option. This

---

[16] Pits were circular areas on exchange floors where the trading of specific contracts occurred.

[17] Floor brokers were exchange members that executed orders on behalf of others and were not assigned a specific options series or space on the exchange.

member was then responsible for selecting a client with the associated short position. The client then bought from or sold to (depending on whether the option was a put or call) the exercising investor the underlying shares at the contract's strike price.[18]

THE ISE EXCHANGE STRUCTURE AND MARKET RULES

The ISE's electronic exchange had an open interface that allowed members to connect their market-quoting, order-routing, and risk-management systems directly to the central exchange. By integrating all these functions with the central exchange, an ISE member was able to manage its positions accurately with greater efficiency. Direct access to the exchange also facilitated greater ease in the execution, amendment, and cancellation of options orders as well. Members were also able to design their own trading applications to interact with the central exchange. To quickly resolve problems and technical issues that came up, the ISE had built an experienced team of professionals to offer technical support to its members.

Trading on the ISE was kept completely anonymous. The identity of each member trading and quoting on the exchange was tracked on the system but unavailable to exchange members. Even after a trade occurred, both the buyer and the seller were unaware of the other's identity. Benefiting from this anonymity, a trader was able to move a large block of options without other exchange members becoming aware that a large order was about to hit the market. Disguising the order provided greater liquidity for large orders and helped avoid a common problem on floor exchanges. When market makers on a trading floor became aware of a large order on the horizon, they were able to adjust their quotes and spreads to take advantage of the transaction size. Conversely, if a large order was individually advertised and blindly auctioned, as occurred on the ISE's system, traders could avoid sending signals to other market players.

The ISE planned on listing the most liquid options in the market, making up 90% of the market's total trading volume.[19] The exchange divided its collection of stock options into 10 evenly distributed subgroups or trading bins. Certain market makers were then delegated the job of providing liquidity for the options trading in specific bins. The market-making function on the ISE was divided into specialized roles to promote the efficient execution of incoming options orders. There were three main categories of market participants, each with a different level of responsibility and certain privileges. The different roles/functions included primary market makers (PMMs), competitive market makers (CMMs), and electronic access members (EAMs).

Primary Market Makers

Similar to specialists on other types of exchanges, PMMs carried the greatest amount of responsibility with regards to providing liquidity on the ISE. PMM memberships had to be purchased or leased. There were 10 PMMs, and each was assigned one of the exchange's trading bins. The PMM was responsible for overseeing the opening and continuous quoting for all the options in its bin. In this manner, there was never a time when an ISE-listed option was without a current price.[20] Furthermore, the PMM was

---

[18] John C. Hull, *Options, Futures, and Other Derivatives, Fourth Edition* (Upper Saddle River, NJ: Prentice Hall), p. 162.

[19] An estimated 600 names made up 90% of the market's total trading volume in 1998.

[20] Without continuous quoting, investors risked receiving "stale" price information. Prices are stale when the current quote is no longer available for trading and no new quote is posted.

EXHIBIT 8

ISE OPTIONS BID-ASK DIFFERENTIAL LIMITS

Bid Price	Maximum Spread Allowed[a]
Below $2.00	$0.25
$2.00 to $5.00	$0.40
$5.01 to $10.00	$0.50
$10.01 to $20.00	$0.80
Greater than $20.00	$1.00

[a]Does not apply to "in the money" series where the underlying security's market is wider than the maximum spread set forth above. For these series, the bid-ask differential may be as wide as the spread for the underlying security on its primary market.

Source: ISE.

obligated to ensure options orders in its bin were being executed at the best price available (i.e., executed at the best price available from all five exchanges). PMMs were bound to quoting a minimum order size of 10 contracts within a maximum bid-ask spread. (See Exhibit 8 for more information about the maximum bid-ask differentials ISE market makers were able to quote.) PMMs were also restricted in their ability to trade contracts outside of their assigned bins. They were only allowed to trade up to 10% of their quarterly contract volume in options from other bins. (See Exhibit 9a for a list of the ISE's PMMs on January 6, 2003.)

Competitive Market Makers

The ISE had 100 CMM memberships, allowing up to 10 CMMs to be assigned to each bin of options. This class of market maker provided additional depth and liquidity in its assigned bin. Each CMM was required to provide continuous quotations for no less than 60% of the options in its bin and was bound to the same spread limitations as PMMs (see Exhibit 8). However, CMMs were given greater freedom to invest across bins. They were allowed to trade up to 25% of their quarterly contract volume in options outside of their designated pool. CMM memberships were purchased/leased similarly to PMM memberships. (See Exhibit 9a for a list of the ISE's CMMs on January 6, 2003).

Electronic Access Members

EAMs were broker/dealers that were allowed to execute their agency orders and proprietary orders on the exchange.[21] Unlike with PMMs and CMMs, there was an unlimited amount of EAMs on the ISE. Instead of purchasing a membership, EAMs paid

[21] A "proprietary order" is a transaction made by a securities firm for its own account that does not affect the accounts of its clients. An "agency order" is a transaction made by a securities firm on behalf of a client; the securities firm is acting as an "agent" for its client, and the transaction will show up in the client's account.

EXHIBIT 9A

ISE PRIMARY MARKET MAKERS (PMMS) AND COMPETITIVE MARKET MAKERS (CMMS)

PMM Members	Bin	CMM Members	Bin(s)
Knight Financial Products LLC	Bin 1	Adirondack Electronic Markets LLC	Bins 1, 4
SLK-Hull Derivatives LLC	Bin 2	Archelon LLC	Bins 4, 6, 7
Adirondack Electronic Markets LLC	Bin 3	Bear, Stearns & Co. Inc.	Bins 1, 2, 3, 4, 7, 8, 9, 10
Timber Hill LLC	Bin 4	Bear Wagner Specialists LLC	Bins 2, 7, 9, 10
Bear, Stearns & Co. Inc.	Bin 5	BNP Paribas Securities Corp.	Bins 1, 2, 8
Bear Wagner Specialists LLC	Bin 6	Citadel Derivatives Group LLC	Bins 1, 3
Timber Hill LLC	Bin 7	Credit Suisse First Boston Corporation	Bins 2, 7, 10
Morgan Stanley & Co. Incorporated	Bin 8	Cutler Group, LP	Bins 5, 6, 8
Deutsche Bank Securities Inc.	Bin 9	Deutsche Bank Securities Inc.	Bins 1, 2, 3, 4, 5, 6, 7, 8, 10
Morgan Stanley & Co. Incorporated	Bin 10	Equitec Proprietary Markets, LLC	Bin 5
		Geneva Trading LLC	Bin 5
		Group One Trading, L.P.	Bin 10
		J.P. Morgan Securities Inc.	Bin 9
		Knight Financial Products LLC	Bins 2, 3, 4, 5, 6, 7, 8, 9, 10
		Lehman Brothers Inc.	Bins 3, 4, 5, 10
		MAKO Global Derivatives LLC	Bin 9
		Morgan Stanley & Co. Incorporated	Bins 1, 2, 3, 4, 5, 6, 7, 9
		SG Cowen Securities Corporation	Bins 1, 6
		SLK-Hull Derivatives LLC	Bins 1, 3, 4, 5, 6, 7, 8, 9, 10
		TD Options LLC	Bins 1,2, 3, 4, 5, 6, 7, 8, 9, 10
		Timber Hill LLC	Bins 1, 2, 6, 8, 9
		Wolverine Trading, L.P.	Bins 1, 2, 3, 4, 5, 6, 7, 8, 9, 10

Source: ISE.

EXHIBIT 9B

ISE ELECTRONIC ACCESS MEMBERS (EAMS)

ABN AMRO Incorporated
ABN AMRO Sage Corporation
Adirondack Electronic Markets LLC
Ameritrade, Inc.
Aragon Investments, Ltd.
Archelon LLC
Banc of America Securities LLC
Bear, Stearns & Co. Inc.
Bear, Stearns Securities Corp.
Bear Wagner Specialists LLC
BNP Paribas Brokerage Services, Inc.
BNP Paribas Securities Corp.
BNY Clearing Services LLC
Brown & Company Securities Corporation
Cantor Fitzgerald & Co.
Carr Futures, Inc.
Casey Securities, Inc.
Charles Schwab & Co., Inc
CIBC World Markets Corp.
Correspondent Services Corporation
Credit Lyonnais Securities (USA) Inc.
Credit Suisse First Boston Corporation
CTC, L.L.C.
Cutler Group, LP
CyberTrader, Inc.

Deutsche Bank Securities Inc.
DRW Securities, L.L.C.
E*TRADE Clearing LLC
Electronic Brokerage Systems, LLC
Equitec Proprietary Markets, LLC
Fimat USA, Inc.
First Albany Corporation
First New York Securities L.L.C.
First Options of Chicago, Inc.
First Southwest Company
Fleet Securities, Inc.
G-Bar Limited Partnership
Gargoyle Strategic Investments L.L.C.
Geneva Trading LLC
Goldman, Sachs & Co.
Group One Trading, L.P.
Helfant Group, Inc.
Highbridge Capital Corporation
Inter-Dealer Brokers LLC
Interactive Brokers LLC
International Correspondent Trading, Inc.
Investec Ernst & Company
Israel A. Englander & Co. Inc.
J.J.B. Hilliard, W.L. Lyons, Inc.
J.P. Morgan Securities Inc.
Jefferies & Company, Inc.
KBC Financial Products USA Inc.
Knight Execution Partners LLC
KV Execution Services LLC

Legent Clearing Corp.
Lehman Brothers Inc.
Lek Securities Corporation
MAKO Financial Markets, LLC
MAKO Global Derivatives LLC
Man Financial Inc.
Maple Securities U.S.A. Inc.
Merrill Lynch, Pierce, Fenner & Smith Incorporated
Merrill Lynch Professional Clearing Corporation
MillenCo L.P.
Miller Tabak + Co., LLC
Morgan Stanley & Co. Incorporated
Morgan Stanley DW Inc.
National Financial Services LLC
National Investor Services Corp.
Nutmeg Securities, Ltd.
O'Connor & Company LLC
OptEx Services, LLC
Option Funding Group, L.P.
optionsXpress, Inc.
Optiver Derivatives Trading - USA, LLC
OTA LLC
Pali Capital, Inc.
Parallax Fund, L.P.
Pax Clearing Corporation
PEAK6 Capital Management LLC

Pershing Division of DLJ Securities Corporation
PFTC L.L.C.
Prebon Financial Products Inc.
PreferredTrade, Inc.
Prudential Securities Incorporated
R.F. Lafferty & Co., Inc.
RBC Dominion Securities Corporation
RedSky Securities, L.L.C.
Refco Securities, LLC
Salomon Smith Barney Inc.
Scottrade, Inc.
SG Cowen Securities Corporation
Spear, Leeds & Kellogg, L.P.
STC LLC
Susquehanna Financial Group, Inc.
Swiss American Securities Inc.
SWS Securities, Inc.
TD Professional Execution, Inc.
The Tiberius Master Fund Ltd.
TJM Investments, LLC
Track Data Securities Corp.
Tullet & Tokyo Liberty Securities Inc.
UBS PaineWebber Inc.
UBS Warburg LLC
Van der Moolen Options U.S.A. LLC
Wall Street Access

Source: ISE.

a nominal access fee that allowed them to place orders in all of the ISE's options bins. The access fee for an EAM, from the time of establishment, was $3,500 per year. In essence, the EAMs were responsible for generating customer order flow on the exchange. However, they were prohibited from quoting their own prices or otherwise serving as market makers on the exchange. (See Exhibit 9b for a list of the ISE's EAMs on January 6, 2003).

An organization was able to hold more than one membership as well as different types of memberships. For instance, a firm was able to be a PMM in one bin, hold two CMMs in other bins, and still be an EAM, allowing it to execute agency and proprietary orders. On the other hand, firms had to keep their EAM business separate from their market-making activities. A PMM was not allowed to manipulate prices in its bin in order to get better prices for its clients' contracts. Therefore, the ISE required a "Chinese Wall" between EAMs and any market-making business.[22]

The ISE's Central Order Book

The ISE had a central order book that tracked each of the options series listed on the exchange. Quotes and limit orders, with their stated prices and sizes, were entered and stored in the central order book according to different measures of priority. Quotes were first sorted according to their price. The best prices (i.e., the highest bid price and the lowest offer price) received first priority. Within a certain price slot, customer orders were prioritized according to their time of entry. In other words, if two customers wished to trade at the same quoted price, the first customer to enter the order received trading priority at that price.

Once all the quote and order information had been entered into the central order book and prioritized, the ISE broadcasted the best bid and offer prices (BBO) to all of its members. The ISE BBO was determined by the highest bid and lowest offer prices available for each options series. For the BBO, bids and offers from market-maker quotes, customer orders, and proprietary orders were all weighed fairly. The BBO was then reported along with the consolidated number of contracts available for that price.[23] In contrast to the ISE, floor exchanges rarely publicized the size of quoted prices to the entire market.

Regardless of timing, all customer orders received priority over market-maker quotes and non-customer orders at any given price level. To ensure customer orders were treated with priority, the ISE required all orders from EAMs to be marked with a "tag" identifying the order as being on behalf of a "customer," a "professional," or an "away market maker." Customer orders were for anyone who was not a registered broker/dealer (e.g., an individual investor). The professional category included the EAM's proprietary trading or any other registered broker/dealer other than an away market maker. Away market makers were market makers from another options exchange. By electronically tracking the source of each order, the ISE ensured customer orders received priority.

The aggregate number of contracts available at the ISE BBO (i.e., the "size" of the quote) was "firm" for all incoming customer orders but might be less for noncustomer

---

[22] The term "Chinese Wall" is widely used to describe procedures used by a securities firm to prohibit nonpublic information from being shared across the firm's different departments.

[23] The size of the ISE BBO was a minimum of 10 contracts. If the BBO was improved on by a customer order and was for fewer than 10 contracts, the PMM was responsible for either executing the order or making up the difference in size. If a non-customer order improved upon the BBO, it had to have a minimum size of 10 contracts.

orders. In other words, EAMs could trade on their customers' behalf up to the full size of a quoted price. However, the same number of contracts might not be available to an EAM for a proprietary trade. Market makers typically reduced the number of contracts available for firms making proprietary trades. There was a deep distrust from market makers, stemming from the belief that securities firms had an unfair advantage due to their proprietary knowledge of their clients' trading activities. Reducing the quote size available for firms to trade on served as protection from these firms taking full advantage of their inside information.

Trade Sharing

The ISE rewarded market makers for creating liquidity by systematically allocating trades based upon the size quoted by a market maker. It was essential for the ISE to offer the best-quality markets defined in terms of both size and spread—the largest size and tightest spread. CMMs quoting the largest size at the BBO received a proportionally larger allocation. In this system, customer orders still received priority, independent of the size they ordered. For example, if an order came in to buy 100 contracts at the BBO and there was a customer order to sell 10 of the same contracts at the BBO, the customer's sell order would be executed before the remaining 90 contracts were divided among the other exchange members.[24] The allocation of the 90 contracts to market makers was dependent upon the size of the markets they quoted at the BBO. Other rules that determined how a trade was executed were:

- If an order was executed across multiple price levels, quotes were given priority at the present price level for the number of contracts executed at the previous price level.

- An original order size of five contracts or fewer was executed against the PMM as long as the PMM quoted a sufficient size at the BBO.

- For an order greater than five contracts, the PMM was guaranteed a certain percentage of the order, depending on how many other noncustomers were quoting at the BBO. The PMM received a minimum of 60%, 40%, or 30% of an order based on whether there were one, two, or three or more other noncustomers, respectively, quoting at the BBO. However, if the PMM's pro-rata share of an order was greater than its minimum percentage guarantee, the PMM was allocated the larger greater pro-rata portion.[25]

- CMM quotes and noncustomer orders were allocated portions of a trade based upon the size of their quotes or orders. After the customers and the PMM had their share of an order, all other members quoting at the BBO received their pro-rata share, determined by the amount of contracts each member quoted/ordered as a percentage of total size outstanding.

(Exhibit 10 gives an example of how a trade would be divided according to the ISE's methodology.)

---

[24] In the same example, multiple customer orders to sell contracts at the BBO were given execution priority based on the order in which they were received.

[25] A market maker's pro-rata share was calculated by dividing the contracts it quoted by the total quote size. Therefore, if a PMM quoted 200 contracts at the BBO and was joined by two CMMs each quoting 100 contracts, the PMM's pro-rata share of an incoming order would be 50% (200/400).

EXHIBIT 10

EXAMPLE OF THE ORDER ALLOCATION AT THE ISE

The ISE BBO for Option XYZ is 6.50. There are six different members willing to buy XYZ options at the ISE BBO. The order book is shown below:

Order	Quantity	Price
Customer (i.e., agency)	5	6.50
PMM	15	6.50
CMM 1	30	6.50
Firm (i.e., proprietary)	20	6.50
CMM 3	10	6.50
CMM 2	10	6.50

The ISE system will display a buy-side quantity of 90 contracts at the BBO 6.50.

If an EAM now decides to enter a market order to sell 21 contracts, the ISE system will execute the order as shown below:

1. The customer's order is executed first. Therefore, the customer receives his full five orders at 6.50.

2. The PMM receives its share of the trade. The PMM's pro-rata share of the remaining trade $(21 - 5 = 16$ contracts) would be 18% (15/85.) However, the PMM is guaranteed a minimum of 30% of a trade when there are three or more other noncustomers participating at the ISE BBO. Therefore, the PMM receives its 30% of the trade, 5 contracts (16 remaining contracts $\times$ 30% = 4.8 contracts, rounded up to 5).

3. The balance of the order, 11 contracts $(21 - 5 - 5 = 11)$ is split up among the remaining CMM and noncustomer orders, pro-rata, based upon the size of their quotes in the order book. The remaining quantity in the order book at 6.50 is 70 contracts. Therefore:

   CMM 1 will buy 5 contracts $(11 \times 30/70 = 4.7$, rounded up to 5).

   The firm will buy 3 contracts $(6 \times 20/40 = 3)$.

   CMM 3 will buy 2 contracts $(3 \times 10/20 = 1.5$, rounded up to 2).

   CMM 2 will buy 1 contract $(1 \times 10/10 = 1)$.

   Note: Even though CMM 3 and CMM 2 quoted equal size, CMM 3 has priority over CMM 2 based upon its time of entry.

4. The EAM that entered the market order is then informed that it has sold 21 contracts of XYZ options contracts at 6.50. After the order is processed, the ISE order book for option XYZ appears below:

Order	Quantity	Price
PMM	10	6.50
CMM 1	25	6.50
Firm (i.e., proprietary)	17	6.50
CMM 3	8	6.50
CMM 2	9	6.50

The ISE system will adjust to display a buy-side quantity of 69 contracts at the ISE BBO 6.50.

Source: Casewriter.

Away Market Price Protection

The ISE did not automatically execute a trade if the ISE BBO was inferior to the NBBO. In other words, the ISE did not allow a customer's order to trade at the best ISE price for an option if another exchange had a better price for the same option. If this situation arose, the order was referred to the PMM in charge of that options series. It was the PMM's responsibility to either match the better price from the other exchange or to attempt to get the better price from the other exchange for the customer. The ISE's trading system provided tools to the PMM for dealing with market prices from other exchanges. Customers had the ability to choose not to receive this price protection for an order. Noncustomer orders were not protected from discrepancies between the ISE BBO and the BBO and were automatically executed at the ISE BBO.

Quoting "Firm" Prices

On the ISE, along with many of the floor exchanges, the size quoted by exchange members did not have to be the same for both customer orders and noncustomer orders. The ISE's trading system allowed for market makers to input quotes of one size for trading against customer orders and a different size for trading against orders on behalf of noncustomer accounts. Many market makers were concerned that the inside information broker/dealers gained from their customers' investing activity gave them an unfair advantage when entering proprietary orders. It was argued that certain broker/dealers were able to track the investing activity done by their clientele in both the options market and the stock market. Using this proprietary information, it was assumed that these broker/dealers had an easier time forecasting trends in the market. Worried that such broker/dealers had an unfair advantage at timing their trading activity, market makers had the ability to limit the amount they would trade with them. Each market marker on the ISE had to set in advance the number of contracts that it was willing to trade with noncustomers, and this amount was monitored in the ISE's central order book.

IMPROVING QUOTE SIZE

So far the ISE had been successful by identifying problem areas in the options market and being the first exchange to execute plans for improvement. The older floor exchanges were fighting hard to keep their market share, but they had shown far less mobility than their all-electronic competitor in adapting to the market's increasing demands. If the ISE was going to remain a pioneer in the options market, the next challenge for the exchange was improving quote size across its customer base. The ISE saw opportunity to increase market share on the exchange by making quote sizes "firm" for all classes of customers. Essentially, if 500 contracts were quoted at the BBO, all 500 contracts were equally available for EAM customer orders and proprietary orders.

By leveling the playing field across customer classes, the ISE wanted to increase the ability of firms to execute their proprietary orders on the exchange. On the other hand, changing the quoting rules could hurt the market as well. The ISE was concerned that by altering its quote size requirements, quote sizes might decrease and/or bid-ask spreads might increase. Such a reaction would decrease liquidity and hurt the quality of the ISE's market.

The ISE had entered into discussions with many of its market makers to get their feedback on the size-quoting process. In the spring of 2002, the ISE launched a pilot study to look at the possible effects of changing to a "one size fits all" system. In this lim-

EXHIBIT 11A

OPTION NAMES MAKING UP THE PILOT GROUP OF THE ISE QUOTE SIZE PILOT STUDY

ISE Rank[a]	Option Symbol	ISE ADV[b]
1	QQQ	32,045
2	MSFT	14,795
3	TYC	14,737
4	CSCO	12,301
5	INTC	10,090
7	AMAT	9,098
8	GE	8,173
9	QCOM	6,953
10	SEBL	6,828
12	C	6,339
13	AOL	6,139
18	SUNW	4,879
20	ORCL	4,554
21	JNPR	4,428
24	BRCM	4,220
25	EMC	4,155
36	NOK	2,752
38	LU	2,714
143	WFC	876

[a]Ranking of options-trading volume on the ISE.

[b]The average daily volume (ADV) on the ISE from January 31, 2002 to April 26, 2002.

Source: ISE.

ited study, the ISE started by creating a minimum quote size for all types of customers for a selection of 19 different options names.[26] For the study, PMMs had to quote a minimum size of 50 contracts for all customer types.[27] While the study's terms allowed for quotes to be larger for customer orders than for firm orders, authorizing a minimum size for all orders allowed the ISE to examine the effect of providing greater size to firms for their proprietary business. The trading activity of these 19 names was tracked by the ISE for three months and compared to a control group of options names over the same period. While the control group included 49 options names, both the pilot group and the control group represented 30.3% of the ISE's trading volume. (Exhibits 11a through 16 present the data collected during the ISE quote size pilot study.)

[26] PMM participation in this study was on a voluntary basis.

[27] The pilot study required PMMs to quote a minimum size of 100 contracts for customer orders and half that size for all other noncustomer parties. Similarly, CMMs participating in the study were required to offer a minimum of 50 contracts for customer orders and half that size for all other parties. Prior to the study, a minimum quote size of 10 contracts was required for customer orders, and no minimum was set for orders coming from noncustomer parties.

EXHIBIT 11B

OPTIONS MAKING UP THE CONTROL GROUP FOR THE ISE QUOTE SIZE PILOT STUDY (COMPARABLE VOLUME WITH THE PILOT GROUP, DIFFERENT NUMBER OF ISSUES)

ISE Rank[a]	Option Symbol	ISE ADV[b]	ISE Rank	Option Symbol	ISE ADV
6	IBM	9,540	44	PSFT	2,563
11	CPN	6,699	45	WMT	2,545
14	VRTS	5,693	46	CA	2,440
15	NVDA	5,372	47	NXTL	2,421
16	JPM	5,287	48	AMZN	2,419
17	MER	5,168	49	AIG	2,403
19	DELL	4,577	50	EDS	2,400
22	ADCT	4,416	51	BAC	2,400
23	BRCD	4,298	52	FNM	2,297
26	TXN	4,134	53	CIEN	2,279
27	WCOM	4,082	54	QLGC	2,275
28	EBAY	4,045	55	JDSU	2,225
29	KLAC	3,832	56	NVLS	2,161
30	JNJ	3,831	57	XOM	2,144
31	AMGN	3,469	58	GMST	2,107
32	GM	3,429	59	MOT	2,091
33	HWP	3,240	60	PFE	2,077
34	MU	3,218	61	AMD	2,076
35	BMY	2,757	62	MRK	2,006
37	XLNX	2,725	63	T	1,997
39	MO	2,687	64	PMCS	1,958
40	BBY	2,685	65	MWD	1,942
41	VZ	2,660	66	LLY	1,939
42	CHKP	2,644	67	CMCSK	1,900
43	HD	2,583			

[a]Ranking of options-trading volume on the ISE.

[b]The average daily volume (ADV) on the ISE from January 31, 2002 to April 26, 2002.

Source: ISE.

CONCLUSION

Krell and Katz were proud of the ISE's recent performance, but both executives understood the importance of staying in the forefront of change in their business. Floor exchanges had become too secure in their ways and, as a result, had been surprised and ill prepared to deal with the introduction of the ISE. Krell and Katz were adamant about not making the same mistake with the ISE. The floor exchanges were all investing heavily to build their own electronic trading capabilities. In Boston, a new all-electronic options exchange was already in the making and claiming it would offer firm quotes for all customer types. The ISE could not let its guard down for a minute. There was a conference call scheduled with the ISE PMMs later in the week, and Krell and Katz were eager to discuss the implications of the pilot study's results.

EXHIBIT 12A

CUMULATIVE TRADING VOLUMES OF OPTIONS IN THE PILOT GROUP DURING THE BEFORE AND AFTER PERIODS OF THE PILOT STUDY

Symbol	Volume Before[a]		Volume After	
	ISE	Industry[b]	ISE	Industry
AMAT	545,878	1,754,313	599,785	1,973,916
AOL	368,340	3,484,711	517,793	3,262,538
BRCM	253,186	946,969	339,240	960,839
C	380,334	1,635,603	544,853	2,119,519
CSCO	738,082	3,769,932	873,131	3,597,588
EMC	249,272	1,566,559	211,098	1,303,649
GE	490,360	3,343,206	709,152	3,011,334
INTC	605,403	4,225,573	603,870	4,007,521
JNPR	265,705	1,046,484	125,361	501,950
LU	162,824	1,086,981	161,353	1,301,161
MSFT	887,725	3,763,855	1,393,418	4,421,499
NOK	165,142	862,435	257,807	1,024,391
ORCL	273,235	1,421,648	326,968	1,817,254
QCOM	417,189	1,474,196	360,715	1,170,252
QQQ	1,922,697	17,398,324	3,411,278	23,046,620
SEBL	409,663	1,433,859	357,763	1,199,689
SUNW	292,735	1,620,600	272,982	1,490,201
TYC	884,229	5,378,551	1,365,993	7,014,407
WFC	52,547	277,657	135,137	573,641

[a]The "Before" and "After" periods for the 60 trading days comparison were January 31, 2002 to April 26, 2002 and April 29, 2002 to July 23, 2002, respectively.

[b]The "Industry" category refers to the volume of the issue traded on all exchanges.

Source: ISE.

EXHIBIT 12B

CUMULATIVE TRADING VOLUMES OF OPTIONS IN THE CONTROL GROUP DURING THE BEFORE AND AFTER PERIODS OF THE PILOT STUDY

Volume Before[a]						Volume After					
Symbol	ISE	Industry[b]	Symbol	ISE	Industry	Symbol	ISE	Industry	Symbol	ISE	Industry
ADCT	264,988	319,416	JPM	317,195	1,342,850	ADCT	14,227	38,508	JPM	294,689	1,295,672
AIG	144,205	607,687	KLAC	229,918	666,349	AIG	288,762	728,879	KLAC	320,047	776,741
AMD	124,589	472,737	LLY	116,337	353,298	AMD	128,646	430,009	LLY	78,787	278,488
AMGN	208,168	754,296	MER	310,063	1,093,976	AMGN	407,604	1,196,033	MER	367,272	996,106
AMZN	145,156	576,370	MO	161,190	1,256,434	AMZN	159,156	560,956	MO	320,372	1,435,337
BAC	143,975	736,709	MOT	125,467	619,628	BAC	190,047	846,080	MOT	191,153	787,367
BBY	161,113	373,538	MRK	120,368	588,431	BBY	136,535	315,693	MRK	150,024	544,781
BMY	165,436	898,544	MU	193,107	1,087,777	BMY	220,366	804,674	MU	231,238	1,095,167
BRCD	257,905	820,930	MWD	116,529	595,209	BRCD	330,725	822,497	MWD	113,210	400,662
CA	146,371	703,771	NVDA	322,329	1,242,527	CA	79,390	291,850	NVDA	261,980	824,877
CHKP	158,661	570,317	NVLS	129,683	337,501	CHKP	131,840	389,437	NVLS	235,633	528,552
CIEN	136,769	503,841	NXTL	145,260	554,056	CIEN	81,820	272,724	NXTL	110,724	536,170
CMCSK	113,982	308,921	PFE	124,610	837,780	CMCSK	199,910	443,252	PFE	254,799	1,257,732
CPN	401,922	1,603,659	PMCS	117,500	328,553	CPN	213,988	819,671	PMCS	74,017	195,974
DELL	274,593	1,325,808	PSFT	153,755	494,781	DELL	520,388	2,061,611	PSFT	131,827	381,646
EBAY	242,679	623,373	QLGC	136,514	487,081	EBAY	361,902	916,338	QLGC	211,689	730,693
EDS	144,029	445,702	T	119,792	729,511	EDS	271,574	612,382	T	210,208	1,336,236
FNM	137,833	470,936	TXN	248,018	1,117,688	FNM	162,924	407,773	TXN	253,875	929,773
GM	205,763	746,800	VRTS	341,578	1,038,027	GM	403,712	1,023,089	VRTS	210,100	755,699
GMST	126,419	550,629	VZ	159,605	515,955	GMST	96,833	409,744	VZ	242,279	767,494
HD	154,994	579,461	WCOM	244,899	1,707,381	HD	252,419	823,178	WCOM	103,917	649,441
HWP	194,396	767,695	WMT	152,723	609,928	HWP	15,642	56,913	WMT	269,406	813,076
IBM	572,372	2,974,790	XLNX	163,527	489,395	IBM	988,820	3,174,798	XLNX	238,901	694,934
JDSU	133,515	634,965	XOM	128,635	717,963	JDSU	85,288	392,976	XOM	146,769	600,607
JNJ	229,864	755,142				JNJ	317,740	856,689			

[a]The "Before" and "After" periods for the 60 trading days comparison were January 31, 2002 to April 26, 2002 and April 29, 2002 to July 23, 2002, respectively.

[b]The "Industry" category refers to the volume of the issue traded on all exchanges.

Source: ISE.

EXHIBIT 13A

**AVERAGE BID-ASK SPREADS
OF OPTIONS IN THE PILOT GROUP
DURING THE BEFORE AND AFTER
PERIODS OF THE ISE PILOT STUDY**

| Symbol | Average Spread | |
	Before[a]	After
AMAT	0.256237	0.200311
AOL	0.154753	0.153109
BRCM	0.304686	0.224097
C	0.208830	0.287995
CSCO	0.155849	0.153266
EMC	0.176151	0.170637
GE	0.186680	0.177007
INTC	0.177284	0.172016
JNPR	0.165925	0.166686
LU	0.139693	0.132556
MSFT	0.229998	0.213468
NOK	0.219971	0.200094
ORCL	0.142552	0.144138
QCOM	0.228256	0.267509
QQQ	0.166466	0.155532
SEBL	0.250986	0.194337
SUNW	0.171187	0.149022
TYC	0.218874	0.242293
WFC	0.210334	0.235397

[a]The "Before" and "After" periods for the 60 trading days comparison were January 31, 2002 to April 26, 2002 and April 29, 2002 to July 23, 2002, respectively.

Source: ISE.

EXHIBIT 13B

**AVERAGE BID-ASK SPREADS OF OPTIONS IN THE CONTROL GROUP
DURING THE BEFORE AND AFTER PERIODS OF
THE ISE PILOT STUDY**

	Average Spread				
Symbol	**Before**[a]	**After**	**Symbol**	**Before**	**After**
ADCT	0.273417	0.215044	JPM	0.208040	0.231776
AIG	0.279945	0.255731	KLAC	0.337145	0.278568
AMD	0.178862	0.179375	LLY	0.384404	0.242584
AMGN	0.260741	0.246430	MER	0.291588	0.258914
AMZN	0.193990	0.219817	MO	0.228883	0.221080
BAC	0.243647	0.264429	MOT	0.205881	0.228424
BBY	0.307273	0.289651	MRK	0.244325	0.251575
BMY	0.237883	0.210987	MU	0.222356	0.218621
BRCD	0.268775	0.232110	MWD	0.247735	0.719355
CA	0.219149	0.203016	NVDA	0.311251	0.259813
CHKP	0.237758	0.190175	NVLS	0.312674	0.260944
CIEN	0.224767	0.178469	NXTL	0.162607	0.177561
CMCSK	0.193823	0.226877	PFE	0.162644	0.187986
CPN	0.245849	0.232031	PMCS	0.199383	0.194199
DELL	0.197761	0.187268	PSFT	0.247779	0.214569
EBAY	0.263828	0.320089	QLGC	0.294791	0.313975
EDS	0.250944	0.271582	T	0.177305	0.176735
FNM	0.274768	0.264015	TXN	0.218192	0.212416
GM	0.295922	0.275100	VRTS	0.341971	0.234305
GMST	0.231557	0.216312	VZ	0.219428	0.338398
HD	0.224697	0.223890	WCOM	0.186911	0.195382
HWP	0.186186	0.171066	WMT	0.256913	0.253952
IBM	0.316485	0.253592	XLNX	0.289292	0.243737
JDSU	0.157842	0.156008	XOM	0.205609	0.191996
JNJ	0.244969	0.287375			

[a]The "Before" and "After" periods for the 60 trading days comparison were January 31, 2002 to April 26, 2002 and April 29, 2002 to July 23, 2002, respectively.

Source: ISE.

EXHIBIT 14A

AVERAGE CUSTOMER QUOTE SIZES FOR OPTIONS IN THE PILOT GROUP DURING THE BEFORE AND AFTER PERIODS OF THE ISE PILOT STUDY

	Average Customer Quote Size	
Symbol	Before[a]	After
AMAT	111.8370	160.0432
AOL	152.8042	176.0139
BRCM	89.1474	103.9345
C	106.4296	103.1877
CSCO	317.2806	341.2030
EMC	124.2425	131.4161
GE	121.1169	140.5144
INTC	135.4023	184.3952
JNPR	186.7560	173.4061
LU	202.0713	214.9513
MSFT	250.7106	259.2182
NOK	79.8389	97.4480
ORCL	346.8327	341.9600
QCOM	120.7746	112.7254
QQQ	935.1981	966.0519
SEBL	100.1585	115.1376
SUNW	165.3190	171.5718
TYC	78.5779	80.9086
WFC	65.4902	74.0298

[a]The "Before" and "After" periods for the 60 trading days comparison were January 31, 2002 to April 26, 2002 and April 29, 2002 to July 23, 2002, respectively.

Source: ISE.

EXHIBIT 14B

AVERAGE CUSTOMER QUOTE SIZES FOR OPTIONS IN THE CONTROL GROUP DURING THE BEFORE AND AFTER PERIODS OF THE ISE PILOT STUDY

	Average Customer Quote Size				
Symbol	**Before T[a]T**	**After**	**Symbol**	**Before**	**After**
ADCT	62.5198	73.2077	JPM	106.8075	126.6057
AIG	61.7713	71.7128	KLAC	49.5668	62.8674
AMD	75.1862	80.7104	LLY	56.3435	57.6586
AMGN	98.3264	87.9201	MER	52.0921	72.8545
AMZN	100.4457	90.3006	MO	58.9348	75.9249
BAC	59.7882	60.3723	MOT	98.9481	88.4896
BBY	72.4032	56.8952	MRK	60.3450	62.7234
BMY	41.1830	51.5647	MU	71.3395	76.9189
BRCD	104.8694	84.5694	MWD	66.0854	69.1702
CA	49.6686	45.9482	NVDA	60.5942	64.5619
CHKP	73.6813	82.2388	NVLS	63.7371	61.0572
CIEN	124.3761	94.6608	NXTL	147.1416	133.1066
CMCSK	57.7283	60.4140	PFE	108.1043	103.2640
CPN	57.4540	60.7489	PMCS	56.5105	57.8521
DELL	192.9845	164.6160	PSFT	76.8148	83.6075
EBAY	106.9790	95.5111	QLGC	62.9766	57.7191
EDS	60.3108	57.6666	T	144.1740	139.3069
FNM	50.3228	54.6034	TXN	69.1881	70.1439
GM	61.9984	69.1247	VRTS	86.2285	77.1045
GMST	58.9093	62.0498	VZ	83.0376	78.9323
HD	79.9851	74.2873	WCOM	112.5917	105.1838
HWP	83.5735	102.2005	WMT	85.4487	70.3896
IBM	79.9007	114.8604	XLNX	57.0739	61.3635
JDSU	148.0352	135.8415	XOM	66.1588	85.3516
JNJ	62.2214	49.3485			

[a]The "Before" and "After" periods for the 60 trading days comparison were January 31, 2002 to April 26, 2002 and April 29, 2002 to July 23, 2002, respectively.

Source: ISE.

EXHIBIT 15

LISTS OF SYMBOLS FOR OPTIONS (PILOT STUDY ISSUES ENLARGED) WHERE THE ISE WAS THE LEADING EXCHANGE (BY VOLUME TRADED) DURING THE BEFORE AND AFTER PERIODS OF THE ISE PILOT STUDY

Symbols With Lead Market Before

ABF	CVS	L	SNDK
ABI	CVTX	LEH	SNPS
ABS	CVX	LGTO	SY
ABT	CY	LLTC	TER
ADBE	DB	LLY	TOY
ADCT	DUK	LMT	UNH
ADI	EBAY	LOW	USB
ADIC	EDS	LSI	UTH
ADVP	EYE	LXK	UTX
AEOS	FD	MANU	V
AETH	FDC	MXIM	VIA
AFFX	FDX	NBR	VRTS
AGE	FITB	NITE	VRTY
AMAT	FMKT	NKE	VSH
AMD	FNM	NSM	VZ
ANDW	FRE	NTRS	WAT
ANF	GILD	NVLS	WMH
BBY	GSPN	ONE	XLNX
BLDP	HD	OPWV	
BP	HDI	PMCS	
BRCD	HGSI	PSFT	
CAH	HON	RATL	
CCU	IDPH	RD	
CELG	INCY	RDC	
CHL	IRF	RFMD	
CLS	JBL	RIG	
CLX	JCP	RKH	
CMCSK	KEG	RMBS	
CMOS	KLAC	SBC	
COF	KMB	SEPR	
CPN	KRB	SII	

Symbols With Lead Market After

A	BDX	CY	HDI	LLTC	OHP	SNE	WTW
ABF	BHI	CYMI	HGSI	LMT	OMC	SNPS	WYE
ABI	BK	DAL	HI	LOW	ONE	SO	XLNX
ABS	BP	DD	HIFN	LXK	OVER	SPLS	YHOO
ABT	BR	DE	HLT	MACR	PCG	SWY	YUM
ADBE	BRCD	DHR	IAH	MAT	PDLI	SY	
ADCT	**BRCM**	DT	IBM	MCDT	PG	SYMC	
ADI	BSX	DUK	IDPH	MCHP	PHA	TDW	
ADIC	CAH	EBAY	IDTI	MDT	PMCS	TER	
ADVP	CBE	EDS	IGT	MEDI	PSFT	TGT	
AEOS	CC	ELX	INCY	MER	PTEN	THC	
AES	CCE	EMR	INET	MERQ	Q	TLAB	
AET	CCMP	EOG	INTU	MLNM	R	TMPW	
AETH	CCU	EXPE	INVN	MMM	RATL	TOY	
AFFX	CDN	EXTR	IP	**MSFT**	RD	TTN	
AGE	CEPH	EYE	IRF	MXIM	RDC	UCL	
AHC	CHIR	FBF	IVGN	MXT	RFMD	UIS	
AIG	CHKP	FCS	JBL	MYL	RIG	UNH	
ALL	CHTR	FDC	JCP	NBL	RIMM	UPS	
ALTR	CIEN	FDX	JNJ	NBR	RKH	USB	
AMAT	CL	FFIV	**JNPR**	NE	RMBS	UTH	
AMD	CLS	FITB	KEG	NET	RMK	UTX	
AMGN	CLX	FMKT	KEY	NEWP	RNWK	V	
AMTD	CMCSK	FNM	KFT	NITE	SANM	VIA	
AMZN	COF	FON	KLAC	NKE	SBC	VRTY	
ANDW	COST	G	KMB	NOC	SGP	VSH	
ANF	CPN	GD	KR	NSM	SHPGY	VZ	
AWE	CSC	GILD	KSS	NTRS	SII	WAG	
AXP	CVC	GM	L	NVDA	SLR	WAT	
AZO	CVS	GP	LEH	NVLS	SMTC	WFT	
BBY	CVX	HD	LLL	NWS	SNDK	WMH	

Source: ISE.

EXHIBIT 16

MARKET ATTRIBUTES OF ALL ISE ISSUES DURING THE BEFORE AND AFTER PERIODS OF THE ISE PILOT STUDY

Category	Before[a]	After	Change
Market Share	17.16%	21.02%	+22.49%
Average Customer Quote Size	54	52	−3.70%
Average Spread	0.2627	0.2570	−2.17%
Lead Market	23.00%	45.00%	+95.65%
Average Listings Per Day	485	509	+4.95%
Average Number of EAMs Trading Per Day	63	71	+12.70%

[a]The "Before" and "After" periods for the 60 trading days comparison were January 31, 2002 to April 26, 2002 and April 29, 2002 to July 23, 2002, respectively.

Source: ISE.

DS-6

REAL OPTIONS

33

RTY Telecom: Network Expansion

On March 5, 2001, Andres Garzon reviewed the pending agreement with Nortel in his office at RTY Telecom (RTY), a U.S. regional telecommunications company, and the subsidiary of European-based international telecom group RTY Global. In the industry, innovation was a company's greatest weapon against insolvency, and RTY had a history of pushing the innovation envelope; from seeking out untapped markets to aggressively marketing new technologies. This deal with Nortel would be no exception: their patented MORail system could provide RTY with as much as 64 times more capacity in their fiber-optic network, a huge boon to meeting the demand of future customers. The demand wasn't there at present, though, and no one knew what future demand would look like. Over the last six months, perceived overcapacity and a lack of demand had caused capital to dry up for telecom providers internationally. As the Chief Financial Officer it was Garzon's job to manage planning for the long run growth of RTY. Without access to needed capital, rationing available funds became critical. Also, telecom technology was developing in months instead of years, and the large scale required to implement this technology raised the decision-making stakes.

Under such turbulent conditions Garzon wanted his technology purchases to be as flexible as possible, while still being consistent with RTY's overall strategy. The MORail system provided that flexibility, allowing RTY to adopt a technology platform that was upgradeable over time and in stages, providing a valuable hedge against loss if it became obsolete. While a strategy of flexibility made sense, selling the approach to the investment community was another matter. To assess his options, Garzon needed a way to estimate the value of this flexibility. Adopting new technology was difficult, and valuing a project when inherent flexibility existed was not always straightforward.

Professor George Chacko, Executive Director of the HBS Europe Research Center, Vincent Dessain, and Research Associates Christopher Smith (MBA '01) and Anders Sjöman prepared this case. It was developed from published sources. The company RTY Telecom and any related company data is purely ficticious. HBS cases are developed solely as the basis for class discussion. Cases are not intended to serve as endorsements, sources of primary data, or illustrations of effective or ineffective management.

THE TECHNOLOGY BEHIND TELECOMMUNICATIONS

The telecommunications industry began in the mid 1800's with the purpose of developing a network of cables designed to carry a series of dots and dashes in electrical form from one telegraph to another. By 2001 this network had become a global infrastructure with the capability to carry all types of information to receiving devices as varied as computers to pay phones. This transition was made possible by a number of technological developments. While the receiving devices themselves precipitated this development, they were alone insufficient to maintain it; a network of computers set up on old telegraph cables would never work. The cable infrastructure behind these devices had to parallel their development in order to keep up with the expanding flow of information and to keep the network operational. This infrastructure development produced a steady increase in network bandwidth, which was the maximum rate at which data could be transferred through the network (also referred to as the capacity of the network per unit time).[1] Increasing bandwidth led to the development of new technologies able to take advantage of this bandwidth, and a cycle of innovation resulted. In the 1990s this cycle led to the development of broadband technologies such as DSL (digital subscriber line) and cable modems, which used telephone and television lines respectively to transfer vast amounts of information at unprecedented speeds.[2] The development of broadband technologies was itself made possible by two previous developments: fiber-optic cable and the digital encoding of information.[3]

A fiber-optic cable, also known simply as fiber, was essentially an insulated cable containing flexible glass fibers designed for the purpose of transmitting light signals over long distances. Before the fiber-optic revolution of the late 1970s and 80s, all information transferred through cables was in the form of varying electrical currents passing through a copper conductor. This form of communication was slower than fiber optics, and the signal was weaker, requiring frequent boosting. In addition, fiber-optic cables had a greater capacity than copper cables and cost less to maintain. Commercial use of fiber-optic systems began in the late 1970s, as improvements in laser technology and fiber cables allowed light signals to be transferred across longer distances without major corruption of the signal. By 2001, fiber-optic cables served as the backbone for most telecommunication networks, and were the primary means of transmitting long-distance information by cable. Copper cables were still used primarily for short-distance transmissions.

Before 1963 electrically encoded information was passed along as an analog signal, which was a continuous stream of information based on the modulation of a constant current of electricity. A digital signal by contrast broke up information into discrete bits of data that approximated the continuous stream of an analog signal. The advantages of digital encoding were that the signal did not degrade over time and was more immune to interference. In addition, digital signals could be greatly compressed in size using

---

[1] Bandwidth rate was measured in bits per second, where "bit" stood for binary digit, and was the basic unit of representation in computer code.

[2] DSL and cable modem technology used electrical cable lines to reach maximum consumer speeds of 1.5 million bits per second, and more advanced technologies using fiber-optic cables could reach transmission speeds as high as 13.21 billion bits per second. For comparison sake, the analog telephone network in use around the world transferred 28.8 thousand bits per second, while original telegraph cables in the mid 1800s could transmit a maximum of 20 bits per second. (Source: Case authors, based on compiled data from public sources such as www.telecommagazine.com (Telecommunications Online) and www.ntia.doc.gov (National Telecommunications and Information Administration).)

[3] http://www.broadbandcompass.com; Broadband FAQ, "How does broadband work?"

pattern-recognition programs, and could also be encrypted for increased security of transmissions. Digital carrier techniques were first introduced in 1963, and soon became widely used throughout the telephone network. By 2001 digital encoding was rapidly becoming the standard for all forms of electrical communication.

As broadband technology gained prominence throughout the late 1990s and new technologies pushed bandwidth transmission rates higher, telecommunication companies continuously upgraded and expanded their cable networks to keep up with the quickening pace of innovation and to remain relevant in the eyes of consumers. Meanwhile, while high prices and transmission limitations had confined wireless technologies mainly to the niche market of cellular phones, emerging technologies were set to make wireless technology a serious future threat to cable-based networks in general.

THE HISTORY OF THE U.S. TELECOMMUNICATIONS MARKET

The U.S. Telecommunications Market Prior to 1996[4]

In 1984, Judge Thomas Penfield Johnson handed down a ruling which dramatically altered the structure of the U.S. telecom industry. His ruling broke AT&T into one major long-distance carrier which kept the name AT&T, and 4 major local carriers which were named regional bell operating companies, or RBOCs. Prior to the MFJ ruling, AT&T dominated both local and long-distance services across the country. While several Incumbent Local Exchange carriers (ILECs) existed in certain rural areas, AT&T was the principal provider of long-distance services across the country.

The MFJ also divided the United States into LATAs—Local Access and Transport Areas—which became regulated jurisdictions. Telephone and data traffic that originated and terminated within a LATA was referred to as intra-LATA traffic and was, more or less, subject to the jurisdiction of the state public service commission as a regulated utility. Traffic that crosses LATA boundaries was referred to as inter-LATA traffic and was heavily regulated by the Federal Communications Commission (the FCC).

This decision altered the landscape because the ruling prohibited AT&T from offering local service. Similarly, the regional bell operating companies (the RBOCs) and Incumbent Local Exchange Carriers (ILECs) could not offer long-distance service. The combination of restrictions on AT&T, the breakup of the long-distance network into smaller jurisdictions, and increased regulations on long-distance traffic served to create competition in the long-distance market for consumer benefit.

The telecommunications industry had effectively operated under this regulatory framework for 12 years. The price of long-distance voice and data communications dropped and new products and services were introduced as highly successful competitors entered the long-distance market. MCI went from near bankruptcy to an industry powerhouse, and other competitors such as Sprint, LDDS, and WorldCom grew rapidly. Beneath the larger national players were the Tier II long-distance providers such as RTY. These serviced a narrow geographical area or a specialized customer niche. By the early 1990s, the long-distance providers were in full competition, yet the RBOC's maintained a strong monopoly in the local-line markets. The next step was to liberalize these local-line monopolies.

[4] This section draws on Peter Temin and Joseph Weber, "The MFJ: Its Logic and Echoes," *Florida Journal of Law and Public Policy,* Spring 1997, pp. 201–17.

The U.S. Telecommunications Market After 1996

With the passage of the 1996 Telecommunications Act, competition within local carriers finally became possible. The powerful RBOCs were required to sell local-line access to competitive local exchange carriers (CLECs) for resale to their customers at below tariff prices. The CLECs providers could then compete for business by offering local-line access services at a price below what the RBOCs could offer (due to the regulatory discounts they received). The law was restructured so that the RBOCs, previously restricted to Intra-LATA business, could now expand into the Inter-LATA and broadband markets. Moreover, firms such as RTY could offer both long-distance and local products bundled, which increased not only the total revenue per customer but also asset utilization. The purpose of this restructuring was to foster competition between the local and long distance markets.

The CLEC market developed into three loose-fitting categories: non-facility, hybrid-facility, and full-facility. The non-facility market was comprised strictly of resellers of RBOC access; they did not own any network facilities themselves. Hybrid-facility providers (often called "smart-builders") first resold RBOC access until concentration within a geographic region was sufficient to justify the creation of their own network facilities. Full-facility describes carriers such as ICG or Quest who typically installed fiber throughout a business district or community and competed primarily on a facility basis with RBOCs and other CLECs.

The Telecommunications Act, coupled with the rise of the Internet and the increasing demand for bandwidth, was expected to generate enormous increases in capital expenditure. The telecom industry was already notoriously expensive. Expansive switch rooms used for rerouting information and fiber facilities dug under city streets pushed the cost of installing a network to exorbitant levels. Upgrading was difficult as well because most (if not all) of the network equipment needed to be upgraded at the same time. Market estimates for installing fiber on land were approximately $30,000 per kilometer.[5] A network spanning North America could cost well over $1 billion.

In 1998 over 1.2 million miles of fiber were installed across the country by CLECs, and 271 new CLEC companies were started to take advantage of the newly competitive local market.[6] CLEC fiber installation represented a 60% jump from the prior year. In competition with the CLECs, annual fiber installation by the RBOCs increased 13% nationwide from 1997 to 1998, to a total of 16 million miles of installed RBOC fiber. Similar developments were seen in the long-distance sector. According to an FCC report, by the end of 1998 United States inter-LATA carriers had installed 3.6 million miles of fiber, a 40% increase over installed fiber in 1997.[7]

Industry-wide spending (including long-distance carriers, CLECs, wireless carriers, and RBOCs) had grown on average nearly 26% annually since 1996, while total revenue on long-distance and local service grew only 10.5% and EBITDA (earnings before interest, taxes, depreciation, and amortization) grew 11.6% annually.[8] In 2000, some

---

[5] David Brown, Schema, LTD (a UK based telecom consultancy), quoted in "Wholesaling for Survival and Growth," Telecommunications Online. Feb. 2000.

[6] Martin, Michael. "Caution Flags Flying as CLEC Woes Mount." Network World. Vol 17, No 47. Nov. 20, 2000. pg. 1.

[7] Dukart, James. "Fiber-Optic Capacity: How Much Is Enough?" Utility Business. Nov. 2000. pg 2.

[8] Bath, Blake. "Telecom Sea Change Creates Overcapitalization." Lehman Brothers. New York: New York. pg. 53.

$128 billion in telecommunication infrastructure bonds were issued and $69 billion in equity was raised in order to finance this disproportionate growth.[9]

The Bandwidth Glut

Over 6 million miles of fiber were installed in all by telecommunication companies in 1998, and by 1999 there was a total of 25 million miles of in-the-ground fiber in the Continental United States. In addition to installed fiber, the introduction of new technologies such as Dense-Wave-Division-Multiplexing (DWDM) further increased the capacity of the network. With DWDM, 8x, 16x, 32x, and even 80x increases in capacity per single strand of fiber were possible with simple equipment upgrades. In addition, fiber projects and facilities were conceived, designed, and initiated simultaneously, seemingly without taking into account the possibility of market saturation. Compounding the problem, projections for Internet and data demand growth appeared to be exaggerated. Originally forecasted to double every 3-4 months for several years, Internet demand growth had scaled back to doubling every 12 months by 1999. In that year, Internet and corporate data represented less than 20% of total traffic, with voice services comprising the remainder.[10] The exaggerated projections were primarily due to the inability of the RBOCs to effectively market DSL and other high-speed services as expected. For example, in January of 1999 SBC Communications forecasted 8.2 million residential and 1.3 million business DSL customers by the end of the year.[11] Only 100,000 total DSL customers were achieved in 1999 and 400,000 in 2000.[12]

As a consequence of these over-optimistic expectations, many analysts believed that too much bandwidth was brought online than was necessary for consumer use. Carriers moved aggressively to court customer volume in order to compensate for the high-fixed costs associated with establishing their networks. This vigorous competition coupled with an overabundance of supply and a lack of demand had prevented many carriers from reaching minimum efficient use of their resources. In the long-distance backbones of major United States carriers, utilization was running as low as 30% in 2000, and the price of long-distance communication had dropped 50% per year over a two year period. This was an increase from a 20–30% year to year drop in the four years prior.[13] A report released in 2000 claimed that if 60% of installed fiber were lit[14] by 2001, the amount of available bandwidth would be 400 times what it was in 1998, and predicted that 64% of lit European capacity and 38% of lit United States capacity would go unused in 2004.[15] Jim Crowe, the CEO of Level 3 Communications, suggested that it could take as long as 38 years to light all available fiber at current growth rates.[16] In-

---

[9] Telecom Financing Week, Sidebar. page 1, January 15, 2001.

[10] Tanner, John C. and Tim Marshall, "The Bandwidth Bubble," America's Network. Feb. 1, 2001, pg. 39.

[11] Dow Jones, "SBC To Offer High-Speed Internet Access by Year-End," New York Times, 13 January 1999, pg. C3.

[12] Edwards, John. "Door Number three: DSL—a new song for old pipes." Upside: Foster City. Nov 2000, pg. 2.

[13] Bluestone Capital Report, et al., 2001.

[14] In industry jargon, installed fiber that is able to be utilized by the network is known as "lit" fiber, while installed fiber still unable to be utilized and requiring further setup is known as "unlit" fiber.

[15] Adventis Consulting quoted in Canadian Business, Sep 18, 2000

[16] CBS Markwatch Report. Comments made at Robertson Stephens "Tech Weekend" held in San Francisco, February 14, 2001.

ternational utilization rates were also low. Telstra, an international communications firm, estimated that only 100 gigabits of bandwidth out of an available 8 to 9 terabits[17] were being utilized on submarine cables linking the United States and Europe in 2001 and that at present growth rates, utilization would reach only 1.6 terabits by 2005.[18] The Yankee group's analysis of European bandwidth forecasted a 500% per annum increase in capacity with only a 50% increase in demand.

The dropping prices had caused problems for CLECs and long distance providers alike. The average CLEC stock price was down over 83% in 2000,[19] and several CLECs had shown significant balance sheet weakness. One of the more prominent failures was ICG Communications, a once highly profitable, full-facility CLEC. ICG's chapter 11 filing in 2000 contributed to an across the board slump of telecommunications stocks in the capital markets. The long-distance market had also seen significant turmoil, reflected in AT&T's announcement in 2000 that it was breaking up its core businesses in order to separate the volatile long-distance business from its other assets.

Remaining Market Uncertainty

While there was little disagreement that prices were dropping, opinions differed as to whether total revenue would decrease. Although price per fiber mile had dropped as new bandwidth capacity became available, analysts and industry insiders were uncertain if increased utilization per fiber-mile would compensate for the drop in price. Perry Cole, SVP of sales at Touch America, a Tier II long-distance provider, commented in November 2000 that he still expected a 30% CAGR (compound annual growth rate) due to high speed access demand. He explained, "We don't see demand drying up any time soon. From what we see, it is more a question of getting it (fiber) lit and provision. . . . We don't see an oversupply of bandwidth." He added, "We don't think it is going to plateau. We think it is going to continue to grow."[20] Similar data reported by AT&T in 2000 stated that demand for voice traffic was estimated to grow at a 9% annual rate, and demand for high speed (and high bandwidth) services was estimated to grow 60% to 70% per year. They also reported demand for Internet protocol services was growing 200% per year. These assumptions were at least somewhat based on observed history. For example, while the average wireless bill in the United States fell from $100 in 1988 to $43 in 2000, the number of customers increased from 250,000 to 100 million.[21]

Meanwhile, the likelihood of innovative, bandwidth-intensive applications being developed further compounded industry uncertainty. Often called "killer apps," these applications could become popular quickly as they spread across the network, and leave companies scrambling to upgrade their own network technologies to a compatible level. For example, as higher bandwidth became available to home users via DSL and other technologies, new applications were developed to take advantage of this higher capacity. These new applications could often utilize more bandwidth than what was currently available, and they pushed the development of bandwidth to meet their new bench-

[17] 1 gigabit = 1 billion bits of information; 1 terabit = 1 trillion bits of information.

[18] Lynch, Grahame. "The coming bandwidth bubble burst," America's Network: Duluth. Feb 1, 2001, pg. 1.

[19] According to Merrill Lynch as quoted in Barron's, 27 September 2000.

[20] Dukart, James. "Fiber-optic capacity: How much is enough?" Utility Business: Overland Park. Nov 2000, pg. 1.

[21] Verburg, Peter. "Can you have too much?" Canadian Business: Toronto. Sep 18, 2000, pg. 2.

mark capacity. Some speculated that this phenomenon had not yet reached its peak due to the slow roll-out of broadband network facilities for home users. Recent data released by the FCC suggested that home and small business broadband access had increased in the first half of 2000 by 57% to a total of 4.3 million lines,[22] indicating that perhaps the industry had turned a corner.

RTY TELECOM COMPANY AND THE NORTEL AGREEMENT

Within this competitive climate, RTY Telecom had faired reasonably well (see Exhibit 1 for financial statements, and Exhibit 2 for historical volatility). An independently operating subsidiary of the Luxembourg-based telecom group RTY Global, RTY Telecom started its first U.S. activities in the early 1990s, offering long-distance services to retail customers as well as running fiber facilities. RTY's later strategy was to focus on business communication needs in less competitive markets and to offer a bundle of stand-alone services including high-speed Internet access, web-hosting, data-networking, voice communication, and video/teleconferencing in both the CLEC and Inter-LATA markets. By 2001, RTY was a full-facility long-distance provider with fiber and switching systems (for rerouting information) that spanned coast to coast. RTY had over 100 co-location and interconnecting agreements with all the major carriers.

Originally established as a voice-only provider, RTY had continuously upgraded and expanded its infrastructure, and was by 2001 offering both wholesale long-distance services to other carriers, as well as enhanced data services (such as web-hosting, co-location and managed services) and Internet security to corporate customers. Given RTY's strategy of focusing on the highly volatile business communication market, it was critical to effectively utilize existing fiber facilities while remaining flexible and open to future customer requirements. It was possible that new multimedia-based applications or technologies could cause demand to rise. In addition, it was also possible that network demand would be more elastic than originally estimated. In either scenario, those carriers without sufficient capacity would be at a significant competitive disadvantage.

Like all facility-based telecommunication service providers, increasing capacity was a function of installing new fiber-optic cabling, installing new equipment, or upgrading old equipment. Often it was a combination of all three. Companies had been established whose main purpose was to supply facility-based service providers with the back-end products and services necessary for maintaining and upgrading their infrastructure, and a large and profitable industry had grown out of this market niche (see Exhibit 3 for a summary of supplier companies, their financial statements, and their current market status). While installing new fiber wasn't necessarily the most expensive choice, laying fiber meant many months or even years of delay, effectively eliminating it from consideration except under very long-term growth horizons.

Description of the Nortel Agreement

As RTY considered how to expand their network in the best and most flexible way, Nortel brought an interesting product to market: the Multi-wavelength Optical Repeater (MORail) 1600-G Plus System which utilized the capacity increasing DWDM

---

[22] FCC, "Trends in Telephone Service," Working Paper, December 2000, pg. 2-1.

EXHIBIT 1

RTY FINANCIAL STATEMENTS

a. Annual Income Statements for RTY Telecom (in $ millions except per share amounts)

Income Statement	Dec-00	Dec-99	Dec-98
Sales	1,042.5	734.4	515.4
Cost of Goods Sold	918.3	646.8	440.4
Gross Profit	124.2	87.6	75.0
Depreciation-Amortization	259.5	161.4	92.7
Operating Income	−135.3	−73.8	−17.7
Interest Expense	166.5	135.9	98.4
Non-Operating Income/Expense	42.9	44.7	22.2
Special Items	48.3	0.0	−3.3
Income Before Taxes	−210.6	−165.0	−97.2
Income Taxes	−1.5	0.3	−19.5
Minority Interest	0.0	0.0	0.0
Net Income After Taxes	−209.1	−165.3	−77.7
Extraordinary Items	−3.9	0.0	−25.2
Adjusted Net Income	−213.0	−165.3	−102.9

b. Annual Balance Sheets for RTY Telecom (in $ millions)

Balance Sheet	Dec-00	Dec-99	Dec-98
Cash	444.3	765.6	595.5
Net Receivables	234.3	154.2	124.5
Inventories	27.6	15.3	4.8
Other Current Assets	16.2	18.0	1.8
Total Current Assets	722.4	953.1	726.6
Net Fixed Assets	2,040.0	1,148.7	786.3
Other Noncurrent Assets	383.1	321.3	249.9
Total Assets	3,145.5	2,423.1	1,762.8
Long Term Debt Due In One Year	6.3	2.4	3.3
Notes Payable	0.0	0.0	0.0
Accounts Payable	229.8	92.7	60.0
Taxes Payable	0.0	0.0	0.0
Accrued Expenses	97.8	79.5	58.5
Other Current Liabilities	132.9	43.8	34.5
Total Current Liabilities	467.1	218.4	156.0
Long-Term Debt	2,135.4	1,548.6	1,250.7
Deferred Taxes	0.0	1.5	1.2
Minority Interest	0.0	0.0	0.0
Other Noncurrent Liabilities	0.0	0.0	0.0
Total Liabilities	2,602.5	1,768.2	1,407.9
Common Stock Equity	543.0	654.3	354.6
Total Liabilities and Stock	3,145.5	2,422.5	1,762.5

Source: Created by casewriters to support the illustration of the fictitious case company.

EXHIBIT 2

HISTORICAL VOLATILITY FOR RTY TELECOM (ONE MONTH ROLLING)

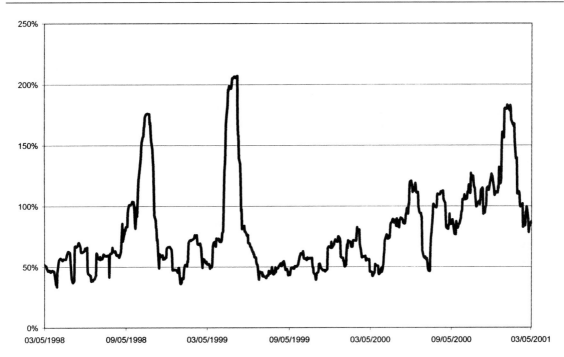

Notes: Historical volatility is normally calculated by taking the standard deviation of the daily net change in value over a thirty day period, and then multiplying this number by the square root of 250 to annualize it.

Source: Created by casewriters to support the illustration of the fictitious case company.

technology. Whereas two strands of fiber originally supported one carrier signal[23] operating at bandwidth speed OC-12 (see Exhibit 4 for bandwidth naming conventions and descriptions), the MORail increased bandwidth of a single strand of fiber to OC-192 speeds. In addition, DWDM technology enabled each of these fibers to support 32 lambdas, or 16 carrier signals. The MORail system was projected to provide up to a 32x or 64x performance increase with upgrades in the foreseeable future (see Exhibit 5 for MORail performance analysis).[24]

[23] A carrier signal actually represents two signals (transmit and receive) that carry information in opposite directions from one source to another, usually in the form of a sinusoidal wave or a predictable series of pulses. Communications through cables always operate using a carrier signal. For example, a home telephone line consists of two copper cables, one for transmitting data and the other for receiving data. Together these two signals make up one carrier signal for the copper network. In a fiber-optic network, one carrier signal consists of two wavelengths of light, one for transmitting data and one for receiving data. A wavelength is called by its industry pseudonym, lambda. Before DWDM, one fiber-optic cable could carry one lambda of light, or $1/2$ a carrier signal. With Nortel's system, one cable could carry 32 lambdas, or 16 carrier signals. (Source: Case authors, based on compiled data from public sources such as Nortel.com's product information, www.telecommagazine.com (Telecommunications Online) and www.ntia.doc.gov (National Telecommunications and Information Administration).)

[24] Nortel press release, "Nortel Introduces New Add-Drop Traffic Capability for More Efficient Optical Networks." June 2, 1998.

EXHIBIT 3

COMPARISON OF A SELECTION OF TELECOM SUPPLIER COMPANIES

a. 2000 Summary Descriptions (in millions of dollars unless ratio or multiple)

	Nortel Networks	Cisco Systems	Lucent Technologies
	The second-largest North American telecom equipment maker. Provides equipment, services, and software for operating networks.	Controls almost two-thirds of the network-linking equipment market. Makes network access servers and management software.	A global leader in telecom equipment and services. Produces transmission and switching, wireless, and optical gear.
Total Assets	42227.00	32870.00	48792.00
Equity Market Value	96236.20	458127.94	102063.83
Debt Book Value	2232.00	0.00	6559.00
Operating Cash Flow	−10.00	6141.00	40.00
Net Income/Total Assets	−0.07	0.08	0.02
ROA[a]	−9.12	11.21	3.84
ROE[b]	−14.54	13.98	8.46
Total Liabilities/Total Assets	0.32	0.19	0.46
Equity Beta[c]	1.75	1.44	1.77
Price/Book	3.35	17.29	3.90
Debt-to-equity[d] (book value)	0.05	0.00	0.12
Debt-to-equity (market value)	0.02	0.00	0.03
Price/Earnings	156.25	97.04	692.50
EBIT[e]/Interest Expense	−8.68	NA	11.01
EBITDA[f]/Interest Expense	20.39	NA	14.73

Notes: Lucent Technologies has a fiscal year ending in September, Cisco Systems has a fiscal year ending in July, and Nortel Networks has a fiscal year ending in December.

[a]ROA is Return on Average Assets. [b] ROE is Return on Average Equity.

[c]Beta is calculated for a 60 month time period, ending in the current month.

[d]As measured by the ratio of long-term debt to shareholders' equity.

[e]EBIT is the Earnings Before Interest and Taxes.

[f]EBITDA is the Earnings Before Interest, Taxes, Depreciation, and Amortization.

Source: Standard & Poor's Compustat data (accessed April 2001), Hoover's Inc, www.hoovers.com, (accessed April 2001), and casewriter calculations.

(Continued)

The technology consisted of an enabling platform chassis connected to the fiber optic cable. Into this chassis were inserted blade pairs which provided high-bandwidth capacity. Each blade pair supported one OC-192 speed carrier signal. With all cards installed, the system could support 16 carrier signals at OC-192 speed per 5,000 fiber miles. Because RTY's network spanned approximately 10,000 fiber miles, two chassis systems would be required and two blade pairs were required per OC-192 speed carrier signal. With this technology RTY could add capacity incrementally by simply adding

EXHIBIT 3 *(Continued)*

COMPARISON OF A SELECTION OF TELECOM SUPPLIER COMPANIES

b. 1999 Summary Financial Statements (in millions of dollars unless ratio or multiple)

	Nortel Networks	Cisco Systems	Lucent Technologies
Total Assets	22597.00	14725.00	38775.00
Equity Market Value	137523.80	199669.75	197803.04
Debt Book Value	1911.00	0.00	7026.00
Operating Cash Flow	973.00	4438.00	−276.00
Net Income/Total Assets	−0.01	0.14	0.12
ROA	−0.93	17.73	10.56
ROE	−1.72	22.32	36.18
Total Liabilities/Total Assets	0.45	0.21	0.65
Equity Beta	1.55	1.36	1.82
Price/Book	11.55	17.10	14.56
Debt-to-equity (book value)	0.14	0.00	0.31
Debt-to-equity (market value)	0.01	0.00	0.02
Price/Earnings	−141.26	105.00	72.08
EBIT/Interest Expense	7.82	NA	13.90
EBITDA/Interest Expense	15.05	NA	16.94

Source: Standard & Poor's Compustat data (accessed April 2001) and casewriter calculations.

c. 1998 Summary Financial Statements (in millions of dollars unless ratio or multiple)

	Nortel Networks	Cisco Systems	Lucent Technologies
Total Assets	19732.00	8916.71	26720.00
Equity Market Value	33173.69	99121.07	90985.02
Debt Book Value	1853.00	0.00	4640.00
Operating Cash Flow	1586.00	2880.52	1366.00
Net Income/Total Assets	−0.03	0.15	0.04
ROA	−3.53	18.79	3.84
ROE	−7.22	23.69	21.75
Total Liabilities/Total Assets	0.41	0.20	0.79
Equity Beta	1.62	1.11	1.74
Price/Book	3.03	13.95	16.44
Debt-to-equity (book value)	0.15	0.00	0.44
Debt-to-equity (market value)	0.05	0.00	0.03
Price/Earnings	156.25	97.04	692.50
EBIT/Interest Expense	6.68	NA	11.30
EBITDA/Interest Expense	10.08	NA	14.04

Source: Standard & Poor's Compustat data (accessed April 2001) and casewriter calculations.

d. Telecom Supplier Companies Market Status on March 5, 2001

	Nortel Networks	Cisco Systems	Lucent Technologies
stock price ($)	17.60	23.08	12.38
shares outstanding (M)	3181.69	7197.15	3403.61
market value of debt ($M)	1098.10	0.00	1060.70

Source: Thomson Datastream (accessed April 2001) and casewriter calculations.

EXHIBIT 4

BANDWIDTH MATRIX: BANDWIDTH NAMING CONVENTIONS, TRANSMISSION RATES, AND PERFORMANCE IMPROVEMENTS ACROSS LEVELS

7	DS-0	DS-1	DS-3/OC-1	OC-3	OC-12	OC-48	OC-192	Aggr. Bandwidth	
DS-0[1]	1	—	—	—	—	—	—	64.000	Kbps[3]
DS-1	24	1	—	—	—	—	—	1.544	Mbps[4]
DS-3/OC-1[2]	672	28	1	—	—	—	—	51.840	Mbps[5]
OC-3	2,016	84	3	1	—	—	—	155.520	Mbps
OC-12	8,064	336	12	4	1	—	—	622.080	Mbps
OC-48	32,256	1,344	144	48	4	1	—	2,488.320	Mbps
OC-192	129,024	5,376	576	192	16	4	1	9,953.280	Mbps

Notes: [1]The basic digital bandwidth rate for electrical signal transmission was known as Digital Signal 0 (DS-0), and was set by convention at 64 kilobits/second (1 kilobit = 1000 bits), corresponding to the capacity of one voice-carrying, digitally-encoded, electrically-transmitted channel. Digital Signal 1 (DS-1) through Digital Signal 4 (DS-4) represented discrete bandwidth increases from this basic rate.

[2]Similar conventions existed for the fiber-optic transmission rates, starting with Optical Carrier 1 (OC-1), which basically corresponded to DS-3, and going up to Optical Carrier-192 (OC-192).

[3]Kbps stands for kilobits per second (one kilobit equals one thousand bits).

[4]Mbps stands for megabit per second (one megabit equals one million bits).

[5]The transition from DC-3 to OC-1 involves an additional increase of 8.6 Mbps.

Source: Casewriter calculations, based on compiled data from e.g. www.juniper.net/techpubs/software/ nog/nog-interfaces/download/overview.pdf, www.telecommagazine.com (Telecommunications Online) and www.ntia.doc.gov (National Telecommunications and Information Administration).

EXHIBIT 5

MORAIL PERFORMANCE ANALYSIS

	Lambda's[1] Per Fiber	Carrier Signal Per Fiber	Speed Per Carrier Signal	Total Capacity Per Fiber
Without MORail:	1	$^1/_2$	622 Mbps[2]	311 Mbps
With 16x:	32	16	622 Mbps	9,952 Mbps/ 1 × OC-192[3]
With 32x (future):	64	32	622 Mbps	19,904 Mbps/ 2 × OC-192

Notes: [1] Lambda corresponds to a single wavelength of light, also known as half a carrier signal in a fiber-optic network.

[2] Mbps stands for megabit per second, where one megabit equals one million bits.

[3] OC stands for "Optical Carrier" and represents different levels of bandwidth transmission rates in a fiber-optic network, ranging from OC-1 to OC-192 (see previous exhibit for a more detailed explanation).

Source: Product information on Nortel company website (www.nortelnetworks.com), accessed April 2001, and casewriter calculations.

cards without having to concern itself with installing new fiber. Garzon faced the dilemma of purchasing the chassis now, giving RTY the option of upgrading the network as capacity was needed, or deferring the purchase of the chassis until later.

If Garzon recommended purchase of the chassis at a later date, RTY could face lead times of six months or more. There was a chance that the technology would not be available at all, for equipment vendors in the past had faced enormous difficulty meeting demand during boom periods. If the demand proved great, RTY would be unable to support its customer base. Customers who elected to order large and expensive broadband packages (the highest margin customers) would quickly turn elsewhere (see Exhibit 6 for a summary of competitors to RTY, their financial statements, and their current market status). If demand did explode, RTY could buy time by buying capacity on the telecommunications spot market. However, in this scenario spot capacity would likely be extremely expensive and limited, if available at all. On the other hand, if the units were purchased and demand did not materialize, $140 million of capital would have been consumed that might have been invested better elsewhere.

Valuation of Agreement

Under the proposed contract between RTY and Nortel, RTY would purchase for $70 million a MORail chassis. It would also purchase the right to acquire the 16 blade pairs (one or more pairs at a time) necessary to fully populate the chassis any time in the next five years for $30 million per pair. (Importantly, the MORail system could not be used in the beginning unless at least one blade pair was purchased to populate it.) The term of the contract was five years. While it was clear that the potential to upgrade in the future was convenient, it was necessary to determine if the chassis was worth the $70 million RTY would be required to commit upfront, in addition to the $30 million it would need to commit in order to start using it.

Consequently, management discussion turned to the strategic and financial implications of such a deal. The ability to expand RTY's capacity and to profit from this expansion was dependent on the future of the telecommunications market and the market overall (see Exhibit 7 for current market indicators), as well as RTY's competitive positioning in the future.

Garzon viewed the MORail chassis as an important project for the future of RTY, and now needed to prepare the analysis of the initiative. As a first step, he had a simple NPV analysis done, but this calculation resulted in the MORail chassis investment being, at best, a marginally positive NPV project relative to some of the other alternatives RTY was considering (Exhibit 8 and Exhibit 9 present some of the information used in the NPV analysis). Intuitively, he knew that the purchase of the MORail system provided a hedge: if demand faltered, RTY had at risk only the investment in the chassis. If demand instead grew unexpectedly, then RTY would be ready to meet customer needs in the future, perhaps even taking market share from competitors who could not meet the increased demand. Accordingly, Garzon viewed this purchase as a strategic move designed more to provide flexibility than a project with well-defined cash flows. However, he wanted to quantify the value of this flexibility, and this value did not seem to be captured in the simple NPV analysis. Was this value $2 million or $200 million? The answer to this would determine the direction of RTY's operational strategy for the next few years.

EXHIBIT 6

FIRMS COMPARABLE TO RTY

a. 2000 Summary Descriptions and Financial Statements for Firms Comparable to RTY (in millions of dollars unless ratio or multiple)

	ITC Deltacom	ALLTEL	BellSouth	Qwest Comm.	SBC Comm.
	Provides long and short distance telecom services to business customers in 9 southern US states.	Provides long distance, short distance, and wireless services to customers in 24 US states.	Provides local access and wireless services to 36 US states and 16 countries. The country's #3 local phone company.	Provides Internet, data, multimedia, and voice services to 14 US states, including parts of Mexico and Europe.	The #2 local phone outfit in the US. Provides local service to 13 states and wireless service to 38 states.
Total Assets	1,048.53	12,182.00	50,925.00	73,501.00	98,651.00
Equity Market Value	331.93	19,521.38	76,389.38	68,138.63	161,632.36
Debt Book Value	713.87	4,680.00	20,032.00	19,066.00	26,962.00
Operating Cash Flow	45.93	1,497.30	8,590.00	3,681.00	14,299.00
Net Income/Total Assets	−0.07	0.16	0.08	0.00	0.08
ROA[a]	−7.50	17.12	8.94	−0.17	8.76
ROE[b]	−34.85	42.26	26.60	−0.38	27.86
Total Liabilities/Total Assets	0.83	0.58	0.67	0.44	0.69
Equity Beta[c]	1.57	0.50	0.50	0.80	0.67
Price/Book	1.95	3.83	4.52	1.65	5.31
Debt-to-equity[d] (book value)	4.19	0.91	0.74	0.37	0.54
Debt-to-equity (market value)	2.14	0.24	0.16	0.23	0.10
Price/Earnings	−5.50	10.15	18.52	116.79	19.25
EBIT[e]/Interest Expense	−0.81	5.45	5.64	3.00	6.35
EBITDA[f]/Interest Expense	0.75	8.43	9.36	5.80	12.10

Notes: All companies have fiscal years ending in December.

[a]ROA is Return on Average Assets.

[b]ROE is Return on Average Equity.

[c]Beta is calculated for a 60 month time period, ending in the current month.

[d]As measured by the ratio of long-term debt to shareholders' equity.

[e]EBIT is the Earnings Before Interest and Taxes.

[f]EBITDA is the Earnings Before Interest, Taxes, Depreciation, and Amortization.

Source: Standard & Poor's Compustat data (accessed April 2001), Hoover's Inc, www.hoovers.com, (accessed April 2001), and casewriter calculations.

(Continued)

EXHIBIT 6   *(Continued)*

FIRMS COMPARABLE TO RTY

b. 1999 Financials for Firms Comparable to RTY (USD mn unless ratio or multiple)

	ITC Deltacom	ALLTEL	BellSouth	RTYst Comm.	SBC Comm.
Total Assets	807.60	10774.20	43453.00	23216.00	83215.00
Equity Market Value	1640.87	25958.08	88194.75	36360.14	96915.00
Debt Book Value	516.91	3821.64	16766.00	13071.00	21849.00
Operating Cash Flow	−5.33	1500.03	8199.00	4546.00	16578.00
Net Income/Total Assets	−0.07	0.07	0.08	0.06	0.10
ROA	−7.88	7.77	8.32	5.30	10.25
ROE	−32.69	20.97	22.30	109.65	33.28
Total Liabilities/Total Assets	0.73	0.61	0.66	0.95	0.68
Equity Beta	1.51	0.44	0.42	0.44	0.76
Price/Book	7.92	6.17	5.95	28.97	3.63
Debt-to-equity (book value)	2.49	0.89	0.62	8.12	0.69
Debt-to-equity (market value)	0.31	0.14	0.10	0.28	0.19
Price/Earnings	−30.69	35.49	26.45	27.91	26.50
EBIT/Interest Expense	−0.54	5.77	6.56	4.37	7.68
EBITDA/Interest Expense	0.65	8.69	11.10	7.48	13.34

Source: Standard & Poor's Compustat data (accessed April 2001) and casewriter calculations.

c. 1998 Financials for Firms Comparable to RTY (USD mn unless ratio or multiple)

	ITC Deltacom	ALLTEL	BellSouth	RTYst Comm.	SBC Comm.
Total Assets	587.52	9374.23	39410.00	18407.00	45066.00
Equity Market Value	782.10	16414.28	97655.25	32447.11	104891.35
Debt Book Value	417.93	3547.24	12169.00	9919.00	14163.00
Operating Cash Flow	9.51	1247.09	7741.00	3927.00	8381.00
Net Income/Total Assets	−0.06	0.06	0.09	0.08	0.09
ROA	−5.32	6.99	9.32	8.46	9.33
ROE	−19.45	19.21	22.56	60.88	35.89
Total Liabilities/Total Assets	0.80	0.65	0.59	0.96	0.72
Equity Beta	NA	0.40	0.59	0.37	0.67
Price/Book	7.29	5.03	6.06	42.98	8.21
Debt-to-equity (book value)	3.89	1.07	0.54	11.45	0.99
Debt-to-equity (market value)	0.53	0.21	0.09	0.27	0.12
Price/Earnings	−39.61	31.82	30.32	22.52	26.95
EBIT/Interest Expense	−0.18	4.54	7.05	5.60	6.81
EBITDA/Interest Expense	0.76	7.06	12.26	9.47	11.75

Source: Standard & Poor's Compustat data (accessed April 2001) and casewriter calculations.

d. Comparable Companies Market Status on March 5, 2001

	ITC Deltacom	ALLTEL	BellSouth	Qwest Comm.	SBC Comm.
Stock price ($)	7.25	53.60	41.00	34.30	45.41
Shares outstanding (M)	61.58	312.75	1872.46	1660.82	3384.97
Market value of debt ($M)	389.00	1230.46	6097.54	2001.09	760.50

Source: Thomson Datastream (accessed April 2001) and casewriter calculations.

EXHIBIT 7

CURRENT MARKET INDICATORS

a. Yields on U.S. Treasury Securities, March 5, 2001

Maturity	Bills, Notes, Bonds	STRIPS
3 month	4.82	5.2085
6 month	4.7	5.0189
1 year	4.51	4.9376
2 years	4.49	5.1925
3 years	4.57	5.3935
5 years	4.78	5.6874
10 years	4.98	6.0549

Source: Thomson Datastream (accessed April 2001).

b. Yields on Industrial Notes and Bonds by Rating Category, March 5, 2001

	2 years	5 years	7 years	10 years	30 years
AAA	5.1	5.55	5.78	5.99	6.4
AA	5.18	5.64	5.85	6.01	6.6
A1-A3	5.35–5.78	5.89–6.31	6.1–6.66	6.23–6.82	6.81–7.42
BBB1-BBB3	5.94–6.35	6.46–6.83	6.74–7.07	6.91–7.23	7.54–7.81
BB1-BB3	7.52–8.35	8.03–9.03	8.26–9.26	8.52–9.48	9.12–10.25
B1-B3	8.88–11.36	9.38–11.93	9.58–12.21	9.84–12.4	10.68–12.68

Source: Bloomberg LP, accessed April 2001.

EXHIBIT 8

INITIAL ASSUMPTIONS FOR RTY'S BROADBAND BUSINESS WITH MORAIL CHASSIS INSTALLED AND ONE BLADE PAIR ADDED

Tax Rate	35.0%
Cost of Sales (as percent of sales)	11.4%
SG&A (as percent of sales)	39.0%
Depreciation (Years)	7.0
Risk Free Rate	4.9%
Discount Rate	15.0%
Initial Price of Bandwidth[1]	$0.02
Initial Demand[2]	25.7%
Projected Annual Change in Bandwidth Demand[3]	75.0%
Projected Annual Standard Dev. In Bandwidth Demand	5.0%
Projected Annual Change in Price	(33.9%)
Projected Annual Standard Dev. in Price	5.0%
Correlation Between Price and Demand Change	−0.4

Notes: [1]Price was measured on a per DS-0 mile basis, where each DS-0 mile represented the capacity of a mile of DS-0 speed transmission cable over a month period, and the total DS-0 miles within a network represented the total bandwidth capacity of that network in one month. Since initial price was $0.02 per DS-0 mile, then RTY would earn $0.02 for each mile of DS-0 speed transmission cable operating at full capacity over a month long period.

[2]Demand is represented as a percentage of total network capacity. Initial demand represented 25.7% of the 645,120,000 available DS-0 miles in RTY's network, or 166,050,125 DS-0 miles used per month. Total monthly revenue could be calculated by multiplying total DS-0 miles × total demand × price per DS-0 mile. Therefore, in the first month revenue equaled 645,120,000 × 25.7% × .$002 = $33,159,168.

[3]Changes in demand reflected a change in the consumption of total available DS-0 miles per month. Normally the network could handle a maximum capacity of 95%. With the chassis added and one blade pair this maximum capacity jumped to 100%, and each additional blade pair after this added an additional 100% capacity.

Source: Casewriter calculations.

EXHIBIT 9

EXPECTED PRESENT VALUE OF INVESTING IN EACH ADDITIONAL BLADE PAIR TODAY

Blade Pair	Expected PV
Blade 2	$35,847,191
Blade 3	$26,070,101
Blade 4	$21,190,914
Blade 5	$18,149,606
Blade 6	$16,035,888
Blade 7	$14,457,468
Blade 8	$13,222,961
Blade 9	$12,225,771
Blade 10	$11,400,911
Blade 11	$10,703,539
Blade 12	$10,103,108
Blade 13	$9,583,656
Blade 14	$9,125,041
Blade 15	$8,719,138
Blade 16	$8,353,958
PV of Assets	**$225,189,251**

Source: Calculated by the casewriters with a Monte Carlo simulation utilizing the numbers in Exhibit 8.

Index